# THE GERMAN LEGENDS OF THE BROTHERS GRIMM

## VOLUME I

*Edited and translated by*
D O N A L D   W A R D

ISHI

*A Publication of the*
*Institute for the Study of Human Issues*
*Philadelphia*

Manufactured in the United States of America

Published in the United States in 1981 by ISHI,
Institute for the Study of Human Issues, Inc.

Published in Great Britain in 1981 by Millington Books,
an imprint of Davison Publishing Ltd.
54 Elgin Ave., London, W9 2HA


Library of Congress Cataloging in Publication Data:

Grimm, Jakob Ludwig Karl, 1785–1863.
    The German legends of the Brothers Grimm.

    (Translations in folklore studies)
    Translation of Deutsche Sagen.
    Bibliography: v. 2, p.
    Includes index.
    1. Tales, German. 2. Legends—Germany. I. Grimm,
Wilhelm Karl, 1786–1859, joint author. II. Title. III. Series.
PT915.G513        1981        398.2'1'0943        80–24596
ISBN 0–915980–72–X (v. 1)                          AACR1
ISBN 0–915980–71–1 (v. 2)

            ISBN 0–915980–79–7 (set)


Publication of this book has been assisted by a grant from the
Publications Program of the National Endowment for the
Humanities.


For information, write:
Director of Publications, ISHI
3401 Science Center
Philadelphia, Pennsylvania 19104

# CONTENTS

## VOLUME I

# FOREWORD

## DAN BEN-AMOS

This publication of *The German Legends of the Brothers Grimm* marks the beginning of a new series entitled "Translations in Folklore Studies." Our purpose in this new venture is twofold: first, we wish to translate the classics of folklore, those works that have withstood time and the trends of scholarship to become the foundation of the discipline; at the other pole of the scholarly spectrum we will translate books of the highest quality that outline new directions for folklore and contribute theoretically and methodologically to current quests and debates.

In its time the *Deutsche Sagen*, the Grimms' collection of German legends, was a truly pioneering work. Together with several of their other publications, it broke ground for a new field of research that years later would be christened "folklore." To be sure, the Grimms were not the only German scholars in the early nineteenth century who were interested in legendry. For example, J. G. Büsching and Friedrich Gottschalk both published separate volumes (in 1812 and 1814 respectively) with the same title, *Sagen und Volksmärchen der Deutschen*. But neither they nor any other scholar of the era looked beyond the amusement value of the tales. It remained for the Grimm brothers to apply a systematic scholarly approach to the study of the folk and their narratives.

It was the Grimm brothers who gave emphasis to the oral nature of the legends and, by comparing them with sources of medieval literature, showed how ancient traditions, which might otherwise have been lost, were preserved through the oral transmissions. The brothers believed their texts to be true reflections of the German national spirit, but they never lost sight of the fact that similar tales could be found throughout the world. Indeed, they made careful comparative annotations of these tales. And throughout their narrative collections, there was always an implicit distinction among the genres; myth was separate from legend which was again separate from fairy tale. All of these concerns provided fertile soil for the growth of folklore scholarship.

In spite of their importance, *The German Legends* have never been translated into English, and their appearance in other languages has been rare. In this regard, the contrast between the legends or *Sagen* and the fairy tales (*Kinder-und Hausmärchen*) is overwhelming, for the fairy tales have been translated into all written languages and have become a classic of childrens' literature.

It may be that the Grimm brothers themselves provided the reason for this disparity when they wrote:

> The fairy tale is more poetic, the legend is more historical; the former exists securely almost in and of itself in its innate blossoming and consummation. The legend, by contrast, is characterized by a lesser variety of colors, yet it represents something special in that it adheres always to that which we are conscious of and know well, such as a locale or a name that has been secured through history. Because of this local confinement, it follows that the legend cannot, like the fairy tale, find its home anywhere. Instead the legend demands certain conditions without which it either cannot exist at all, or can only exist in less perfect form.

Subsequent generations upheld the Grimms' original insight and found in it the explanation for the worldwide acceptance of the *Märchen* and the relative neglect of the *Sagen*. The local nature of the legend, the known personality, and the belief in its historicity have limited the legend's appeal and distribution. In contrast, the anonymity, the timelessness, and the indefiniteness of locale in the fairy tale enabled listeners and readers from other nations to relate to these stories.

Yet the specificity of the legends is deceptive. While these tales are often told about particular places or particular persons, tales with almost identical themes and structures are told about other locations and other individuals. Thus, the legends only appear to be specific. In truth, they are really local or national examples of historical stories as they are told around the world. Tales about Ghosts and Goblins, about Giants and Gnomes that people encounter on their way in the dark, by the cemetery, through a narrow alley, or in a forest are told by many in terms of their own traditions, beliefs, and landscapes. Thus, although the legends do concern specific events, they nevertheless demonstrate the universal principles that people follow when they tell what they believe to be true and hope to convince their listeners of the veracity of their experience. It is the universality of general themes and the narrative principles that make *The German Legends* a cornerstone of modern folklore scholarship.

In the first English translation of this classic work, Donald Ward provides us with an excellent rendering of the original texts. He demonstrates sensitivity to stylistic nuances, dialectical variations, and historical changes in the language. In addition, he has included an informative commentary for each legend, a bibliography of the sources used by the Grimm brothers, and an index that will be of immense importance for future comparative studies. More than a scholarly translation, *The German Legends of the Brothers Grimm* is destined to become the definitive edition of the *Deutsche Sagen*.

# FOREWORD

## 1. The Essence of the Legend

Every time a man journeys out into life he is accompanied by a good angel who has been bestowed upon him in the name of his homeland, and who accompanies him in the guise of an intimate companion. He who does not sense the good fortune that this companion brings him will nevertheless feel a sore loss the minute he crosses the border leading from his fatherland, where the angel will then forsake him. This benevolent companion is none other than the inexhaustible store of tales, legends, and history, all of which coexist and strive to bring us closer to the refreshing and invigorating spirit of earlier ages.

Each of them has its own realm. The fairy tale is more poetic, the legend is more historical; the former exists securely almost in and of itself in its innate blossoming and consummation. The legend, by contrast, is characterized by a lesser variety of colors, yet it represents something special in that it adheres always to that which we are conscious of and know well, such as a locale or a name that has been secured through history. Because of this local confinement, it follows that the legend cannot, like the fairy tale, find its home anywhere. Instead the legend demands certain conditions without which it either cannot exist at all, or can only exist in less perfect form.

There is scarcely a spot in all of Germany where one cannot hear elaborate fairy tales, locales on which legends are usually sown only quite sparsely. This apparent inadequacy and insignificance is conceded, but in compensation we find legends far more intimately representative. They are like the dialects of language, in which time and again one encounters the strangest words and images that have survived from ancient times; while the fairy tales, by contrast, transport a complete piece of ancient poetry to us from the past in a single breath.

Curiously, narrative folk songs resemble the legends considerably more than they do the fairy tales, which again have preserved the tendencies of the earliest poetry in their content more purely and more vigorously than even the surviving great songs of ancient times have been able to do. Because of this, one can explain without any difficulty whatsoever why the fairy tale, almost alone, has preserved portions of proto-Germanic heroic material, without names to be sure (except in cases where the names themselves have acquired significance in their fixed form, as is true for example, of "Old Hildebrand"), whereas so many individual, almost withered names, locales, and customs have tenaciously held on from the earliest of times in the songs and legends of our people.

The fairy tales are thus destined, partly because of their external distribution and partly because of their innermost essences, to capture the pure thoughts of a childlike world view. They nourish us directly like milk, mild and delicate, or like honey, sweet and satisfying, but without the burden of earthly gravity. The legends, by contrast, serve as a far richer diet, bearing simpler yet therefore more pronounced colors, and demanding more serious contemplations and reflection.

To try to debate the advantages of both genres would be crude and awkward, and even in this discussion of their differences one should neither overlook nor deny their common properties, nor the fact that they intermingle with one another in infinite combinations and intertwinings, often resembling one another to a greater or lesser degree. Both forms, the fairy tale and the legend, set themselves up in opposition to history inasmuch as they constantly combine the perceptible and conceivable natural world with the inconceivable, uncanny world. History does not, as appears commensurate with our education, tolerate the incredible in its presentations; but it is able, in its own way and in its observance of the totality, to seek it out and to honor it.

While it is the children alone who believe in the reality of fairy tales, the folk have not yet stopped believing in their legends; and the collective understanding does not attempt to differentiate between the real and the unreal. The reality of the wondrous is established sufficiently for the folk by the details that accompany narration, that is, the undeniable familiarity with the nearby events and the visible existence of the site together outweigh any doubts about the wondrous events associated with the location. It follows that it is this very "cooperative union" of the legend that is its true characteristic. There is actually nothing that the folk can gain from what is called "true history" (lingering as it does behind certain contemporary circles and behind that which every royal family has lived through) that has not already been conveyed to them by means of the legend. The people will either remain alienated from an historic event that has been transported through time and space if it does not fulfill this condition, or they will simply ignore it.

Yet how unswerving is their allegiance to the legacy of the legends that tradition has given them, that follow them from remote times, and that have become attached to their most intimate concerns. They are never bored by them, for they do not perceive them as mere idle play to be cast aside when they are through with them. Instead the legends are considered a necessary part of their households, to be discussed on the proper occasion with all the reverence that is inevitably accorded all righteous things.

When we consider the matter carefully, we can determine that the constant motion and lasting security of folk legends represent the most reassuring and most refreshing of God's gifts to man. Around everything that appears extraordinary to the human senses—existing either as part of nature's possessions in a given landscape, or as something that history calls to man's attention—there gathers the scent of song and legend, much the way the distant heavens appear to be blue, or the way an aura of fine, delicate dust surrounds fruit and blossoms. From the coexistence and cohabitation with rocky crags, lakes, ruins of castles, and with trees and plants there soon emerges a kind of union founded upon the features peculiar to each of these objects, and at certain hours, one is permitted to hear of their wonders. The power of this bond is felt in the heart-rending homesickness known to all normal people. Without this poetry that is their companion whole peoples would have languished and faded into oblivion, for language, customs, and habits would have become empty and meaningless to them. Indeed, without the poetic element, all a people's possessions would exist without firm borders to enclose them.

Thus, we can understand the essence and the virtue of the German folk legend that proffers fear and warnings of evil together with a joyous appreciation of the good from the same hands. It ventures into places and locales that have long since become inaccessible to our official history. But for the most part, history and legend flow together, intermingling with one another as in rivers where the greener waters of a tributary stream can long be discerned after the two rivers have joined together.

## 2. *The Truth and Reliability of the Collection*

The first and foremost requirement of a collection of legends, and one we never lost sight of, is truth and reliability. The need has always been recognized as the most important element in all histories. But we also demand the truth of poetry, and we recognize it in its pure form in all true poetry. Lies are false and evil, as is all that comes from lies. However, we have never encountered any lies in the songs and legends of the folk. They leave the contents of these tales just as they found them and have always known them.

On the other hand, certain elements will drop off in the course of time, much in the same way otherwise healthy trees will slough off dead branches. For with legends, too, nature protects the organism with eternal, self-generating renewals. No single human hand is capable of feigning the fundament and workings of a poem. The individual who attempted to do so would be expending the same fruitless energy as if he were seeking to devise a new language (even one consisting of small simple words) or to establish a new law or custom, or to have a deed that never occurred entered into history.

Poetry can only be composed from that which the poet feels and experiences truthfully within his heart, whereby the language will reveal the words to him half consciously and half unconsciously. But where the poet, who works alone, can easily—and almost always does—go astray is in the sense of the right proportion of all the elements. This sense of proportion is, however, instilled by itself in all folk poetry. Over-refined foods are repugnant to the members of the folk, who are considered unpoetic because they are fortunately not consciously aware of their own quiet poetry. Educated people who are never satisfied have sought not only to mix untruths with history, they have also sought to do the same with the inviolable store of legends, overstuffing it with untruths in the attempt to pass it off for something it is not. Yet the appeal of indomitable truth remains infinitely more powerful and longer lasting than all fabrication because it never compromises itself and it remains undaunted.

There is such a refreshing power of surprise inherent in these folk legends that the most extravagant power of an individual's imagination would ultimately be put to shame by it. And a comparison of the two would produce a difference as pronounced as comparing two plants, one thought up and designed by an individual, and a newly found real one not yet observed by botanists, but one that could justify itself by producing the most singular borders, petals, and pistula, or that could confirm what had already been observed in other plants. The legends offer an abundance of similar comparisons among themselves and with others that have been preserved by ancient writers. For this reason their innermost essence must never be violated, not even in trivial details, and all material and all circumstances must be faithfully recorded. It has thus been our task to follow the exact words as faithfully as was feasible, but not necessarily to adhere slavishly to them.

### 3. *The Diversity of the Collection*

The second main requirement, and one that was already included in the first in regard to a collection of legends, consists of guaranteeing both the diversity and the characteristic nature of the materials. For the depth and breadth of the collection are based thereon, and from this alone will the investigator be able to probe its very nature.

In epics, in the folk song, and in language itself the same elements recur incessantly; sometimes an epic and a song will share an entire sentence in common, other times it will be individual lines and expressions. Sometimes the opening lines, and other times the closing lines, will be different, paving the way for new measures and transitions. No matter how great the similarity may be, in no case is one totally identical to another. In one case the song will be fully developed and long, in another it will be shorter and exist in underdeveloped poverty. Yet this very poverty—since it is innocent—always finds compensation in its own distinctiveness, and it becomes a blissful poverty.

If we observe language closely, we see that it is graduated in infinite, immeasurable rows and series, revealing extinct roots alongside prospering ones. Language also shows us compounded words next to simple ones and others that have acquired new meanings as well as those that have yielded their place to words with related meanings. This dynamic quality of language can be traced down to the tone and color of individual syllables and sounds.

Which elements among this great diversity are better or more to the point can scarcely be determined, and any attempt to do so may be impossible, and even sinful, inasmuch as we do not wish to lose sight of the fact that the source from which they have all flowed is none other than the divine spring, beyond comprehension in its dimensions, infinite in its emanations. And since the sunlight shines upon the great and the small, helping all as much as is fitting, then the strong and the weak, the sprouts and buds, ruin and decay exist alongside of and intermingled with each other. It is therefore of no particular import that one encounters similarities and repetitions in our book, for the idea that an imperfect diversity could have worked its way free from complete perfection seems to us extremely reprehensible as that kind of perfection does not belong to this world, but must necessarily be God himself from whom, flowing, everything returns.

Had we not rescued these legends that were similar to others, their special nature and their very lives would have been lost. Nor have we attempted to make the poor legends rich—neither by joining several short ones together, which to be sure, would have preserved the contents but lost all the tailoring and the coloring, nor by illicit garnishing, which can neither be justified nor excused—and which will necessarily remain forever alienated from that inscrutable idea of the complete original form from which these fragments have come.

This collection is not intended to be a reading text in the sense that one might sit down and read it from cover to cover. Rather, each of the legends is an entity unto itself and has no actual connection with those preceding and following it. He who seeks out and selects materials from the collection will find both satisfaction and pleasure. Incidentally, it hardly need be said that—as much as we sought to preserve the living diversity of the collection—the rendering of a complete legend from several versions by eliminating all nonessential varying forms was left to the unerring critical sense that became instilled in us automatically.

## 4. The Arrangement of the Collection

In the arrangement of the individual legends of the collection, we would once again have preferred to follow in the footsteps of Nature herself, who never marks off rigid and easily recognizable borders. In the realm of poesie there are only a few general categories; all others are simply wrong and forced, and even those main categories touch upon and overlap one another. The separation of history, legends, and fairy tales is obviously justified and necessary. Yet, there are times when one cannot determine to which of these categories a given narrative belongs, as for example, when Mother Holla appears in both legends and fairy tales, or when a legendary circumstance might also have actually occurred in history.

In the legends themselves, only one criterion—one that would have to be taken into consideration in any superficial classification of legends—was considered. It involved separating those legends associated more with history from those associated more with specific locales. The former we have set aside to be included in the second volume of our collection. The local legends, however, could have been further divided along the lines of regions, periods, or content. A classification by regions would have formed groups of legends classified by landscape, which in turn would have called attention to the migration that some kinds of legends have undergone. Yet in this procedure it is evident that one would at least have had to rely upon the present-day division of Germany. According to this, for example, Meißen would now be considered part of Saxony, whereas a large portion of the actual Saxony—now called Hannover—is all jumbled into smaller individual units.

We also would have liked to base a regional classification not on mountain ranges and rivers, but according to the regions inhabited by the various branches of the Teutonic peoples, regardless of political boundaries. In this regard, however, there has been so little solid and reliable study carried out that one would first have to help pave the way for such an undertaking with a far more careful investigation of regional dialects and legends, which until now have, for similar reasons, been so maligned and neglected. That which might ultimately result from this kind of investigation obviously cannot be used at this time to determine its direction.

Furthermore, the attempt to attribute a greater antiquity to some legends over others would be very difficult and would, for the most part, lead to misconceptions since legends are constantly being reborn. The Dwarf legends and the Giant legends, for example, clearly have the tinge of a heathen past. However, in the many legends about structures built by the Devil, one merely need substitute the word *Thurst* or Giant for Devil in order to bestow upon such tales the status of great antiquity.

In actuality this antiquity is determined by features other than names. The same can also be said of the feminine personal name Jette, reminiscent of the older form *Jöten*, or Giants. By the same token, the legends of witches and spooks could be labeled the most recent since they are the ones that are most frequently brought up to date, and when observed locally, appear to be less fixed in form than others. In actuality, however, they are basically the most ineradicable of all legends because of their constant and close relationship with the activities of humans. This factor can in no way serve as proof of their recent origin. It would merely prove that these legends will outlast all others, chiefly because of the superstitious proclivity of human nature which expects more in the way of good and evil from witches and sorcerers than from Dwarfs and Giants. But it is precisely these legends, almost alone, that have found their way from the folk to educated classes. These examples suffice to show why it would be untenable to attempt a chronological classification of legends.

There is, moreover, the difficulty occasioned by the fact that, in each legend, the most diverse elements have grown together organically, and it would take continuing investigation to sort them out. This kind of study would not merely conclude with the differentiation of individual legends but would, in turn, have to concern itself with the details within the legends to cast true light upon the problem.

Finally, this last reason also speaks out decisively against a classification based on content, according to which, for example, one would list all the Dwarf legends, or all the legends about sunken cities, etc., under individual headings. Obviously, only a very few of the legends are concerned with just one of these themes. In actuality, each legend shows manifold relationships and connections with others. Therefore the arrangement of legends that seemed to us the most natural and advantageous was one that would, while providing the requisite freedom and alleviating the need to grope around, lead one unaware to those obscure yet strangely prevailing transitions.

The classification scheme is also entirely in character with the necessarily incomplete nature of the collection. Thus, one will frequently encounter a legend that has either a distinct or a faint allusion to the preceding one, and those that bear a superficial resemblance will be grouped together. Yet, a grouping will also come to a sudden halt, only to re-emerge, for various reasons, elsewhere in the volume.

Many other arrangements of the same body of tales could have been attempted without hesitation, if other relationships had been taken into account. All of them, however, would yield only a few examples of that inexhaustible force which shapes and differs one legend from another, one trait from another, as organically as Nature herself.

## 5. Explanatory Commentary

We have chosen to dispense with an addendum of commentary of the kind that we provided for the two volumes of the *Kinder- und Hausmärchen* (*Household Tales*) because our space was too limited, and also because a number of the relationships will not be immediately and easily discernible until we have reached a tentative conclusion to our collecting activity. An exhaustive treatise on German legendry, as much as will remain within our powers, will be reserved for the future and for the publication of a separate volume. It is our plan not only to attempt a comprehensive survey of all of German legendry in the three unities of time, place, and action but also to pursue our analysis in other directions as well.

## 6. The Sources of the Collection

It has been ten years since we laid the groundwork for this collection (see *Zeitung für Einsiedler oder Trösteinsamkeit*, 19–20, Heidelberg, 1808), and we have worked incessantly ever since. We have collected from written sources, excerpting materials from books of the sixteenth and seventeenth centuries—many of which have since become exceedingly rare—and, above all, from oral sources as well, where we acquired living narrative traditions.

Among the written sources, the most significant for us were the works of Johannes Prätorius, who wrote in the second half of the seventeenth century. With tasteless yet perspicacious erudition, he was able to combine his sense for legends and for superstitions, which led him to draw materials directly from bourgeois life itself. Indeed, without the legends and superstitions—and he was certainly never aware of this fact—his countless works would have seemed barren and worthless to later generations. To him we owe our knowledge of many of the interrelated legends that follow the course of the Saale River to the shores of the Elbe, where the rivers join, and of those legends that were extant among the folk of the regions of Magdeburg and the Altmark. Many later writers have copied material right out of Prätorius without bothering to mention his name, and only rarely do we find someone achieving similar distinction by gathering his own materials from the oral tradition.

In the long period between Prätorius and the collection by Otmar (1800), for example, there appeared not a single significant book with folk legends, and only occasionally do we find an individual item here or there. A few years before Otmar, we do find Musäus and Lady Naubert at least drawing attention to a few basic legends in their literary treatment of material that came in part from written sources and in part from oral tradition.

Otmar certainly deserves much praise for the refreshing and reliable quality of his collection of legends from the Harz Mountains. His accomplishment most certainly outweighs the chidings he received for having added unnecessary trimmings and stylistic adornments. Many of his legends are—even in the details of wording—beyond reproach, and one may place one's full trust in them.

Ever since Otmar published his collection, interest in legends has been fermenting, and on occasion, demands for collecting activity have been sounded. But nothing of significance has been collected until now—disregarding the quite recent (1815) publication of a dozen Swiss legends by Wyß, who wove the narratives skillfully into longer poems. Despite the talent he revealed in so doing, we nevertheless discern a dulling effect on what was once exquisitely simple poetry that was in no way in need of this kind of help.

In accordance with our own objectives, we have endeavored to deliver these legends from their new costumes and to return them to their naked truth and innocence, a task made considerably easier by the commentary that Wyß appended. These legends, together with an equal number—or even a few more—that we extracted from the Otmar collection, proved to be indispensable for our objective and our ideal of completeness. Some, however, had to be compared with legends from other sources and corrected and returned to their original, simple style.

There are, in addition, two new collections to be mentioned, one by Büsching (1812) and one by Gottschalk (1814). The former has been extended to cover foreign legends as well as indigenous fairy tales, saints' legends, songs, and even some speculations about other legends, such as the one about Spangenberg. It thus covers a very broad and ill-defined expanse.

Taken together, both collections owe no more than twelve legends, not previously known, to oral sources. These would have been worked into our collection if the collecting activity for both works were not still in progress, and if plans did not already exist for continuing work on both editions. We thus have kept our hands off of both collections. However, in cases where we had already copied legends from the same sources that both men used, or the same legends from other sources, we certainly did not want to discard these excerpts.

After giving the matter sincere consideration, we found that we had collected with greater rigor and with greater care than had they. Both of them, moreover, have presented historical legends mixed in with local legends, whereas we have set aside several hundred of the former for publication in the next volume. We have no intention of interfering in or of disturbing other people's work and instead wish them both fruitful continuation of their efforts. But we also wish them—especially Gottschalk—greater critical facility for deleting false and counterfeit items. The treatise by Dobeneck (1815) on superstition in the Middle Ages, which covers all of Europe, generally has objectives different from our own. Moreover, it restricts itself—much to its own detriment—to so-called superstitions. In summary, one can say the work is a significant, if immature, survey of folk poetry and is only incidentally a collection. We have not rejected any of those items excerpted from Prätorius that happen to overlap with those published by Dobeneck. In the meantime the work will suffice to inspire and recommend others to study this poetry.

Finally, we wish to state expressly that we intentionally did not make use of the many legends of the mountain spirit Rübezahl, which we felt could be more suitably published in a separate work. We furthermore decided not to publish a large body of Rhine River legends in our collection after we received word from Voigt that he was planning to publish an edition of such materials in Frankfurt during the current year.

## 7. Hopes and Objectives

We recommend our book to devotees of German poesie, history, and language and hope that it will be welcome to all as purely German fare. For it is our firm belief that nothing is as edifying or as likely to bring more joy than the products of the Fatherland. Indeed, an apparently insignificant, self-occasioning discovery and endeavor in the study of our own indigenous culture can in the end bring more fruit than the most brilliant discovery and cultivation of foreign fields. In the latter case, there is always an element of uncertainty in the harvest that tends to become intensified and that is cold to human embrace. We feel that now is the time for us to step forth with our collection and to adjudge it to be sufficiently complete and diverse, first, to excuse any unavoidable deficiencies; second, to awaken in our readers an awareness of the degree to which we need their assistance in finishing our work; and third, to assure them that we will not abuse their trust.

All beginnings are difficult, and we feel that our collection is indeed quite deficient in a significant portion of German legends. And even among those we have included, many would have been better and more precisely recorded from the mouths of the folk. We may also have missed some important materials scattered in travel journals of the preceding century. Our experience has also shown us that the attempt to gather materials through letters and circulars yields little or nothing until we can show through the example of a published collection the kinds of apparently trivial things, formerly held in contempt, with which we are concerned.

But the business of collecting, as soon as one has acquired the sincere desire to engage in it, is soon worth the effort. And the discoveries border on the innocent joy of childhood, surprising a bird brooding on its nest amid moss and shrubbery.

In regard to our legends, here too one must quietly lift the leaves and carefully bend back the bough so as not to disturb the folk, if one wishes to steal a furtive glance into the strange yet modest world of nature, nestled into itself, and smelling of fallen leaves, meadow grass, and fresh-fallen rain. We will be grateful for any communication in this regard, and take this opportunity to publicly thank our brother, Ferdinand Grimm, as well as our friends August von Haxthausen and Carove, for supporting us so diligently.

Kassel, 14 March 1816

# PREFACE TO THE THIRD EDITION

## HERMAN GRIMM

Jacob and Wilhelm Grimm did not want their *German Legends* to be known as an entertaining reading text. And, indeed, it has not been regarded as such from the time it appeared until the present. A period of almost fifty years elapsed from the time of its initial appearance to their deaths. Then another quarter of a century passed before the reprint of 1865 was exhausted. This new edition, however, is being directed at a different audience, indeed, perhaps to that audience that the brothers had quietly hoped for in 1816. It is my wish that the book will now be read by Germans everywhere, and that it will open our world of legends especially to German-Americans.

In order to offer the work to the people more as a reading text, I have taken the notations of sources, originally listed after each individual title (and where they also appeared in the 1865 edition), and moved them to the table of contents. I have furthermore appended additional commentary that the brothers themselves assembled through the years and have furnished them with square brackets.* The few additions that had been appended to the notes of the 1865 edition are also repeated here, but without any identifying marks. The consecutive numbering system of the legends also follows the 1865 edition, when a number of legends the brothers assembled after the appearance of the first edition were added. Most of the

*Since these addenda have been culled from the posthumous papers of the brothers themselves it was felt that the brackets were superfluous, and they have not been included in this English translation.—*D. W.*

additional notes found were written in Jacob's hand, and most of them are from the earlier period. *The German Legends* appeared in those years when the brothers were still working exclusively as a team, so that the participation of each on the works of that period can indeed be recognized by their individual thoughts but not by the materials. Had they later revised the work, which they hardly considered seriously, it perhaps would have been undertaken exclusively by Wilhelm, inasmuch as it was he alone who was responsible for the later editions of the fairy tales.

The Brothers Grimm turned early in their careers to Berlin for the publication of their books. The first edition of the fairy tales appeared there. *The German Legends* too were, from the beginning, handled by the Nicolai Publishing House. Volume I appeared in 1816 ("typesetting finished in early May" is written in Jacob's hand on the title page), and the second volume in 1818.

There is nothing on the title page of the first volume to indicate that it is Volume I in a series, yet the "Foreword" states explicitly that the brothers considered it the beginning of a longer work. When Wilhelm was in Kassel in 1815 attending to the publication of the first volume, Jacob was in Paris, where he purchased editions of Gregory of Tours and of other early authors. Deeply stirred by their contents, he immediately resolved to include them in the next volume of the legends. The planned third volume, discussed in the foreword to the second volume and which was to include a critical analysis of the entire corpus (as was the case in the third volume of the fairy tales), never materialized.

The special place the work still occupies today results above all from the manner of narration, for there was no one who could recite the epic events of the Fatherland with such conviction as Jacob and Wilhelm Grimm. Each of them had his own style of narrating. The most perfect of Jacob's compositions of this kind was his summary of the contents of *The Lay of Waltharius*, while it was Wilhelm who endowed the fairy tales with their characteristic style. Each of their styles, as different as they appear when compared, complement each other, as when the separate tones of two bells join together in harmony. *The German Legends* will live on into future centuries in the language that Jacob and Wilhelm Grimm have bestowed upon them.

I now conclude by repeating the words that the Nicolai Publishing House used when they announced the publication of the first volume in 1816:

> Much in the way the child has his own fairy-tale world and believes in it—and into whose realm of marvels even the adult longingly seeks to transport himself in his thoughts—the folk too have their own

characteristic world of legends bestowed upon them as a companion of
their homeland, and to which they are attached in intimate love. These
venerable and delightful tones echoing from an earlier existence of the
folk speak to us as friendly companions wherever we set our wandering
staff in German lands. In this volume the Brothers Grimm have presented the myriad abundance of their collections. Around four hundred
legends of dwarfs, giants, mountain spirits, hobgoblins, nixies, witches,
elves, princes, legends of dragons, werewolves, of sunken palaces, and
many more are told in exquisite fashion.

Three things distinguish this collection from all others. First is the
fidelity and truth of the tales, reproduced as they were told in their
home settings, even to details of the words and the style. Second is the
diversity and breadth of the material. Third is the precise indication of
all the sources, whither they have come, and places where they are at
home. No other work is able to awaken and nurture both fear and
warning of evil and the most intimate joy in the good and the beautiful.
No other work can penetrate so deeply into the most intimate secrets
and the stirrings of the daily life of the folk. Many people will find
renewed devotion for their beloved German land through these legends.

This contemporary appraisal of the book reflects the joyous
spirit of the age in which it appeared. The succeeding years that
were to be marked by distrust of feelings and emotions, to which
Germany owes its liberation, had not yet dawned. In 1816, under
the aegis of the triumphs that had been fought for and won in
France, there prevailed an optimistic faith in the dawn of a new era
of intellectual and political greatness for the Fatherland, against
which, however—and now it can be said—the whole world of that
day had allied itself.

The age of the succeeding defeats of the nation would never
have been possible if German historical essence and German
thought and consciousness could have been made the foundation for
the education of the German people.

# THE GERMAN LEGENDS

## THE BROTHERS GRIMM

‡‡ 1 ‡‡

## THE THREE MINERS IN THE KUTTEN MINE

Three miners once worked the Kutten Mine in Bohemia. They toiled faithfully for many long years earning honest bread for their wives and children. Each morning when they left home for the mine they took three things with them: their prayer books, their lamps, with only enough oil for one day, and their day's bread. Before they began working, they prayed to God that he might protect them from the dangers of the mine, and thus comforted, they went on to perform their work diligently.

One day, just as they were finishing their work, the whole face of the mountain caved in, burying the entrance to the mine. Knowing they were trapped, they exclaimed: "O Lord! We poor miners have but one day's supply of oil in our lamps and only enough bread for one day. We must surely starve!" They then commended themselves to God and prepared to die. Yet they did not want to idle away their last hours, so they continued to do their work and to pray. And it came to pass that their lamps kept burning for seven years. And the small piece of bread, from which they ate daily, was never totally consumed. And they thought the seven years were only one day. Yet since they could cut neither their hair nor their beards, these grew very long. In the meantime their wives, convinced their husbands were dead, considered remarrying.

It then came to pass that one of the three miners made a wish from the bottom of his heart. "If I could only see the light of day once more, I would die happily." Then the second miner said, "If I could only sit with my wife once more at my table and eat with her, I would happily die!" And the third one spoke, "Oh, if I could only live one more year peacefully and happily with my wife, I would be happy to die."

No sooner had they uttered these words than the mountain thundered with great force and split asunder. The first miner ran to where the mountain had opened, looked up, and saw the blue sky above him. Standing there, overwhelmed by the beauty of the light of day, he suddenly sank to the ground—dead. Then the mountain gave another roar, and the split opened wider. The other two miners began digging stairs into the side of the mountain, and finally they crawled out.

They proceeded hastily to their village. But when they reached their homes they found that their wives did not recognize them. "Did you not have a husband?" each miner asked. "Yes," answered the wives, "but they have been dead for seven years, buried deep under the earth in the Kutten Mine!" The second miner then said to his wife, "I am your husband." But she did not believe him because his long beard made him look quite different than she remembered. He then said, "Fetch me the razor high in the wall cabinet, and bring me a piece of soap." Then he shaved off his beard and washed and combed his hair. And when he had finished, his wife saw that he was indeed her husband. She was overjoyed and brought food and drink to the table, and they sat down together and enjoyed their meal. The man ate his fill. But then, as he was swallowing the last bit of bread, he fell over dead.

The third miner lived a whole year in peaceful joy with his wife. But one year to the hour and day that he had crawled from the mine, he and his wife both sank to the floor dead.

Because the three miners had been pious and good, God granted each of them his final wish.


‡‡　2　‡‡

## THE MINE SPIRIT

From time to time, deep in the shafts of mines, there appears a gigantic figure clad in the black robe of a monk. He is called Meister Hämmerling, or more frequently Mine Monk.

He frequently appeared in the mine in the Graubünden Alps—especially on Fridays. There he was seen emptying the ores from one bucket into another and then back again. The owner of the mine was careful not to object to this activity, and the spirit responded in kind by never causing any trouble. But one miner became upset at this seemingly wasted effort, and he scolded and cursed at the spirit, whereupon the spirit grabbed the man and shook him violently. The man survived the attack, but from that day on he walked around with his face turned inside out!

Then there was this incident in the Anna Mine. Twelve men were working the Rosencranz shaft when the spirit suddenly appeared and breathed on them. All the miners dropped dead on the spot. This explains why this particular shaft, although rich in silver deposits, has never again been worked.

In the Anna Mine he appeared in the shape of a steed with a long neck and terrifying eyes, but in the St. George Mine in Schneeberg he appeared again as a black-clad monk. Here he seized an apprentice, lifted him up into a shaft rich in silver deposits, and set him down so violently that the youth injured all his limbs.

Another time in the Harz Mountains, the spirit punished a mean foreman who tormented the unfortunate miners. When the foreman was emerging from the shaft, the spirit positioned himself above the entrance where the man could not see him. As the foreman left the shaft, the spirit caught the man's head between his legs and crushed his skull.

‡‡　3　‡‡

## THE MINE MONK OF THE HARZ MOUNTAINS

There were once two miners who always worked as a team. One day when they arrived at the shaft where they were to work, they noticed that they didn't have enough oil in their lamps to last their shift. "What can we do?" they asked. "If we run out of oil before we get to the surface, we'll be in serious trouble, for the shaft is very dangerous. But if we run home for more oil, the foreman will punish us. And he'll enjoy it because he doesn't like us."

As they stood there wondering what to do, they saw a light coming toward them out of the distance. At first they were happy to see the light. But as it came closer, they received a terrible fright, for a monstrous figure, crouched over, was making his way up the shaft toward them. He wore a large hood and was clad like a monk, but he was carrying a large miner's lamp in his hand.

When he reached the two men, who stood frozen in fear, he straightened up and spoke to them. "Do not fear, I shall do you no harm, but rather good." He then poured oil from his lamp into theirs. Then he grabbed their tools and began to work the mine. In one hour he had mined more ore than they could have done in a week of diligent work. He then said, "Tell no one that you have seen me here," and he slammed his fist against the shaft wall, which shattered, revealing a long vein sparkling with pure gold and silver.

The unexpected glitter blinded the men and they turned their faces away. But when they turned to look again at the treasure—it had disappeared! Had they but thrown in a pick, or any one of their tools, the treasure chamber would have remained open. Fortune and honor would have been theirs. But all that passed when they turned their eyes away. Nevertheless, the oil from the spirit remained in their lamps, and the supply never diminished. This gave the two men a considerable advantage over the other miners.

One Saturday night, however, as the two of them were drinking with their friends in the tavern and having a good time, they told their whole story. Monday morning, as they prepared themselves for work, they saw that their supply of oil was exhausted. And from then on they had to replenish their lamps every day, just like all other miners.


## ‡‡ 4 ‡‡

## MOTHER HOLLA'S POND

Many landmarks in the Meißen Mountains of Hesse give testimony to great antiquity by their very names, such as Devil's Hole or Battle Meadows. But of all such places, the strangest is Mother Holla's Pond. It lies in one corner of a swampy meadow and is only about forty or fifty feet across. The entire meadow is encircled by a stone wall that has sunk halfway into the marshy ground. It is no rare occurrence for a horse to venture beyond the wall, only to sink out of sight.

The people tell many things about Mother Holla, both good and bad. Women who visit her by climbing into the spring have been made healthy and fertile. She is said to deliver newborn children from her well. She has flowers, fruits, and cakes in her underground realm. She distributes these and the produce from her marvelous gardens to those whom she meets—if she finds them to her liking.

Mother Holla is very tidy and keeps a neat household. When it snows in man's world then everyone knows that Mother Holla is shaking out her feather beds until the flakes drift around in the wind.

She punishes girls who are lazy at the spinning wheel by soiling their linens, tangling their yarn, even setting fire to their flax.

However, she rewards the hard-working girls by presenting them with new spindles and by doing their spinning for them at night. When these girls wake in the morning, they frequently find their spools full of newly spun yarn. But she also visits the lazy girls at night. She pulls the covers off their beds, carries them out into the night, and places them on cold, hard cobblestones where they wake up freezing.

Mother Holla also rewards hard-working maidens who at dawn fetch water from the wells in finely polished pails, by placing silver coins in their buckets. She likes to lure children into her pond—the good ones she rewards with success and fortune; the evil ones become changelings.

Each year, Mother Holla wanders around the countryside bestowing fertility on the fields. However, she can also strike terror into the hearts of the people when she roars through the forests, leading raging hordes.

Sometimes she appears as the beautiful White Woman, floating or hovering above the surface of her pond. At other times, however, she is invisible. Then one hears only the pealing of her bells and other dark rumblings from deep beneath the surface.


## ‡‡ 5 ‡‡

## MOTHER HOLLA ROAMS ABOUT

At Christmastime Mother Holla begins to roam the countryside. It is then that all village maidens remount the distaffs on their spinning wheels and wind new flax or tow onto them. They then let them stand over night. Mother Holla rejoices when she sees such things, and she exclaims:

> As many hairs as I can see,
> So many good years there will be!

She continues her nightly wanderings until the Great New Year, that is, the Holy Day of the Three Kings, at which time she must return to her home in Horsel Mountain. If at this time she encounters a distaff with flax on it she becomes angry, and says:

> As many hairs as I can see,
> So many bad years there will be!

This is why all girls will carefully remove from their distaffs all the flax that has not yet been spun at the end of the day. For if even one strand remains, evil may befall a girl. Best of all, however, is when they manage to spin all the flax from the distaff before their day's work is done.

## ‡‡ 6 ‡‡
## MOTHER HOLLA'S BATH

Near the Meißen Mountains in Hesse there lies a large muddy pond, or lake, called Mother Holla's Bath. According to the stories of old people, Mother Holla is sometimes seen at midday, bathing in this pond. When she finishes, she always disappears.

The mountains and the moors of this entire area are filled with spirits. Many a traveler and hunter have been led astray or otherwise harmed by them.

## ‡‡ 7 ‡‡
## MOTHER HOLLA AND FAITHFUL ECKART

There is a village in Thuringia called Schwarza where Mother Holla was seen at Christmastime, leading her hordes through the area. At the head of the troop was Faithful Eckart, who warned all the people to get out of the way so no harm would befall them.

At the local tavern two peasant youths had just bought some beer that they were going to carry home, when Mother Holla's horde came into view. The troop of ghosts filled the wide street so the two youths, still holding their beer pitchers, cowered in a corner. Various women from the horde approached them, took the pitchers, and drank from them. The youths remained silent out of fear, but they worried about what would happen to them when they arrived home with empty pitchers.

Finally, Faithful Eckart stepped forward and spoke, "God commanded you not to say a word, otherwise your necks would have been wrung. Now hasten home. Tell no one what has happened and your pitchers will always be full of beer and will never break."

The youths did as they were told, and it came to pass that the pitchers remained full. The boys maintained their silence for three days, but finally they could keep their secret no longer. Curious to see what would happen, they told their parents all that had transpired. That did it! The beer dried up in the pitchers.

Others have reported that the event occurred not at Christmas but at some other time.

## MOTHER HOLLA AND THE PEASANT

Mother Holla was once abroad in the countryside when she encountered a peasant with an ax. She addressed the man, instructing him to wedge and board up her carriage. The worker did as he was commanded, and when he was finished, she said, "Gather up the shavings and take them as your reward." Then she rode off in her carriage.

The wood shavings seemed worthless to the man, so he left most of them lying there and took only two or three with him. When he arrived home and reached into his sack, the shavings had become pure gold. The man immediately went back to gather up the shavings he'd left. But search as he might, it was too late. None could be found.

‡‡  9  ‡‡

## THE SPURGE ROOT

Many years ago a shepherd was tending his flock on Köter Mountain. Turning, he saw a splendid royal maiden standing before him. She spoke, saying, "Take the spurge root and follow me."

The spurge root can only be obtained by going to the nest of a green flicker—or a magpie, or hoopoe—and wedging it shut with a piece of wood. When the bird sees this it will fly away, for it knows where to find the wondrous root that man seeks in vain. It will fly back, bringing the root in its beak in order to gain entry to its nest. When it holds the root before the wooden wedge, the wedge jumps out as though it had been struck by the hardest blow. If one hides and waits until the bird returns and then makes a great noise, the bird will drop the root in fear. One can also spread a white or red cloth under the nest, and the bird will drop the root after using it to dislodge the wedge.

Now, the shepherd, who owned such a root, let his flock roam by itself and followed the maiden. She led him through a cave and into the mountain. Whenever they came to a door or sealed passage, the shepherd would hold out his root and the entrance would crash open.

And thus they continued until they entered a chamber about midway into the mountain. Two maidens were sitting there, spinning industriously. The Evil One was also there, but he was powerless for he lay bound beneath the table where the girls worked. All around were baskets filled with gold and brilliant gems, and the royal maiden spoke to the shepherd who was eyeing the treasures greedily. "Take as much as you want." With hesitation the shepherd dug into the baskets and filled his pockets as full as he could.

Richly laden, he was about to depart, when she said, "But do not forget the best of all." He thought she meant the treasures, and he felt he had already provided himself with sufficient riches. However, it was the spurge root she had meant. When he left the chamber without the root, the door slammed behind him with such a crash it almost caught his heels. He was unharmed, but it could have cost him his life.

The shepherd succeeded in bringing his riches home. But never again was he able to find the entrance to the mountain chamber.

## ‡‡  10  ‡‡

### THE MAIDEN OF BOYNE CASTLE

Many years ago the fortress at Boyne was inhabited by three young maidens. One night the youngest sister dreamed that it was fated by God himself that one of the three was to die in a storm. When morning came, the youngest told her sisters what she had dreamed. And by midday clouds were forming in the heavens, growing even larger and darker. By evening a threatening thunderstorm was moving across the skies, covering them completely.

When lightning filled the heavens with fire, the oldest sister said, "I wish to obey God's will, for I am fated for death." She had a chair carried outside, and she sat in it for a day and a night waiting for the lightning to strike her. But not a single bolt hit.

The following day, the second sister descended the stairs, saying, "I will submit to God's will, for I am fated for death." She spent the second day and the second night in the chair, but the lightning did not strike her either.

On the third day the youngest sister spoke. "I see it is God's will that I am the one to die." She sent for the priest, who administered the Sacrament to her. Then she made her last will and testament, which provided that the entire community would be given food and drink on the day of her death. Having done this, she descended the stairs peacefully and sat down in the chair. Within a few moments a bolt of lightning flashed down and killed her.

In later times, when the castle was no longer inhabited, she appeared time and again as a benevolent spirit. Once, a good shepherd, who had lost all his wealth and possessions, and whose very last belongings were about to be repossessed for debts, was tending his flock near the castle of Boyne. He turned his glance to the castle and there, sitting in front of the entrance, was a young maiden, white as snow. She had spread a white cloth before her upon which she scattered flower buds so they would open in the sunlight.

The shepherd wondered at seeing a maiden in such a lonesome place. He walked up to her and said, "What beautiful blossoms." Taking a few buds in his hand, he looked at them and then put them down again. The maiden gave him a friendly yet sad look but did not respond to his words. Then fear overtook the shepherd, and he ran away without turning around, driving his flock home before him.

However, a few of the buds had fallen into his shoes while he was standing among them. Soon they began to hurt his feet, and he stopped along the way to empty his shoes. As he did so, five or six gold nuggets fell into his hand. The shepherd hastened back to the castle, but the white maiden and her flower buds had disappeared. The shepherd still had enough gold to pay all his debts and set up house again.

Many treasures are said to be still hidden in the castle. One man was particularly fortunate. He saw a pigeonhole in the wall of the castle and opened it. It was full of gold.

A widow, who had only a cow and goat to her name, once went to the castle wall to gather some sweet nettles for fodder. But as she was reaching for a cluster of the greens, she slipped and fell deep into the earth. She screamed and called for help, but there was not a single soul in the desolate region. That evening, her children became frightened when she did not return, and they went to the castle. And there they heard her voice. When the children pulled her to the surface with ropes, she told them that down deep where she had fallen there was a door of iron bars behind which she had seen a table completely covered with riches and wares of solid silver.

‡‡ 11 ‡‡

## PIEL MOUNTAIN

Outside the town of Annaberg in Meißen, there is a high peak called Piel Mountain where a beautiful maiden was cursed and burned to death. She is said to appear there frequently at midday—and that is the reason no one ever goes there at that time. The maiden is a beautiful figure and wears her long golden hair tied behind her.

## THE MAIDEN OF THE CASTLE

It is said that a maiden appears from time to time at Castle Mountain not far from the town of Ohrdruf in Thuringia. She is reported to carry a large ring of keys. At twelve noon she always appears and comes down the mountain. She proceeds to Hörling Spring in the valley below, where she bathes herself, and then goes back up the mountain. A number of people claim to have seen her and to have watched her closely.

## THE SNAKE MAIDEN

In the city of Basel around the year 1520 there lived a young man named Leonhard, commonly called Lienimann. He was the son of a tailor and was a foolish, simple fellow. He stuttered, and speaking was a real problem for him.

Lienimann once wandered through the underground vault or tunnel that leads from Augst, above Basel, deep into the earth. He went further through this passageway than anyone had ever thought possible, and when he returned he told of many wondrous happenings.

He reported—and there are people still around who heard it from his own mouth—that he took a consecrated candle, lit it, and descended into the vault. First he passed through an iron gateway, and then through one vault after another, and finally through beautiful and cheerful green gardens. In the center of the gardens stood a splendid palace. Within, there was a beautiful maiden. On her head she wore a crown of gold, and her hair flowed to the ground. Her body was human to her waist; but from there down she was a dreadful snake.

The Snake Maiden led the youth by the hand to an iron chest upon which lay two black dogs who barked so threateningly that no one could come near. The maiden, however, quieted the dogs and kept them in check so that Lienimann could approach the chest unhindered. She then took a ring of keys from around her neck and opened the chest. She lifted out coins of silver and other precious metals, and with remarkable kindness, presented him with no small amount. He brought the coins with him when he emerged from the vault and showed them to people.

The maiden is also said to have spoken to him. She told him that she came of a royal family and dynasty but had been transformed by a wicked spell into a monster. The spell could only be broken if a youth, whose chastity was pure and undefiled, kissed her three times—only then would she regain her human form. She would then present the entire treasure buried there to her deliverer.

He told how he kissed her two times. Each time, in great anticipation for the unhoped-for miracle, the maiden made such dreadful gestures that he feared she was going to tear him to pieces. He, therefore, did not dare kiss her a third time and instead departed in haste.

It then happened that a few youths took him to a brothel where he sinned with a frivolous woman. Thus tainted with sin, he was never again able to find the entrance to the underground vault, and he often lamented this tearfully.

## ‡‡   14   ‡‡

### THE HEAVY CHILD

On the eighth day of June in 1686 two noblemen were on their way to the city of Chur in Switzerland when they spied an infant wrapped in linen lying under a bush. One of the pair, feeling compassion, ordered a servant to climb down from the carriage and fetch the child so they could bring it to the next village and arrange care for it. But when the servant seized the child and tried to lift it, he found that he could not.

The two noblemen were astonished to see this, and they ordered a second servant to step down and help. But both together could not move the child.

After they had labored for some time, heaving and tugging, the child began to speak. "Let me lie here, for I cannot be moved from the earth. I will, however, tell you that this will be a rich and fruitful year—but few people will live to see it!" No sooner had the child spoken these words than it disappeared.

The two noblemen and their servants reported the incident to the officials in Chur.

## ‡‡   15   ‡‡

### THE OLD WINE CELLAR OF SALURN

In the City Hall of the small Tyrolean village of Salurn on the Etsch River, there are two wine bottles on display. The following story is told about them.

In the year 1688, Christoph Patzeber was walking from St. Michael to Salurn to take care of some business. When he passed the ruins of the old castle, he felt a yearning to have a closer look inside the stone walls. While looking around in the upper part, he found a stairway leading underground. It appeared to be well illuminated, so he descended and soon found himself in an attractive cellar, lined with large casks. Rays of sunlight shone through cracks in the wall, so he was able to count exactly eighteen barrels. He calculated that each contained at least one hundred gallons. Each cask was equipped with a spigot and a spout, and in his playful inquisitiveness he turned the handle of one. To his amazement wine flowed as rich as oil. He found it to have a splendid flavor, the likes of which he had never tasted before. He would have been delighted to take some home to his wife and children, but he had no container for carrying it.

A familiar legend crossed Patzeber's mind that told of riches being bestowed on many an unsuspecting man in this castle. He wondered and wondered if he could make his fortune off this happy discovery. He took the road to town, completed his business, and then he purchased two large earthenware bottles and a funnel. He then returned to the castle, arriving before sunset. He found everything just as it had been before. Without hesitation, he filled both bottles, each holding about twenty measures.

But as he turned to leave, he suddenly saw three old men seated at a small table blocking the stairs. On the table was a black slate covered with chalk marks. Patzeber gave a terrible start and would gladly have left all the wine if he could have escaped. He began to pray fervently and asked the masters of the cellar for their forgiveness. One of the three, who had a long beard and wore a leather cap and a black coat, spoke to him. "Come as often as you like, and you shall receive what you and your family need." And then the entire apparition disappeared.

Patzeber left the cellar without hindrance, arrived home safely, and told his wife everything that had happened. At first she would not touch the wine, but when she saw her husband delighting in it without the slightest harm, she too tried it. Soon she was serving it to everyone in the house. When the supply ran out, he simply took the bottles to the cellar and refilled them. This continued for a whole year. The splendid beverage, fit for a king's table, cost him not a penny.

One day, however, three neighbors visited him. When they found his wine so excellent, they grew suspicious and wondered if he had acquired it by evil means. Since they were ill-disposed toward him anyway, they went immediately to the City Hall and filed a complaint against him. The citizen appeared when he was summoned and did not conceal how he had acquired the wine, although

he thought to himself that he had n...
council sent for the wine and the jud...
another like it in the land.

Although Patzeber was released a...
court ordered him to retrace his steps,...
the castle cellar. But when he got ther...
the cellar could be found. He then fell...
by some invisible hand. Lying there...
again saw the cellar, but it was far aw...
He could see the three men sitting th...
ing by lamplight on the slate with...
though they had to close an important...
all the figures, drew a cross on the sla...
of them got up, unlocked three locks on an iron door, and one could
hear the sounds of clinking coins. This same old man then climbed
another stairway, walked up to Patzeber, who was lying there, and
dropped thirty taler into his hat, still without uttering a sound. The
apparition disappeared just as the City Hall clock struck eleven.

Patzeber dragged himself to his knees and crawled through the
walls of the castle. Outside he saw a funeral procession with lanterns moving up the hill, and he realized this was an omen of his
own death.

By and by, he made it to the road, and he waited for someone to
help him home. When he arrived, the council was waiting for him.
He told them what had happened and showed them the thirty ancient coins. They proved beyond question that he was telling the
truth, for it was clear the coins were from no earthly source.

The next day the council sent eight bold men to the castle to
investigate. They found no trace of stairway or cellar. However, in a
corner of the courtyard, they found two earthenware bottles and
brought them back as evidence.

Ten days later Patzeber died. He had paid the bill for his wine
with his life. Perhaps that cross on the slate foretold the ten days left
to him on earth.


‡‡ 16 ‡‡

## THE GAME OF THE GIANTS

Near the town of Höxter, between Godelheim and Amelunxen, lie
the two mountains of Brunsberg and Wiltberg. It is said the Saxons
built twin fortresses here during their struggles with Charlemagne.
According to the legend told by the people of Godelheim, Giants
once lived there. These Giants were so enormous that when they got

, they greeted each other by shaking hands across
rating the two castles. They played ball by throwing
each other from mountain to mountain. One of these
nce fell into the valley and left a huge hole in the ground
still be seen. It is called Boulder Meadow.
These Giants reigned supreme in that land, until a powerful,
arlike people arrived and did battle with them. The war was so
terrible that blood flooded the valley, until the Weser River ran
bright red. The Giants were all slain and their fortresses conquered.
The invaders then reigned over the entire region.

According to another tale, each day, the Giant of Brun Mountain sent the Giant of Wilt Mountain a letter wrapped in a huge ball of yarn. And thus they corresponded by throwing the ball back and forth across the valley. One day, however, the ball of yarn fell into the Lauh Forest near Braunberg, and a large pond formed in the depression where hundreds of white lilies still grow. To this very day, the White Woman comes to the pond at Easter to wash herself.

‡‡ 17 ‡‡

## THE GIANT'S TOY

Next to a waterfall on a high mountain in Alsace stands Nideck Castle. In early times the knights who inhabited this castle were Giants. One day a Giant maiden, who decided to see what life was like down in the valley, walked down the mountain almost as far as Haslach. Hard by the forest she came to a field just being plowed by some farmers. Her eyes filled with wonderment as she stopped to look at the plow, the horses, and the men. The whole tableau was quite new to her. "Oh," she said as she approached, "I'm going to take it all home with me." She knelt down, spread out her apron, and stroked her arm along the ground, sweeping everything into her apron. She then made her way happily back to the castle, leaping up the steep cliffs. Near the summit, where the face of the mountain is so sheer a man could scale it only with great difficulty, the Giant maiden gave a single bound and was at the top.

The knight was sitting at the table when she entered the castle. "Ah, my child," he said, "what have you there? You can't hide the joy in your eyes." She quickly opened her apron and let her father look in. "What are those wiggly things you have there?"

"Oh, Father, it's such a marvelous toy! I have never had anything like it in my whole life." She then removed each item one by one—the plow, the farmers, the horses—and set them on the table. Then she ran to the other side to look at her display. When the little creatures began moving back and forth she clapped her hands together and laughed with great joy.

However, her father spoke sharply to her, "Child, that is not a toy. Quickly now, carry them back down to the valley." The maiden began to weep, but to no avail. "For me, child, the farmer is not a toy," said the knight grimly, "and I will have no more of your whimpering! Pack all these things gently into your apron and return them to the exact place from which you took them. If the farmer cannot plow his fields we Giants up here in our mountain nest will have nothing to eat."

‡‡   18   ‡‡

## THE ONE-MAN-ARMY GIANT

During the time of Charlemagne there lived a Giant, who was a knight by the name of "One-Man-Army." He was a Swabian, born in Thurgau, which is now in Switzerland. He was so big he never needed to use a bridge. He would simply wade across all lakes and rivers, pulling his horse by the tail behind him, while calling out, "Now, fellow, you'll just have to come along too."

The knight rode in Charlemagne's campaigns against the Wends and the Huns. In battle he mowed soldiers down like grass with his giant scythe. He would then skewer them on his spear and carry them over his shoulder as if they were foxes or hares.

Whenever he returned from battle, his neighbors and friends would ask what he had done and how the battle had gone. This always annoyed him and made him angry, and he would reply, "What am I to say about these little frogs? I carried seven or eight of them on my spear; don't know what they were croaking about. It's a waste of time and effort for the Emperor to assemble such a large army to fight such vermin. I could have done it much better all by myself."

The Giant was called One-Man Army because in battle he could accomplish as much as a whole army. All the enemy would flee when they saw him, and the Wends and Huns were convinced he was the Devil himself.

‡‡   19   ‡‡

## THE COLUMNS OF THE GIANTS

Near Miltenberg, or Kleinen-Haubach, one can see nine gigantic stone columns on a mountainside in the forest. One can also see the handholds the Giants used to turn the columns when they were building the bridge over Main River. Old people have been telling children this story for years, and they also say that once, many years ago, numbers of Giants lived in this region.

‡‡   20   ‡‡

## KÖTER MOUNTAIN

Köter Mountain, which lies on the border between the regions of Paderborn, Lippe, and Corvey, was once called Idol Mountain because the heathens used to worship their gods there. The interior of the mountain is full of gold and treasures that could make a poor man very rich—if he could get to it.

There are caves on the north side of the mountain, and a shepherd once found the entrance leading to the treasures. But just as he was about to enter, a horrible man, covered with blood, came running across a field and frightened the shepherd away.

To the south, on a forested hill, stood Harz Castle, the ruins of which can still be seen today. Not long ago someone found keys there. The castle used to be inhabited by Giants. On Mt. Zieren, two hours away, stood another castle also inhabited by Giants. These Giants used to amuse themselves by throwing their hammers back and forth between the two castles.

‡‡   21   ‡‡

## THE PALACE OF GEROLDSECK

In Wasgau there is an old palace called Geroldseck, and many a tale has been told concerning it. For example, it was said that ancient German heroes—the kings Ariovist, Hermann, Wittekind, the horned Siegfried, and many many others—could be seen there at certain times of the year. It was also said that they would appear with the old armies of the German nations to help whenever the Germans were in distress and faced defeat.

‡‡   22   ‡‡

## CHARLEMAGNE IN NÜRNBERG

According to legend, Charlemagne is condemned by his own curse to remain in the deep well at the castle in Nürnberg. His beard is said to have grown right through the stone table at which he sits.

## FREDERICK BARBAROSSA AT MT. KYFFHAUSEN

Many legends are told about Emperor Barbarossa. It is said that he is not yet dead; that no true emperor has ruled since his reign; and that he will live until Judgment Day. Until then he will remain concealed in Mt. Kyffhausen. When he emerges, he will hang his shield on a leafless tree, the tree will sprout green leaves, and a better age will begin.

Occasionally, he will talk to people who enter the mountain; at other times he can be seen on the outside. Usually, he sits on a bench at a round stone table, resting his head in his hand, sleeping—nodding his head and blinking his eyes. His beard has grown long, according to some, right through the stone table. But according to others, the beard grows around the table, and when it has encircled the table three times, it will be the time of his awakening. It has now grown around twice.

In 1669, a peasant was transporting grain from the village of Reblingen to Nordhausen. Along the way he was stopped by a Dwarf and led into the mountain. He was instructed to empty his grain sacks and fill them with gold. He saw the emperor sitting there, quite motionless.

Similarly, a shepherd, who was whistling a tune the emperor liked, was led into the mountain by a Dwarf. The emperor rose and asked him, "Are the ravens still flying around the mountain?" When the shepherd assured him that they were, he cried, "Now I am going to have to sleep for another hundred years."

## THE PEAR TREE OF WALSER FIELDS

A terrible battle is said to have been fought on Walser Fields near Salzburg. When the two armies collided, there was such a dreadful bloodbath that the blood on the ground filled the boots of the combatants—but the bad men were slain by the good.

A wizened pear tree still stands on Walser Fields as a remembrance of this final battle. Three times the tree has been chopped down, but each time its roots have produced new shoots and a full-grown tree has reappeared.

The tree remains bare for many years; but when it begins to sprout new leaves, a new battle is about to begin, and as soon as the tree bears fruit, the fighting will start. Then the Prince of Bavaria will appear and hang his coat of arms on the tree. No one will know what this means.

‡‡   25   ‡‡

## THE ENCHANTED KING OF SCHILDHEISS

In a desolate mountainous area of the German-speaking part of Bohemia stood the ancient castle of Schildheiß, which was to be rebuilt and restored. When the master builder and his workmen examined the foundation of the ruins, they discovered far more vaults, cellars, and passageways than they had anticipated.

In one of the vaults a powerful king, who glittered with jewels, sat in a large chair. At his right hand a beautiful maiden stood motionless, holding his head in such a way that it appeared to be resting in her hands. But when the workers approached, full of curiosity and greedily anticipating a rich booty, the girl changed into a fire-breathing serpent, and the men were forced to flee.

They reported the incident to the lord of the manor who went to investigate. Standing before the vault, he heard a woman's bitter sigh from within. Later he returned to the cave with his dog. But the cave was immediately filled with smoke and flame, and the knight, thinking his dog was lost, had to retreat. However, when the flames subsided, he saw the maiden holding the dog unharmed in her arms, and writing appeared on the stone wall threatening his life.

Later, his bravado drove him to dare the adventure again, but this time he was consumed by the flames.

‡‡   26   ‡‡

## CHARLEMAGNE'S EXODUS

Between Gudensberg and Besse in Hesse lies Mt. Odenberg, into which Emperor Charlemagne disappeared with his whole army. Before a war is to break out, the whole mountain will open up. Charlemagne will then come forth, blow on his horn, and move with his entire army into another mountain.

‡‡   27   ‡‡

## WONDER MOUNTAIN

On the shores of the bottomless Moos, just a short German mile from Salzburg, there lies Unter Mountain, or Wonder Mountain, as it is also called. Many years ago it was the site of the principality of

Helfenburg. The interior of the mountain has been hollowed out and equipped with palaces, churches, cloisters, and fountains of gold and silver. Dwarfs guard great treasures there, and they often venture into the city of Salzburg at midnight to hold their church services in the cathedral.

## ‡‡ 28 ‡‡
### EMPEROR CHARLES IN WONDER MOUNTAIN

Within Wonder Mountain Emperor Charles waits with other princes and eminent men. He wears his golden crown upon his head and holds his scepter in his hand. He sits upon the meadows of Walser Fields, and he has retained the human form he had during his life on earth. His grey beard is so long that it covers his golden breastplate completely. On special days and feast days his beard is parted in two halves, one on his right side and one on his left side, and both halves are entwined with strings of precious pearls. The countenance of the emperor is both keen and profound, and he is friendly and engaging toward his subjects, who walk with him back and forth across the beautiful meadow. Why he resides in the mountain and the purpose of his mission are unknown. These are among God's secrets.

According to Franz Sartori, it is Emperor Charles V—according to others it is Emperor Frederick—who sits at the table around which his beard is wrapped twice. However, as soon as his beard grows long enough to reach the last corner of the table for the third time, the days of the world will be at an end. The Antichrist will appear, a battle will rage on Walser Fields, the trumpets of the angels will sound, and the Day of Judgment will have begun.

## ‡‡ 29 ‡‡
### VON SCHERFENBERG AND THE DWARF

Mainhard, Count of Tyrol, following the orders of Emperor Rudolf von Hapsburg, conquered Styria and Carinthia, for which he was named Duke of Carinthia. But he feuded constantly with Count Ulrich von Heunburg. With treachery and disloyalty, Wilhelm von Scherfenberg went over to Ulrich's side during the battle. Afterward, von Scherfenberg was reported missing, and Konrad von

Aufenstein, who had been fighting for Mainhard, began looking for him.

Von Scherfenberg was found lying in the sand with a spear through his chest. He had seven wounds but felt only one pain. Von Aufenstein asked if he was Wilhelm von Scherfenberg. And he replied, "Yes. And if you are von Aufenstein then bend down to me." With failing strength he continued, "Take this ring. As long as it is in your possession your wealth and worldly honor will never dissipate." Then he handed von Aufenstein the ring.

At this moment Henry the Tall rode up and heard that it was von Scherfenberg who was lying there. "So he is the one who broke his word and betrayed my lord," he said. "May God take his revenge upon him in this hour." A squire draped the mortally wounded man over the back of a horse, but before they could ride off, von Scherfenberg died. Henry the Tall ordered the body placed on the ground again, where it was mourned by both men and women.

Von Scherfenberg acquired the ring he gave von Aufenstein in the following manner. One day, while looking at his fields from a window in his castle, von Scherfenberg saw a strange sight. Four Dwarfs were carrying a celestial canopy of fine noble cloth upon four long golden rods. Beneath it rode a Dwarf with a golden crown upon his head. His every gesture betrayed his kingly nature. The saddle and the reins of his horse were covered with gold and studded with the finest gems. His clothes were of similar grandeur. Von Scherfenberg stood and watched for a while. Finally, he rode thither and doffed his hat. The Dwarf gave him good morning and then continued, "Wilhelm, may God greet you!"

"How do you know me?" asked von Scherfenberg.

"Do not be offended that you are known to me or that I call you by name," said the Dwarf. "I seek your valor and your loyalty, of which much has been reported to me. A powerful king and I both covet a great land. My enemy is attempting to win it from me by trickery. War has been declared between us for six weeks, but he is too powerful, thus all my friends have counseled me to win you for my cause. If you agree to do battle for me I will make you so strong, that even if he sends a Giant against you, you will triumph. Know this, good hero, I shall protect you with a magic belt that will give you the strength of twenty men."

Von Scherfenberg replied, "Because you have shown me such trust and are counting on my valor, I enlist in your service. No matter what happens to me, I shall venture my all."

The Dwarf replied, "Fear not, Lord Wilhelm, that I am some demonic creature. No. Christian faith in the Holy Trinity and in the incarnate birth of God through the Virgin Mary resides within me." Von Scherfenberg rejoiced at these words and assured him that only death or illness would prevent him from appearing when he was needed.

"Then return to this spot with horse, armor, and a squire," said the Dwarf, "but tell no one a word of this, not even your wife, or else everything will be lost." Von Scherfenberg swore a vow of silence.

"Look here," said the Dwarf, "this ring shall be witness to our conversation. You shall possess it with joy, for if you live for a thousand years, with this ring in your possession, no worldly goods of yours will dissipate. So be off in good spirits and remain loyal to me." Thereupon he rode off across the heath, and von Scherfenberg watched as he disappeared into the mountains.

When von Scherfenberg arrived at home, dinner was waiting. Everyone asked where he had been, but he revealed nothing. Yet his bearing showed that he was not as carefree as he had been before. He ordered his horse taken care of, had his breastplate prepared, and sent for the priest. In seclusion he confessed his sins and partook reverently of the Holy Eucharist. His wife sought to learn the truth of the affair from the priest, but he sent her away without saying a word. Then she called for four of her closest friends who led the priest into a private chamber, set a knife to his throat, and threatened him with death until he revealed what he had heard.

When the wife learned what had happened, she sent for her husband's best friends. They took him aside secretly and demanded to know his intentions. When he said nothing, they told him to his face that they knew all, and he realized they were telling the truth. Since it was now useless to continue in silence, he told them his story. His friends tried to deter him from his word and to weaken his intent. They pleaded with him to refrain from the campaign. He was unwilling to break his word and told them that if he did as they wished his good fortune would evermore turn to bad. However, his wife consoled him and did not relent until she convinced him with tearful pleas to remain at home.

More than six months had passed when he rode out with his family and entourage to his castle at Landstrotz. He chose to ride behind all the others. The Dwarf then rode up beside him and said, "Whoever praises your valor is a liar! How you have deceived and betrayed me! For what you have done to me you deserve the wrath of God and of all women! Know this: Victory in battle will never again be yours. Were it not for the ring I foolishly gave you, you and your wife and children would have to live evermore in wretched poverty." The Dwarf then grabbed for the knight's hand and tried to pull the ring off his finger, but von Scherfenberg withdrew his hand and placed it inside his coat. The Dwarf then rode silently away. None of those riding ahead saw what had transpired.

‡‡ 30 ‡‡

## THE SILENT FOLK OF PLESSE

On a high cliff in the Hessian mountains there stands a castle called Plesse. According to legend Dwarfs, who are called the Silent Folk, reside in the surrounding springs, wells, and caves. They never speak, but they are benevolent and gladly serve the people whom they like. If a human mistreats them they will not avenge their anger on him, but will torment his poor farm animals. Actually, the dwellers of this underground community have little contact with people; they carry on their daily lives inside the mountain where they have rooms full of gold and precious gems. If they have some task to perform on the outside, they will avoid the daylight and work only at night. These mountain dwellers are made of flesh and blood like humans, and like humans, they produce children and they die. They do, however, possess special gifts. They can make themselves invisible and they can pass through walls and rocks as easily as we move through air. Occasionally they appear to humans and lead them inside their caves. If these people are to their liking, they present them with priceless treasures.

The main entrance to their mountain is through a deep well near an inn called the Rustling Waters.

‡‡ 31 ‡‡

## THE WEE PEOPLE'S WEDDING

The wee people of Eilen Castle in Saxony wanted to celebrate a wedding and one night stole into the giant hall through keyholes and window cracks. They jumped down like peas bouncing on the floor of the threshing barn. This sound awoke the old count who was sleeping in his great canopied bed in the hall, and he marveled at the throng of little fellows. One of them, dressed like a herald, stepped forward and addressed the count in a most courtly manner, inviting him to join in their festivities. "But we must make one request of you," he added. "You alone shall be present. None of your retinue may look at the celebration, not even a single glance."

The old count answered with friendly words, "Since you have interrupted my sleep, I shall gladly join you." A tiny woman was led forth and was presented to the count, little lamp bearers formed a circle, and the music of crickets began to play.

The count had to expend a great deal of effort to keep from losing his tiny dancing partner. She sprang in all directions and turned pirouettes so fast he could hardly catch his breath. But, suddenly, in the middle of the joyful dance the music stopped and everyone stood still. Then the whole throng ran to every doorjamb, mousehole, and window crack—wherever they could find an opening.

The wedding couple, the heralds, and the dancers turned their eyes toward an opening in the ceiling where the face of the aged countess could be seen looking down with amazed curiosity at the merry celebration. Then they all turned to the count, bowed most graciously, and the herald who had delivered the invitation stepped forth again. He expressed his gratitude for the hospitality, but continued, "Because our joy and wedding celebration have been interrupted and other human eyes have fallen upon us, the family of the Eilenburgs shall never again number more than seven." When he finished speaking, they all rushed to the exit, and all was soon very still. The aged count found himself once again alone in the dark hall.

The curse remains in effect even now. Each time a seventh Eilenburg is to be born, one of the six living knights of the castle must die.

## ‡‡  32  ‡‡

## THE DWARFS WHO WERE TURNED TO STONE

Near the town of Elbogen in Bohemia the Eger River winds its way through a steep, isolated canyon almost as far as Karlsbad. Here among the rocky cliffs lies the famous Cave of the Dwarfs, about which the inhabitants of the region tell the following story.

Many years ago these cliffs were inhabited by Mountain Dwarfs. They lived in tunnels and shafts within the cliffs and went silently about their business. They never caused anyone any harm. Indeed, they had even been known to help people in distress. For many years they were under the control of a powerful sorcerer. But one day, just as they were about to celebrate a wedding and had formed a procession to march to their church, the sorcerer flew into a violent rage and turned them all to stone—or rather, since they were indestructible spirits, imprisoned them in stone columns.

Today these rows of stone columns are known as the Enchanted Wedding Procession of the Dwarfs. One can still see their diverse forms at the top of the cliffs. And in the middle of the cliffs one can just make out the image of a Dwarf who tarried too long in his chamber while the others were trying to get away. He was turned to stone as he leaned out the window seeking help.

In the City Hall of Elbogen one can still see today the wicked and greedy burgraves who were bewitched and changed into ingots of clanging metal. According to legend, no one contaminated by sin can raise these clumps of metal into the air.


‡‡  33  ‡‡

## DWARF MOUNTAIN

Not far from the city of Aachen there is a mountain in which Dwarfs once lived. When they wanted to celebrate a wedding, they would borrow kettles, brass pots, dishes, and frying pans from the city dwellers. But they would always return them in good condition.

There are similar Dwarf mountains near the city of Jena and also in the county of Hohenstein.


‡‡  34  ‡‡

## THE DWARFS BORROW BREAD

In 1684 Father Hedler, the priest in Selbitz and Marlsreuth, reported this story.

Between these two towns lies an opening in the forest known to everyone as the Cave of the Dwarfs, because a hundred years earlier Dwarfs lived there underground. Certain inhabitants of nearby Naila would bring them enough food to survive. Two men, Albert Steffel, who was seventy years old and died in 1680 and Hans Kohmann, who was sixty-three years old and died in 1679—both of them quite credible men—frequently told of the following course of events.

Kohmann's grandfather was plowing his field, which bordered upon the cave, when his wife brought freshly baked bread for his breakfast. She wrapped it carefully in a cloth, carried it out to the field, and placed it on the edge of the plot he was plowing. Along came a Dwarf Woman who spoke to the plowman. She too had bread in the oven, but her children were so hungry they could not wait. If he would give her his loaf she would replace it at midday with hers. The grandfather agreed to this.

Precisely at noon she returned, spread out a white cloth, and placed a warm loaf upon it, expressing her deep gratitude. After assuring him he could eat the bread without fear, she said she would return later for the cloth. When she came again, she explained to him that so many ironworks had been built in the area she would soon have to move away, leaving her beloved underground home. She added that the people's cursing and swearing were also driving her away, as was their blasphemous behavior such as going out to check their fields on the Sabbath—a grievous sin.

Not long ago several farm youths went to the Cave of the Dwarfs on a Sunday. Taking torches with them, they entered it and found a crumbling low passageway that threatened to collapse. Eventually they came to a large rectangular chamber that had been carved from the rock with great industry. The roof was higher than a man, and in each wall were many tiny doors. A feeling of dread overcame the boys and they left quickly without examining the many small chambers.

## ‡‡ 35 ‡‡
## THE COUNT OF HOIA

A tiny Dwarf once appeared in the middle of the night to the Count of Hoia. When the count drew back in fear, the Dwarf told him not to be alarmed. He simply had a request to make of the count, would he please not reject it. The count replied that if no harm came to him and his family he would gladly do as requested.

The Dwarf then said, "Tomorrow night a large party of my people will come here to hold a feast. They request the use of your kitchen and your large dining hall for the night. Please instruct your servants to retire; they are not to get up to view our activities. Moreover, you are the only one who may know of this. Gratitude for this service will be demonstrated in due time. You and your family will enjoy a reward and not the slightest harm will come to any of you." The count agreed to everything.

It came to pass the following night that an entourage of tiny Mountain Dwarfs came marching up the bridge and into the house. They looked just as people have described them. They proceeded into the kitchen where they chopped, cooked, and served just as though they were preparing a large feast.

On toward morning, as they were about to leave, the tiny Dwarf appeared again to the count. With words of gratitude, he handed the count a sword, a festive cape, and a golden ring engraved with a red lion. The Dwarf told him that he and his progeny should guard the three items with care, for as long as the family had them in its possession, all in the county would be prosperous and peaceful. But if the items became separated, ill would befall the county. And whenever a member of the family was to die the red lion would turn pale.

There was a later time, however, when Count Jobst and his

brothers were too young to rule. The government fell into the hands of a viceroy, and it was then that two of the items, the sword and the cape, were taken away. However, the ring remained with the brothers until they died. No one knows the whereabouts of the ring today.

‡‡  36  ‡‡

## THE MIGRATION OF THE DWARFS

When the iron forges and stamping mills were built in the Erz Mountains, the noise drove the Dwarfs out. They complained bitterly about the situation but told the people they would return once the noisy works were removed.

There used to be a settlement of Dwarfs in the caves under Mt. Sion near Quedlinburg. These Dwarfs would loan their pewter dishes, utensils, and other items to the villagers in the region when they celebrated wedding feasts.

‡‡  37  ‡‡

## THE LITTLE PEOPLE

The Little People, or Gnomes, look almost the same as Dwarfs, but they are only about ten inches tall. They have the figures of old men with long beards, dress like miners with white hoods attached to their shirts, and carry lanterns, picks, and hammers. They never harm the miners. And even when they occasionally throw rocks, it's rare that anyone gets hurt—unless the Gnomes have been angered by abusive language and cursing. They especially like to appear in shafts rich in ore or where the prospects for making a strike are good. Because of this the miners are not afraid of Gnomes. In fact they consider it such a good omen when they appear that the miners work harder and are happier.

The little creatures like to roam through mine chambers and shafts and appear to be working very hard, when in truth they never do anything at all. Sometimes the miners think the Gnomes are tunneling out a new shaft or a vein; at other times they seem to be filling their buckets with ore or working the lift as though they want to send something to the surface. But they are really only teasing the miners, driving them to distraction. Occasionally they will call out from one of the chambers, but when one goes to investigate, no one is there.

At the Kutten Mine in Bohemia, Gnomes have been seen marching in and out in great numbers. When the mine is unoccupied, they can be hard shoveling, picking, hammering, pounding, and otherwise simulating miners' work. This activity often indicates an imminent disaster or accident. The Gnomes can also prophesy a miner's death by knocking three times. At other times they will work and hammer iron the way blacksmiths do on their anvils. And they have often been heard knocking, and picking, as if three or four blacksmiths were pounding something out. Thus, the Bohemians frequently call them the Little Housesmiths.

In Idria the miners set out a little pot of food for them every day in a special place. Each year at a certain time the Idrians purchase a child's red coat and present it to the Gnomes. If they fail to do this, the Little People become angry and wreak harm.

‡‡ 38 ‡‡

## CONJURING THE GNOMES

In Nürnberg there once lived a man by the name of Paul Creuz who possessed the remarkable ability to invoke spirits. He went to a certain meadow where he set up an unusual table. He spread a white cloth over it on which he placed two bowls of milk, two pots of honey, two small plates, and nine little knives. Then he held a black hen above a pot of cabbage and tore off its head so that the blood dripped into the food. Thereupon he cast one piece toward morning and the other toward evening and began his invocation. After completing it, he ran behind a green tree and watched as two Gnomes emerged from the ground, sat down at the table near some precious incense burners that had been placed there, and acted as if they were eating.

From behind his tree, the man began asking questions, which they answered. Yes, if he did this often enough, the little creatures would become so trusting that they would come as guests into his house. Had he not set up the table in the proper manner, they would either not have appeared or they would have soon disappeared again. Later, the man was even able to summon forth their king who appeared in a scarlet robe under which he carried a book. He brought it forth, placed it on the table, and permitted the conjurer to read from it as long as he wished. And it was thus that Paul Creuz acquired great wisdom and powerful secrets.

‡‡   39   ‡‡

# THE GNOME AT THE DANCE

Old people state with conviction that some years ago in the village of Glaß, which lies an hour from Wonder Mountain and an hour from the city of Salzburg, a wedding celebration was held. As evening approached, a Gnome appeared from the mines beneath Wonder Mountain. He instructed all the guests to be joyful and merry and requested permission to join in the dancing. It was not denied him. He then approached the honorable maidens of the village and danced three dances with each of them, demonstrating such elegance that all the guests at the wedding took notice and watched with amazement and joy.

After the dance he expressed his gratitude and presented the bride and groom each with three pieces of gold. No one recognized the coins, but the guests considered them worth at least four crowns. The Gnome admonished the newlyweds to live in peace and harmony like good Christians, to remain pious and good for the rest of their lives, and to raise their children to recognize right. If they put the coins away with the rest of their money, and if they thought of him constantly, they would never be in need. However, they should never become arrogant in their prosperity, but should always use it to help their neighbors.

The Gnome remained with the party until midnight, and he accepted food and drink from everyone who offered it, taking only a wee portion each time. He then thanked one and all and asked if one of the bridesmen might take him to the Salzach River and ferry him across. One of the guests was a ferryman by the name of Johann Standl; he eagerly volunteered and they proceeded together to the landing. As they were crossing the stream, the ferryman demanded his pay. The Gnome gave him three pennies. The ferryman looked with scorn upon the poor reward for his services, but the Gnome told him not to be distressed by this payment. If he kept the three pennies he would never lack for material goods, especially if he kept his youthful zeal in check. He also gave the ferryman a small stone and said, "If you wear this around your neck you will never lose your life in the waters." And the prophecy came true within that same year. As he was departing, the Gnome admonished him to lead a pious and humble life, and then he disappeared in an instant.

## ‡‡ 40 ‡‡
## THE CELLAR DWARF

The following events occurred in the town of Lützen in the year 1665. A small Dwarf emerged from the cellar of one of the houses and sprinkled water from a can in front of the house. He then stole silently back into the cellar. However, a maid had witnessed this. She became so frightened that she fell to her knees and began reciting a psalm. Seeing this the Dwarf reemerged, fell to his knees beside her, and prayed as long as the girl did.

Not long after, a terrible fire broke out in the town, destroying many of the newly constructed houses. But the house with the Dwarf in the cellar remained unharmed.

Once after that event, the Dwarf is said to have appeared again— he sprinkled water as before, but this time nothing happened to the town.


## ‡‡ 41 ‡‡
## THE MATRIARCH OF THE FAMILY VON RANTZAU

The members of the noble family of von Rantzau tell the following legend. One night the grandmother of the house, who was sleeping beside her husband, was awakened by a small Dwarf carrying a tiny lantern. The Dwarf led her out of the palace, into a hollow mountain, and then to the side of a woman in labor. The grandmother placed her right hand as requested on the head of the suffering one, whereupon the woman gave birth to a child. The tiny guide then led her back into the palace and presented her with a gold piece and suggested that she have three things made from it—fifty coins, a herring, and a spindle—corresponding to the number of her children, two sons and a daughter. He also warned that she should protect these items well, for their loss would see the family fall into bad times and begin to decline.

A newly wedded countess from a Danish family was sleeping beside her husband when she suddenly heard a rustling sound. Then the curtains of her bed were drawn apart and she saw an amazingly beautiful little lady, barely one ell tall. She was standing next to the bed, holding a lantern. The tiny woman spoke to the countess, saying, "Do not be afraid. I will do thee no harm but can bring thee good fortune if thou wilt come to my aid. Stand and follow me where I lead. Guard against eating anything offered thee, and accept no other gift than the one I shall give thee—but that one thou mayest certainly keep."

The countess followed, and the way led underground. They came to a chamber shimmering with gold and precious gems, which was filled with scores of tiny men and women. Before long the King of the Dwarfs appeared and led the countess to a bed where his queen was lying in labor. He asked the countess to help her. The countess performed the task to the best of her ability, and the Dwarf Queen happily gave birth to a son. There arose great joy among the guests, and they led the countess to a table of magnificent foods and urged her to eat. But she touched not a single morsel, nor did she take any of the precious gems heaped in the golden bowls on the table.

Finally, the first Dwarf Lady returned the countess to her bedside. The Dwarf Lady then told her, "Thou hast performed a great service for our people, and thou shalt be rewarded. Take these three sticks of wood and place them beneath thy pillow. Tomorrow morning they will have changed to gold. Have the following items made from the gold: first a herring, then coins, and from the third a spindle. Reveal nothing of this to anyone in the world except thy husband. Together thou wilt bring three children into the world who will establish the three branches of your house. The one who receives the herring will have good fortune in battle; the one who is given the coins will, together with his children, occupy high state offices; and the one who receives the spindle will be blessed with many children."

When she finished speaking, the Dwarf Lady departed, and the countess fell asleep. When she woke she told her husband the whole story as though it had been a dream. The count made fun of her, but when she reached under her pillow, she found three gold bars. They were both quite astonished but did exactly as they had been instructed.

The prophecy came true, and the diverse branches of the family guarded the precious items with great care. Those who lost their tokens died off.

The family of the coin branch tell this story. The King of Denmark once demanded one of the coins from a member of the family, and at the moment he handed it to the king, he felt a sharp pain in his abdomen.

According to another version of the story, the countess received an apron full of wood shavings and emptied them all into the fireplace. The next morning, when it all seemed to have been a dream, she looked at the fireplace and saw that it was full of gold. The following night the Dwarf Lady returned and told her she should have three things made from the gold: a spindle; a chalice [beaker]; and a sword. If the sword turned black it meant that someone in the family would die by the sword; if it disappeared entirely, it meant that he had been murdered by his brother. The countess had the gold worked as she had been instructed.

Years later the sword turned black and then disappeared entirely. One of the counts von Rantzau had been murdered, and as it later came out, the murderer had indeed been his own brother who had not recognized his victim.

## ‡‡ 42 ‡‡
### HERMANN VON ROSENBERG

When Hermann von Rosenberg celebrated his nuptials, he and his bride were visited in their wedding night by countless little earth spirits, barely a foot tall. They had brought their musicians with them and requested permission to celebrate the wedding of one of their own bridal couples. After their petition was granted, they proceeded to hold their celebration.

## ‡‡ 43 ‡‡
### THE DWARFS OF MT. OSEN

When Winkelmann traveled from our Hessian countryside to Oldenburg in 1653, he was overtaken by darkness just as he was crossing Mt. Osen, and he stopped for lodgings in the village of Bümmerstedt.

The aged innkeeper, nearly a hundred years old, told Winkelmann that in his own grandfather's day the inn had served splendid food, but now it was quite bad. He said that when his grandfather brewed beer, Dwarfs would come from Mt. Osen, take the warm beer right out of the vat, and pay him for it with unknown coins of good silver.

One hot day in summer an old Dwarf fetched himself a large mug of warm beer, and he was so thirsty he drank it all in one swallow. But it was too much beer, and it made him fall asleep. Later, when he woke up and saw how late it was, he began to weep bitterly, "Now my grandfather will beat me for staying out so long!" In dismay he ran off, forgetting to take his beer mug with him, and he never returned for it.

The mug later came into the possession of the innkeeper's father and was subsequently inherited by the innkeeper himself in exchange for his daughter's dowry. As long as the mug remained in the house, the food was plentiful at the inn. But not long ago, the innkeeper said, the mug was broken, and the spell of good fortune was broken too, for nothing had gone right since.


‡‡ 44 ‡‡

## THE DWARF AND THE SHEPHERD

In 1644 a youth was tending the village flock not far from Dresden when right next to him a stone of moderate size suddenly lifted itself into the air. It repeated this several times, and the youth finally picked it up. As he did so, a young Dwarf popped out of the ground, stood himself directly in front of the young shepherd, and said, "I was spellbound here under the ground and thou hast released me. In return for thy good deed, I shall serve thee. Give me work so I have something to do."

Somewhat dismayed, the youth replied, "Well now, you could help me tend the sheep."

The Dwarf performed this task until nightfall, at which time he said, "Wherever thou goest, I will go too."

But the youth objected, "I can't take you home with me, I have brothers and sisters and a stepfather. He would give me a terrible beating if I brought someone home who took up room and made the house even smaller."

"Thou hast accepted me once already," said the spirit. "If thou wouldst not have me thyself, then thou must secure lodgings for me elsewhere."

The youth then directed the Dwarf to a neighbor's house where there were no children. The Dwarf moved right in, and the neighbor was never able to get rid of him.


‡‡ 45 ‡‡

## THE DWARF WHO CAME TO VISIT

There is a story told of the villages of Ralligen on Thun Lake and of Schilling in Grindelwald Valley after Schilling was buried under a landslide from the mountains above.

One day in a heavy rainstorm a wandering Dwarf came into the village. He was dripping wet, and he went from hut to hut pounding on each door, but none of the villagers would take mercy on him and let him in. At the edge of the village there lived two poor but pious people, a man and his wife. The Dwarf, who was now quite weary, dragged himself up with his staff and knocked gently at the window. The old shepherd opened the door without hesitation, invited him in, and offered him all that his poor house had. The old woman brought out bread, milk, and cheese; the Dwarf took a small sip of milk and some crumbs of bread and cheese. "I am not accustomed," he said, "to eating such coarse food. But I thank you from my heart, and may God reward you for your kindness. Now that I am rested I shall be on my way again."

"Oh, take care," cried the woman. "Do not go out at night in weather like this. Please accept the offer of our bed for the night."

But the Dwarf shook his head and smiled. "I still have all kinds of tasks to perform up among the cliffs. I must not stay away any longer. Tomorrow morning you shall think of me." With that he took his leave, and the old couple retired for the night.

At the break of dawn they were awakened by a terrible storm. Lightning flashed across the red sky and torrents of water came rushing down. The water tore a giant boulder loose from the top of the cliff and came crashing down along with trees, rocks, and earth, burying everything in its path—people, farm animals, and soon the whole village.

The wall of water quickly reached the hut of the old couple. Trembling, they stepped through their door. In the middle of the stream they saw a giant boulder; perched on top of it was the little Dwarf, bouncing happily as if he were enjoying the ride. He appeared to be paddling and guiding the boulder with the trunk of a fir tree. The boulder stopped the flow of water and turned it away from the hut. The hut remained unharmed, and the old couple were out of danger. The Dwarf began to swell, growing larger and taller, until he was a huge Giant. Then he disappeared. The old couple fell to their knees, praying to God and thanking him for their deliverance.


## ‡‡ 46 ‡‡

### THE FOREST OF ZEITEL MOSS

Between Wunsiedel and Weißenstadt in the Fichtel Mountains there lies a great forest called Zeitel Moss. Many Dwarfs and mountain spirits reside in that region.

Once, a man was riding through this forest late in the evening when he saw two children sitting next to each other. He admonished them to go home and not to tarry any longer. But the two began laughing loudly.

The man rode on and after a while he encountered the same two children who began laughing again.

## ‡‡ 47 ‡‡

## THE MOSS WOMAN

One afternoon in the year 1635 a peasant named Hans Krepel, who came from the area around Saalfeld, was out chopping down trees on the heath. Suddenly, a small Moss Woman approached him and said, "Father, when thou art finished with thy work and call it a day, taketh thine ax, and after felling the last tree, maketh three crosses on its trunk—it will do thee well." She then disappeared.

The peasant, a coarse and rough fellow, thought to himself: What use is all this rubbish? What do I care about that spook! He thus failed to chop the crosses into the tree trunk and made his way home that evening.

The next day at the same time he returned to the forest to fell more trees. Again the Moss Woman appeared and said, "Alas, man, why hast thou not chopped the three crosses into the tree? It would have helped both thee and me. Now the Wild Huntsman will pursue us day and night, and he will not desist until he hath slain us both in miserable fashion. He will never leave us in peace for we do not have a tree trunk with three crosses on which to seat ourselves. He is powerless to remove us from such a tree, and we would have been safe."

But the peasant just laughed. "What use can three crosses be? I am not going to cut them just to please you." At this, the Moss Woman fell upon the peasant and pressed him so hard that, although he had a strong constitution, he nevertheless became sick and miserable. After that, the peasant followed the instructions to the letter. He never again forgot to chop the three crosses into the last tree—and he suffered no further harm.

## ‡‡ 48 ‡‡

## THE WILD HUNTSMAN PURSUES THE MOSS PEOPLE

Upon the heath, in the forest, in all dark places, even in holes in the ground, live little men and women who lie upon green moss and are clothed all over in green moss. They are so familiar that craftsmen and lathe operators make little statues of them to sell. These Moss People are pursued by the Wild Huntsman, who frequently moves through the region. The local inhabitants are often heard to say, "The Wild Huntsman was out hunting again last night with all that racket and roaring."

Once, a peasant from Arntschgereute near Saalfeld went out into the mountains to fell trees. The Wild Huntsman was out too, and although he was invisible, the peasant could hear the resounding noise of the hunt and the barking of the dogs. The peasant instantly expressed his intention of wanting to help in the chase and began yelling like a hunter. But then he continued his work, and returned home when he was done.

The following morning, just as he entered his stable, he saw a quarter of a Moss Woman hanging there as though she were his share of the catch. Greatly shocked, the peasant ran to the town of Wirbach to seek advice from the nobleman, Lord von Watzdorf. When the peasant finished his tale, the nobleman advised him, for his own welfare, not to touch the meat, otherwise the Huntsman would contest him for it. Instead, he should just let it hang there.

The peasant did as he was advised, and the piece of wild game soon disappeared as mysteriously as it had appeared. The peasant was never again challenged by the Huntsman.


‡‡  49  ‡‡

## THE WATER NIX

Around the year 1630, in the parsonage of Breulieb, half a mile from Saalfeld, an old midwife, in the presence of her priest, told the following story about her mother, who had also been a midwife.

Awakened in the middle of the night, the mother was told to get dressed and attend a woman in labor. It was very dark, but she dressed and went downstairs where she found a man waiting for her. She asked him to excuse her a moment while she found a lamp, then she would be prepared to follow him. However, the man said the matter was too urgent to wait. He would show her the path without a light, and he assured her she would not lose her way. But then he tied a blindfold around her eyes and the midwife became so frightened she wanted to cry out. Again the man reassured her, saying no harm would come to her, that she should proceed without fear. And thus they went off together.

Along the way the midwife heard the man strike water with a twig. Then she noticed that they seemed to be descending, going

deeper and deeper until they entered a small room. The man removed the blindfold and the midwife saw that there was no one in
the room except the pregnant woman. The man led her to the bed,
entrusted his wife to her care, and left. Thereupon the midwife
brought the mother to bed and helped deliver the child. Then she
bathed the infant and performed all the other necessary tasks.

Filled with secret gratitude, the mother began to whisper warnings to the midwife. "Like you," she said, "I am a Christian, but I
have been abducted by a Water Nix. He left his own child in exchange for me. On the third day after I bring a child into the world
he devours it. Just come to your pond three days from now and you
will see the water change to blood. When my husband returns, he
will offer you money. But do not take more from him than your
normal fee or he will wring your neck. Please—take heed."

Just then the Nix returned, his face angry and evil. Looking
about, he saw that everything had transpired successfully, and he
praised the midwife. Then he threw a vast number of coins on the
table and said, "Take as many as you wish."

But the midwife was clever and she replied, "I wish no more
from you than from anyone else. Mine is a small fee; but if it is too
much for you, then I ask only that you see me home again."

The Water Nix replied, "God commanded you to speak so." He
then paid her the usual fee and guided her safely home again.

The midwife was too frightened to return to the pond on the
appointed day.


‡‡  50  ‡‡

## THE WILD WOMEN OF WONDER MOUNTAIN

The townspeople and farmers of Grödich reported that around the
year 1753 the Wild Women would emerge from Wonder Mountain
and give bread to the boys and girls who were tending cattle in the
meadows of Glanegg Valley.

The Wild Women also appeared frequently while the grain was
being harvested. They would come down from the mountain early in
the morning and return in the evening when the work was done.


Once, right next to this mountain, a small boy was sitting on a
horse that his father had harnessed for plowing. The Wild Women
came out of the mountain and tried to abduct the boy by force. The
boy's father was well acquainted with the mysteries of this mountain. He bravely approached the Wild Women, took the child from

them, and said, "What do you think you're doing? You keep coming out of the mountain, and now you attempt to take my boy away. What do you want with him?"

The Wild Women replied, "We can care for him better than you. He would be very dear to us, and no harm would befall him." But the father did not let go of the child, and the Wild Women departed in tears.

Another time the Wild Women came out of Wonder Mountain near Kugel Mill, or as it is also called, Kugeltown, which lies on a plateau near the mountain. They abducted a boy who was tending the sheep. A year later the boy, who was known to all, was seen dressed in green sitting on a ridge of the mountain.

The following day his parents set out to find the boy on the mountain, but they did so in vain—the boy was never seen again.

Several times a Wild Woman from Wonder Mountain made the journey to the village of Anif, which lies a good half hour from the mountain. Along the way she dug holes in the ground where she could rest. She had unusually long and beautiful hair that hung down to her ankles.

A farmer from the village frequently saw this woman and he fell in love with her, chiefly because of the beauty of her hair. He could not resist going to her, and he would watch her with pleasure. Finally, he innocently lay down beside her in one of her resting places. Neither of them spoke or did anything unseemly. But the second night, the Wild Woman asked the farmer did he not have a wife. Denying his own wife, the farmer replied no.

The farmer's wife, however, began to wonder where her husband was spending his nights. And so one night she decided to follow him and see for herself. She came upon him in the field sleeping next to the Wild Woman.

"May God preserve your lovely hair," she said to the Wild Woman. "What are you doing there with one another?" Having spoken these words, the farmer's wife left the two of them alone. The farmer was very upset at what had transpired.

The Wild Woman reproached the farmer for his faithless denial of his wife. "Had your wife shown me hatred and anger," she said, "you would not have left this spot alive. But since your wife was not angry, you must love her evermore and live with her faithfully. You must never attempt to come here again, for it is written: 'Let every man live faithfully with his wedded wife.' Some day the power of this commandment will greatly decrease, and when it does, the worldly prosperity of all married couples will also decrease. Take this shoe full of gold and go away. Do not look back."

## DANCING WITH THE MERMAN

In the Laibach River, near the city of the same name, there once lived a water spirit called a Nix, or Merman. At night he would appear to fishermen and boatmen; but to all others he would appear during the day. Everyone was familiar with the tale of how he would emerge from the water from time to time and appear in human form.

According to ancient custom, the citizens of Laibach come together every year on the first Sunday of July to celebrate a community festival. In the year 1547 the whole community gathered at the old market place next to the fountain, which was shaded by a beautiful linden tree. After everyone had enjoyed the traditional feast, resounding chords of music were struck and the people got up to dance.

Suddenly there appeared a handsome, well-dressed youth, who asked to join in the dancing. He greeted the entire gathering with courtesy. But when people touched his hand, they found it limp and cold, and they were struck with a strange feeling of dread. The youth then led a young girl by the name of Ursula Schäferin to the dance floor. She was well dressed and had a pretty figure, but she was also quite frivolous.

For a time the pair danced wildly around the dance floor. Then they began to swing farther and farther away from the other dancers. They twirled past the linden tree and out toward the Sittich farm and beyond. They danced until they reached the Laibach River where, in full view of many boatmen, the youth jumped in with the girl and both of them disappeared.

The linden tree stood by the fountain until the year 1638, when it had to be chopped down because of its great age.

## THE MERMAN AND THE FARMER

The Merman looks just like any other man; the only difference is that when he opens his mouth, one can see his green teeth. And he always wears a green hat. When a pretty girl walks past his pond, he appears, measures out a length of ribbon, and tosses it to her.

For a time a Merman and a farmer, who lived not far from his lake, enjoyed a good neighborly relationship, and the Merman often visited him. One day the Merman asked the farmer if he would not like to visit him in his house. The farmer agreed and went with him.

Everything under the water was as magnificent as if it had been in a splendid palace on earth. There were rooms, halls, and chambers full of diverse treasures, wealth, and decorations. The Merman led his guest around all of his palace and showed him everything.

Finally, they came to a small room where many pots stood upside down, their openings resting on the floor. When the farmer asked what they were, the Merman replied, "Those are the souls of the drowned. I keep them here under the pots and thus hold them captive so they cannot escape." The farmer remained silent, and later he ascended again to the surface.

For a long time the affair of the drowned souls plagued the farmer, and he paid close attention to the Merman to see when he would leave his watery home. When this came to pass, the farmer, who had made careful note of the right path under the water, descended once more into the watery place. He was fortunate enough to find the little room again and he turned up all the pots, one after the other. And so it was that the souls of the drowned rose up through the water to the surface and were thus delivered.

## ‡‡ 53 ‡‡
### THE MERMAN AT THE BUTCHER'S STALL

There was a Merman who came into town every week and went to a butcher's stall where he made some purchases. Although his clothing was somewhat different from other people's, everyone let him do as he wished, and no one gave the matter any particular thought. However, the Merman always paid for his purchases with old coins with holes drilled through their centers. This oddity finally attracted the attention of the butcher who said, "Just wait, I'll mark him so that he'll never come again."

The Merman returned and asked to buy meat, but just as he was handing over his money, the butcher took his knife and jabbed him in the fingers, so that his blood flowed. From that day to this, the Merman has never returned.

## ‡‡ 54 ‡‡
### THE SWIMMER

During one Pentecost holiday in Meißen three baker's apprentices slipped out of church during the sermon and went swimming in the Elbe River just above the brick barn across from the Arboretum. One of the youths was over-proud of his swimming prowess. He told his comrades that if they were willing to put up a silver taler, he would swim the Elbe back and forth three times without stopping. The challenge seemed incredible to the other two, and they agreed.

The daring young man had made it back and forth twice and was just starting to swim across to the Castle of the Seven Oaks a third time, when a giant fish, resembling a salmon, leaped into the air, dragged him down under the water, and drowned him. Search parties set out that same day and the body was discovered just below the bridge. They found little pinch marks with hemorrhages beneath them all over the corpse. It was easy to tell that these scars had been made by the Nix or Water Spirit.

## ‡‡ 55 ‡‡

## BROTHER NICKEL

In the middle of the dense forest on the Isle of Rügen there is a deep lake full of fish. However, the waters of the lake are so clouded that no one can fish there. Yet many years ago a group of fishermen wanted to try it. They carried their boat to the lake and then went home to get their nets. But when they returned the next day, their boat had disappeared. One of the fishermen happened to glance skyward and he saw the boat lodged in the top of a tall beech tree.

"Who were the devils who put the boat up in the tree?" he shouted angrily. Nearby, where there was no one to be seen, a voice replied, "The devils did not do it. My brother Nickel and I did it!"

## ‡‡ 56 ‡‡

## THE SPRING OF THE NIXIES

In Hesse, not far from Kirchhain, there is a very deep lake called the Spring of the Nixies. The Nixies can frequently be seen there sunning themselves on the banks. The mill there is similarly called the Mill of the Nixies.

In Marburg, too, a Water Nix is reported to have been seen in the Lahn River near Elisabeth Mill.

# THE NIXIES OF MAGDEBURG

There is a spot on the Elbe River in Magdeburg where Nixies can frequently be seen. There they drag swimmers into the depths and drown them. Shortly before the city was destroyed by Tilly, an accomplished swimmer struck out across the river on a wager for money. When he approached a certain spot, however, he was held fast and dragged down beneath the surface. No one was able to save him, and his corpse finally floated up to the shore.

There are times when the Water Wonder reveals himself in the light of day, sitting sometimes on the shore, sometimes in the branches of the trees that line the banks. There he can be seen combing his long golden hair much as a maiden would do it.

The water from the wells of this region is hard to boil, and though the water from the river is of a better quality, it takes great effort to carry it into the city. For this reason the city fathers decided to build a water pipeline from the river to the city. They began the project by driving great piles into the river floor, but the work did not proceed for long. For suddenly, a naked man rose up in the stream, forcefully pulled out all the piles that had been driven, and hurled them in all directions. Thus the construction plans for the pipeline had to be abandoned.

# DÖNGES LAKE

In Hesse, near the town of Dönges, lies Dönges Lake, or as it is also called, Haut Lake. On a certain day every year the waters turn blood red. The following story is told about this lake.

Once there was a church fair in the village of Dönges at which two beautiful but unknown maidens appeared. They danced with the peasant youths and had great fun. But at midnight—even though the church fair went on day and night—they disappeared. The next day, however, they returned, and one youth, who would have had them stay forever, stole a glove from one of the maidens while he was dancing with her.

The maidens kept on dancing until midnight approached. They were about to depart once again when the one noticed her glove was missing. She looked for it everywhere but was not able to find it, and she became frightened. When it began to strike twelve, they both ran to the lake in great fear and plunged in. The next day, the lake turned blood red, and it has done so on that day every year since.

On the cuff of the glove that was left behind small gold crowns had been embroidered.

It is also said that one night two riders appeared before the house of a midwife of the village. They awakened her and ordered her to accompany them. When she refused, they tied her to one of the horses. They then rode with her beneath the waters of Dönges Lake. There she helped deliver the child of their queen. The midwife saw many wondrous things there—great treasures, riches, and gems. However, she was made to swear she would never tell anyone what she had seen. She spent the whole day there, was richly rewarded for her services, and was brought again to the surface. Many years later she fell ill and could not die in peace until she had confessed everything to her priest.


‡‡  59  ‡‡

## LAKE MUMMEL

High in the mountains of the Black Forest, not far from Baden, lies a lake whose depths are unfathomable. If one were to tie an odd number of peas, pebbles, or some such into a cloth and lower it into the lake on a rope, they would change into an even number; similarly, an even number changes to an odd. If one casts stones into the lake, the clearest sky will immediately cloud over and a great storm will arise with gale-force winds and hail. All stones cast into these depths are carefully carried back to the shore by the Mermen who live there.

Once some cowherds were tending their cattle on the shores when a brown bull emerged from the lake and began to graze with the other cattle. However, a man soon came from the lake to drive the bull back. When it did not obey, he began cursing at it until it finally returned to the lake with him.

Once in midwinter, a farmer crossed the frozen lake with a team of oxen who were hauling fallen trees. But when the farmer's dog ran after them, the ice beneath him collapsed, and the dog fell through and drowned.

A rifleman was walking past the lake one day when he saw a Forest Dwarf sitting there, playing with gold coins that filled his lap.

When the rifleman raised his gun and was about to fire, the Dwarf dove into the water and called out that had the rifleman asked, the Dwarf could have made him very wealthy. But now, he and his descendants would have to live in poverty.

Late one evening a Dwarf came to a farm and asked the farmer for lodgings for the night. The farmer, not having enough beds, offered the Dwarf the window seat in his living room, or the hayrick in the barn. But the Dwarf requested permission to sleep in one of the hemp-soaking beds. "It's all right with me," replied the farmer. "For all I care, you may sleep in the fish pond or the water trough."

Having received permission, the Dwarf thus proceeded to submerge himself between the rushes and the water, as if he were lying in hay and warming himself. Early the next morning he emerged with his clothes completely dry. When the farmer expressed amazement at his wondrous guest, the Dwarf replied that it was quite possible that his kind had not spent the night there for more than a hundred years.

The Dwarf soon became trusting enough of the farmer to confide that he was a Merman who had lost his wife. He wanted to look for her in Lake Mummel, and he asked for directions. On the way to the lake the Dwarf confided more wondrous things: How he had sought his wife in many lakes but had not found her; and what lakes look like beneath the surface.

When they arrived at the shores of Lake Mummel, the Dwarf asked the farmer to wait until he either returned or sent him a signal. After the farmer had waited a few hours he saw pools of blood surface in the middle of the lake, followed by a number of shoes springing from the water into the air. The farmer assumed that this was the signal the Dwarf had mentioned.

A duke of Württemberg once had a raft built and anchored on the lake so he could sound its depth. But when the measuring rope sank nine fathoms without touching bottom, the raft began—against its very nature—to sink. The duke and his party gave up their plan as they attempted to save themselves. Pieces of the raft can still be seen on the shores of the lake.

‡‡　60　‡‡

## THE ELBE MAIDEN AND THE SAALE WOMAN

At Magdeburg, people know about the beautiful Elbe Maiden who sometimes emerged from the river to shop at the meat market.

She bore herself as a well-mannered bourgeoise, was neat and clean, and carried a shopping basket. One could not tell her from any other maiden unless one paid close attention and saw that a corner of her snow-white apron was always damp—a sign of her watery origin.

A young journeyman fisherman fell in love with her, and he followed her until he learned whence she came and wither returned. He finally worked up his courage and plunged into the water after her. She called to another fisherman, who was standing on the shore waiting for his comrade, that if a wooden platter with an apple on it came to the surface, everything was fine, otherwise not.

But shortly after, a red gusher burst forth. This was a sign that the maiden's relatives had not been pleased by the suitor and had killed him.

There are, however, divergent tales about this event, according to which the maiden descended into the stream while the youth sat on the shore waiting for her word. She was to ask her parents' permission to marry, but she told her brothers first. Instead of an answer from her, the youth saw a gusher of blood rush to the surface. The brothers had killed her.

Occasionally Nix Women were seen emerging from the Saale River at the city of Saalfeld, where they would go to the market and buy fish. One could recognize them by their dreadful eyes and the hems of their skirts which were dripping wet. These were said to have once been mortal children for whom the Nixies had left changelings.

Outside the city gate at Halle there is a pond called Nix Pond, from which Nix Women emerge and enter the city to buy staples. They can be recognized by the wet hems of their skirts. Otherwise their dress, language, and money are the same as everyone else's.

Not far from Leipzig a Nix Wife was often seen on the street. She wandered with her shopping basket among the other peasant women at the weekly market, and bought groceries. She returned every week but never spoke to a soul, never greeted or thanked anyone on the street. However, when it came to making purchases, she knew as well as any of the women how to haggle and bargain. One day two people followed her. They saw her come to a small pond and set her shopping basket down, and then, in an instant, both the woman and her basket disappeared. None of her clothing distinguished her from other women, except that the hems of her undergarments were always wet.

## WATER RIGHTS

In the summer young people like to swim in the Elster River, right
where it joins the Pleisse River near Leipzig. But the water there is
treacherous. In some places there are deep holes, in others sand-
banks, especially at a place called the Students' Pool. There, as with
other rivers, it is often said that the waters have to have a human
offering every year, and nearly every summer someone drowns
there. It is commonly believed that the Water Nix pulls his victims
beneath the surface. It is also said that the Nixies dance on the
surface of the water everytime someone drowns.

In Hesse, when children who want to go swimming stand on the
shore, their parents yell a warning to them: "The *Nöcken* [Nix] will
pull you in!"
And the following children's rhyme is also known:

> Nixie in the grave,
> Thou art a naughty knave.
> Thou washeth thy legs the while
> Using red pieces of tile!

## THE DROWNED CHILD

Many tales are told about bodies of water, and it is said that every
lake or river must have an innocent child as an offering every year.
But the water will not abide a dead body, and sooner or later will
cast it upon the shore. Indeed, even the last bone, after it has sunk to
the bottom, will eventually be cast out again.
    Once, a mother lost her child when it drowned in a lake. She
prayed to God and his saints to at least grant her the skeletal
remains for burial. The next storm brought forth the skull, the
following one the torso. And when all the bones had been retrieved,
the mother wrapped them in a cloth and carried them to the
church.
    Wonder of wonders—when she entered the church, the bundle
began to grow heavier and heavier. Finally, as she placed it upon the
steps of the altar, the child began to cry, and to everyone's amazement it crawled forth from under the cloth. Only a small bone from
the little finger of the right hand was missing, which the mother

carefully sought and found. This little bone was preserved in the church along with other relics in memory of the event.

Boatmen and fishermen near Küstrin in Neumark also speak of an unknown creature that rules the Oder River. It too must have its human offering every year. Death by drowning is inevitable for whomever this fate is intended.

The salt workers of Halle are especially fearful of St. John's Day. A certain Count Schimmelmann went swimming on this day against warning—and he drowned.

‡‡  63  ‡‡

## LITTLE SLIT-EARS

People who cross the bridge below Mellrichstadt on the River Streu are often pulled into the water by a Water Spirit called Slit-Ears, and they frequently drown.

‡‡  64  ‡‡

## THE WATER NIX AND THE MILLER'S APPRENTICE

Two miller's apprentices were walking along a riverbank, when one of them, looking out over the water, saw a Nix Maiden sitting on the surface combing her hair. He grabbed his rifle and loaded it, intending to shoot her. But the Nix Maiden sprang into the river, waved with her fingers, and disappeared. All of this happened so fast that the apprentice who was walking ahead never saw what had happened. He learned of it only when his companion told him. Three days later, when the first apprentice went swimming in the river, he drowned.

‡‡  65  ‡‡

## DOSTEN AND DORANT
## SAVE PEOPLE FROM THE NIXIES

A midwife from Halle told this story that happened to the woman from whom she learned her trade. One night, the woman was called upon by a man who led her through the city gate, which stood open, down to the Saale River. She dared not speak a single word as they walked, otherwise he would have wrung her neck. She also knew she must remain hopeful. She thought of God, who would protect her, and devoted herself to her task, for it was after all her trade.

When they came to the edge of the river, the waters parted and they descended. When they reached the riverbottom, the earth itself opened, and they continued to descend until they entered a splendid palace. There a tiny sweet-faced woman lay in labor. The man left, and the midwife helped deliver the child.

After she had performed her work successfully, the little woman spoke to her with compassion. "O dear woman, it grieves me that you must remain here until Judgment Day. Now please take heed! My husband is going to set a whole trough of ducats before you. Take no more than the usual fee for your help. Furthermore, when you leave this room and are underway, dig your fingers into the earth and quickly pluck the Dosten (*Origanum*) and Dorant (*Marrubium*) you find there. Clasp them firmly and do not let them out of your hand! Only thus will you be set free and able to return home."

Scarcely had she finished than the Water Nix, with his golden locks and bright blue eyes, stepped into the chamber. He had an entire trough filled with gold that he set at the feet of the midwife in the middle of the beautiful room. "Cast thine eyes on this," he said, "and take as much as thou wisheth." At this, the midwife reached in and took but a single gold coin. The Nix made a face and his eyes grew angry as he said, "If thou hadst not plowed with another woman's heifer, thou wouldst not have known this—and she will certainly pay for it. Come with me!"

As he led her out, the woman quickly bent over and grabbed the Dosten and Dorant with both hands. "God himself commanded thee," said the Nix. "This too hast thou learned from my wife. Now return whither thou camest!" Forthwith, the midwife found herself out of the river, standing on the shore, and she returned to the city.

Another midwife, who was born in Eschätz near Querfurt, told the following story. In her hometown a man had to go out and leave his wife, who was in her ninth month, at home alone.

Around midnight the Nix appeared before the house. He mimicked the voice of her husband as he called through the garden window, "Come out quickly! I have something unusual to show you."

This request seemed a bit strange to the woman, and she answered, "You come in here. Why should I get up in the middle of the night and go out in my condition? You know the key is hidden in the hole above the front door."

"Yes, I know. But you're still going to have to come out here," he called. He plagued her so long with these words that finally she got up, opened the door, and stepped out into the yard. The spirit led her to a stream that flowed near the house, and then it said:

> Raise up your gown,
> So you do not fall down
> in the Dosten and the Dorant.

There herbs grew profusely in the garden. The moment she cast her eyes on the water, she hurled herself onto the ground in the bed of herbs. The Nix disappeared immediately, for he had no more power over her.

After midnight the husband returned home, found the front door and bedroom wide open, and the expectant mother missing. In his sorrow, he began to call out until he heard her gentle voice coming from the garden. He picked her up from the bed of herbs and led her back to the bedroom.

Midwives think a great deal of these herbs and they place them all over the house—in beds, in cradles, in the cellar. They wear them on their dresses and give them to others to carry with them. The herb wives of Leipzig frequently bring them to the market place to sell.

It is also said that a woman once went into her cellar at noon to tap some beer. A spirit in the cellar began to speak:

> Were you not wearing Dosten on you,
> I would help you drink your brew.

This rhyme can be heard repeated in other stories.

## ‡‡ 66 ‡‡
## THE LEGS OF THE WATER NIX

A midwife, who was born in Eschätz, half a mile from Querfurt, told the story of a woman who appeared at midnight before the house of a barber who lived near the water. The woman cried at the window, calling for the barber's wife, a midwife, to come out. At first the midwife refused, but then the barber agreed to accompany her. He brought a lamp with him and instantly caught sight of the Nix's legs. Immediately, the Nix Woman began to cower, and when the barber noticed this he began to curse her in a terrible fashion and ordered her to leave. Thereupon, she disappeared.

## THE MAID AND THE WATER NIX

The following occurred in a village near Leipzig. A maidservant descended beneath the river and served for three years in the home of the Water Nix. Her life was good and she had all she wanted, except for the fact that all her meals were unsalted. She finally used this as an excuse to leave but added, "After this time I still had not more than seven years to live, and now only three remain." Otherwise, she was always simple, yet sad.

Prätorius heard the story in 1664.

## LADY VON ALVENSLEBEN

Several hundred years ago an aged, pious noble lady of the family von Alvensleben lived on an island in the river near Kalbe. She showed kindness to everyone and was always willing to help when help was needed. Above all, she was always there to help the citizens' wives in childbirth. Indeed, her services were highly desired in such cases and she was greatly honored. Once, however, the following events happened to her.

A maidservant appeared in front of the castle one night, and she knocked and cried out anxiously that the lady should not become angry with her, but should get up and follow her outside the city gates to attend a woman who was in labor. It was, she said, the time of highest danger, and her lady had not the slightest idea what to do.

But the lady replied, "It is the middle of the night, all the gates are closed. How can we possibly get outside the city walls?"

The maidservant replied that the city gate had been opened, all she had to do was to follow. But as some people tell it, the maidservant also advised her to take heed not to eat or drink anything and not to touch anything that was offered to her.

The noblewoman rose and dressed, went downstairs, and accompanied the girl who had knocked. She indeed found the city gate open, and they made their way—which was indeed very long—across the fields until they came to a mountain. The mountain stood open, and although she well knew there was something strange about this whole affair, she nevertheless resolved to proceed without fear.

Finally, they arrived at a bed on which lay a small woman in painful labor. The noblewoman helped her (according to some, she only needed to place her hand on the woman's abdomen), and the woman successfully gave birth to her child. After performing all necessary chores, the noblewoman wished to leave the mountain and return home. She took leave of the woman without touching any of the food or drink that was offered to her, and the maidservant brought her back to the castle unharmed.

Just outside the castle gate, however, the maidservant stopped and thanked the noblewoman in her lady's name. She then drew a gold ring from her finger and presented it to her with the following words, "Pray accept this precious pledge, but take heed never to let it out of the possession of your family. The von Alvenslebens will enjoy great prosperity so long as they have this ring. If, however, it should ever fall into someone else's hands, the noble lineage will come to an end." With these words the maidservant disappeared.

This ring is said still to be in the possession of the von Alvenslebens to this very day, and it is kept safely locked away in the city of Lübeck. Others maintain that the ring was carefully halved when the family split into two separate lineages. Still others contend that one of the halves was melted down. Subsequently, that half of the lineage has suffered only misfortune, while the other half of the ring is carefully kept by the other lineage in Zichtow.

One also hears the story that the noblewoman was married, and that the next morning when she told her husband what had transpired during the night, he did not believe a word of it. She then replied, "Ah, so you won't believe me. Then just get the key from the desk and open that chamber over there, and you will find the ring." And, indeed, the ring was found there just as she said.

It is truly a wondrous thing, the way people have been given gifts by the spirits.

‡‡  69  ‡‡

## LADY VON HAHN AND THE NIX

An aristocratic lady from the noble lineage von Hahn was once awakened at night by the calls of the maidservant of a Water Nix and urged to go as a midwife with her beneath the river. As they approached the river, the waters parted and they entered a cheerful hallway that led deep into the interior of the earth. There, she performed her helpful services for a tiny woman in advanced labor.

After she had performed all the necessary tasks and was ready to hasten home, a small Water Nix entered the room and handed her a bowl full of ashes and told her that she should take as much as she wanted in payment for her efforts. She refused and took nothing.

The Nix then said, "God bade you to speak so, for had you taken something I would have had to take your life."

She was then permitted to leave and was led home by the maidservant along the same route they had come. When they arrived at their destination, the maidservant brought forth three pieces of gold. She presented these to the noblewoman with a warning to guard the treasure carefully and never to let it fall into anyone else's hands. If this happened the noble house would go to ruin and poverty. However, so long as the treasure remained in the family's possession, they would enjoy a rich abundance of all things. The maidservant then left.

The three gold pieces were eventually divided among the three sons. Today, two of the lineages of the family who carefully put away the treasure for safekeeping enjoy prosperity. The third piece of gold, however, was treated carelessly and lost by a woman who died in poverty in Prague. She was the last member of that lineage.

## ‡‡ 70 ‡‡
### LADY VON BONIKAU

Once when Lady von Bonikau was lying in childbed alone in her home in Saxony, a tiny woman came to her and asked for permission to hold a feast in her chamber. The woman told her to take heed that only she and no one else be present during the celebration. No sooner had Lady von Bonikau consented than a whole party of tiny Dwarf Men and Women entered the chamber. They brought with them a small table, spread a cloth upon it, and set many dishes upon it. Then the entire party of celebrants sat down at the table. When they had eaten their fill, one of the tiny women called out in a loud voice:

> God be praised, God be thanked.
> We came here in great sorrow
> For old Schump is dead.

## ‡‡ 71 ‡‡
### THE MEASURING CUP, THE RING, AND THE CHALICE

In the Duchy of Lorraine, at a time when it still belonged to Germany, there reigned over the cities of Nancy and Luneville, the last Count von Orgewiler. He had no male heirs, and so, on his deathbed, he divided his lands among his three daughters and his sons-in-law. The eldest daughter had married Simons von Bestein, the second, Lord von Crony, and the youngest had married a German count from the Rhineland. In addition to all his lands, the count bequeathed three gifts to his heirs. To the oldest daughter he gave a measuring cup; to the second a chalice; and to the third he gave a ring. He warned them that they and their progeny should guard the gifts with great care, thus, their respective houses would enjoy constant good fortune.

The story of how the count came into possession of the three objects was told by Marshall de Bassompierre (von Bassenstein), the great-grandson of none other than Simons himself. The count was married, but he had a secret love affair with a wondrously beautiful woman, who rendezvoused with him every Monday at the summer cottage in the palace gardens. This arrangement was kept successfully hidden from his wife for many years, for everytime he absented himself he convinced her that he was out in the forest in his hunting blind. However, after a few years, the countess became suspicious and was determined to learn the truth.

One summer morning she followed him, creeping silently through the garden. When she came to the arbors by the cottage, she saw her husband asleep in the arms of a most radiantly beautiful woman. She did not wish to disturb them and instead took the veil from her head and spread it over the feet of the sleeping couple.

When the lovely mistress woke and became aware of the veil, she let out a scream and began to weep bitterly. "Henceforth, my beloved," she said, "we can see each other nevermore. I must travel far, far from here and remain separated from you forever." She then took her leave. But before she departed, she presented the count with the three objects, telling him that they were for his three daughters, and that they must always keep them in their possession.

For many years thereafter the city of Épinal had to pay a duty to the house de Bassompierre for which the measuring cup was always put to use.

## ‡‡ 72 ‡‡

## THE COBOLD

In some villages nearly every peasant, along with his wife, sons, and daughters, has a Cobold who performs all kinds of domestic chores. He carries water into the kitchen, chops wood, fetches beer from the cellar, cooks, brushes the horses in the stable, clears the manure out of the stalls and the like. When the Cobold is present, the cattle increase in number and the whole farm is successful and prospers. Even today, when a maidservant accomplishes her tasks with dispatch, this proverb is recited: "She has a Cobold." But whoever vexes the Cobold had best take care!

Before they choose a house in which to settle, Cobolds conduct a test. They carry sawdust into the house at night and put dung from the different farm animals into the milk cans. If the farmer sees to it that the sawdust is not scattered, that the dung is left in the milk cans and the milk is consumed, then the Cobold will stay in the house as long as at least one member of the family is still alive.

If a cook has accepted a Cobold as a secret helper, she must put a dish full of good food in a chosen place every day at the same time and then go back to her chores. If she does so, then she can be lazy, go to bed early, and still find that all her work has been done for her by early morning. But if she once forgets to put out the food, then she must not only do all the work herself in the future, she also finds she has acquired a most unlucky hand—it gets burned in hot water, drops and breaks pitchers and dishes, and spills food. Thus, she will constantly be reprimanded by her employers. When this happens, the Cobold is frequently heard snickering and giggling.

If the service personnel of the house should change, the Cobold will nevertheless remain. But the departing maidservant must recommend him to her successor and make certain that she will continue to set out his food. If the new servant is not willing to do this, she will have constant misfortune until the day she decides to go elsewhere.

Some believe that Cobolds are, in essence, human, much like children in form, and that they wear colorful cloaks. Others contend that some Cobolds have knives stuck in their backs, and that some are terribly misshapen due to the weapon that killed them in their former human existence. These people consider Cobolds to be the souls of people who were murdered in the house years before.

Sometimes the maidservant is curious to see her *Kurd Chimgen* or *Heinzchen*, however her Cobold is called. If she is persistent, the spirit will finally name the site where she will be able to see him. However, he also instructs her to bring a bucket of cold water with her. It invariably happens that she sees him lying naked on a pillow on the floor with a butcher knife stuck in his back. Most of the time she becomes so frightened by this sight that she faints. Thereupon, the Cobold jumps up and dumps the bucket of cold water over her so she comes to again. Afterward, the maidservant loses all desire ever to see the Cobold again.

## THE FARMER AND HIS COBOLD

One farmer had had enough of his Cobold, who was always up to nothing but mischief. Yet no matter what he did, he could not get rid of him. At last the farmer was advised to burn down the barn because that is where the Cobold resided. First, the farmer carted all the straw out of the barn. Then, as he was carrying out the last load, he locked the spirit inside and set the barn afire. When the structure was completely in flames, the farmer glanced around—and lo and behold! There was the Cobold sitting on the back of the cart saying over and over, "It's about time we got out of there! It's about time we got out of there!" All the farmer could do was return to the house and keep his Cobold.

## THE HOBGOBLIN OF THE MILL

Once there were two students from Rinteln who decided to go on a walking tour. They planned to find lodgings in a particular village but were overtaken by a heavy rainstorm and darkness and could go no further. Instead, they went to a nearby mill, knocked on the door, and asked for lodgings. At first, the miller acted as though he hadn't heard them. But, finally, he gave in to their pleas, opened the door, and led them to a room. They were both hungry and thirsty, and since a dish of food and a mug of beer were sitting on the table they asked the miller if they could have them, expressing their willingness to pay. The miller, however, refused. He would not give them a single piece of bread and only offered them the hard bench as a resting place. "The food and drink," he said, "belong to the house spirit. If your life is dear to you leave both untouched. If you do as I say you have nothing to fear here. If there is any disturbance during the night just lie still and go back to sleep." With these words the miller departed, closing the door behind him.

The students lay down for a night's sleep, but after an hour or so, one of them had such hunger pangs that he sat up and began feeling around for the plate. The other, who was a magister, warned his friend that he should leave to the Devil that which is entrusted to the Devil. But his friend replied, "I have more right to it than the Devil!" He then sat down at the table and ate to his heart's content, so that very little of the food was left. Next, he grabbed the mug of beer and took a long draft from it. After his desire had been quenched somewhat, he lay down again next to his friend. But after a while his thirst began to plague him once more, and once again he got up and took another hearty swig, leaving only the dregs for the house spirit. After he had congratulated himself, and had drunk to his own health, he lay down and fell asleep at last.

Everything was quiet and peaceful until midnight, but scarcely had the twelfth bell rung, when the Hobgoblin entered with a tremendous racket, frightening both of the students. He roared up and down the room a few times and then sat down at the table to enjoy his meal. The two students heard him slide the dish over to himself and then slam it down as if he were angry. He next grabbed the mug and lifted the lid, but snapped it shut again immediately.

He then began to perform his chores. He carefully wiped off the table and then the table legs and began to sweep the floor. When he had finished, he returned to his dish and the mug to see if things had improved any, but he shoved them away again in anger. Then he went back to his work. He came to the benches and began washing, scrubbing, and rubbing them down, and when he got to the place where the students were lying, he skipped over them and continued his work on the part that lay below their feet. When he reached the end of the bench, he returned to the other end and began the cleaning process anew, and for the second time he skipped over the two of them.

The third time, however, when he came to the student who had not eaten anything, he stroked him from head to toe without doing him the slightest bit of harm. But he grabbed the other one by the feet, pulled him off the bench, dragged him around the floor a few times, and finally left him lying behind the stove. The Hobgoblin then began laughing at him derisively. The student crawled back to the bench, but, after about a quarter of an hour, the Hobgoblin began his chores anew—sweeping, scrubbing, dusting.

Both of the students lay there trembling in fear. When he had scrubbed down to the spot where the two of them lay, he felt the one over carefully, but the other one he again cast down onto the floor and finally left him lying behind the stove amid coarse, derisive laughter.

The students no longer wanted to lie on the bench, so they got up and began shouting at the locked door, but no one listened to them. They finally decided to lie down on the floor next to each other, but still the Hobgoblin did not leave them in peace. For the third time he began his drama, dragging the guilty one once again round the room while continuing his mocking laughter.

The guilty student now fell into a rage. He drew his rapier, lunged and stabbed into the corner where the laughter echoed, and challenged the Hobgoblin to come forth. Then he took his weapon and sat down on the bench to see what would happen. But the racket stopped and everything was quiet.

In the morning, the miller reproached them for not having heeded his warning. It could easily have cost them their lives.

‡‡ 75 ‡‡

## CAPPY

At the country estate of Bishop Bernhard of Hildesheim a spirit once resided who let himself be seen in peasant dress by everyone, appearing quite amiable and pious. He wore a felt hat, from which he got the name of Cappy (or in Low German, *Hödeken*). He wanted to convince people that he had their best interests at heart, that he wasn't out to cause harm. And so, sometimes he would warn of an impending disaster, other times he helped in a difficult enterprise. He appeared to take pleasure and joy in human company. He talked with everyone, asked and answered questions in an uninhibited, friendly manner.

At this time a certain count named Hermann, born in Swabia, lived in Winzenburg Castle. He owned the estate as his own county. Now, one of his courtiers had a lovely wife, upon whom the count cast a lustful eye, and whom he began to pursue in his passion. She, however, paid him little mind.

But he did not relent and began to devise evil plans. The count sent her husband away to a distant place and took by force what he could not have with assent. As long as her husband was away she was forced to endure the injustice in silence. But when her husband returned, she revealed all to him with great pain and suffering gestures.

The nobleman knew that this outrage could only be washed away with the blood of the culprit. Since he had the freedom of the count's chambers at any time, he took advantage of an hour when the count was sleeping with his wife. The nobleman entered the room, walked over to the bed, and with harsh words accused the count of the crime.

When he saw that the count was about to try to defend himself, he took his sword and stabbed the count to death in bed right next to the countess. She became enraged and violently cursed the perpetrator of this crime. As she was pregnant at the time, she uttered the curse: "The child I carry here beneath my belt shall avenge this murder on thee and on thy family, so that all posterity may be served by the example." When the nobleman heard these words, he returned to the bed and stabbed the countess to death as he had done the count.

Count Hermann von Winzenburg was the last of his lineage, and after his and his pregnant wife's deaths, the land was without a ruler. At the very hour of the morning that the deed was committed, Cappy appeared before the bed of the sleeping Bishop Bernhard, awoke him, and said, "Get up, baldy, and bring your people together! The countship of Winzenburg is vacant due to the murder of its lord, and you can annex it as a part of your dominion with little effort." The bishop got up, assembled his army quickly, and immediately occupied the land. With the assent of the emperor, he was able to annex the land for the diocese of Hildesheim.

The oral tradition of the area tells another, probably earlier, version of this story. A count of Winzenburg had two sons who lived in enmity. In order to avert a fight over the inheritance an agreement was made with the Bishop of Hildesheim that the first son to report to the bishop after the death of his father was to be made sole heir to the count's property. When the count died, the older son immediately mounted his horse and rode off to the bishop. The younger son had no horse and was at a loss about what to do.

It was then that Cappy appeared to him and said, "Write a letter to the bishop and tell him that you are ready to accept the fief. It will arrive there before your brother on his swift horse." The younger son wrote the letter as instructed, and Cappy sped off with it straight over the mountains and through the forests. Within thirty minutes he was in Hildesheim—long before the elder brother came racing into the town. Thus it was that Cappy gained the count's lands for the younger son.

This trail is very hard to find, but today it is still called Cappy's Racetrack.

Cappy often appeared at the bishop's court and frequently volunteered warnings of impending danger. He also imparted revelations of the future to famous men. At times he would appear before people when he spoke, at other times he was invisible. But he always had his large cap pulled down over his eyes so no one could ever see his face. Cappy kept a close eye on the city watchmen to make sure that they didn't sleep during their watches. He never harmed anyone unless someone was foolish enough to abuse him. In that case he never forgot and always returned the ridicule at an appropriate time. He frequented the kitchens to chat about all kinds of things with the cooks and the kitchen personnel. He made his bed in a tub in the cellar, but he also had a hole in the ground into which he liked to crawl.

Once, when people had grown accustomed to him and were no longer afraid, a scullery boy began to heap abuse on him and to ridicule and vex him with curses. Moreover, as often as he had the chance, the boy would throw garbage from the kitchen at him or pour dishwater on him.

Cappy became quite annoyed at this behavior, and he finally asked the kitchen master to mete out appropriate punishment so the youth would stop his tomfoolery; otherwise, he himself would have to avenge these humiliations on the youth. But the kitchen master laughed at Cappy and said, "Ha! You're supposed to be a demon, and you're afraid of a little kitchen boy!"

To which Cappy replied sternly, "Because you have refused my request to punish the youth, you will see in a few days how afraid I am of him," and he left in anger.

A short time later, the boy was sitting alone in the kitchen after supper when he became weary and fell asleep. Cappy appeared, choked the boy, and cut him into pieces, which he placed in a large kettle, and set over the fire. When the kitchen master returned, he saw that the spirit was evidently cooking something for himself. But then he looked in the kettle and saw human limbs cooking. When he perceived that the spirit was about to prepare a weird meal, he began to scold and curse him in a terrible fashion.

Cappy became even more embittered at this behavior. He took some ugly toads and squeezed them all over the roasts on spits over the fires until the meat was dripping with blood and vile poison. The cook, of course, became even more furious, and while cursing the spirit stepped out of the kitchen onto a small bridge. Cappy then pushed him into the moat, which lay far below.

Now everyone became frightened that the enraged spirit would try to set fire to the bishop's castle and to all the houses of the city. Thus, all the watchmen had to stand guard at their posts on the walls of the city and of the castle. Because of this event and for other reasons the bishop wished to rid himself of the spirit, and he finally forced him to leave through exorcism.

The spirit enjoyed playing diverse, adventurous tricks that rarely harmed anyone. There was, for example, a man in Hildesheim who had a wife who was not always faithful. Once, when the man had to go on a trip, he came to Cappy and said, "My good friend, could you do me the favor of keeping an eye on my wife while I am gone and see to it that all is as it should be." Cappy agreed, and when the woman sent for her lover immediately after her husband's departure, Cappy was on hand. Just as the two of them were about to make merry, Cappy popped between them and frightened them with apparitions of horrible demons. And when one of the lovers would get into bed, the invisible Cappy would kick him out again with such force that his ribs would crack on the floor. This humiliation was experienced by one lover after another that the frivolous wife invited into her chamber, so that no one could touch her.

Finally, when the husband returned, the overjoyed Cappy ran out to meet him. "Your return is a most welcome sight to me, for I am now relieved of all the trouble and effort you've caused me."

"Who are you?" asked the man.

Cappy replied, "I am Cappy to whom you entrusted your wife's safekeeping before your departure. For your sake I have watched over her this time and have kept her from adultery, but it took great and incessant effort to do so. And now I ask that you never again place her in my charge, for I would rather watch over all the swine in Saxony than to guarantee the chastity of one such woman ever again. She invented countless schemes and ruses in the attempt to fool me."

Another time there was a cleric in Hildesheim who managed to get through seminary without having learned very much. It soon became his turn to be sent by the other clerics to attend a church congress. But he was afraid of humiliating himself among such a learned and distinguished group because of his ignorance.

Cappy helped him out of this dilemma by giving him a ring woven of laurel leaves and other things. It had the magical ability to make the cleric, for a short time, so learned and articulate that everyone at the congress marveled at his great wisdom and they ranked him among the most famous orators.

Cappy once left a bar of iron for a poor nail smith from which the smith could make nails of gold. To the man's daughter he gave a roll of lace from which she could measure off as much as she wanted, without its ever diminishing in size.

‡‡ 76 ‡‡

## HINZELMANN

In the region near Lüneburg, not far from the Aller River, there once stood Hude-Mill Castle, of which only the walls remain today. Long ago a strange house spirit lived in the castle. He first attracted attention in 1584 when he made his presence known by pounding on the walls and making a general racket. After that he began carrying on conversations with the servants in the middle of the day. At first they were quite terrified of the voice, which could be heard when there was no one to be seen. In time, however, they became used to the voice and scarcely paid it any heed. Finally, the spirit became quite bold and even began speaking to the lord of the house. He carried on all kinds of conversations with those who were present at the noon and evening meals, whether they were inhabitants of the castle or guests.

As soon as people stopped being afraid, he became very confiding and friendly. He sang, laughed, and performed all kinds of amusing tricks—as long as no one did anything to make him angry. He had a very gentle voice, like that of a boy or a young woman. When people asked him where he came from and why he was living in the castle, he replied that he came from the mountains in Bohemia and that his kind still lived there in the Bohemian forests. However, he had fallen out of favor with them and he had been forced to leave and find asylum with good people until his comrades would again receive him. He said his name was Hinzelmann, but that he was also called Lüring. He had a wife who was called Hille Bingels. He also said that when the time was right, he would show himself to everyone in his true form, but he wasn't ready to do so yet. But he assured them that he was as fine and honest a fellow as anyone else.

The lord of the manor, however, soon began to notice that the spirit was spending more and more time with him. This made him feel very uncomfortable, but he didn't know how to get rid of the spirit. On the advice of his friends, he decided to leave his castle for a time and move to Hannover. Along the route, his party noticed a white feather flying alongside the carriage, but no one knew what it meant.

When the nobleman arrived in Hannover, he suddenly realized that a valuable gold chain he'd been wearing around his neck was missing, and he cast suspicion on the servants in the new household. The chamberlain, however, took the side of his personnel and demanded redress for this insult to their—and his—honor. The nobleman, who had no proof, sat disgruntled in his room, wondering how he could get out of this distasteful affair.

Suddenly, he heard Hinzelmann's voice next to him saying, "Why are you so sad?" Did something unpleasant happen to you? If so, just tell me, and maybe I can help you. Or should I guess what's wrong and say that you are unhappy because of a lost gold chain?"

"What are you doing here?" the nobleman replied in great surprise. "Why have you followed me here? Do you know anything of the chain?"

Hinzelmann answered, "Of course I followed you. I kept you company all during the trip and was present at all times. Didn't you see me? I was the white feather flying beside your carriage. If you want to know where your chain is, all you have to do is look under the pillow on your bed and you'll find it."

When he found the chain, the nobleman was even more upset at the spirit, who was indeed becoming quite a pest. He spoke to him sternly, asking why he had caused all the trouble with the chamberlain, particularly after he had left the castle because of the spirit in the first place.

Hinzelmann replied, "Why are you trying to get away from me? I can easily follow you wherever you go! It would be best for you to return to your own property and not try to get away from there because of me. You can see how easy it would be for me to rob you of all your possessions. But I have no intention or desire to do so."

The nobleman thought over what the spirit had said and decided to return. He vowed to God that he would never again be chased away by the spirit.

Hinzelmann proved himself reliable and industrious in all kinds of tasks in the castle. He bustled around the kitchen at night, and whenever the cook left a stack of unwashed dishes after a dinner, she would find them washed, dried, polished, and neatly stacked in the morning. Thus she was always able to count on his help and could retire to bed after dinner without worry. And if something was lost or misplaced in the kitchen, Hinzelmann always knew where it could be found and would return it to the lord. Whenever guests were expected for dinner, the spirit could easily be heard working through the night, scouring kettles, washing dishes, and scrubbing buckets and tubs. The cook was very grateful to him. Not only did she do everything he requested, but she also prepared sweet milk for him every morning for breakfast.

The spirit also assumed supervision of the scullery boys and maids. He paid attention to what work was assigned to them and kindly admonished them to be industrious in their work. But if one of them did not heed his advice, he would take a stick and teach his lesson with it. He warned the maidservants whenever their mistress was displeased at something, and he was always reminding them to get to work on this or that task.

The spirit proved to be equally efficient in the stables. He took care of the horses and brushed them so vigorously that they glistened. They began to increase their number so rapidly that everyone marveled.

Hinzelmann's chamber was in the attic, and his furniture consisted of three pieces. First, there was an easy chair. He had made it from multicolored straw, artistically woven in many decorative figures and crosses that could not be viewed without much admiration. Second, there was a small round table that had been made for him at his repeated request. Last of all, there was a bed that he had also requested. There was hardly any evidence that he ever slept in it except for a small depression, as though a cat had curled up there.

The house servants—especially the cook—had to prepare for him each day a dish of sweet milk and bread crumbs or white bread and set it on the table. At the end of the day it would all have been consumed. Occasionally, he would join the table of the lord of the manor, at which time a special place would be set for him and an extra chair brought in. Whoever served dinner had to put a small portion on his plate, and if this was forgotten, the spirit would become quite angry. The food on his plate would soon vanish. And his full glass of wine would disappear for a short time and then reappear—empty. The food was usually found later under the benches or hidden in a corner of the dining room.

In the presence of young people Hinzelmann would become very jolly, and he liked to sing and make verses. One of his favorites was:

> Master, if here you let me stay
> Good fortune will come your way;
> But if you show me the gate
> Misery will be your fate!

But he also enjoyed repeating the songs and verses of others, either to entertain or to anger them.

Once when Pastor Feldmann had been invited to Hude-Mill Castle and was approaching the front door, he heard a lot of noise coming from the hall upstairs. Someone was singing and whooping and yelling—raising all kinds of racket. The pastor thought that a group of travelers had acquired lodging during the night and were now celebrating in the upstairs rooms. He asked the steward, who was chopping wood in the courtyard, who the noisy guests were upstairs. The steward replied, "Those are not guests; that's just our Hinzelmann acting so merry. Otherwise there's not a soul up in that hall."

When the pastor climbed the stairs and approached the hall entrance, he was greeted with Hinzelmann's song.

> Domino, Domino,
> Benny licked us at dominoes.

The pastor was perplexed by this curious song and said to Hinzelmann, "What kind of music are you prancing to?"

"Oh," answered the spirit, "I learned that little verse from none other than you. You have sung it often enough. Indeed, I just heard it a few days ago while you were baptizing a child."

Hinzelmann loved to tease people but never did anyone any real harm. His teasing often resulted in workers and servants getting into scuffles at the inn in the evening when they sat down to drink. When one of them would consume a bit too much and sometimes knock an object to the floor, then reach down to pick it up, Hinzelmann would box his ears, while at the same time pinching his companion's leg. This would, of course, result in an argument, first with words, then with deeds. Then others would join in, and soon everybody would be brawling. The next day, when they were walking around with black eyes and swollen faces, one could see what had happened. Hinzelmann was greatly amused by all this, and he loved to tell how he had mischievously set up the melee. But he always made sure that no one suffered any serious injuries.

At this time Otto Aschen von Mandelslohe lived at the royal castle of Ahlden. He was Councilor and High Bailiff of Brunswick. Hinzelmann loved to play tricks on him. Once, when he was having a party, Hinzelmann started an argument among the guests, some of whom became enraged and grabbed for their sabers. But as they did, they found that their weapons were gone, and thus they had to fight with their fists. Hinzelmann took great delight in telling, with much laughter, how he had been the instigator of the argument and how he had first removed everyone's weapon. He then told how he sat back to witness the success of his prank as the guests tore into each other with a vengeance.

One time, however, a nobleman came to the castle at Hude-Mill and volunteered to drive the house spirit out. When he knew the spirit was in a room with all the windows and doors locked, he had the room and the entire castle occupied by armed soldiers. The nobleman then drew his saber, and with armed soldiers beside him, he entered the room. They looked around, and seeing nothing, began to slash and stab everywhere in the room with their swords. They thought that because the spirit could be seen in the flesh he could also be slain. Nevertheless they struck only empty air as they swung their swords wildly. Weary of the sword play, and convinced that their task had been completed, they were about to leave. But, suddenly, the door of the chamber swung open, and a black marten sprang from the room as they heard the words, "Oh, ho, how nobly you have caught me."

However, Hinzelmann had been grievously insulted by their action. He lamented bitterly, saying he would easily take the opportunity to avenge himself were it not for the two young ladies of the house whom he would like to spare this vexation.

Not long after, the same nobleman, upon entering one of the empty chambers of the castle, saw a snake curled up on the bedding that lay in a deserted corner. The snake vanished immediately, but the nobleman heard the spirit say mockingly, "You almost caught me that time!"

Another nobleman had heard many stories about Hinzelmann and was eager to experience his presence in person. No sooner had he arrived at Hude-Mill Castle than his wish was fulfilled. Hinzelmann let himself be heard in the corner of his room where a large cupboard stood, full of empty pitchers with long necks. Since the voice was soft and fine though a little hoarse—as if it were coming from an enclosed, hollow chamber—the nobleman became convinced that Hinzelmann was hiding in one of the pitchers. He grabbed the one from which he thought the voice had come and stopped it up with his fist, thinking to catch the spirit.

Hinzelmann broke into loud laughter and said, "If I had not already learned from others that you are a fool, I could now see it for myself, since you think I am crouching in an empty wine jar, and you are trying to cover it with your hand. I really wanted to tease you for a while, but it wouldn't be worth the effort. Nevertheless, I believe you will soon be taking an unexpected bath."

He then became silent and never let his presence be felt as long as the nobleman was there. Whether the man actually fell into water is unknown, but it can be assumed that he did.

Once, an exorcist came to the castle to chase the spirit away. When the man began to chant his magic formulae, which were supposed to conjure the spirit, Hinzelmann remained silent and did not reveal his presence. But when the sorcerer was about to pronounce his most powerful charms against him, Hinzelmann tore the book from his hands, ripped it to shreds, and sent them flying around the room. He then grabbed the exorcist and squeezed and scratched him until he fled in great fear. Thereupon, Hinzelmann cried out bitterly, "I too am a Christian like any other man, and I too hope one day to achieve salvation."

When someone asked him one day if he were acquainted with Hobgoblins and Poltergeists, he replied, "What have I to do with such creatures? They are demons of the Devil, and I do not number among them. No one should expect anything evil from me, only good. Just let me go unchallenged and you will experience good fortune in all things. The farm animals will prosper, the supplies will increase, and everything will be successful."

Hinzelmann was repelled by vice and sinful behavior. He used harsh words to punish one household member for stinginess, letting everyone else in the house know that he did not like this man because he was such a miser. He also rebuked another man for his vanity and pride.

When someone once told him that, if he wanted to be a good Christian, he would have to appeal to God and recite Christian prayers, he began reciting the Lord's Prayer, repeating the first five petitions out loud; but when he came to the words "deliver us from evil," he mumbled them softly. He also recited the Apostles' Creed, but did so in a stammering, hesitating fashion. When he came to, "I believe in the forgiveness of sins, the resurrection of the body and in life everlasting," he uttered them in a hoarse, scarcely audible voice, so that the words could not be understood.

The Pastor of Eickelohe, the late Reverend Marquard Feldmann, reported that his father had once been invited to Hude-Mill during Pentecost. On this occasion Hinzelmann sang the hymn "Now We Ask the Holy Ghost" from beginning to end in a pleasant soprano voice, like that of a young woman or boy. It is said that he could sing not only this hymn but many others as well upon request, especially when the people who asked him were his friends, people with whom he felt comfortable.

The spirit would become terribly enraged if one did not treat him honorably or as a Christian. Once a nobleman from the lineage of Mandelslohe came to Hude-Mill. He was a highly respected man because of his great learning. He was a canon of the Verden Seminary as well as an envoy to the Elector of Brandenburg and to the King of Denmark. When he was informed that the house spirit wanted to be treated like a Christian, the man replied that he could not believe that this was true; rather, he was compelled to regard him as an evil fiend or as the Devil, for God has not created creatures of such shape and kind. The angels praised God the Lord and watched over and protected men on earth. The racket-making, the frenzy, and the generally mischievous nature of the spirit were just not in harmony with this view.

Hinzelmann, who had so far not revealed his presence during the nobleman's visit, made a noise and then spoke, "What are you trying to say, Barthold (for that was the envoy's name)? That I am the Evil Fiend? I urge you not to say too much or I shall be compelled to show you otherwise and prove to you that you should form a better opinion of me."

The man became so frightened when he heard a voice without seeing anyone that he immediately broke off the conversation. He did not want to hear another word from the spirit, preferring to leave him unchallenged in his laurels.

Another time, when a nobleman came to dinner, he saw the place and chair that had been set for the spirit, and he refused to drink to him as the others were accustomed to doing. At this the spirit became quite angry, complaining, "I am as honest and as good a comrade as he. Why does he pass me by while drinking to everyone else?"

The nobleman replied, "Get thee out of here and go drink with thine own infernal companions. Thou hast nothing to seek here."

When Hinzelmann heard these words, he became so violently embittered that he grabbed the man by the strap under his chin (which people used, according to the customs of the day, to fasten their cloaks). He dragged him down to the floor and began to squeeze and choke him so that all those present were afraid that the spirit would do the man in. But the spirit finally let him go, although it took several hours before he recovered.

Another time, a good friend of the lord of the manor came by, but he had heard so much of the mischievous nature of the spirit that he hesitated to enter the house. Instead, he sent his servant in to report that he was unable to pay his visit. The lord sent repeated invitations to join him at the noonday meal, but the friend politely excused himself, saying that he did not have time to stay. But he also added that it terrified him to think of dining at the same table with a diabolic spook.

Hinzelmann overhead this conversation, for no sooner had the visitor expressed his feelings than a voice was heard to say, "Just wait, my good fellow, you shall pay dearly for these words."

The traveler then departed, but when he came to the bridge across the Meiße River, the horses reared so high in the air that their front legs became entangled in the harness—and horses, carriage, and passenger nearly tumbled into the water. Then the horses and harnesses were set back in order, and they got underway again. However, as they were traveling further along the route between Hude-Mill and Eickelohe where the earth was quite flat, the carriage wheels hit deep sand and the carriage tipped over. Still, none of the party suffered injury.

Hinzelmann enjoyed being among people and being present at social occasions. But, above all, he liked to spend time with the ladies, and he was quite friendly and convivial toward them. There were two young ladies at Hude-Mill, Anna and Katharine, to whom he was especially attracted. He would tell them of his sorrows whenever he had been angered and would engage them in all kinds of conversation. Whenever they traveled across country he did not wish them to be alone, so he accompanied them in the shape of a white feather. When they lay down at night to sleep, he would rest on top of the blanket at their feet, and in the morning one could tell that he had slept there by the little depression in the blanket that looked as if a small dog had lain on the spot.

Neither of the young ladies married, for Hinzelmann frightened all prospective suitors away. On several occasions a courtship developed far enough to schedule the announcement of an official engagement, but the spirit always knew what to do to have it called off. He caused one suitor, who was about to deliver his proposal, to become so confused that he forgot what he wanted to say. He caused another to become so terrified that he could do nothing but quake and tremble. His usual trick, however, was to cause golden letters to appear on the wall in front of the suitor spelling out: "Take Miss Anna and leave Miss Katharine for me." But if a suitor appeared with the intention of gaining the favor of Miss Anna, the spirit would change the letters to read: "Take Miss Katharine and leave Miss Anna for me."

If a suitor, however, paid no attention to the letters and remained firm in his resolve, perhaps even remained in the house overnight, then Hinzelmann would torment him and fool him by pounding, and throwing things, and making such a great racket that by morning the poor fellow abandoned all thoughts of marriage and was relieved to escape in one piece. The spirit caused some of the suitors to be thrown time and again from their horses as they were riding them, until they thought they would surely break a leg or their necks, and they did not know what had happened to them.

Thus it was that the two maidens never married. They lived to a ripe old age and finally died within a week of each other.

Once, one of these ladies sent a servant to the town of Rethem to purchase this and that. While he was gone, the spirit began to make clattering sounds like a stork and said, "Miss Anna, by the end of the day you will be seeking your things in the millstream." She had no idea what that was all about, but a short time later the servant returned. He told her that he had been riding home and had seen a stork standing not far from the road and had shot at it out of sheer boredom. He thought he'd hit the stork, but the stork stood where it was, and then began to clatter loudly, finally flying away.

It soon became apparent that Hinzelmann had been aware of all that had happened, for later his prophecy came true. The same servant, somewhat intoxicated, wanted to wash the sweat and dust from his horse, and he rode it down to the millstream that flowed near the castle. However, in his drunken state, he made a wrong turn and rode his horse over a steep embankment. There, unable to maintain his seating, he fell into the water far below and drowned. He was still carrying the items he had purchased on his body, and thus they, together with the corpse, had to be fished from the stream.

Hinzelmann also prophesied the future to others and warned them of impending dangers. Once, a colonel, who enjoyed especially high esteem with King Christian III of Denmark, and who had fought most courageously during the battles with the city of Lübeck, came to Hude-Mill. He was a superb marksman and a passionate huntsman, and he spent many hours pursuing wild sow and stag in the surrounding forests.

One day, as he was again preparing himself for the hunt, Hinzelmann appeared before him and said, "Thomas (that was his name), I warn thee, take special caution in thy shooting, otherwise an accident will befall thee shortly." The colonel paid no heed to the warning, for he thought it meaningless. A few days later, while he was firing at a deer, the musket exploded and tore the thumb off his left hand. No sooner had it happened than Hinzelmann appeared and said to him, "Look now, what have I told thee? Hadst thou refrained from shooting during this period, this misfortune would not have befallen thee."

Another military officer, Lord von Falkenberg, also came to Hude-Mill for a visit. He was a vivacious fellow with a merry nature, and he soon began to tease Hinzelmann and make all kinds of jokes. After a while the spirit tired of all this frivolity and began to show his displeasure. Finally, he stormed out with the words, "Falkenberg, now thou canst excel at making fun of me. But when thou arrivest outside the gates of Magdeburg, they will give thy cap a good brushing, so that thou wilt forget thy words of ridicule."

The nobleman was frightened, convinced that there was more behind these words, and broke off his conversation with Hinzelmann. Shortly thereafter he left the castle. Not long after, the siege of Magdeburg began under the leadership of the Elector Moritz. Lord von Falkenberg was present under the command of a distinguished German prince. Those under siege defended themselves with great courage, and day and night they fired their artillery at their attackers. During the battle, a missile from a falconet struck Lord von Falkenberg, tearing his chin away, and after three days in great agony he died.

Another time a man from Hude-Mill was out in the fields with other workers and servants cutting the grain. He had no thoughts of misfortune when suddenly Hinzelmann came running up to him in the field, yelling, "Run! Run! Run home in all haste and help thy youngest son who has fallen into the hearth and whose face is badly burned!"

The man, greatly shocked, dropped his scythe and raced home

to see if Hinzelmann had told the truth. No sooner had he crossed the threshold than someone ran up to him and told him of the accident, and he saw his child with terrible burns over his face. He had been sitting on a small stool next to the fire where a large kettle was hanging. As he reached into the kettle with a spoon, his stool tilted, and he fell forward, landing with his face in the fire. His mother, who was nearby, ran and pulled him from the flames. Although he was badly burned, he had been saved from certain death. It was remarkable that at the very instant the accident happened, the spirit appeared to the father in the field, urging him to hasten to the rescue.

If the spirit took a dislike to someone, he would pester him constantly or punish him for his vices. For example, he accused the clerk of Hude-Mill of being vain and pretentious and thus became spiteful toward him, plaguing him day and night with annoyances and vexations. Once he bragged quite merrily about boxing the ears of the arrogant clerk. When someone asked the clerk if this were true—had the spirit visited him—the clerk replied, "Yes, indeed, he has visited me too many times. Last night he tormented me so much I didn't know how to escape him."

The clerk had been having an affair with the chambermaid, and one night he had gone to her and they were engaged in an intimate conversation. While he sat next to her, thinking in lustful anticipation that only the four walls were witness to them, the cunning little spirit arrived, drove them apart, and kicked the clerk through the door in a most ungentle fashion. He even took after him with a broomstick, chasing him back to his room where he soon forgot his beloved. It is said that Hinzelmann composed a satiric song making fun of the unlucky lover that he often performed amid much laughter for the entertainment of guests.

Once, toward evening, someone at Hude-Mill was seized by painful stomach cramps. He sent a maidservant down to the cellar to fetch wine, for he was supposed to take his medication with a glass of wine. While the girl sat before the keg and began to tap it, Hinzelmann appeared next to her and said, "You will remember how you scolded me and cursed at me a few days ago. As punishment you are going to have to spend the night sitting here in the cellar. Don't fret about the sick man. Within a half hour the pains will be gone, and the wine you would have taken to him would have done more harm than good. Stay seated here until the cellar door is opened again."

The sick man waited for a long time; but when the girl did not appear with the wine he sent another girl down to the cellar. When she came to the cellar door, she found that it was locked with a padlock and that the other maidservant was still inside. She called out that Hinzelmann had locked her in. They wanted to open the cellar to let the maid out, but they could not find a key for the lock anywhere in the castle, no matter how hard they looked. By morning, however, the cellar door stood open, and the padlock and the key lay before the door so that the girl was free to go. The man's stomach cramps totally disappeared just as the spirit predicted.

The spirit had never let himself be seen in the flesh by the lord of the manor, and each time the lord would ask to see him, especially since he was supposed to have human form, the spirit would reply that the time had not yet arrived and that his lordship should wait until he considered it the proper time.

One night, as the lord was lying in bed unable to sleep, he heard a noise at one side of his bedchamber, and he suspected that the spirit was present. He thus said aloud, "Hinzelmann, if that is you, then answer me."

"Yes," the spirit replied, "it's me. What do you want?"

As the chamber was illuminated to some degree by moonlight, the lord thought that he could see the shadow of a child's figure in the part of the room from which the voice had emanated. When he noticed that the spirit was acting quite friendly and trusting, he engaged him in a conversation, and finally said, "Do let yourself be seen and felt by me." But Hinzelmann did not want to. "At least give me your hand so that I can see that you have flesh and bone like a human."

"No," said Hinzelmann, "I do not trust you. You are a rascal. You want to grab hold of me and you won't want to let go."

After a long discussion, during which the lord swore by trust and faith not to hold on to him, but to let go of his hand immediately, the spirit said, "Look, here is my hand!"

When the lord reached out and touched it, it seemed to him as though he were feeling the hand of a small child. But the spirit quickly withdrew it. The lord did not relent and expressed his desire to touch the spirit's face. The spirit finally relented, and as the lord groped for it, he felt as though he were touching bare teeth or a fleshless skull. But the spirit again quickly pulled his head back so that the lord was not able to perceive what the face actually looked like. All that he could conclude was that it, like the hand, was cold and without the warmth of human life.

The cook, who was on quite familiar terms with Hinzelmann, believed that she could make requests of him that others would not dare. The urge overcame her to see the spirit she had heard talking every day and for whom she provided food and drink. And so she begged him incessantly to grant her the wish. However, he refused to give in, saying that the opportunity was not yet right.

After a certain time had passed, he assured her, he would let himself be seen by everyone. But the cook's curiosity was only enhanced by this refusal, and she pleaded with him more and more not to deny her request. He warned her that she would surely come to regret her excessive curiosity if he did relent.

But when this too failed and she would not give up, he finally said to her, "Tomorrow morning come to the cellar before sunrise and hold a bucket of water in each hand. Your wish will be granted."

The woman asked, "What is the water for?"

"You will find out," replied the spirit, "for without the water the sight of me would cause you harm."

The following morning the cook was up and ready at the earliest hour. She filled the two buckets with water, and carrying one in each hand, she descended into the cellar. She looked around but couldn't see a thing. Then, she glanced down at the floor and saw, lying in a trough, a naked child who appeared to be about three years of age. Two crossed knives were stuck in its heart, and its body was covered with blood. This terrible sight gave the woman such a fright that all her senses left her and she fell to the floor unconscious. The spirit then took the buckets of water and poured them over her head and she regained consciousness. She looked at the trough, but everything had vanished.

Then she heard Hinzelmann saying, "Now you see the purpose of the water. If it had not been within reach, you would have died here in the cellar. I do hope your passionate curiosity to see me has now cooled off some."

Afterward he frequently teased the cook about this episode, and he often told it amid laughter for the entertainment of guests.*

Pastor Feldman von Eickelohe wrote in a letter on December 15, 1597, that Hinzelmann had frequently permitted people to see his small hand, which was like that of a boy or a young woman, but that otherwise no one had been able to catch sight of him.

He did show himself, however, to innocent, playing children. Pastor Feldman, for example, recalled that when he was fourteen or fifteen years old and not particularly concerned with the spirit, he once saw it running up the stairs in the form of a small boy. When-

---

*Told somewhat differently about the spirit "Heinzlein" in Luther's *Tischreden*, ed. Aurifaber, 1571, p. 441a.

ever children gathered outside the house at Hude-Mill to play games, Hinzelmann would appear among them in the form of a handsome child, and all the other children saw him clearly. Later, they would tell their parents of this unknown child who came to them and joined in their play.

A maidservant confirmed this story. Once when she came into a room where five or six children were playing, she saw among them an unknown little boy, dressed in red velvet. He had a beautiful face and long curly golden hair that hung down over his shoulders. When she approached to get a closer look, he left the group of children and vanished.

Hinzelmann also revealed himself to a fool named Klaus, who was staying at the castle, and on whom he played all kinds of tricks. Once, the fool was missing for a long time. Later, when he was asked where he had been, he replied, "I was with the little man, and I played with him." And when they further asked how big the man was, he held out his hand to about the height of a four-year-old child.

When it was time for the house spirit to move away, he came to the lord of the manor and said, "Look here, I want to present you with something. Guard it carefully and think of me every time you look at it." He then handed him first a small crucifix (it is uncertain from the words of the informant whether it was made of silk or of cord), woven quite exquisitely. It was of a finger's length, hollow inside, and when one shook it, it made a ringing noise. Second, he presented the lord with a straw hat that he had also made himself. On it he had woven artistic figures and pictures with colored straw. Third, he gave him a leather glove, set with pearls that formed wondrous figures.

Finally, the spirit added the prophecy: "As long as these objects remain intact within thy house, the entire lineage will prosper and thy good fortune will continue to increase. But if these gifts are divided, lost, or squandered, the lineage will decrease in number and finally sink into oblivion." When Hinzelmann perceived that the lord did not seem to place particular value on the gifts, he spoke further, "I fear that thou dost not esteem these things very highly and that thou wilt let them fall from thy possession. Therefore I advise thee to hand them over to thy two sisters, Anna and Katharine, for safekeeping. They will take better care of them."

And so the lord gave the items to his sisters, who took them and put them carefully away. They showed them to others only as a gesture of special friendship. After the death of the sisters, the objects fell to their brother and remained with him throughout his life.

He once showed them to Pastor Feldmann at the latter's request after they had been mentioned during an intimate conversation. When the brother died, the objects came into the possession of his only daughter, Adelheid, who was married to L.v.H., and they remained for some time in her possession.

After this, their location was unknown for a time. But the son of Pastor Feldmann made many inquiries and learned the following. The straw hat was presented to Emperor Ferdinand II, who esteemed it as an object of wonder. At this same time the leather glove was still in the possession of a nobleman. It was short and just barely covered his hand; the top of the glove was embroidered with pearls in the figure of a snail. The fate of the small cross is still unknown.

After spending four years, from 1584 to 1588, at Hude-Mill, the spirit departed voluntarily. Before he left, he said that one day when the lineage was on the decline he would return, and once again everything would prosper, and the family would enjoy a new ascendance.


## ‡‡ 77 ‡‡
### KNOCKER

There lived in the castle at Flügelau a good spirit who did many things as a favor to the servant girls. All they had to say was, "Knocker, fetch it!" and the desired item would appear. He delivered letters; rocked the children to sleep; and picked the fruit. But once, when someone demanded that he reveal himself in the flesh and would not relent until he gave in, he turned himself into a ball of fire, flew up the chimney, and disappeared. The castle burned to the ground and has never been rebuilt. This happened just before the wars with Sweden.


## ‡‡ 78 ‡‡
### BOOTS

There once lived in the castle of Calenberg a small spirit by the name of Boots. He had once received an injury to his leg, and ever after he wore a large boot that covered the entire leg. He was afraid it might otherwise be torn away.

## SQUIRREL

A spirit once lived near the town of Elten, about half a mile from Emmerich in the Duchy of Cleves. The common people named him *Ekerken*, which means Squirrel in the local dialect. He would run and jump across the highway, and he would mock and plague all the travelers in every possible way. He would often strike some riders, throw others from their horses, and turn carts and carriages upside down. Nobody ever saw anything of him with their own eyes, other than a small human hand.

‡‡  80  ‡‡

## THE NIGHT SPIRIT OF KENDENICH

On Kendenich, the old estate of the Teutonic Knights, situated about two hours from Cologne on the Rhine, there is muddy swamp, densely overgrown with rushes and alder shrubs. A nun hides in the rushes there, and no one can pass the area at night without her trying to jump on his back. If she succeeds, the victim is compelled to carry her, and she will ride and drive him the whole night until he falls to the earth unconscious.

‡‡  81  ‡‡

## THE NIGHTMARE

Even if one closes all windows and doors securely against Nightmares they can still enter through the tiniest of openings, which they seek out with peculiar glee. In the still of the night one can hear the noise they make as they pass through the wall. If one gets up quickly and stuffs the hole shut, they are compelled to remain inside and cannot leave, even if all the doors are opened. Before they are released, one must extract a promise from them never to bother this place again. When they are thus trapped, they will lament pitifully that they have children at home who will waste away if they do not return.

The *Trud*, or Nightmare, will travel very far during the nocturnal rounds. Late one night some shepherds were tending their flocks in a field near some water, when the Nightmare appeared, climbed into a boat, and rowed itself across the water with a paddle that it had brought along. Once on the other side, the Nightmare climbed out, secured the boat, and continued on its way. After a time it reappeared and rowed back across the water. After witnessing this event for several nights without doing anything, the shepherds decided to remove the boat. When the Nightmare reappeared the next night, it began to wail pitifully and threaten the shepherds that unless they wanted trouble, they had best return the boat immediately—and they did so.

One man, who was being plagued by the Nightmare, placed a flax comb with very sharp points on his chest in order to repel the spirit. But the Nightmare turned it around and pressed the sharp points into the man's chest. A better method of repelling the spirit is to turn one's shoes around by the bed, so that the heels are right at the baseboard and the toes are pointing outward. Also, if the Nightmare is plaguing someone and the victim can grab hold of its thumbs and squeeze them it will have to flee.

At night they like to ride horses, and in the morning one can see that they have done so because the horses are exhausted. The spirit can also be repelled and driven off by a horse's head. If a sleeper goes to bed at night without changing the position of the chair in the room, he will be ridden in the night by the Nightmare. They like to tangle their victims' hair into elflocks, or as they are also called, tangle locks, or mare's braids. They do this by sucking on the hair and twisting it.

When a nursemaid puts diapers on a child, she must make a cross and a corner on the diaper, otherwise the Nightmare will redo the job.

If one can say the following verse to the Nightmare

> *Trud*, come in the morrow
> for something to borrow

then the spirit will have to flee, but it will return in the morning in the shape of a human in order to borrow something. Or if one can yell at it, "Come in the morning and have a drink with me," then the person who sent the spirit will have to appear the next day.

According to Prätorius, you can tell a Nightmare when you see one because its eyebrows join together in a single line. However, others say that people whose eyebrows are joined together can with mere thoughts send Nightmares to plague people with whom they are angry. The Nightmare that emerges from their eyebrows looks like a small white moth and lights upon the breast of the sleeping victim.

## THE CHANGELING

A clerk who lived in Heßloch, near Odernheim in the Gau, had a servant and a cook who lived together as man and wife, the only difference being that they were not able to have their relationship publicly consecrated. They produced a child, but it neither grew nor gained weight. It would scream day and night and constantly wanted to eat. The woman finally sought counsel and accordingly wanted to take the baby to Cyriak Meadow near Neuhausen to have it weighed and to give it water from Cyriak Spring. Only then would it get better. At that time it was believed that such a treatment would either lead to a cure or to the child's death after nine days.*

The woman tied the child to her back and started out on her journey. But by the time she arrived at the valley near Westhofen the child had become so heavy that she was gasping for breath and sweat was rolling down her face. There, however, she encountered a traveling student who said, "Woman, what a vile creature you are carrying! It wouldn't be surprising if he crushed your neck."

She replied that it was her dear child. And she told him how the child would not grow and prosper and that was why she was taking it to Neuhausen to have it weighed.

But the student replied, "That is not your child. That is the Devil himself.† Cast him into the stream!" But when she refused and insisted it was her child and kissed it and hugged it, the student continued to speak, "Your child is home. You will find it in the storage room behind the hamper in a new cradle; cast this monster into the stream."

The woman, amid tears and wailing, did so. As soon as she threw him in, a howling and grumbling noise as if from wolves and bears was heard beneath the bridge on which she was standing.

When the mother returned home, she found her own child, happy, healthy, and laughing in a new cradle.

## THE CHANGELINGS IN THE WATER

A farmer near Halberstadt had a changeling at home that had sucked its mother and five wet nurses dry. It had consumed inordinate amounts of food (for such creatures eat as much as ten

---

*A changeling does not generally live more than seven years. According to others, however, it will live to be eighteen or nineteen years of age.

†The Devil steals the real children from their cradles and replaces them with his own. From this comes the term "changeling."

normal children) and behaved in such a fashion that they grew weary of it.

The farmer was advised to take the child on a pilgrimage to Heckelstadt to entrust it to the Virgin Mary and to have it weighed. The good farmer followed this advice; he placed the child in a basket, which he bore on his back, and took it on the pilgrimage.

But when he was crossing a bridge over a stream, he heard a voice call out from the water below, "Changeling! Changeling!" The farmer was quite unaccustomed to such a thing, and it gave him quite a fright.

Then the devil in the water asked, "Where are you going?"

The little monster replied, "I'm on my way to Heckelstadt to Our Dear Lady—

Me they want to weigh
And for my good health pray."

When the farmer heard the changeling speak so well, he became furious and cast the child and the basket into the water. The two devils then swam off together, calling "Ho! Ho! Ho!" They played together, had words with one another, and then they vanished.

‡‡ 84 ‡‡

## THE MANDRAKE

Legend has it that when an inveterate thief is hanged—one for whom stealing is an innate quality; or whose mother when pregnant either stole or had a great urge to do so; or, according to some, if he was innocent but confessed to stealing under torture; and if he is still an otherwise chaste youth—if he lets water and sperm fall to the ground (*aut sperma in terram effundit*) then a Mandrake or a Gallows Manikin will grow from the earth at that spot.

The plant has broad leaves and yellow flowers on top. There is great danger involved in trying to remove it, for if it is pulled up, it will groan and howl and scream so frightfully that the person who pulled it up will soon die.

In order to get the plant one must go out before sunrise on a Friday, stop up one's ears with cotton, wax, or pitch, take an all-black dog—he cannot have a single spot on his body—and proceed to the gallows site. One makes three crosses over the Mandrake and digs a ring all around it so that the roots are attached to the earth only by tiny fibers. One then takes a string and ties one end to the Mandrake and the other end to the dog's tail. Next, one takes a piece of bread, shows it to the dog, and then one runs off. The dog, hungry for the bread, will follow, pulling the root out. However, he will then be struck by the groaning cries and will drop dead. One then removes the Mandrake, washes it clean in red wine, wraps it in red and white silk, and places it in a small chest. One must bathe it every Friday, and at each new moon give it a new white shirt.

If the owner of the Mandrake asks it questions, it will answer, and it will reveal all kinds of secret things about the future and how to attain prosperity and good fortune. The owner will have no enemies, cannot become poor, and if he has no children, a blessed event will soon occur. If one places a piece of money with the Mandrake at night it will have doubled by morning. However, if one wants to enjoy its services for a long time and insure that it will not decay or die then one must take care not to overload it. One can safely place a half taler with it every night. But no more than one ducat may be left, and then only on rare occasions—and by no means every night.

Whenever the owner of a Mandrake dies, the youngest son inherits it. But he must place a piece of bread and a piece of money in his father's casket to be buried with him. If the heir should die before the father, then the Mandrake will go to the oldest son, but the youngest must also have already been buried with bread and money.

‡‡   85   ‡‡

## SPIRITUS FAMILIARIS

The familiar of sorcerers is usually kept in a sealed glass bottle. He looks like something between a spider and a scorpion and is always moving. Whoever purchases him will find that the familiar is always present in his pocket. Even if he mislays the bottle somewhere and forgets it, it will return to him all by itself. He brings much good fortune, reveals hidden treasures, makes one beloved by one's friends and feared by one's enemies. He is as strong as iron and steel in war, and thus insures that his owner always emerges the victor. He also protects his owner against arrest and incarceration. One does not need to care for him or bathe or clothe him.

Whoever dies with the spirit still in his possession must accompany him into Hell. For this reason the owner always seeks to sell him to another. But he can only be sold at a price cheaper than that for which he was purchased. He must remain finally in the possession of the one who purchased him with the smallest possible coin.

There was once a soldier who purchased a familiar for one crown and learned only later how dangerous it was to possess this spirit. He took it to its previous owner, threw it at his feet, and then raced away in great haste. When he arrived home, he found the spirit back in his pocket. He fared no better when he cast him into the Danube.

A man from Augsburg, who was a horse trader and a wagon driver, once traveled to a famous German city. The trip was very hard on his horses. One fell dead at the city gates, another at the inn, and within a few days the remaining six were also dead. He was desperate and did not know what to do. He walked around the city in tears, lamenting his losses to anyone who would listen.

It then came to pass that he met another wagon driver, to whom he told the story of his great misfortune. The second wagon driver replied, "Don't fret. I'm going to tell you a way to help yourself that you'll thank me for." The horse trader was convinced that the man was only speaking empty words of condolence, but the man insisted, "No, no, comrade! You're indeed going to be helped. Go into that house and ask for a certain group of men," whom he named. "Tell them about your stroke of misfortune and ask for help."

The horse trader followed the man's advice, entered the house, and asked a boy who was there about the men. He had to wait for an answer. Finally, the boy returned and led him into a room in which a group of old men were sitting at a round table. They addressed him by name and said, "Thou hast lost eight horses and that has made thee despair. Now, on the advice of thy comrade, thou hast come to us for help. Thou shalt be granted what thou desireth." He was directed to sit at a small table, and after a few minutes had passed, he was handed a little box with the words "Always carry this box with thee, and thou wilt from this moment on acquire wealth. But take care never to open it if thou dost not wish to become poor again." The horse trader asked what he would have to pay for the box, but the men would take nothing for it. The only thing they demanded was that he enter his name into a large logbook, which he was able to do with someone guiding his hand.

The horse trader left to return home, but no sooner had he left the house than he found a leather sack with three hundred ducats. He took the money and bought new horses. Before he left the city, he found a large pot of money in the stalls where his new horses were quartered. He soon discovered that wherever he went, if he set the box down on the ground, a light would begin to glow, signaling a place where someone had either lost money or buried some treasure long ago that could be easily recovered. In this manner he was able to acquire great treasures of wealth without having to resort to thievery or murder.

When the horse trader's wife heard what had transpired, she became frightened and said, "Thou hast received something evil; it is not God's will that a man should become rich through such forbidden things. Thou shouldst earn thy bread by the sweat of thy brow. I beg thee, for the sake of thine immortal soul, return to this city and give the box back to the men." The man, moved by these words, resolved to do so, and he sent a stableboy back to the city to return the box. But the boy returned with the report that the men in question were no longer in the house, and that no one knew of their present whereabouts.

The wife of the horse trader then paid very close attention to see where her husband kept the box. She saw him place it in a special pocket he had made in his trousers under his belt. One night, while her husband was sleeping, she got up, found the box, and opened it. A black buzzing fly flew out and found its way to the open window. She closed the lid of the box and put it back where she'd found it, unconcerned about what would happen next.

From that time on, all their good fortune turned to the most wretched misfortune. The horses fell dead or were stolen, the grain in the attic rotted, their house burned down three times, and their acquired wealth disappeared before their eyes. The man went into debt and became so poverty stricken that, in total despair, he killed his wife with a butcher knife and then put a bullet through his head.

## ‡‡ 86 ‡‡

## THE BIRD'S NEST

In some regions one still encounters the belief that there are certain bird's nests, often called Twaleaf or Sisken Nests, which, usually being invisible themselves, have the power to make the man who carries one invisible. In order to find such a nest, one must glimpse the reflection of one, by chance, in a mirror or in the water. It is possible that the name Twaleaf relates the legend to the belief concerning the double-leaf growth (*Bifolium*) that bears the name Bird's Nest in almost all European languages. This growth appears to have many of the same characteristics as the Mandrake. A seventeenth-century novel, which is clearly based on popular tradition, gives us the most complete description of the legend.

While this conversation was going on, I looked out over the water and saw the reflection of a tree. I also saw something sitting on the fork of a branch, which, however, I could not see when I looked directly at the tree. I showed this wondrous apparition to my wife, and when she saw it, she made note of precisely where in the tree the forked branch was, on which the nest sat. She then climbed the tree in order to bring down that which we had seen in the water. I was watching her closely and noticed how she disappeared at the moment she took hold of that thing we had seen in the water. But I could see the reflection of her figure in the water as she was climbing down from the tree, holding a small bird's nest in her hand that she had taken from the forked branch.

I asked her what kind of bird's nest she had. She, in turn, asked if I could see her. I answered, "I cannot see you in the tree, but I can see you in the water."

"That's fine," she replied, "when I get down you will see what I have."

It seemed miraculous to me that I could hear my wife speaking and yet not see her, and it was even more wondrous to see her shadow moving toward me but not her! And when she moved into the shade and came closer, so that she herself cast no shadow at all because she was now out of the sunlight and in the shade, I could perceive nothing of her at all, except for the slightest rustling noise made both by her feet and by her dress while she was walking. It was as if a spook had been hovering around me.

She sat herself down where I was sitting and handed me the nest. The moment I took it from her hand I could see her again, but she could not see me. We tried this procedure a number of times, and we determined that each time the one who had the nest in his hand was totally invisible. She then wrapped the nest in a handkerchief, so as to insure that the stone, herb, or root in the nest that possessed this strange power would not fall out and be lost. And after she set it aside, we could see each other again as we did before she had climbed the tree. However, we could not see the handkerchief in which the nest was wrapped. But when we moved our hands to the place where she had set it down, we could feel it.*

## ‡‡  87  ‡‡

### THE BROOD PENNY

The Brood Penny, or as it is also called, the Hatching Coin, can be acquired in the following blasphemous manner. The man who wants to join up with the Devil should go to a crossroad on Christmas Eve

*The story took place in Bavaria. S. *Simplicissimus*, II, 92, 94, 277, 288, 340, 362. Cf. also *Simpl.* II, 229.

just as it begins to turn dark. Standing under the open skies, he should take thirty pennies or other coins and place them, one after the other, in a round circle and then begin counting them first in one direction and then the other. The counting must be in progress at precisely the time when the church bells ring for mass. The Infernal Spirit will do everything he can to disturb the man in his counting, producing all kinds of frightful visions of glowing furnaces, curious carriages, and headless ghosts. If the man hesitates for an instant in his counting, or stammers, his head will be twisted off. But if he continues his counting correctly in both directions, the Devil will eventually throw the thirty-first coin in with the other thirty. This thirty-first coin has the magic power to breed a new coin each and every night.

A farmer's wife in Pantschdorf near Wittenberg, who possessed such a brood penny, was discovered to be a witch by the following incident.

One day she had some compelling business to take care of. But before leaving she instructed the maidservant to take the milk from the first cow she milked and—before she milked the others—to boil it immediately and pour it over the slice of white bread she would find in a dish. She was then to place the dish in a wooden box that the farmer's wife pointed out to her.

The maid either forgot the instructions, or thought it made no difference whether she boiled the milk before or after milking the other cows, and she went about all the other chores first. Afterward she took the boiling milk from the fire and, holding the kettle in one hand, she opened the box with the other. In the box she saw a pitch-black calf, which opened its mouth wide. She was so frightened that she poured the hot milk down its throat, and the calf jumped up and fled, setting the whole house afire.

The farmer's wife was apprehended and she confessed. The farmers of the village kept her Brood Penny for many years in the village treasury.

‡‡   88   ‡‡

## BEATING THE CHANGELING WITH SWITCHES

The following true story took place in 1580. Near Breslau there lived a well-known nobleman who every summer had large harvests of hay and grass. Each year, his subjects were required to work the harvest for him as part of their servitude. One year, included among those called there was a new mother who had given birth to her child less than a week before. When she saw that the lord insisted on her services and that she could not refuse, she took her child to the fields with her, placed it on a small stack of hay, and then proceeded with her work. After she had worked for some time, she returned to her child to nurse it. But when she looked at it, she gave a loud scream and put her hands together in despair, lamenting to everyone there that this child was not hers because it sucked the milk from her so greedily and because it howled in such an inhuman way, making noises that she had never before heard from her own child.

As always happens in such cases, the woman kept the child for several days, but it behaved in such unseemly fashion that the poor woman was close to despair. Finally, she went to the lord and amid tears told him all. He said, "Woman, if you think this child is not yours, then there is only one thing to do. Take it out to the field where you left your own child and begin to beat it severely with a switch. Then you will witness wonders."

The woman did as he said. She went out and beat the child with a switch until it screamed. The Devil then returned her stolen child, saying, "There, you have it!" And he then disappeared, taking his own child with him.

This story is widely told by young and old in the area in and around Breslau.

## ‡‡ 89 ‡‡

## WATCHING OUT FOR THE CHILDREN

A reliable citizen of Leipzig told the following story. When his first son was just a few weeks old, he was found uncovered and lying crosswise in his cradle on three successive nights, even though the cradle stood right next to the mother's bed. On the fourth night, the father decided to stay up all night and keep watch over his child. He watched and waited for a long time, staying constantly awake until some time after midnight. Of course, nothing happened to the child because he had been watching it the whole time. But then his eyes closed for a moment, and when the mother woke shortly thereafter, she found the child once again lying crosswise in the cradle, and its blanket had been thrown over the middle of her bed. The blanket had been tucked in at the foot of the cradle, where it could be folded back. It all happened so fast, everyone was quite amazed. Otherwise the evil spirit seemed to have no power over the child.

## THE NURSEMAID-IN-THE-RYE

Among the rural folk in Mark Brandenburg the legend of the Nurse-maid-in-the-Rye is still current. She hides in grain fields and that is the reason children are afraid to venture into such places. In Alt-mark one can quiet children down by saying, "Shut up, or the Rye Woman with her long black teats will get you!"

In the regions around Brunswick and Lüneburg she is called the Grain Wife. When children are out picking cornflowers they remind each other that she comes and steals children, and thus they do not venture too far into the planted fields.

In the year 1662 a woman from Saalfeld told the following story to Prätorius. A nobleman who once lived there forced a woman to get up from childbed and help bundle the sheaves during harvest. The woman had to take her newborn with her into the fields, and she laid it on the ground next to her and proceeded with her work. After a while the nobleman who was supervising the work saw the Earth Woman come with another child and exchange it for the woman's. The false child then began to scream, and the mother came running in order to nurse it. But the nobleman stopped her and ordered her to stand back, he would let her know when the time was right. The woman thought that he only did so because he didn't want her to stop working, and she returned to her work greatly troubled. In the meantime the child screamed incessantly, and finally the Rye Woman appeared again, picked up the screaming child, and put back the stolen child. After the nobleman witnessed all this, he called to the peasant woman and told her to take her child and return home. From that time on he never again forced a woman to get up from childbed to perform service.

## TWO WOMEN FROM THE UNDERWORLD

Prätorius learned of the following occurrence from a student, whose mother said it had taken place in Dessau.

A woman brought a child into the world, but before it had been baptized, she fell into a deep sleep. At midnight two women from the Underground World appeared. They made a fire in the stove, heated water upon it, took a child that they had brought with them and bathed it, and then they exchanged this child for the other one.

They then departed, but at the next mountain they got into an argument over the child and began throwing it back and forth like a ball. In the meantime the child in the house began to cry, which awoke the maidservant. When she saw the child of the woman in the bed, she knew it had been exchanged. She ran from the house and found the women haggling over the stolen child. She moved close to them as they were throwing it back and forth, and as soon as it came her way she took it in her arms and raced home. She then took the changeling brat and set it on the doorstep. The Underground Women soon came and took it back.

## ‡‡ 92 ‡‡

### KING GREEN FOREST

Many years ago a king lived on Mt. Christen in Upper Hesse, where he had his castle. He had an only daughter of whom he thought very highly and who possessed wondrous gifts. Once, his enemy, King Green Forest, came with his army and besieged his castle. After the siege had gone on for some time,* the king in the castle spoke words of encouragement to his daughter. By May Day, however, the siege was still going on, and as day broke the daughter saw the enemy army approaching with green trees. She became frightened at this sight for she knew that everything was lost, and she said to her father:

> Give up, O Father dear,
> the green forest is near!

The king then sent his daughter to King Green Forest who agreed to grant free passage from the embattled castle for herself and all the belongings she could load on a single jackass. She took her own father† and loaded him onto the animal, together with her most prized treasures and left the castle.

After they had traveled a long while and were weary, the king's daughter said, "Let us rest here!" That is why the village is called Wollmar‡ (one hour from Mt. Christen, in the plains). Soon they moved on through wilderness areas and into the mountains, until finally they came to a spot, where the king's daughter said, "Here is a field!" And there they remained and built a castle, which they

---

*Nine years. On one occasion he deceived the enemy with cakes that he rolled down the hill from the bastions while the besiegers went hungry. From this episode comes the name Hunger Valley, which lies nearby.

†According to others, it was the queen who did this and not the daughter.

‡In German her words were: "Hier *wollemer* ruhen." Wollemer is the colloquial pronunciation of "*wollen wir.*"—D. W.

called Hatzfeld.* The remains of the castle are there to this very day. And the nearby village takes its name from the castle. (Hatzfeld, a town on the Eder River, lies about four hours west of Mt. Christen.)

## ‡‡ 93 ‡‡

## BLÜMELISALP

More than one region of Switzerland knows the legend of the fertile Alpine meadow that was once magnificently full of flowers but which today is covered over with ice and boulders.

For example, in the Bernese Highlands the following story is told of the Klaride Alps. Years ago the Alpine meadow here was glorious in its richness. The cattle prospered beyond all expectations, and each cow had to be milked three times a day and gave two full buckets at each milking.

Up on the mountainside at that time there lived a very wealthy herdsman who became proud and vain, and he began to ridicule the simple old customs of the countryside. He decorated and furnished his cabin in a most luxurious fashion, and he began to have a love affair with Kathrine, a beautiful milkmaiden. In arrogant presumption he built a stairway in his house entirely out of large cheeses. Moreover, he would display his cheeses and his butter for show, and he washed his paths with milk, over which walked his beloved Kathrine, Brändel his cow, and Rhyn his dog.

His pious mother was quite unaware of his sins, and one Sunday she decided to visit the pastures of her son. When she arrived, she was quite weary and asked for a drink for refreshment. The mistress talked the herdsman into putting sour milk and sand into the mug of milk he handed to his mother. Astonished at the shameful deed, the old woman quickly left. She descended to the valley, where she turned and cursed her godless son, asking God to punish him.

Suddenly a storm arose, and powerful thunder, lightning, and torrential rains laid waste the glorious meadows. Alpine pastures and cabins were buried under landslides, and people and cattle perished.

The ghosts of the herdsman and his servants are damned to wander the mountains until they are delivered. He can be heard calling, "I and my dog Rhyn and my cow Brändli and my Kathy are doomed eternally on Klaride!" Their deliverance can only take place if a herdsman, on Good Friday, can milk the cow dry without saying

*In German her words were: *"Hier hat's Feld!"*—D. W.

a word. But since the cow's udder is enveloped in thorns that constantly pierce it, the cow cannot hold still and is quite wild. Thus, the task is not an easy one.

A cowherd was once able to milk half a bucketful when, suddenly, a man tapped him on the shoulder and asked, "Is it nice and foamy?" Without thinking the herdsman replied, "Oh, yes!" It was too late! Brändli, the cow, vanished before his very eyes.

## ‡‡ 94 ‡‡

### THE LILY

In the country of H. there once lived a nobleman, named A.v.Th., who had the amazing ability to chop off heads and then replace them. However, he made a firm resolution to desist in this dangerous, diabolic business before something terrible happened—but too late.

During a party he let his friends talk him into performing this diversion one last time. Quite understandably, no one was willing to lend his own head for this purpose. Finally, the houseboy was talked into it, but only on the firm condition that his head would be restored properly to its place.

The nobleman then proceeded to chop the boy's head off. But this time, he could not succeed in replacing it. He then turned to the guests and said, "There is one among you who is preventing me from completing this act. I warn him not to do so any longer." He then tried again to complete his trick, but he was unable to do so. He warned and threatened his guests again not to hinder him. But again it did no good.

When for the third time he failed to replace the head, he caused a lily to grow from the table, and he then chopped off the flowering head. At that very instant one of the guests, who was sitting on a bench behind him, fell to the floor with his head rolling beside him. The nobleman then successfully replaced the head of the houseboy. Afterward he fled the country and did not return until things had been smoothed over and he had been granted a pardon.

## ‡‡ 95 ‡‡

### JOHANN VON PASSAU

Doctor Martin Luther told the following story. A nobleman once had had a beautiful young wife, but she died and was buried. Not long after, when the lord and his servant were sleeping in the same room, the deceased woman appeared and leaned over her husband's bed, as though to speak to him. The servant observed this occurrence two nights in a row, and he asked his master why a woman in a white dress came nightly to his bed. The man said that was impossible, for he slept soundly every night and saw nothing.

When the third night came, the lord decided to pay attention and remain awake in bed. And when the woman came to the bed again, the lord asked who she was and what she wanted. She replied that she was his wife, and he said, "But you are dead and buried."

To this she replied, "Yes, because of your cursing and for the sake of your sins I have had to die, but if you want me, I shall become your wife again."

The man then said, "Yes, if it could only be!"

But she had one condition. She warned him never to curse again, even when he had something to curse about, for she would then have to die once more. The man agreed, and the deceased wife remained with him. She ran the household, slept with him, ate and drank with him, and together they produced children.

It came to pass that one evening the nobleman had guests. After dinner the woman left to get some gingerbread from a box to go with the fruit, and she was detained in the kitchen for a long time. The man became grumpy and abusive and began to curse in his former fashion. When the woman did not return, they went into the kitchen to see where she was. Her dress was there with the sleeves in the box, the remainder on the floor, just the way she had been standing as she bent over and reached into the box. She was gone and was never seen again.

## ‡‡ 96 ‡‡

## THE PUPPY OF BRETTA

In the Rhine Palatinate, especially in Kraichgau, there is a proverb current among the people. When someone's trust and fidelity are ill rewarded, people say, "You have been treated like the puppy of Bretta." The folk legend must be very old, since the sixteenth-century author Fischart makes reference to it on two occasions.

In the city of Bretta many years ago there lived a man who had a very faithful dog he had trained to perform several chores. The man would give him a basket in which there was a written note and sufficient money, and the dog would take it to the butcher and bring home meat and sausage without ever touching it.

Once, however, the master, who was Protestant, sent the dog out on Friday to a butcher who was Catholic and paid strict observance to fasting. When the butcher found the order for meat on the note, he grabbed the dog, cut off its tail, put it in the basket, and wrote on the note, "Here you have your meat!"

The puppy, mistreated and wounded, carried the basket faithfully home, but then lay down and died. The whole city mourned, and a statue of the dog without a tail was carved in stone and placed over the city gate.

Others, however, say that the puppy stole meat and sausage for his poor hungry master until the butcher finally caught him and cut off his tail as punishment.

‡‡　97　‡‡

## THE VILLAGE BY THE SEA

A woman saint walked along a beach, looking toward Heaven and praying. It was Sunday afternoon, and the villagers were all dressed up in their silken clothes walking about with their sweethearts on their arms. They saw the saint and made fun of her pious ways. She paid them no heed, other than to pray to God not to hold them accountable for this sin.

The next morning, however, two oxen appeared and dug into a giant sand dune with their horns until evening. That night a powerful gale hit the area and blew the loosened sand over the entire village until it had been totally buried, and everything that breathed perished. When people from neighboring villages attempted to uncover the town, all the sand that they dug out during the day would be blown back at night. It is still that way to this very day.

‡‡　98　‡‡

## THE BURIED SILVER MINE

The two richest silver mines in the Harz Mountains, both of which long ago ceased to operate, were the Big John and the Golden Altar (near Andreasberg?). The following legend is told about them.

Many years ago when the mines were still being worked, a foreman was placed in charge. When the mines were prosperous and profits were great, he had two rich veins sealed off so that when the yield was down and the remainder of the mine nearly exhausted, he could use them to replace the loss. Thus, the profits would remain at the same high level. He did this with the best of intentions, but his actions were misunderstood by others, and they accused him of a crime and sentenced him to death.

As he knelt down for his beheading, he protested and swore his innocence saying, "As sure as I am innocent, my blood shall change to milk, and work in the mines will cease. Then a son will be born with glass eyes and deer hooves. If he lives, work in the mines will begin again. But if he dies after his birth, then the mines will remain buried forever."

When the executioner let the ax fall and the head dropped, two streams of snow-white milk burst forth from his body like a fountain, thus testifying to his innocence. Soon both mines closed down, and a young count with glass eyes and deer hooves was born, but he died immediately after his birth. The silver mines have never again been opened up, and they remain buried to this very day.

## ‡‡ 99 ‡‡

## THE PROSPECTORS

The richest veins are usually found by the poorest and the least-respected prospectors, and many legends report such findings. In the Bohemian Mine on the Owl Plateau, for example, there was a miner who was known as the Red Lion. He became so rich that he invited King Wenceslaus as a guest and presented him with a ton of gold. He also equipped King Charles' army with a hundred knights in armor.

When he first began, however, the Red Lion lost all his money and his wife even had to sell her wedding veil, which was part of her dowry. One day, his wife hit her heel so hard on a sharp rock that she bled from the wound. When the miner took his hammer to knock the sharp point off the rock, he struck solid gold.

He became very wealthy from this strike. But he fell victim to pride and vanity, and soon everything in his house had to be fashioned from silk, gold, and silver. His wife said that God would never permit them to become poor again. But by and by the Red Lion became poor as a beggar, and he died on a dung heap.

There once lived a powerful prospector named Old Weinmoser, who worked the Salzburg mines at Gastein and Rauriß. Once, things were so bad that he decided to flee his debtors. He was standing in his door about to depart when someone brought him samplings and nuggets from a new vein. It was rich in gold and silver, and when it was processed it yielded enough to make him and others very wealthy. Yet, when he was on his deathbed and someone brought him even more splendid nuggets from the mine, he said, "The righteous and most beautiful vein is Jesus, my Lord and my Savior. To him I shall soon depart in eternal life."

‡‡   100   ‡‡

## THE GHOSTLY HORSEMAN

Toward the end of the seventeenth century, an unknown man appeared at the court of a Count von Roggendorf and claimed he was a horse trainer. After he passed some tests, he was engaged in the count's service and was officially installed. It came to pass, however, that a member of the nobility arrived at the court and was placed at the same table with this horse trainer. The stranger looked at the trainer in amazement, then became very despondent and refused to eat anything even though the count encouraged him in a most friendly manner.

After the food had been carried away, the count again asked the stranger the cause of his despondency. The man replied that this horse trainer was not a normal man—he had been shot to death when standing next to him during the siege of Ostende, and he himself had been present at the burial. The stranger reported everything he knew about the man, his homeland, name, and age. Everything agreed completely with what the horse trainer had said about himself, of that there was no room for doubt.

The count then found reason to dismiss the horse trainer on grounds that his own income had diminished greatly and that he was forced to reduce his court expenditures. The horse trainer said that the guest had been telling stories and added that the count had no cause to dismiss him. Since he had been faithful in his service and wished to serve further, he asked the count to retain him at his court. The count, however, remained steadfast and said that the dismissal was still in effect. The horse trainer then requested not money, but rather a horse and a fool's costume with silver bells, which the count gladly gave him. He even offered the trainer many other things, which, however, he refused to accept.

It so happened, though, that the count traveled to Hungary. And in the vicinity of Raab he encountered his horse trainer, still wearing the fool's costume. He had several strings of horses with him. The trainer greeted the count with much joy and offered him a horse as a gift. The count expressed his gratitude at the offer but refused to accept it. But when the trainer spotted a servant whom he had known well at the count's court, he gave him the horse. The servant mounted the horse with joy, but he had no sooner seated himself in the saddle than the horse bolted and reared into the air, throwing his rider to the earth, half dead. At the same instant the horse trainer and all his strings of horses vanished from sight.

## ‡‡ 101 ‡‡

## THE FALSE OATH

Near the monastery of Schönau in the Odenwald there is a town called False Oath. Some time ago a farmer there swore an oath that a certain piece of property belonged to him. Instantly, the earth beneath his feet opened up and swallowed him completely—nothing remained but his staff and shoes. That is how the town got its name.

It is also said of perjurers that they cannot bend the fingers they raised while swearing false oath, or that their fingers turn black. It is further said that the fingers of perjurers grow from the grave after they are dead and buried.

## ‡‡ 102 ‡‡

## THE TWELVE UNFAIR JURISTS

Near Minden in Westphalia there is a piece of land about which the local people tell the following story. Twelve jurists awarded the land to a man to whom it did not rightly belong. The earth then opened and swallowed them up to their knees. One can still see the holes in the ground there.

## ‡‡ 103 ‡‡

## THE SACRED SPRINGS

Country people in Switzerland still talk of the sacred springs that suddenly gushed forth in Rütli. While the Great Oath was being sworn, the man who had betrayed the Confederation began to breath fire from his mouth and nose. His house also burst into flames all by itself and burned to the ground.

## THE GUSHING SPRING

There is a spring that gushes from the earth at the foot of a mountain in Franconia. It was there that a royal family built their residence. The spring furnishes pure, crystal-clear, bubbling water in great quantity throughout the year. Only when someone in the family dies does the spring stop gushing. In such cases it dries up immediately and there is scarcely a sign that a spring was once there.

Once, the aged lord of this family lay mortally ill in a foreign land, and since he was already in his eighties, he sensed his impending death. He thus sent a messenger to his homeland to ask if the spring had gone dry.

When the messenger arrived, the water had just stopped flowing, but fearful that the news would make the lord morose, the family urged the messenger not to tell him the truth, but rather to say the spring was doing well and was full of water.

When he heard this, the old gentleman laughed out loud and reproached himself for seeking to learn through the superstition of the fountain what was God's will alone. He thus prepared himself for a peaceful departure. But, suddenly, the illness of the man began to abate, and he soon rose from his sickbed, fully recovered.

But the spring had not dried up without reason—its oracular powers, which had stood the test of time, proved to be as true as ever. For at the same time that the spring had dried up a young nobleman of the lineage was thrown from a horse and killed.

## HUNGER FOUNTAIN

There is a spring-fed fountain next to the Red Tower in the market place of Halle from which the water flows on its north side. It is known as Hunger Fountain, for the common man divines times of plenty or famine from the strong or weak flow of the water. When the farmers come to town, it is their custom to go to the fountain to watch the flow. If it is strong they will say:

This year, the food is dear.

Those fountains that usually trickle in the summers of most years flow fully only in wet, unfruitful years. The farmers say when the year is warm and sunny and thus good:

Year of sun,
Year of fun!

## STREAM OF LOVE

The City of Spangenburg in Hesse is supplied with water by a brook that carries it from a bountiful spring on the mountainside across the valley. The following story is told about the brook.

A youth and a maiden of Spangenburg were very much in love, but their parents would not agree to a marriage. Finally, both sets of parents relented, on the condition that the wedding would take place only after the two lovers had succeeded in diverting the flow of water from the fresh spring in the mountains to the city. Thus, the city would be provided with drinking water, of which there was a serious shortage at that time. The two sweethearts began to dig the waterway, and they worked without interruption for forty years. The moment it was completed the two of them died.

## HELPERS' BLUFF

On Giant Mountain in Bohemia, just a mile from Trautenau, lies Helpers' Bluff—a high cliff where there once stood a castle occupied by robber barons, but which has since disappeared.

In 1614 a young maiden was tending sheep near the village of Mäschendorf, just a quarter mile from the bluff, and she asked the children who were with her, "Come, let's go to Helpers' Bluff and see if it is open. If it is, we'll be able to see the giant wine cask."

When they arrived there the cliff was indeed open, and inside was a steel door with a lock on which hung many keys. Full of curiosity, they approached the door, opened it, and entered. They found themselves in a rather large antechamber at the end of which stood another door, through which they also passed.

In the second room they found all kinds of furniture and household effects, but they also found a giant wine cask from which most of the barrel staves had fallen away. Through the years, however, the barrel had developed a coating nearly half an inch thick, and the wine had remained sealed within. When the four of them grabbed hold of the keg and shook it, it wobbled like an egg with a soft shell.

As they were watching the keg, a well-dressed gentleman wearing a red feather in his hat emerged from a lovely adjoining room. He held a pewter pitcher in his hand and had come to fetch more wine. When he opened the door they could see that there was a merry time going on in there. Handsome men and beautiful women were seated at two tables. There was music, and everyone was having a good time.

The man drawing the wine gave them a hearty welcome and invited them into the room. They were quite frightened and wished themselves well away from there, but the girl said they were too filthy and poorly dressed to join such an elegant group. But the man offered them wine to drink and told them to wait until he could get another pitcher.

While he was gone, the oldest girl said to the others, "Let's get out of here. This can come to no good, for it is said that people have been condemned here for their sins." Thus, they made haste for the exit. But as they were leaving they heard loud banging and crashing noises just a few steps behind them, which gave them a terrible fright.

After an hour had passed, the oldest girl said to the others, "Let's go back and find out what made that loud noise." The others did not want to return, but since the girl was so brave in going alone, they followed behind. When they reached the cliff they could find neither the iron door nor the opening, for the cliff had closed behind them.

After they drove the sheep back home, they told their parents what had transpired. The parents in turn reported it to the authorities. But whenever anyone went to look at the cliff, it was always sealed shut.

‡‡ 108 ‡‡

## THE CRADLE FROM THE SAPLING

Near the city of Baden in Austria one can still see the ruins of the old castle of Rauheneck atop the mountain. It is said that a great treasure lies buried there. However, it can only be recovered by a man who has been rocked in a cradle made from the wood of the tree that is now only a tiny sprout growing from the wall of the high tower of Rauheneck Castle. If the sapling should die or be chopped down, then the recovery of the treasure will have to wait until it sprouts again and a new tree grows.

‡‡ 109 ‡‡

## HESSIAN VALLEY

The old castle of Schellenpyrmont lies in ruins. According to legend the throne of Queen Thusnelda was located there. Thusnelda possessed a marvelous talking bird, and one day it came flying from Hessian Valley, a forested area at the foot of Castle Mountain, crying over and over again:

> It's shiny in Hessian Valley!
> It's shiny in Hessian Valley!

The bird thus revealed that the Romans with their shining armor had invaded the valley. This gave the Germans time to arm themselves against the attack and they were saved.

‡‡ 110 ‡‡

## REINSTEIN

Beneath the ancient castle of Reinstein, not far from Blankenburg in the Harz Mountains, there is a very large cave in the side of a cliff. This cave is filled with many small pebbles of the kind not usually found in the mountains but rather in the flatlands. If one carries away some of these pebbles, whether just a few or sackfuls, they always return to the place from which they were removed—thus, the cave always remains full of pebbles. No one has yet profited from gathering the stones and hauling them away.

Around the noon hour one can hear the strange sounds of ringing bells coming from the cliff near the cave, and occasionally one hears a hammering noise as though many smiths were at work.

‡‡ 111 ‡‡

## THE RIVER THAT STANDS STILL

It is said that whenever a prince, a ruling lord, or his wife is about to die in the land of Hesse, the Fulda River—in contrast to its normal flow—will stand still as though the stream were expressing sorrow. Each time this happens it is considered a certain omen of death; and the inhabitants of this valley have observed this phenomenon several times.

## ‡‡ 112 ‡‡

## LAKE AREND

The following episode is told about Lake Arend in the Altmark section of Brandenburg. On the same site where the town and the lake of this name are now located, there once stood a great castle. One day, the castle suddenly sank from sight. No one survived except for a man and his wife. They had just left the castle when the woman turned around, and perceiving the sudden disappearance, she screamed, "Arend, look!" (for her husband's name was Arend). That is why the town that was later built by this lake was called Arend See [Lake Arend].*

The bottom of the lake is covered with the finest white sand, and when the sun is shining brightly, it is said that one can see all the old walls and the structures of the sunken castle. Some people have attempted to fathom the depths of the waters and have lowered long ropes toward the bottom. But each time the rope was pulled back up there was a note attached to it with the warning: "Give up your attempt or else the same thing will happen to your town as happened to us."

## ‡‡ 113 ‡‡

## OX MOUNTAIN

In the region of Altmark, not far from the ruins of Alvensleben, there is a large cheerful village called Ursleben. A rifle's shot away from the village lies a large lake, called Brock Lake, where once there stood a beautiful castle that sank out of sight and was then replaced by the water. It is reported that all the people in the castle went under except for one young noblewoman, who was warned in advance by a dream. When the farm animals and the chickens began making strange mourning sounds, the way they do before an impending disaster, the maiden mounted an ox and rode away. She reached the top of a nearby hill just in time, for behind her the castle collapsed and sank. Still sitting on the ox, she turned around to look and saw water rising where the castle had been. This is why that hill is still called Ox Mountain to this very day.

*In German she cried, "Arend seh!" a homophon of Arend See.—D. W.

## THE MAIDENS OF THE MOORS

In the Rhön Mountains there is a swamp called the Red Marsh. According to folk legend, the village of Poppenrode that was once located at that site sank into the ground. At night small lights can be seen hovering above the surface of the marsh.

Not far away there is a similar swamp called the Black Marsh, which is mentioned in old documents. Local legend reports another sunken village of which only one piece of stone has survived. The village was called Stony Bridge.

## ST. ANDREAS' EVE

According to folk belief, a maiden is supposed to be able to conjure up her future lover on the eves of St. Andreas, St. Thomas, Christmas, and New Year's. She must set a table for two people, but there must not be forks among the cutlery. And should her lover leave something behind, it must be carefully put away for safekeeping, for he will return to the one who possesses it and will love her passionately. But he must never be permitted to see the item, for he would be reminded of the torment he suffered that night because of supernatural forces, and he would be aware that sorcery was used. Terrible misfortune would then result.

In Austria it is said that a lovely maiden once desired to see her future beloved, and she performed the necessary rituals at midnight. A shoemaker appeared to her with dagger in hand. He threw it in her direction and then vanished. She picked up the dagger and put it in her chest for safekeeping. It was not long before that very shoemaker began courting her. Some years after they had been married, on a Sunday after mass, she went to her chest looking for something she wanted to work on the next day. Just as she opened the chest, her husband entered the room and wanted to look in. She held him back, but he shoved her aside, looked into the chest, and saw his long lost dagger. He picked it up and wanted to know how she had acquired it. In her state of dismay and fear she could not think of any other explanation so she openly confessed that it was the dagger he had left in her room the night she had desired him. The man became enraged and shouted a terrifying curse at her: "Whore! So you're the bitch who caused me such wretched terror that night!" And he plunged the dagger into her heart.

This same legend is told in diverse locations about various people. One oral version tells of a hunter who left his hunting knife behind at a maiden's house. They had not been married a week when the woman sent her husband to her chest to get some fresh bedding, forgetting that the item of sorcery was lying there. He found it and killed her with it.

‡‡   116   ‡‡

## INVITING HER BELOVED TO DINNER

There was a woman who worked as a tax collector in Saalfeld in Thuringia. She was secretly in love with her clerk and decided to try to win him by sorcery. She had a fresh loaf of bread baked, and at midnight on Christmas Eve she placed two knives crosswise into the loaf while muttering a number of words. Immediately the clerk came from his sleep and sprang into the room totally naked. Then he sat down at the table and gave her a piercing look. As she leapt up and hastened away, he snatched the knives from the bread and threw them at her, nearly causing her severe injury. Then he returned home. The woman's aunt, who had been in the room at the time, received such a shock that she took to her sickbed for several weeks.

The following day the clerk is said to have remarked to the family with whom he lived that he would certainly like to know who the woman was who gave him such a terrible fright during the night! He was so completely worn out that he was practically speechless. He added that he was compelled to go there, and that he was unable to resist. Had he prayed—as fervently as he was able—he still would have been forced to go there.

The same old woman who told this story also added the following tale. Several young maidens of nobility who lived in Coburg saved portions from nine different meals, put them on the table at midnight, and then sat down. In short order, all their lovers appeared, each one bringing a knife with him. They were all about to sit down at the table together when the maidens suddenly became frightened and fled. One of the men, however, took his knife and threw it toward them. One of the maidens turned, looked at the man, and picked up the knife.

On one occasion Death himself appeared at the meal instead of the desired lover. He brought his hourglass with him and set it down next to one of the girls, who died before the year was out.

According to another story, three young ladies of the court of Silesia sat down one Christmas Eve at a table they had prepared, and they waited for their future lovers, for each of whom a place had been set. But only two lovers appeared, and they joined two of the maidens at the table. The third maiden, saddened and impatient, got up from the table and sat by the window. Across the street she saw a casket in which lay a young woman who seemed remarkably like herself. This gave her such a fright that she soon became very ill, and within a short time she was dead.

According to one oral version, the casket enters the room all by itself, she approaches it, the lid opens, and she falls in dead.

## ‡‡ 117 ‡‡

### CHRISTMAS EVE

Superstitious maidens who wish to dream of their beloved purchase on the morning of the day before Christmas a penny's worth of bread, always including its end piece, or heel. They proceed to cut a piece of the crust off the bottom, tie it under their arm, and carry it there all day long as they go about their chores. Then on Christmas Eve, when it is time for bed, they place the crust under their pillow and chant the following words:

> Now I lay me down and the bread with me,
> If only my true love would come and eat with me!

If all works as it is supposed to, some of the crust will be nibbled away at midnight. If that happens it is a sign that her beloved will marry her before the next year is out. But if the crust remains untouched she has little hope.

According to one story that is the way it happened in Leipzig in 1657. Two maidens were lying next to each other in a single bed, and one of them had such a crust beneath her and the other did not. The latter was awakened during the night by gnawing and crunching sounds and she became frightened. She shook her bedmate, who had been deep in sleep and noticed nothing, and awoke her from her dreams. When she looked at the bread crust in the morning, a cross had been nibbled into it. Soon thereafter the girl acquired a soldier for a husband.

The old woman of Saalfeld also tells of other girls who take a vessel filled with water and carefully measure it into a second vessel. They continue doing this several times, all the while taking careful note whether, in any of the repeated measurings, they record more water than the first time. If so, they believe that their material possessions will increase during the following year. If the quantity of water does not change, then they believe that their fate will be at a standstill, and that they will have neither better nor worse fortune than before. But should the quantity of water diminish, they then deduce that their good fortune and prosperity will likewise diminish. The woman of Saalfeld met with the second result herself on one occasion.

Others take an antique key and a ball of twine and tie the key to it. Next, they let the twine out a couple of yards and tie it so that it can't unwind any farther. Then they dangle the key out the window and swing it back and forth along the exterior wall of the house, saying, "Hark, hark!" They are then supposed to hear a voice coming from one direction or the other. If they do, they will eventually be courted from that direction and go there to live.

Other maidens stick their hand out the front door and grab at the air. When they withdraw their hand they find they are holding a few hairs from their future beloved.


‡‡  118  ‡‡

### CASTING THE PETTICOATS AWAY

In Coburg, several maidens sitting together on Christmas Eve were curious to learn who their future husbands might be. The day before, they had gone out and cut nine different kinds of wood, and when midnight came they built a fire. The first maiden removed all her clothes and cast her petticoat out through the front door. Then, sitting before the fire, she sang:

> Here I sit, quite naked without wrap,
> If only my beloved would come
> And throw my petticoat into my lap!

When she completed the chant, the petticoat was thrown back in, and she recognized the young man who had done so by the look on

his face. They later came to an understanding, and he began courting her.

The remaining girls then disrobed too. But they made a mistake
and wadded all their petticoats together and threw them, all entangled, out the door. The spirits were unable to sort them out and
began to fuss and make such a racket that the maidens shuddered in
fear. They quickly poured water over the fire and crawled into bed.
In the morning they found their petticoats outside—shredded into
thousands of tiny pieces.


‡‡ 119 ‡‡

## CRYSTAL GAZING

A lovely young lady of nobility and a young nobleman fell passionately in love with each other, but their step-parents would not grant
them permission to marry. They were both very saddened by the
situation.

It then came to pass that an old woman, who had access to the
house, came to the maiden, consoled her, and said that the man who
loved her would certainly be hers someday. The maiden, overjoyed
to hear this, asked her how she could be so certain. "Aye, milady,"
said the old woman, "I have the gift from God of seeing the future,
and therefore this, as well as many other events, cannot be concealed from me. To remove all your doubts, I shall reveal everything
to you in my crystal so clearly that you will have nothing but praise
for my talents. But we must choose a time when your parents are
away, and then you will see many wonders."

The maiden waited until her parents traveled to a country estate, and then she went to her brother's tutor, Johann Rüst, who
was later to become a famous poet. She told him her plan and asked
him to accompany her when she gazed into the crystal. He tried to
convince her that it was sinful, that it could be the occasion of great
misfortune, but in vain. She remained steadfast, and he finally let
himself be moved by her incessant pleadings.

When they entered the room, the old woman was busy removing her implements from a small basket. She was displeased when
she saw the tutor accompanying the maiden, and she said that she
could tell from his eyes that he did not think highly of her art. She
then took a blue tablecloth, on which were embroidered wondrous
pictures of dragons, serpents, and other creatures, and spread it over
the table. Next she took a green glass bowl, set it on the tablecloth,
and then placed a gold-colored silk cloth inside the bowl. Finally,

she brought forth a rather large crystal ball and placed it upon the silk cloth. She covered the crystal with a white cloth and then began murmuring some words to herself, while making wondrous gestures. When she finished, she lifted the crystal ball with great reverence and walked with it to the window where she invited the maiden and the tutor to come and gaze into it.

At first they saw nothing. But then an image of the maiden as a bride clad in an exquisite gown formed in the crystal. She was so beautifully dressed that it could have been her wedding day. And yet, although she looked splendid and beautiful, she nevertheless wore an expression of sadness and misery on her face. Indeed, her pallor was so death-like that one could not see her without compassion.

The maiden looked at her own image in terror. And then the image of her beloved appeared, standing before her. He, who was otherwise a kindly fellow, had such a gruesome, brutal look on his face, it made them all tremble. He was wearing boots and spurs as if he had just returned from a journey and he was dressed in a grey overcoat with gold buttons. He drew two new shiny pistols, and holding one in each hand, he aimed one at his own heart and the other he held to the temple of the maiden.

As the three of them witnessed this scene they didn't know what to do and felt helpless. Then they saw the beloved pull the trigger of the gun he was holding against the head of the girl, and they heard a distant, somewhat muffled shot ring out. They were so utterly terror-stricken by this scene that they couldn't move. Finally, trembling, they stumbled into the adjoining room where they recovered their composure to some degree. But the old woman, who had been unaware that this scene would appear, was so distressed that she rushed in great haste from the house and it was a long time before she ever returned.

The terror the girl felt could not erase her love for the man, but her step-parents remained steadfast in their resolve to withhold their permission. Indeed, with threats they forced her to become engaged to an aristocratic court official from a nearby manor. This situation tormented the maiden and she grew sick at heart and spent all her time crying and sighing. Her beloved also fell into extreme despair.

Meanwhile, the date of the wedding was set, and since members of the royal house were to be present, it was to be celebrated in great splendor. When the day arrived, it was arranged that the bride would be transported in great pomp and circumstance in the prince's own royal carriage, drawn by six horses and attended by royal servants and riders. The most prominent and eminent of all the relatives and friends of the bride joined them in their carriages as they traveled in glorious procession.

The lover had inquired about all of this, and in despair he was resolved not to allow his beloved to become the wife of another. With this in mind, he purchased a pair of pistols and planned to use one to kill the bride and the other to kill himself. Outside the gate of the residence where the marriage was to take place stood a cottage that the wedding procession had to pass—and this he selected as his site. When the splendid procession of riders and carriages approached, followed by a crowd of spectators, he drew one of the pistols and put a shot into the bridal carriage. But he acted too hastily, for the bullet missed the bride and hit, instead, the elevated coiffure of the lady sitting next to her. The woman fainted, and everyone rushed to her aid, thus giving the attempted assassin opportunity to flee through the back door of the cottage. He saved himself by jumping across a ravine so wide that no one could follow.

As soon as the woman regained consciousness, the procession moved on, and the wedding was celebrated in great splendor. But the bride participated with heavy heart. She thought back on the day she had gazed into the crystal, and now took the prophecy to heart.

Her marriage proved to be an unhappy one, for her husband was a heartless, cruel man. And, in spite of the fact that she bore him a handsome son, he always treated his lovely and virtuous wife in a most despicable manner.

‡‡ 120 ‡‡

## PREPARING MAGIC HERBS

In 1672 a maidservant and a dyer's apprentice who worked in the same household in Erfurt began a love affair, which they carried on in a rather reckless manner for some time. But the youth began to tire of her, so he wandered off and found a new master in the town of Langensalza.

Meanwhile, the maidservant could not get over her thoughts of love; she wanted desperately to have her beloved back again. So, on Holy Pentecost, when all the house servants and apprentices were in church, she took certain herbs, placed them in a kettle, and set them over the fire. Her boyfriend was supposed to appear when the pot came to a boil.

Now, it so happened that one of the apprentices, who was still in the house, came to the fire in order to heat a pan. Unaware of what was in the kettle, he shoved it out of his way and over the glowing coals. Just then the kettle with the herbs began to boil, and he heard a voice coming from it, crying, "Come, come, Hansel, come! Come, come, Hansel, come!" While the youth was stirring his lime, he heard something behind him fall to the floor like a heavy sack. Turning, he saw a young fellow lying there clad only in a nightshirt. The apprentice let out a pitiful scream.

The maidservant came running—and so did the other people living in the house. They found the good apprentice in his nightshirt, lying there as though he'd been suddenly awakened from a deep sleep. When he was asked what had happened, he explained that he'd been sleeping when a large black animal, all shaggy and matted and shaped like a billy goat, came up to his bed and gave him such a fright that he grabbed hold of its horns and it flew with him out through the window. From that point on he could not recall what happened, only that he felt nothing unusual. But how did he get so far away? At eight o'clock he'd been lying in bed in Langensalza, and here he was in Erfurt, and it was scarcely eight thirty. He had no choice but to believe that Katharine, his former sweetheart, had been the cause, for when he left her she warned him that if he didn't return soon, she'd send the billy goat for him.

The maidservant, under threat of being turned over to the authorities as a witch, began to weep pitifully. She confessed that an old woman, whom she named, had convinced her to do it and had given her the herbs with the instructions that if she boiled them gently, her beloved would have to appear, no matter how far away he was.

## ‡‡  121  ‡‡

### THE YOUNG SALT WORKER IN POMERANIA

A woman in Pomerania once had a young salt worker in her service. He soon discovered that she was a sorceress, and he did not wish to remain with her any longer. He therefore asked for leave to visit his homeland in Hesse to see his friends. Because she was afraid that he would not return she refused him permission. But he left anyway. After he had been wandering for several days, a black billy goat appeared on the road behind him. It slipped its head between his legs, picked him up, and carried him back—but not by land. Rather, the goat took him through thick and thin, over fields and forests, and streams and lakes until it set him down outside the gate of the woman's estate. He lay there trembling in fear and covered with sweat, and he finally lost consciousness. The woman then appeared and bade him welcome in a taunting, mocking tone, saying, "Well, look here! Are you back so soon? Maybe this will teach you to stay home!" She then gave him some fresh clothes and something to eat so that he recovered his composure.

## MAID ELI

More than a hundred years ago an abbess, a very pious woman, lived in the minster convent at Frekenhorst. A servant girl by the name of Eli worked for her. She was a wicked, greedy girl, and when the poor came begging for alms, she took a whip and drove them away. Then she would take a ribbon and tie up the bell so that the poor could not ring. One day, Eli became very ill, and the priest was called to administer last rites. When he arrived at the convent and was walking through the abbess's garden, he saw Eli sitting in the apple tree wearing a green hat with a white feather. And yet, when he entered the house, he found her in bed. She was as wicked and impious as ever, and she had no interest in bettering her ways. When the priest tried to address some kind words to her, she turned her back, faced the wall, and died. The moment her eyes closed the bell in the convent cracked. She has haunted the convent from that day on.

One day, when the maids were in the kitchen cutting string beans, she came rushing into the room, just as she had done in real life, and called out, "Now don't cut your fingers! Now don't cut your fingers!" And when the maids went out to do the milking, Eli sat in the middle of the path. She refused to let any of them pass until they called out, "In the name of God, get thee hence!" Whereupon she was forced to make way. But then, she ran after them, holding out a beautiful cake and yelling, "Cake, cake!" When the maids refused to take it, she cast it on the ground amid diabolic laughter and it instantly turned to cow dung.

The male servants also saw her when they went out to chop wood. She always flew from one tree branch to another. At night she would raise a racket all around the house, knocking over vases and pots, mixing up the dishes, and disturbing people in their sleep.

Finally, she appeared to the abbess herself on the way to Warendorf. She stopped the horses in their tracks and tried to get in the carriage. But the abbess said to her, "I have no business with you. If you have done wicked things, it was against my will." But Eli would not let herself be turned away so easily. The abbess then cast one of her gloves onto the ground and ordered the maid to pick it up. As she bent over, the abbess cried to the coachman, "Drive off as fast as you can, even if you have to run the horses into the ground!" The coachman raced his horses, and they arrived safely in Warendorf.

Eventually, the abbess became tired of all the noise and disturbance, and she called all the clergy of the whole region together, asking them to join in exorcising Eli. They gathered together in the gallery of the cathedral and began to chant the verses to summon the ghost, but she refused to appear. Then a voice was heard snickering. The head priest then said, "Someone must be in the church listening!" They looked and found a small boy who must have hidden himself there out of curiosity. As soon as they had chased the boy out, Eli appeared, and they banished her to Davert Forest near Münster. This is a place where many ghosts roam and to which evil spirits are committed.

Once every year, according to the legend, Eli comes flying with a terrifying roar over the convent and smashes a couple of windowpanes or engages in similar mischief. However, after every fourth wedding, she is permitted to advance the length of one chicken step closer to the convent.


‡‡   123   ‡‡

## THE WHITE WOMAN

The Snow-White Woman appears in forests or on meadows, and occasionally she is seen in stables carrying burning candles. She cleans and brushes the horses and drops of wax fall on their manes. When she goes out at night she can see clearly, but in her own abode she is said to be blind.


‡‡   124   ‡‡

## A DOVE DISCOVERS A TREASURE

When Duke Henry of Breslau conquered the city of Krakow, he entered the cathedral and knelt down before the altar of Our Lady, just like a simple, pious man. He thanked her for bestowing her grace upon him and for turning his suffering to joy. As he rose, he spotted a dove and followed its flight. He saw it land on the cornice of an arch above a large column. He then watched as it began to peck at the wall with its bill and push away pieces of falling mortar and stone with its feet. Within a short time, a gold piece fell to the floor from above. The duke picked it up and said, "The dove has uncovered this; there could easily be more." He had someone bring a ladder, and he sent for a stonemason to see what else was there. The mason climbed up the ladder, took out his chisel, and with the first blow discovered a large treasure of gold behind the wall. He called down, "My Lord, reward me well, for here lies glittering gold in enormous quantity." The duke had the wall torn out and removed the treasure that God had bestowed upon him. When it was weighed it came to fifty thousand marks.

## ‡‡ 125 ‡‡

## A DOVE HOLDS OFF THE ENEMY

During the Thirty Years' War, the city of Höxter in the region of Corvey in the Weser Valley was surrounded by imperial troops, but it could not be taken. Finally, the order came to bombard the town with heavy artillery to terrify the inhabitants and force them to surrender. But, at the onset of darkness, when the artilleryman was about to set off the first cannon, a dove flew down and pecked at his hand and he missed lighting the fuse. He then said, "It is God's will that I should not fire the cannon," and he desisted. During the night the Swedish army arrived, and the imperial army was forced to retreat. Thus, on this occasion, the city was spared.

## ‡‡ 126 ‡‡

## CASTING THE BELL OF BRESLAU

When the bell of St. Mary Magdalena in Breslau was to be cast, and everything was nearly ready, the caster went off to have lunch. Before he left he forbade his apprentice on pain of death to touch the tap on the smelting vat. However, the apprentice, who was an inquisitive and curious sort, wanted to see what the molten metal looked like. But when he touched the tap and moved it, the metal came pouring forth against his will. Try as he might he could not stop it, and the molten metal ran and ran into the prepared mold. Dismayed, the youth didn't know what to do, until finally, amid tears, he dared to go into the room and confess all to his master, from whom for the sake of God he asked forgiveness.

The master, however, became enraged; he drew his sword and stabbed the youth then and there. Then he ran to see if anything could be salvaged from the job. He waited until the metal had cooled and then removed the mold. Lo and behold, the entire bell had been cast perfectly and without flaw. Full of joy, the master hastened back to the room. Only then did he realize what a wicked thing he had done—the apprentice had bled to death. The master was arrested and sentenced to die by the sword. In the meantime the bell was installed in the church.

At his execution the caster pleaded with the authorities to let him hear the bell peal just once, since he had prepared the mold for it—if only the gentlemen would grant this final honor before the end! The authorities granted his wish, and ever since, this bell is rung for all poor sinners who are led from the City Hall to the executioner's block. The bell is so heavy that if one rings it fifty times, it will ring fifty more times all by itself.

‡‡   127   ‡‡

## CASTING THE BELL AT ATTENDORN

Many years ago in the city of Attendorn in Westphalia there lived a widow who sent her son to Holland to learn commerce. He was so successful that he was able to send his mother a portion of his earnings each year. Once, he sent her a plate of pure gold, but it was painted black and had been sent together with a number of other items. His mother, not realizing the great value of the piece, placed it beneath a bench in her shop, where it remained until a bell caster arrived in the city. He had been commissioned by the city fathers who agreed to have a bell cast, but first the citizenry had to go around begging for sufficient metal for the casting. As they went around collecting pieces of metal, they were mostly given broken brass pots until they came to the widow's house. She gave them the gold plate her son had sent because she did not know what it was and because she had no other old vessels.

The bell caster moved on to Arensberg where he was to finish a few bells, but he left a journeyman behind with orders to complete the mold and make all the other preparations. However, he was not to pour the metal until his master returned.

But when the master did not return, the journeyman, who wanted very much to try his own hand at bell casting, went ahead and poured the metal. He succeeded in making a splendid bell for the citizens of Attendorn. It was so fine in form and sound that they let it peal as long as he wanted to hear it at his departure, for he wanted to journey to Arensberg to bring news of the successful casting to his master. A number of the citizens accompanied him at the start of his journey and they carried full pitchers of drink, which they repeatedly offered him along the way.

When he arrived, amid honor and joy, at the stone bridge that lies between Attendorn and the royal castle of Schnellenberg, he met the master, who cried out in anger, "What have you done, you beast!" Then he drew his pistol and shot the young man in the head. The master then turned to the entourage and said, "That fellow cast a bell no better than any rascal. The only honorable thing to do is to melt it down and recast it, then the city will have a fine new bell." At this, he rode off and repeated his contention as though the matter were settled.

Instead, he was arrested for murder, and they asked him what had motivated him to do it since the townspeople had been completely satisfied with the young man's work. He finally confessed that when he heard the sound of the bell he could tell immediately that a goodly portion of gold had been cast into it. He had not wanted to leave the gold in the bell but wanted to make off with it himself, and that is why he did the journeyman in. The master craftman's head was then chopped off. As an eternal memorial for the journeyman, an iron cross was placed on the bridge where he was slain.

In the meantime, people wondered where the gold could have come from, for no one remembered having gathered any. It was all made clear, however, when the widow's son returned home amid great joy, laden with many riches. He later mourned the fact that his gold had caused the death of two men, one innocent and one guilty. But he never asked that the gold be returned because he was grateful that God had blessed him richly in other ways.

Many years later, lightning struck the belfry, destroying everything except the masonry, even melting the bell. The citizens later found molten metal among the ashes which had the approximate gold content of gulden. They later used this metal to restore the belfry, and they covered it with lead.

‡‡   128   ‡‡

## THE MILLER'S WIFE

In a lonesome mill located between Ems and Wels in Austria there once lived a miller. One Sunday morning he went to church with all his apprentices in the usual manner, leaving behind only his wife, who was heavy with child and close to confinement. As the miller's wife was sitting alone, the midwife dropped in to visit and to see how the expectant mother was doing. The miller's wife was polite, served the midwife something to eat, and they sat together at the table. While they were eating, the midwife dropped a knife and said, "Pick up the knife for me!"

"Ay!" answered the miller's wife, "You must be crazy. You know that bending over is more difficult for me than for you." But she decided to let it be and bent over to pick up the knife. But as she was handing it to her, still bending, the midwife grabbed the knife, pointed it toward her, and said, "Now give me all the money that you have in this house, or I'll plunge this cold blade into your breast!"

The miller's wife was greatly alarmed, but she regained her composure and said, "Come with me into the bedchamber. All the money we have is in the closet there, and you can take it." The midwife followed her and took the money from the closet. But since her greed was not yet satisfied, she rummaged through all the drawers and shelves looking for more. The miller's wife took this opportunity to slip out of the room, and she closed the door behind her and locked it. Since all the windows were covered with iron bars, the midwife was trapped.

The woman then called her seven-year-old son and told him, "Run fast and get your father from the church. Tell him to hasten home with his apprentices, for I am in great danger!" The child did as he was told, but not far from the mill he ran into the husband of the midwife, who was arriving as planned to help carry off the booty. When he saw the child, he grabbed him and dragged him back to the mill. The miller's wife, expecting her husband, was standing by the windows and saw the man approaching. She locked the door and bolted it. When the man got to the door he shouted at her to open it, but when she refused, he gave the door a furious kick, hoping to break it in. The miller's wife screamed from one of the windows, but since the mill was so isolated and surrounded by brush and forest, no one heard her cries.

In the meantime, the man kept trying to break down the door, but it was too sturdy. He realized what a dangerous situation he and his wife would be in if the miller returned from church, and he drew his knife and called to the miller's wife, "If you don't open up immediately I am going to stab your son to death before your eyes and burn your mill down to the ground."

The miller's wife ran to the door and was about to open it, but she stopped, for the thought struck her that the murderer only wanted to lure her out to kill her and the child within her womb. And so she vacillated for a moment. The man, however, did not hesitate. He plunged the knife into the child's breast. Then he ran around the house, seeking another entrance.

It suddenly occurred to the miller's wife, who was quite unaware of what was happening, that if she set the mill wheel in motion, the unaccustomed clattering on a Sunday might attract some people to help her. The murderer, however, was just about to climb through the wheel to enter the mill, and he would no doubt have succeeded. But the wheel, set free, began to move according to God's wondrous ways, and since the man had a foot on one of the blades it dragged him under, crushing him in a most wretched manner.

A short time later the miller and his apprentices returned home.

When he opened up the room in which the midwife was imprisoned, she was lying dead on the floor. Fear and terror had caused her to have a stroke.

‡‡  129  ‡‡

## JOHANN HÜBNER

On Mt. Geißen in Westphalia the ruins of a fortress can still be seen today. Many years ago robbers lived there. They roamed about the countryside at night and stole cattle from the farmers and drove them into the courtyard of their fortress where they had their stalls. Later, they would sell them to strangers in distant regions. The last robber to have lived here was called Johann Hübner. He wore armor made of iron, and he was stronger than all the other men in the entire land. He had only one eye and wore a long curly beard. During the day he used to sit drinking with his robber band in a corner of the castle where one can still see the broken window.

Johann Hübner could see with his one eye far out into the countryside. Whenever he would spy a rider far below, he would cry, "Hello! Look, there goes a rider! What a splendid horse! Hello!" Then they would ride out, wait for the rider to come, strike him dead, and take his horse.

Now, there reigned at this time Prince von Dillenburg, called Black Christian, who was a very strong man. He had heard a great deal about the robberies of Johann Hübner, for the farmers always came to him to lament their losses. Black Christian had a very clever servant by the name of Hanns Flick, whom he sent out into the countryside to keep a watch on the activities of Johann Hübner. The prince, however, remained behind with his knights, hiding in the forest at Giller, where the local farmers brought him and his men bread, butter, and cheese.

Hanns Flick had never seen Johann Hübner and wasn't sure he would recognize him, so he went about the countryside inquiring about him. Finally, he came to a smithy, where horses were being shod and many wagon wheels were hanging on the walls waiting to be repaired. Leaning up against the wheels was a man who had only one eye and wore an iron doublet. Hanns Flick walked up to him and said, "Greetings, iron-doublet man with one eye! Are you perchance Johann Hübner of Mt. Geißen?"

The man replied, "Johann Hübner of Mt. Geißen is on the wheel."

Hanns Flick thought he meant the wheel at the place of execution, and said, "Was that recently?"

"Yes," replied the man, "it was just today."

Hanns Flick did not quite believe him, and he stayed at the smithy, keeping watch on the man leaning against the wheels. The man whispered in the smith's ear that he should shoe the horse backward, so the front of the horseshoe pointed to the rear. The smith did as told, and Johann Hübner rode off. But before leaving he called to Hanns Flick: "May God be with you, fine fellow. Tell your lord that he may send strong fists against me but not flea brains!"

Hanns Flick stood and watched him ride off over the fields and into the forest. He then tried to follow the man's trail, but Johann Hübner rode back and forth and around in circles, and Hanns Flick soon became quite confused following the tracks because wherever the horse rode, its tracks pointed in the opposite direction. He soon lost the trail and did not know where the man had ridden off to.

But he persevered. Finally, he discovered the clearing in the forest where Johann Hübner and his men had camped, and where they were letting their stolen cattle graze. He then hastened to report the location to Black Christian, who came riding quietly through the forest with his knights. The prince and his men had tied moss to their horses' hooves and were thus able to stage a surprise attack on the robber and his men. Johann Hübner and Black Christian fought in their iron helmets and doublets, and the ringing noise resounded through the forest. But finally Johann Hübner lay dead and the prince occupied the castle at Mt. Geißen.

They buried Johann Hübner in a corner of the castle grounds. Then they cleared the forest around the tower and undermined it. In the evening, when the cows were being milked in the village below, the tower toppled, and the entire countryside shook from its fall. One can still see the stones of the tower scattered down the mountainside.

Johann Hübner often appears there at midnight. He can be seen, his one eye shining in the dark, sitting on a black horse, riding around the old fortress wall.

‡‡  130  ‡‡

### EPPELA GAILA

Not long ago one could hear the street urchins in Nürnberg singing the following old verses:

> Eppela Gaila of Dramaus
> Rides out the fourteenth of the month.
>
> The enemy of Nürnberg is riding out,
> Eppela Gaila of Dramaus.

In ancient times there lived in Drameysel, a tiny village in the parsonage of Muggendorf in the region near Bayreuth, a bold and venturesome knight by the name of Eppelin von Gailing. He used to roam the countryside robbing and pillaging. He was especially ill-disposed toward the citizens of Nürnberg, and he would do them harm whenever he had the chance. He was also versed in sorcery, and moreover, possessed a marvelous horse, which he could make jump over cliffs and ravines and over the Wiesent River without touching the water. The horse could also clear tall hay wagons in the fields and his hooves never touched a single straw.

The knight's headquarters were located at the fortress at Gailen-reuth, but he had other fortresses all around the countryside, and he could fly like the wind from one to the other in no time at all. He would be on one side of a mountain one moment, and the next on the other side. He often rode to St. Lorenz in Muggendorf.

In Nürnberg, neither the fortress walls nor the city moat could keep him out, and he had many an adventure there. Finally, how-ever, the citizens of Nürnberg caught up with him, and he was hanged with all his men on the gallows at New Market. His wea-pons are still on display in the fortress of Nürnberg, and one can still see the print of his horse's hoof in the fortress wall where he and his horse once sprang over it.

‡‡ 131 ‡‡

## BLUMENSTEIN

A band of knights once lived at the fortress of Blumenstein near the city of Rotenburg in Hesse. One evening an adventuresome young peasant girl bet her friends that she could go out in the moonlight at midnight and bring back a piece of tile from the dreaded fortress. She set off and succeeded in getting the piece of tile as proof, but when she was about to make her way back she heard the sound of hooves resounding in the still night air. She quickly darted under the drawbridge just as a knight rode over it. A lovely maiden he had abducted was with him on his horse, and all her precious gowns were tied on behind. As he rode over the bridge, the bundle of clothing fell from his horse. The peasant girl grabbed it and ran off. But she was scarcely halfway over the hill that lay between Blumen-stein and Hohnebach, when she heard the knight again riding out over the drawbridge. She thought he was probably going back to look for the lost bundle, and she had no choice but to leave the trail and hide in the dense forest until he rode past. Thus, she saved her booty and was able to bring the proof of her adventure back home.

Others tell of similar adventures at different sites, such as the following story. The girl witnessed the knight murdering the abducted maiden. The maiden dropped a bundle of clothes, which the knight did not notice. The girl picked it up and took it with her, and when she opened it later, she discovered precious gowns and jewelry. She kept silent about her find, telling everyone that she had become frightened, had turned back, and had never made it to the castle. In time, however, she began to wear an item here and there, as though she had just acquired it. Finally, she wore the whole splendid outfit to a dance. A stranger was there who fixed his eyes upon her and who danced with her and finally asked to accompany her home. On the way he drew his knife and was about to kill her, when the girl screamed for help. He was then arrested and was discovered to be the knight who had murdered the other girl.

## ‡‡ 132 ‡‡

## SEEBURG LAKE

Located just two short hours from Göttingen is Seeburg Lake. It is growing smaller every year, and is now only thirty to forty feet deep and about half an hour in circumference. There are many cave-ins and deep holes in the earth around the lake, which indicate a possible underground river. The local fishermen tell the following legend.

In the old days a majestic castle stood where the lake is now, in which a count by the name of Iseng lived. He led a wild and wicked life. Once, he even forced his way through the sacred walls of a convent in Lindau, abducted a nun, and raped her. Scarcely had he completed the blasphemous act when it was revealed that the woman, whom he had so disgraced, was his own sister whose existence had been kept secret from him. While it is true that his revelation was a terrible shock to him, and he sent her back to the convent with rich atonement, he nevertheless did not convert to God and continued to lead his life of vain and sinful desires.

One day he sent his servant out to the fishmonger's to get a fresh eel, but the fishmonger gave him a shiny silver serpent instead. The count, who was versed in the language of animals, was not at all displeased, for he knew that anyone who ate from such a snake would acquire all the secrets of the animal language. He ordered the snake prepared for dinner but forbade his servant, under threat of death, to eat any of it. He then consumed as much of the snake as he was able, but he left a small portion on his plate, which was carried away. The servant, who had been prompted by the strange interdiction, could not resist the temptation and ate the remainder.

After the meal, the count was suddenly struck by the thought of all the sins and blasphemies he had committed, taking them all to heart, for they became so clear in his mind that he could not drive the thoughts away nor get rid of his growing fear. "It's so hot in here!" he cried. "I feel as if I had blown into the fires of Hell!" He went out into his garden, where a messenger approached him and said, "Your sister has just died as a result of the sins you forced upon her." In growing fear, the count ran into the courtyard. But there, all the farm animals were running up and down—chickens, ducks, and geese—and they were speaking of the wicked life he had led and of the frightful blasphemies he had committed. The sparrows and the doves on the roof joined in the chorus and called out, "Now is the time for the sinner to receive his full measure, for the end has come. In a short time all the splendid towers here will topple, and the entire castle will sink out of sight."

Just as the rooster was crowing mightily from the rooftop, the servant who had eaten some of the snake appeared, and the count, who wanted to test him, asked, "What is it that the rooster is crowing?"

The servant, forgetting himself, but understanding the words perfectly, replied, "He cries, 'Run, run! Before the sun goes down, if thou wisheth to save thy life. Run, run! But go alone!'"

"O you traitor," cried the count, "you ate from the snake. Pack your things and let us flee!"

The servant raced back into the castle, and while he was gone, the count began to saddle his horse. He was already in the saddle and about to leave when the servant, quite pale and out of breath, returned. He grabbed hold of the reins and pleaded with the count to take him along. The count looked up and saw that the last rays of the sunset were glowing on the peaks of the mountains, and he heard the rooster crowing, "Run, run, before the sun goes down— but go alone." Then he drew his sword and struck his servant such a blow that it severed his head.

He raced his horse across the drawbridge and rode beyond the town of Gieboldehausen, then he turned and looked back. Seeing the towers of his castle glowing in the setting sun, he thought that everything must have been either a dream or that his senses had been playing tricks on him. But, suddenly, the earth beneath him began to shake and tremble. Quite frightened he rode off again. When he stopped and turned around a second time, the walls, masonry, and towers had disappeared, and in their place was a large lake.

After this wondrous deliverance, the count converted and devoted himself to God. He atoned for his sins in the monastery of Gieboldehausen, presenting them with all his remaining properties.

By his decree, masses are still read for repentant sinners on a specific day every year. His endowment also provided the church in the town of Berenshausen with a new altar and a new choir, and it is said that the letter of endowment can still be seen there. Moreover, it is reported that even today masoned stonework and carved wooden beams are still hauled out of the lake on occasion. Not long ago, two silver pots with finely worked decorations were fished from the lake, and the innkeeper in Seeburg bought one of them.

## ‡‡ 133 ‡‡

## THE CASTLE LAKE AND THE CASTLE WALL

On the Pomeranian island of Rügen, in a region called the Stubnitz, there can be seen a mighty earthen wall. It forms a large circle and is now overgrown with beech trees. The inside of the circle is filled with tree roots and scattered stones. Hard by the east rim of the wall lies a deep round depression in which there is a lake, called Black Lake, or Castle Lake. According to local legend, a devil was worshipped within these walls in ancient times and a maiden was kept there in his service. When he grew tired of her, his priests took her to Black Lake and drowned her.

## ‡‡ 134 ‡‡

## ST. NICHOLAS AND THE THIEF

In the St. Gertrude Chapel in Greifswald in Pomerania stood a statue of St. Nicholas. One night a thief broke into the church intending to rob the donation box, and he called out to the saint, "Hey, St. Nicholas, is the money yours or mine? Come, let's have a race and whoever gets to the donation box first wins!" He then began running. But the statue started running too, three times as fast as the thief, who said, "My, St. Nicholas, you won fair and square. But the money isn't any use to you. You're made of wood and have no need of money."

Soon after, the robber died and was buried. Then devils appeared from Hell, dug up the body from its grave, threw it next to the stolen donation box, and finally hung it on a windmill outside the city gate and spun it against the wind on one of the blades.

The mill still was standing on that site in 1633, and it always turned against the wind, in contrast to the other mills around it, which turned in the normal fashion.

According to others, it was the sexton who stole the offerings, or rather, who had a race with the statue of Mary.

When the Devil's feet touched the earth, they burned the grass in that spot and left deep prints. Grass never grew there again until the entire church, which was the goal of many pilgrimages, was buried, together with the cemetery. It was later rebuilt into the wall of the local fortification.

## ‡‡ 135 ‡‡

## GIANT STONES

Now and again one finds dreadful-looking boulders in which the shapes of hands and feet have been imprinted. According to legend, these were put there by Giants, who tossed them or stood on them. One such stone lies along a road running past the Cow Tower in Leipzig. Imprinted in it is the form of a large hand with six fingers. Another large stone can be seen on the road from Leipzig to the village of Hohentiegel, closer to the village than to the city. There is a huge slash in the rock that looks as though it had been made by a battle sword.

Many years ago Salzwedel was besieged by a fierce enemy army, but they could not take the city because angels were patrolling the city walls, walking back and forth and snatching arrows out of the air, and otherwise protecting the city. The enemy general became enraged, and as he paced through his camp, he came upon a large boulder. He drew his battle sword and cried, "If I am not to take this city, then may God let me slash this stone as if I were slicing a soft bread roll." When he struck, the stone gave way as though it were quite soft. This very stone was pointed out on this spot to Prätorius in 1649. It lies along the road from Salzwedel to Tielsen, and Prätorius felt it and saw with his own eyes the deep slash that went right through the middle of it.

## ‡‡ 136 ‡‡

## IMPRINTS IN THE STONE

There is a forest near the glass foundry in Minden called Geismar Forest. A city called Geismar stood there before the Thirty Years' War. Hard by the forest stands a mountain called the Mountain of the Dead. A terrible battle was once fought there. The general of one of the armies was beaten during the initial encounter, and he re-treated into the Geismar Forest. He was sitting on a boulder contem-plating his best course of action, when one of his captains came to him and tried to convince him to take up the battle again and to attack the enemy courageously. If only he could win this one battle, the captain told him, then everything would be saved. However, the general replied, "No, I have about as much chance of victory as this stone has of turning soft." After speaking these words he got up—but his legs, and even his hand on which he had leaned while getting up, left a clear imprint in the stone. As soon as he beheld this wonder, he had his bugler summon the army to battle. He attacked the enemy with courage and was victorious. The stone is still there and the imprints in it can still be seen.

## ‡‡ 137 ‡‡
## THE GIANT'S FINGER

A wild and wicked Giant once lived on the shores of the Saale River not too far from Jena. He often went up into the mountains to eat his meals, and a butte on Mt. Landgraf is still called the Spoon because he once dropped his spoon there. Whenever his mother scolded him for his terrible behavior, he would even become wicked toward her, cursing and insulting her. He expressed only rage to-ward humans, calling them Dwarfs. Once, when his mother was admonishing him again, he became so enraged that he struck her with his fist.

With this act of brutality the day darkened into night, a storm moved in over the mountains, lightning flashed, and there was such a furious crack of thunder that the Giant fell to the ground. In-stantly, the mountain collapsed and buried him. As further punish-ment, his little finger grew from his grave. The finger can be recog-nized as a tall thin tower on the top of House Mountain. Today it is called Fox Tower.

## ‡‡ 138 ‡‡
## THE GIANTS FROM WONDER MOUNTAIN

The old men of the village of Feldkirchen, which lies two hours from Salzburg, say that in the year 1645, when they were still innocent boys, they saw Giants coming out of Wonder Mountain. The Giants proceeded to the chapel of Grödich, which is the closest church to

Wonder Mountain. They leaned up against the church and spoke with the men and women who were there. They warned the people that if they wished to escape an impending disaster they should lead good Christian lives and raise their children with good manners. The Giants then returned to their homes in Wonder Mountain. The people of Grödich had often been warned by the Giants to continue in their pious ways to protect themselves against misfortune.

‡‡   139   ‡‡

## JETTA HILL IN HEIDELBERG

The hill in Heidelberg on which the castle now stands used to be called Jetta Hill. An old woman by the name of Jetta used to live in a chapel there, the remains of which can still be seen. When Count Palatine Frederick became Elector in 1544, he built a splendid castle there on the hill, which was called New Court. Jetta had become quite famous because of her ability to give prophecies, but she hardly ever left her chapel, and when people came to hear her prophecies she would give answers to those who asked through the chapel window without letting anyone see her.

Among other things she foretold—expressing the prophecy in memorable verse—that the hill would one day be enclosed in walls, that in future years royalty would live there, and she even named them. She told how the place would be decorated and honored and how the valley below would become heavily populated. At that time the valley floor was covered with forest.

One day, Jetta was very happily walking along the trail that led down to the well at the foot of Goat Mountain near the village of Schlürbach, half an hour from Heidelberg, to get a drink of water. Suddenly, she was attacked and killed by a wolf with young. That is why this well is still called Wolf Fountain today.

There is a vaulted passageway under the mountain there, which the people call Heathen Cave.

‡‡   140   ‡‡

## GIANT HAYM

There lived many years ago a Giant by the name of Haym, or as he was also called, Haymon. At that time, a poisonous dragon was on the loose in the wilds of the Inn Valley, wreaking great damage upon the inhabitants. Haymon sought him out and killed him. Because of this deed the inhabitants of the valley declared the Giant their leader, and they became his subjects.

Later, Haymon acquired even greater fame when he rebuilt the bridge over the River Inn, making it stronger. It is from this bridge—the Inn Bridge—that the city of Innsbruck takes its name.

The Bishop of Chur converted him to Christianity and baptized him. Haymon then built the monastery at Wilten in honor of Christ, where he lived until his death, and where he is buried. His grave can still be seen at Wilten; it is fourteen feet and three fingers long. A figure in armor carved of wood is on the tomb. The dragon's tongue, together with an old chalice, is still on display in the sacristy.

Scenes from Christ's Passion are depicted on the chalice found there more than 1100 years ago when the foundation for the monastery was being excavated. It is thus estimated that the chalice was made shortly after Christ's Ascension.

A plaque can be seen next to Haymon's tomb on which are written the events of his life.

‡‡ 141 ‡‡

## THE DRIPPING RIB

In the Ciller region of Styria there is a village by the name of Oberburg, called Gornigrad in the Slavic tongue. On display in the church there is a huge rib, of a kind no land animal is known to possess. It is not known when the rib was excavated. Folk legend attributes it to a Heathen Maiden (Slavic: *Ajdowska Dekliza*). The legend also maintains that each year one drop falls from it, and when it stops dripping it will be Judgment Day.

‡‡ 142 ‡‡

## MAIDEN'S LEAP

Not far from Graz in Styria there is a high cliff, usually called the Wall, which has also borne the name of Maiden's Leap for several centuries. Many years ago a wicked, arrogant youth had long been pursuing a maiden and he had even made rude, impestuous advances toward her. One day after spying on the maiden and following her, he caught her on top of the cliff. Seeing herself trapped, and frightened of him, she ventured a leap over the Mur River to a hill on the other side—and she made it! That is why this cliff is called Maiden's Leap.

## BULL CREEK

There is a creek that runs through a valley in the Suren Alps. It is called Bull Creek and it is fed from Lake Suren up in the mountains. According to a well-known legend, told both by the people of Uri as well as by those from Engelsberg, the creek got its name in the following manner.

Several centuries ago, an Alpine shepherd lived in the area, and in his flock he had a lamb of which he was especially proud. Indeed, he was so devoted to this lamb that he decided to have it baptized and to give it a Christian name. What happened? The heavens, to avenge themselves for this blasphemy, changed the lamb into a frightful specter. It roamed the fertile Alpine pastures day and night, grazing away all the grass and herbs, until the Engelsberg farmers could no longer use the pastures for their own sheep and cattle.

One day, a wandering student came to Uri, and he told the people how to get rid of the monstrous animal. They should raise a bull calf for nine years on nothing but pure milk—the first year with the milk from one cow, the second with the milk of two cows, the third of three cows, and so on. After nine years, the bull that had been raised on milk should be led over the pastures by a chaste maiden. The farmers from Uri hoped to get a reward from the farmers of Engelsberg, and so they raised such a bull in the pasture of Waldnacht, where today one can still be directed to the Bull Stall.

When the bull had been raised on the milk for nine years, a chaste maiden led it across the high ridge of a cliff and then let him run loose. As soon as the bull saw that he was free, he took off after the specter, and they engaged in a fierce struggle. The fight was so wild and furious that the bull, although victorious, was exhausted and covered with sweat. He then raced for the stream rushing nearby, plunged in, and drank so much water that he dropped dead on the spot. Ever since, the stream has borne the name of Bull Creek. The inhabitants of the area can also point to the imprints in the rock where the bull dug himself in for the valiant struggle.

## THE MEN IN ZOTTEN MOUNTAIN

In the sixteenth century a man by the name of Johannes Beer lived in the city of Schweidnitz. He liked to wander about Mt. Zotten, not far from the city. But one day in 1570, as he was taking his accustomed walk on the mountainside, he noticed for the first time an opening in a cliff. As he entered, he felt a strong wind blowing against him and, frightened, he quickly withdrew.

Soon thereafter on Low Sunday, the first Sunday after Easter, he resolved to return to investigate the cave. Again he entered and soon found himself in a long narrow passageway. He began to follow a ray of light that glimmered far ahead of him. Finally, he came to a closed door into which was set a pane of glass that cast the wondrous light. He knocked on the door, and after the third time it opened. Upon entering he saw a large round table at which were sitting three emaciated men in ancient German dress. They looked quite distressed and were trembling. On the table before them lay a book, bound in black silk on which were stamped gold letters.

He then addressed them with the words *"Pax vobis"* [Peace unto you].

He received the reply *"Hic nulla pax!"* [There is no peace here].

Stepping closer, he spoke again, *"Pax vobis in nomine domini!"* [Peace unto you in the name of the Lord].

Trembling, they replied in weak voices, *"Hic non pax"* [No peace here].

Stepping right up to their table, he repeated, *"Pax vobis in nomine domini nostri Jesu Christi!"*

They did not reply to these words. Instead, they shoved the book toward him, opened to the title, *Liber obedientiae* [Book of Obedience]. Beer asked who they were, to which they replied that they themselves knew not who they were. What were they doing here? They were waiting in terror for Judgment Day when they would be rewarded for their deeds. What was their work on earth? They pointed to a curtain behind which lay all kinds of instruments of murder, human skeletons, and skulls. He asked if they confessed to these wicked works. "Yes!" Had they done good or evil? "Evil!" Did they repent? To this they said nothing, simply sat there, trembling. They did not know.

A Silesian chronicle records that the castle of some robber barons was once located on Zotten Mountain, and the ruins can still be seen.


‡‡ 145 ‡‡

## THE PRONOUNCEMENT OF DOOM

On September 22, 1550, the army of Magdeburg was preparing to do battle with Duke George of Mecklenburg. As they marched past the village of Barleben, just a mile from the city, they encountered a tall, stately old man dressed like a peasant. He asked the leaders where they thought they were going with all their soldiers and armor. When they informed him of their intentions, he raised his hands into the air. He pleaded with them and warned them to stop and return home to protect their own city, not to undertake a campaign at that place and especially not at that time. It had been just two hundred years before, on the day of St. Moritz, that the army of Magdeburg had been defeated along the Ohra River. This fact could be read by everyone on a plaque in St. John's Church in Magdeburg. He warned them that if they continued they would surely fare no better than before.

Although a number of the soldiers marveled at the man's appearance and at his words, many of them nevertheless made fun of him and laughed off the warning with scorn. None of those who ridiculed the prophecy would later escape the battle; they were either killed or captured.

It is said that the man appeared as an extremely aged, white-haired man, but that his face sparkled wondrously with the color and vitality of youth. And since his prophecy unfortunately came true, they began investigating to find out who he might have been. But no one could find out anything about him, nor locate anyone who had seen him before or since.

‡‡　146　‡‡

## THE DWARF ON HIS BACK

In March 1669 a rope maker was walking on the road that led to Torgau when he met a boy who was sitting in a field, playing with a board. The rope maker inadvertently kicked the board aside as he was walking, and the boy said to him, "Why are you kicking my board away? My father will get you for this!"

The rope maker continued on his way, but not a hundred steps farther he encountered a little man of considerable age with a grey beard. The old man asked him to carry him along the way because he had become so wearied from walking. The rope maker laughed at the presumption of the little man, but then he jumped up on his shoulders and would not get off, and he was forced to carry him to the next town. Ten days later, the rope maker died.

While the man's son was pitifully lamenting the sudden death, the small boy came up to him and told him to be content for the father had received his due. He also said that he would soon return for him and his mother, for Meißen would be struck by disastrous times.

## GOTTSCHEE

In the Lower Krain region of Slovenia there is the town of Gottschee. The many Germans who live there are quite different from the surrounding Krainians in dress, language, and customs. Not far away lies the old castle of the same name, which belongs to the princes of Auersperg. The people in the area tell many stories about this castle. A hunter and his servants still occupy the inhabitable portion of the crumbling structure, and spirits are known to reside there. The following story is supposed to have happened to one of the hunter's ancestors.

The wife of the hunter had gone down to the town while he, having become sleepy, lay down under a large oak tree outside the castle. Suddenly, he saw the elder of his two sons, whom he had left sleeping inside the house, come walking toward him as though he were being led. Although the hunter could see no one else, the five-year-old held his left arm out as though someone were holding on to it. Walking at a fast clip, the child was heading straight for a steep cliff overlooking a deep ravine. Frightened, the father jumped up. Trying to save his child, he grabbed him and attempted to free his left hand from the invisible leader. With great effort he succeeded in pulling the hand of the child free from another hand, which the hunter could not see, but which he felt to be ice cold. The child was not frightened at all. He calmly told his father how an old man with a long beard all dressed in black clothes had come to him. He had been quite friendly, promising the boy many nice things if he would come along, and then led him by the hand.

The evening of that same day, the hunter heard himself being called by name. When he opened the door, he saw the same old man standing outside waving to him. The hunter followed and was led to that same ravine. The wall of the cliff opened and they descended a stone stairway into the cliff. Along the way he encountered a snake, and then they came to a large vault. As they walked, it grew lighter and lighter. Then they came to a long hallway where seven aged men with bald heads were sitting in deep silence. From there they proceeded through a narrow passageway into a small vault where he saw a little coffin. Then they went into a larger vault where he saw twenty larger coffins in which lay corpses of both sexes. Among the deceased he saw several faces that he recognized, but he could not recall where he had seen them.

He was then led into a large, brightly illuminated hall, where thirty-eight people were sitting, including many young women. They were celebrating a festive occasion. But they were all as pale as death, and no one spoke a word. The old man then led the hunter through a red door where he saw a row of people in Old Franconian dress, several of whom the hunter thought he recognized. The old man kissed the first one and the last one in the row.

Finally, the hunter implored his guide to tell him who all these people were, and was it possible for a mortal to grant them the eternal peace they were lacking.

"They are all former residents of this castle," he replied in a hollow voice. "Additional particulars cannot be disclosed to you at this time, but you will learn more before long."

The hunter was then gently nudged out another door and he found himself alone in a damp vault. He discovered an old, crumbling stairway, which he carefully ascended, and then came to another, somewhat larger chamber. From there he could look up through a small round opening and happily see the skies and the stars. He then bumped into a heavy rope and heard the sound of rushing water, which led him to conclude that he was behind the castle, at the bottom of a cistern where water was drawn up by a crank. Unfortunately, no one in the castle came to get water for three whole days. Not until the evening of the fourth day did the hunter's wife go there. She was astonished when she hauled up her husband, whom she thought dead, in the heavy water bucket.

The old man's promise to reveal the secrets to the hunter one day remains, for the time being, unfulfilled. Nevertheless, the hunter did discover that the old man's information about the spirits being former inhabitants of the castle was indeed true. For later, when he walked into the royal hall and looked at the portraits of his ancestors, he recognized the same faces he had seen on the corpses and spirits in the cave.

## ‡‡  148  ‡‡

## THE DWARFS IN THE TREE

In summer, hordes of Dwarfs used to come down the mountainsides into the valleys to join humans, either to help or to watch them at their work. They especially liked to be around when it was time to make hay. Often they would sit happily among the shady leaves of the long, heavy branches of a maple tree. Once, however, some wicked people sawed through one of the heavy branches at night so that it was barely held in place on the trunk of the tree. And the next morning, when the unsuspecting little creatures climbed up on the branch, it came crashing down throwing all the Dwarfs onto the ground where they were laughed at. They became quite enraged and cried:

Oh, how high are the heavens,
And how great is man's treachery!
We are here today, but nevermore!

They kept their word, and never again were they seen in that land.

## THE DWARFS ON THE BOULDER

It used to be the custom of the Dwarfs to come during hay harvests to sit on top of a large boulder and watch the workers in the fields. Once, however, a pair of rascals built a fire on top of the boulder, and they left the glowing coals there for quite a while before sweeping them away. When the Wee Folk appeared in the morning, they burned themselves pitifully and cried out angrily, "Oh, wicked world! Oh, wicked world!"

They swore revenge and then vanished evermore.

## THE FEET OF THE DWARFS

In olden times humans lived only in the valleys, and all around them on the cliffs and peaks lived the Dwarfs. They were friendly and good to people, and they would often help them on difficult chores during the night. When the farmers would go out into their fields early in the morning, riding with all their farm implements in their wagons, they would often be pleasantly surprised to find that all the work had already been done. The Wee Folk, who were hiding in the bushes, would begin laughing out loud as the farmers exclaimed in surprise.

Sometimes, however, farmers would become angry if they found that all their grain, which had not quite become ripe, lay in the fields already cut. But after thunderstorms and hail struck the countryside, they realized that they would not have been able to save a single stalk of grain. Then they expressed their heartfelt gratitude to the prophetic Dwarfs.

Through sin and wickedness, however, people ultimately forfeited the favor and good will of the Dwarfs. The Wee Folk fled the countryside and no human being has laid eyes on them since. It all came about like this.

A shepherd up on the mountains once owned a splendid cherry tree. One summer, when the fruit had become ripe, he awoke one morning to find that the tree had been picked clean during the night, and that all the fruit had been carefully deposited in the storage bins. This strange event was repeated three summers in a row.

The people in the village said, "That can only have been the good Dwarfs. They always come prancing out at night with their long cloaks covering their feet, and they are as quiet as the birds as they perform the day's work for humans. Many a time we have listened to them secretly, but one should never disturb them in any way—just let them come and go as they please."

These words aroused the shepherd's curiosity, and he wondered why the Dwarfs were so careful to conceal their feet. And he wondered further if their feet might not be different from those of humans.

When summer came around the following year, and it was again time to harvest the cherries and store them in the bins, the shepherd took a sack full of ashes and spread them all around the trunk of his tree. The next morning at the break of dawn he hurried out and found that the tree had again been picked clean, and he saw the prints of many geese feet in the ashes under the tree. The shepherd laughed out loud, and he made fun of the fact that the secret of the Dwarfs was a secret no longer.

Soon thereafter the Dwarfs destroyed their houses and moved far inside the mountains. They became ill-disposed toward humans and forevermore denied them their help. The shepherd who had betrayed them became increasingly feeble and demented until he died.


‡‡   151   ‡‡

## THE WILD SPIRITS

Among the Germans living in Vicentia and Verona there is not a single one, not even the bravest hunter, who would risk going up to the high hunting grounds between mid-December and mid-January. They fear the Wild Man and the Forest Woman. The shepherds do not move their flocks during this period. Instead, children haul water from springs in clay pots and carry it to the animals in their stalls. In order to placate the Forest Woman, the women of the village used to spin some hair on their distaffs and then cast it into the fire. On Christmas Eve, the ashes are then spread around the kitchen and around every chimney and opening leading inside from the open air. One can then look at the ashes and tell by the foot-prints—their position, size, whether they were coming or going—which spirits, good or bad, visit the house.

‡‡   152   ‡‡

## THE DWARFS OF HEILING

Along the Eger River between the Court of Wildenau and Aicha Castle there are gigantic cliffs rising high above the water that ages ago were named Heiling Bluff. At the foot of the cliffs a cave can be seen. Inside, there is a high vaulted chamber. But on the outside there is only a very small opening, and one must bend over and crawl to enter. The cave used to be inhabited by tiny Dwarfs, who eventually came to be ruled over by an old, unknown man called Heiling.

A long time ago a woman who was born in the village of Tasch-witz wandered into the forest on the Eve of St. Peter and Paul to pick wild berries. She was overtaken by night but then she saw a pretty cottage right next to the cliffs. She opened the door, and upon entering she saw a man sitting at the table writing fast and busily. The woman asked for lodging for the night and it was willingly granted.

Other than the old man there seemed to be no living creature in the room, but the woman heard bustling noises from every corner. She shuddered with fear and finally asked the old man, "Where am I anyway?" The old man told her that his name was Heiling, and that he was soon going to be leaving this region, "for two-thirds of my Dwarfs have already fled these parts." This strange reply made the woman even uneasier, and she wanted to ask more questions. But he told her to remain silent and added, "Had you not arrived precisely at this rather remarkable time, you would not have been able to find lodging here." Somewhat intimidated and fearful, the woman crawled humbly into a corner and fell peacefully asleep.

When morning came to the foot of the cliff and awakened her, she believed that she had been dreaming, for there was no building to be seen anywhere. Content and happy that no harm had come to her in this dangerous region, she proceeded to hurry back to her village. But when she arrived, everything looked different and strange. The houses of the village were new and built differently. She didn't recognize the people she encountered, nor did they know her. With some effort she located the hut where she lived. It too had been rebuilt, but she recognized the giant oak tree, which shaded the house, and which her grandfather had planted there. When she tried to enter the front room, she was turned away as a stranger by people she didn't even know, and she ran weeping and lamenting around the village.

The people who saw her thought she was insane, and they took her to the authorities where she was interrogated and her case investigated. And behold, they found in old logs and church records that on that precise day, just one hundred years before, a woman of the same name had gone into the forest to pick berries. She had never returned home and had never been found. It thus became clear that she had slept inside the cliff for a hundred years and had not grown any older during that time.

She lived her remaining years in peace and without need, for she was cared for by the whole community as repayment for the sorcery she had been forced to endure.

## ‡‡ 153 ‡‡

## THE DEPARTURE OF THE DWARF NATION OVER THE BRIDGE

On the south side of the Harz Mountains, and especially in certain regions in County Hohenstein, one can see many small caves in the cliffs, which for the most part are so small that grown men have to get on their hands and knees to enter them. Other caves, however, have spacious chambers where whole parties of people could meet. These caves were once inhabited by Dwarfs and are therefore called Dwarf Holes. The Dwarfs used to have two whole kingdoms in the area between Walkenried and Neuhof in County Hohenstein.

Once, an inhabitant of that region became aware that fruits and vegetables were being taken from his farm at night, but he was never able to catch the culprit. On the advice of a wise woman, he finally walked up and down the rows of his pea patch at the onset of darkness, swinging a stick back and forth through the air over his plants. Before long, two Dwarfs were standing in the flesh in front of him. He had succeeded in knocking off their fog caps that made them invisible. Trembling, the Dwarfs fell to their knees and confessed that their people had been robbing his fields, but that they had been forced to do so by extreme need.

The news of the captured Dwarfs stirred the whole countryside. The Dwarf People sent envoys and bargained for release for themselves and their captured brothers. It was agreed that they were to leave this region forever. Yet, the manner in which they were to depart occasioned new bickering. The inhabitants did not want to permit the Dwarfs to depart with their collected and hidden treasures, and the Dwarf People did not want to be seen during their departure. Finally, it was agreed that the Dwarfs, without any of the citizens being present, would depart over the narrow bridge near Neuhof, and that each of them, as a toll for free passage, would deposit a certain portion of his wealth in a large kettle set out there.

The departure took place as planned. But a few curious people hid themselves under the bridge in order to at least hear the Dwarfs as they passed. Thus, they heard the clippety-clop of the feet of the tiny men for many long hours. It was as if they were listening to a very large herd of sheep crossing over the bridge.

Ever since this final great migration of the Dwarf Nation, only a few individual Dwarfs have been sighted on rare occasions. Nevertheless, a few of the Dwarfs who remained behind in the mountain caves were known on occasion to have stolen newborn babies from the houses of the farmers, leaving their own children as changelings.


‡‡　154　‡‡

## THE PARADE OF DWARFS OVER THE MOUNTAIN

On the north side of the Harz Mountains there once lived thousands of Dwarfs, or as they were also called, *Kröpel*. They lived in crevices and small caves called Dwarf Holes. Near Seehausen, a town belonging to Magdeburg, the people can point to a number of such *Kröpel* holes. However, the Dwarfs appear to the country people in visible form only on rare occasions, preferring to wander around among people unseen, invisible in their fog caps.

Many of these Dwarfs were quite benevolent, and under certain circumstances, very helpful to humans. They would lend their utensils and china to people for weddings and baptisms. But one had to take care not to incite them to anger, for then they could become malicious and cunning, and they could do all kinds of harm to the person who offended them.

A baker who lived in the valley between Blankenburg and Quedlinburg noticed one day that a few of his breads were always missing. Yet try as he would he could not uncover the thief. This unrelenting thievery was gradually driving the man into poverty. Finally, he began to suspect that perhaps the Dwarfs were responsible for his misfortune. He took a swatter of supple twigs and began swinging it back and forth through the air in his bakery until he finally struck a few fog caps, knocking them off so the Dwarfs were no longer invisible.

There arose quite a disturbance and, when the baker caught a few more Dwarfs in the act of stealing bread, it finally became necessary for the entire Dwarf Nation to migrate from that region. It was also agreed that there should be recompense for the victims of the Dwarfs' thievery, and that there should be some control over the number of Dwarfs emigrating. Therefore, a large pot was set out along the trail over Church Mountain near the village of Thale, and it was agreed that each Dwarf was to throw a coin into the vessel. After the departure of the Dwarfs, the pot was filled to the top with old coins, they were so many in number!

The Dwarf Nation gradually moved eastward beyond Warnstedt, not far from Quedlinburg. Since this migration, the Dwarfs have disappeared from this region, and there is only a rare sighting of an individual Dwarf.

‡‡ 155 ‡‡

## THE DWARFS OF DARDESHEIM

Dardesheim lies between Halberstadt and Brunswick. Directly north of the city limits there is a large spring of the finest water called Smans Spring. The spring's source lies deep within the mountain where Dwarfs once lived. If the people who lived in the region at that time needed a dress for a special occasion, or if they needed a special utensil for a wedding, all they had to do was walk up the mountain, knock three times, and state their needs in loud, clear voices. They were also required to say:

> Before sunrise on the morrow,
> We'll return all we do borrow.

The Dwarfs were perfectly content when a portion of the leftovers from the festive banquet was left as payment when the borrowed items were returned.

Later, however, arguments gradually upset the fine understanding that existed between the Dwarfs and the inhabitants of the countryside. At first, the disputes did not last long. But finally the Dwarfs emigrated from the region because the taunting and ridicule of many of the farmers proved to be as unbearable as their ingratitude. Since then no Dwarfs have been seen or heard there.

‡‡ 156 ‡‡

## RIECHERT THE SMITH

There is a farmer's field that covers the base of the east side of Dwarf Mountain near Dardesheim. A smith by the name of Riechert once planted peas in this field. When the peas were about ripe, he began to notice that some of them had already been picked. To catch the thief in the act, Riechert built a little hut on his field and kept watch day and night. All day long he didn't see a thing. But each morning he saw that in spite of his standing guard the field had been robbed again during the night. Angry at spending so much time and effort in vain, he decided to harvest the remainder of his pea crop. He had scarcely finished half of the field when he suddenly heard pitiful screams. When he investigated, he found a Dwarf lying on the ground under the pea vines. The threshing stick had smashed his head in, and since his fog cap had been knocked off he was now visible. The Dwarf got up and hurried back into his mountain.

## ‡‡ 157 ‡‡
### GRINKEN THE SMITH

In olden times in the Detter Mountains, just three hours from the city of Münster, there lived a Wild Man. He was called Grinken the Smith, and he lived in a cave deep under the earth. The entrance to the cave is now completely overgrown with grass and brush, but one can still see where it used to be. The Wild Man had his smithy in this cave and the things he made were very fine and lasted forever. He also made locks that no one could open without the keys. The lock on the door of the church in Nienburg is said to have been made by him. Thieves once tried to get in but they could not break the lock. Whenever there was a wedding, the farmers would come and borrow a spit from Grinken, and they would give him one of the roasts in exchange.

Once, a farmer came to Grinken's cave and said, "Grinken the Smith, give me a spit!"

"You won't get a spit. Give me a roast."

"You'll get no roast—go fetch your spit!"

By then Grinken was as furious as he could get and he yelled, "Try and stop me from taking my roast!"

The farmer then walked along the foot of the mountain back to his house. But when he arrived, he found his best horse lying in the stall with one of its legs torn off. That was Grinken's roast.

## ‡‡ 158 ‡‡
### THE SHEPHERD BOYS

Two shepherd boys who were out chasing birds on St. John's Day found themselves at the foot of Heiling Bluff. At the base of the cliff they found a small door standing open. Curiosity drove them inside, and in one corner they saw two large chests—one open and the other closed. The open chest was filled with money, and they reached in and filled their lunch packs with coins. Then a feeling of dread came over them both, and they raced for the door. The first one made it through. But as his friend followed, the hinges began to creak with a frightening sound. The boy leaped over the threshold just as the door slammed shut. But it caught his left shoe and tore off the wooden heel as he crossed over, barely managing to escape. The boys then brought the money home to their delighted parents.

‡‡ 159 ‡‡

## THE NUT KERNELS

Two youths, Peter and Knipping, from Wehren in the region around Corvey, were out looking for birds' nests. Peter was remarkably lazy and he only looked around for a bit and then lay down under a tree and fell asleep. Suddenly, in his sleep, he felt as though someone had grabbed him by the ears, and he woke with a start and looked around. But he saw no one, so he lay down and went back to sleep. Once again something grabbed him by the ears. He still couldn't see anyone, so he fell asleep for the third time. But when something jerked his ears for the third time, Peter figured he'd had enough, and he got up and looked around for some other place to nap without disturbance.

But as he walked, he suddenly saw the Maiden of Will Mountain walking in front of him. She was cracking nuts, placing the shells in her sack, and throwing the kernels away. When all the nuts had been cracked, she vanished. Peter had followed her the whole time, picking up the nut kernels and eating them. Then he turned around, found Knipping, and told him all that had happened to him.

They went home, found others to help them, and then returned to the spot where Peter had seen the maiden vanish. They began digging there and found an underground kitchen equipped with all kinds of cooking utensils. They continued digging, and they came to a cellar with vats full of money. They took as much money as they could carry, planning to return the next day. But when they did, everything had vanished. Try as they might, they could not locate the site where they had dug before.

Peter built himself a house with his money, and he still lives there today.

## THE TREASURE OF SOEST

At the time of the Thirty Years' War there was an old wall standing not far from the city of Soest in Westphalia. According to legend, an iron chest filled with money had been hidden in that wall and it was guarded by a black dog and a maiden under a spell.

The older people of the area say that a nobleman from a foreign country once came there and tried to deliver the maiden and to open the chest with a flaming key.

A number of traveling students and exorcists also came there and began to excavate. But so many strange and terrible things happened to them in the process that, no one since has had the desire to try again—especially since it is also said that even if the chest is opened, no one who has ever tasted mother's milk, even once, can partake of the treasure.

Not long ago, a girl from a nearby village was grazing her goats along the wall. One of them ran into an opening and she followed. She saw the maiden standing in a courtyard. The maiden asked the girl what she was doing there. The girl told her, and then the maiden pointed to a basket of cherries and said, "Take what you want of what you see there and let your goat do the same, but do not return or turn around or evil will befall you." The frightened child took seven cherries and then fled in great fear. The cherries then changed to gold.

## THE SPRING OF SILVER

In February 1605, during the reign of Duke Henry Julius of Brunswick, the following event occurred in a valley just a mile from the city of Quedlinburg.

A poor farmer sent his daughter into some brushland to gather firewood. The girl took a large pack basket and a smaller hand basket and set out. When she had filled both baskets and was about to return home, a Dwarf, dressed all in white, stepped forth and asked, "What have you there?"

"The wood I have gathered," replied the girl. "It's for heating and cooking."

"Dump the wood out," said the Dwarf. "Bring your baskets and follow me; I'll show you something better and more valuable than wood." He then led her to a spot at the foot of a hill. There he showed her a depression in the ground, nearly as wide as two tables, filled with silver coins—some large and some small, and moderately thick. Stamped on them was a picture reminiscent of the Virgin Mary surrounded by an inscription in an ancient tongue.

This silver seemed to come bubbling out of the ground, and the girl, overcome by a feeling of dread, stepped back, unwilling to empty her basket of wood. The Dwarf took the basket from her, emptied it, and refilled it with the silver coins. "That is better for you than wood," he said.

In consternation, she took the basket from him. But when the Dwarf urged her to dump out her pack basket as well, she told him that she had to take the wood home, for there were little children there and they had to have a warm room. She also told him that they had to have wood for cooking. The Dwarf was satisfied with that explanation, and he said, "Fine, take it home then." And he vanished.

The girl brought the basket of silver coins home and told what had happened. Before long, all the peasants were running into the forest with their rakes and shovels to claim a portion of the treasure—but no one could locate the spot where silver coins bubbled out of the ground.

When the Duke of Brunswick heard about it, he demanded a pound of the silver; and a citizen of Halberstadt named N. Everkan once had one coin melted down.


## ‡‡ 162 ‡‡
### GOLDEN SAND ON WONDER MOUNTAIN

In 1753 a very poor servant by the name of Paul Mayr, who worked for the court farms in St. Zeno, went for a hike up a mountainside in the area near Fountain Valley. When he was about halfway up, he came to a steep bluff with a pile of sand at its base. Because he had heard stories of such things and hadn't a doubt that it was pure gold, he filled all his pockets with the sand. Overjoyed, he was about to return home when he saw a strange man standing right in front of him, asking, "What are you carrying there?" The servant was so shocked and frightened he couldn't answer. But the man seized him, turned out his pockets, and said, "Now go home, but not by the path you came—find another one. And if you ever show yourself around here again you won't get away alive."

The good servant returned home. But as time passed, thoughts of the gold grew more and more enticing, and finally he decided to try to find the sand. But it was all in vain. Neither he nor the friend who accompanied him could locate the spot again.

On another occasion, a master woodsman was caught on the mountain by darkness and had to spend the night in a cave. In the morning he came upon a cliff from which heavy, glittering gold sand was flowing. Since he had nothing to carry it in, he ran down to the valley for a pitcher, returned, and set it under the cliff. When the pitcher was full of the running sand, he picked it up and headed back. But then he saw a door open into the cliff. He looked inside, and the scene was as natural as if he were looking at a special world inside the mountain that had daylight just like we have. However, the door only remained open a moment, and when it slammed shut, the inside of the mountain reverberated like the inside of a great empty wine barrel. The woodsman could have returned any time he wanted to fill his pitcher, but after his death, the gold proved to be no blessing. Since then, no one has ever seen the door in the cliff again.

## ‡‡ 163 ‡‡

## COALS OF GOLD

In 1753 an old woman walked from Salzburg to Wonder Mountain to collect herbs. After she had been gathering for some time, she came to the foot of a steep cliff where some broken pieces of rock were lying. They were greyish black and looked like pieces of coal, so she took several home with her. But when she took them out and looked at them again, she saw that they all had pure gold running through them. She immediately went back to the mountain for more of the rocks, but try as she might, she could not find the site again.

## ‡‡ 164 ‡‡

## THE FOUNTAIN OF STEINAU

In 1271, the subjects of Abbot Berold of Fulda plotted to assassinate him. One day, as he was reading mass in St. James Chapel, he was attacked and slain by the lords von Steinau, von Eberstein, Albrecht von Brandau, Ebert von Spala and by the knight Konrad. A short time later the whole band of robbers—thirty men with twenty horses—were apprehended as they attempted to rob a church in

Hasselstein. They were executed by the sword and their houses were razed. Because of the deed, the lineage von Steinau was forced to depict three wheels and three razors on their coat of arms. The site where they formed their conspiracy to assassinate the abbot lies near Steinau,* on the road to the Hanau region. On this spot there is a fountain surrounded by a meadow where to this day no grass grows.

## ‡‡ 165 ‡‡
## THE FIVE CROSSES

Just outside Klaus Gate in Höxter, on the left-hand side of the road to Pyrmont, stand five large stones called the five crosses, probably because they are the tops of old crosses that have sunk into the ground. Legend has it that five Huns were slain on this spot. According to others, however, the crosses mark the grave of the five counts von Reischach. Still another tradition says this is where Tilly had hanged five citizens during the Thirty Years' War.

## ‡‡ 166 ‡‡
## THE SWORD DANCE AT WEISSENSTEIN

Not far from Marburg, on the road to Wetter, there is a small village called Wehre. Near it, lies a mountain with a pointed peak on which a robber's castle is supposed to have stood in olden times. It was called Weißenstein, and its ruins can still be seen there. The robber knights of the castle inflicted great harm on the inhabitants of the surrounding territory. Yet, because of the strength of the castle walls and the steepness of the mountain, no one could attack the robbers. Finally, the farmers from the village of Wehre devised a plan. Secretly arming themselves with all kinds of weapons, they went to the castle and announced to the courtiers that they wanted to perform a sword dance in their honor. This ruse got them inside the gates, where they drew their weapons and fought so valiantly that the courtiers surrendered and begged for mercy. The farmers turned them, as well as their castle, over to the reigning prince.

*The town of Steinau on the Haun River, about one hour from Fulda, is probably meant.

## THE STONE TABLE OF BINGENHEIM

In the town of Bingenheim, in the Wetterau region of Hesse, the Hundred Court used to be held three times a year under the linden tree in front of the City Hall. It was attended by all the noble families from the Mark of Fulda. A stone table stood under the linden tree, and according to legend, it came from Hohenberg, a forest located on the plateau near Stade. The forest used to be inhabited by Wild People, and one can still see the handholds they dug into the side of the cliffs as well as three stone benches they carved there. In the summer of 1604 three figures in white were seen roaming about that area.

## THE TALL MAN OF MURDERER'S ALLEY IN HOF

In 1519, just before the plague killed many people in the city of Hof, a very tall thin man dressed all in black was seen in Murderer's Alley. With his legs spread, he stood with one foot on each side of the alley, while his head rose far above the housetops.

My own* great-grandmother, Wallburg Widmann, saw him herself as she passed through that alley one night. He had one foot planted in front of the carriage entrance to the inn and the other foot right in front of the house on the other side of the street. She was so frightened she didn't know whether to go on or turn back. Finally, calling on God to protect her, and making the sign of the cross, she walked down the alley, right through his legs. She was convinced that, had she done otherwise, the spirit would have followed her. She had scarcely passed through when the giant figure slammed his legs together so hard that all the houses in Murderer's Alley shook as though they were about to collapse.

Soon after, the great plague hit the city, and the first fatalities were registered in Murderer's Alley.

## WAR AND PEACE

On the eighteenth of August in 1644, as the army of the elector Johann Georg I marched passed the city of Chemnitz, they captured a Wild Woman in the forest. She was only about two feet tall but otherwise human. Her face, hands, and feet were smooth, but the

*The speaker is Widmann writing in the *Chronicle of Hof.—D. W.*

rest of her body was covered with hair. She began to speak, saying, "I proclaim to you that I am bringing peace to this country." The elector gave the order to set her free because just twenty-five years before, a male creature of the same kind had been captured, and he foretold the coming of a long war.

‡‡  170  ‡‡

## RODENSTEIN ON THE MOVE

Not far from the village of Oberkrainsbach, which belonged to the residence of the counts of Erbach at Reichenberg near the Oden Forest, there stands a mountain on which the remains of the old castle of Schnellert can still be seen. Across from this mountain, about an hour away, there once resided the lords of Rodenstein, whose line has since died out, but the ruins of their robbers' castle still stand there. The last resident of this castle was especially renowned for his impressive power, for the vast number of his servants, and for his ill-gotten wealth. The following legend is still told about him.

Whenever a war was about to be declared, the lord would depart—to a trumpet fanfare—from Schnellert Castle at the onset of night with his retinue of servants. He and his party would travel through the brush, over hedges, and through the farmyards and barns of Simon Daum's farm in Oberkrainsbach, and continue until they came to Rodenstein. He seemed to be retreating as if he wanted to bring his family to safety before the battles started. Witnesses are reported to have heard the rumblings of the wagons, the cries of "Hoho!" driving the horses on, and even the precise commands of the leader of an advancing army.

If there were signs of peace, the lord would then repeat the march from Rodenstein back to Schnellert, but always in silence. One could then be certain that peace was about to be concluded.

Before Napoleon appeared, in the spring of 1815, the legend was circulating that the lord of Rodenstein had returned to his fortress of war.*

*Many witnesses were interrogated in the Reichenberg offices in Reichelsheim in Erbach county. The reports begin with those dated in 1742 and end with 1764. There was an evacuation in July of 1792. In 1816 similar reports and rumors began to multiply. Instead of Lord Rodenstein, a few reports mention the name of Lindenschmied. This name is also mentioned in the familiar folksong which begins:

> It happened not long ago
> That Lindenschmied was seen riding
> High upon his horse
> Riding up and down the Rhine
> Enjoying it all so.

Still others report that the lord of Schnellert moved from his fortress toward Rodenstein, in order to engage his sworn mortal enemy, the lord of Rodenstein, in

# TANNHÄUSER

Noble Tannhäuser, a German knight, traveled through many lands. He even visited the lovely women in Lady Venus' Mountain to see what great wonders transpired there. But after he had tarried there for a time in joy and contentment, his conscience finally urged him back out into the world, and he thus asked for leave.

Lady Venus, desiring him to stay, offered him everything she could think of to weaken his resolve. She offered him one of her ladies as a wife, tempting him with her smiling red mouth. Tannhäuser replied that he desired no other woman than the one he had already chosen in his thoughts; that he did not wish to burn in Hell for eternity; that red lips meant nothing to him; and that he could stay no longer, for if he remained his spirit would sicken. Then the diabolic temptress used all her seductive powers to lure him into her chamber where they could engage in passion, but the noble knight cursed her in a loud voice and called upon the Heavenly Virgin to help him escape.

Filled with remorse, he traveled on foot to Rome. And there he sought to confess his sins to Pope Urban and do penance for the salvation of his soul. Yet, when he confessed to the pope that he had spent an entire year with Lady Venus in the mountain, the pope said to him, "Your sins will be forgiven only when this dried-up twig in my hand begins to grow green leaves and not before."

Tannhäuser replied, "If I had but one year remaining to me on earth, I would spend it in repentance, doing penance in the hope of attaining God's mercy." Then, filled with misery and pain because the pope had condemned him, he left the Holy City and returned to the diabolic mountain, resolved to spend all eternity there. Lady Venus bade him welcome as she would a returning lover.

On the third day after his departure from Rome, however, the dried-up twig began to sprout green leaves, and the pope sent messengers to all lands to learn where noble Tannhäuser had gone. But it was too late, for he was once again inside the mountain where he had taken a lover. And there he will stay until Judgment Day, when perhaps God will direct him elsewhere.

---

battle, even when the latter was a ghost. A depiction of the ruins of Rodenstein, painted by Theodor von Haupt in 1816, is called "Gleaning the Grain in Times Gone By."

A priest should never discourage a sinner. Forgiveness should be granted when a person offers himself for penance.


‡‡  172  ‡‡

## HACKELBERG, THE WILD HUNTSMAN

Many years ago in the lands of Brunswick there lived a master huntsman by the name of Hackelberg. He was said to have been so devoted to the hunt that when he lay on his deathbed he couldn't bear to take eternal leave from it. He begged God to allow him to exchange his place in Heaven for permission to engage in the chase in Solling Forest until Judgment Day (no doubt because he had led a God-fearing, Christian life). He also asked that he be buried in the wilderness of Solling, and the request was granted.

His irreverent, even diabolic wish was evidently also granted, for four times every night the terrifying echo of the hunting horn signaling the chase and the baying of hounds can be heard in the wilderness. One time the sounds will ring out from here, another time from there. All this was reported to me by those who have heard these threatening sounds themselves. It is also said that if someone hears these sounds during the night and still goes hunting the following day, he will invariably suffer a broken arm or leg, even a broken neck or some other terrible misfortune.

I myself,* I believe in 1558, was riding through Solling on the way from Einbeck to Ußlar when I became lost and chanced upon Hackelberg's grave. It was located in a clearing something like a meadow, but it was covered with a wild growth and with reeds. It measured about an acre and was somewhat longer than it was wide. Though the area was surrounded by trees, none grew on this clearing. One end extended toward sunrise, and at the other end there was a raised, flat red stone about eight or nine feet long, and about— as it seemed to me—five feet wide. The stone did not face toward the east as gravestones usually do, but instead one end pointed south and the other north.

I was told that no one would ever be able to find this grave— whether from inquisitiveness or from a sense of purpose—no matter how determined and adventurous he might be. But if someone should chance upon the site, he would find a pack of frightful black dogs next to it. I, however, saw no such spooky apparition, and if I had, the few hairs I have on my head would surely have stood on end.

*The narrator is Hans Kirchhof in *Wendunmuth.*—D. W.

## THE WILD HUNTSMAN AND THE TAILOR

A tailor was once sitting at his work bench next to a window when the Wild Huntsman and all his dogs came flying over the house making such a great racket and barking that it sounded as though the world were coming to an end. It is said that tailors are cowardly. But this one was not, for he mocked the Wild Huntsman, crying out, "Hoho! Hoho! Kliffklaff, kliffklaff!" And he baited the dogs even more. Then a horse's hoof came flying through the window, striking the tailor and knocking him to the floor as though dead. When he regained consciousness, he heard a frightful voice ring out:

> If thou wouldst hunt with me,
> Then thou wilt suffer with me!

I am certain that the tailor never again mocked the Wild Huntsman.

## HÖSEL MOUNTAIN*

Not far from the city of Eisenach in Thuringia lies Hösel Mountain. The Devil lives inside the mountain, and all the witches of the area make pilgrimages there. Occasionally, the pitiful shrieks and moanings of the Devil and the Poor Souls can be heard emerging from the mountain.

In 1398, in the light of day, three large fires erupted near Eisenach. Each of them rose into the air, joined one another, became separated again, and then all three, one after the other, flew into this mountain.

On another occasion some carters were delivering wine, and as they drove their wagons past the mountain, the Evil One produced a vision that lured the men inside the mountain. The Devil then showed them a group of well-known citizens who were already sitting in the infernal flames.

A legend reports that the King of England took a wife who was called Reinschweig [Silentpure]. He had found her among lowly

*One finds mountains with names of the same meaning: Hörsel, Hursel, Hösel, and Osel Mountain. A derivation from *Ursel, Usel (favilla)* ashes is apparent. Also known is Hiesel Mountain. There is a small river called the Hörsel, which flows into the Werra River, and is called the Leine at its source.

people and had elevated her to queen because of her great virtue. When the king, whom she loved beyond all measure, died, she could not forget her love and loyalty, and she gave alms and prayed for the deliverance of his soul.

It was said that the king had found his purgatory in the flames of Hösel Mountain. Thus, the pious queen moved to Germany and had a chapel built at the foot of the mountain where she prayed every day. A village grew up around the chapel. But evil spirits appeared to her there, and she called the place Satan's City, which later became Saddle City [Sattelstadt].

‡‡　175　‡‡

## LORD RECHENBERG'S SERVANT

In the year 1520, Lord Hans von Rechenberg told Sebastian Schlich and other respected and honest citizens about a servant who had served his father and himself with great loyalty for many years during the time King Matthew warred with the Turks in Hungary. He said that they had never known a better, more loyal servant.

On one occasion the servant was entrusted with a message to deliver to a powerful lord. Thinking the servant long underway, Lord von Rechenberg went to the stables where he found the man sleeping on the straw among the horses. The lord became angry and asked what was going on. The servant jumped up, drew a letter from his jacket, and said, "This is the answer." Now, the way there and back was very long. It was impossible for a man to have gotten there and back in that time. It now became apparent that the servant was a spirit.

A short time later, when the lord and his men were besieged by the enemy, the servant said, "Do not fear, My Lord. Retreat quickly while I go back and scout the enemy." When the servant finally returned his heavily laden bags made loud clinking and clanking noises.

"What do you have there?" asked the lord.

"I removed all the iron from the horses' hooves and I bring it to you," replied the servant. He then shook out his bags and horseshoes fell onto the ground. The enemy was thus unable to follow in pursuit.

Lord Hans von Rechenberg also said that the servant disappeared once his true identity became known, and no one knew where he had gone.

Kirchhof tells of another nobleman who had to improvise to make ends meet and adds the following incidents to the story.

Once, when the nobleman had to be absent for a time, he called the servant to him and instructed him to take special care of his favorite horse. In his lord's absence, the servant took the horse up to a tall tower, over ten stories high. When the nobleman returned, the horse recognized him as he entered and it stuck its head out the tower window and began to whinny. The nobleman was greatly amazed by this, and the horse had to be lowered from the tower with ropes and pullies.

On another occasion, the nobleman was being held prisoner because he had slain another man in a fight, and he sent for his servant and implored him to help. The servant said, "Although it will be difficult, I will do it. But you must promise not to wave about with your hands and make protective gestures in front of me." (He meant that the nobleman should not make the sign of the cross and bless himself in the servant's presence.) The nobleman replied that the servant should proceed, he would keep the promise.

What happened?

He picked him up—chains, fetters, and all—carried him up into the air, and flew away. But when the nobleman grew dizzy and fearful of the great height, and he cried out, "God help me, where am I?", the servant dropped him into a cesspool. Then he proceeded to the nobleman's wife, showed her where he was, and instructed her to have him hauled out and to heal his wounds, which she did.


‡‡  176  ‡‡

## THE GHOST CHURCH

Around the year 1516 a wondrous, yet true story occurred in the cemetery of the Church of St. Lorenz.

A devout old woman departed early in the morning before daybreak, as was her custom, to attend the Angel's Mass in St. Lorenz; however, it was around midnight when she came to the upper gate of the city. Finding it open, she went out through it and from there into the church. Inside, she found an old priest, whom she did not recognize, conducting the mass before the altar. Many people were scattered throughout the pews, most of them unknown to her, and some of them were headless. Others among them had died a short time before, and she had known them well when they had been alive.

The woman, in great fear and terror, took a seat in one of the pews, and since she saw only deceased people around her, both known and unknown, she concluded that they were the souls of the dead. Since she had arrived much too early, she could not decide whether to remain in the church or flee, and her hair stood on end. One woman, whom she recognized as a neighbor who had died only a few weeks before, rose from the ghostly group and approached her. The deceased woman, who was clearly one of God's good angels, took hold of her coat, bade her a good morning, and said, "Ay, dear neighbor, may the almighty God protect thee! What art thou doing here? I bid thee, for the sake of God and thy beloved mother, take care to do precisely as I say. Just as the priest is about to bless and transform the wine, get up and run as fast as thou canst. Do not turn around or it will cost thee thy life."

When the priest began the blessing, the old woman got up and ran from the church as fast as she could. But no sooner was she outside than she heard a tremendous crash, as though the church had collapsed. All the ghosts from the church were pursuing her, and when she got to the cemetery they caught up with her and began tearing the cloak from around her neck. But she left it behind and thus managed to escape unharmed.

When she reached the upper gate to re-enter the city, she found it locked, for it was now one hour past midnight. She thus had to spend three hours in a little hut until the gate was opened. It was then that she realized that it was no good spirit who had let her pass through the gate the first time. And she now understood that the swine she had seen and heard outside the gate earlier, which had led her to believe that it was the time when animals were driven out to pasture, had been none other than the accursed Devil himself. But since she was a courageous woman, and since she had escaped the great danger, she did not pursue the event. She returned home and, though not physically harmed by the terrible experience, she did have to take to bed for two days because of her terrible fright.

The following day, however, after it became light, she sent someone to the cemetery to see if they could find her cloak. It was discovered torn into tiny shreds, with at least one shred lying on each of the graves. On hearing the story, the citizens proceeded to the cemetery in great numbers, and they marveled at the appearance of the shredded cloak.

This story was very well known to our parents, since the story was told not only here in the city but in the country and in neighboring villages and remote areas as well.

According to oral narratives, these events occurred the night before All Souls' Day, when the church solemnly celebrates the memory of departed souls. When the mass was over, all the people vacated the church quite suddenly, and as full of people as it had been, it now became quite deserted and dark. Full of fear, the woman sought her way in the dark to the church door. As she left, the church bell struck one A.M. and the door slammed shut behind her with such force that her black raincoat was caught in it. She left it behind and hastened away. When she returned for it the next morning, it had been torn apart and a piece of it lay on each grave.

‡‡ 177 ‡‡

## THE BANQUET OF GHOSTS

After King Frederick III proclaimed a public assembly in Flensburg, a nobleman from afar arrived late at night and was unable to secure lodgings at the local inn. The innkeeper informed him that all the rooms were occupied. He did have one large room still empty, but he would not advise him to spend the night there, for the room was haunted by spirits. The nobleman only smiled and said he was not afraid of spooks, just give him a light so that he could see anything that showed itself. The innkeeper brought him the light, and the nobleman set it down on the table, intending to remain awake just long enough to make sure no spirits were visible.

The night was not yet half over when things began to move and shift here and there around the room, and he heard one rustling noise after another. At first, the nobleman mustered his courage and remained steadfast in the face of these frightful horrors. But before long, as the racket grew in intensity, fear mastered him, and no matter how hard he resisted, he began to tremble.

After this prelude of rumbling and rattling, a man's leg plunged down the chimney into the fireplace. Then came an arm, the torso, the breast, and all the remaining limbs. Finally, when nothing else was lacking, the head came tumbling down. The separate parts joined themselves together, and a court servant stepped forth. Then, more and more limbs clattered down the chimney, and they too joined themselves into human shape, until finally the door of the room opened and the whole retinue of a royal state court entered.

The nobleman, who had been standing paralyzed at the table, fled into a corner of the room as he saw the retinue walking in his direction. He was unable to escape through the door because the entire crowd blocked his path. He watched as the ghostly figures set the table with incredible dexterity. They then brought forth delicious dishes and set out beakers of gold and silver.

After they completed this task, one of them walked over to the nobleman and invited him, as a stranger and guest, to join them at table and accept their hospitality. When he declined, they offered him a giant silver chalice and bade him partake of it. The nobleman was so distressed that he didn't know what to do. Finally, he accepted the chalice, for it appeared they were going to insist that he drink with them. But as he set the beaker to his lips, a feeling of dread penetrated so deep into his bones and marrow that he cried out to God for protection and deliverance.

Scarcely had he finished uttering his prayers aloud than, in the bat of an eyelash, all the splendor, pomp, and noise, along with the sparkling table and all the splendidly attired proud spirits, disappeared.

After all had passed, the nobleman noticed that the silver chalice was still in his hand, and even though all the splendid dishes had disappeared, the silver utensils remained on the table as well as the lamp the innkeeper had given him. The nobleman was overjoyed, for he believed that he could rightfully take possession of this windfall. But the innkeeper objected so loud and long that word of the strange event reached the ears of the king, who declared that all the silver belonged to him and ordered it delivered to his palace. The origin of the treasure remains unknown, since neither the customary name nor the crest was engraved on the items.

## ‡‡ 178 ‡‡
### THE ROOFER

A young roofer was scheduled to complete his masterpiece and to make his acceptance speech from the pinnacle of the newly completed tower. In the middle of his speech, however, he began to falter. Suddenly, he cried to his father, who was standing below in the crowd of people, "Father, the towns and hills and forests out there—they're moving in on me!" On hearing these words, the father fell to his knees and began to pray for the soul of his son, and he implored the others to do the same. The son then fell to his death.

According to the rules of the roofer's trade when the son climbs up before the father and then begins to blabber incoherently, the father has the right to grab the son and hurl him to earth so that he himself will not be pulled down by the son when he falls.

## ‡‡ 179 ‡‡
### THE SPINNING WOMAN AT THE CROSS

Just outside the city of Vienna, where one leaves the suburb on the main highway, there stands a beautifully worked stone statue of a saint, undoubtedly over two hundred years old. Legend has it that a poor woman wanted to have this holy image erected for the honor of

God, and that she spun and spun until she had saved enough money from her efforts to commission the statue.*

Beside the road that leads from the town of Calw to Zabelstein there stands a stone crucifix upon which is engraved a spinning distaff and the date 1447. A seventy-year-old man reports that he once heard from a one-hundred-year-old that a poor old spinning woman suffocated at that spot in a snowdrift.

## ‡‡ 180 ‡‡
### BUTTERMILK TOWER

The following story is told about Buttermilk Tower in the town of Marienburg in Prussia.

The Grand Master of the Teutonic Order of the region once demanded some buttermilk from the farmers of a neighboring village. But the farmers mocked and ridiculed the messenger who brought the demand, and the following day they sent two men to the palace with a whole keg of buttermilk. Enraged, the Grand Master had the two farmhands locked up until they had consumed the entire quantity of buttermilk from the keg. The castle tower has borne this name ever since.

Others, however, report the following. The inhabitants of a neighboring village had to pave a road leading to the construction site of the tower with coins of Our Lady. They were also required to procure a sufficient quantity of buttermilk instead of water to mix with the quicklime to make the mortar used in constructing the masonry of the tower.

According to Fürst, however, the peasants of Great Lichtenau were so blasphemous that they put a sow to bed and called the village priest to administer extreme unction to the supposedly mortally ill patient. As punishment for their thoughtless frivolity, they were ordered to erect the tower at their own expense and to prepare the mortar for the construction by mixing quicklime with buttermilk.

## ‡‡ 181 ‡‡
### SAINT WINFRIED

When St. Winfried, who was called Boniface, wanted to convert the Hessians, he came to a mountain on which stood a heathen temple. He ordered it torn down and had the first Christian church built on

*This is a story of how a poor spinning woman with a halfpenny completed a king's cathedral. Colocz XXXVI.

the site. The mountain, which lies four hours from Marburg, has been called Christian Mountain ever since. Two hundred steps from the church, the local people point out a footprint embedded in the stone where Boniface is said to have stamped his foot into the rock and said, "As certain as I am that my foot will penetrate this stone, thus certain will be the conversion of the heathens." The heathen name for the mountain had been Castor Mountain. Boniface wanted to retain the C of this name by renaming it Christian Mountain.

The people of the region still tell of the Boniface Path on which he arrived and departed through the woods. The fields adjacent to this path are still free from tithe, while all others must bear this burden. Any blasphemies committed on the Path or the adjacent fields must be severely atoned for. Farmers of the neighboring villages are still buried in the cemetery that surrounds the chapel on Christian Mountain, but the caskets are borne up the mountainside only through great effort.

When Boniface came to Thuringia, it is said that he had a church built at Großvargula, which he dedicated himself. He is reported to have stuck his bare staff into the ground and entered the church to read the mass. After the holy services were over, the staff was found to have produced green sprouts.

## ‡‡  182  ‡‡

## HELP MOUNTAIN

One hour from Wanfried, on the border of the Eichsfeld region, lies Mt. Hülfen, or Help Mountain, where St. Boniface ordered a chapel built. While construction was underway, a man came by frequently and asked what it was going to be. One of the carpenters invariably answered, "Oh, it's going to be a barn." Then the man would continue on his way. Finally, however, the church neared completion—the altar was built, and the cross was successfully set. When the Evil One returned and saw this, he became enraged and took off into the air right through one of the gables. The hole he left can still be seen today, and try as one might, it cannot be patched. He also went underground inside the mountain and attempted to destroy the church from below, but all in vain.

It is also said that an oak tree, sacred to the heathen deity, was bricked into the wall. The hole in which the oak was encased is called Stuffen's Hole, and the mountain is called Mt. Stuffen. At times, clouds of mist and fog are said to emerge from that hole.

It is also said that this chapel was dedicated to a woman

saint, and that, if a sick person touches her cloak, he will be cured immediately.

It is further said that this saint had once been a beautiful princess with whom her own father had fallen in love. In her distress, she prayed to God in Heaven for assistance, and she immediately grew a beard. Thus, she never again had to be concerned with the problems of earthly beauty.

## ‡‡ 183 ‡‡

## THE DEVIL'S HOLE IN GOSLAR

There is a crack in the wall of the church in the city of Goslar, and the following story is told about it.

The Bishop of Hildesheim and the Abbot of Fulda were once engaged in a bitter struggle over who had the right to occupy the pew next to the emperor. When the bishop declared this place of honor for himself for the services on the first day of Christmas, the abbot ordered some of his men, who were secretly armed, to enter the church in the morning and secure the honored place with force. The bishop, however, got word of the plot, and he also ordered armed troops into the church.

On the following day the argument broke out, first in words, and then with violence as the armed knights of both parties stepped forth and engaged in combat. The church soon resembled a battlefield, and blood flowed in streams from the church, down the steps, and into the graveyard.

During this bloody battle, which continued for three days, the Devil came crashing through the wall and confronted both groups of knights. His appearance enraged the men even more, and the Evil One was able to gather up many a soul from the fallen heroes. The Devil remained there as long as the battle lasted. But when it finally ended, he vanished, for there was no longer any reason for his presence.

Later, attempts were made to repair the hole the Devil had made in the wall when he entered the church. The workers were successful until they got to the last stone. But then, every time they tried to set it, all the stones fell out and the hole gaped anew. They tried time and again, and priests chanted over it and sprinkled holy water on it, but each time the stones collapsed.

Finally, they asked the Duke of Brunswick to send his master builders. The masters came, took a black cat, and enclosed it in the wall. As they set the last stone, they uttered these words, "If thou wouldst not stay in the name of God, then stay in the name of the

Devil!" It worked, and the Devil left the wall in peace. The following night, however, a crack opened in the wall, and it can still be seen today.

According to August Lercheimer's *Bedenken von der Zauberei*, an argument developed between the bishop and the abbot over sorcery and over who had the right to occupy the place of honor next to the Archbishop of Mainz. After the argument had been settled, the lines *Hunc diem gloriosum fecisti* [Thou hast made this day glorious] were sung during the mass. At this time, the Devil appeared beneath the vaulted ceiling, singing in a loud, coarse voice, *"Hunc diem bellicosum ego feci"* [I have made this day for war].

‡‡ 184 ‡‡

## THE DEVIL'S MILL

On the top of Ramm Mountain near Haberfeld there are large granite blocks that have crumbled and weathered with the years. These are called Devil's Mill.

A miller once built a windmill on the side of the mountain, but there were occasions when there was no wind to turn it. He often wished he had a mill on the peak of the mountain that would operate constantly, but because of the location such a mill could not be built by human hands.

Still, the miller could not get the thought out of his mind. And so, one day, the Devil appeared to him, and they negotiated with each other for many hours. Finally, the miller signed over his soul to the Devil in exchange for thirty years of life and a mill with six gears on the peak of Ramm Mountain, which would always have enough wind to drive it and would never break down. However, the miller insisted that it had to be constructed and in operation by the time the cock crowed the following morning. The terms were quite agreeable to the Evil One, and he immediately began to construct the mill.

When the miller became aware of the great speed with which the Devil worked and saw that the mill would indeed be finished before the agreed-upon deadline, he stole to the mountaintop, lifted the giant millstone the Devil had already made, stood it on end, and sent it rolling down the side of the mountain. When the Devil saw the stone rolling down the mountain, he wanted to stop it and took out after it. But the millstone picked up speed. It began bouncing along in greater and greater leaps, and the Evil One could not catch up to it until it came to rest at the bottom of the mountain. He then set about rolling the heavy stone back up the mountain as fast as he could. He was almost to the top when the cock crowed and the contract became invalid.

In a rage, the Evil One seized the structure and tore out the windmill's blades, gears, wheels, and drive shafts. And then he cast them in all directions down the mountainside to prevent the miller, who thought he had acquired a nearly finished mill for nothing, from rebuilding it. He then smashed the great cliffs on the peak so the pieces covered the entire mountain, leaving only a small part of the original foundation as a memorial to the mill he constructed. It is said that the millstone can still be seen at the foot of the mountain.

‡‡ 185 ‡‡

## THE LORD'S JOURNEY

The ruins of Rosenstein Fortress lie on the top of a cliff overlooking a beautiful valley near Heuberg in the German Jura Mountains. Not too many years ago, one could still see the imprint of a human foot in the rock of the cliffs, but the government had that portion of the cliff blasted away with gunpowder because it inspired much superstition.

On the other side of the valley, on the cliffs of Mt. Scheul,* a similar footprint could be seen pointing away from the valley, whereas the print at Rosenstein pointed toward the valley. Not far away, in a small forest, there lies the chapel of the miracle worker, Mary of Beisswang.† To the left of the chapel there is a ravine, called the Devil's Marsh, where muddied waters flow after a steady rain. Behind the castle there is a hollowed-out cliff called Scheuer Cliff.

In ancient times, the Tempter of Christ showed this beautiful region—the Rems Valley, the Leine River, Rech Mountain, Ellwangen, and all—to Prince von Staufen from the top of Mt. Scheul and offered it all to him if the prince would only kneel before him. No sooner had the Devil made the offer than Christ appeared and ordered him to depart. Satan plunged down the side of the cliff and was condemned to spend a thousand years in chains and fetters at the bottom of Devil's Marsh. The muddied waters that still flow from this ravine are the tears of the Devil. Christ then took a giant

*According to Seyfried, Schawel Mountain, and it was the left foot of the former, and the right foot of the latter.
†Founded by Frederick-with-the-Bitten-Cheek *(Bißwang).*

step across the valley, and where he set his feet down the prints became embedded.*

Many years later, the knights von Rosenstein built a fortress there from which they operated as robber barons, and they used to conceal their booty on Mt. Scheul. Once, the Devil inspired them to raid and pillage the forest chapel. But no sooner had they returned to their castle with the booty from the church than a terrible storm erupted and reduced the robbers' castle to rubble. And all the while one could hear the Devil laughing loudly.

## ‡‡ 186 ‡‡
## THE BRIDGE TO SACHSENHAUSEN

In the middle of the bridge over the Main River from Frankfurt to Sachsenhausen there are two arches. The tops of these arches are constructed of wood so that they can be dismantled in time of war, thus preventing passage across the river without blowing up the bridge. The following legend is told about this bridge.

The master builder made a contract to finish the bridge by a certain time. But as the deadline grew near, he realized that it would be impossible to finish it in the remaining two days. In his distress he called out to the Devil and asked for his support. The Devil appeared and offered to complete the construction of the bridge in one night if the master builder would deliver to him the first living creature that crossed the bridge. The pact was agreed upon. And on the last night, when it was so dark that no one could see what progress was being made, the Devil set to work on the bridge and completed it.

When the morning dawned, the master builder showed up with a rooster, which he proceeded to drive across the bridge before him. This he delivered to the Devil. When the Devil saw the rooster, he knew he had been tricked out of a human soul. He became so enraged that he grabbed the rooster and threw it with great force against the bridge foundation, ripping two large holes in the masonry.

These holes can still be seen today, and every effort to seal them with masonry is in vain, for the stones set into the holes during the day always fall out again at night. A rooster of gold mounted on an

*Zeiler gives a varied account. Christ in fleeing from the Jews left his footprints there. People used to go there to find eye-healing waters. His source is *Crusii Liber paral.*, p. 48.

iron pole was made to commemorate the incident, and it can still be
seen on the bridge.

## THE WOLF AND THE PINE CONE

A crack runs across one of the great brass doors of the cathedral in
Aachen, and next to the door stand the statues of a wolf and a pine
cone, both cast in fine metal. The following legend is told about
these figures.

Many decades ago when the cathedral was being built, construction had to be halted before the church was finished because
the city ran out of money. The desolate construction site stood there
for some time until the Devil reportedly appeared before the city
fathers and offered them the money they needed. But he added a
condition—he would take possession of the first soul to enter the
church during the dedication ceremonies. The council deliberated
and hesitated for a long time. But they finally decided to accept the
offer, and they all agreed to keep the terms of the agreement a
secret. The acquisition of the infernal money enabled them to complete the cathedral.

In the meantime, however, rumors of the terms of the agreement spread around the city, and no one wanted to be first to enter
the cathedral. Finally, someone thought of a trick. Some men went
out in the forest, trapped a wolf, and brought it back to the main
entrance of the church.

On the day of the dedication when the bells began to peal, the
wolf was set loose and chased into the church. The Devil then
swooped down like a tornado, roared through the church doors, and
seized what belonged to him by the terms of the agreement. But as
soon as he realized he'd been tricked, that only the soul of a wolf
had been delivered to him, he flew into a rage and slammed the
brass door shut with such force that a crack developed in it that
remains to this day.

In commemoration of this event, statues of the wolf and his soul,
which resembles a pine cone, were cast. When the French occupied
the region they had both antique statues shipped to Paris. But in 1815
they were returned to the city and mounted on pedestals on both
sides of the door. The wolf, however, lost two of his paws.

Others say that a sinful woman was offered to the Devil for the
sake of the whole city. They believe the figure to be an artichoke,
which is supposed to symbolize the poor soul of the woman.

## THE DEVIL OF ACH

In Aachen there is a large tower in the city wall called Ponelle Tower. The Devil has been seen and heard there many times, emitting weird screams, ringing bells, and engaging in all kinds of foolery. According to local legend, he was condemned to the tower till Judgment Day.

When the people of this region want to indicate that something is impossible, they say, "That will happen when the Devil comes from Ach!"—meaning never.

## DEVIL'S WALL

The peasants of Obernfeld and Otmannsfeld tell the following legend about the palisades at Nordgau, which lie between Ellingen and Pleinfeld, about an hour and a half from Weißenburg. The Devil wanted some land of his own and he requested some from the Lord God, who agreed on the following terms. The Devil would fall heir to as much land as he was able to enclose in walls before the cock crowed. The Evil One immediately went to work setting stones. But just as he was about to set the final stone and complete the wall, the cock crowed. Furious that his hopes had been dashed, he tore into his own structure with rage and scattered the stones in all directions. The ruins of Devil's Wall are still said to be haunted by spirits.

## THE DEVIL'S DANCE FLOOR

There is a rocky plateau south of the village of Thale, between Blankenburg and Quedlinburg, on the north side of the Harz Mountains. The local people call this plateau the Devil's Dance Floor. Not far away lie the ruins of a stone wall that runs from an outcrop of rocks on the north side of the village. These ruins, and the rocks as well, are called Devil's Wall.

The Devil had long been engaged in a struggle with God over who had the right to rule the earth. Finally, they agreed upon a division of the inhabited parts of the world. The cliff on which the Dance Floor is now found was to mark the border, and the Devil, dancing in jubilation, constructed a wall. Soon, however, the insatiable demon began the quarrel again. As a result, God also gave him the valley at the foot of that cliff. And the Devil then constructed a second wall.

## ‡‡ 191 ‡‡
## THE DEVIL'S PULPIT

In the Murg Valley, not far from Baden, there stands a row of steep cliffs that the people of the area call the Devil's Pulpit. They believe the Devil once delivered sermons from the top.

## ‡‡ 192 ‡‡
## DEVIL'S PILLOW

There are some strange smooth cliff formations beneath the castle of Bentheim. One of these is flat on top and looks like a round upholstered cushion standing on end. It is called Devil's Pillow because the Devil reportedly slept on it once. The outline of his ear is still stamped in the rock, and it can be seen there today.

## ‡‡ 193 ‡‡
## DEVIL'S BLUFF

The inhabitants of the Fichtel Mountains tell this story of how the Devil led our Christ to the Kößein Cliffs to show him the riches of the world. He also promised that if Christ would only worship him, he would give away everything—except for the towns of N. and R., which were to provide his annuity. The inhabitants of these towns are coarse and misshapen. In fact, the whole area has a hostile character, and it is called Turkey or Tartarland by some people.

## ‡‡ 194 ‡‡
## DEVIL'S WALL

This Devil's Wall runs along the Danube River downstream from Melk in the direction of Vienna. The Devil once tried to channel the whole Danube River by building masoned walls along its shores, but the stones slipped away every time he tried to mortar them together.

## ‡‡ 195 ‡‡
## DEVIL'S LATTICE

In St. Mary's Church in the town of Wismar there is an exceptionally elaborate iron lattice around the baptismal font. A smith was commissioned to forge it, but he could not get the parts to join as he wished. Finally, he cried out in anger, "I wish the Devil would complete this work!" No sooner had he said this than the Devil came and joined the lattice work. It is said that no one will ever be able to copy it or even find the seams—even though it is not attractive.

## ‡‡ 196 ‡‡
## DEVIL'S MILL

In the region around the city of Wolfenbüttel, between Pestorf and Grave, there is a mill on the Weser River. Local folk legend reports that it was built by the Devil, and that it is driven by water running off the cliffs. There is also a Devil's Mill in the Rhön Mountains.

## ‡‡ 197 ‡‡
## DEVIL'S CHURCH

High in the Rhön Mountains, black basalt cliffs tower above the valley below. When the Devil discovered that the inhabitants of the valley planned to build a church there, he grew angry and made off with all the construction stones. He took them up the cliffs and piled them on top. No one has ever been able to get the stones down again.

People say that once the Devil sets a stone down somewhere, no one can move it again. And even if someone does manage to cart it away, the Devil will come and put it right back in place.

## ‡‡ 198 ‡‡
## DEVIL'S ROCK AT REICHENBACH

In a forest near Reichenbach, in the county of Lichtenau, a large boulder called Devil's Rock stands facing a cliff. This rock and the area around it look as though they were created by the delivery of several hundred carts' worth of stones, artistically arranged to form wondrous halls, chambers, and cellars. The inhabitants of the region might well have moved here with their entire households during times of prolonged war. According to local legend, the Devil formed these marvelous stone structures in a single night.

## ‡‡ 199 ‡‡
## DEVIL'S ROCK IN COLOGNE

Near the church in Cologne one can see a large stone. It is called Devil's Rock because imprints of the claws of the Evil One became embedded in it when he threw it at the Chapel of the Three Holy Kings. The Devil was trying to destroy it,* but the attempt failed.

## ‡‡ 200 ‡‡
## SÜNTEL ROCK IN OSNABRÜCK

Near the city of Osnabrück an ancient rock protrudes thirteen feet out of the earth. The farmers call it Süntel Rock† and say that the Devil carried it through the air and dropped it here. They can also point to the place where the Devil attached a chain to haul it.

## ‡‡ 201 ‡‡
## LIAR'S ROCK

There is a round rock of considerable size located in the market place in front of the cathedral in the city of Halberstadt. The citizens call it Liar's Rock. When the Devil, the Father of Lies, saw the ground being excavated for the foundation of the cathedral, he thought that a palace was being constructed for his realm and he carried many large rocks to help with the construction. When the building began to take shape, however, and he realized it was going to be a Christian church, he resolved to destroy it. He came flying through the air on a giant boulder and was just about to let it drop into the structure to destroy the scaffolding and masonry when the citizens of the city dissuaded him by promising to build a wine tavern right next to the church. He

*According to Berkenmeyer—October 30, 1414, during a windstorm.
†Probably "Sacred Rock" from *sünt, sant, sanctus.* Cf. Süntel, Süntelberg in the Schaumburg region of Westphalia.

then steered the boulder away from the cathedral and let it fall to earth in front of the church. One can still see the indentations where his glowing thumbs burned into the rock.


## ‡‡ 202 ‡‡

## THE BRIDGE OVER THE CANYON

One evening a shepherd set out to visit his beloved. The path led him to a place where the Visper River flowed through a deep canyon and the only way across was a narrow planked suspension bridge. Before he started to cross, the young lover saw a pile of hot black coals lying in the middle of the bridge blocking his way, something he had never seen before. He knew that something was amiss, so he braced himself and gave a great leap over the deep abyss from one side to the other. The Devil, rising from the steam of the scattered coals, called out to him, "That move was well advised. Had you stepped back, I would have wrung your neck, and had you proceeded and stepped on the coals, you would have plunged to the bottom of the chasm."

Fortunately for the shepherd, he had not forgotten, in spite of his thoughts for his beloved, to pray an Ave when he came to the Chapel of the Mother of God, which lay along his route, behind St. Niklas.


## ‡‡ 203 ‡‡

## DEVIL'S BATH NEAR DASSEL

Not far from the city of Dassel there is a bottomless lake called Bedessic or Bessoic Lake. It is said that a beautiful pure-sounding bell lies in the lake, and that it was the Devil himself who stole it from the belfry of the church in Portenhagen and brought it there. The old people of the region tell wondrous things about the bell. It is supposed to be made of pure gold, and the Evil One took it away out of pure envy, especially since it was particularly sacred and powerful, so that people could no longer make use of it for divine services.

A diver once volunteered to descend into the lake and tie ropes around the bell so the people on the shore could pull it up to the surface and thus recover it. Alas, the diver had to return to the surface with his task incomplete. He reported that there was a green meadow in the depths of the lake in which there was a large table on which the bell rested. A black dog lay next to it and it would not permit the bell to be touched. An ugly, frightening Mer Woman was also there, and she said that it was still much too early to retrieve the bell from the site.

An eighty-year-old man also told a story about the Devil's Bath. There once was a farmer who kept plowing one Saturday much longer than was customary. He even continued after the evening Vespers had sounded, whipping and cursing both his horse and his boy.

Suddenly, a giant black plow horse emerged from the lake and climbed up the shore and into the field. The blasphemous, cursing farmer grabbed the horse and in the Devil's name harnessed him in front of the other horses, intending to continue until the entire field had been plowed. The boy began to cry and wanted to go home, but the farmer cursed him severely.

The huge black plow horse is then said to have pulled the poor exhausted horses, along with the plow, the farmer, and the boy, into the depths of the bottomless lake called the Devil's Bath—they were never again seen by human eyes. Whoever summons the Devil will have to provide work for him.

## ‡‡ 204 ‡‡

### THE TOWER OF SCHARTFELD

It is reported by the old people of Schartfeld that the tower in the town will not tolerate any roofing. The Devil himself lives in the tower, and rumblings and racket can be heard from there at night.

Many years ago Emperor Henry IV developed a highly improper passion for the wife of a gentleman from Schartfeld, but he was not able to fulfill his desire for her. Once, when he was lamenting his plight to a monk in the Pölde Monastery in the county of Lutterberg, the monk suggested what he might do.

The emperor thus ordered the gentleman of Schartfeld to come to him in the monastery and dispatched him to a distant place on an assignment. The knight was a subject of the emperor's and he obeyed the orders. The following day the emperor was joined in the hunt by the monk, who was wearing worldly attire, and as planned, they stole away to the knight's house in Schartfeld. There, the monk led the emperor to the woman's chambers, where Henry overpowered her and forced her to submit to him.

It was then that the Devil is said to have torn the roof off the tower and to have cast it down. As he departed, flying through the air, he is said to have screamed aloud that the monk was far more guilty of this outrage than the emperor. The monk spent the remainder of his life in the monastery in misery and sorrow.

## COLOGNE CATHEDRAL

Just as construction on the Cathedral of Cologne began, the citizens of the city also started work on an aqueduct. However, the master builder of the cathedral audaciously proclaimed, "There is not to be the slightest work on the water system until the cathedral is finished!" Now, he could say this because he alone knew where the water source could be found, and he told no one his secret except his wife, warning her not to reveal it to anyone if she held her life dear.

The work on the cathedral began and progressed rapidly, but the construction of the aqueduct never got started because that builder didn't know where to look for the source. When his wife perceived how greatly this situation was troubling him, she promised to help him and went to the wife of the master builder of the cathedral. By trickery, she was able to draw from her the secret that the spring was located directly beneath one of the towers of the cathedral. The master builder's wife even described the stone that covered the water source.

This knowledge proved to be invaluable to the builder of the aqueduct, for when he went to the site, he struck the stone with his hammer and water immediately gushed forth. When the master builder discovered that his secret had been betrayed, and that his public vow had been reduced to mockery because the aqueduct obviously could now be built in a short time, he screamed angrily at his structure, cursing it never to be finished. Shortly thereafter he died of a broken heart.

From then on when the workers tried to continue their work on the structure, they found that the stones they set during the day would invariably crumble away by morning—no matter how tightly they fit, or how securely they had been mortared. So it came to pass that not a single additional stone was added to the structure.

Others, however, tell a different version. The Devil was envious of the proud sacred structure that Master Gerhard, the master builder, had designed and begun. Not wanting to come away completely empty-handed, and hoping to prevent completion of the structure, the Devil made a wager with Master Gerhard. He bet the master builder that he could finish an aqueduct from Trier to Cologne before the builder could finish his cathedral. If he should lose, the master's soul would be forfeited to the Devil.

Herr Gerhard was by no means lazy, but the Devil was able to work with diabolic speed. One day Master Gerhard climbed up the tower, which was then as high as it is today. The first thing he saw were ducks cackling loudly as they took off from the water the Devil had brought via his aqueduct from Trier. The master builder then said with grim fury, "Thou hast, to be sure, won thy wager, Devil. But thou shalt not take me alive!" With these last words, he plunged headfirst from the tower. The Devil, taking the form of a dog, jumped right behind him.

To this day, both their figures can be seen embedded in the stone at the foot of the tower. If one places an ear to the ground, one is supposed to be able to hear water flowing under the cathedral.

There is also a third version of the legend. According to this one, the Devil was carrying on an affair with the wife of the master builder. It was presumably thus that he learned the master's secret of the water beneath the tower, as in the first version.

‡‡ 206 ‡‡

## DEVIL'S CAP

There is a giant boulder near Altenburg, in the region of Ehrenberg. It is so large and heavy that a hundred horses could not move it from this spot. Many years ago the Devil used to play games with this boulder. For example, he would place it on his head and run around wearing it as a hat.

Once, he boasted in vain arrogance, "Who else can wear this stone as I do? Even he who created it cannot lift it, for he leaves it here where it lies!" Christ the Lord then appeared, placed the stone on his little finger, and wore it as a ring. Shamed and humiliated, the Devil disappeared from the scene, and he has never been seen there since. The outline of the Devil's head and the mark left by the Lord's finger can still be seen in this boulder today.

‡‡ 207 ‡‡

## DEVIL'S FIRE

There was a little town in Switzerland called Schiltach. On April 10, in the year 1533, the whole town suddenly burned to the ground. It is said that the fire started at a time when the citizens of the town had been called before the authorities in Freiburg.

The master of a house in the town heard some strange sounds, as if someone were whispering in a soft voice, signaling to another to keep silent. At first, the master of the house thought a thief was hiding there, and he went upstairs to look but found no one. No sooner had he gone downstairs than he heard the same noises coming again from one of the rooms at the top of the house. He went back up, thinking he would surely catch the thief this time. Again, he found no one. But just as he was about to descend once more, he finally heard the voice coming from the chimney.

He then surmised that he had a devil haunting his house, and he reported this to his family, who were all quite fearful. He told them that they need not be afraid, for as long as they trusted in God, the Almighty would protect them. He then had two priests come and exorcise the demon. When they asked the spirit who he was, he replied, "The Devil." When they further asked what his mission here was, he replied, "I am going to destroy this town!" The priests then began to menace the demon, but the Devil laughed and said, "Your threatening words have no effect on me, for one of you is a dissolute scoundrel and both of you are thieves!"

A short time later he went to the woman one of the priests had been living with for fourteen years, bore her through the air, and set her down on top of the chimney of the house. He then gave her a kettle and told her to turn it over and pour its contents out. When she did as she was told, fire came roaring out. Within an hour the entire town had been consumed by flames.

‡‡  208  ‡‡

## DEVIL'S HORSESHOE

In the village of Schwarzenstein, which lies half a mile from Rastenburg in Prussia, there is a church where two large horseshoes are hanging on the wall. The following legend is told about them.

There was once a woman innkeeper who constantly cheated her customers when she drew beer. One night, the Devil came and rode her to the blacksmith's. He woke the smith, calling in a blustering voice, "Master, come and shoe my horse!"

It so happened that the smith was a godfather of the innkeeper, and as he was about to shoe her, she whispered to him, "Godfather, not so fast, not so fast!" The smith had only seen a horse, and he gave a terrible start, trembling with fear when he heard this voice that sounded so familiar to him. Because of his great fear his work was delayed, and before he could drive the first nail, the cock crowed. Although the Devil was forced to flee, the innkeeper fell ill and took to her bed for a long time.

If the Devil shoes all the innkeepers who are stingy drawing beer, iron will become very dear.

## THE DEVIL ABDUCTS THE BRIDE

In Saxony there was once a very wealthy maiden who wanted a certain youth, who was handsome but poor, to marry her. However, he knew she had a tendency to be fickle, and seeing what would happen, he told her that she would not remain faithful. She, in turn, swore fidelity and said, "If I ever forsake you for another, may the Devil come and get me at my wedding!"

Not long thereafter, she changed her mind and betrothed herself to another man, showing contempt for her first fiancé. He reminded her several times of her previous promise and of the oath she had sworn. She, however, cast all such thoughts to the winds, deserted the youth, and celebrated her marriage to the second man.

On the day of the wedding, when all the guests, friends, and relatives were of joyful spirit, the bride suffered an awakening of conscience and was in sadder spirits than was her usual nature. Finally, two noblemen came riding up to the house in which the wedding was being celebrated; they were received as guests from afar and were led to the table. After the wedding banquet was over, the bride was led to the place of one of the noblemen, and in honor of his being a foreign guest, he was offered the opening dance with her as was the custom. He led her around the dance floor in one or two dances. And then he danced her right past her parents and friends, out the door, and flew with her into the air, where they disappeared amid the screams and gasps of parents and guests.

The following day the grieving parents and friends began searching the countryside in hopes of finding her body so they could at least give her a decent burial. Lo and behold, they encountered the two companions who handed them her clothing and jewelry, explaining, "We have received no power over these things from God, only over the bride."

## THE WHEEL OF FORTUNE

Twelve foot soldiers were discharged from the army after the Ditmar wars, and having acquired neither money nor booty, wandered aimlessly about the countryside. Sad and discouraged, and not knowing where their next meal was coming from, they encountered a strange man in a grey cloak, who greeted them politely and asked, "Whence come you, and whither leads your path?"

"We come from the wars," they replied, "and we're going some-place to get rich, but we don't know where."

Greycloak then told them, "The art of getting rich will be re-vealed to you if you are willing to follow me, and I ask for nothing in return." The soldiers asked what they had to do, and he continued, "I have in my possession a marvelous thing called the Wheel of Fortune; whoever I set upon this wheel acquires the ability to read the future and to locate buried treasures in the earth. But I will set you upon the wheel only on the condition that I be granted the power and the right to take one of you away with me." When they asked which one of them he wanted, he replied, "I cannot tell you now. When the time comes, I will know which one I desire."

The soldiers conferred for a long time; should they accept the offer or forget it? Finally, they decided to accept, saying, "Everyone has to die sometime, just as we could have fallen in the battle of Ditmar or could have been snatched away by the plague. Yes, we'll take a chance—it's no worse than what we've already faced, and it will only affect one of us." Thus, they asked the man to take them to the Wheel of Fortune, accepting his condition that he could take away any one of them he chose.

When all was agreed, Greycloak took them all to the place where the wheel rested. It was so large that when all of them were sitting on it, they were separated from each other by a distance of three fathoms. The man forbade the soldiers to look at one another while they were on the wheel, for if any of them failed to heed his warning, he would wring his neck. When all the men had taken their positions on the wheel as he instructed, the master grabbed the wheel with his claws (which, incidentally, he had on both hands and feet) and began to turn the wheel until it had made one complete revolution. Then, he began anew, continuing to turn the wheel for twelve straight hours—one revolution every hour.

It seemed to the men that a large body of water was located directly beneath them. And, mirrorlike, it reflected everything that was going to happen to them, both good and bad. They also saw reflections of people they recognized and could call by name. Above, there seemed to be fires whose sharp flames reached down toward them.

After they had withstood this ordeal for twelve hours, the Master of Fortune grabbed a handsome young man from the wheel—the son of the Lord Mayor of Meißen—and took him through the roof of flames. The eleven others, not knowing what was happening to them, sank to the ground as if drugged and fell into a deep sleep.

After they had lain beneath the open sky for several hours, they awoke to discover that the clothes they wore had become very brittle, and when they touched the fabric, it disintegrated beneath their fingers. This change had occurred because of the great heat to which they had been subjected while sitting on the wheel.

Then they got up, and each went his own way in the hope that he would have good fortune and wealth for the rest of his life. But, in fact, they were as poor as they had been before and had to beg for bread from door to door.

‡‡  211  ‡‡

## THE DEVIL AS ADVOCATE

There once was a soldier who, when called to war, left all his money with an innkeeper in the Mark for safekeeping. When the soldier returned for it, the innkeeper denied ever having received any such thing. The soldier realized that he was being cheated and tried to force his way into the house to search for his money. The innkeeper, however, had him arrested and taken to jail. Since he planned to keep all the money himself, he decided to take the offensive away from the indignant soldier. He therefore accused the soldier—head to toe, up and down—of having breached domestic peace by forcibly entering his home.

That night, the Devil came to the soldier in his prison cell and said, "Tomorrow you'll be sentenced and then they're going to chop off your head for your breach of domestic peace. But if you agree to be mine, body and soul, I'll get you out of this mess." But the soldier refused the offer. Then the Devil said, "Do as I tell you. When you are called before the court and accused of the crime, insist that you gave the money to the innkeeper. Also tell them that you have since received bad advice, therefore the court should grant you the right to a defense counsel who can plead your case. You'll then see me standing close by in a blue hat with a white feather, and I'll assume your defense."

It happened just as the Devil predicted. The innkeeper, however, continued to deny fervently that he had ever received the money. The soldier's defense counsel in the blue hat then said, "My dear innkeeper, how can you deny it when the money lies hidden in your bed under your pillow? Judge and jury, I bid you send someone there—he'll surely find it."

In desperation, the innkeeper swore, "If I ever received that money, may the Devil sweep me away from this very spot!"

When the money was found in the bed and brought to court, the man in the blue hat with the white feather said, "I knew I was destined to get one of you, either the innkeeper or his guest." He then wrang the innkeeper's neck and led him away through the air.

## THE DREAM OF THE TREASURE AT THE BRIDGE

A long time ago, a man in Regensburg had a dream that if he went to the bridge in that city he would become rich. He thus went to the Regensburg bridge every day.

After fourteen days, a rich merchant saw him and asked what he was doing on the bridge every day, and what he sought there. He answered, "I dreamed I should go to the Regensburg bridge and there I would find my fortune."

"Oh," said the merchant, "what is all this nonsense about dreams? Dreams are illusions and lies. I too had a dream that there was a kettle of gold buried beneath that large tree," and he pointed to the tree. "But I paid it no heed, for dreams are illusions."

The man went immediately to the tree and began digging beneath it. There he found a great treasure that made him very rich. Thus, his dream was confirmed.

Agricola adds to this report, "I heard this story several times from my beloved father."

The story is also reported to have taken place in several other cities, such as Lübeck (Kempen), for example. There, a baker's apprentice dreamed that he would find a treasure on the bridge. He had been going there every day for some time when a beggar addressed him and asked him his reason for going to the bridge all the time. After he told his story, the beggar said that he too had dreamed that in the cemetery in the town of Mölken a treasure lay buried beneath a linden tree (also told about the town of Dordrecht, beneath a bush). The baker's apprentice replied, "Indeed, one often dreams very foolish things. I shall renounce my dream and bequeath my treasures of the bridge to you." Then he immediately proceeded to Mölken, dug beneath the linden tree, and recovered the treasure.

## THE POT OF GOLD

Many years ago, in the town of Großbieberau in the Oden Forest, the master wainwright was sitting with his children and apprentices one winter evening, speaking of this and that. Suddenly, a very strange noise was heard. Behold, a great pot of gold jumped out from under the stove. Had one of those present immediately, without saying a word, cast a little bread or a clod of earth upon it, then everything would have been fine. But no, the Evil One was there, and all went amiss.

The wainwright's little daughter had never seen so much money all at once, and she cried out, "Father, look at all that money! There's so much money!" The father paid little heed to her, for he knew what had to be done. He quickly grabbed the clamp from his axel borer and stuck it through the handle of the kettle. Too late— the kettle sank through the floor and only the handle remained behind. As recently as twenty years ago, people still showed the handle of the pot.

There is a house in Quedlinburg in whose cellar, it is said, a great treasure is buried. Years ago the wife of a coppersmith who lived there ordered the apprentice to see to the various tools and utensils. Above all, he was supposed to clean out a large kettle in one of the work huts.

Toward evening, when the boy had finished all of his other tasks and went to fetch the large kettle, he found it filled to the top with shining pieces of gold. Nearly overcome with joy, he grabbed a couple of coins and hastened to his master's wife to tell her what he had seen. Both hurried back, but no sooner had they crossed the threshold of the work hut than they heard a sudden crashing, crackling noise, and they saw the great kettle moving back and forth. When they approached, the kettle came to a stop. But as they looked in, it was once again empty—the gold had sunk out of sight.

## ‡‡ 214 ‡‡

## THE WEREWOLF

This story was told by a soldier, who claimed it had happened to his own grandfather when he went to the forest one day to chop wood. A neighbor went with him and another man who had always been suspected of not being entirely honest, although no one had ever been able to accuse him of anything with certainty. The three of them got on with their work, and were quite tired by the time they had finished. The third man suggested that they all nap for a while, and all three of them lay down on the ground. The grandfather, however, only pretended to be sleeping and opened his eyes ever so slightly.

The third man sat up and looked around to make sure the others were sleeping. When he was certain, he got up, removed his belt,* and was suddenly transformed into a Werewolf! A Werewolf does not look exactly like a normal wolf; it is somehow different. He then headed off for a nearby meadow where a young foal was grazing, and he attacked and ate it, hide and hair. Then he returned, put his belt back on,† and returned to his sleeping position—in human form.

After some time, they all got up and proceeded back to town. When they arrived at the turnpike, the third man complained bitterly of a terrible stomachache, and the grandfather whispered in his ear, "That's quite understandable after eating a whole horse, hide and hair."

The man replied, "Had you said that while we were still in the forest, you would never have had the chance to say it again!"

A woman once assumed the shape of a Werewolf, and she attacked the flock of a shepherd whom she hated, causing him great losses. When the shepherd saw the wolf, he threw his ax at it and hit it on the hip. It then crawled into the brush, and the shepherd followed, thinking to finish it off. Instead, he found a woman busily trying to stanch the flow of blood with a piece of cloth that she had torn from her dress.

In Lüttich, two sorcerers were executed in 1610 because they had transformed themselves into Werewolves and killed many children. Every time they went out on one of their hunts to tear up and consume their prey, they were accompanied by a twelve-year-old boy whom the Devil would transform into a raven.

‡‡  215  ‡‡

### WEREWOLF ROCK

There is a large rock jutting into a meadow near the Magdeburgian village of Eggenstedt, not far from Sommerschenburg and Schöningen. It is called Wolf Rock, or sometimes, Werewolf Rock.

A long time ago, a stranger was seen loitering around the forest of Brandsleber. No one knew who he was or where he came from. Known everywhere simply as Old Man, he would appear time and again without notice in the villages, where he offered his services and performed them to everyone's satisfaction. He was most often assigned the task of watching over the flocks of sheep.

*Or as others say, put on a belt.
†Or took it off.

It came to pass that a pretty little lamb was born in the flock that belonged to shepherd Melle of Neindorf. The stranger pleaded incessantly with the shepherd to give him the lamb, but the shepherd refused. When shearing time came, Melle engaged the Old Man to help with this task. When Melle returned, he found everything in order and all the work done, but he could find neither the Old Man nor the lamb.

Nothing was seen of the Old Man for a long time, but then one day he came up quite unexpectedly to Melle, who was grazing his flock in Katten Valley. Mockingly, he said, "Good day, Melle. Your little lamb sends his greetings." Angrily, the shepherd grabbed his crook to avenge himself. But the stranger suddenly changed his shape and sprang forth as a Werewolf. The shepherd was terrified, but his dogs attacked the wolf with fury. It fled, pursued by the dogs, through the forests and valleys until it neared Eggenstedt. There, the dogs surrounded it and the shepherd cried, "Now thou shalt die!"

Suddenly, the Old Man changed back into his human form and pleaded fervently for his life. But the shepherd attacked him furiously with his crook. Instantly, a thorn bush stood before him. Even then the vengeful one did not spare the Old Man, but beat the branches of the bush with his staff.

Once again the stranger changed into human form and pleaded for his life. But the shepherd was merciless. Old Man then changed himself back into a Werewolf and tried to flee, but Melle struck him dead with a single blow. A large stone marks the spot where he fell and was buried, and to this day the stone bears the name of Werewolf Rock.

## ‡‡ 216 ‡‡
### THE MIGRATION OF THE WEREWOLVES

The following legend is told in Livonia.

After Christmas had passed, a youth who limped on one leg went around to all those who were devoted to the Evil One, of whom there were a large number, and bade them to follow him. If any of them balked or hesitated, a huge man appeared and beat them with a whip of wire and chains, driving them along with brute force. He was said to have whipped people so cruelly that after a while one could see great welts all over their bodies, from which they suffered terribly. As soon as they began to follow him, they appeared to lose their former shapes and become transformed into Werewolves. Before long, several thousand people had joined together, and leading them was the man with the iron whip.

They came to a meadow where they attacked the cattle in a gruesome fashion, ripping the animals apart, making off with whatever they could grab, and causing great damage. They were not, however, permitted to injure human beings. Whenever they came to a body of water, their leader would strike at it with a switch or with his whip. The waters then parted, and they all crossed on dry ground.

After twelve days, the people were released from their Werewolf shapes and changed back into human form once again.

‡‡ 217 ‡‡

## THE EMERGENCE OF THE DRAGON

The Alpine people of Switzerland have preserved many legends of terrible dragons and mighty serpents that once lived in the mountains many years ago. They frequently descended into the valleys, where they wreaked havoc and destruction. Even today, whenever a mountain stream floods its banks and roars over the cliffs, sweeping boulders and trees along with it, the people utter the ancient proverb, "The dragon has come out." One of the most remarkable stories is the following.

A cooper from Lucerne once went out into the forest to gather wood for barrel staves. He lost his way in a desolate region and was overtaken by night. In the darkness, he suddenly fell into a deep hole whose sides were as damp and slimy as a well. At the bottom there were two entrances to huge caves on either side. When the cooper investigated these, to his terror he encountered two dreadful dragons. The man fell to his knees and began praying fervently while the dragons coiled themselves around his body a number of times but did him no harm.

One day went by, another, and another. Indeed, he was forced to live from the sixth of November to the tenth of April in the company of the dragons. He was able to sustain himself by doing as they did, consuming a moist, salty substance that oozed from the rocky walls.

When the dragons sensed that winter had passed, they prepared to fly from their den. The first one flew away with great roaring sounds. But just as the other dragon made ready to do the same, the plucky cooper grabbed hold of its tail, held on tight, and was pulled from the well. When they reached the surface, he let go and was thus liberated. He then returned to the city.

As a memorial to his escape, he had the entire story embroidered on a priest's cloak, which is still on display in the parish church of Leodagar in Lucerne. According to the church register, the event took place in the year 1420.

## ‡‡ 218 ‡‡
## WINKELRIED AND THE DRAGON

In ancient times, near the village of Wyler in Unterwalden, there lived a frightening dragon that killed everything it encountered, both men and cattle. The dragon so ravaged the area that the village was soon named Desolate Wyler. It then came to pass that a native of the area, by the name of Winkelried, was banished from that land because of a murder he was said to have committed. He offered to challenge the dragon and kill it on condition that afterward he would be allowed to return to his homeland. The citizens of the region were overjoyed at this, and they granted his terms.

Winkelried then set about his dangerous task. He took a bundle of thorns, and when the threatening dragon opened its mouth wide, he thrust the bundle between its jaws. While the dragon sought in vain to spit out the thorns, it neglected to defend itself. The hero took advantage of his opening and cut the dragon's head off. In jubilation he showed the inhabitants his triumphant deed by holding the dragon's head in one hand, and brandishing the dripping sword in the other. But the poisonous dragon blood ran down his arm onto his bare skin, and he died soon after. However, the region was saved, and even today the inhabitants still point to the place in the cliff where the dragon had its den. It is called Dragon Cave.

## ‡‡ 219 ‡‡
## THE DRAGON AT THE WELL

There is an old castle called Frankenstein which lies an hour and a half from Darmstadt. Many years ago three brothers lived there, and their gravestones can still be seen today in the cemetery of the Ober-birbacher Church. One of the brothers was called Hans and an image showing him standing on a dragon is engraved on his headstone.

Down in the village there is a well that the inhabitants of both the village and castle used for their water. Right next to the well, a dreadful dragon had his den. The only way the people could get water was to bring a sheep or a cow every day to feed to the dragon. As long as it was busy eating, the inhabitants could get to the well safely.

In order to put an end to this intolerable situation, the knight, Hans, resolved to challenge the dragon. The battle lasted a very long time, but he finally succeeded in cutting the dragon's head off. However, the body of the monster kept on wiggling and writhing, so Hans attempted to spear it with his lance. As he did so, the spiked tail of the creature wound around the knight's leg and struck him in the knee cap, the only place he was not covered with armor. Since the dragon was poisonous all over, Hans von Frankenstein lost his life.

## ‡‡ 220 ‡‡

### DRAGON CAVE

There is a cave near the village of Burgdorf in the Bern region of Switzerland where two terrible dragons were supposedly found many years ago while the castle was being constructed. Legend has it that in the year 712 two brothers named Sintram and Beltram (others say they were called Guntram and Waltram), dukes of Lenzburg, embarked on a hunt. They soon found themselves in a wild, desolate forest where they came upon a hollow mountain. Inside lay the frightful dragon who had ravaged the whole countryside. When he saw the two brothers outside his cave, he came at them in leaps and bounds and in no time had swallowed Beltram, the younger brother. Sintram, however, boldly took up the battle and after a long struggle defeated the wild beast. Cutting open its body, he found his brother still alive. As a memorial to this event, the princes of the region had a chapel built and dedicated to St. Margareta. They also had the whole story painted in frescoes, which can still be seen today.

## ‡‡ 221 ‡‡

### THE SNAKE QUEEN

A shepherd's daughter, while wandering along a trail through some cliffs, came upon a mortally ill serpent that seemed near death. Out of pity, she gave it her milk pitcher, and the snake drank the milk eagerly and appeared to feel stronger.

The girl departed, and soon thereafter it came to pass that her beloved began to court her. But he was too poor for her proud, wealthy father. He rejected the youth with much mockery, telling him to come back only when he had as many herds as he himself. From that time on, the old shepherd met nothing but misfortune.

People claimed they had seen a fiery dragon above his grazing lands at night and soon all his property had been laid waste.

During this same period, however, the poor youth prospered and became quite wealthy. He once again courted the girl, and this time she was granted to him.

On the day of the wedding, a large serpent entered the room, and on the end of its coiled body sat a splendid maiden. She said that she was the one to whom the shepherd girl had given milk when she was starving. Out of gratitude she took a dazzling crown from her head and laid it in the bride's lap. She then disappeared. Thereafter, the young couple was blessed with great fortune and increase in their flocks, and they soon became very wealthy.


## ‡‡ 222 ‡‡
### THE MAIDEN OF OSEL MOUNTAIN

Between Dinkelsbühl and Hahnkamm lies Osel Mountain, and there, many years ago, stood a castle. A lovely maiden lived there with her father, a widower. She ran the entire household for him, and had access to the keys for every room in the castle. One day the walls of the old castle disintegrated. They came crashing down, taking the lovely maiden with them. Soon thereafter, a rumor began to circulate that her ghost was hovering around the walls of the ruins. It was said that during the four fasting periods called Ember Days she appeared at night as a lovely maiden, carrying a ring of keys at her side.

On the other hand, some of the farmers of this region claimed to have heard from their fathers that this maiden had been the daughter of a heathen, and that she had been transformed by a curse into a terrifying serpent. They also reported that from time to time she could be seen in the shape of a large serpent with a woman's head and breasts, and with a ring of keys around her neck.


## ‡‡ 223 ‡‡
### THE TOADSTOOL*

Near the Alsatian town of Wasgau there is a castle called Notweil where many years ago there lived the beautiful daughter of a duke. However, she was so proud that she considered none of her many suitors worthy of her hand, and this cost many of them their lives.

*In common dialect, the forest mushroom is called a toadstool.

As punishment for this she was cursed to live out her time among the desolate cliffs of the mountain until someone delivered her. She could be seen only one day of the week—on Fridays. The first time she would appear in the figure of a snake, the next time as a toad, and a third time in her natural shape, as a maiden. She can still be seen every Friday, washing herself on a cliff still called the Toadstool. She sits by a mountain stream looking far and wide for someone to deliver her.

If anyone should choose to undertake this task, he will find a shell on the Toadstool upon which will be three signs: the scale of a snake, a piece of toad skin, and a lock of yellow hair. Carrying these three things with him, the rescuer must climb this desolate mountain at noon on Friday for three consecutive Fridays and wait at the spring until the maiden comes to wash. He must kiss her on the mouth in each of her three forms without becoming frightened and fleeing. Whoever can accomplish this will give her eternal peace and will also receive all the treasure in her possession.

Several men have found the three signs and have ventured into the ruins of the old castle. Many, too, have died in fear and terror. Once, a bold youth actually pressed his lips to the mouth of the snake and was prepared to wait for her in her other forms. But suddenly, he was overcome by terror and ran down the mountainside. Furious, she pursued him in the shape of a toad until they reached the Toadstool.

Through the years she has retained her original appearance and never grows old. She is most frightening in her serpent form, and local proverb has it that she is "as long as a hay pole." As a toad she is "as large as a baking oven," and she spits fire.


‡‡   224   ‡‡

## THE WOMAN OF THE MEADOW

Near Auerbach, along the mountain road, a youth used to watch over his father's cattle in the narrow valley meadows where he could see the old castle. Once, as he was standing there, he felt a soft hand reach around him and stroke him on the cheek. When he turned around, he saw a wonderfully beautiful woman standing before him, clothed head to foot in white. Just as she was about to speak to him, the boy became frightened and took off for his village as though he had seen the Devil himself.

However, since his father owned only one meadow, he always had to drive the cows to this place for them to graze whether he wanted to or not. After a time the youth forgot the apparition, until one warm summer day when he heard a rustling noise in the leaves. Looking about, he saw a serpent creeping along, carrying a blue flower in its mouth. Suddenly, it began to speak, "Listen well, my boy, you can deliver me if you will take this flower. It is the key to my chamber in the castle. There you will find gold in abundant measure." But the shepherd boy became frightened when he heard the snake speaking, and once again he bolted for home.

Then, on one of the last days of autumn when the youth was again watching the cattle on the meadow, she appeared to him for the third time, once again in the shape of the White Woman. She stroked him on the cheek and, pleading fervently, told him that he could deliver her and that she would give him all the means and instructions for doing so. But all her pleading was in vain. Fear again overcame the youth, and he crossed himself and blessed himself and would have nothing to do with the spirit.

Then the woman gave a deep sigh and said, "Oh, woe, that I have placed my trust in thee. Now I must once again wait until a cherry tree grows in this meadow, and a cradle is made from the wood of this tree. For only a child who is first rocked in that cradle will someday deliver me." With these words she disappeared, and the boy, so it is said, did not grow to be very old. No one knows the cause of his death.

## ‡‡ 225 ‡‡

## THE SNEEZES FROM THE WATER

A man who was crossing a small bridge that spanned Auer Brook heard someone below sneezing three times. Each time, he said, "God bless you." With these words, the spirit of a boy, who had waited thirty years to hear them, was delivered.

According to a different tale, there was another man, in an area not far from this bridge, who heard three sneezes coming from the brook. Twice he said, "God bless you." But the third time he said, "May the Devil take you!" Suddenly, a wave moved across the brook, as though someone had violently turned over in the water.

## ‡‡ 226 ‡‡

## THE LOST SOUL

There is a bridge outside of Haxthusen-Hofe near Paderborn. Beneath it lives a poor soul who sneezes from time to time. If someone in a wagon crosses over the bridge at just that moment, and the driver does not say, "God bless you," then the wagon will tip over. Many a man has broken an arm or leg from such an accident.

## ‡‡ 227 ‡‡
## THE ACCURSED WOMAN

Not far from Eisenach there is a cave in the side of a cliff. From time to time a woman is seen there at midday. She can only be delivered if someone says, "God bless you," after she has sneezed three times. She was a headstrong daughter who was caught in a spell when her own mother cursed her in anger.

## ‡‡ 228 ‡‡
## THE MAIDEN OF STAUFEN MOUNTAIN

Staufen Mountain lies near the village of Sorge in the Braunschweig region of the Harz Mountains. A mighty castle once stood on the mountaintop, and one can still see the print of a human foot in a cliff on the side of the mountain. This print was left by the daughter of the lord of the castle. She often stood there because it was her favorite place. From time to time an enchanted maiden with long golden hair can be seen there.

## ‡‡ 229 ‡‡
## MAIDEN ROCK

There is a large cliff not far from the fortress of Königstein called Maiden Rock, and also Pastor Rock. Once a mother cursed her own daughter who went into the forest to gather blueberries instead of going to church on Sunday. The daughter was turned to stone, and her image can still be seen there at noon.

During the Thirty Years' War, people fled to this site to escape enemy soldiers.

## ‡‡ 230 ‡‡
## THE STONE BRIDAL BED

In German Bohemia there stands a high cliff whose top is divided into two peaks that form a large bed. The following legend is told about it.

There used to be a castle at the top of the cliff, and there a noblewoman lived with her only daughter. The maiden, against the will of her mother, fell in love with a young gentleman from the region, but the mother would not permit her to marry him. The daughter, however, disobeyed her mother's commandment and secretly promised herself to her lover on condition that they not marry until after her mother's death.

However, the mother found out about the engagement before her death. She uttered a curse, praying fervently to God to hear her and to turn her daughter's bridal bed to stone. And then she died.

The disobedient daughter gave her hand to her fiancé, and the wedding was celebrated in great splendor in the castle on the cliff. However, when they entered the bridal chamber around midnight, everyone in the whole region heard a terrifying clap of thunder. The next morning no trace of the castle could be seen. No road, no path led up the cliff. But there, on the peaks, sat the bride in her stone bed. It can still be seen clearly today.

No one was able to save her, for every man who tried to scale the cliffs plunged to his death. Thus, she languished until she finally starved to death and the ravens consumed her corpse.

‡‡ 231 ‡‡

## CURSED TO REMAIN STANDING

The following occurred in the town of Freiberg in the region of Meißen in the year 1545.

A weaver named Lorenz Richter, who lived in Weingasse, ordered his son, a boy of fourteen, to do some chores with dispatch. The boy, however, tarried and remained standing in the room instead of doing as he was told. The father then lost control of himself and angrily cursed his son, saying, "All right then, just keep standing there, and you'll never move from that spot!"

No sooner had the father finished uttering the curse than the boy froze to the spot and was unable to move a step. And he stood thus for three whole years, until his feet wore deep grooves in the floor. Later, a lectern was set before him so he could lean his arms and head on it.

However, since the place where he was standing was not far from the entrance to the room and also close to the stove, he was a hindrance to people coming in and out of the room. The clergy of the city, after much fervent praying, picked him up from the spot and moved him to another corner of the room without harming him, although it took great effort. They had tried to move him once before, but he had been struck with indescribable pain and had flown into a rage.

After he was placed in the new location he remained standing for four more years, and his feet made even deeper impressions in the floor. Still later he was covered with a cloth so that people coming in and out would not be able to see him. He requested this himself. Because of his habitual melancholy he liked to be alone and did not like to talk to others. Finally, the Merciful Lord mitigated his punishment somewhat. In his last six months he was able to sit down, and he was also able to lie down in a bed that was placed next to him.

Whenever anyone asked him what he was doing, he usually replied that he was suffering God's punishment for his sins—he entrusted all to God's will, and he hoped to achieve salvation by devoting himself to the service of his Lord Jesus Christ. His appearance reflected his misery. He was pale of countenance, and his body was wasting away for he would accept only the bare necessities of food and drink.

He was mercifully delivered on the eleventh of September, 1552, at the end of his seventh year of suffering. He died a peaceful and natural death in true conversion and faith in Jesus Christ. The grooves worn by his feet can still be seen today in the above-named house on the above-named street (whose owner at the present time is Severin Tränkner) in the upstairs room in which the event occurred. The first pair of footprints are next to the stove, the others are in the next room, for a wall has since been built separating the two rooms.


‡‡  232  ‡‡

## THE PEASANTS OF KOLBECK

In the year 1012, in the village of Kolbeck, near Halberstadt, there was a peasant named Albrecht who held a dance with fifteen other peasants on Christmas Eve while mass was being said. The dance was held outside the church in the cemetery, and there were three women among the dancers.

When the priest stepped forth from the church to punish the sinners, the farmer said, "They call me Albrecht, let them call you Ruprecht. You are happy inside, so let us be happy out here. You are singing your hymns in there, so let us sing our dance songs out here."

The priest then said, "May God and St. Magnus force you to dance for a whole year."

It came to pass that God gave power to these words. Neither rain nor frost touched the dancers' heads, neither did they feel heat, hunger, or thirst. And though they danced ceaselessly, their shoes did not wear out. The sexton ran up to the group and tried to pull his sister away from the other dancers, but only her arms followed him.

When a year had passed, Bishop Heribert of Cologne came and freed them from the curse. Four of them died immediately and the others became very ill. It is said that they danced themselves into the earth up to their waists and hollowed out a deep hole, which can still be seen there. The lord of the land had as many stones as there had been dancers set up as a memorial.

## ‡‡ 233 ‡‡

### HOLY SUNDAY

There was a spinner in the city of Kindstadt in Franconia who used to spin all day on Sunday, and she forced her maids to do the same. One day they all had a vision that fire sprang from their distaffs, but none of them was the least bit harmed. The next Sunday, fire indeed leaped from the distaffs, but it died out again by itself.

The woman paid no heed to these warnings, and on the third Sunday the entire house burned to the ground—with the spinning wheel, the flax, the woman, and her two children. Only by the grace of God was a small child in its cradle saved.

It is also said that a farmer who used to go to the mill on Sunday to grind his grain saw it turned to ashes. Another one had to watch his barn filled with grain burn to the ground.

Yet another farmer wanted to plow his fields on the Holy Day. But as he began to sharpen his plow blade, the iron file grew into his hand. He had to carry it around for two whole years in great pain until—after he had prayed fervently—God took mercy on him and delivered him from his agony.

## ‡‡ 234 ‡‡

### MOTHER HÜTT

In the mountains overlooking Innsbruck in Tyrol there lived many years ago a powerful Giant Queen called Mother Hütt. The mountains today are grey and bare, but at that time they were covered with forests, fertile fields, and green meadows.

One day her small boy came home crying and weeping, his hands and face covered with mud, and his clothes as black as a charcoal-maker's apron. He had been trying to break off a fir tree to make a hobbyhorse for himself. But as the tree was growing right next to a marsh, the ground gave way beneath him as he tried to break it, and he sank up to his neck in slimy mud. Fortunately, he managed to make his own way out of the muck.

Mother Hütt consoled and comforted him and promised him some new clothes. She then called a servant and instructed him to clean the boy's hands and face with some soft bread crumbs. However, he had scarcely begun this blasphemous task of wasting God's sacred gift when a terrifying black thundercloud appeared on the horizon and grew until it covered the whole sky. There followed dreadful flashes of lightning and roars of thunder.

When the skies finally cleared, the fertile fields of grain, the green meadows and forests—even the house of Mother Hütt—had all disappeared. Instead, there was only a desert of scattered stones and cliffs, not even a blade of grass grew there. In the midst of all this desolation stood Mother Hütt. She had been turned to stone, and there she will stand until Judgment Day.

This story is told in many regions of Tyrol, especially around Innsbruck, to bad and mischievous children as a warning not to waste or throw away bread or to otherwise misbehave. "Save your crumbs for the poor," their parents say, "or you will end up like Mother Hütt!"


‡‡ 235 ‡‡

## MT. KINDEL

Towering over the countryside behind Mt. Geißen in Westphalia are three high peaks. The middle one is called Mt. Kindel, and many years ago, a castle stood there that also bore the name Kindel. A group of knights who were blasphemous and ungodly lived there. To the right of their castle they had a silver mine so rich that they became very wealthy. Indeed, they had so much silver that they were able to make a bowling game with silver pins and silver balls. Their wasteful arrogance, however, went even further. They took the finest flour and baked giant cakes in the shape of carriage wheels, then they drilled holes in the middle of them and mounted them on the axles of their carriages. That blasphemy screamed to the heavens, for in those days many, many people had no bread at all to eat.

Before long, God grew weary of these antics. And late one evening a Dwarf, who was white from head to toe, appeared in the castle and prophesied that they would all die within three days. As proof of his accuracy, he foretold that a cow would bear three lambs that very night. And it came to pass that the cow did give birth to three lambs, but no one in the castle paid heed to the event except for the youngest son, who was called Knight Siegmund, and one daughter, who was a lovely maiden. The two of them knelt and prayed day and night. The plague then descended upon them and killed everyone in the castle except for these two.

At this same time, there lived in the castle on Mt. Geißen another young bold knight who always rode about on a large black steed. He was thus named the Knight of the Black Horse. He too was a blasphemous man, always engaged in pillage and murder.

When this knight met the lovely maiden of Mt. Kindel, he fell in love with her and wanted to marry her. But she always refused him, for she was already engaged to a young count of the Mark, who had gone off with her brother to war, and to whom she was resolved to remain true. But after many months, with the count still away at the wars, she said to the knight who had been courting her so intensely and incessantly, "When the green linden tree outside my window withers, then shall I feel more kindly disposed toward you."

The Knight of the Black Horse searched long through the countryside until he found a withered linden tree the same size as the one in the maiden's garden. Late one night, by the light of the moon, he uprooted the girl's tree and replaced it with the withered one he had found.

When the lovely maiden awoke the next morning, the sun was shining outside her window, so she went there to enjoy the warm sunlight. Then, to her shock, she saw the withered linden tree. Seating herself beneath the withered tree, she began to weep. And when the knight appeared to demand her heart, she cried out in distress, "I shall never be able to love you." The knight became so enraged that he took his sword, and stabbed her to death.

On that very day, her fiancé returned. He dug her grave and planted a linden tree next to it, and then he erected a giant tombstone, which can still be seen today.

‡‡ 236 ‡‡

## THE BREADROLL SHOES

In Klatauer County, just a quarter of an hour from the village of Oberkamenz, a castle once stood on Hradek Mountain and a few of the ruins can still be seen there. Many years ago the lord of the castle had a bridge built all the way to Stankau, an hour away, to make it easier to go to church.

Now, the lord of the castle had an arrogant young daughter,

who was so possessed by pride that she took breadrolls, hollowed them out, and wore them as shoes. Once, while wearing such shoes, she crossed this bridge on her way to church. She was halfway across when, suddenly, the bridge and the castle collapsed and sank out of sight. Her footprint can still be seen on one of the stone stairs leading down from the bridge.

## ‡‡ 237 ‡‡

## THE CAVE-IN AT HOCHSTÄDT

In Klettenberg County, near the Lower Harz Mountains in Brandenburg, stands the village of Hochstädt. Not far from there is a small lake that lies in a deep depression in the earth. The inhabitants of the region tell the following legend about this site.

Many years ago, when there was pasture where the lake is now, several stableboys were grazing their horses there. One of the boys took out his lunch, which consisted mainly of fine white bread, and began to eat. The other stableboys developed an appetite for that white bread and they demanded some from the youth. But he said no, he needed what he had to still his hunger.

The others then grew angry and cursed their master for giving them common homemade black bread. They threw their bread on the ground in blasphemous anger, stomping it with their feet and smashing it with their whips. But no sooner had they done this than blood began to flow from the bread.

When they saw this, they became terribly frightened and did not know where to turn. The boy who was innocent, however (some say that he had been warned by a strange man who appeared on the scene), mounted his horse and escaped with his life. The others tried to follow him, but it was too late. Before they could ride off, the entire earth caved in all around them. The sinful youths and their horses were swallowed up deep beneath the surface of the earth, and not one of them ever again appeared in the light of day.

According to others, the plants that grow around the lake have leaves shaped like horseshoes.

## ‡‡ 238 ‡‡

## SHOES OF BREAD

There once was a woman whose young child was the apple of her eye, but it died. Still, she wanted to show it all the love and kindness she could before it was buried beneath the earth, never again to be seen. So she dressed the corpse in the very finest clothes and set it in its casket. It then occurred to her that the little shoes were not elegant enough, and she took the finest white flour that she had and made dough with it. From this she baked a pair of shoes in which the child was then buried. But the child kept appearing to the mother in great misery and it left her no peace. Finally, they had to dig up the casket and remove the shoes of bread from the corpse and replace them with regular shoes. The spirit of the child was at peace from that time on.

## ‡‡ 239 ‡‡

### DEAF GRAIN

The citizens of the town of Stavoren in Frisia became very wealthy. They grew so proud and arrogant that they had their doors and entryways plated with solid gold just to spite the citizens of the poorer cities of the region. Because of this behavior they came to be known as "the spoiled children of Stavoren."

Among them there lived an especially stingy old widow. She commissioned a ferryman from Danzig to bring her the best of goods that he could fit in his ship and to charge them to her account.

The ferryman thought to make her a fine profit by taking aboard a few tons of fine Polish grain, for at the time of his departure the price of grain in Frisia was very high. En route, however, he encountered nothing but gales and storms until he was forced into the port of Bornholm, where he wintered over. When he finally arrived in the spring the price of grain had fallen, and the widow was so angry that she had the entire cargo of grain dumped into the sea just outside the city.

What happened?

A giant sandbank rose to the surface. It was afterward named Lady's Sand, and nothing ever grew there except deaf grain, (wonder grain or dune grass, *Arundo arenaria*, which protects the dunes from the sea). The sandbank blocked the entrance to the harbor and thus rendered it useless. Upon the sins of the old woman grew retribution for the whole city.*

---

*The sandbank was the retribution. Upon it grew the grain, which prevented the sea from eroding the sandbank. There is a play on words, *Sand/Sünde* (sand and sin). "Upon the 'sinbanks' of the old woman grew retribution for the whole city."—D. W.

# LADY'S SANDBANK

On the west side of the Zuyder Zee there is a place where grass and reeds grow right out of the water. On this site once stood the proud houses and church towers of the city of Stavoren, which is now buried deep beneath the sea. Excessive wealth made the citizens of the city profligate and wicked, and when they had done their full measure of evil deeds, they suffered their just fate. The fishermen and sailors along the shores of the Zuyder Zee have preserved this legend and passed it on by word of mouth.

The wealthiest of all the inhabitants of the city of Stavoren was a certain young woman whose name is nevermore mentioned. Overproud of her wealth and property, ruthless in her dealings with others, she wanted only to increase her hoard of money. And she was frequently heard to curse and blaspheme. However, the other citizens of this excessively rich city—which existed long before anyone heard the name of Amsterdam, and when Rotterdam was still a tiny village—had also forsaken the straight and narrow path of virtue.

One day, the young woman ordered her captain to set out to sea and to return with a cargo of the most precious and noble goods available in the world. The captain, who was accustomed to receiving more precise and definite orders, sought in vain for further instructions. For the young woman became angry, and remaining steadfast in her wishes, ordered him immediately to sea.

The captain set sail with indecision and uncertainty, for he had no idea how he would be able to fulfill the wishes of the woman, whose fury and stubborn nature he knew only too well. And he thought and thought of what he should do. Finally, he said to himself, "I'll bring her a cargo of the finest wheat, for what is more precious and noble on earth than this splendid grain, without which man cannot survive?" Thus, he steered a course for Danzig where he loaded his ship with choice wheat. Then he set sail again for home, but he was still fearful and troubled.

"Ay, Captain," called out the woman, "you're back already? I thought you would still be on the coast of Africa bargaining for gold and ivory. Let's see what you have loaded in your hold."

Seeing immediately that she was not going to be pleased with his purchase, he hesitatingly replied, "My lady, I bring to you the most precious wheat that can be found anywhere in the world."

"Wheat!" said she. "You dare to bring me such miserable stuff?"

"I thought it not so miserable, for it provides us with our daily and nutritious bread," he replied.

"I'll show you how contemptible your cargo is to me," she said. "On which side did you load your hold?"

"From starboard," replied the captain.

"Well then, I command you to unload all of the cargo immediately from the port side into the sea. I shall return myself to see if my command has been obeyed."

The captain shuddered at the thought of carrying out an order that would so hideously denigrate God's gift to man. He immediately called out all the poor and needy people of the city in the hope that the sight of them would move his lady to change her mind. When she returned to ask whether her order had been carried out, a crowd of poor and needy fell upon their knees before her and begged her to divide the grain among them rather than let it be swallowed up by the sea. But the heart of the young woman remained as hard as stone, and she repeated her command to dump the entire cargo overboard.

The captain, no longer able to restrain himself, cried out, "No! God cannot allow this sin to remain unavenged. If it be true that Heaven rewards good and punishes evil, then the day will come when to still your hunger you will be happy to pick up kernel by kernel the precious wheat you now cast away so frivolously."

"What?" she shouted, laughing diabolically, "I'm supposed to become a beggar and suffer from hunger and starvation! That will never happen, as sure as I will never again cast my eyes upon this ring I now throw into the depths of the sea." With these words she removed the precious ring from her finger and cast it into the waves. Then all the wheat in the hold and on the deck of the ship was dumped into the sea.

What happened?

A few days later, the woman's maidservant went to the market, bought a haddock, and brought it back to the kitchen. When she opened up the fish, she found a precious ring inside, and she showed it to her lady. The young woman immediately recognized the ring as the one she had recently thrown into the sea. She grew pale and felt the forebodings of her punishment in her conscience. Imagine her shock and terror when at the same moment she received the message that her entire fleet sailing from the Orient had been washed ashore in a storm! A few days later there came a second report of the sinking of other of her ships on which many riches had been loaded. Yet another ship had been pirated by Turks and Moors. And the collapse of the commercial houses in which she had major investments completed her misfortune.

Scarcely a year had passed when all the conditions of her captain's terrible curse had been fulfilled. Pitied by no one and scorned by many, she became poor and sank further and further into need and misery until she had to beg hungrily from door to door for bread, frequently receiving not a single crumb. Finally, in total despair, she withered and starved to death.

The wheat that had been dumped into the sea sprouted and grew the following year, but it bore only deaf ears [no grain]. However, no one paid any heed to this warning. Instead, the profligate and wicked ways of the citizens only increased from year to year, until God finally withdrew his protecting hand from the evil city.

It soon happened that people began to draw up flounder and herring in the water from their wells. And then one night a roaring tidal wave swept over three-quarters of the city. Hardly a year goes by without several more cabins and houses sinking beneath the surface. Ever since that time there has been nothing but ill fortune in Stavoren, and not a single wealthy person is now to be found there.

And each year grass sprouts from the water at that spot. It is a kind of grass that no connoisseur of herbs recognizes, it bears no blossoms, and its like is to be found nowhere else on earth. The stems shoot up long and tall and the ears look like wheat, but they are deaf, that is, without kernels. The sandbank on which this grass grows, runs along the city of Stavoren, and it is known only as the Lady's Sandbank.


‡‡ 241 ‡‡

## BREAD TURNED TO STONE

In many places, especially in Westphalia, there is a legend about a hardhearted woman. During a period of great famine, she is said to have replied to the pleas of her poor sister for bread for herself and her children with the words "Even if I had bread, I'd rather it turned to stone!" And behold, her entire store of bread changed immediately to stone. A stone loaf of bread is on display in the Church of St. Peter in Leiden, Holland, and it is shown to people as proof of this story.

In the year 1579, during a great famine, a baker in Dortmund bought up all the grain in the area and looked forward to making great profits. However, one day in the middle of this enterprise, all the bread that he had stored in his home turned to stone, and when he tried to slice one loaf with a knife, blood flowed from the bread. He immediately retired to his room and hanged himself.

In Landshut, in the church dedicated to St. Kastulus, there hangs a round stone framed in silver, which has the shape of a loaf of bread. On the surface of the bread there are four small depressions, and the following legend is told about it. Shortly before his death, St. Kastulus appeared in this town as a beggar and went to a widow to ask for a handout. The woman ordered her daughter to take the only bread she still had and give it to the needy man. The daughter, however, was reluctant to give the bread away and wanted to break off a few pieces for herself first. In that instant the bread intended for the saint turned to stone, and one can still clearly see the finger depressions in it.

Once, during a great famine, a poor woman with one child on her arm and another running along beside her was walking along a street in the city of Danzig, crying loudly for bread. A monk from the Monastery of Oliva encountered her and she pleaded fervently with him for a bit of bread for her children.

The monk said, "I have none."

"Ah, but I see that you have a loaf of bread hidden beneath your cloak," said the woman.

"Oh, that's just a stone I carry to throw at dogs," replied the monk, and he departed.

A little later, when he wanted a bite of his bread, he discovered it really had turned to stone. A feeling of dread overcame him, and he confessed his sin and gave up the stone, which can still be seen hanging in the chapel of the monastery.

## ‡‡  242  ‡‡

### THE MOUSE TOWER OF BINGEN

In the middle of the Rhine River, near the city of Bingen, a large tower can be seen, and the following legend is told about it.

In the year 974 a great famine prevailed throughout Germany. In their need, the people were forced to eat dogs and cats, and still many starved to death. At that time the archbishop in Mainz was Hatto the Second, a miserly man whose only thought was to increase his great fortune. He used to watch poor people collapsing on the street and mobbing the bread market where they would take bread by force.

The bishop felt no pity whatsoever, saying instead, "Let all the poor and needy gather in a barn outside the city. I shall feed them." After they had entered the barn, he locked the doors, set fire to it, and burned the barn along with all the poor people, young and old, men and women. As the people were shrieking and screaming amid the flames, Bishop Hatto cried out, "Hear, hear, how the mice squeak!"

But soon thereafter, God, our Lord, saw to it that he was tormented day and night by mice. They ran over him and bit him until, with all his might, he was unable to hold them off. Knowing no other way to escape from the torment, he had a tower built in the middle of the Rhine near Bingen, which can still be seen today. There he thought he could escape the mice. But they swam through the current, climbed the tower, and ate the bishop alive.

## ‡‡ 243 ‡‡

## THE CHILD'S MARSH

On the commons of Großbieberau there is a valley opposite Überau that local people call the Child's Marsh. One cannot walk by there at night without getting goose flesh all over.

Many years ago when war and famine raged in the Empire, two beggar boys were returning from Überau. They had always been together and had always shared the handouts they received in that valley. That day they had only received a few tin pennies, but a rich man named Schulze had given one of the boys a whole loaf of bread to share with his companion.

After everything else had been divided honestly, the one boy took the bread from his sack. But it smelled so good to him that he wanted to keep it all for himself and not share any of it with the other boy. And now the peace that had reigned between them came to an end, for they began to quarrel. After exchanging harsh words, they began exchanging blows, but since neither could defeat the other, they both grabbed fence posts. The Evil One guided their clubs, and thus each boy slew the other.

For three nights after the double murder, not a leaf moved, not a bird sang in the marshland. And ever since that time it has been spooky there, and one can still hear the boys whimpering and whining.

## ‡‡ 244 ‡‡

## CHILDREN'S BRIDGE

In Thuringia there is a country village called Children's Bridge. It is said to have acquired this name many years ago when two small children were riding their hobbyhorses across the bridge over the Wipper River. They fell from the bridge into the water.

## THE CHILDREN OF HAMELN

A wondrous man appeared in the town of Hameln in the year 1284. He wore a coat of many bright colors from which he is said to have acquired the name Pied Piper. He proclaimed himself a ratcatcher, and he promised to rid the city of all mice and rats in exchange for a certain sum. The citizens accepted his offer and promised him the requested amount of money as his reward.

The ratcatcher then drew out a small fife and began playing. The rats and mice immediately came creeping out of all the houses and gathered around him. When he was certain that none remained behind, he began marching out of town with the entire horde following after him. He led them down to the Weser River where he rolled up his clothes and marched right into the water, followed by all the creatures, who then drowned.

After the citizens had been delivered from this plague, they regretted having promised so much money. Using all kinds of excuses, they denied the man his reward, and he departed in bitterness and anger. Then, on the morning of June twenty-sixth, St. John's and St. Paul's Day—some say at seven o'clock, others say at noon— he reappeared as a hunter with a terrifying countenance, wearing a strange red hat.

Once again the sounds of his fife were heard in the streets and alleys. This time, however, instead of rats and mice came children. Boys and girls from four years of age on ran after him in great numbers, among them the grown daughter of the town mayor. The troupe of children followed him as he played, and he led them outside the town where they disappeared with him into a mountain.

A nurserymaid with a child in her arms, who had been approaching the town from afar and witnessed all this, brought the report to the city. The parents ran en masse to the gates, seeking their children with grieving hearts. All the mothers were weeping and wailing. Messengers were sent out in all directions by land, sea, and riverways to discover if anyone had seen or heard of the children—but all in vain.

Altogether, one hundred and thirty children were lost. Some people say that two of them returned some time later, but one was blind and the other dumb. The blind one could not point out the place but was able to tell how they had followed the Piper, and the dumb one could point out the place though he had heard nothing. One child joining the others was in his nightshirt and turned around to get his coat. He thus escaped the tragedy, for when he returned, the others had already disappeared into a cave in the hillside, which people still point out today.

The street on which the children marched out through the gate was still called—in the middle of the eighteenth century and probably still today—the Silent Street because no dance could be held and no musical instrument could be played there. Indeed, even when a bride was led to church in a procession, the musicians had to cross that street in complete silence.

The mountain near Hameln where the children disappeared is called Mt. Poppen. Two stone crosses have been erected to the right and to the left of the mountain. Some say the children were led into a cave and emerged again in Transylvania.

The citizens of Hameln recorded the event in their city register, and ever since have been in the habit of dating all their announcements from the day that their children were lost.

According to Seyfried, the date recorded in the city register was the twenty-second, not the twenty-sixth, of June. The following lines are inscribed on the City Hall:

> In the year of our Lord 1284
> from Hameln were led away,
> 130 children who here were born,
> lost by a piper inside the mountain.

And on the new gate are the lines:

> *Centum ter denos cum magnus ab urbe puellos*
> *Duxerat ante annos CCLXXII condita porta fuit.**

In 1572 the town mayor had the entire story illustrated in stained glass windows for the church with an accompanying text inscription. This, however, has become largely illegible. A coin commemorating the event was also printed.†

‡‡ 246 ‡‡

# THE RATCATCHER

The ratcatcher knows how to blow a certain tone on his fife, and when he pipes it nine times, all rats follow him wherever he wants to take them—into ponds and puddles.

---

*"This gate was built 272 years after the sorcerer abducted 130 children from the city."—*D. W.*

†Cf. the similar legend in the *Adventures du Mandarin Fum Hoam*, 44 soirée, German translation, Leipzig, 1727, II, pp. 167–172. Chardin records only the name of the Tower of Forty Virgins.

Martin Schock, *Fabula hamelensis*, rejects the truth of the story, opposing Erich.

An inscription in gold letters on a building in Hameln reads: "Anno 1284 on the day of John and Paul, the 26th of June, 130 children, all of them born in Hameln, were led away by a Piper clothed in all kinds of colors, and taken to Calvary at the Koppen (Schöppach.)"

Once a certain village could not get rid of all the rats, so they finally called for the ratcatcher. He prepared a hazel branch in such a fashion that all the rats would be held spellbound by it and would have to follow whoever picked up the stick. The ratcatcher waited until Sunday and then placed the stick outside the door of the church.

As people returned home from services, a miller who was among them saw the stick lying there and said to himself, "That would make a fine walking stick." So he picked it up, walked through the village, and headed for his mill.

As he did so, a few individual rats came out of their corners and holes and began to run, jumping across the fields, coming closer and closer. When the unsuspecting miller came to the meadow still holding onto his stick, all the rats dashed out of their holes, and ran after him across the fields and meadows. Soon, they were all around him, some even running before him, and they arrived at his house before he did. Thereafter, they remained in his home as an intolerable plague.

## ‡‡ 247 ‡‡

## THE SNAKE CATCHER

There was once a sorcerer in Salzburg who boasted that he could conjure all the snakes in a one-mile radius of the city and that he would then lead them to a large hole where he would kill them. He succeeded in conjuring all the snakes into the hole, but crawling behind all the others, there came a giant venerable old serpent. When the sorcerer tried to entice it too into the hole, it whipped itself around his waist like a giant belt, dragged him into the hole, and killed him.

## ‡‡ 248 ‡‡

## THE LITTLE MOUSE

The following event took place at the beginning of the seventeenth century in the splendid noble residence at Wirbach, near Saalfeld in Thuringia. The servants were busy peeling fruit in one of the rooms when one of the maids became very sleepy. She left the others and lay down on a nearby bench in order to rest. After she had been lying there for a while, a small red mouse crawled out of her open mouth. Most of the other servants witnessed this event, and they commented on it to each other. The mouse then ran to the open window and crawled through to the out-of-doors.

After the mouse had been gone for some time, one of the other maids became inquisitive. She approached the soulless girl on the bench and began shaking her, but she could not be awakened. The maid then shoved the lifeless body to another place on the bench. Soon thereafter the mouse returned to the spot from which it had emerged from the girl's mouth. It ran back and forth, seeking in vain to return, and then the mouse disappeared. However, the girl was dead, and dead she remained. The meddlesome maid regretted what she had done, but it was too late.

Prior to this event, one of the farmhands at the residence had often been plagued by a Nightmare, finding no peace. But with the death of the maid, the attacks suddenly ceased.

## ‡‡ 249 ‡‡

## THE EMERGING PUFF OF SMOKE

In Hersfeld there were two maids serving in a certain household. They were in the habit of staying up in the parlor every evening after everyone else had retired, where they would sit quietly. The lord of the house grew curious about this odd behavior, and one evening he decided to stay awake and see what they were up to. Hiding himself in the room, he witnessed the two maids sitting quietly at the table. Finally, one of them stood up and uttered the words:

> Spirit, seek thine own joy
> And weigh upon yonder boy!

When she finished speaking, a puff of black smoke emerged from her mouth and from the mouth of her companion, and it disappeared out the window. The two maids sank immediately into a deep sleep. The lord of the house approached one of the maids, called her by name, and began shaking her, but she remained motionless. Finally, he turned and departed, leaving them alone in the room. The next morning the girl that he had shaken was dead. However, the other maid, the one he had not touched, was still alive.

## ‡‡ 250 ‡‡

## THE CAT IN THE WILLOW

A servant boy who worked for a farmer in Straßleben told of a certain maidservant who lived in the village. On occasion the girl disappeared from the dance, and no one knew where she went. However, after a time she would find her way home again.

One day the boy conspired with the other servants to follow this maid. The next Sunday she came to the dance and was having fun with all the servant boys when she again stole away. A number of them crept after her and they saw her leave the inn, run across the field, and without looking around, crawl into a hollow willow tree and hide herself. The boys, eager to see how long she would remain hidden in the tree, followed and spied on her from a place where they were well concealed.

After a short while they saw a cat dash out of the willow and run across the fields toward Langendorf. The boys then approached the willow and looked inside where they saw the girl, or rather her body which was quite stiff, leaning against the wall. Try as they would, poking and shaking her, they could not bring her to life.

Then, a feeling of dread came over them, so they left the body where it was and returned to their hiding place. After a while, they saw the cat return along the same path and crawl back into the hollow tree. The girl then emerged from the willow and returned to her village.

<br>

‡‡   251   ‡‡

## CREATING STORMS AND HAIL

In 1553 two sorceresses were arrested in Berlin, and they confessed to creating freezing weather in order to destroy the fruit crops. They had also stolen an infant from a neighbor, and chopped it up and cooked it. It came to pass through the will of God that the mother, while looking for her child, came to their house and saw a limb of her lost child sticking out of a pot. The two women were then taken into custody and interrogated, and they said that had they been permitted to continue cooking, a great cold spell with frost and ice would have set in, and the entire fruit crop would have been destroyed.

On another occasion two such sorceresses met in a tavern. They took two large tubs, filled them with water, and set them out in a special place. Then they proceeded to argue over whether they should make the wheat crop or the grape crop their target. The innkeeper, who had concealed himself around the corner, overheard the whole conversation. And that evening, after the two women had retired, he took the tubs and poured their contents over the women. The water instantly turned to ice and both women froze to death.

Once there was a poor widow who, while contemplating how to find some food for her children, went into the forest to gather wood.

As she walked along, thinking of her misfortune, she encountered the Evil One, who appeared before her disguised as a forester. He asked her why she was so sad. Had her husband died? She replied, "Yes." And he said, "If thou wouldst take me and be obedient to me, I will give thee money in abundance." After much persuasion, she finally gave in, denied God, and became the mistress of the Devil.

After a month's time her lover returned and handed her a broom. On this they rode through the air, through thick and thin, through sunshine and rain, arriving finally at a dance on top of a mountain. There were other women there, only two of whom she recognized. One of them gave the musician a fee of twelve pennies. After the dance all the witches came together. They took ears of grain and leaves from grapevines and oak trees, planning to wreak havoc on the grain, grape, and acorn crops. But they were not successful, for the hailstorm did not strike the targets it was destined for, drifting past them instead.

The widow herself killed a sheep by this method because it was so late returning home.

## ‡‡ 252 ‡‡

### THE WITCHES' SABBATH

A woman from the town of Hembach took her sixteen-year-old son, Johannes, to a Witches' Sabbath. Since he knew how to play the fife, she commended him as an accompanist for their dance. So that everyone could hear him better, she instructed him to climb to the top of the tallest tree. He obeyed and did so. As he was playing and watching the dance, and perhaps because he considered their actions weird and strange—for foolish behavior prevails at such meetings—he spoke out, saying, "Protect me, Dear Lord. Where have all these foolish and nonsensical people come from!" No sooner had he uttered these words than he fell from the tree, dislocating a shoulder. He called out for someone to help him, but other than himself there was no one there.

## ‡‡ 253 ‡‡

### THE GRAPEVINE AND THE NOSES

At the court of H. there was a fellow who was accustomed to entertaining the guests with strange and disgusting tricks of magic. After they had eaten they asked him, since they had come for that purpose, to perform one of his magic tricks for their enjoyment. He then caused a grapevine to grow from the table with bunches of grapes hanging from it, one for each guest. He commanded each of them to take a bunch of grapes in one hand and a knife in the other, placing the knife on the stem as if to cut it off. But he insisted that no one should actually cut the vine. He then left the room and returned somewhat later. They were all still sitting there, each one holding his own nose with a knife resting on it. Had they not followed his instructions, they would have done severe injury to their noses.

## ‡‡ 254 ‡‡

### HANGING FAST

There was at one time a mysterious sorcerer in Magdeburg. He once, in the presence of a large crowd of spectators from whom he had first collected a substantial amount of money, displayed a wondrous miniature horse that danced around in a circle. Just as the act was coming to a close, he began lamenting that he was unable to accomplish anything of use in this ungrateful world, that he was almost reduced to begging because of everyone's miserliness. He then explained that he wanted to take leave of this world and seek the most direct route to Heaven to see if his lot would not be better there. No sooner had he spoken these words than he threw a rope into the air upon which the little horse, without hesitation, proceeded to gallop skyward. The sorcerer caught the horse by the tail, the sorcerer's wife caught him by the feet, the maid caught the wife by the hem of her dress, and all of them, as if glued together, disappeared up the rope and into the sky.

As the crowd stood there, open-mouthed in astonishment at this strange series of events, a citizen chanced by and asked what they thought they were doing, standing around gaping like that. They replied that they had just seen the magician disappear into the sky with his horse. The citizen, however, told them that he had just seen the magician a moment before, walking toward his lodgings.

## ‡‡ 255 ‡‡

### THE SHIRT OF NEED

The Shirt of Need is prepared in the following manner. On Christmas Eve two innocent girls who are not yet seven years of age must spin some yarn and weave a shirt from it. Two heads are to be woven on the front of the shirt—one with a long beard and a helmet on the right side, and one with a crown something like the one the

Devil wears on the left. On each side there is to be a cross. The shirt should be long enough to cover half the body.

Whoever wears such a shirt into battle will remain protected from lances, swords, bullets, and all other harm. Because of this, the shirt is highly cherished by emperors and princes. Women in childbirth also wear this shirt to deliver with greater ease. *Contra vero tale indusium, viro tamen mortuo ereptum, a foeminis luxuriosis quaeri ferunt, quo indutae non amplius gravescere perhibentur.* *

## ‡‡ 256 ‡‡
## FATE SECURED

Once, during the siege of a fortress, a noble soldier was seen dodging back and forth with two others just across the moat, while shots rained down on him from the walls. But he was zigzagging from left to right with his adjutants, and he ordered both of them to stay close to him and not to duck the shots. The volleys of bullets all fell to one side, wounding neither him nor the other two.

There was also once a general who had to flee from a battle, seeking haven in a city. He then shook the musket bullets from his sleeves like split peas. None of them had been able to wound him.

Master Peter, a barber in Wittenberg, had a son-in-law who was an infantryman in the war. He understood the art of making himself invulnerable to all weapons. Moreover he was able to prophesy his own death, saying: "My brother-in-law is going to do it." That very day he told his wife, "Go shopping, for you are going to receive some guests today, or rather, they will be spectators." This also came to pass, for after his brother-in-law stabbed him to death, everyone ran into the barber's house wanting to see the corpse of the murdered man.

## ‡‡ 257 ‡‡
## THE CRACK SHOT

A master gunsmith I knew once boasted that he could hit everything in range of his rifle even if he couldn't see the object, and that he had made use of this skill during the siege of the city of W.

The Colonel, a noble gentleman who was the leader of the attack, was lurking in the forest outside the city. Although the gun-

---

*It is also said that when this article of apparel has been removed from a corpse, it is especially desired by sensuous women, for when they wear it, they are protected from pregnancies.— *D. W.*

smith could not see him, he declared that he wanted to shoot him dead. Even though he was told not to, he fired at the tree behind which the colonel was sitting on his horse, casually eating his breakfast. The bullet hit the Colonel and saved the city.

Valvassor* recalls a noble gentleman who had been granted three shots a day that would never miss. With these he was able to hit without fail any target one suggested. Such a marksman only needs to let someone declare what he should shoot—a stag, a deer, a hare—and then all he has to do is to point the gun out the window, fire at random, and the game will drop dead.

## ‡‡ 258 ‡‡
## THE NOMADIC HUNTSMAN

It came to pass that a forester in charge of a huge forest preserve was shot to death. The nobleman who owned the forest commissioned a replacement, but he too fell victim to the same fate, as did several others who followed. Finally, no one was willing to take charge of this dangerous forest. No sooner would a new forester assume his position than a shot would ring out from afar and he would drop dead, shot through the forehead. And there was never a trace of where or from whom the shot came.

Nevertheless, a few years later a nomadic hunter applied for the position. The nobleman did not conceal from him what had happened to the others. He even added that happy as he was to have the forest again under supervision, he could not in all honesty counsel him to accept the dangerous office. The hunter replied confidently that he would devise a means of protecting himself from the invisible marksman, and he took charge of the forest.

The next day when he, accompanied by several others, was first led into the forest, a shot rang out from afar. The hunter immediately threw his hat in the air, and when it fell to earth it had been hit by a bullet.

"Now," he said, "it's my turn." He loaded his rifle, and as he fired into the air he said, "My bullet will deliver the answer!" Thereupon, he bade his companions to accompany him on the search for the culprit.

After roaming around the forest for a long time, they finally found a mill at the other end of the forest. Inside, they found the miller, shot through the forehead by the hunter's bullet. The nomadic huntsman remained in the service of the nobleman for some

*Ehre von Crain, I, 676.

time. But since he was able to keep the game spellbound when he wished, could conjure partridges out of his pocket, was able to hit his target from quite incredible distances, and was the master of many another similar trick, the nobleman began to develop a dread of him, and he used a clever ruse to release him from his service.

‡‡  259  ‡‡

## THE DOUBLE

A vagabond once approached a nobleman who had been suffering for some time from fainting spells and loss of strength. He said to him, "You have been cast under an evil spell. Should I bring the woman responsible for this before your very eyes?" When the nobleman gave his assent, the man said, "The woman who comes to your house in the morning, makes a fire in your hearth, and grabs the kettle hanger in her hand and holds onto it is the one who is causing all your suffering."

The following morning the wife of one of his subjects, who lived next to him—a pious and honest woman—arrived and did exactly as the vagabond had predicted. The nobleman was quite mystified as to how such an honorable and God-fearing woman, to whom he wished no evil, could be capable of committing such evil deeds.

He began to doubt if things were as he had been led to believe. And he therefore gave a servant the secret command to run next door and see if the neighbor woman was home or not. When the servant arrived, the woman was sitting at her work, combing flax. He instructed her to come with him to her lord, and she replied, "It is not proper that I should appear before the nobleman so unkempt and dirty." The servant assured her that it was all right in this case, that she should hasten and accompany him there.

The moment she stepped through the door of the squire's house, the imposter disappeared from the hall like a ghost. The squire thanked God that he had given him the presence of mind to send the servant to the woman. Otherwise he would have trusted the Devil's illusion and would have had the innocent woman burned at the stake.

‡‡  260  ‡‡

## THE GHOST POSING AS A WIFE

Back in the days when Duke Johann Casimir of Coburg was still ruling, his stablemaster, G. P. v. Z., lived in town, first on Spitalgasse, then in the house that was later occupied by Dr. Frommann, and subsequently in a large suburban villa called Rosenau. From there, he finally moved into the castle itself, where he became major domo. He was forced into these many changes of residence by a ghost identical in appearance to his wife who was still living. The situation grew so bad that when he came into his new home and sat down at the table, he was never certain whether the woman sitting across from him was his own living wife.

The ghost followed him everywhere, even when he moved from one house to another. When his wife suggested that they move into the home that later belonged to the doctor in order to escape the ghost, it began speaking in a loud voice, telling them, "You can move wherever you wish, for I shall move right behind you, anywhere in the whole world." These words were no empty threat, for after the stablemaster moved out, he had the entrance to the rear building bricked up. But the ghost was never again reported in this house; instead, it appeared in the house into which he had just moved.

Whatever clothes his wife put on, the ghost appeared in the same garments, whether formal evening dress or everyday attire, nor did it matter what color it was. For this reason the wife never went about her household duties alone but always made sure she had someone with her. Usually, the ghost appeared around midday, between eleven and twelve o'clock. If a clergyman was in the house, however, it did not put in an appearance.

On one occasion the priest, Johann Prüscher had been invited, and when it came time for him to leave, the nobleman, his wife, and sister accompanied him to the top of the stairs. The ghost then began to ascend the stairway from below, grabbed the sister's skirt through the wooden railing, and then disappeared when she began to scream.

Once, it was seen at the kitchen threshold, leaning against the doorframe. The cook asked, "What do you want?" And it replied, "I want your lady." Otherwise, it did the noblewoman no harm. However, it did remain a threat to the nobleman's sister. On one occasion it slapped her across the face so hard that her cheek became swollen and she had to return home to her father's house. Finally, though, the ghost vanished, and the house became peaceful once again.

## ‡‡ 261 ‡‡

## THE DEATH OF THE FIRSTBORN

Several hundred years ago, the first child, an infant son, of a noble family was found one morning dead in bed, lying next to the nurse-maid. She was suspected of having suffocated the child intentionally, and even though she insisted on her innocence, she was sentenced to death. As she knelt down and was about to receive the death blow, she spoke one last time, "My innocence is as certain as the fact that from now on every firstborn child in this family will die." After she had spoken these words, a white dove flew above her head, whereupon she was executed. The prophecy was fulfilled, and the oldest son of this house has always died in his early years.

‡‡ 262 ‡‡

## THE BOY OF COLMAR

In the Pfeffel house in Colmar there once lived a child who refused to walk across a certain spot in the family garden, although his companions played there without concern.

No one understood why the child behaved this way, and on one occasion they pulled him forcefully to this spot. His hair stood on end and a cold sweat broke out over his whole body. When he finally regained his senses, they asked him the reason for his fear. For a long time he refused to speak up. But finally, after much persuasion, he said, "A man was buried on this spot. His hands are crossed like this, and his legs are like this (he described the positions in detail), and there's a ring on one of his fingers."

The others began to dig beneath this grassy spot. Barely three feet down, they found a skeleton lying in the very position the child had described, and there was a ring on the finger the boy had named. Then they gave the remains a decent burial. The child, who was told nothing about their digging up the corpse, played on the site without concern from that time on.

This child had the ability to see the figures of corpses in the haze over the site where they lay, and he could recognize all the details. Because he saw so many of these terrifying apparitions, the boy began to pine away and soon died.

‡‡ 263 ‡‡

## THE DEATH OF THE CANON OF MERSEBURG

Many years ago in the cathedral of Merseburg, the following events used to occur three weeks before the death of a canon. A great racket would be heard during the night. Then a violent blow, as though from the clenched fist of a mighty man, would strike the chair of the one who was to die. Many guards made their rounds through the church day and night because of the splendid treasures there. And as soon as they perceived this activity, they would report it to the church authorities. The canon whose chair had received the blow interpreted the report as a personal notice that his time was due, that in three weeks he would join the pale ranks.

## ‡‡ 264 ‡‡

### THE LILY IN THE MONASTERY OF CORVEY

The monastery of the Abbey at Corvey on the Weser River received a strange dispensation from God. Whenever one of the monks was to die, he received a warning three days prior to his departure. A lily would appear on a brass wreath that hung in the choir. Each time, the lily descended wondrously upon the chair of the brother whose end was at hand. Thus, he could not fail to perceive it, and he knew he must depart the world in three days.

This miracle is said to have continued for several centuries. But then, a young brother of the order, who had been warned of his approaching hour of death in this fashion, showed contempt for the omen. He moved the lily to the chair of an elderly monk because it seemed to him more appropriate for an old man to die than a young one. When the kindly elderly monk saw the lily he took such a bad turn, perhaps from the smell of death, that he became very ill. But instead of going immediately to his grave, he recovered completely. However, the young man who had shown contempt for the warning was torn away on the third day by a miserable death.

## ‡‡ 265 ‡‡

### CANON REBUNDUS OF THE CATHEDRAL IN LÜBECK

In olden times, when a canon of Lübeck was soon to die, he would find a white rose beneath the cushion of his chair in the choir. It soon became the custom of the monks, upon arriving, to turn over their cushions to see if this omen of the grave was lying underneath.

It came to pass that one of the canons, whose name was Rebundus, found this rose beneath his cushion one morning. Because it appeared to his eyes to be more a tormenting strip of thorns than a rose, he removed it with trembling hands and placed it beneath the cushion of his neighbor, although the latter had already looked under his cushion and found nothing. Thereupon Rebundus asked him, didn't he want to turn his cushion over. The other replied that he had done so already. But Rebundus continued. No doubt he hadn't looked carefully enough, perhaps he should look once again, for Rebundus believed he had seen something white glimmering there when he looked in that direction.

Whereupon the canon turned his cushion over and found the grave flower. He then spoke angrily, saying that this was deceit, for he'd looked carefully enough the first time and he'd found no rose beneath his seat. And he shoved it back under Rebundus' cushion. The latter, however, not wanting it forced upon him again, cast it back at the other canon. And then a heated argument ensued.

When the head canon intervened and separated them, Rebundus completely refused to confess that he had received the rose first. Instead he persisted in his untruth. Finally, the other canon became bitterly impatient and he delivered a curse, saying, "May God grant that whichever of us is wrong become the omen himself and replace the rose. When a canon is to die, may he signal from his grave by knocking, and may he continue to do this until Judgment Day."

Rebundus, who respected this curse about as much as the empty wind, added blasphemously, "Amen! So be it!"

Soon thereafter Rebundus died. And from that time on, whenever a canon neared his end, there was a frightful knocking from beneath Rebundus' gravestone. Thus arose the proverb: "Rebundus has moved in his grave and a canon shall die."

Actually, it is not merely knocking that one hears. Instead, three great roars resound from beneath his massive gravestone—and these are about as soft as striking thunderbolts or large cannon saluting three times. With the third roar, the sound reverberates through the entire vault of the cathedral with such great fury and duration that one is certain the entire vault together with the cathedral is about to collapse into a pile of rubble. The sound can be heard not only in the cathedral but also in the surrounding houses.

On a certain Sunday, between nine and ten in the morning, Rebundus began to roar with great fury during the sermon. A number of journeymen who were standing on the stone listening to the sermon were—partially from shock and partially from the quaking motion of the gravestone—knocked down and scattered as though they had been struck by lightning. At the third terrible blow, everyone was ready to flee from the church, believing it was about to collapse. But the priest gathered his courage and told his congregation to remain seated and not be afraid for it was only a diabolic spook intent on disturbing the divine service. They should show contempt for him, and offer him faith not spite. However, a few weeks later death struck the son of the deacon, for Rebundus also raged when a near relative of a canon was to go to his grave.

## THE BELL THAT RINGS ITSELF

On the twenty-seventh of March in the year 1686 in a famous imperial city, the market bell struck three times all by itself. Soon thereafter, the Lord of the Council, who was also Chief Market Inspector,
died.

On two other occasions, six or seven weeks before the death of
the head of the house, a shrill bell began to peal within the house.
Since the head of the house at that time was in good health, although his wife was confined to bed, he forbade the servants to
mention the occurrence to her. He feared it might frighten her, and
that her melancholy imagination would give her a turn for the
worse, perhaps even cause her death. But this sign had been intended for him alone, for he soon came to his grave, while his wife
recovered her full health.

Seventeen weeks later, as she was busy cleaning and brushing
her late husband's suits and coats, the farm bell began swinging all
by itself and before her startled eyes and ears it rang out its usual
sound. One week later her eldest son fell ill, and within a few days
he died. Soon thereafter, this widow remarried and had several
children by her second husband. But all of them withered like the
flowers of March and were buried within a few weeks. In each case,
the bell rang three times, although the room in which it hung was
locked to prevent anyone from touching the rope.

Some people believe that the bell ringing (which is usually not
heard by those who are ill or lie dying but rather by others) is
caused by evil spirits. Others believe it comes from good angels. Still
others maintain that the ringing is caused by protective spirits who
seek to remind people to prepare for the end toward which we all
hasten.

## SPIRIT OF DEATH

A spirit appears in the cities of Schwaz and Innsbruck in Tyrol,
when a death is imminent—sometimes he is small, sometimes he is
as large as a house. Whenever he appears and looks in at a window,
the people in that house will die.

## MOTHER BERTHA OR THE WHITE WOMAN

The White Woman appears in the castles of a number of royal families, especially at the residences of Neuhaus in Bohemia, Berlin, Bayreuth, Darmstadt, and Karlsruhe, and over the years in all residences of families that have become related to these houses by marriage. She does no one any harm, and when she meets someone she bows her head and says nothing. But her visit means that a death is near. Yet, when she is not wearing a black glove, her appearance can mean joyful news. She carries a ring of keys and wears a veiled white hood.

According to some people, when she was still living she was called Perchta von Rosenberg. She lived in Neuhaus in Bohemia and was married to Johann von Lichtenstein, an evil, stubborn man. After the death of her husband, she lived as a widow in Neuhaus and began—much to the chagrin of her subjects, who were obliged to serve her—to build a palace. While they were working, she constantly called out to them to work hard, telling them, "When the palace is finished, I shall serve you and your families a sweet porridge," for the elderly frequently used this proverb when they invited someone as a guest.

In the fall, after the completion of the structure, she not only was as good as her word—she made provision for all the Rosenbergs to give their people such a meal for all eternity. And, indeed, this event has taken place ever since.* If the family fails to provide the meal, she appears before them with an angry countenance.

At times she is said to appear in the royal nurseries when the nursemaids are asleep at night, to cradle the children and carry them around. Once a shocked uninformed nursemaid asked her, "What concern of yours are these children?" and began scolding her with angry words.

The White Woman replied, "I am not, like you, a stranger in these walls. I am a member of the family, and this child is descended from the children of my children. But since you refuse to pay me homage, I shall nevermore return."

## WILD BERTHA WILL COME

In Swabia, Franconia, and Thuringia, obstinate children are chided with these words: "Be silent or Wild Bertha will come!" She is called Bildaberta, and Hildaberta by others, and even Iron Bertha.

*The porridge is prepared from peas and wild groats, and fish is always served with it.

She appears as a Wild Woman with shaggy hair, and she befouls the dresses of maidens who do not finish spinning all their flax on the last day of the year. Many people eat dumplings and herring on this day, believing that, if they don't, Perchta or Prechta will cut their stomachs open, remove the contents, and fill them with chopped straw. Then she will sew up the incision, using a plowshare instead of a needle and an iron chain instead of thread.

## ‡‡ 270 ‡‡
### THE TÜRST, THE POSTERLI, AND THE STRÄGGELE

When storms rage and howl through the forest at night, the people in the region around Lucerne say, "The Türst (or the giant) is hunting!"

In Entlebuch one speaks instead of the Posterli, a female monster who, according to the local people, goes hunting on the Thursday before Christmas, leading a vast horde and making a tremendous noise and racket.

In the city of Lucerne, the name Sträggele refers to a witch who is up to no good on the holy fasting night of the Wednesday before Christmas Eve. She is also known to plague girls who have not spun their daily allotment in a number of ways. For this reason this night is also known as the Night of the Sträggele.

## ‡‡ 271 ‡‡
### THE NIGHT HUNTER AND THE SHAKING WOMEN

At night the inhabitants of the Giant Mountains of Silesia often hear the call of the Huntsman, the sounding of the horn, and the roaring of the wild animals. At such times they say, "The Night Hunter is hunting!" Small children are afraid of him, and they can be silenced by shouts of, "Be still! Don't you hear the Night Hunter hunting?"

Above all he hunts the Shaking Wives, supposedly small women clothed in moss. He terrifies them, and pursues them relentlessly, unless they can first reach a felled tree over which a woodsman has spoken the words "God disposes!" On such a log the creatures find sanctuary. However, should the woodsman say, when he first strikes the tree with his ax, "It disposes God," so the word "God" comes at the end, then such a tree cannot provide peace and asylum for a Shaking Woman. Instead, she must flee constantly from the Night Hunter.

## THE MAN IN THE SLOUCH HAT

A few years ago there was an old woman who still lived in one of the rooms of the castle of Freienstein. One evening a man entered the room quite nonchalantly. He was wearing a grey cloak and a large slouch hat, and he had a long beard. He hung his hat on a nail, and paying heed to no one, sat himself down at the table. He then pulled a small pipe from his sack and began smoking and he remained sitting thus at the table. The old woman did not wish to wait for his departure so she went to bed. In the morning the ghostly figure had disappeared.

The mayor's son tells the following story. "On the morning after Christmas, while church services were being held, my grandmother was sitting in our parlor praying. As she looked up from her book and glanced into the palace garden, she saw a man in a grey cloak and a slouch hat standing there. From time to time she saw him hoeing in the garden. Later we, and all the neighbors as well, saw him too. Just as the sun was going down, he disappeared."

## THE GREY HOCKELMAN

One evening many years ago, a farmer from Auerbach was walking past Castle Mountain. Suddenly, he was stopped by a grey man and forced to carry him on his shoulders up the hill to the castle. The farmer was found the next day upon a dark stairway in the castle, suffering from overexhaustion. A short time later, he died.

## CHIMMEKE OF POMERANIA

A Poltergeist, whom the old people of Pomerania called Chimmeke, is said to have chopped up a kitchen boy at the castle of Loyz and to have stuffed him into an earthenware jar because he drank the milk that was set out for the spirit every night in the age of superstition. For many years the inhabitants of the castle displayed the pot Chimmeke used to cool his temper.

## THE SHRIEKER

On the twelfth of March, 1753, Johann Peter Kriechbaum, mayor of the village of Zent in the region of Oberkrainsbach, told the following story.

In the region called the Spreng there lives a spirit or ghost, who makes all kinds of animal noises, such as those of a deer, fox, jackass, hound, swine, and many other animals and birds. Because of this, the local inhabitants call him the Shrieker. He has led many people astray, and no one, not even a shepherd, dares to remain long in the meadows of his territory.

Mayor Kriechbaum himself encountered the spirit recently as he was walking across the meadow of the Spreng one evening, making plans to channel his waters for irrigation. As he approached the forest on the side facing Langenbrombach, he heard a wild boar screaming as though it had just had its throat cut with a knife.

The spirit continued until it entered Holler Forest, where charcoal was still being made sixteen years ago. The charcoal burners used to complain frequently about the ghost, and they told of being frightened many times by him in the shape of a jackass.

A similar report was given by the late Johann Peter Weber. He used to load charcoal in the forest at night to transport it to the forge in Michelstadt.

Heinrich Germann, the former Mayor of Zent, confirmed that once, while tending his oxen in the meadows of the Spreng, a fox came running toward him. But after he cracked his whip in its direction, it vanished instantly.

## FERRYING THE MONKS

Many years ago in the city of Speyer there lived a fisherman. One night, just as he came to the Rhine River and was about to set out his lines, a man wearing a black monk's cloak stepped up to him. After the fisherman greeted him politely, he said, "I come as a messenger from afar and would like to be transported across the Rhine."

"Step into my boat," said the fisherman, "and I will ferry thee across."

After he had taken him across and returned, five more monks were standing on the bank, and they too desired to be ferried across the river. When the fisherman asked them why they were traveling in the dark of night, one of the monks replied, "We are driven by need. The world is our enemy, so please accept us and God's reward for the deed." The fisherman demanded to know what they were willing to give him for his work. "Now we are poor," said the monk, "but when things go better for us, thou shalt perceive our gratitude."

The boatman shoved off, but when the boat reached the middle of the Rhine, a terrifying storm blew up and huge waves crashed over the boat. The fisherman turned pale. "What can this be?" he asked himself. "When the sun went down, the skies were clear and bright and the moon shone beautifully. Whence comes this furious storm so suddenly?"

And as he raised his hands to pray to God, one of the monks called out, "What art thou doing filling God's ears with prayers? Steer thy ship!" With these words he tore the oar from the poor fisherman's hands and beat him with it. As he lay half dead in his boat the day began to dawn, and suddenly the men in black disappeared and the heavens were as clear as they had been before. The boatman pulled himself together, rowed back, and managed to reach his home only with great difficulty.

The next day a messenger who had departed early from Speyer met these same monks as they were riding in a rattling carriage covered all in black. It had only three wheels and was driven by a coachman with a long nose. The messenger stood there silently aghast as the carriage drew past. Shortly, he saw it disappear into the air in roaring flames, and then he heard the clanging noises of swords, as though an army were going into battle. The messenger turned around, returned to the city, and revealed all he had seen. One concluded from this vision that there was discord among the German princes.

‡‡　277　‡‡

## THE WILL-O'-THE-WISP

In Hänlein on the Mountain Highway, and also in the region of Lorsch, Will-o'-the-Wisps are called the Heerwische. They are said to appear during Advent, and there is a verse customarily directed at them:

> Heerwisch! Haw, Haw!
> Burn like oat straw!
> Strike me lightning fast!

It is said that more than thirty years ago a girl saw a Heer-wisch, and she taunted it with the rhyme. It flew directly at the girl, who turned and fled home to her parents. But it followed right on her heels into the room. There, it struck everyone present with its fiery wings and they lost both sight and hearing.

## ‡‡ 278 ‡‡
## THE FLAMING CARRIAGES

Konrad Schäfer from Gammelsbach tells the following story.

"A few years ago I used to keep fruit trees on the Hirschhorn Plateau, not far from the old castle of Freienstein. One night at midnight I encountered two fiery carriages that were making a terri-fying clatter. Each was harnessed with four fiery steeds. The proces-sion was coming directly from Freienstein. I have encountered it often, and each time I have been terror-stricken, for there were people sitting in the carriages and fire and flame leaped from their mouths and from their eyes."

## ‡‡ 279 ‡‡
## RÄDER MOUNTAIN

A butcher from Nassau once went out on foot to make some pur-chases. Upon the highway he soon encounters a coach driving along, and he walks behind it on foot, following the wheel ruts while in-volved in his own thoughts.* Without warning, the coach stops in front of a large beautiful villa by the highway. As often as he has traveled this route, he has never seen it before. Three monks climb out of the carriage, and the astonished butcher follows them unno-ticed into the well-lit house. First they enter a room and offer some-one communion, and then they go into a hall where a large party is seated around a table, devouring a meal with great clamor and revelry.

Suddenly the man seated at the head of the table notices the butcher, and all at once everything becomes still and quiet. Then, the foremost member of the party rises and offers a beaker of wine to the butcher, saying, "One more day!" The butcher feels a dreadful trembling overcome him, and he does not want to drink. But shortly

*The sudden change to the present tense is a characteristic trait of the oral narra-tion of legend texts. Narrators frequently switched to the present tense at the moment of highest suspense and excitement.—D. W.

after, a second member of the party rises and approaches the butcher also carrying a beaker of wine and saying, "One more day." The butcher again refuses. Thereupon, a third person approaches with a beaker and repeats the words, "One more day!"

This time the butcher drinks. But no sooner has he done so than a fourth member of the party approaches him, again offering wine. The butcher becomes terribly frightened and makes the sign of the cross. Instantly, the entire apparition disappears and he is plunged into impenetrable darkness.

When dawn finally breaks, the butcher finds himself on Räder Mountain, far from the highway. He proceeds down the difficult rocky path back to his native city. There, he recounts the entire episode to his clergyman and within three days he is dead.

An old legend has it that a monastery once stood on that mountain, and its ruins can still be seen. The religious order, however, long ago died out.


‡‡   280   ‡‡

## THE LIGHTS ON THE HALBERDS

An hour from Ingweiler on a high cliff in the lower Alsace, stands the ancient Hanauan castle of Lichtenberg. The following story is told about it.

Everytime it storms with thunder and lightning, one can see upon the roofs and turrets of the castle, indeed, even upon the points of the halberds, scores of tiny blue flames. This phenomenon has continued for many long years and according to some it is responsible for the name of the old castle.*

Two farmers were once traveling on foot from the village of Langenstein (located near Kirchhain, in Upper Hesse) on their way to Embsdorf, carrying pitchforks on their shoulders. Along the way one of them chanced to notice a small flame on his companion's halberd, and he smilingly stroked the glittering spot with his fingers until it vanished.

They had hardly traveled another hundred steps when the small flame once again flickered on the same spot. And, once again, it was wiped off. Soon thereafter it appeared on the same spot for the third time. The first farmer then uttered a few coarse words and wiped the blade once more. This time the flame did not return.

A week later, at the very spot where the first farmer had wiped

---

*Lichtenberg translates as Mountain of Lights.—D. W.

the flame away for the other, the two farmers, who had until then been the best of friends, met and fell into an argument. It grew into a fight wherein one of the friends stabbed the other to death.

## ‡‡ 281 ‡‡
## WAFELING

Along the Baltic Sea people believe that ships about to sink or become stranded can be seen in advance as they often haunt the sites where they will meet their doom for some days or weeks. They appear at night as dark silhouettes with all parts of the ship—the hull, the rigging, the masts, and the sails—enveloped in fire. The people call this phenomenon "Wafeling."

People who will drown, houses that will soon burn down, and cities that will sink also "wafel." And on Sundays one can still hear the bells of sunken cities tolling beneath the surface of the water.

## ‡‡ 282 ‡‡
## THE CASTLE OF FLAMES

There is an old castle situated upon a high mountain in Tyrol. Every night a fire burns in the castle and the flames leap so high above the castle walls that they can be seen far and wide.

It once came to pass that a poor woman in need of firewood was gathering fallen brushwood on the mountainside until she reached the castle gate. She grew curious and looked around. And then she entered, but not without difficulty, for everything was in ruins and it was not easy to advance on foot. When she came to the courtyard, she saw a party of gentlemen and ladies sitting at a large table eating. Servants were waiting upon them, changing plates, carrying food to and fro, and pouring the wine. As she stood there, one of the servants approached and led her to the others. Someone then threw a gold piece into her apron—and in an instant everything vanished.

Quite frightened, the poor woman sought the way back. But as she attempted to leave the courtyard, a warrior with a burning torch appeared before her. His head was not sitting upon his neck; instead he held it beneath his arm. He began to speak, forbidding the woman to reveal to anyone what she had seen and learned there, otherwise great evil would befall her.

The woman returned home still full of fear. She brought the gold piece with her, but she told no one where she had gotten it.

When the authorities got word of this she was called before them, but she refused to utter a word, explaining that if she did, great harm would befall her. After they began to deal with her more severely, however, she revealed everything that had happened to her in the flaming castle, down to the smallest detail. But the moment she finished her statement she was swept away, and no one ever discovered where she had gone.

During the second year after this event, a young nobleman spent some time in this town. He was a knight and well experienced in all matters. When he learned the details of this episode, he set out on foot late at night with his servant to climb the mountain. They made the ascent with great difficulty, and while they were underway they were warned six times by a voice which said that if they continued they would learn the truth only at the cost of great harm to themselves. Paying no heed, they continued on their way and finally arrived at the gate.

The same warrior as before was standing there as sentry, and he called out the customary "Who goes there?"

The nobleman, being a bold gentleman, replied, "It is I!"

The ghostly warrior again challenged, "Who art thou?"

This time the nobleman did not reply but ordered his servant to hand him his sword. As he did, a black knight came riding out of the castle on horseback, and the nobleman made ready to fight him. However, the knight pulled him up on his horse and took him back to the courtyard, while the sentry chased the servant down the mountain.

The nobleman was never seen again.

## ‡‡ 283 ‡‡

### FIRE MOUNTAIN

A few hours from Halberstadt lies a mountain that is now covered with tall fir and oak trees. But it was formerly quite bare, and called by many Fire Mountain. The Devil is said to conduct his diabolic affairs deep within this mountain, where everything burns in bright flames.

In olden times in the region of Halberstadt there lived a count who was evil and rapacious, and who sorely oppressed the inhabitants of the land. For many years he had owed a large sum of money to a shepherd, but whenever the man came to remind him, the count dismissed him with vicious contempt. Suddenly, the count vanished from sight and was said to have died in a foreign land. The shepherd wandered his meadows in distress, lamenting his loss, for the heirs and descendants of the count claimed to know nothing of his demand. They chased him down the mountain from the castle whenever he came to see them.

Once, when he was in the forest, it came to pass that a figure approached him and said, "If you want to see your old debtor, then come with me." The shepherd followed, and they walked through the woods until they came to a large bare mountain, which opened up before them with a great roar. The mountain accepted them and then closed behind them.

Inside, everything was flame and fire, and the shepherd saw the count sitting on a chair surrounded by a thousand flames dancing and shimmering off the glowing walls and floor. The sinner cried, "Wouldst thou have thy money? Then take this cloth and bring it to my family and tell them that thou hast seen me in the fires of Hell where I must suffer for all eternity." He then tore a cloth from his head and gave it to the shepherd, who saw sparks shooting from the count's eyes and hands.

With trembling legs, the shepherd hastened with his guide back the way they had come. The mountain again opened and closed behind them. He then went to the count's castle with his cloth. He showed it to the count's family, and told them what he had seen, and they gladly gave him his money.

## ‡‡ 284 ‡‡

### THE MAN OF FIRE

"In this year (1125) we* saw a fiery man walking between the two castles called Gleichen. It was right at midnight. The man walked from the one castle to the other, and he burned like a bright flame."

The sentries who tell this story report that he did this for three nights and no more.

Georg Miltenberger, who lived in the so-called Hoppelrain† near Kailbach in the region of Freienstein, tells the following story. "It was on the first Sunday of Advent between eleven and twelve o'clock when I saw, not far from my house, a man who was completely enveloped in fire. One could count all the ribs in his body. He remained on the road from one milestone to the next until right after midnight, when he vanished."

*The "we" in the legend is not identified. See, however, Sources and Addenda and Source Bibliography for the sources used by the Grimms.— D. W.

†"Hoppelrain" is evidently a local name. The region is referred to as the "so-called" Hoppelrain because the name is not official.— D. W.

Many people have been struck with fear and terror at the sight of this man because he spews fire from his nose and mouth, and because he can fly back and forth, here and there, at great speed.

## ‡‡ 285 ‡‡
## THE ACCURSED SURVEYORS

The Will-o'-the-Wisps that are seen at night flying back and forth around riverbanks and hedgerows are said to have once been land surveyors who practiced deceit when measuring the boundaries of property. In their afterlife they are condemned to wander around and watch over those very boundaries.

## ‡‡ 286 ‡‡
## THE DISPLACED BORDER STONE

A ghostly spirt in human form is frequently seen around fields and grazing lands near the town of Eger, and he is called by the local people Squire Ludwig. It is said that a man by this name once lived here, and that he deceitfully displaced field and boundary stones. Soon after his death he began wandering around, and many a person has been terror-stricken after encountering him.

Even recently, a girl from the city had such an experience. She was walking alone outside the town gate and chanced into the infamous region. At the site where the border stone is said to have been moved, a man came walking toward her. He looked just the way people had often described the evil squire. He lunged at her and grabbed one of her breasts in his fist and then vanished. In deep shock, the girl ran home to her family and said, "I have received my share." It was discovered that her breast had become black where the spirit had grabbed her. She immediately took to her bed, and within three days she departed this life.

## ‡‡ 287 ‡‡
## THE BOUNDARY DISPUTE

A dispute over their boundary once arose between the Hessian village of Wilmshausen, not far from Münden, and the neighboring village. There was no apparent way to reconcile the matter to everyone's satisfaction, so the villagers agreed to let a crayfish run across the disputed property. They were to follow it and then set the boundary stones accordingly. But because the crayfish wandered back and forth in a curious manner the border there is very strange, with all kinds of sharp angles and corners and it remains that way to this very day.

## THE RACE FOR THE BOUNDARY

Over Klausen Pass, beyond the watershed and Schächen Valley, there is a large stretch of land along Fletsch Creek called Uri. This extends as far as the region of Glarus. The inhabitants of Uri once had a dispute with the inhabitants of Glarus over the boundary separating them, and people began to heap insults and wreak harm on each other daily.

Finally, the righteous leaders proclaimed that at the equinox, at the moment the cock crowed in the morning, each side would send a robust, skillful mountain climber running toward the boundary territory. At the point where the men met, the boundary line was to be drawn, no matter if the shorter part fell on one side or the other. The contestants were chosen. And special heed was paid to finding a cock that would not fail to crow and that would announce the morn at the earliest possible moment.

The inhabitants of Uri took their cock and placed it in a basket. In the belief that hunger and thirst would make it waken earlier, they gave it very little to eat or drink. The inhabitants of Glarus, by contrast, fed and fattened their cock so that he would be able to greet the dawn with joy and glory, and they were convinced that they would fare better by this method.

When fall came and the chosen day arrived, it came to pass that in the village of Altdorf, the hungry cock crowed first, right at the crack of dawn. The mountain climber of Uri took off happily, racing toward the boundary territory.

In the Lin Valley, by contrast, full dawn had already lit the whole sky and the stars had disappeared, but the fat cock still slept in blissful peace. Sadly, the entire community surrounded him, but honesty prevailed and no one dared awaken him. Finally, he began flapping his wings, and then he crowed.

Now it would be difficult for the runner from Glarus to make up the advantage gained by the man from Uri! Anxiously, he started off. But woe! Looking up at the brow of the ridge, he saw the other man already coming down the mountain. The man from Glarus pushed himself to the limit in hopes of saving as much territory as possible for his people. Before long the two men met, and the man from Uri cried, "This is where the boundary will be."

"Neighbor," said the man from Glarus sadly, "be just. Grant me still a portion of the grazing land that thou hast acquired."

The man from Uri stood firm. But the man from Glarus left him no peace until he finally showed compassion and said, "I shall grant thee land as far as thou canst carry me on thy back up the mountainside."

The righteous herdsman from Glarus took him on his back and climbed up the cliff with him. He was about to drop, but managed to stagger a few more steps, until finally his breath ran out, and he sank to the ground dead.

To this very day people still point to Boundary Creek, where the dying man from Glarus carried the triumphant man from Uri. Great joy reigned in Uri over their victory. But in Glarus the inhabitants paid deserving honors to their herdsman, and they preserved his great loyal deed in everlasting memory.

## ‡‡ 289 ‡‡
### THE ALPINE BATTLE

Once the herdsmen of Obwalden had a dispute with the herdsmen of Entlebuch over some pasture land, but the Obwalden cowherds were in possession of the land, and they continued to drive their cattle there. Still they were worried that their bold opponents might attack, so they set out sentries to guard their herd. Meanwhile, the clever, quick-witted inhabitants of Entlebuch thought up a ruse. They feigned a neighborly peace for a time, until the trusting herdsmen from Obwalden, who suspected nothing, began to combat their boredom by playing games instead of keeping watch. The daring cowherds of Entlebuch then stole secretly to the poorly guarded meadow, quietly removed all the cowbells from the cattle, and quickly led their booty away. However, one of them had to remain behind to keep ringing the cowbells until the rustlers had reached safety. He did so, and then he threw the whole pile of bells on the ground and took off at a run while laughing tauntingly at his enemies. The herdsmen of Oberwalden were alarmed by the racket, but they discovered their misfortune too late.

In revenge they gathered together a troop of their own people and staged a sudden attack on the inhabitants of Entlebuch. But the latter were ready and waiting. Not only were the people of Oberwalden unable to erase their disgrace, they were once again humiliated in defeat.

The people of Entlebuch still keep the banner they won in the encounter in a hiding place in the old tower in the village of Schüpfen. The site where the battle took place is still called the Alpine Battlefield.

## ‡‡ 290 ‡‡
## THE ROCK OF WENTHUSEN

Many years ago there was a convent at Wenthusen in the region of Quedlinburg. It later became the property of the counts of Regenstein, but after their line died out, it fell to other noblemen. A large rock on the property is thought to be left from the days of the convent. The rock must remain unmoved and undamaged, otherwise great harm will befall the owner. It is said that one of the owners had it carted away simply out of curiosity. But he was subsequently tormented by every possible kind of misfortune until the rock lay once again in its correct place.

## ‡‡ 291 ‡‡
## THE CHURCH OF ALTENBERG

Above the village of Altenberg in the Thuringian Forest there is a chapel pleasantly situated among the trees on a high mountain. It is the Church of St. John. The path leading there was quite difficult to travel—especially when it was icy in winter, or when bodies of the deceased had to be carried up for burial, or when babies were taken there for baptism.

According to the legend, because of this difficulty, the people of Altenberg wanted to tear down the church and rebuild it in their village. But they were not able to do so, for whatever they carried down the hill during the day was found the next morning back in its accustomed spot in the chapel on the mountain. They thus had to abandon their plans.

The church was founded by St. Boniface, and he himself frequently delivered sermons there on the mountain. Once, as he was preaching under open skies, it came to pass that a large number of ravens, jackdaws, and crows flew over, making such a raucous din that the words of the saint could no longer be heard. Boniface then asked God nevermore to allow such birds in this region. His plea was granted, and they have never again been seen here.

## THE KING IN LAUENBURG MOUNTAIN

In the year 1596 a tremendous chasm was found in a mountain not far from Lauenburg in the region of Kassuben. At this time the city council of Lauenburg had sentenced two criminals to die. But they were ready to commute the sentence if the two convicts were willing to descend into the chasm and explore it. When the two of them had reached the bottom they saw a lovely garden. In it there stood a tree with beautiful white flowers, but they were not permitted to touch them. A child who was standing nearby then led them across a wide meadow to a castle, from which came the music of stringed instruments. As they entered, they saw a king sitting on a silver throne, holding a scepter in one hand and a letter in the other. The child then took the letter from the king and handed it to the two criminals.

## SWAN MOUNTAIN

Although no one knows where the saying comes from, as far back as anyone can remember people have said, "Swan Mountain will one day lie in the middle of Switzerland." In other words, all of Germany will become part of Switzerland. The legend is crude, and no one pays it any heed.*

## THE SPRING OF ROBBEDISSEN

If one wished to walk from Dassel over Bier Plateau and Church Mountain, one would pass on the left a town by the name of Robbedissen, where there is a fountain fed by a spring. The people of the region share a firm belief about this spring, the dark hill behind the courthouse, and the giant poplar that stands outside of Eilenhausen.

One day the spring of Robbedissen will change its location, the dark hill will become level with the ground around it, and the giant poplar of Eilenhausen will wither and die. Then a great bloody battle will be fought on the Schöffe, a large field located between Eilenhausen and Markoldendorf.

*Swan Mountain (Schwanberg, Schwanberger Alpen) is located in Styria.

## THE SCALES OF BAMBERG

In Bamberg on the tombstone at the grave of Emperor Henry, there is a carving of Justice holding scales in her hand. However, the pointer on the scales is not in the middle; instead, it leans off to one side. An ancient rumor has it that as soon as the scales are balanced the world will come to an end.

## EMPEROR FREDERICK IN KAISERSLAUTERN

A number of people claim that after Emperor Frederick was released from imprisonment by the Turks, he came to Kaiserslautern and maintained a residence there for a long period of time. He is said to have built his palace there next to a beautiful lake now called Emperor's Lake. He is also said to have caught a giant carp there, and to commemorate the event he took a gold ring from his finger and wore it as an earring. It is believed that this fish remains in the lake, not to be caught until Emperor Frederick reigns again.

Back when people still fished in the pond, two carp were caught which were joined together by a golden chain around their necks. This scene has been carved on Metzler Gate in Kaiserslautern since human memory.

Not far from the palace, a splendid zoological garden was laid out so the emperor could see all kinds of wondrous animals from the windows of his palace. However, it has long since been made over into a pond and a moat.

The emperor's bed is said still to be in the palace, hanging from iron chains. And it is also said that although the bed is still neatly made in the evenings, it is found disarranged again in the morning. Clearly, someone lies in it during the night.

There is a cliff in Kaiserslautern in which there is a cave so large and mysterious that no one has discovered how deep it goes. The rumor is widespread that Emperor Frederick, the missing one, has his residence there. Someone once attempted to descend into the cave on a rope tied at the surface to a bell. He could thus ring the bell when he could proceed no farther. Descending to the bottom, he saw Emperor Frederick wearing a long beard and sitting on a golden throne. The emperor spoke to him and told him that as long as he did not speak to anyone there nothing would happen to him, but he should tell his master that he had seen him. The explorer then looked around and saw a wide, beautiful lawn on which there were many people standing about the emperor. Finally, he rang his bell and returned unharmed to the surface where he delivered his message to his lord.

## ‡‡ 297 ‡‡

## THE SHEPHERD ON MT. KYFFHAUSEN

Many people say that near Frankenhausen in Thuringia there is a mountain in which Emperor Frederick has his residence, and that he has been seen there many times.

A shepherd, who tended his flock on the side of the mountain and who had heard the legend, began one day to play on his bagpipe. When he felt that he had performed his courtly duties in good fashion, he called out in a loud voice, "Emperor Frederick, this tune is presented to you!"

The emperor is then said to have stepped forth and revealed himself to the shepherd, saying, "May God greet thee, my little man. May I ask in whose honor thou hast played?"

"I played for Emperor Frederick," replied the shepherd.

The emperor continued, "If thou hast done that then come with me; thou wilt be rewarded for it."

But the shepherd said, "I dare not leave my sheep."

"Follow me, and no harm will come to thy sheep," the emperor replied.

The shepherd followed Emperor Frederick, who took him by the hand and led him to a cave in the side of the mountain nearest the sheep. Entering the mountain, they came to an iron door that opened immediately. Behind it lay a large and splendid hall where many gentlemen and servants paid honor to the shepherd.

The emperor also showed him kindness and asked what reward he desired for his playing. The shepherd replied, "None."

"Go and remove one of the supporting feet from my golden cask as thy payment," said the emperor. The shepherd did as he was told, and he was about to depart when the emperor began showing him many wondrous weapons—armor, swords, and muskets—and he told the shepherd to tell his people that he would use these weapons to regain the Holy Sepulchre. Thereupon, he permitted the shepherd to find his way out again.

The following day the shepherd took the cask foot to a goldsmith who recognized it as genuine gold and bought it from him.

## THE THREE TELLS

According to the beliefs of local citizens and shepherds, in the rugged Swiss mountain region around Waldstätter Lake there is a cliff with a cave in it. There the three liberators of the land—the three Tells—are sleeping. They are dressed in ancient clothing, and they will rise and emerge as liberators should a time of need for the Fatherland come again. Access to the entrance of the cave can be attained only through good fortune.

A shepherd youth once told the following story to a traveler. His father, while seeking a runaway goat in the mountain ravines, came to this cave. As soon as he realized that the men sleeping there were the three Tells, old William Tell himself sat up and asked what time it was out in the world. When the shocked shepherd replied, "It is high noon," Tell said, "It is not yet time for us to return," and went back to sleep.

The father returned there with his apprentices in a time of distress for the Fatherland in order to wake the Tells. But though he looked everywhere for the cave, he was never able to find it again.

## THE MOUNTAIN DWARF

In Switzerland there are many tales of mountain spirits current among the folk—and not just in the mountains but also in the valleys, along the River Belp, at Gelterfingen and Rümlingen, and in the Bernerland.

These mountain people are shepherds, but goats, sheep, and cows are not their cattle, for they raise chamois and make cheese from chamois milk. After one has butchered and eaten from the chamois, they regenerate and become whole again—unless one carelessly consumes them entirely, leaving nothing behind.

The Dwarf Folk live quietly and peacefully in the innermost ravines of the cliffs, where they work industriously and appear only rarely to humans. When they do appear it often means suffering and tragedy, unless one sees them dancing upon the Alpine meadows—that is the sign of a bountiful year. They will often return stray lambs to the people in their houses. And poor children who gather wood often find bowls of milk awaiting them in the forest along with little baskets full of berries that the Dwarfs set out for them.

Many years ago there was a shepherd who was plowing his land with his farmhand, when suddenly they saw smoke and steam coming from the wall of the cliff. "Look, the Dwarfs are baking and cooking," said the farmhand, "and we suffer from severe hunger. If only we had a bowlful from them!"

Just as they were turning their plow around—behold, a white cloth lay across the furrow before them, and upon it they saw a plate of freshly baked cake. They ate with gratitude, and their hunger was stilled. In the evening, when it was time to return home, the dish and the knife had disappeared; only the tablecloth was still lying there, and the farmer brought it home with him.

‡‡ 300 ‡‡

## THE CEMBRA NUTS

The fruit of the cembra pine *(Pinus cembra)*, a variety of conifer that grows in the Alps, has a reddish nut that tastes sweet and delicious, almost like an almond. However, one can seldom reach them and then only with great effort, for the trees usually grow isolated upon the sides of cliffs or ravines; only rarely are they found in groups in the forest. The local inhabitants contend that the masters put a spell on this tree and made it infertile, because instead of working hard in the fields, their servants would spend their time climbing trees after these nuts and eating them because of their delicious flavor. And thus the servants would be negligent in performing their tasks or they would do them poorly.

‡‡ 301 ‡‡

## THE PARADISE OF ANIMALS

There is said to be a region located high atop the towering, unscalable cliffs and snow-covered ridges of Mt. Matten where the most beautiful chamois and mountain goats and many other rare and wondrous animals live and graze as if in Paradise. Only once every twenty years is it possible for a human to reach this site, and then only one out of every twenty hunters. But he who succeeds is not permitted to bring any game down with him. The hunters tell a number of things about the splendor of this place, and it is said that the names of those who have been there through the years are carved in the trees. One hunter is said to have brought the magnificent hide of a mountain goat home with him.

## THE CHAMOIS HUNTER

A chamois hunter once scaled a ridge of a high mountain, climbing farther than he had ever been before. Suddenly, an ugly Dwarf appeared before him and said angrily, "Why hast thou been killing my chamois for so long? Why dost thou not leave my herd for me? Thou shalt now pay dearly for all the kills with thine own blood!"

The hunter grew pale and almost plunged to his death, but he quickly recovered. He then begged the Dwarf for forgiveness, for he had not known that the chamois belonged to him.

"Very well," said the Dwarf, "but I commend thee, let thyself be seen here nevermore and thou shalt find every seventh day early in the morning a butchered chamois hanging before thy cabin. But beware of me and leave the other animals unharmed." With these words the Dwarf disappeared.

The hunter returned home pensively, for the quiet life suited him not at all. On the seventh morning he found a fat chamois hanging in the branches of the tree in front of his cabin, and he ate from it with pleasure. The next week the same thing happened, and so it went for a few months. But the hunter gradually became disgusted with his own indolence, and he finally decided that he much preferred to hunt his own chamois come what may, rather than have his roasts delivered to him.

Thus, he once again ascended the mountains, and within a short time he spotted a proud lead buck. He raised the gun to his shoulder, took aim, and was just squeezing the trigger, when the Dwarf crept up from behind and pulled him by the ankle. He plunged to the bottom of a ravine where his body shattered on the rocks.

Other people say the Dwarf presented the hunter with a small chamois cheese that could have fed him for the rest of his life. But once he—or an ignorant guest—carelessly devoured it all. Reduced to poverty, he resumed hunting chamois and was shoved over a cliff by the Dwarf.

## THE CAVES OF THE DWARFS

In the Harz Mountains, between Elbingerode and Rübenland in the county of Hohenstein, one can see small round holes and other openings high up in the cliffs. The common folk call these the Caves of the Dwarfs. It is said that in olden times the Dwarfs used ladders to climb in and out of the holes.

The Dwarfs were good to the citizens of Elbingerode in every way. If a wedding was to take place in the city, the parents or relatives of the engaged couple would go to the caves and ask the Dwarfs for brass and copper kettles, iron pots, tin plates and bowls, and other kitchen equipment. Then they would stand to one side and shortly thereafter the Dwarfs would place the desired objects outside the entrances to their caves. The people would then take them home. When the wedding was over, they would return these things to the same place, adding an offering of food out of gratitude.

‡‡   304   ‡‡

## THE DWARF AND THE WONDER FLOWER

There was once a poor young shepherd who lived in Sittendorf, which lies on the south side of the Harz Mountains in a region called the Golden Aue.

One day he was driving his flock along the foot of Mt. Kyffhausen, and as he climbed up the slope he began to grow more and more melancholy. Then, high up on the mountainside, he found a wondrously beautiful flower, the likes of which he had never seen before. He picked it and stuck it in his hat, intending to present it to his fiancée. As he continued on his way, he found an opening to an underground chamber amid the ruins of an old castle at the top of the mountain. The entrance was only partially blocked with rubble, so he climbed in. There, he saw many glittering stones lying on the ground, and he filled his pockets with them.

Just as he was about to leave, a muffled voice rang out, saying, "Forget not the best thing!" However, he did not comprehend what was happening to him nor how he found his way out of the chamber. No sooner had he seen the sun and his flock again than the door, which he had not even noticed before, slammed shut behind him.

When the shepherd grabbed his hat, he saw that he had lost the flower when he stumbled. Suddenly he saw a Dwarf standing before him. "What hast thou done with the flower that thou hadst found?" asked the Dwarf.

"Lost," said the shepherd gloomily.

"It was destined just for thee," said the Dwarf, "and it was worth more than the whole castle of Rothen!"

Back home, the shepherd reached into his pocket and found that the glittering stones were pieces of pure gold.

*The German Legends* · 242

The flower was gone. But it is sought by miners to this very day, and not only in the caverns of Mt. Kyffhausen but also at Questen Castle, and even on the north side of the Harz Mountains where hidden treasures make the ground tremble.

‡‡   305   ‡‡

## THE NIX OF LAKE KELLE

Nixies used to live at the Kelle, a small lake not far from Werne, in the Hohenstein region. One night, a Nix fetched a midwife from a village, making her many promises as he led her down to great depths under the lake where he lived with his wife. He took her to an underground chamber where the midwife performed her services, and the Nix then rewarded her handsomely. But before she departed, the woman in childbed signaled to her and secretly lamented that the Nix would soon strangle the newborn child. Sure enough, a few minutes after she arrived at the surface, the midwife saw a blood-red stain spread across the lake—the child had been murdered.

‡‡   306   ‡‡

## SCHWARZACH

There are two separate legends told about the old Schwarzach Castle in the Rhine Palatinate. Many years ago a knight lived there whose daughter, while playing in the meadows bordering the lake, was dragged into the water by a giant serpent that emerged from the walls of a cliff. The father went to the shores of the lake every day, lamenting bitterly. On one occasion he thought he heard a voice coming from the water, and he cried in a loud voice, "Give me some sign, my little daughter!" He then heard a bell peal, and from that time on he heard the pealing of the bell every day. Once, when it sounded louder than usual, the knight heard a voice saying, "I am alive, my father, but I am now bound by a spell to the world of water. For a long time I resisted, but my first drink robbed me of my freedom. Beware of this first drink."

Standing there in deep sadness, the father was approached by two boys who handed him a drink in a golden beaker. No sooner had he tasted it than he plunged into the lake and sank into its depths.

The second story tells of an old knight who was blind and who lived with his nine daughters in Schwarzach Castle. In a forest nearby there was a robber who had long been attracted by the daughters, but all his efforts to win them had been in vain. One day he appeared at the castle disguised as a pilgrim and said to the maidens, "If you wish to heal your father of his affliction, I can help you. There is a powerful herb that only grows at the bottom of the cold ravine. It has to be picked before sunrise." The daughters begged him to show them where they could find it. When they arrived before sunrise in the cold ravine, the scoundrel murdered all nine of them and buried them there. Shortly thereafter the father died. Thirty years later remorse plagued the murderer and drove him to dig up the corpses of his victims and to have them buried in hallowed ground.

‡‡  307  ‡‡

## THE THREE MAIDENS FROM THE LAKE

In the town of Epfenbach near Sinsheim, as long as anyone could remember, three lovely maidens dressed in white had come every evening to the village spinning room. They always brought new songs and melodies with them, and they told marvelous tales and taught many new games. Their spindles and bobbins were also quite special, and no other woman of the village could spin so fine and nimbly as they. However, every evening at the stroke of eleven, they rose, gathered up their distaffs, and departed. Not once did they allow themselves to be detained by the pleas of the others. No one knew whence they came or whither they went; and they were called simply the Maidens from the Lake or the Sisters of the Lake.

The village youths liked to see them and they fell in love with them, especially the son of the schoolmaster. He never tired of listening to them and speaking with them. Nothing saddened him more than to see them depart so early every evening. Then he got the idea of setting the village clock back an hour. That evening, amid the ceaseless chatter and joking, no one noticed the loss of an hour, for when the clock struck eleven it was actually already twelve. The three maidens stood up, folded their distaffs, and departed.

But the next morning, a number of people walking along the lake heard whimpering noises and saw three bloody spots on the surface of the water. From that time on the sisters returned nevermore to the spinning room. The son of the schoolmaster began to pine away, and shortly thereafter he died.

## THE DEAD BRIDEGROOM

A nobleman in Magdeburg became engaged to a beautiful young lady. But then it came to pass that the nobleman fell into the Elbe, and although people searched for him for three days, they could not locate his body. All the relatives went into deep mourning.

Finally, a sorcerer came to the parents of his beloved and said, "The Water Sprite is holding the one you seek beneath the waters. She will not release him alive unless your daughter and her beloved swear themselves body and soul to the Sprite, or unless your daughter immediately lets the Sprite take her life in place of his, or unless the bridegroom promises himself to the Sprite, which he refuses to do." His betrothed immediately wanted to sacrifice herself in his place, but her parents would not allow it. Instead, they urged the sorcerer to conjure up the bridegroom dead or alive.

Soon thereafter they found his corpse, covered with bruises, lying on the shore.

A similar fate is said to have befallen the fiancé of a Fräulein von Arnheim; he too lost his life in the waters of the river. No one knew the spot where he had gone under, so a sorcerer was employed who used his art to make the body leap out of the water three times. They dragged the river at that spot and found the body of the deceased lying at the bottom.

## THE ETERNAL HUNTSMAN

Count Eberhard von Württemberg once felt the urge to go hunting for his amusement, and he rode out alone into the green forest. Suddenly, he heard a tremendous uproar as though a hunter were riding past through the sky. He was greatly frightened, and, after the apparition had dismounted onto a tree top, he asked the spirit if the intended to do him any harm.

"No," replied the figure, "I am, like you, a human being and stand before you quite alone; I, too, was once a nobleman. However, I found so much joy in the hunt that I begged God to let me continue hunting until Judgment Day. Unfortunately, my wish was granted. I have now been pursuing the same stag for five hundred and fifty years. And until now my royal line and family have never been revealed to anyone."

Count Eberhard replied, "Show me your face, perhaps I will recognize you." The spirit then revealed himself—his face was no larger than a fist, and it was as withered as a dried turnip and as wrinkled as a sponge. He then remounted his horse, continuing his pursuit of the stag, and vanished. The count then returned to his estate.

‡‡ 310 ‡‡

## HANS JAGENTEUFEL*

It is believed that if a man commits a crime punishable by decapitation, and it remains undiscovered during his lifetime, he will have to wander around after his death with his head under his arm.

In the year 1644 a woman from Dresden went out early one Sunday morning to gather acorns in a nearby forest. At a spot on the heath not far from the place called Lost Waters, she heard someone blowing loudly on a hunting horn. This was followed by a heavy falling sound, as though a tree had fallen. The woman became very frightened and hid her sack of acorns in the brush. Soon after, the horn sounded again, and when she turned around she saw a headless man in a long grey coat sitting on a grey horse. He wore boots and spurs and a hunting horn hung behind his back. But he rode past peacefully, so she regained her courage, gathered up her acorns, and returned home that evening unharmed.

Nine days later the woman returned to the same region with the same intention. As she sat at the foot of Förster Mountain to peel an apple, she heard a voice cry out behind her, "Thou hast a sack full of acorns and hast not been apprehended!"

"No," replied the woman, "the foresters are pious and have done nothing to me, may God have mercy on me, poor sinner!" As she finished speaking she turned around, and there stood the same man in the grey coat, this time without his horse but with his head and its curly brown hair again held under his arm.

The woman gave a start, but the spirit continued, "Thou dost well to beg God's forgiveness for thy sins. I did not get off so easily." He then told her of his fate—he had lived in the region a hundred and thirty years before, and had been called, just like his father, Hans Jagenteufel. His father had often warned him not to be too severe with the poor. But he cast this advice to the winds, and dedicated himself to drinking and carousing and committing evil deeds. Now, because of this, he was condemned to wander around as a spirit.

*The name translates roughly as 'Jack, the-Hunting-Devil'.—D. W.

## HACKELNBERG'S DREAM

Hans von Hackelnberg was chief hunting master and an accomplished huntsman. One night at Harz Castle he had a bad dream. He seemed to be engaged in battle with a terrible wild boar that finally defeated him after a long struggle.

He was not able to forget this dream and a short time later, while he was in the foothills of the Harz Mountains, he actually encountered a wild boar similar to the one in his dream. It attacked him, and for a long time the outcome was doubtful. But in the end, Hans triumphed and laid his opponent out on the ground. Overjoyed as he viewed him stretched out at his feet, Hans kicked at the terrible tusks of the boar and cried, "Thou shall not do me in after all!"

However, Hackelnberg had kicked the boar with such force that a sharp tusk had penetrated his boot, wounding his foot. At first he paid little heed to the wound and continued the chase. But by the time he returned home the foot had become so swollen that the boot had to be cut away. He then hastened back to Wolfenbüttel, but the effect of the shaking carriage was so damaging that he was barely alive when they reached the hospital in Wülprode, near Hornburg. Shortly after he died.

On his gravestone there is a carving of a knight in full armor sitting on a mule.

## TOOT OSEL

Hackelnberg, the Wild Huntsman, is often seen at midnight in his carriage, rushing through storm and rain. His barking hounds lead the way through the Thuringian Forest, the Harz Mountains, and especially through his favorite area—the Hackel. A night owl is sometimes said to fly before him. The local people call the owl Toot Osel, and wanderers who encounter the owl throw themselves face down on the ground and let the Wild Huntsman ride by above them. Soon after, they hear the barking of the hounds and the huntsman calling, "Hoho! Hoho!"

Many years ago, in a distant convent in Thuringia, there lived a nun by the name of Ursel. She had a terrible voice and upset the choir with her hooting sounds. Because of this she was called Toot Ursel. Things got worse after she died, for every night at eleven o'clock she would stick her head through one of the openings of the belfry of the church and hoot in a wretched fashion. Every morning at four A.M. she would join uninvited in the hymns of the sisters.

They put up with it for a couple of days. But on the third morning one of them, full of fear, said to her neighbor, "That can only be Ursel!" Suddenly, everyone stopped singing, their hair stood on end, and they rushed out of the church screaming at the top of their voices, "Toot Ursel! Toot Ursel!"

No threat of punishment would make any of them enter the church, until finally a famous exorcist from a Capuchin monastery on the Danube was sent for. He banished Toot Ursel in the form of a horned owl to Dumm Castle in the Harz Mountains. There she met Hackelnberg and found as much joy in his cry of "Hoho!" as he did in her "Hoohoo!" Thus, the two of them banded together in their chase through the sky.

## ‡‡ 313 ‡‡
### THE BLACK HORSEMEN AND THE RIDERLESS HORSE

Many years ago a robber knight by the name of Rechenberg is said to have ridden out at night with his squire in search of plunder. Soon they encountered a horde of black horsemen. The knight yielded the way to them, but he could not refrain from approaching the last one in the entourage, who was leading a beautifully saddled horse. He asked him who had just ridden by. The horseman replied, "The Raging Horde."

The squire then interrupted and asked to whom the beautiful horse he was leading belonged.

In reply he was told, "It belongs to your master's most loyal squire, who will be dead within the year and who will ride upon this horse."

Rechenberg's squire thus tried to change his ways, and he signed on as the stableboy of an abbot. But within a year he got into an argument with another stableboy and he was stabbed to death.

## ‡‡ 314 ‡‡
### FAITHFUL ECKHART

It is said that Faithful Eckhart can be seen sitting outside Venus Mountain, or Hösel Mountain, warning all those who are about to enter. Johann Kennerer, the minister in Mansfeld, who was over eighty years of age, told the following story.

In Eisleben, and in the entire region of Mansfeld, the Raging Horde would ride past every year on the Thursday of Carnival. The people would run out and wait for it, just as though a mighty emperor or king was about to pass by. At the head of the Horde rode an old man carrying a white staff, and he called himself Faithful Eckhart. He warned the people to clear the way, and he told a number of them to go home lest harm befall them.

Following this man, there was a horde of others, some riding, some walking. Among them were seen some who had recently died in that village—and even a few who were still among the living. One person was riding upon a two-legged horse. Another was seen strapped to a wheel, and the wheel was rolling all by itself. A third was carrying the leg of his booty upon his shoulder and running with it. Still another had no head, and there were scores of others like them.

The Raging Horde has recently been seen in Franconia, and it has been spotted many times this year in Heidelberg on the Neckar. The Raging Horde always appears in remote, desolate places, flying through the air in the darkness of night, accompanied by the barking of hounds, the sounding of hunting horns, and the roaring of wild animals. Hares can be seen fleeing, and wild boar are heard grunting.

‡‡ 315 ‡‡

## THE YOUNG LADY OF WILL MOUNTAIN

A man from Wehren, near Höxter, went to the Amelung Mill to grind some grain. While returning home, he stopped at the pond in Lau in order to rest for a while. A young lady from Will Mountain, opposite Godelheim, came down and approached him, saying, "Bring two buckets filled with water up to the peak of Will Mountain for me, and thou shalt be richly rewarded." He carried the water up the mountain, and when he reached the top, she spoke again, "Come again tomorrow at this same time and bring with thee the bunch of flowers the shepherd of Osterberg wears on his hat, but take care that you acquire it from him with kindness."

The man asked the shepherd of Osterberg for the flowers the next day, and he got them, but only after much pleading. He then returned to the peak of Will Mountain where the young lady was standing. She led him to an iron door and said, "Hold the bunch of flowers before the lock." As he did so, the door sprang open immediately and they entered. There, within the mountain, a Dwarf was sitting at a table. His beard had grown completely through the stone table top, and all around him were magnificent treasures.

Overjoyed, the young man set the bunch of flowers down on the table and began filling his pockets with gold. However, the young lady said to him, "Don't forget the best of all!" The man looked around and thought she had meant a massive candelabra. But as he reached for it, a hand emerged from beneath the table and struck him across the face. Again the young lady said, "Don't forget the best of all!" But thoughts of the treasure filled his mind, and he thought not at all of the bunch of flowers. After he had filled his pockets, he was ready to leave. Scarcely had he passed through the door than it slammed shut behind him.

Now wanting to unload his treasures, he found, alas, that his pockets were only stuffed with paper. Then he remembered the flowers, realizing too late that they were the best of all. Despondent, he descended the mountain and returned home.


‡‡   316   ‡‡

## THE SHEPHERD AND THE OLD MAN OF THE MOUNTAIN

In a valley near the city of Wernigerode there is a depression in the stony earth. It is called the Wine Cellar Hole and great treasures are said to be buried there.

Many years ago a poor shepherd, who was a quiet and pious youth, used to graze his flock there. Once, just as darkness was about to set in, an old man approached him and said, "Follow me and I shall show thee treasures from which thou mayest take as much as thou wisheth."

The shepherd then entrusted the tending of the flock to his dog and followed the old man. After a short distance, the ground opened up before them. They both entered and descended into the depths of the earth until they came to a cavern in which there were magnificent treasures of gold and rare gems piled up all around. The shepherd chose a large gold nugget for himself, and a voice said to him, "Take the gold to the goldsmith in town, and he will pay thee well for it." His guide then led him back to the entrance.

The shepherd did as he had been directed, and he received a large sum of money from the goldsmith. Overjoyed, he brought the money to his father who said to him, "Try once again to descend into the depths." "Yes, Father," replied the shepherd. "I left my gloves lying there. If you want to go with me, then I shall go fetch them."

At night they both set out and found the opening in the earth. When they arrived at the cavern of underground treasures everything was there as before, and the shepherd's gloves were there too.

They both loaded as much treasure in their pockets as they could carry, and they then climbed back up to the surface where the entrance slammed shut behind them with a great din.

The next night they wanted to try a third time, but though they looked high and low, they could not find a trace of the entrance. The old man then stepped forth and said to the shepherd, "Hadst thou not taken thy gloves with thee and left them there instead, thou wouldst have found the entrance a third time, for it was destined to open to thee three times. But now it shall remain invisible and locked to thee evermore."

It is said that spirits cannot keep in their abode that which earthly visitors leave behind, and that they have no peace until someone returns to retrieve it.


‡‡ 317 ‡‡

## MAIDEN ILSE

Ilse Rock is one of the large bluffs of the Harz Mountains. It lies on the north side of the mountains not far from Ilse Castle in the county of Wernigerode, and its sides are washed by the Ilse River. Across from the bluff is a very similar rock formation whose strata fit the former so perfectly that they appear to have been separated during an earthquake.

During the primordial flood, two lovers were fleeing toward the Brocken, the highest mountain in the Harz range, in hopes of escaping the great floods whose waters surged ever higher. Climbing toward the peak, they reached a bluff that split beneath them and threatened to separate them. The girl was standing on the left side facing the Brocken, and the boy was on the right. Embracing each other, they plunged into the rising waters below.

The maiden was called Ilse. And every morning she emerges from Ilse Rock in order to bathe herself in the Ilse River. Only a few people have been blessed with the ability to see her, but whoever knows her, cherishes her.

A charcoal maker saw the maiden early one morning, greeted her kindly, and followed her beckoning right up to the edge of the bluff. Standing before the rock wall, she removed his knapsack, carried it inside, and then returned with the sack filled. She handed it to him and instructed him not to open it until he was back in his hut.

He felt its great weight, and crossing Ilse Bridge, he could not control himself no longer. But when he opened his knapsack he found only acorns and pine cones. Indignant, he held the sack over the water and shook it out. No sooner had the contents touched the rocks of the river than he began to hear clinking sounds. With dread he discovered that he had cast away pure gold. However, the one remaining nugget stuck in the corner of the sack made him rich enough.

According to another legend, the castle of the King of the Harz once stood on Ilse Rock. He had a daughter named Ilse who was very beautiful, while nearby there lived a witch whose daughter was ugly beyond description. Many suitors sought the hand of Ilse, but no one was interested in the witch's daughter. This so angered the witch that she used her magical powers to turn the castle into a huge rock. At its foot she put a door visible only to the princess.

Every morning the enchanted princess emerges from this door to bathe herself in the river, which is also named after her. If someone is lucky enough to see her bathing, she leads him into her castle, regales him royally, and sends him away richly rewarded. But the jealous witch has arranged it so that she is only visible a few days of the year. She can be released from the spell only by a man who bathes in the river at the same time as she and who is her equal in beauty and virtue.

## ‡‡  318  ‡‡

### THE HEATHEN MAIDEN OF GLATZ

The people of Glatz, young and old, tell the following story.

Back in heathen times the land was ruled by a godless, bewitching maiden. On one occasion she made a wager with her brother as to who could shoot an arrow the farthest. And then she took her great bow and shot an arrow all the way from the castle to the great linden tree in Eiserdorf. Her brother's arrow traveled scarce half the distance, and the maiden won the contest.

The linden tree that marks the boundary is said to be as old as the Heathen Tower in Glatz, and although it has now and then withered and dried up, it has always grown back again and is still standing today. A seeress once sat in this tree and prophesied many things that were to happen to the city. The Turks, she said, would invade as far as Glatz, but when they crossed the stone bridge onto the Ring, they would suffer a great defeat at the hands of the Christians who would attack from the castle. But such would not occur until a flock of cranes came flying through the bread stalls of the market place.

In commemoration of the fact that the maiden had outshot her brother with bow and arrow, two pointed columns of stone were erected on a spot located a mile beyond the moat. Because the maiden engaged in forbidden love with her brother, she was abhorred by the people, and attempts were made on her life. However, she was able to escape because of her sorcery and great strength. Once she even tore a horsehoe apart just for amusement. Finally, she was captured and walled up in a long hall in the castle that had been a passageway near the gate from the lower to the upper castle. And here she perished.

In her memory, her likeness was carved in stone. It can still be seen to the left of the same gate in the wall over the moat where it is pointed out to visitors. A painting of her also hangs in the green palace hall, and a braided lock of her beautiful golden hair hangs on an iron nail in the wall of the palace chapel. People call it the hair of the Heathen Maiden. It hangs three steps from the entrance at a height a tall man can just reach with his hand.

The maiden is said to appear from time to time in the castle wearing the same clothes and looking just as she does in the painting. She causes no one harm unless she is mocked or made fun of, or unless someone has thoughts of stealing her lock of hair from the chapel.

On one occasion a soldier began making fun of her, and she came to the guard station and slapped him across the face with her cold hand. On another occasion a solider stole her hair, and she appeared to him at night and began to scratch him and choke him. She probably would have done him in had he not had his comrade take the lock of hair back to its old place.

‡‡  319  ‡‡

## THE HOOFPRINT AND THE DEVIL'S POND

Behind the town of Thale, in the high foothills on the north side of the Harz Mountains, there is an egg-shaped depression in a stone cliff called the Hoofprint because it resembles the impression of a gigantic horse hoof. Several conflicting legends are told about it.

(1) In ancient times a Giant Princess made a wager that she could jump her horse across a deep chasm, called the Devil's Pond, from one cliff to the next. The first two times she performed the jump with success, but on the third time the horse reared and plunged with her into the canyon. She remains down there to this day. Once, for the amusement of others and for a small reward, a

diver was able to bring her close enough to the surface of the water so the crown she wore on her head was visible. When he was asked to do it a third time, he at first refused but finally decided to try, telling the others, "If you see a stream of blood gush from the water then you will know the maiden has killed me. If this happens, get out of here quickly so harm does not also befall you." A stream of blood did indeed gush forth, just as he had said.

(2)   Many years ago, a king who had a lovely daughter lived in the ancient palaces surrounding the region. A prince who was in league with the Devil fell in love with her and wanted to abduct her. Through the black arts of the Devil, he acquired a horse from Hell, on which he abducted the princess. As the horse was springing from cliff to cliff, it left the hoofprint in the rock.

(3)   A princess who lived in the Harz Mountains was carrying on a secret love affair against the wishes of her father. She fled to save herself from his fury, but she also took the royal crown with her and planned to hide it among the cliffs of the mountains. The tracks of the wheel nails of her carriage are still said to be visible in the rocks across from the Hoofprint. She was pursued and surrounded until her only means of escape was a leap across the canyon. When the maiden saw that, she turned and began to dance as if performing her wedding dance. This is why this cliff is still called the Dance Floor. Then she climbed on her horse and made the great leap successfully. Where her horse landed, it left the print of its hoof, and that is why the cliff is still called the Hoofprint. While she was in the air, however, the priceless crown she was wearing on her head fell into a deep whirlpool at the bottom of the canyon. That is why the place is called Crown Hole, and to this very day the crown is lying there on the bottom.

(4)   A thousand or more years ago, before the robber barons built the castles of Hoym, Leuen, Steckeln, and Winzen, the land around the Harz Mountains was inhabited by Giants. They were heathens and sorcerers and devoted themselves to plunder, murder, and other acts of violence. They would rip sixty-year-old oak trees from the ground and use them as clubs to fight with, and they would beat down whatever ventured to oppose them. They also dragged women away and forced them to serve day and night in captivity.

One of these Giants, who resided at that time in the Bohemian Forest, was called Bodo. Everything and everybody was his subject—except Emma, the princess from the Giant Mountains. He could not force her to accept his love, and neither his strength nor his wiles were of any avail to him, for she was in league with a powerful spirit.

Once, however, while Bodo was out hunting, he spied her upon Snowcap Mountain. He immediately threw a saddle on his ambling horse that could cover miles in the bat of an eyelash, and swearing that he would either capture her or die, Bodo began the pursuit. He was just two miles away when she spotted him and recognized the picture of the gate of a destroyed city he bore on his shield. She quickly turned her horse around, and driven by her spurs, it flew over hills, cliffs, and forests, through all of Thuringia and finally into the Harz Mountains. Often she could hear the snorting of Bodo's horse behind her, but she merely urged her tireless horse on to greater speed and longer leaps.

Finally, she let her horse catch its breath, stopping atop the terrible cliff called the Devil's Dance Floor. Fearfully, Emma looked down into the depths, for the wall of the cliff fell away beneath her more than a thousand feet to the bottom of the canyon. Far below, the stream roared, and roiled in dreadful whirlpools. The cliff across from her appeared so distant, and it scarcely offered enough room for one of the front hooves of her horse.

But then she heard the snorting of Bodo's horse approaching once again, and in her fear she cried out to the spirits of her father for help. Then, without realizing what she was doing, she dug her giant spurs into her horse's flanks. The steed leaped the deep abyss and happily reached the other side, digging its hoof four feet into the hard rock so that sparks flew.

That hole in the cliff is the aforementioned Hoofprint. Time has made the depression somewhat shallower than it was, but no rainstorm can erase it completely. Emma was saved, but the heavy royal crown she wore toppled from her head during the leap and fell into the depths below. Pursuing her in blind rage, Bodo plunged into the raging current and thus gave the river its name (the Bode River, together with the Emme and the Saale, flows into the Elbe). He has been transformed into a large black dog, and he guards the princess' crown to prevent some greedy person from making off with it.

A diver once ventured to retrieve it. He plunged into the depths, found the crown, and brought it to the surface. The people gathered there could just see the golden point, but it was too heavy for him and twice it sank from his hands. The people shouted encouragingly to him to try a third time. But when he did, a stream of blood gushed from the depths, and the diver never surfaced again.

Now, silence and darkness of the night prevail at the bottom of the chasm. No birds fly over the site. No sound escapes from there except at midnight, when the muffled howling of the heathen can frequently be heard. The whirlpool is called the Devil's Pond, and the cliff where Emma pleaded for the intervention of the diabolic spirits is called the Devil's Dance Floor.

(5) In Bohemia, many centuries ago, there lived a princess who was courted by a Giant. The king, who was fearful of the Giant's strength and power, gave his consent to the marriage. But the princess loved another man, who was of the human race, and so she resisted both the suitor and the command of her father. Enraged, the king was determined to enforce his will, and he set the wedding for the next day. Weeping, she lamented her fate to her beloved, and he urged her to flee, arranging to meet her that night and escape with her.

It was, however, quite difficult for her to get away because the royal stables were locked at night and all the stablemen were loyal and devoted subjects of the king. To be sure, the Giant's great black steed was there in a stall specially constructed for it, but how was a frail woman to control a beast that stood 10 ells [twenty feet] tall? And how was she to gain access to it? It was secured with a heavy, powerful chain that served as a halter, with an equally heavy lock whose key the Giant carried on his person.

Her beloved, however, provided the necessary aid. He found a ladder, held it against the horse, and told the princess to climb up and mount. Drawing his sword, he struck the chain a blow so mighty that it sprang apart. He then mounted the horse himself and away they rode. The clever maiden took her jewels with her and also set her father's crown upon her head.

While they were speeding aimlessly through the countryside, the Giant suddenly thought how nice it would be to go out riding in the night. As he prepared to saddle his horse in the bright moonlight, he was quite shocked to find the stall empty. He immediately sounded the alarm throughout the castle, and when they went into the princess' chamber to awaken her, they discovered that she too had disappeared.

Without hesitation, the intended bridegroom mounted the best horse available and began pursuing her over hill and dale. Leading the way was a giant bloodhound that had picked up the scent of the fleeing couple.

As they neared the Harz Forest, the Giant was close behind them. The maiden saw her pursuer, and she turned her horse and rode through the dark forest until she reached the abyss through which the Bode River cuts its path. The mighty steed hesitated for a moment, placing the lovers in great peril. But then the princess looked behind her and saw the Giant approaching at a rapid gallop, and she dug her spurs into her steed. With one mighty leap, gouging its hoof into the cliff, the great horse vaulted to the other side, and the lovers were saved. But the mare that was carrying the pursuing Giant was so overburdened with his weight that she jumped short, and they both plunged with great clatter into the abyss.

The princess, safe on the other side, began to dance in her great joy. That is why this site is still called the Dance Floor. In the exuberance of the great leap, however, the golden crown had tumbled from her head and fallen into the waters of the rushing stream below. It still lies there, guarded today by a giant hound with glowing eyes. Dazzled by the great value of the treasure, swimmers have sought to fetch it from the depths. But when they come ashore, they reveal how useless it is to try, for whenever anyone approaches, the great hound dives to greater depths, and thus the golden crown will remain evermore inaccessible.

‡‡   320   ‡‡

## THE GIANT MAIDEN'S LEAP

In the Selke Valley, between Ballenstedt and Harzgerode, the local people point out to visitors a high cliff with a formation that looks like a great column, and a depression in the rock that bears a certain resemblance to a human footprint, and another such print about eighty to a hundred feet away. Diverse legends are told about the site.

A Giant Maiden was once wandering along the saddle of the Harz Mountains, having just come from Peter's Mountain. When she reached the cliffs that now stand above the smelting works, she spotted her playmate waving to her from the top of Ramm Mountain. She remained standing there for some time, hesitating, for a wide valley lay between her and the next mountain peak. She stood there so long that her foot sank several feet down into the rock—and faint traces of her footprint can still be seen today.

A farm boy, who was plowing in the fields near Harzgerode, laughed mockingly at her hesitation. The Giantess reached out and with one hand picked up the boy, the horse, and the plow and tucked them into her blouse. She then leaped across the valley and reached her playmate in just a few steps.

A story that is also heard quite frequently concerns a princess who approached in her carriage and wanted to travel to that distant mountaintop. The Giantess quickly picked up the carriage, horses and all, placed them in her apron, and sprang from one mountain peak to the other.

And finally, the footprints have been ascribed to a peasant girl who leaped across the valley to reach her beloved, a shepherd youth. She landed with such force that her feet gouged holes in the rock. A mountain goat is also said to have played a role in the event.

## ‡‡ 321 ‡‡

## MAIDEN'S LEAP

In the Lausitz region, not far from the Bohemian border, a steep cliff called Oybin juts out. The people of the region point out a place on the cliff called Maiden's Leap and tell the following story about it.

Many years ago a maiden paid a visit to the mountain monastery, which now stands in ruins. One of the monks was to show her around and point out the passes and wonders of the remote region. However, the great beauty of the maiden awakened sinful lust within him, and he made improper advances to her.

Cursing him, she began to flee along the winding mountain path still pursued by the monk. Suddenly, she found herself standing on the rim of a deep mountain canyon, and being both courageous and chaste, she leaped into the abyss. The angels of the Lord caught her and bore her unharmed gently to earth.

Others contend that a hunter once saw a lovely peasant girl wandering up on the Oybin, and he hastened after her. Like a hunted doe, she darted along the rocky trails, and when the canyon yawned before her, she leaped unharmed to the canyon floor.

Still others report that a nimble maiden once bet her playmates that she could jump across the canyon. However, as she leapt, her foot slipped out of her smooth shoe. She would have been dashed to bits on the rock, but her crinoline ballooned out and brought her gently to earth.

## ‡‡ 322 ‡‡

## HARRAS' LEAP

Near Lichtenwalde, in the Erz Mountains of Saxony, the local people point out a cliff in Zschopau Valley called Harras' Leap. Many years ago a knight who was being pursued by his enemies rode his horse down the steep cliff into the canyon. His horse was dashed to pieces on the rocks, but the hero escaped safely to the other side.

## ‡‡ 323 ‡‡
## HIDDE THE GIANT

In the days of the reign of Charlemagne there lived a Frisian by the name of Hidde, who was immense in size and possessed of great strength. He once traveled to Brunswick, where the duke made him overseer of his forests. Once, when he was out wandering through the wilderness, he came upon a lioness in her den with her cubs. Slaying the old one, he brought the young ones, which he called "wolves," back with him to the court where he presented them to the duke. The simplicity of a man who could not tell the difference between lions and wolves pleased the duke, and he bestowed many estates in the Elbe Valley upon him. The Giant built himself a house there and called it Hiddesacker, after his own name.

## ‡‡ 324 ‡‡
## THE EYE-OF-THE-NEEDLE AT ILEFELD

Near the Monastery of Ilefeld, there is a high mountain to the left of the Harz Highway. Upon it stands a large stone through whose center runs a narrow hole. When venturing out for the first time into the Harz Forest to gather firewood, all the youths from Nordhausen and other surrounding villages are required to crawl through this hole three times. They do this only with great effort and difficulty, especially since the other boys beat them with whips as they crawl in and out. If they are not able to withstand the torment, they have to purchase their way free. The authorities have several times sought to abolish this custom under penalty of a heavy fine, but to no avail. Any youth who tries to escape the initiation receives no peace from his comrades and they will not abide him.

According to the local people, the rock came there in the following manner. Many years ago a Giant who had been traveling for a number of miles came to Ilefeld. He then felt something in his shoe, removed it, and found this rock. He cast it away and it came to rest just where it stands today.

# THE GIANTS OF LICHTENBERG

There is a mountain castle called Lichtenberg that was rebuilt from its ancient ruins, and the following legend is still told about it in all the surrounding villages. Back in ancient times there were Giants in the region. Among the stones of the original castle are some that are so heavy they could not have been transported up the steep mountain by human strength.

Once a Giant was carrying a huge boulder weighing over eighty hundredweights on his shoulder up the side of the mountain, but along the way he dropped it and it broke in two. It still lies on the plateau an hour from Lichtenberg, and is still called Giant's Rock today.

In the castle a huge bone is preserved that is a foot and a half wide and still attached to another that is half a foot wide and a foot long. It is said that twenty-five years ago a gigantic bedframe was still to be seen there.

It is also said that a Giant Woman once wandered farther from Lichtenberg than was her usual wont and she met a peasant who was plowing his field with oxen. She had never seen the likes of that before, so she gathered up the farmer, the plow, and the oxen in her apron. She brought them back to her husband in the castle and said, "Look here, Husband. What fine little beasts I have found!"

# GIANT'S BLOOD

Between the city of Egeln and the village of Westeregeln, not far from the Hackel in Magdeburg, there is a depression in the earth filled with red water that the local people call Giant's Blood. A Giant who was being pursued by another Giant took a great step across the Elbe River to the area where Egeln now stands. But he failed to lift his foot high enough and caught the top of the tower of the old fortress there. He tripped, kept his balance as he stumbled a few thousand feet, but then he finally plunged to the earth. He fell so hard that he broke his nose on a large boulder near Westeregeln. A stream of blood gushed out, and the remains can still be seen today.

According to another tale, the Giant lived in the region near Westeregeln. He used to take pleasure in jumping over the entire village and its tiny inhabitants. During one leap, however, he caught his big toe on the top of a tower, and blood from the wound spurted out in an arc a thousand feet long. Finally, the blood collected into a depression in the earth—forming a pond which will never dry up.

## ‡‡ 327 ‡‡
### THE NOISE FROM THE TOMB OF THE GIANTS

Attention is often called to Giant's Mountain near Köslin in Pomerania. Excavations there are said to have turned up a gigantic horn, a very large sword, and an immense bone. Giants are also said to have lived in Hither-Pomerania in ancient times.

In 1594, in the region around Greifswald, someone broke into such a Giant's tomb and carted the contents away. Masons working at the site found bodies that were from eleven to sixteen feet long, and they also found jugs next to them. They then discovered a second grave site, much like the first, and were about to excavate it. But suddenly, according to their own words, they heard a tremendous din, as though something with a ring of keys was clattering and cavorting around them. They disturbed the grave no further.

## ‡‡ 328 ‡‡
### THE DEAD FROM THE GRAVES REPEL THE ENEMY

According to legend, the village of Wehrstadt, located near Halberstadt, received its name after it had been besieged by foreign heathens.* The inhabitants had already been subdued by the superior forces when their dead rose from the grave and courageously repulsed the enemy, thus rescuing their descendants.

## ‡‡ 329 ‡‡
### THE CLIFFS OF HANS HEILING

On the Eger River, just opposite the village of Aich, strange cliffs called the Cliffs of Hans Heiling jut high into the sky. It is said that ages ago a man by the name of Hans Heiling lived in the region. He had money enough and owned a farm, but every Friday he would lock himself in his house and remain invisible for the entire day.

*The name Wehrstadt is apparently related to the verb *wehren* 'to repel.'—D. W.

This man Heiling was in league with the Evil One, and he fled everytime he saw a cross. He is once said to have fallen in love with a pretty maiden. In the beginning she gave him her consent, but later she refused to have anything to do with him.

Sometime after, when she was celebrating her marriage to another man and there were many guests present, Heiling suddenly appeared in their midst at twelve midnight and cried out, "Devil, I will release thee from thy servitude if thou wilt destroy all this!"

The Devil, replying, "And thus thou art mine," transformed the entire wedding party into columns of stone.

The bride and bridegroom still stand there embracing one another while the others stand around them with folded hands. Hans Heiling plunged from the cliff into the Eger, which swallowed him up in its hissing waves, and no one ever laid eyes on him again. People still point out the stone images of the bridal pair, the father of the bride, and the guests. They also point to the spot where Heiling fell to his death.

## ‡‡ 330 ‡‡

### THE MAIDEN WITH THE BEARD

At Saalfeld there is a church which stands in the middle of the river, and which can only be reached by crossing a nearby bridge. Services are no longer held there. There is a seal engraved in stone on that church, and it shows a crucified nun before whom a man with a violin is kneeling. The following story is told about it.

The nun had once been a princess and she lived in a convent in Saalfeld. Because of her great beauty a king had fallen in love with her, and he would not leave her in peace until she consented to take him as her husband. However, she was true to her vows and continued to refuse him. But he remained relentlessly persistent until, finally, she reached her wit's end.

Thereupon, she prayed to God to rescue her by taking away her physical beauty and granting her some disfigurement. God heard her pleading and from that moment she began to grow a long ugly beard. When the king saw her, he became enraged and had her crucified. She did not die immediately but was forced to languish on the cross in indescribable pain for several days. A compassionate minstrel appeared at that time, and he sought to salve her pain and sweeten her mortal despair. He began playing his fiddle to the best of his ability, and when he could no longer stand because of weariness, he knelt down and continued playing his consoling music without interruption. The holy virgin was so pleased that she let fall from her foot a shoe embroidered with precious gold and gems as a memento and reward.

## ‡‡ 331 ‡‡
## THE WHITE VIRGIN OF SCHWANAU

The Free Swiss destroyed the castle at Schwanau on Lake Lowerz because the evil and cruel overseer of the emperor resided there. Once every year in the silence of night a rap of thunder shakes the ruins, and a cry of distress rings out from the tower. The overseer can be seen being pursued around the tower by maidens dressed in white whom he had dishonored. They pursue him to cliff's edge where he finally plunges screaming into the lake below.

Three sisters once fled from his lust into the canyons of Rigi from which they never emerged. The Chapel of St. Michael now marks this spot.

## ‡‡ 332 ‡‡
## THE FORTRESSES OF SCHWARZKOPF AND SEEBURG AT LAKE MUMMEL

Lake Mummel lies deep in the Murg Valley, ringed by the ruins of ancient castles and fortresses. Across from each other are the remains of the once mighty fortresses of Schwarzkopf and Seeburg. Legend reports that every day when dusk first envelops the mountainpeaks, thirteen deer can be seen at the side of the courtyard at Seeburg. They enter through a small gate, cross the plaza, and then hasten out the archway that was once the main gate to the fortress.

Practiced marksmen have been able to bring down one of these animals but never more. Their remaining bullets either missed their mark or struck the hounds. No hunter of the region ever shot at any animal other than those that ran with this herd; and an animal of great size and beauty was invariably selected. Fridays, however, were exempted from this daily procession; this day is still commonly known as Hunters' Sabbath, and no one sets foot in the Fortress of Seeburg then.

Around midnight on Fridays, however, another apparition can be seen. Twelve nuns surrounding a bloodied man with twelve daggers in his body come through the small forest gate, wander into the courtyard, and march silently toward the large main gate. At this instant a similar column consisting of twelve men dressed all in black appears at the main gate. Sparks fly from their bodies and flames spurt from burning spots all over them. As they march past the nuns and their bloody companion, a female figure can be seen creeping along in their midst. A legend explains this vision in the following manner.

Twelve brothers, all of them robber barons, once lived in Seeburg, and with them lived their sister—a good woman. In Schwarzkopf a noble knight lived with his twelve sisters. It came to pass one night that the twelve knights of Seeburg abducted the twelve sisters of Schwarzkopf, and the knight of Schwarzkopf retaliated by taking the only sister of the twelve robber barons by force.

Both parties met on the plains of the Murg Valley and a battle ensued from which the knights of Seeburg emerged victorious. They took the knight of Schwarzkopf prisoner and led him into their fortress. There, each of the robbers plunged a dagger into his body before the eyes of their sister, his beloved. Shortly after, the abducted sisters escaped from their captivity, removed the twelve daggers from the breast of their brother, and in the dark of night slew all the murderous robber barons. After this deed they fled. But the servants of the brother pursued, caught them, and killed them all.

The castle was then destroyed by fire. But during the blaze, the walls within which the maidens had been languishing opened up and twelve female figures, each holding a child in its arms, stepped forth, walked directly to Lake Mummel, and jumped into its waters. Later, the water swallowed up the remains of the crumbling castle, but fragments of it can still be seen protruding from the surface.

A poor man who lived near Lake Mummel and who often prayed for the souls of the spirits in the water lost his wife through death. That evening he heard music coming from the room where she lay upon her bier. He opened the door a crack, and looking in he saw six maidens with lamps in their hands standing over the body. On the following evening he saw six more of them keeping watch over the corpse, beholding her with sadness.

‡‡  333  ‡‡

## THE PEDDLER AND THE MOUSE

Many years ago a poor peddler was walking through the Bohemian Forest on his way to Reichenau. He grew weary and sat down to eat a piece of bread, which was all that he had to still his hunger. While he was eating, he saw a small mouse crawling around at his feet, and it finally sat down before him as if it were expecting something. As needy as he was, he unselfishly tossed a few crumbs of bread to the mouse, and it immediately gobbled them up. He kept giving the mouse more crumbs as long as he still had some, until together they had consumed all the bread.

The peddler then got up and drank from the spring nearby. When he returned, behold, there lay a piece of gold. Then the mouse brought a second piece, set it down, and ran off to fetch a third. The peddler followed and saw it run into a hole and then emerge with another piece of gold. He then took a stick and dug into the hole, where he found a great treasure of pure gold coins. He removed the gold and looked around for the mouse, but it had disappeared. He took the gold joyfully to Reichenau, distributed half of it among the poor, and had a church built with the other half.

The story was engraved in stone as an eternal memorial, and it can still be seen to this very day in Holy Trinity Church in Reichenau in Bohemia.

‡‡　334　‡‡

## THE THREE TREASURE SEEKERS

A great treasure is said to lie buried beneath the Church of St. Dionysius, not far from Erfurt. Three men once tried to dig up the treasure—a blacksmith, a tailor, and a shepherd—but the evil spirit protecting it killed all three.

Their heads were carved in stone on the cornice of the church beneath the roof. Next to them can be seen a horseshoe, a pair of scissors, and a shepherd's staff or a vintner's scoop.

‡‡　335　‡‡

## AN INVITATION TO APPEAR
## BEFORE THE JUDGMENT OF THE LORD

There was a very deft thief living in Leuneburg in Prussia who could steal a horse from anyone, no matter how much care was taken to prevent the theft.

Now, it so happened that the village minister had a beautiful horse he had purchased from the fish commissioner of Angerburg. The thief bet someone that he would steal the horse and thereafter desist from thievery. The minister, however, learned of these plans and had the horse locked up and guarded to prevent the thief from getting to it.

But then the minister had to ride the horse into town, and the thief, dressed in beggar's rags and supporting himself on two crutches, came to the hostel. When he overheard the minister saying he would soon be leaving town again, he left first and went out to a field alongside the road. There, he threw the crutches into a tree and lay down beneath it, waiting for the minister to ride by.

Shortly after, the minister appeared—quite in his cups. He saw the beggar lying there and said, "Up, brother, get up! Night is approaching, go join the townspeople or the wolves will devour you."

The thief replied, "O dear master! Two wicked boys were here and they threw my crutches up in the tree. Now I must sit here and rot and starve, for I cannot go anywhere without my crutches!"

The minister took mercy on him and handed the scoundrel the reins of the horse to hold while he removed his riding cloak and placed it across the back of the horse. He then proceeded to climb the tree to fetch the crutches. But while he was climbing, the thief leaped onto the horse and rode off, casting his beggar's clothes away—and the minister returned home on foot.

The sheriff, learning of this misdeed, had the thief apprehended and hanged on the gallows. But by this time everybody was talking about his cleverness and skill.

On one occasion several noblemen, well in cups, were riding past the gallows, talking and laughing about the thief's cunning. One of them, a dissolute and acrimonious man, cried out to the gallows, "O deft and clever thief, come Thursday with thy friends as guests to my place and teach me thy skill and cunning!" The others laughed heartily at this.

The nobleman had been drinking all night, and he had been dead to the world for some time when, at the stroke of nine on Thursday morning, the thieves arrived wearing their chains. They entered through the courtyard, went in and greeted the man's wife, and said that the squire had invited them as guests and that she should awaken him. This was a dreadful shock to her and she went to the squire's bed and said, "I have told you many times that you would cause us great harm someday with your drinking and taunting. Now get up and receive your guests." She then told him what they had said in the antechamber.

Startled, the nobleman rose, bade them welcome, and asked them to be seated. He had a meal served to them—as much as could be prepared in haste—and all of it was consumed. In the meantime, the nobleman said to the horse thief, "My dear man, your talents have given us much laughter, but I do not find them funny at the moment. I'm amazed that you could have been so adept, for you appear to be such an ill-bred fellow."

The thief answered, "When Satan sees that you have forsaken the word of the Lord, he can easily make you adept."

The nobleman asked other things, and the thief answered him until the meal was finished. Then the guests rose, expressed their gratitude, and said, "We bid you appear before God's judgment in Heaven. We have been condemned for our misdeeds by a worldly court, but you must join us before the court of worldly disgrace. The session will be held four weeks from today." They then took their leave and departed.

The nobleman was terrified and grew very despondent. He told many people what had transpired, and one person advised this and another that. But he consoled himself with the fact that he had never stolen anything, and that the fateful day was All Saints' Day, and the courts were not in session then because of the Festival of the Saints. Still, he remained home that day and invited guests over so that if anything did happen he would have witnesses.

At that time theft ran rampant throughout the land, and especially active was the Gregor Matternen gang, one of whom had stabbed to death the Imperial Commander, D. Eberhard of Emden. Because of this, an order was issued stating that if any member of the gang was found, he should be sentenced on the spot without even a hearing.

Meanwhile, the murderer's whereabouts were reported and the commander rode out with his men to find him. Since it was the last day of the four-week period for the nobleman, and since it was the Festival of the Saints, he thought he'd gotten off free. Toward evening he craved some enjoyment, so he went riding through the fields.

When the commander's men caught sight of the nobleman, they were certain he was riding the horse and wearing the clothes of the murderer, and they came riding directly toward him. The lone rider tried to defend himself, but in so doing, he stabbed a young nobleman, a friend of the commander's, to death, and he was taken into custody.

They brought him to Leunebrug, where a Lithuanian was paid to hang him alongside his guests. It did him no good to insist that he had just ridden directly from his house, for the commander's men cried out, "Hang him quick before the others come and take his side. He's only faking an alibi!"

‡‡  336  ‡‡

## GUESTS FROM THE GALLOWS

An innkeeper from a respectable city was returning one evening with two wine dealers from the vineyard country where he had purchased a considerable amount of wine, and their route led them past the gallows. Although they were intoxicated, they noted the gallows well, and saw the three criminals who had been hanged there many long years before.

One of the two wine dealers called out, "Hey, innkeeper, the three fellows hanging there used to be your guests."

"Aha," replied the innkeeper in foolhardy extravagance, "they can join me again tonight and have dinner with me!"

What happens?*

When the innkeeper arrives home drunk, he dismounts, goes into his living room, and sits down. But suddenly, he is overcome with a fear so great that he cannot even call for help. In the meantime when the houseboy comes in to remove his master's boots, he discovers him lying in his armchair half dead, and calls the innkeeper's wife. She soon revives him a bit with the help of some strong drink, and asks him what happened.

He tells her how he invited the three hanged men as he rode by. But then, he says, when he entered the room, there were the three of them, looking as wretched as they had upon the gallows. They came into the room, sat down at the table, and beckoned to him to join them. But then, when the houseboy finally entered, all three spirits vanished.

This episode was at first thought to have been simply imagined by the innkeeper, that what he had thought was real had been triggered in his drunken mind by his invitation to the sinners at the gallows. However, he immediately took to his bed, and he died the third day thereafter.

‡‡  337  ‡‡

## THE DEVIL'S BRIDGE

A Swiss shepherd, who liked to visit his girl friend frequently, had to make his way through a marsh with great effort to get to the other side, otherwise he had to take a very long detour. It came to pass that while he was standing at an extraordinary altitude, he cried out in anger, "I wish the Devil were here and would build me a bridge across this!" In an instant the Devil was standing next to him, and he said, "Promise me the first living thing that crosses and I'll build thee a bridge on which thou canst cross back and forth." The shepherd agreed, and in a few moments the bridge was completed. He then drove a chamois across the bridge before him. Soon thereafter the cheated Devil rained down shredded bits of chamois from the mountaintops.

---

*The change to the present tense at the moment of highest suspense is typical of legend narration.—D. W.

## THE TWELVE JOHANNESES

There once was a Franconian king who had twelve youngsters called the German Students, and each one of them was named Johannes. They would travel everywhere on a magic disk and thus could discover what was happening anywhere in the world within twenty-four hours. They would then report what they had learned to the king.

Each year, however, the Devil would make one of them fall from the disk and take him as tribute. He caused the last one to fall on Peter's Mountain near Erfurt, which had previously been called Berber Mountain.

The king wanted to know where the last one had landed, and when he learned the boy had fallen on a beautiful mountain, he had a chapel built there. He called it Corpus Christi and moved a hermit into it.

At that time the land around the mountain was covered by navigable waterways and none was farmed. A lantern used to be hung from the chapel so that people could take their bearings from it. But then the waters were channeled off to Saxon Castle.

## THE DEVIL'S DITCH

Near the village of Rappersdorf, not far from the city of Strehlin in Lower Saxony, there is a deep ditch that runs down to a creek some distance away. The local people call it the Devil's Ditch.

A farmer from Rappersdorf was once in serious distress because he had no means of draining the excess water from his fields and it was now getting the upper hand. The Devil then appeared before him and said, "If thou canst provide me with seven workers to help, then before dawn breaks I will complete a ditch that will drain all the water from thy fields." The farmer agreed and delivered the workers and their tools to the Devil. When he stepped out the following morning to look over the work, he discovered that the wide ditch had been completed—but the workers had disappeared. Later, the torn limbs of the unfortunate souls were found scattered around the fields.

## CROSS MOUNTAIN

Many years ago a princess lived in a castle in the area near Baden, in the Aargau region. She frequently wandered to a nearby hill to rest in the shadow of the bushes growing there.

The inside of this hill, however, was inhabited by spirits, and once, during a terrible storm, they tore up and laid waste to the area. When the princess returned, she decided to climb down to the depths through an opening that was now there for a look around.

She entered at nightfall and was immediately seized by wild, terrifying figures who bore her over a great number of kegs, deeper and deeper into the abyss. She was found the following day on a plateau near the devastated hill with her foot rooted in the earth. Her arms had grown into two tree branches, and her body had been turned to stone. However, she was released from this frightful state by means of a miraculous icon, which was fetched from a nearby monastery, and she was then led back to the castle.

A cross was placed at the top of the hill, and it is called Cross Mountain to this very day. The abyss with the kegs is called the Devil's Cellar.

## ‡‡ 341 ‡‡

## THE HORSES LOWERED FROM THE HAYLOFT

Richmuth von Adocht, the wife of a rich mayor of Cologne, died and was buried. The gravedigger noted that she wore a precious ring on her finger, and greed drove him back to the grave at night. He reopened it, intending to steal the ring. But he had no sooner opened the lid of the coffin than he saw the corpse press her hands together and try to climb out of the coffin. He fled in terror.

The woman unwound herself from her shrouds, stepped out, and walked directly to her house. There, she called to the houseboy by name and told him to open the door quickly. She then briefly related what had happened to her.

The houseboy went to his master and said, "Our lady is waiting outside at the door and wants to be let in."

"Ah," said the man, "that is not possible. Before such a thing could happen my white horses would be standing in the hayloft."

No sooner had he uttered these words than the sound of hooves echoed from the stairs and above, and behold, the six white horses were standing there in the hayloft.

The woman had continued knocking the whole time, and now the mayor believed that she was really there. The door was opened with joy, for she had been brought back to life. On the following day the horses were still there looking out the window of the hayloft, and a large hoist had to be erected so that they could be lowered to earth safely and without harm.

In memory of the event, the horses that had looked out the window of the house were stuffed. A painting of them was made in the Church of the Apostles, where one can also see a long linen curtain that Frau Richmuth spun with her own hands and donated to the church. She lived another seven full years.

## ‡‡ 342 ‡‡

## THE MEETING OF THE DEAD

A queen had died and was lying on the bed of state in a hall draped with black cloth. At night the hall was brightly illumined with wax candles, and in an antechamber a watch was posted, consisting of a captain and forty-nine men.

Toward midnight the captain heard a carriage drawn by six horses approach at high speed and stop before the palace. The captain goes down to investigate, and a woman of noble and aristocratic bearing, dressed in mourning, approaches him and asks for permission to spend some time with the deceased. He explains to her that it was not in his power to grant such permission. She then reveals her name, which was well known, and says that as Mistress of the Robes for the deceased, she was entitled to see her before she was interred. The captain vacillates, but she remains so persistent that he runs out of fitting and appropriate reasons for refusing, and he leads her into the hall.

He closes the door behind her, and assumes the watch himself, marching up and down outside the door. After a while, he stops in front of the door, listens, and then looks through the keyhole. He sees the dead queen sitting straight up in bed and talking to the woman in a soft voice. Her eyes, however, remain closed, and her face shows no sign of life other than her lips moving slightly. He orders all the soldiers, one after the other, to look—and every one of them sees the same thing. Finally, he returns and watches as the deceased woman slowly lowers herself back into the bed of state.

Thereupon the other woman leaves the room and the captain leads her back downstairs. As he helps her into the carriage, he feels her hand and it is cold as ice. The carriage then speeds off as rapidly as it came, and from afar the captain sees the horses exhaling sparks of fire.

The next morning the news arrives that the Mistress of the Robes, who lived in a country estate several hours away, had died around midnight, precisely the time she had been with the deceased.

# THE BIRD OF PROPHECY

In the year 1624 a voice coming from the sky was heard to cry, "Woe, woe to Pomerania!"

On the fourteenth of July the weaver's wife, whose name was Barbara Sellentins, walked from Colbatz to Selow to buy some fish. On the way back to Colbatz, while walking on the path down the hill, she heard the crying of birds, and as she came closer, a voice rang out in her direction, saying, "Hark, hark!" She then saw a small white bird, about the size of a swallow, sitting in an oak tree. It spoke to her in clear, distinct words, "Tell the captain that he should tell the prince to bear the attack that is coming with good spirits, otherwise it will mean his doom. He should comport himself in a manner that will answer to God and the world!"

# THE ETERNAL JEW ON THE MATTERHORN

Mt. Matter, beneath the Matterhorn, is a high glacier of the Valais region from which the Visper River springs. According to a popular legend, a splendid city was situated on that site ages ago. The Wandering Jew once came to the city and said, "The next time I come through here, trees will grow and rocks will stand where there are now houses and streets. And the third time my wanderings bring me through here there will be nothing but ice and snow." Now, nothing but ice and snow can be seen on that site.

# THE POT OF BUTTER

An entire village with its church and homes is said to lie buried beneath the earth at the foot of a mountain in the Visper Valley, not far from Altesch. The following reason is given for this catastrophe.

There was once a farmer's wife who was about to melt some butter, and she had it in a pot hanging above the hearth fire. Just as the boiling foam filled the kettle halfway, a man came walking by and spoke to her, saying he would like to taste some of her melted butter. The woman, however, was cruel and unfeeling and replied,

"I am going to need it all for myself. I cannot afford to give any away."

The man then turned to go, saying, "Hadst thou given me even the smallest amount, I would have granted thee the gift of a kettle always full to the brim and never empty."

The man was none other than Our Lord himself. And from that time on the village was cursed. It was completely buried by a landslide so that nothing was visible except the top of the altar that had been in the village church. A brook that once flowed beneath the village, now flows over it, winding its way through a canyon in the cliffs.

## ‡‡ 346 ‡‡
### THE WEEPING WILLOW

As he was being crucified, Our Lord, Jesus Christ, was lashed with twigs from a willow tree. Ever since this time, the willow lowers its branches toward the earth as though it were in mourning—and it can no longer lift them toward the heavens. This tree is the weeping willow.

## ‡‡ 347 ‡‡
### THE STATUE OF CHRIST IN WITTENBERG

A statue of Christ stands in Wittenberg. It has the wondrous power of always being an inch taller than whoever is standing before it and looking at it, no matter whether the person is short or tall.

## ‡‡ 348 ‡‡
### THE STATUE OF THE MADONNA ON THE CLIFF WALL

There is a steep, towering cliff on the side of Räti Mountain in the Visper Valley near St. Niklas. High up, in a little opening in the cliff wall, there stands a small statue of the Virgin Mary, scarcely visible to the eye. It used to stand in the small chapel on the road below so that people could pray to her as they passed by, but the chapel is now empty.

It came to pass once that a godless man, whose wishes had not been answered, took some dung and besmirched the sacred statue with it. The statue shed tears, and when he repeated the blasphemy, it fled high up the wall of the cliff. No matter how the people pleaded, she refused to return to the chapel.

It was not possible to climb up the cliff wall to bring it back. But it might be possible, so the people thought, to retrieve it from above. So they climbed to the top where they wound a strong rope around a man and tried to lower him down the side of the cliff right next to the statue so he could retrieve it.

But as they lowered him down the cliff, the rope by which he was suspended began to grow thinner and thinner until, as he neared the statue, it was no thicker than a human hair. The man became terribly frightened and cried out to those above, for God's sake, pull him back up or he was doomed. So they hauled him back up, and as they did, the rope regained its previous strength. Thus, the people had to abandon their plan, and they were never to retrieve their statue.

## ‡‡ 349 ‡‡

## THE HOLY ICON IN THE LARCH TRUNK OF WALDRAST

In the year 1392 the Great Lady of Heaven sent forth an angel to Waldrast on Serles Mountain in Tyrol. He approached the hollow trunk of a larch tree and addressed it in the name of the Mother of God, saying, "Thou shalt yield the image of Our Lady in Heaven!"

The image then grew in the trunk, but it was not discovered until the year 1407, when it was found by two pious shepherd boys, Hänsle and Peterle from the village of Mizens. Struck by the wonder of it, they raced back down to the villagers, telling them, "Quick! Go up the mountain. Something truly wondrous is there in the hollow tree, but we were afraid to touch it!"

The sacred icon was found and carefully cut from the tree with a saw. Then it was brought to the church in Matrey, where it remained until its own chapel was built in Waldrast.

For this purpose, Our Dear Lady engaged a poor woodsman by the name of Lusch who resided in Matrey. One night during Holy Pentecost he was lying asleep in his bed when a voice came to him and spoke to him three times, saying, "Art thou asleep or art thou awake?"

The third time, he awoke and asked, "Who art thou, and what wouldst thou of me?"

The voice said, "Thou shalt build a chapel in honor of Our Dear Lady in Waldrast." The woodsman, however, replied, "I do not wish to do so." But the voice returned on the next night of Pentecost and again delivered the same message, to which he replied, "I am too poor to do so." The voice returned on the third night of Pentecost and again delivered the same message. He had thus no sleep for three nights because of his worries, and so this time he replied to the voice, "Why dost thou continue to plague me?"

The voice replied, "Thou shalt do it."

He answered, "I do not wish to do so!"

Then it seized him and lifted him high into the air and said, "Thou shalt do so, be well advised!"

He then thought to himself, "Alas, I am a wretched man, how do I know I can do it right?" He then told the voice that he would do it only if he knew the right place to build it.

The voice answered, "In the forest there's a patch covered with green moss. Go there and lay thyself down to rest, and the right place will be revealed to thee."

The woodsman set out for the bed of moss and when he found it he lay down upon it to rest (which is why the place is called *Waldrast* or Forest Resting Place.) After he had fallen asleep, he heard two small bells ring in his dreams. He woke and saw a woman in white standing on the spot where the chapel now stands. She was holding a child in her arms, but he perceived the vision for only an instant before it vanished. Then he thought to himself, Almighty God, that must be the right spot.

He then proceeded to the place where he had seen the figure, and he paced off the area on which the church was to stand. The bells continued to ring until he had finished, and then he heard them no more. Then he spoke, "Dear Lord in Heaven, how shall I accomplish this? I am but a poor man and have not the means to build such a structure."

The voice then spoke once more, "Go to the pious people. They will give thee what thou must have to accomplish the task! But when the time of the dedication approaches, all work will come to a halt for thirty-six years. It will then start up again and a symbol will be produced that will last for all eternity."

When the time came for him to begin work on the chapel, he went to his priest, who arranged a hearing with the Bishop of Brixen. Five times he had to travel to Brixen before the bishop granted him permission. But the bishop finally did so, and that came to pass on the Tuesday before St. Pancratius' Day in 1409.

‡‡ 350 ‡‡

## OXEN REVEAL THE SACRED SITE

The ruins of a tremendous stone structure can still be seen near Matten, a village located near the mouth of Fermel Valley in Switzerland. The following legend is told about the place.

In ancient times the community wanted to construct a church in honor of St. Stephan, and they chose the site where the masoned walls were to be built. But every night all the work that had been accomplished during the previous day by the hard-working inhabitants of the valley would be destroyed. The community members then decided after much prayer to attach the construction tools for the church to the yoke of a pair of oxen and turn them loose. Where the beasts came to a stop, they would recognize the intervention of God and would build their church on that site. The two animals crossed the river and came to a halt on the spot where St. Stephan's church was later to stand.

‡‡   351   ‡‡

## ST. NOTBURGA

The palace of Rottenburg is located in the lower Inn Valley in Tyrol. Many years ago a pious maid by the name of Notburga worked there, serving a royal family. She was gentle and kind and shared everything she had with the poor. But since the greedy family could not abide this behavior, they beat the pious girl and finally sent her away. From there she went to some poor peasants who lived nearby on Mt. Eben.

God, however, soon punished the wicked woman of Rottenburg Palace, and she died a wretched death. Her husband was now remorseful and felt guilty about the wrongs that had been heaped upon Notburga. He brought her back from Mount Eben to the palace, where she was able to live a pious life until the angels came and bore her off to heaven.

Two oxen carried her body across the Inn River, and though its waters usually raged in fury, they became quite peaceful and quiet as the holy maiden approached. She was buried in the Chapel of St. Ruprecht.

In the Neckar Valley another legend is told.

The remains of the ancient towers and walls of the castle of Hornberg still rise high above the river. Many years ago a powerful king lived there with his beautiful and pious daughter, Notburga. She was in love with a knight and became engaged to him; however, he rode off into foreign lands and never returned. She wept day and night, mourning his death, and she rejected every other suitor who appeared.

Her father, however, was unfeeling, and he thought little of her mourning. One day he told her, "Prepare thy wedding clothes and jewelry, for a bridegroom whom I have chosen for thee will be here in three days."

But Notburga said within her heart, "I would sooner run away to the farthest limit of the blue sky than to be untrue."

The next night, after the moon had risen, she called to a faithful servant, telling him, "Lead me across the forest plateau to the Chapel of St. Michael so that I might hide there from my father, and spend the rest of my life in the service of Our Lord."

When they came to the top of the plateau, they heard the rustling of leaves, and when they looked up they saw a snow-white stag approaching them. It walked right up to Notburga and stood next to her. She climbed up on its back and held on to its antlers, and it bore her rapidly away. The servant saw the animal swim easily across the Neckar and disappear with her on the other side.

The next day, when the king could not find his daughter, he had messengers sent out seeking her in all directions, but they returned without finding any trace of her; and the faithful servant said nothing. At midday the white stag appeared to the servant at the castle of Hornberg, and when he handed it bread, it nodded its head, letting him know he should stick the bread on its antlers. Then it bounded away and brought the bread to Notburga in the wilderness. Thus, it appeared at the castle every day and fetched food for her. Many witnessed it, but no one other than the faithful servant knew the meaning of the visits.

Eventually the king became aware of the white stag, and he obtained the secret from the old servant through force. The next day at noon he mounted his horse, and when the stag appeared again for food and then hastened away with it, the king gave chase on his horse. He followed it across the river and then to a cave in the side of a cliff, into which the animal disappeared. The king dismounted and entered the cave where he found his daughter kneeling before a cross, her hands folded in prayer. The white stag lay quietly beside her. Since she had not been touched by sunlight, she was as pale as death, and he took fright when he saw her.

Then he said, "Return with me to Hornberg."

But she replied, "I have entrusted my life to God and have nothing to seek among men."

No matter how he argued he could not move her, and she had no other reply. He then became enraged and tried to drag her away by force, but she held fast to the cross. As the king pulled harder, the arm he was pulling became separated from her body and lay dangling in his hand. Overcome with dread, he raced away and never again approached the cave.

When the people heard what had happened, they revered Notburga as a saint. Repentant sinners who came to the Chapel of St.

Michael seeking help were sent to her by the hermit. She prayed with them and removed the burden of guilt from their hearts.

In the autumn, as the leaves were falling, the angels came and bore her soul to Heaven. They wrapped her body in a shroud and decorated it with fresh roses (although all the flowers had wilted by then). Two snow-white bulls, who had never before had a yoke attached to them, bore her across the river without getting their hooves wet. And the bells of all the churches in the area began to peal all by themselves. Thus was her body brought to the Chapel of St. Michael and buried there.

A statue of St. Notburga carved in stone still can be seen in the church in the village of Hochhausen on the Neckar. The Cave of Notburga, also called the Virgin's Cave, can still be seen and is known to every child of the region.

According to another tale, the king was Dagobert, who held court in Mosbach. His daughter, Notburga, fled when her father tried to force her to marry a heathen Wend. She was nourished upon herbs and roots, brought to her in her cave by a serpent, until she finally died.

The presence of will-o'-the-wisps revealed the site of the hidden grave, and the princess was found there and recognized. Two bulls then pulled the carriage bearing her body until they reached a certain spot and stopped, and that is where she now lies buried. A church was later constructed over her grave, and many miracles still occur there. The image of the serpent is likewise engraved in stone in Hochhausen. A portrait of Notburga can be seen on the altar. It shows her with her long hair, just as she appeared when her cruel father had her beheaded to satisfy his lust for revenge.

‡‡ 352 ‡‡

## MORTAR SLAKED WITH WINE

In 1450 the grape harvest in Austria was so sour that most of the citizens emptied their wine kegs into the streets, for the wine was much too bitter to drink. This wine was called *Reifbeißer*, some say because the frost [*Reif*] spoiled the grapes. Others say because the wine had bitten the barrel staves and hoops [*Reifen*] with its sharp edge.

It was then that Frederick III, ruler of the Holy Roman Empire, gave the order that no one was to pour out the gift of God. Whosoever was unable to drink the wine was to transport it to the construction site of the Cathedral of St. Stephan. There, the wine was to be used to slake the mortar, and the church was to be built thus.

There is an ancient tower still standing in Glatz near the Bohemian Gate. It is called the Heathen Tower because it is said to have been built in ancient times by the heathens. The walls are very strong, and it is believed that the mortar was prepared with pure wine.

## ‡‡ 353 ‡‡

## THE ROCK OF THE JEWS

In the year 1462 it came to pass in the village of Rinn in Tyrol that a number of Jews convinced a poor farmer to deliver his own small child over to them in exchange for a large sum of money.

They took the child out into the forest to a large boulder on which they martyred it, killing it in the most wretched fashion. The boulder has been known ever since as the Rock of the Jews. They then took the battered and stabbed body and hung it from a birch tree not far from the bridge.

The child's mother had been working in the field at the time the murder took place. Suddenly, her thoughts turned to her child, and she became very fearful without knowing why. It was then that three drops of blood fell from her hand. Full of terror, she raced home, desiring her child. Her husband pulled her inside and confessed what he had done, and was about to show her all the money that would now free them from oppressive poverty, when it changed to dead leaves.

At that moment the father went mad and grieved himself to death. The mother, however, ran out seeking her child. And when she found it hanging from the tree, she took it down amid tears and bore it to the church in Rinn.

Its body still lies there, revered by the people as a sacred child. The Rock of the Jews was also brought there. According to local legend, a shepherd chopped down the tree on which the child had hung, but when he sought to carry it home, he broke his leg and died from the injury.

## ‡‡ 354 ‡‡

## THE MAIDEN WHO WAS KILLED BY THE JEWS

In the year 1267 a greedy old woman who lived in Pforzheim sold an innocent seven-year-old girl to the Jews. The child was gagged so that she could not scream, her arteries were opened, and she was wrapped in a cloth to catch all the blood. The child soon died from this martyring, and the body was cast into the Enns River, weighed down with a sack of stones.

A few days later Margaretchen raised her hand above the surface of the water. Some fisherman saw it and were terribly shocked. Soon, all the people ran down to the river, including the count himself. The boatmen pulled the child from the water, and she was still alive, but, after crying out for revenge, she died.

Suspicion for the deed fell upon the Jews, and all of them were ordered to appear on the site. As they approached the corpse blood began to gush from its open wounds. The Jews and the old woman confessed their wicked deed, and they were executed.

The child's coffin, together with an inscription, can be seen inside the entrance to the palace chapel, right next to the bell rope.

The legend is widespread among the children of the members of the Fishermen's Guild that at the very time the count granted their ancestors freedom from sentry duty "as long as the sun and moon still shine," in the city of Pforzheim. They were also granted the privilege of having twenty-four of their number march with their weapons and musical instruments every year at Carnival, and they were also to guard the city and the market place on that day. This provision is still in force to this very day.

‡‡ 355 ‡‡

## THE FOUR HORSESHOES

Some years ago there used to be four gigantic horseshoes nailed above the door of the old church in Ellrich, and all the people marveled at them. After the church collapsed, the horseshoes were kept in the minister's dwelling where they remain today.

Count Ernst von Klettenberg is said to have ridden out one Sunday morning many years ago, heading for Ellrich, to try for the prize of a gold chain in a drinking contest. He won over many competitors, and with the chain around his neck he set out on the ride back to his castle at Klettenberg.

While riding through the suburbs he heard vespers being sung in the Church of St. Niklas, and he drunkenly rode his horse into the church, past the congregation, and right up to the altar. Scarcely had the horse reached the altar steps when all four of its horseshoes fell to the floor, and the horse and its rider sank to the floor dead.

## THE ALTAR IN SEEFELD

Not far from Innsbruck in Tyrol lies the ancient castle of Seefeld, where Oswald Müller, a proud and impious knight, lived in the fourteenth century.

He finally went so far astray that while he was attending church on Maundy Thursday in the year 1384 he refused, in the presence of all the people and servants, to accept the sacramental host that was offered him. Instead he insisted on having the larger kind that priests usually receive. No sooner had he taken it than the stone floor beneath his feet began to quake. Terrified, he tried to save himself by grabbing onto the iron railing with both hands, but it melted beneath his grip like wax, and the marks left by his fingers clearly showed in the iron.

Before the knight sank completely out of sight, he was overcome by repentance and remorse, and the priest removed the host from his mouth. As soon as it had touched his tongue it had become covered with blood.

Soon after, he founded a monastery on that site, and he himself was accepted there as a lay brother. The iron railing with the marks of his fingers on it can still be seen there today, and the entire episode has been depicted on a mural.

When the knight's wife learned of the event, encountering some churchgoers on their way home, she at first refused to believe what had happened. She said, "I'll believe that when roses bloom from that withered, rotting pole over there." But God gave her a sign of his omnipotence, for the dry pole sprouted green twigs, and beautiful snow-white roses began to bloom upon it. The sinner tore the roses from the pole and cast them on the ground, but that very moment she went mad. She began to race up and down the mountainside, and she continued to do so until she dropped dead in her tracks the next day.

## THE STONE OF DEATH

In Oberhasli, on the way to Gadmen, not far from Meiringen, there is a narrow mountain canyon, called the Kirchetbuel, through which the muddied waters of the Aar River have been raging for centuries. Next to this canyon there is a stone, on which can be seen the print of a human hand, and several finger marks show quite distinctly. The local people say that many years ago there was a murder at this site. As the unfortunate victim grabbed at the rock, he left a record of his violent death gouged in the surface of the stone.


## ‡‡  358  ‡‡

### SINFUL LOVE

On Peter's Mountain near Erfurt there is a tombstone on which is depicted in high relief the burial of a brother and sister. The sister was so beautiful that her brother, after spending some years in a foreign land, returned and fell passionately in love with her and sinned with her. The Devil appeared and tore their heads off. A similar fate befell the depiction of them carved on their tombstone. Here, too, the heads disappeared from the bodies—and only the spike on which they had been mounted remained. New heads made of brass were attached to replace them, but these vanished too. Indeed, even when people tried to draw in the heads with chalk, they would be erased the next day.


## ‡‡  359  ‡‡

### THE COUNCILMAN OF SCHWEIDNITZ

Many years ago there lived in Schweidnitz a councilman who loved gold more than God. He had trained a jackdaw to fly through a broken pane in the barred window of the City Treasury, which was just across the street from his own house. The jackdaw would pick up a gold piece and fly back with it to the councilman's house. And every night the jackdaw would pick up a piece of gold or silver from the city's latest collection that was lying on the table, and it would carry away the coin in its bill.

Finally, the other council members perceived that their city treasury was dwindling, and they resolved to hide and catch the thief. They soon discovered that a jackdaw came flying in after sundown and made off with one of the coins. They marked a few coins and set them out on the table, and by and by these were picked up by the jackdaw.

Later, as the entire city council sat in session, the matter was brought up. They resolved that if the thief were caught he was to be set out on the cornice of the City Hall tower, there to die of hunger or to try to climb down on his own.

In the meantime, investigators were sent to the residence of the suspicious councilman. Not only was the flying accomplice discovered there but the marked gold pieces as well. The culprit confessed his crimes and subjected himself to the sentencing of the court. Because of his advanced age they wanted to lessen the severity of the penalty. He would have none of it. Instead, he climbed with fear and trembling up to the cornice of the tower before the eyes of all the others. But when he attempted to climb down, he found himself on a narrow ledge from which he could neither advance nor retreat. And so he had to remain where he was.

For ten days and nights the old man stood there, a pitiful figure, without food or drink. Finally, he began to gnaw his own flesh from his hands and arms out of starvation. Repentant and remorseful, he died a cruel and ugly death.

Later, a stone statue of him and his jackdaw was set out on that ledge. In 1642 a gale is said to have toppled it to the ground, but the head of the statue is still said to be in the City Hall.

## ‡‡ 360 ‡‡

### A RAINBOW APPEARS ABOVE THE SENTENCED MEN

Twenty-six esteemed men became involved in the Bohemian conspiracy and were condemned to be executed in Prague in June of the year 1621. As they stood before the executioner, one of them, a Johann Kutnauer who had been Captain of the Citizens' Militia in the old quarter of the city, prayed incessantly to Heaven for a sign of forgiveness and mercy for himself and his fellow citizens. He prayed with great trust and confidence, never doubting that such a sign would appear. After a short rain, just as the execution was about to begin, a rainbow appeared above Mt. Lorenz in the form of a cross. It remained there for an hour as a consolation for the condemned men.

## ‡‡ 361 ‡‡

### GOD WEEPS WITH THE INNOCENT

In Hanau there was once a woman who was accused of a serious crime and sentenced to death. When she appeared before the executioner, she said, "Although circumstance condemned me, I am as innocent as I am certain that God will weep for me." And, indeed, it began to pour down from a perfectly clear sky. She was executed, but later her innocence was revealed.

## FOOD FROM GOD

In a village not far from Zwickau in the Vogtland region it once came to pass that the parents of a very young boy sent him out to the forest to drive home the oxen that had gone there to graze. He tarried a little on his way and was overtaken by darkness. During the night a heavy snowfall covered all the mountains and hills around, and the boy was trapped in the forest.

When he did not come home the following day, the parents were greatly concerned, not so much for the cattle as for the boy. But because the snow was so deep, they could not penetrate the forest. Finally, on the third day, after the snow had partially melted, they were able to search for the boy. They found him at last on top of a sunny hill where no snow had fallen at all.

When the boy saw his parents he smiled and laughed. They asked him why he had not come home, and he told them that he had been waiting until evening. He had not known that more than a day had passed or that harm could have befallen him. When they asked him if he had eaten anything, he reported that a man had come to him and given him bread and cheese.

There can be no doubt that the boy had been fed and cared for by an angel of God.

## THE THREE OLD MEN

In the Angeln region of the Duchy of Schleswig there are people still living who remember hearing the following story told by the late Pastor Oest, a man well known for several learned works he had published. However, no one can now recall whether the experience happened to the pastor himself or to a minister from a neighboring town.

It all took place back in the middle of the eighteenth century when the new pastor set out on horseback to ride the borders of his diocese to acquaint himself with his territory. In a remote area he found a lonesome farm along the road. On a bench in front of the house sat an old man with snow-white hair who was crying bitterly.

The pastor wished him a good evening, and asked him what was wrong. "Alas," replied the old man, "my father has given me a beating." Astonished, the pastor tied up his horse and entered the house. In the hall he met a man who was even older than the man outside, and he was beside himself with rage.

The pastor addressed him in a polite manner and asked what had caused his anger. The old man replied, "Oh, that boy. He let my father fall." He then opened the door to the living room and the pastor, speechless with amazement, saw an ancient man, withered with age but still active, sitting in an armchair behind the oven.

# SOURCES AND ADDENDA

## THE BROTHERS GRIMM

In their first edition of the legends (1816–18) the Brothers Grimm provided information on their sources. They planned to update this edition eventually and to provide it with a third volume consisting solely of sources, notes, and commentary, much as they had done in the case of the *Kinder- und Hausmärchen*. Through the years they thus assembled a considerable amount of notes and data for this purpose, but they never had the time for a second edition. So, when Herman Grimm re-edited the collection in 1865 and again in 1891, he worked through all the notes his father and uncle had left behind and incorporated them into the commentary. In the interest of completeness, I have included these additional notes. Thus, when the reader encounters such entries as "written in Jacob's hand," he or she will realize that these are Herman Grimm's references to the posthumous notes of the Brothers Grimm.—*D.W.*

1. THE THREE MINERS IN THE KUTTEN MINE *(Die drei Bergleute im Kuttenberg)* Collected orally in Hesse.

2. THE MINE SPIRIT *(Der Berggeist)* Prätorius, *Weltbeschreibung*, I, 110 and 127–128. Bräuner, *Curiositäten*, 203, 206. G. Agricola, *De animalib. sub-terr.* from an oral narrative. Lavater, *De spectris*. (The following additional commentary is written in Jacob's hand:)

A very busy Mine Spirit was observed some time ago in the Graubünden Alps. He ran to and fro through the mine shafts and hauled out the newly excavated ore in a basket. The mine owners let him do as he pleased, harmed him in no way, and made the sign of the cross whenever he left. However, on one occasion he raised such a racket that one of the miners lost control and cursed the Dwarf violently. The spirit then seized the miner's head and twisted so hard that the man's face was on backward. Many people saw him in this condition. He lived only a short time after this episode. Whenever there was going to be a mining accident, the racket, rustling, and hammering of the Mine Spirits was always heard.

3. THE MINE MONK OF THE HARZ MOUNTAINS *(Der Bergmönch im Harz)* Recorded orally in the Harz Mountains.

4. MOTHER HOLLA'S POND *(Frau Hollen Teich)* Schaub, *Beschreibung des Meißners*, Kassel, 1799, 8, pp. 12–14. Münchhausen, "Abh. über den Meißner in Hinsicht auf myth. Alterthum," *Hess. Denkwürdigkeiten*, II, 161–202. (There are additional notes in Jacob's hand on this topic that were later worked into *Deutsche Mythologie*. The same applies to Legends No. 5, 6, and 7.)

5. MOTHER HOLLA ROAMS ABOUT *(Frau Holla zieht umher)* Prätorius, *Weihnachtsfratzen, propos.*, 54.

6. MOTHER HOLLA'S BATH *(Frau Hollen Bad)* Zeiller, *Sendschreiben*, II, 533, 695. Prätor., *Weltbeschreibung*, I, 476.

7. MOTHER HOLLA AND FAITHFUL ECKART *(Frau Holla und der treue Eckart)* Prätor., "Weihnachtsfratzen," *propos.*, 55. Falkenstein, *Thüring. Chronik*, I, 167. The latter used Waldenfels, *Sel. antiq.*, Norimb. 1677, p. 376, who in turn had used Prätorius.

8. MOTHER HOLLA AND THE PEASANT *(Frau Holla und der Bauer)* Prätor., "Weihnachtsfr.," *propos.*, 56.

9. THE SPURGE ROOT *(Der Springwurzel)* Recorded orally from a shepherd on Köter Mountain. Cf. *Altdeutsche Wälder*, II, 95.

10. THE MAIDEN OF BOYNE CASTLE *(Fräulein von Boyneburg)* Recorded orally in Hesse. For a more complete version see Bechstein, *Museum*, I, 184 ff.

11. PIEL MOUNTAIN *(Der Pielberg)* Prätorius, *Glückstopf*, p. 506.

12. THE MAIDEN OF THE CASTLE *(Die Schloßjungfrau)* Falkenstein, *Thüring. Chronik*, I, 172.

13. THE SNAKE MAIDEN *(Die Schlangenjungfrau)* Prätor., *Weltbeschr.*, 661–663. Seyfried in *Medulla*, pp. 477–478, 1609. Kornmann, *Mons Veneris*, cap. 34, pp. 189–192. Prätor., *Glückstopf*, 489–490. *Rübezahl*, I, 187–192.

14. THE HEAVY CHILD *(Das schwere Kind)* Bräuner, *Curiosit.*, p. 274.

15. THE OLD WINE CELLAR OF SALURN *(Der alte Weinkeller bei Salurn)* *Nachr. von Geistern*, Frankfurt, 1737, pp. 66–73.

16. THE GAME OF THE GIANTS *(Hünenspiel)* Recorded orally in the Corvey region of the Weser Valley.

17. THE GIANT'S TOY *(Das Riesenspielzeug)* Recorded orally from a forester. Arthur von Nordstern composed a ballad based on this topic: *Dresdner Abendzeit.*, (1817), No. 8.

18. THE ONE-MAN-ARMY GIANT *(Riese Einheer)* Aventin, *Bair. Chronik,* Frankfurt, 1570, p. 285b. *Monachus Sangallensis,* Dippoldt, pp. 116–117. *Al. Cishere Aenothere. 1. Eishere + Egishere, terribilis.* Pertz, II, 756. Crusius, *Ann. suev. dod.,* I, 337. Αἰνόϑηρος, *horribilis venator.*

19. THE COLUMNS OF THE GIANTS *(Riesensäulen)* Winkelmann, *Hessische Chronik,* p. 32. Melissantes in *Orograph,* quoted from Malchenverg. Bader, No. 387.

20. KÖTER MOUNTAIN *(Der Köterberg)* Recorded orally from a shepherd tending his flocks on Köter Mountain.

21. THE PALACE OF GEROLDSECK *(Geroldseck)* J. Moscherosch, *Philander vom Sittewald: Gesichte,* pp. 32–33, and *Philander vom Sittewald: Soldatenleben,* pp. 276–277, edit. lugdun., tom. 4.

22. CHARLEMAGNE IN NÜRNBERG *(Kaiser Karl zu Nürnberg)* Melissantes, *Orogr.* Francof., 1715, p. 533. Cf. Struve, *Hist. polit. Archiv,* I, 14.

23. FREDERICK BARBAROSSA AT MT. KYFFHAUSEN *(Friedrich Rotbart auf dem Kyffhäuser)* Agricola, *Sprichwort,* 710. Melissantes, *Orogr. v. Kyffausen.* Tenzel, *Monatl. Unterr.,* 1689, pp. 719–720. Prätorius, *Alectryomantia,* p. 69. Prätorius, *Weltbeschr.,* II, 306–307. Behrens, p. 151. Cf. *Curiosit.,* IV, 170–171. Cf. the ancient song published by Gräter, *Odina,* pp. 197–198.

24. THE PEAR TREE OF WALSER FIELDS *(Der Birnbaum auf dem Walserfeld)* *Brixener Volksbuch vom Untersberg,* pp. 38–39.

25. THE ENCHANTED KING OF SCHILDHEISS *(Der verzauberte König zu Schildheiß)* *Volksbuch vom Ritter Eginhard,* pp. 42 ff.

26. CHARLEMAGNE'S EXODUS *(Kaiser Karl des Großen Auszug)* Recorded orally in Hesse. For information on *Gudensberg, Udenesberg, Wuodenesberg,* see Wenk, III, pp. 79, 86. See also Engelhard, *Erdbeschreibung,* I, 391. Charlemagne is said to have fought and won a memorable battle against the Saxons at Gudensberg. Wondrous tales about his existence in the nearby Oden Mountains still circulate today.

27. WONDER MOUNTAIN *(Der Untersberg)* *Sagen der Vorzeit oder ausführliche Beschreibung von dem berühmten salzburgischen Untersberg oder Wunderberg, wie solche Lazarus Gitschner vor seinem Tode geoffenbart,* Brixen, 1782 (chapbook). Franz Sartori, *Naturwunder des österr. Kaiserthums,* Wien, 1807, I, No. 7 *(Helfenburg 'Iuvavia').*

28. EMPEROR CHARLES IN WONDER MOUNTAIN *(Kaiser Karl im Untersberg)* Brixener *Volksbuch* of 1782, pp. 28–29.

29. VON SCHERFENBERG AND THE DWARF *(Der Scherfenberger und der Zwerg)* From Ottokar von Horneck, cap. 573–580, pp. 539a–544a. Cf. Rauch, I, 36.

30. THE SILENT FOLK OF PLESSE *(Das stille Volk zu Plesse)* Joh. Letzner, *Plessisches Stammbuch: Wunderbare Begebenheiten eines göttingischen Studenten auf dem alten Schlosse Plesse,* 1744, pp. 15 ff. See also p. 34 for additional information.

31. THE WEE PEOPLE'S WEDDING *(Des kleinen Volks Hochzeitfest)* Collected orally in Saxony.

32. THE DWARFS WHO WERE TURNED TO STONE *(Steinverwandelte Zwerge)* Spieß, "Vorrede," to *Hans Heiling.*

33. DWARF MOUNTAIN *(Zwergberge)* Agricola, *Sprichw.*, 171b.

34. THE DWARFS BORROW BREAD *(Zwerge leihen Brot)* Joh. Wolfgang Rentsch, *Beschreibung merkwürdiger Sachen und Antiquit. des Fürstenthums Baireuth.*

35. THE COUNT OF HOIA *(Der Graf von Hoia)* Hammelmann, *Oldenb. Chronik*, 21–22. Tenzel, *Monatl. Unterr.*, 1609, p. 525. Prätorius, *Glückstopf*, 489–490, and *Weltbeschr.*, I, 95. Bräuner, *Curiosit*, 622–624. Cf. Spiel's *Archiv.* III, 157–158.

36. THE MIGRATION OF THE DWARFS *(Zwerge ausgetrieben)* Christ. Lehmann, *Erzgebirg. Schauplatz*, cap. 2, pp. 187–188.

37. THE LITTLE PEOPLE *(Die Wichtlein)* Prätorius, *Weltbeschr.*, I, 129–132. Bräuner, *Curiosit.*, 205–209. G. Agricola, *De re metallica.* Valvassor, *Ehre von Crain*, I, 417.

38. CONJURING THE GNOMES *(Beschwörung der Bergmännlein)* Prätorius, *Im Glückstopf*, p. 177.

39. THE GNOME AT THE DANCE *(Das Bergmännlein beim Tanz)* Brixener Volksbuch.

40. THE CELLAR DWARF *(Das Kellermännlein)* Prätor., *Weltbeschr.*, I, 172–173 and 319–320.

41. THE MATRIARCH OF THE FAMILY VON RANTZAU *(Die Ahnfrau von Rantzau)* Seyfried in *Medulla*, p. 481, No. 10. Cf. Prätorius, *Weltbeschr.*, I, 104–105. Cf. Happel, I, 236. The following introduction should have been included: A more precise and complete version of this legend is contained in an anthology of French novellas published in Brussels in 1711 under the title *L'amant oisif.* See the next-to-last tale from this collection, pp. 405–411: *La comtesse de Falinsperg* (Falkenberg?), *nouvelle allemande.* The third version is in Wilhelm's hand and it bears the title "Fräulein von Calenberg."

42. HERMANN VON ROSENBERG *(Hermann von Rosenberg)* *Unterred. vom Reich der Geister*, I, 223. A more detailed version can be found in the *Bibliothek des. rom. Wunderbaren*, Lfg. 1803, I, 204–210.

43. THE DWARFS OF MT. OSEN *(Die Osenberger Zwerge)* Winkelmann, *Beschr. des oldenb. Horns*, Bl. 15. Happel (a native of Hesse), *Rel. cur.*, II, 525.

44. THE DWARF AND THE SHEPHERD *(Das Erdmännlein und der Schäferjung)* Prätor., *Weltbeschr.*, I, 122.

45. THE DWARF WHO CAME TO VISIT *(Der einkehrende Zwerg)* A folk legend from the Bernese Alps. See Wyß, *Volkssagen*, Bern, 1815, pp. 62–79. Cf. p. 315 and *Alpenrosen*, 1813, pp. 210–227.

46. THE FOREST OF ZEITEL MOSS *(Zeitelmoos)* *Beschreibung des Fichtelbergs,* Leipzig, 1716, p. 90.

47. THE MOSS WOMAN *(Das Moosweibchen)* Prätorius, *Weltbeschr.*, I, 691–692, collected orally from an old woman in Saalfeld. Cf. Jul. Schmidt, p. 143.

48. THE WILD HUNTSMAN PURSUES THE MOSS PEOPLE *(Der wilde Jäger jagt die Moosleute)* Prätorius, *Weltbeschr.*, I, 691–694, collected as an oral legend in the region of Saalfeld. See *Schw. Mundarten*, p. 530, the Devil pursues the Wild Woman through the forest on Ash Wednesday.

49. THE WATER NIX *(Der Wassermann)* Prätor., *Weltbeschr.*, I, 480–482. Collected as an oral legend.

50. THE WILD WOMEN OF WONDER MOUNTAIN *(Die wilden Frauen im Untersberge)* Brixener *Volksbuch.*

51. DANCING WITH THE MERMAN *(Tanz mit dem Wassermann)* Valvassor, *Ehre von Crain*, Vol. 2 and Vol. 15, cap. 19.

52. THE MERMAN AND THE FARMER *(Der Wassermann und der Bauer)* Collected orally in German Bohemia.

53. THE MERMAN AT THE BUTCHER'S STALL *(Der Wassermann an der Fleischerbank)* Collected orally in German Bohemia.

54. THE SWIMMER *(Der Schwimmer)* Bräuner, *Curiosit*, p. 37.

55. BROTHER NICKEL *(Bruder Nickel)* Cluver, *German. antiq.*, lib. 3, cap. 27. Prätorius, *Weltbeschreibung*, I, 487–488. Cf. Micrälius, Vol. I, 16. Zöllner, *Reise*, p. 259. For another legend on Nickel, see I. A. E. Göze, *Natur, Menschenleben und Vorsehung*, Leipzig, 1796, Teil 4, pp. 96–101.

56. THE SPRING OF THE NIXIES *(Nixenbrunnen)* Kornmann, *Mons veneris,* cap. 43, p. 215. Wormius, *Mon. danica.* Hornung, *Cista medica,* p. 191.

57. THE NIXIES OF MAGDEBURG *(Magdeburger Nixen)* Prätor., *Weltbeschr.*, I, 497–498.

58. DÖNGES LAKE *(Der Döngessee)* Collected orally in Hesse.

59. LAKE MUMMEL *(Mummelsee)* *Simplicissimus*, Bk. 5, cap. 10. Cf. cap. 12, "From the Tales of Old Peasants." Cf. Gottschalk, pp. 252 ff. Schreiber, *Rheinreise*, 23–24. There is more than one Lake Mummel. See Schreiber, p. 29. *Mummelchen, Mühmchen* 'young lady,' 'elf lady.' At the end of the second paragraph Schreiber remarks, "A longer account can be found in *Simplicissimus*." Included here is an excerpt from a newspaper from the year 1849.

A Legend from the Black Forest

The people here guard their world of legend and fairy tales as if they were guarding a hidden treasure. They have an insurmountable yet natural shyness that prevents them from communicating this lore to educated people. Did they not in the past have to see their most beloved lore damned or ridiculed as blasphemous or simple-minded superstition? Yet it is this very timidity that has preserved many of these charming legends. The man who is not discouraged by the great effort needed to collect this material will be rewarded when he raises a few pearls from this hidden treasure. He will owe his success to the people's timidity since not everyone has the good fortune of the Brothers Grimm in finding a Frau Viehmann (the Hessian peasant woman from whom they have collected a large number of their fairy tales). Even fewer have the gift of making the fairy-tale fountain flow freely with all its force.

I discovered this fact one brisk morning in the fall of 1845 when I set out on foot for the Black Forest from Achern. I wandered over Hornisgrinde and then into the Murg Valley. I had been told not to miss seeing the renowned Lake Mummel, which was nearby. When we asked a quarryman near the village of Seebach for directions, he obligingly informed us that he was much more inclined to take a morning walk than to dress stones, and he joined us as a guide.

I was eager to learn something of the superstitions surrounding this mysterious lake so frequently used as the setting for modern fairy tales. Thus, after we had become friends, I asked the quarryman for information. Although he was too honest to deny familiarity with the wonders of this lake, I was still unable to entice an organized, continuous narrative from him. Each individual element of the tale had to be pumped out of him with great effort. As we walked through a dense fir forest and started to climb a mountain, I subjected him to a veritable cross-examination, and I shall now relate the information he finally confessed to me. Fortunately, we still had some way yet to go, so by the time I finally coaxed the entire delightful fairy tale from him we found ourselves standing before the lake itself.

Lake Mummel lies hidden in the midst of a dense forest high above the Rhine. It is surrounded on all sides by the highest peaks of the Black Forest. Tall black fir trees cast their long shadows across the clear deep water, and the impression the lake gives is one of gloom and dread. Scarcely noticeable is a small creek that flows from the lake between some cliffs and pines, finally descending to Lake Creek Valley and on to the Rhine. Only rarely is this desolated wilderness visited by a curious wanderer, or by a cowherd and his grazing cattle with their clanging bells, or by some robust woodsman. But it is not always so quiet there. The people roundabout often speak of the Hobgoblins that live there, and of the hauntings that occur all around the lake at night. They speak of those strange days when, just before a storm strikes and the skies are yet sunny and the air still, suddenly a dull roar boils up from the depths and great waves begin to pound against the shore. For this reason it is called "Murmur Lake" or Lake Mummel.

The lake has not always been there. In olden times a splendid convent was located on this site and it was inhabited by pious nuns. One day the convent simply sank out of sight to be covered by the waters of the lake that filled the depression. The convent is still there, completely intact, more than a hundred leagues beneath the surface of the water, and it is still inhabited by the nuns. Many people have seen them, and everyone in Seebach can tell stories about the Water Sprites that live there. Many years ago these creatures used to descend the mountain and visit the peasants, helping them work their fields, or watching the small children at home. They would arrive early in the morning, but they all had to be back in their lake by the time it grew dark.

One of the Water Sprites, a kind and lovely maiden, won the love of a peasant youth. Once during the annual village festival, the Water

Sprites came down into the valley and joined in the festivities in the dance hall behind the village tavern. And the Sprite who loved the peasant youth danced one dance after another with her beloved. They were the handsomest couple of all; and the youth himself was so appealing that many of the other Water Sprites were as attracted to him as the first. Far and wide there was no maiden as beautiful as she, and no other who could dance with such nimble grace.

When it began to grow dark all the others climbed the mountain to their lake, but the lovely maiden was not able to tear herself away—she wanted to dance just one more time with her beloved. She thought that since it grew dark earlier in the valley than up in the mountains she could just make it in time if she ran.

Thus, she danced one more dance, then another, and another. In her bliss she did not realize that time was flying by. Suddenly, the prayer bell began to ring and the dance came to a stop. Everyone began to pray in a quiet murmur, saying, "Oh do not forsake us Lord Jesus." Suddenly her foolhardy frivolity began to weigh heavily on her heart, and quickly she drew her beloved outside. The stars were already in the heavens. They both began to climb the mountain in silence but great haste. When they came to the lake she turned to him and said with great sadness, "We shall never see each other again, for I must now die. Wait here a quarter of an hour. If blood gushes up in the water, you will know they have killed me. If there is none, then I shall be with you again soon." After she had spoken, she took a twig and struck the water three times. The waters parted and there appeared a sparkling staircase of polished stone leading down to the bottom of the lake where the old convent could be seen in its splendor. The Water Sprite descended the beautiful stairs, and when she reached the bottom the water closed over her and all the splendor vanished.

The night was dark and still; not a fir branch moved and there was not a single wave upon the surface of the water. Suddenly, a whirlpool spun silently out of the depths below and red blood spurted up in the middle of it. It was the blood of the Water Sprite who had been executed. Ever since that time—and that was hundreds of years ago—the Water Sprites have never returned to the valley. Only now and again will a shepherd, driving his flock up there, see one of them from afar, sitting by the shore. But no sooner does he draw near than she quickly disappears beneath the surface. But they still live down there at the bottom of the lake, and their splendid convent still stands there to this very day. And when the weather is calm and clear, and the water is very still, one can still see it glittering at the bottom of the lake.

60. THE ELBE MAIDEN AND THE SAALE WOMAN (Die Elbjungfer und das Saalweiblein) Collected orally in Magdeburg. The same story in Prätorius, Weltbeschreibung, I, 482–483, recorded in Saalfeld and Halle. See also Bräuner, Curiositäten, pp. 33–34, recorded in Leipzig.

61. WATER RIGHTS (Wasserrecht) Bräuner, Curiositäten, p. 31. Schönfeld, De spectris, Marburgi, 1685, p. 19. From an oral source.

62. THE DROWNED CHILD (Das ertrunkene Kind) Wilh. Meister, III, 501. Nationalzeitung der Deutschen, 1796, p. 74.

63. LITTLE SLIT-EARS (*Schlitzöhrchen*)  Jäger, *Briefe über die hohe Rhön*, 1803, Part 3, p. 12.

64. THE WATER NIX AND THE MILLER'S APPRENTICE (*Die Wassernixe und der Mühlknappe*)  Prätorius, *Im Glückstopf*, pp. 505–506, from an oral legend.

65. DOSTEN AND DORANT SAVE PEOPLE FROM THE NIXIES (*Vor den Nixen hilft Dosten und Dorant*)  Prätorius, *Weltbeschreibung*, I, 106–108; 531–535. A similar account in Bräuner, *Curiositäten*, pp. 34–36. Cf. Jul. Schmidt, p. 132.

66. THE LEGS OF THE WATER NIX (*Des Nixes Beine*)  Prätorius, *Weltbeschr.*, I, 533.

67. THE MAID AND THE WATER NIX (*Die Magd bei dem Nix*)  Prätorius, *Weltbeschr.*, I, 498–499.

68. LADY VON ALVENSLEBEN (*Die Frau von Alvensleben*)  Tenzel, *Monatl. Unterr.*, 1698, p. 525. Hammelmann, *Oldenb. Chronik* ("Der vielförmige Hinzelmann"), pp. 313–316. Prätorius, *Weltbeschr.*, I, p. 95; pp. 101–104, and also *Im Glückstopf*, p. 488, recorded both from oral legends and from Cyriak, *Edinus' poematische Bücher, die er vom Geschlecht der Alvensleben*, 1581, quarto edition. Neocorus, I, 543.

69. LADY VON HAHN AND THE NIX (*Die Frau von Hahn und der Nix*)  Prätorius, *Weltbeschr.*, I, 100–101.

70. LADY VON BONIKAU (*Frau von Bonikau*)  Anecdoten der Charlotte Elisabeth von Orleans, Straßburg, 1789, pp. 133–134 (first written down in 1719). (Added here as No. 70 in Jacob's handwriting.)

71. THE MEASURING CUP, THE RING, AND THE CHALICE (*Das Streichmaß, der Ring und der Becher*)  Mémoires du maréchal de Bassompierre (died 1646), Cologne, 1666, Vol. I, pp. 4–6. See Goethe, *Werke*, XII, 220–221. Cf. *Curiositäten*, pp. 271–272.

72. THE COBOLD (*Der Kobold*)  Unterredungen vom Reich der Geister, I, 503. Prätorius, *Weltbeschr.*, I, 315–320. Luther, *Tischreden*, p. 103.

73. THE FARMER AND HIS COBOLD (*Der Bauer mit seinem Kobold*)  Tenzel, *Monatl. Unterred.*, Jan., 1689, p. 145.

74. THE HOBGOBLIN OF THE MILL (*Der Kobold in der Mühle*)  Valvassor, *Ehre von Crain*, Vol. III, cap. 28, I, 420–421. From an oral narrative.

75. CAPPY (*Hütchen*)  From oral narratives. *Der vielförmige Hinzelmann*, pp. 39–50. Erasm. Francisci, *Höll Proteus*, 792–798. Prätorius, *Weltbeschr.*, I, 324–325. Joh. Weier, *De praestig. daemon.*, cap. 22 (German transl., pp. 64–66). Happel, *Relat. curios.*, IV, 246. *Stiftische Fehde*, Leibnitz, *S.S. R.R. brunsvic.*, II, 791; III, 183, 258b. *Volkssagen*, Eisenach, I, 127–170; IV, 209–237. Pomarius, *Sächsische Chronik*, Wittenb. 1588, p. 253, relates the legend up to the point where Bishop Bernhard occupies Hildesheim. Pomarius has the spirit say, "Wake up! The county of Winzenberg is free for the taking."

76. HINZELMANN (*Hinzelmann*)  From the book *Der vielförmige Hinzelmann oder umständliche und merkwürdige Erzählung von einem Geist, der sich*

*auf dem Hause Hudemühlen und hernach zu Estrup im Lande Lüneburg unter vielfältigen Gestalten und verwunderlicher Veränderung—sehen lassen,* 379 pp. in 12, first composed by Pastor Feldmann of Eickelohe.

77. KNOCKER *(Klopfer)* *Fränkische Sage,* Reizenstein, Leipzig, 1778, I, 76.

78. BOOTS *(Stiefel)* Collected orally.

79. SQUIRREL *(Ekerken)* Weier, *Von der Zauberei,* VI, 15.

80. THE NIGHT SPIRIT OF KENDENICH *(Nachtgeist zu Kendenich)* Oral version from Cologne.

81. THE NIGHTMARE *(Der Alp)* Oral narratives. Prätorius, *Weltbeschr.,* I, 1–40; II, 160–162. Bräuner, *Curiositäten,* 126–137.

82. THE CHANGELING *(Der Wechselbalg)* Bräuner, *Curiositäten,* pp. 6–7. Prätorius, *Weltbeschr.,* I, 363–364.

83. THE CHANGELINGS *(Die Wechselbälge im Wasser)* Kirchof, *Wendunmuth,* V, 314, Nr. 258. Bräuner, *Curiositäten,* 9. Hildebrand, *Entdeckung der Zauberei,* p. 109. Fischart, *Im wilden Teufels Heer.* Luther, *Tischreden,* 105b, 106a. Also known orally.

84. THE MANDRAKE *(Der Alraun)* "Galgenmännlein," in Part III of *Simplicissimus.* Israel Fronschmidt, *Vom Galgenmännlein.* Rollenhagen, *Indian. Reisen,* Magdeb., 1605, pp. 271–272. Bräuner, *Curiositäten,* pp. 226–235. Prätorius, *Weltbeschr.,* II, 215–216. *Weihnachtsfr.,* pp. 155–156. Harsdörfer, *Mordgeschichten,* No. 45, p. 151. Chr. Gotfr. Roth, *Diss. de imagunculis Germanor. magicis, quas Alraunas vocant,* Helmst., 1737, 8. Cf. Vulpius, *Vorzeit,* III, 46–54.

85. SPIRITUS FAMILIARIS *(Spiritus familiaris)* Trutz Simplex, *Leben der Landstörtzerin Courage,* cap. 18 and 22. *Der Leipziger Aventurieur,* Frankfurt and Leipzig, 1756, Part 2, pp. 38–42.

86. THE BIRD'S NEST *(Das Vogelnest)* Michaeler, "Vorrede" to *Iwein,* Wien, 1786, p. 54. *Simplicissimus Springinsfeld:* cap. 23. For information on the *bifolium,* see *Franz. hermin* and *nid d'oiseau.* Cf. *Simplicissimus,* II, 229.

87. THE BROOD PENNY *(Der Brutpfennig)* Happel, *Relat. curios.,* I, 522.

88. BEATING THE CHANGELING WITH SWITCHES *(Wechselkind mit Ruten gestrichen)* Prätorius, *Weltbeschr.,* I, 365–366.

89. WATCHING OUT FOR THE CHILDREN *(Das Schauen auf die Kinder)* Prätorius, *Weltbeschr.,* I, 124.

90. THE NURSEMAID-IN-THE-RYE *(Die Roggenmuhme)* Tharsander (G. W. Wegner), *Schauplatz,* I, 433–434. Prätorius, *Weltbeschr.,* I, 125–126. See also Prätorius, *Rübezahl,* II, 135, who had it from an oral source.

91. TWO WOMEN FROM THE UNDERWORLD *(Die zwei unterirdischen Weiber)* Prätorius, *Weltbeschr.,* I, 123–124.

92. KING GREEN FOREST *(König Grünewald)* *Hess. Denkwürdigk.,* IV, 2, pp. 295–297, recorded by Prof. Schwarz from the legends of the elderly. The

addenda are from the schoolmaster of Christenb. An Arabian legend relates that everyone in the army carries tree branches to conceal himself. And here too a female sentry cries: "The trees, the enemy of Hemjar, are coming." Fr. Rückert, *Hariri*, I, 651. Cf. *Macbeth*, and *Graf Rudolf*, and my review (written in Jacob's hand).

93. BLÜMELISALP *(Blümelisalp)* Scheuchzer, *Naturgesch. der Schweiz*, Zürich, 1746, II, 83. Wyß, *Volkssagen*, Berlin, 1815, collected from oral tradition.

94. THE LILY *(Die Lilie)* Aug. Lerchenheimer, *Bedenken von der Zauberei*, Bl. 14–15.

95. JOHANN VON PASSAU *(Johann von Passau)* Luther, *Tischreden*, 105. Prätorius, *Weltbeschr.*, I, 357–358. *Wendunmuth*, V, 312, No. 256.

96. THE PUPPY OF BRETTA *(Das Hündlein von Bretta)* Collected orally. See *Gargantua; Aller Praktik Großm.*, "All night long they chased the puppy from Bretta, so that it left its weak tool hanging on the fence" [nontranslatable proverb].

97. THE VILLAGE BY THE SEA *(Das Dorf am Meer)* Collected orally in Holstein.

98. THE BURIED SILVER MINE *(Die verschütteten Silbergruben)* Collected orally in the Harz Mountains. Cf. the Legend of St. Paul, *Mem. celt.*, III, 56.

99. THE PROSPECTORS *(Die Fundgrübner)* Happel, *Relat. curios.*, I, 758–760.

100. THE GHOSTLY HORSEMAN *(Ein gespenstiger Reiter)* H. Speidel in *Notabil. polit.*, f. 397. Prätorius, *Im Glückstopf*, pp. 173–174. Happel, *Relat. curios.*, III, 521.

101. THE FALSE OATH *(Der falsche Eid)* M. Schneider, *Titius contin.*, lib. II, sect. 2, cap. 3, p. 416.

102. THE TWELVE UNFAIR JURISTS *(Zwölf ungerechte Richter)* Zeilleri, *epist.*, 58. Hilscher, *Zungensünde*, p. 455.

103. THE SACRED SPRINGS *(Die heiligen Quellen)* *Morgenblatt*, 1808, No. 247, p. 987.

104. THE GUSHING SPRING *(Der quillende Brunnen)* Happel, *Relat. curios.*, V, 43, from Mich. Piccard, *Orat. acad.*, 4.

105. HUNGER FOUNTAIN *(Hungerquelle)* Dreyhaupt, *Hall. Chronik*, I, 1106. Cf. Stalder, *Schweiz. Idiot.*, "Vom Hungerbrunnen." *Allg. Anz. d. Deutschen*, 1816, No. 220, p. 2287. Cf. the evil springs of Sulzbach, the Hunger Fountain in the church drama of Nykerke in Ostgotland, and Hunger Lake in the Harz Mountains. The legend associated with the lake was reported by Behrens, p. 97. In the village of Rosia, in the Italian province of Siena, there are springs (called *lucales*) that only flow at certain times. When this happens, the surrounding towns know that without fail there will be a period of severe famine. If the springs then dry up again the famine will ease. See Berkenmeyer,

p. 409. Near Chateaudun, in the Orleans region of France, there is a lake. Whenever it is in flood the people there also expect famine, *idem*, p. 124. Many such hunger fountains were reported in the year 1816.

106. STREAM OF LOVE *(Der Liebenbach)* Collected orally in Hesse.

107. HELPERS' BLUFF *(Der Helfenstein)* Grundmann, *Geschichtschule*, Görlitz, 1677, pp. 779–782.

108. THE CRADLE FROM THE SAPLING *(Die Wiege aus dem Bäumchen)* *Wiener Litter. Zeitung*, Sept., 1813, p. 227. Cf. Gottschalk, *Ritterburgen*, II, 103–105, who quoted Gaheis, *Wanderungen um Wien*, 1803. Cf. Büsching, No. 34, with variations.

109. HESSIAN VALLEY *(Hessental)* *Münchhausen im Freimüthigen*, 1806, No. 47, p. 186. Collected orally in the 1780s from two elderly country-dwellers named Thusnelde and Römer (written in Jacob's hand).

110. REINSTEIN *(Reinstein)* Happel, *Relat. curios.*, III, 784. Cf. Behrens, p. 162.

111. THE RIVER THAT STANDS STILL *(Der stillstehende Fluß)* Winkelmann, *Beschr. von Hessen*, p. 59.

112. LAKE AREND *(Arendsee)* Prätorius, *Weltbeschr.*, I, 97. Collected orally. Cf. *Annales fuld. ad a. 822* (Pertz, I, 357):

> Item in parte orientalis Saxoniae, quae Soraborum finibus contigua est, in quodam deserto loco, juxta lacum qui dicitur Arnseo, terra in modum aggeris intumuit et limitem unius leugae spatio porrectum sub una nocte, absque humani operis molimine, ad instar valli surrexit.

The same report in *Ann. Einhardi* ad a. 822, Pertz, I, 209.

113. OX MOUNTAIN *(Der Ochsenberg)* Prätorius, *Weltbeschr.*, I, 96, who heard it orally from his mother, a native of the region.

114. THE MAIDENS OF THE MOORS *(Die Moorjungfern)* Jäger, *Briefe über die hohe Rhön*, I, 144; II, 36–39.

115. ST. ANDREAS' EVE *(Andreasnacht)* Collected orally. Erasm. Francisc., *Höll. Proteus*. Bräuner, *Curiositäten*, pp. 91–93. Goldschmid, *Höll. Morpheus*, Hamburg, 1698, pp. 173–174.

116. INVITING HER BELOVED TO DINNER *(Der Liebhaber zum Essen eingeladen)* Prätorius, *Weihnachtsfratzen*, prop. 53. Bräuner, *Curiositäten*, p. 97. Valvassor, *Ehre von Crain*, II, 479.

117. CHRISTMAS EVE *(Die Christnacht)* Prätorius, *Weihnachtsfratzen*, Nos. 60, 61, 64.

118. CASTING THE PETTICOATS AWAY *(Das Hemdabwerfen)* Prätorius, *Weihnachtsfratzen*, No. 62.

119. CRYSTAL GAZING *(Kristallschauen)* Joh. Rüst, *Zeitverkürzung*, pp. 255 ff. Erasm. Francisc., *Sittenspiegel*, Bl. 64 ff. Bräuner, *Curiositäten*, pp. 72–80.

120. PREPARING MAGIC HERBS *(Zauberkräuter kochen)* Bräuner, *Curiositäten*, pp. 58–61, collected as an oral narrative.

121. THE YOUNG SALT WORKER IN POMERANIA *(Der Salzknecht in Pommern)* Bräuner, *Curiositäten*, pp. 67–68.

122. MAID ELI *(Jungfer Eli)* Collected orally in the Münster area.

123. THE WHITE WOMAN *(Die weiße Frau)* Scotus, *Magia univers.*, p. 339. Bekker, *Bezauberte Welt*, I, 289.

124. A DOVE DISCOVERS A TREASURE *(Taube zeigt einen Schatz)* From Ottokar von Horneck, p. 197a, cap. 225.

125. A DOVE HOLDS OFF THE ENEMY *(Taube hält den Feind ab)* Collected orally in Höxter in the Weser Valley.

126. CASTING THE BELL OF BRESLAU *(Der Glockenguß zu Breslau)* Ungarischer *Simplicissim.*, 1683, pp. 43–44.

127. CASTING THE BELL AT ATTENDORN *(Der Glockenguß zu Attendorn)* Simplicissimus, *Rathsübel*, cap. 8. A related yet different version of the legend is told about a church in Wien-Neustadt, in Löw von Rozmital, *Denkw. und Reisen*, published by Horky, Brünn, 1821, II, 137–139. See also the Swedish bell legend "In the Village of Örkeljunge in Schonen There Is a Deep Valley Called Fantehalle" ( *Mon. Scanensia*, pp. 309 and 318):

*Vallis haec ab hujusmodi casu denominata est: Artifex quidam in ecclesiae usum campanam fabricarat, qui famulum habuit nomine Fante. Artifex vero peregre profectus, cum diutius abesset, famulus ejus Fante opus confecit et mercedem pro labore a parochianis reportavit. Sed decedens domino obviam factus est, qui cum campanae pulsum audiret, a famulo sciscitatus est, quid novi accidisset, cum ita pulsarent oppidani, respondit campanam fabricandam a se confectam esse operisque peracti se mercedem reportasse, unde dominus indignatione aestuans, jussit ut lapidem pedi suo adjungeret, quare cum caput reclinaret, malleo militari cum interfecit. In hujus necis memoriam cumulus lapidum ab agricolis coacervatus est, qui adhuc dicitur Fantonis monumentum.*

128. THE MILLER'S WIFE *(Die Müllerin)* Collected orally and also recorded on a broadside. Cf. *Wiener Friedensblätter*, 1874, No. 74, which records a similar legend but with slightly different details.

129. JOHANN HÜBNER *(Johann Hübner)* Stilling, *Leben*, I, 51–54.

130. EPPELA GAILA *(Eppela Gaila)* Fischart in *Garg.* mentions jumping over Eppelin's haywagon. Rentsch, *Antiquitäten des Burggrafthums oberhalb Gebirg, aus einer ihm 1684 vom Pfarrer Meyer zu Muggendorf mitgeteilten Nachricht: Beschreibung des Fichtelbergs*, Leipzig, 1716, p. 149. Edward Brown, *Sonderbare Reisen*, p. 67. E. M. Arndt, *Bruchst: einer Reise von Baireuth nach Wien im Sommer 1798*, Leipzig, 1801, Teil 8, pp. 27–28 and 96. *Eppelein von Gailingen* (a play by Hansing), Leipzig, 1795, 8. Cf. a letter from Count von Platen, May 7, 1824. A sixteen-page folksong about the sorcerer Eppo is said to be located in the Munich library.

131. BLUMENSTEIN *(Der Blumenstein)* *Kurhess. Magazin*, 1804, No. 30. (The addendum written in Jacob's hand.)

132. SEEBURG LAKE *(Seeburger See)* *Neues hanöv. Magazin*, 1807, St. 13 and St. 40.

133. THE CASTLE LAKE AND THE CASTLE WALL *(Der Burgsee und Burgwall)* Kosegarten, *Rhapsodien*, II, 110.

134. ST. NICHOLAS AND THE THIEF *(Der heilige Niklas und der Dieb)* Prätorius, *Weltbeschr.*, I, 200–201, who knew it orally, and from Michael Saxe, *Alphab. hist.*, p. 383. Micrälius, VI, 573. (Last entry in Jacob's hand.)

135. GIANT STONES *(Riesensteine)* Prätorius, *Weltbeschr.*, I, 591–593.

136. IMPRINTS IN THE STONE *(Spuren im Stein)* Collected orally in Hesse. (Addendum written in Wilhelm's hand:) During the night in which the prophet Mohammed was taken from Mecca by the angel Gabriel and led to Jerusalem, the prophet went to the cliffs of *al Sáffara* to pray. As he stood upon the rocks the solid stone gave way as though it were wax, and the blessed footprint of the prophet became embedded in the southwest corner of the rock. Later, this impression of the prophet's foot was protected with a structure of golden wire. See also Ali Bey, as quoted by Bertuch, II, 402. "When I climbed to the peak of Mount *Djebel Tor*, which the Christians call the Mount of Olives, I came upon a Christian chapel where the footprint of Christ, embedded in marble, is revered. The impression was made when Christ ascended to Heaven after his resurrection. Ali Bey, II, 415.

137. THE GIANT'S FINGER *(Der Riesenfinger)* Cf. *Taschenbuch für Freundschaft und Liebe*, 1815, pp. 279–281.

138. THE GIANTS FROM WONDER MOUNTAIN *(Riesen aus dem Untersberg)* *Brixener Volksbuch.*

139. JETTA HILL IN HEIDELBERG *(Der Jettenbühel zu Heidelberg)* Freher, *Orig. palat.*, I, 50. Kaiser, *Schauplatz von Heidelberg*, pp. 19–20, 169–170, and *passim*. Cf. *Idunna*, 1812, p. 172. Cf. the song "Corydon" by Martin von Opitz:

*Geh jetzund hin zu dem Brunnen*    Go now to the spring
*da des Wolfes strenge Macht*    where the wolf's powerful strength
*Mutter Jetten umgebracht.*    killed Mother Jette.

Freher reports the tale of Hubertus Thomas Leodius (*De Heidelbergae antiquitatibus*, 1624, 4, p. 296) who lived around 1540, and who excerpted the legend from an old book lent to him by Johannes Berger. This is the source for the whole legend (notated in Jacob's hand):

> *Non procul inde et satis magnus pagus Heydesheim est quoque oppidum, quod ibi habitarint Romani, qui Germanis Heyden appellabantur. Quo tempore Velleda virgo in Bruchteris imperitabat. Vetula quaedam, cui nomen Jettha, cum collem, ubi nunc est arx Heydelbergensis, et Jetthae collem (sic!) etiam nunc nomen habet, inhabitabat vetustissimumque phanum incolebat, cujus fragmenta adhuc nuper vidimus, dum comes palatinus Fridericus factus Elector egregiam domum construxit, quam novam*

*aulam appellant. Haec mulier vaticiniis inclyta, et quo venerabilior foret, raro in conspectum hominum prodiens, volentibus consilia ab ea petere de fenestra, non prodeunte vultu respondebat. Et inter caetera praedixit, ut inconditis versibus canebat, suo colli a fatis esse datum, ut futuris temporibus regiis viris, quos nominatim recensebat, inhabitaretur, coleretur et ornaretur, vallisque sub ipsa multo populo inhabitaretur et templis celeberrimis ornaretur.*

*Sed ut tandem fabulosae antiquitati valedicamus, lubet ascribere, quae is liber de infelici morte ipsius Jetthae combinebat. Egressa quondam amoenissimo tempore phanum, ut deambulatione recrearetur, progrediebatur juxta montes, donec pervenit in locum, quo montes intra convallem declinant et multis locis scaturiebant pulcherrimi fontes, quibus vehementer illa coepit delectari, et assidens ex illis bibebat, cum ecce lupa famelica cum catulis e sylva prorupit, quae conspectam mulierem nequicquam Divos invocantem dilaniat et frustillatim discerpsit. Quae casu suo fonti nomen dedit, vocaturque quippe in hodiernum diem fons luporum, ob amoenitatem loci omnibus notus.*

140. GIANT HAYM *(Riese Haym)* Matth. Holzwart, *Lustgarten newer deutscher Poeterei*, Straßb., 1568, f., pp. 164–166. Pighius, *Hercules prodic.*, p. 167. Cf. Joh. Müller, *Schweiz. Gesch.*, I, 98, Note 81. Cf. *Tyroler Almanach 1804*, p. 245, and *1805*, pp. 225–232. Bartholdy, *Tyroler Krieg*, Berlin, 1814, p. 145. Cf. the addendum to *Heldensage*, p.m. 430, excerpted from Albertus Stadens.

141. THE DRIPPING RIB *(Die tropfende Rippe)* *Wiener Litterar. Zeitung*, Feb. 1813, col. 191–192. Cf. the masc. name *Ribbentrop*.

142. MAIDEN'S LEAP *(Jungfrausprung)* Reported by Abraham a Santa Clara. Berkenmeyer, p. 491, also reports the name.

143. BULL CREEK *(Stierenbach)* Scheuchzer, *Itin. alp.*, p. 12, and *Kupfertafel 11*. *Alpenrosen*, 1813, pp. 28–29. Cf. Eyerbygg, cap. 63, and *Von einem zauberhaften Kalb Gläsir und der Quelle Gläsiskellda*.

144. THE MEN IN ZOTTEN MOUNTAIN *(Die Männer im Zottenberg)* Seyfried, *Medulla*, pp. 478–481. Nic. Henelius ab Hennenfeld, in *Silesiographia renovata*, cap. II, para. 13. *Beschreibung des Fichtelbergs*, Leipzig, 1716, pp. 59–63. Valvassor, *Ehre von Crain*, I, 247.

145. THE PRONOUNCEMENT OF DOOM *(Verkündigung des Verderbens)* Prätorius, *Weltbeschr.*, II, 38.

146. THE DWARF ON HIS BACK *(Das Männlein auf dem Rücken)* Prätorius, *Weltbeschr.*, II, 584–585.

147. GOTTSCHEE *(Gottschee)* *Volkssagen*, Eisenach, 1795, pp. 173–188.

148. THE DWARFS IN THE TREE *(Die Zwerge auf dem Baum)* Collected orally in the Hasli Valley. Wyß, *Volkssagen*, p. 320.

149. THE DWARFS ON THE BOULDER *(Die Zwerge auf dem Felsstein)* Collected orally in the region of Gadmen and reported by Wyß, *Volkssagen*, p. 320.

150. THE FEET OF THE DWARFS *(Die Füße der Zwerge)* Collected orally from a peasant in the region of Bern and reported by Wyß, *Volkssagen*, pp. 101–118.

151. THE WILD SPIRITS *(Die wilden Geister)* Hormaier, *Geschichte Tyrols,* I, 141–142.

152. THE DWARFS OF HEILING *(Die Heilingszwerge)* Spieß, Prologue to his *Hans Heiling.*

153. THE DEPARTURE OF THE DWARF NATION OVER THE BRIDGE *(Der Abzug des Zwergvolks über die Brücke)* Otmar, *Volkssagen.*

154. THE PARADE OF DWARFS OVER THE MOUNTAIN *(Der Zug der Zwerge über den Berg)* Otmar, *Volkssagen.*

155. THE DWARFS OF DARDESHEIM *(Die Zwerge bei Dardesheim)* Cf. Otmar, No. 302.

156. RIECHERT THE SMITH *(Schmied Riechert)* Otmar.

157. GRINKEN THE SMITH *(Grinkenschmidt)* Collected orally in the area of Münster. See also *Münstersche Sagen,* p. 175.

158. THE SHEPHERD BOYS *(Die Hirtenjungen)* Spieß, Prologue to *Hans Heiling.*

159. THE NUT KERNELS *(Die Nußkerne)* Collected orally from the region near Corvey in the Weser Valley.

160. THE TREASURE OF SOEST *(Der Soester Schatz)* *Simplicissimus,* Book III, cap. 13.

161. THE SPRING OF SILVER *(Das quellende Silber)* Grundmann, *Christl. und weltl. Geschichtschule,* p. 184. Happel, *Relat. curios.,* III, 529. Prätorius, *Rübezahl,* I, 401–403. Cf. Lessing, *Collect.,* I, 122. See pp. 56–58 of the first printing.

162. GOLDEN SAND ON WONDER MOUNTAIN *(Goldsand auf dem Untersberg)* *Brixener Volksbuch.*

163. COALS OF GOLD *(Goldkohlen)* *Brixener Volksbuch.*

164. THE FOUNTAIN OF STEINAU *(Der Brunnen zu Steinau)* Bange, *Thüring. Chronik,* Bl. 105.

165. THE FIVE CROSSES *(Die fünf Kreuze)* Collected orally in Höxter in the Weser Valley.

166. THE SWORD DANCE AT WEISSENSTEIN *(Der Schwerttanz zu Weißenstein)* Winkelmann, *Hess. Chronik,* p. 375, who collected it orally from the elderly.

167. THE STONE TABLE OF BINGENHEIM *(Der Steintisch zu Bingenheim)* Winkelmann, *Beschr. von Hessen,* p. 184, who collected it orally from Pastor Draud of Dauernheim. Cf. Wenk, II, 508.

168. THE TALL MAN OF MURDERER'S ALLEY IN HOF *(Der lange Mann in der Mordgasse zu Hof)* Widmann in the *Chronik* of Hof.

169. WAR AND PEACE *(Krieg und Frieden)* Gottfr. Schulz, *Chronik,* p. 542. Bräuner, *Curiositäten,* p. 279. Prätorius, *Weltbeschr.,* p. 665.

170. RODENSTEIN ON THE MOVE *(Rodensteins Auszug)* Collected orally. Cf. *Zeitung für die eleg. Welt*, 1811, No. 126. Also *Reichsanzeiger*, 1806, No. 129, pp. 160, 198, 206 and 1515–1521; 1816, No. 94. Also *Morgenblatt*, 1816, No. 48. *Besondere Schrift*, 1816, and Darmstadt, 1824. For North Frisian beliefs about hordes in the sky, see Heinrich (ed. Falk), II, 93.

171. TANNHÄUSER *(Der Tannhäuser)* Based on the ancient folksong publ. by Prätorius, *Blocksberg*, Leipzig, 1668, pp. 19–25. Agricola, *Sprichwort*, 667, p.m. 322b. Jewish Legend, *Helvicus*, 2, No. 46.

172. HACKELBERG, THE WILD HUNTSMAN *(Der wilde Jäger Hackelberg)* Hans Kirchhof, *Wendunmuth*, IV, No. 283, pp. 342–343. Kirchhof was nearly contemporary with the historical Hackelberg, who died in 1581. For the Wild Huntsman in Prussian legends, see Baczkos, *Märchen und Sagen*.

173. THE WILD HUNTSMAN AND THE TAILOR *(Der wilde Jäger und der Schneider)* Collected orally in Münster.

174. HÖSEL MOUNTAIN *(Der Höselberg)* Bange, *Thüring. Chronik*, fol. 57. Kornmann, *Mons Veneris*, cap. 74, p. 374. Seyfried, *Medulla*, p. 482. Cf. Agricola, *Sprichwort*, 301. Cf. Legend No. 5. NB., and Toot Osel, who is also a member of the Raging Horde (cf. Legend No. 312). She is sometimes called Ursel and at other times Osel. There is an Osel Mountain near Dinkelsbühl. See also Legend No. 222, "The Maiden of Osel Mountain," and Legend No. 43, "The Dwarfs of Mt. Osen."

175. LORD RECHENBERG'S SERVANT *(Des Rechenbergers Knecht)* Agricola, *Sprichwort*, 301, Bl. 172. Kirchhof, *Wendunmuth*, V, Nos. 247–249, pp. 304–305. Luther, *Tischreden*, 106.

176. THE GHOST CHURCH *(Geisterkirche)* Widmann, *Höfer Chronik*. From oral tales collected from the region around Paderborn.

177. THE BANQUET OF GHOSTS *(Geistermahl)* Bräuner, *Curiositäten*, pp. 336–340. Erasmus Francisc., *Höll. Proteus*, p. 426.

178. THE ROOFER *(Der Dachdecker)* Collected orally.

179. THE SPINNING WOMAN AT THE CROSS *(Die Spinnerin am Kreuz)* Collected orally in Austria. See also Crusius, *Ann. suev. dod.*, III, 387. Cf. the woodcut showing St. Elisabeth as a spinning woman (added by Wilhelm).

180. BUTTERMILK TOWER *(Buttermilchturm)* See Fricke's copper etching of Marienburg, which was taken from an oral legend. See also Fürst, *Reisen*, Sorau, 1739, pp. 12–13, and Berkenmeyer, *Curieus. antiq.*

181. SAINT WINFRIED *(Der heilige Winfried)* Ges. *Denkwürdigk.*, II, 3–4, and collected orally. (The addenda within the legend text are in Jacob's hand.)

182. HELP MOUNTAIN *(Der Hülfenberg)* Collected orally in Hesse. Cf. Sagittarius, *Thür. Heidenthum*, pp. 165–166.

183. THE DEVIL'S HOLE IN GOSLAR *(Das Teufelsloch zu Goslar)* Müchler, *Spiele müß. Stunden*, 1810, Part 4. It occurred under Henry IV (*anno* 1063), cf. Schlosser, II, 2, p. 672. According to Vincent, *bellov.*, lib. 26, cap. 19, it was

Henry III. A similar dispute regarding rank occurred later, during the reign of Frederick Barbarossa, when the contingents from Fulda and Cologne quarreled at the famous gathering in Mainz in 1184. See V. Rommel, *Hess. Gesch.*, I, 267 (note on page 219 also). See also Koberstein, p. 14. Lamb, *Schafnab, Ad a 1063*, relates a complex version of the incident in which there is no mention of the Devil. Since Lamb was contemporary with the event it is evident that the popular legend that included the Devil was a later development. The conflict here was also *de positione sellarum*, but the place of honor was next to the Archbishop of Mainz, not the emperor.

184. THE DEVIL'S MILL *(Die Teufelsmühle)* Otmar, pp. 189–194. Quedlinburg collection, pp. 97–98. (Changes made in this version were done in Jacob's hand on the basis of the Quedlinburg collection.)

185. THE LORD'S JOURNEY *(Der Herrgottstritt)* Würtemberg. Lang, *Taschenbuch für 1800*, pp. 129–136. Prätorius, *Weltbeschr.*, II, 599. Zeiller, Vol. II, epist., No. 60. Seyfried, *Medulla*, p. 429. Cf. Sattler, *Topographie Würtembergs*.

186. THE BRIDGE TO SACHSENHAUSEN *(Die Sachsenhäuser Brücke zu Frankfurt)* Collected orally in Frankfurt. According to Löw von Rozmital, *Reisen*, I, 225–226, *El puente de Segovia* was built by the Devil in a single night.

187. THE WOLF AND THE PINE CONE *(Der Wolf und der Tannenzapf)* Collected orally. (The addition *"in fine"* in regard to the French is written in Jacob's hand. Jacob also added the note that J. Jansen calls her Frau Abo in his edition of *Volkslieder*.)

188. THE DEVIL OF ACH *(Der Teufel von Ach)* Agricola, *Sprichw.*, p. 301; Schottel, *Grammat.*, p. 1134.

189. DEVIL'S WALL *(Die Teufelsmauer)* Döderlin, *De antiq. in Nordgavia romanis*, p. 29. See also Falkenstein, *Nordg. Alterthümer*, II, 61. The walls are said to go around the whole world.

190. THE DEVIL'S DANCE FLOOR *(Des Teufels Tanzplatz)* Otmar, pp. 175–178. See also the Quedlinburg collection, pp. 122–123.

191. THE DEVIL'S PULPIT *(Die Teufelskanzel)* *Homilien des Teufels*, Frankfurt, 1800.

192. DEVIL'S PILLOW *(Das Teufelsohrkissen)* *Morgenblatt*, 1811, No. 208, p. 830.

193. DEVIL'S BLUFF *(Der Teufelsfelsen)* *Beschreibung des Fichtelberges*, Leipzig, 1716, pp. 128–129.

194. DEVIL'S WALL *(Teufelsmauer)* Arndt, *Reise von Baireuth nach Wien*, Leipzig, 1801, pp. 169–170. See also Arndt, *Reise nach Deutschland, Italien und Frankreich*, I, 113.

195. DEVIL'S LATTICE *(Teufelsgitter)* Collected orally. See Berkenmeyer, p. 702.

196. DEVIL'S MILL *(Teufelsmühle)* *Tradit. Corbeienses*, p. 559. Jäger, *Briefe über die hohe Rhön*, II, 51.

197. DEVIL'S CHURCH *(Teufelskirche)* Jäger, *Briefe über die hohe Rhön,* II, 49. Melissantes, *Bergschlösser,* p. 181.

198. DEVIL'S ROCK AT REICHENBACH *(Teufelsstein bei Reichenbach)* Winkelmann, *Hess. Chronik,* p. 34.

199. DEVIL'S ROCK IN COLOGNE *(Teufelsstein zu Köln)* Rhein. *Antiquarius,* p. 725.

200. SÜNTEL ROCK IN OSNABRÜCK *(Süntelstein zu Osnabrück)* Strodtmann, *Idiotikon,* p. 236.

201. LIAR'S ROCK *(Der Lügenstein)* Otmar, *Volkssagen.*

202. THE BRIDGE OVER THE CANYON *(Die Felsenbrücke)* Collected orally in Oberwallis.

203. DEVIL'S BATH NEAR DASSEL *(Das Teufelsbad zu Dassel)* Letzner, *Dasselische Chronik,* Erfurt, 1596, Book V, cap. 13; Book VIII, cap. 9.

204. THE TOWER OF SCHARTFELD *(Der Turm zu Schartfeld)* Letzner, *Dasselische Chronik,* Book VI, cap. 1.

205. COLOGNE CATHEDRAL *(Der Dom zu Köln)* Oral narratives current in Cologne. Cf. the account of the aqueduct by Schreiber, *Handbuch für Rheinreisen,* p. 274. Cf. *The Lay of St. Anno,* 510–516. See also Gelenius, *De admir. Colon. magnit,* 1645, quarto, p. 254: *"De aquaeductu ubio-romano treverico,"* which also makes mention of a *"continua a majoribus accepta narratio, fabellis, tamen quibusdam a plebe inspersa."* *Weltchronik,* Heidelberg, 361, folio 3, p. 2, col. 2, reports on the founding of Cologne and of the construction of an underground aqueduct.

206. DEVIL'S CAP *(Des Teufels Hut)* Cf. *Taschenbuch für Liebe und Freundschaft,* 1816, pp. 237–238.

207. DEVIL'S FIRE *(Des Teufels Brand)* Erasmus Rotterodam, *Epist. fam.,* lib., 27, c. 20. Nic. Remigii, *Daemonolatria,* pp. 335–336.

208. DEVIL'S HORSESHOE *(Die Teufelshufeisen)* Prätorius, *Weltbeschr.,* II, 362. Essentially the same story but more detailed and set in a different context can be found in Francisci, *Lust. Schaubühne,* Part I, p. 801. See also the Dutch folksong in Garekeuke, pp. 12–13.

209. THE DEVIL ABDUCTS THE BRIDE *(Der Teufel führt die Braut fort)* Godelmann, *Von Zauberern, Hexen und Unholden,* translated by Nigrin, 1592, p. 9. Latin edition, *De magis,* etc., Francof., 1591, pp. 12–13. Hilscher, *Zungensünde,,* pp. 200–201. See Dobenek, I, 161, for the text of a folksong on the theme.

210. THE WHEEL OF FORTUNE *(Das Glücksrad)* Grundmann, *Geschichtschule,* pp. 228–230. D. Siegfried Saccus, from an oral tale told by a treasure seeker in Magdeburg. Prätorius, *Wünschelruthe,* pp. 88–90. See *Froschmäuseler,* 1595, 0, VI. Book 1, Part 1, cap. 18.

211. THE DEVIL AS ADVOCATE *(Der Teufel als Fürsprecher)* D. Mengering, *Soldatenteufel,* cap. 8, p. 153. Hilscher, *Zungensünde,* p. 189. Luther, *Tischreden,* p. 113. Prätorius, *Wünschelruthe,* 101–103.

212. THE DREAM OF THE TREASURE AT THE BRIDGE *(Traum vom Schatz auf der Brücke)* Agricola, *Sprichwort*, p. 623. *Der ungewissenhafte Apotheker*, p. 132. Prätorius, *Wünschelruthe*, pp. 372–373. Cf. Musäus, *Stumme Liebe.* Abraham a Santa Clara, *Judas*, I, 4, Kempen and Dordrecht. Kulda, No. 89. *Prag. Menevi*, 6, 87. Cairo (Sitzungsber., 7, 829); on the bridge into Paris, see the *Karlmeineit.*

213. THE POT OF GOLD *(Der Kessel mit dem Schatz)* Collected orally in both Bibesheim and Wernigerode.

214. THE WEREWOLF *(Der Werwolf)* Orally from both Bibesheim and Wernigerode. 253. Nic. Remigii, *Daemonolatria*, etc., Francof., 1598, pp. 263–264.

215. WEREWOLF ROCK *(Der Werwolfstein)* Otmar, pp. 270–276.

216. THE MIGRATION OF THE WEREWOLVES *(Die Werwölfe ziehen aus)* Casp. Peucerus, *De divinatione*, p. 170. Bräuner, *Curiositäten*, pp. 251–252.

217. THE EMERGENCE OF THE DRAGON *(Der Drache fährt aus)* Scheuchzer, *Itinera per alpinas regiones*, III, 386–387, 396. Valvassor, *Ehre von Crain*, III, cap. 32. Seyfried, *Medulla*, p. 629, No. 5. Cf. *Gesta rom.*, cap. 114.

218. WINKELRIED AND THE DRAGON *(Winkelried und der Lindwurm)* Etterlin, *Chronik*, Basel, 1764, pp. 12–13. Stumpf, *Chron. Helvet.*, VII, cap. 2. Joh. Müller, *Schweizer Geschichte*, I, 514. Scheuchzer, cap. I, pp. 389–390.

219. THE DRAGON AT THE WELL *(Der Lindwurm am Brunnen)* Collected orally from a peasant from Oberbirbach.

220. DRAGON CAVE *(Das Drachenloch)* Scheuchzer, cap. III, pp. 383–384. Cysati, *Beschr. des IV. Waldstädtersee*, p. 175, in turn from Jac. Man., *Hist. Austriae.* Athanas Kircher, *Mund. subt.*, VIII, p. 94, from Cysat. Wagner, *Hist. nat. Helvetiae*, p. 246. Joh. Müller, *Schweizer Gesch.*, II, 440, Note 692. Cf. *Alpenrosen*, 1817, pp. 120–127. Justinger, p. 8.

221. THE SNAKE QUEEN *(Die Schlangenkönigin)* Wyß, pp. 148–184.

222. THE MAIDEN OF OSEL MOUNTAIN *(Die Jungfrau im Oselberg)* Crusii *Analecta paralipom.*, cap. 17, p. 68, according to G. Widemann.

223. THE TOADSTOOL *(Der Krötenstuhl)* Die Brautschau: ein Mährlein von C. F. W., Magdeburg, 1796.

224. THE WOMAN OF THE MEADOW *(Die Wiesenjungfrau)* Collected orally in Hesse.

225. THE SNEEZES FROM THE WATER *(Das Niesen im Wasser)* Collected orally in Hesse.

226. THE LOST SOUL *(Die arme Seele)* Collected orally in Paderborn.

227. THE ACCURSED WOMAN *(Die verfluchte Jungfer)* *Eisenacher Volkssagen*, II, 179–180.

228. THE MAIDEN OF STAUFEN MOUNTAIN *(Das Fräulein von Staufenberg)* Otmar's collection.

229. MAIDEN ROCK *(Der Jungfernstein)* Melissantes, *Orograph. h.v.*

230. THE STONE BRIDAL BED (*Das steinerne Brautbett*)  Spieß, *Biograph. der Wahnsinn.*, Parts 3 and 4; Spieß acquired the story from a folk legend.

231. CURSED TO REMAIN STANDING (*Zum Stehen verwünscht*)  Prätorius, *Weltbeschr.*, I, 659–661.

232. THE PEASANTS OF KOLBECK (*Die Bauern zu Kolbeck*)  Bange, *Thüring. Chronik*, Bl. 39. Becherer, *Thüring. Chronik*, pp. 193–194. Gerstenberg as quoted in Schminke, *Mon. hass.*, I, 88–89. Spangenberg, *Brautpredigt*, 45. Henr. hervord., *anno 1009*. Cosner, p. 564. *Lübeker Rymböklin*, Bogen K, 3b:

In Colbeke, in the Meydeborg [Magdeburg] region, a dance was arranged for the Holy Evening of Christ's birth. The participants continued to dance for a whole year. There were fifteen women and eighteen men. The dance took place in the cemetery of the church of St. Magnus.

233. HOLY SUNDAY (*Der heilige Sonntag*)  Harsdörfer, *Mordgeschichten*, No. 120, 3.

234. MOTHER HÜTT (*Frau Hütt*)  Cf. *Morgenblatt*, 1811, No. 28.

235. MT. KINDEL (*Der Kindelsberg*)  Stilling, *Leben*, II, 24–29.

236. THE BREADROLL SHOES (*Die Semmelschuhe*)  Collected orally in German Bohemia.

237. THE CAVE-IN AT HOCHSTÄDT (*Der Erdfall bei Hochstädt*)  Behrens, *Curiöser Harzwald*, pp. 85–86. See Gottschalk, pp. 36–40, for a varying account.

238. SHOES OF BREAD (*Die Brotschuhe*)  Collected orally in German Bohemia.

239. DEAF GRAIN (*Das taube Korn*)  A well-known legend in Holland. Grabner, *Reise in die Niederlande*, Gotha, 1792, pp. 58–60. Winsheim, *Fries. Chronik*, Bl. 147–148.

240. LADY'S SANDBANK (*Der Frauensand*)  Communicated orally from Holland. Cf. Nemnich, *Catholikon v. arundo*, I, 486.

241. BREAD TURNED TO STONE (*Brot zu Stein geworden*)  Melissantes, *Handb. für Bürger und Bauern*, Frankfurt und Leipzig, 1744, p. 128. Ernst, *Gemüthsergötzlichkeit*, p. 946. *Rheinischer Antiquar.*, p. 864. Legend collected orally in Landshut. Another version from Danzig is printed in Mart. Zeiler, *Handbuch von allerlei nützl. Sachen und Denkwürdigkeiten*, Ulm, 1655, p. 27.

242. THE MOUSE TOWER OF BINGEN (*Der Binger Mäuseturm*)  Bange, *Thüring. Chronik*, Bl. 35b. *Froschmäuseler*, Book 3, Part 1, cap. 13. Cf. Bodmann, *Rheingau*, pp. 148–150. Becherer, pp. 183–184.

243. THE CHILD'S MARSH (*Das Bubenried*)  Collected orally in the Oden Forest.

244. CHILDREN'S BRIDGE (*Kindelbrück*)  Collected orally.

245. THE CHILDREN OF HAMELN (*Die Kinder zu Hameln*)  Samuel Erich, *Der hamelschen Kinder Ausgang*. Kirchmayer, *Vom unglücklichen Ausgang der ha-*

*mel. Kinder*, Dresden und Leipzig, 1702, p. 8. Joh. Weier, *Von Teufelsgespenstern*, l.c., 16. Meibom, *SS.RR. GG.*, III, p. 80. Hondorf, *Prompt. exempl. Tit. de educ. liberor.* Becherer, *Thüring. Chronik*, pp. 366–367. Seyfried, *Medulla*, p. 476. Hübner, *Geogr. Hamb.*, 1736, III, 611–613. Verstegan, *Decayed Intelligence*, London, 1634, pp. 84–86. *Die hamel. Chron., passim. Froschmäuseler*, III, 1, 13.

246. THE RATCATCHER *(Der Rattenfänger)* Collected orally in German Bohemia.

247. THE SNAKE CATCHER *(Der Schlangenfänger)* Joh. Weier, *Von Teufelsgespenstern*, p. 95.

248. THE LITTLE MOUSE *(Das Mäuselein)* Prätorius, *Weltbeschr.*, I, 40–41. Cf. II, 161.

249. THE EMERGING PUFF OF SMOKE *(Der ausgehende Rauch)* Prätorius, *Weltbeschr.*, II, 161.

250. THE CAT IN THE WILLOW *(Die Katze aus dem Weidenbaum)* Der ungewissenhafte Apotheker, p. 895.

251. CREATING STORMS AND HAIL *(Wetter und Hagel machen)* Godelmann, *Von Zauberern*, translation by Nigrin, V, 1, p. 83. Luther, *Tischreden*, 104. Kirchhof, *Wendunmuth*, V, No. 261, p. 316. Lercheimer, pp. 50 ff.

252. THE WITCHES' SABBATH *(Der Hexentanz)* Nic. Remigii, *Daemonolatria*, p. 109.

253. THE GRAPEVINE AND THE NOSES *(Die Weinreben und Nasen)* Aug. Lercheimer, *Bedenken von der Zauberei*, Bl. 19.

254. HANGING FAST *(Festhängen)* Joh. Weier, *Von Teufelsgespenstern*, p. 105.

255. THE SHIRT OF NEED *(Das Nothemd)* Joh. Weier, *Von Teufelsgespenstern*, Bk. 8, cap. 13. Zedler, *Universallexicon*, h.v. *Der ungewissenhafte Apotheker*, p. 650.

256. FATE SECURED *(Fest gemacht)* Bräuner, *Curiositäten*, p. 365. Luther, *Tischreden*, p. 109.

257. THE CRACK SHOT *(Der sichere Schuß)* Aug. Lercheimer, *Bedenken von der Zauberei*, Bl. 12.

258. THE NOMADIC HUNTSMAN *(Der herumziehende Jäger)* Collected orally in Paderborn and Münster.

259. THE DOUBLE *(Doppelte Gestalt)* Erasm. Francisci, *Höll. Proteus*, p. 1097. Bräuner, *Curios.*, pp. 351–352.

260. THE GHOST POSING AS A WIFE *(Gespenst als Eheweib)* Bräuner, *Curios.*, pp. 353–355. Erasm. Francisci, *Höll. Proteus*, pp. 1097–1098.

261. THE DEATH OF THE FIRSTBORN *(Tod des Erstgeborenen)* Collected orally. It is also told in the Hessian royal residence itself. According to others,

the obstinancy of the firstborn, Landgrave Henry the Child, occasioned the curse. Cf. Rommel, *Hess. Geschichte*, II, note on p. 72.

262. THE BOY OF COLMAR *(Der Knabe zu Kolmar)* Collected orally.

263. THE DEATH OF THE CANON OF MERSEBURG *(Tod des Domherrn zu Merseburg)* Erasm. Francisci, *Höll. Proteus*, p. 1056.

264. THE LILY IN THE MONASTERY OF CORVEY *(Die Lilie im Kloster zu Korvei)* Gab. Bucelin, *Germania sacra*, II, p. 1642. *Notitiae S.R.I. procerum*, III, cap. 19, p. 334. *Höxar in elegiis*, Paderborn, 1600. Erasm. Francisc., *Höll. Proteus*, pp. 1054–1055. *Altdeutsche Wälder*, II, 185–187.

265. CANON REBUNDUS OF THE CATHEDRAL IN LÜBECK *(Rebundus im Dom zu Lübeck)* Ph. H. Friedlieb, *Medulla theologica*. Erasm. Francisc., *Höll. Proteus*, pp. 1057–1065, who recorded it from an oral legend.

266. THE BELL THAT RINGS ITSELF *(Glocke läutet von selbst)* Erasm. Francisc., *Höll. Proteus*, pp. 1035–1036, 1039.

267. SPIRIT OF DEATH *(Todesgespenst)* Erasm. Francisc., *Höll. Proteus*, pp. 419 and 1044. Presumably deals with Margareta Maultasch.

268. MOTHER BERTHA OR THE WHITE WOMAN *(Frau Berta oder die weiße Frau)* Joh. Jac. Rohde, *De celebri spectro, quod vulgo die weiße Frau nominant*, Königsberg, 1723, p. 4. Stilling, *Theorie der Geisterkunde*, pp. 351–359. Erasm. Francisc., *Höll. Proteus*, pp. 59–92. Cf. *Volksmärchen der Frau Naubert*, Vol. III.

269. WILD BERTHA WILL COME *(Die wilde Berta kommt)* Crusii, *Annal. suev.*, Part I, lib. XII, cap. 6, p. 329. Part II, lib. VIII, cap. 7, p. 266. Flögel, *Gesch. des Grotesken*, p. 23. *Journal von und für Deutschland*, II (1790), 26 ff.

270. THE TÜRST, THE POSTERLI, AND THE STRÄGGELE *(Der Türst, das Posterli, und die Sträggele)* Stalder, *Idiot.*, I, 208–209, 329; II, 405.

271. THE NIGHT HUNTER AND THE SHAKING WOMEN *(Der Nachtjäger und die Rüttelweiber)* Prätorius, *Rübezahl*, II, 134–136.

272. THE MAN IN THE SLOUCH HAT *(Der Mann mit dem Schlack-hut)* Collected orally in the town of Beerfelden in the region of Erbach.

273. THE GREY HOCKELMAN *(Der graue Hockelmann)* Collected orally along the "Mountain Highway" *(Bergstraße)*.

274. CHIMMEKE OF POMERANIA *(Chimmeke in Pommern)* Micrälius, Bk. III, cap. 64. Studemund, *Mecklenb. Sagen*, II, No. 7.

275. THE SHRIEKER *(Der Krischer)* From a report made by the municipal treasury of the city of Erbach. Cf. the French folk legends of the *Criard*. See *Mem. celt.*, V, 109.

276. FERRYING THE MONKS *(Die überschiffenden Mönche)* Taken from a tale in the writings of Ph. Melanchthon, set to rhyme by Georg Sabinus, and printed in Weier, *Von der Zauberei*, I, cap. 17. Reported differently by Büsching, *Leipz. Lit. Zeitung*, 1812, No. 314. See also *Melandri jocos.*, I, 709.

277. THE WILL-O'-THE-WISP (Der Irrwisch)   Collected orally in Hänlein.

278. THE FLAMING CARRIAGES (Die feurigen Wagen)   Collected orally in the Oden Forest.

279. RÄDER MOUNTAIN (Räderberg)   Collected orally.

280. THE LIGHTS ON THE HALBERDS (Die Lichter auf Hellebarden)   Happel, Relat. curios., II, 771–772.

281. WAFELING (Das Wafeln)   Kosegarten, Rhapsodien, II, 76. Zölner, Reise durch Pommern, 1797, I, 316 and 516.

282. THE CASTLE OF FLAMES (Weberndes Flammenschloß)   Der abenteuerliche Jean Rebhu, 1679, Part II, pp. 8–11.

283. FIRE MOUNTAIN (Der Feuerberg)   Collected orally in Wernigerode.

284. THE MAN OF FIRE (Der feurige Mann)   Bothonis, Chronicon brunsvic. pictur., quoted by Leibnitz, SS. RR. BB., III, 337. From oral legends from the region of Erbach.

285. THE ACCURSED SURVEYORS (Die verwünschten Landmesser) Collected orally in Mecklenburg.

286. THE DISPLACED BORDER STONE (Der verrückte Grenzstein)   Erasm. Francisc., Höll. Proteus, p. 422. See also Gargant., 23b: "Old stone markers are not to be displaced."

287. THE BOUNDARY DISPUTE (Der Grenzstreit)   Collected orally in Hesse.

288. THE RACE FOR THE BOUNDARY (Der Grenzlauf)   Wyß, ibid., pp. 80–100. Cf. Legend No. 317.

289. THE ALPINE BATTLE (Die Alpschlacht)   Stalder, Fragmente über Entlebuch, Zürich, 1797, I, 81–85.

290. THE ROCK OF WENTHUSEN (Der Stein bei Wenthusen)   Quedlinburg collection, pp. 150 and 154.

291. THE CHURCH OF ALTENBERG (Die Altenberger Kirche)   J. C. Geller, Merkwürdigk. Thüringens, I, 59 and 466. Falkenstein, Thür. Chronik, II, 273. See also the note in Vol. III, 1272.

292. THE KING IN LAUENBURG MOUNTAIN (Der König im Lauenburger Berg)   Kornmann, Mons Veneris. Seyfried, Medulla, p. 482. Valvassor, Ehre von Crain, I, 247.

293. SWAN MOUNTAIN (Der Schwanberg)   Agricola, Sprichw., pp. 389–390.

294. THE SPRING OF ROBBEDISSEN (Der Robbedisser Brunn)   Letzner, Dasselische Chronik, B. VIII, cap. 10.

295. THE SCALES OF BAMBERG (Bamberger Waage)   Manlii, Loc. comm. collect., p. 46.

296. EMPEROR FREDERICK IN KAISERSLAUTERN (Kaiser Friedrich zu Kaiserslautern)   Georg Draud, Fürstl. Tischreden. Cf. Fischart, Gargantua, 266b.

There is a similar legend about Trifels near Anweiler. Cf. Zeiller, *Reisebuch*, II, 395. Schlegel, *Mus.*, I, 293.

297. THE SHEPHERD ON MT. KYFFHAUSEN *(Der Hirt auf dem Kyffhäuser)* Georg Draud, *Fürstliche Tischreden*, Frankfurt, 1621, I, 322.

298. THE THREE TELLS *(Die drei Telle)* *Journal des Luxus und der Moden*, January, 1805, p. 38. Cf. Ranke, Part 1, p. 396. According to a review *(Erg. Blätter Jen. L.Z.* 1818, No. 84, col. 185) and a folk legend told by the people of Lake Urn, the three champions of Swiss freedom have been sleeping for centuries inside the cliffs of Mt. Salis above Grütli. One day they will awaken in order to save Switzerland once again. See the translation of the *Tuti Nameh* by C. Iken for an account of "The Seven Sleepers," pp. 288–311.

299. THE MOUNTAIN DWARF *(Das Bergmännchen)* Wyß, *ibid.*, pp. 1–12. Cf. pp. 306 and 308. From an oral legend.

300. THE CEMBRA NUTS *(Die Zirbelnüsse)* Collected orally in Oberwallis.

301. THE PARADISE OF ANIMALS *(Das Paradies der Tiere)* Collected orally in the Visper Valley of Oberwallis.

302. THE CHAMOIS HUNTER *(Der Gemsjäger)* Wyß, *ibid.*, pp. 43–61. Cf. 312. See also *Mem. celtiq.*, V, 201.

303. THE CAVES OF THE DWARFS *(Die Zwerglöcher)* Behrens, *Curiöser Harzwald*, pp. 37 and 75–76.

304. THE DWARF AND THE WONDER FLOWER *(Der Zwerg und die Wunderblume)* Otmar, pp. 145–150.

305. THE NIX OF LAKE KELLE *(Der Nix an der Kelle)* Otmar, *Volkssagen*. Cf. Behrens, p. 82.

306. SCHWARZACH *(Schwarzach)* *Badische Wochenschrift*, 1807, St. 17, col. 268, and St. 34, col. 543.

307. THE THREE MAIDENS FROM THE LAKE *(Die drei Jungfern aus dem See)* *Badische Wochenschrift*, 1806, St. 21, col. 342.

308. THE DEAD BRIDEGROOM *(Der tote Bräutigam)* Prätorius, *Weltbeschr.*, I, 105–109.

309. THE ETERNAL HUNTSMAN *(Der ewige Jäger)* Based on a *Meistergesang* by Michael Behams, *MS. Vatic.*, 312, Bl. 165, published in the *Sammlung für altdeutsche Lit. und Kunst* by von Hagen *et al.*, pp. 43–45. Hackelberg is also reported to have uttered the following words on his deathbed: "I will gladly relinquish whatever God has in store for me in Heaven if I can hunt for all eternity." See Weidmann, *Feierabende*, Marburg, 1816, II, 5. Cf. Legend No. 172.

310. HANS JAGENTEUFEL *(Hans Jagenteufel)* *Journal von und für Deutschland*, 1787, II, No. 27. Prätorius, *Weltbeschr.*, II, 69–72.

311. HACKELNBERG'S DREAM *(Des Hackelnberg Traum)* Otmar, pp. 249–250. Weidmann, *Feierabende*, pp. 4–9, born in 1521 and died in 1581. Cf. *Freimüthiger*, 1815, Nos. 143–144 *(Die Dornburg* by Ferdin. von Knesebeck). *Jugendzeitung*, 1812, No. 104 (by D. Nagel of Hornburg). His gravestone is said to be located in the garden of a tavern called Klapperkrug, three hours from Goslar.

312. TOOT OSEL *(Die Tut-Osel)* Otmar, pp. 141 ff. See *Feierabende*, p. 8: Dummburg = Dornburg?

313. THE BLACK HORSEMEN AND THE RIDERLESS HORSE *(Die schwarzen Reiter und das Handpferd) Hanauischer Landcalender vom Jahre 1730.* Hilscher, *Vom wütenden Heer*, Dresden, 1702, pp. 31–32.

314. FAITHFUL ECKHART *(Der getreue Eckhart)* "Vorrede" to the *Heldenbuch* (toward the end). Agricola, *Sprichw.*, 667. *Hanauischer Landcalender*, ibid.

315. THE YOUNG LADY OF WILL MOUNTAIN *(Das Fräulein vom Willberg)* Collected orally from the Corvey region of the Weser Valley.

316. THE SHEPHERD AND THE OLD MAN OF THE MOUNTAIN *(Der Schäfer und der Alte aus dem Berg)* Collected orally in Wernigerode.

317. MAIDEN ILSE *(Jungfrau Ilse)* Otmar, pp. 171–174. Quedlinburg collection, pp. 204–205.

318. THE HEATHEN MAIDEN OF GLATZ *(Die Heidenjungfrau zu Glatz)* Älurius, *Glätzische Chronik*, Leipzig, 1625, 4, pp. 124–128. Cf. p. 86. Prätorius used this source in his *Rübezahl*, I, 176–185.

319. THE HOOFPRINT AND THE DEVIL'S POND *(Der Roßtrapp und der Kreetpfuhl)* Behrens, *Harzwald*, pp. 121 and 130. Seyfried, *Medulla*, p. 428. Melissantes, *Orograph.* h.v. Otmar, pp. 181–186. Quedlinburg collection, pp. 125–128 and 147–148.

320. THE GIANT MAIDEN'S LEAP *(Der Mägdesprung)* Quedlinburg collection, p. 67. Otmar, pp. 195–198. Cf. p. 53. See also Behrens, *Harzwald*, p. 131, and Seyfried, *Medulla*, p. 428. Melissantes, *Orograph* h.v.

321. MAIDEN'S LEAP *(Der Jungfernsprung)* Peschek, *Oybin bei Zittau*, Leipzig, 1804, pp. 33–34.

322. HARRAS' LEAP *(Der Harrassprung)* Körner, *Nachlaß*, II, 71–74.

323. HIDDE THE GIANT *(Der Riese Hidde)* Pierius Winsemius, *Geschiedenisse van Friesland*, Franeker, 1622, fol. Bk. III, p. 93.

324. THE EYE-OF-THE-NEEDLE AT ILEFELD *(Das Ilefelder Nadelöhr)* Behrens, *Cur. Harzwald*, pp. 126–127.

325. THE GIANTS OF LICHTENBERG *(Die Riesen zu Lichtenberg)* Collected orally in the Oden Forest.

326. GIANT'S BLOOD *(Das Hünenblut)* Otmar, pp. 267–270.

327. THE NOISE FROM THE TOMB OF THE GIANTS *(Es rauscht im Hünengrab)* Micrälius, *Pomm. Gesch.*, II, K. 52.

328. THE DEAD FROM THE GRAVES REPEL THE ENEMY *(Tote aus den Gräbern wehren dem Feind)* Otmar's collection.

329. THE CLIFFS OF HANS HEILING *(Hans Heilings Felsen)* Körner, *Nachlaß*, II, 132–152. It is from a German Bohemian folk legend. Cf. 174. (Cf. Legend No. 32.)

330. THE MAIDEN WITH THE BEARD *(Die Jungfrau mit dem Bart)* Prätorius, *Wünschelruthe*, pp. 152–153, who had it from an oral narrative. Cf. *Kinder- und Hausmärchen*, II, 66.

331. THE WHITE VIRGIN OF SCHWANAU *(Die weiße Jungfrau zu Schwanau)* Joh. Müller, *Schweiz. Gesch.*, II, 3.

332. THE FORTRESSES OF SCHWARZKOPF AND SEEBURG AT LAKE MUMMEL *(Schwarzkopf und Seeburg am Mummelsee)* Gustav, *Erzählungen und Märchen*, Leipzig, 1804.

333. THE PEDDLER AND THE MOUSE *(Der Krämer und die Maus)* Wenzel, *Dramat. Erzählungen.*

334. THE THREE TREASURE SEEKERS *(Die drei Schatzgräber)* Falkenstein, *Thüring. Chronik*, I, 219.

335. AN INVITATION TO APPEAR BEFORE THE JUDGMENT OF THE LORD *(Einladung vor Gottes Gericht)* Casp. Henneberg, *Chronicon Prussiae*, p. 254. Prätorius, *Weltbeschr.* I, 285–288.

336. GUESTS FROM THE GALLOWS *(Gäste vom Galgen)* Bräuner, *Curiositäten*, pp. 296–298.

337. THE DEVIL'S BRIDGE *(Teufelsbrücke)* Collected orally.

338. THE TWELVE JOHANNESES *(Die zwölf Johannesse)* Falkenstein, *Thüring. Chronik*, I, 218.

339. THE DEVIL'S DITCH *(Teufelsgraben)* Collected orally.

340. CROSS MOUNTAIN *(Der Kreuzliberg)* Kleine Reminissenzen und Gemälde, Zürich, 1806.

341. THE HORSES LOWERED FROM THE HAYLOFT *(Die Pferde aus dem Bodenloch)* Merssaeus (Cratepolius), *Catalogus episcop. Coloniens.* See also Greg. Horst's *addendum* to March Donatus, *Hist. medica mirabl.*, cap. 9, p. 707. See also Balthasar Bebelius, *Diss. de bis mortius*, p. 9. *Rhein. Antiquarius*, pp. 728–730. *Cölner Taschenbuch für altdeutsche Kunst*, 1816.

342. THE MEETING OF THE DEAD *(Zusammenkunft der Toten)* Collected orally in Hesse.

343. THE BIRD OF PROPHECY *(Das weissagende Vöglein)* Micrälius, *Pomm. Gesch.*, Book IV, p. 159.

344. THE ETERNAL JEW ON THE MATTERHORN *(Der Ewige Jud auf dem Matterhorn)* Collected orally in Oberwallis. Cf. Thiele, II, p. 50.

345. THE POT OF BUTTER *(Der Kessel mit Butter)* Collected orally in Oberwallis.

346. THE WEEPING WILLOW *(Trauerweide)* Collected orally.

347. THE STATUE OF CHRIST IN WITTENBERG *(Das Christusbild zu Wittenberg)* Collected orally from a pastor near Goßfelden who had been introduced to Clemens and Savigny by Bang. Cf. Savigny, *Vom Beruf*, p. 160.

348. THE STATUE OF THE MADONNA ON THE CLIFF WALL *(Das Muttergottesbild am Felsen)* Collected orally in Oberwallis.

349. THE HOLY ICON IN THE LARCH TRUNK OF WALDRAST *(Das Gnadenbild aus dem Lärchenstock zu Waldrast)* *Tyroler Sammler*, V (1809), 151–265. Taken from a folk legend and also recorded in the *Waldraster Protokoll*. Cf. Büsch, *Wöch. Nachr.*, III, 95–98.

350. OXEN REVEAL THE SACRED SITE *(Ochsen zeigen die heilige Stätte)* Kasthofen, *Alpenrosen*, 1813, p. 188.

351. ST. NOTBURGA *(Notburga)* Notburga was a holy virgin who lived in the castle of Rottenburg. Her martyrdom was portrayed on the stage in public on September 17, 1738. *Süddeutsche Miscellen*, 1813, März, No. 26. *Miscellen für die neueste Weltkunde*, 1810, No. 44.

352. MORTAR SLAKED WITH WINE *(Mauerkalk mit Wein gelöscht)* Cuspinianus, *Hist. Austr. ex relatione seniorum*. Älurius, *Glätzische Chronik*, Bk. II, cap. 2, p. 97. According to Dillich, *Hess. Chronik*, p. 144, the year 1166 was so bad for wine that the vintage was undrinkable and it was used instead to prepare mortar for masonry.

353. THE ROCK OF THE JEWS *(Der Judenstein)* Collected orally in Vienna. F. A. Graf von Brandis, *Des tirol. Adlers immergrünendes Ehrenkränzel*, Bozen, 1678, IV, p. 128. Schmiedt, *Heiliger Ehren-Glanz der Grafschaft Tirol*, Augsburg, 1732, 4, II, 154–167.

354. THE MAIDEN WHO WAS KILLED BY THE JEWS *(Das von den Juden getötete Mägdlein)* Thomae Cantipratani, *Bonum universale de apibus*, Duaci, 1627, 8, p. 303. Cf. Gehre, *Pforzheimer Chronik*, pp. 18–24.

355. THE FOUR HORSESHOES *(Die vier Hufeisen)* Otmar, pp. 115–118. There is a similar legend about the church in the town of Wittingen in the Lüneburg Heath.

356. THE ALTAR IN SEEFELD *(Der Altar zu Seefeld)* Collected orally in Vienna. *Von dem hoch und weit berühmten Wunderzeichen, so sich mit dem Altar in Seefeld in Tirol im Jahre 1384 zugetragen*, Dillingen, 1580. Reprinted, Innsbruck, 1603, 4.

357. THE STONE OF DEATH *(Der Sterbensstein)* *Kleine Gemälde der Schweiz* (von Appenzeller), Winterthur, 1810, p. 172.

358. SINFUL LOVE *(Sündliche Liebe)*   Falkenstein, *Thüring. Chronik*, I, 218–219.

359. THE COUNCILMAN OF SCHWEIDNITZ *(Der Schweidnitzer Ratsmann)* Lucä, *Schlesische Denkwürdigkeiten*, Frankfurt, 1689, 4, pp. 920–921. From Naso, *Phoenix redivivus*, Breslau, 1667, 4, pp. 91–94. Cf. Büsching, *Wöch. Nachr.*, III, 105–109.

360. A RAINBOW APPEARS ABOVE THE SENTENCED MEN *(Regenbogen über Verurteilten)* Westenrieder, *Histor. Kalender*, 1803.

361. GOD WEEPS WITH THE INNOCENT *(Gott weint mit dem Unschuldigen)* Collected orally in Hesse.

362. FOOD FROM GOD *(Gottes Speise)* Luther, *Tischreden*, pp. 90b–91a.

363. THE THREE OLD MEN *(Die drei Alten)* Reported by W. Schmidt from Lübeck in *Freimüthigen* (1809), No. 1. Cf. Joh. Gundlach, *Algebr. Aufgaben*, Kassel, 1804, p. 5. See also H. Hebel, *Schatzkästlein*, I, 185. Cf. *Beg. des Stud. zu Plesse*, I, 22. Holberg, *Ud en Hoved og Hale*, I, 6.

# COMMENTARY

D O N A L D   W A R D

The commentaries are organized by legend numbers. For a list of the abbreviations used, see page 430.

LEGEND NO. 1. This narrative belongs to the category of legends of mines and miners. The largest single compilation of German mining legends was made by Gerhard Heilfurth, *Bergbau und Bergmann in der deutschsprachigen Sagenüberlieferung Mitteleuropas*, vol. 1 (Marburg, 1967). Heilfurth brought together 1,210 texts of mining legends divided into 66 separate types. He classified this legend, "The Three Miners in the Kutten Mine," as Type E-5. The letter E designates the group of legends dealing with "Miraculous Rescue and Preservation." Heilfurth lists seven variants (Nos. 467–473) of this legend, including this one from the Grimm collection. In Heilfurth's Legend No. 468, from the Harz Mountains, the miners feel a terrible dread on the morning of the disaster. After they utter their devout wishes, the Mine Monk (see Grimm No. 3) comes and leads them to the surface. It is apparent in this variant that the Mine Monk becomes a servant of God, representing a curious syncretism of demonic and Christian elements. There are variants from Upper Silesia, Styria, the Erz Mountains (in present-day Czechoslovakia), and others from the Harz. In some variants an angel leads men to safety, in others it is a Mine Spirit, and in still others the mountain simply opens up above them (as in this legend).

Related to this legend is Type E-6, the "Prolonged Stay in the Underground." In this group, men are either trapped by a landslide or misled by mischievous spirits. They then discover that they have spent a hundred years (Heilfurth, No. 474), two hundred years (No. 475), three generations (No. 476), several hundred years (No. 478), seven years (Nos. 479 and 486), one year (No. 480), twenty-five years (No. 484), etc., beneath the earth before they once again re-emerge on the surface.

Legends dealing with mining disasters frequently involve the theme of crime and punishment. In such accounts the miners, after striking rich veins of valuable ore, become haughty and wasteful in their conspicuous consumption of wealth. The collapse of their mine is then punishment for their wicked ways.

Other legends tell of miners who failed to respect the auguries of impending disaster and were punished for their lack of faith. Such tales are reminiscent of the widespread sunken-city legends (Grimm Nos. 59, 114, 132, 236, 239, 240, and 281). See G. Korson, *Minstrels of the Mine Patch: Songs and Stories of the Anthracite Industry* (Philadelphia, 1943), pp. 167–168. Korson was a pioneer in the study of American mining lore. See also W. D. Hand, "George Korson and the Study of American Mining Lore," *Keystone Folklore Quarterly*, 16 (1971), 65–68. See also commentary to No. 37.

LEGEND NO. 2.    Mining legends constitute one of the largest single categories of European legends (see the commentary to No. 1), and within this category, the legends dealing with Mine Spirits make up the largest subcategory. Mine Spirits are also well known in the Anglo-Welsh-American tradition where Tommy Knockers inhabit the shafts and caverns of the underground world. Such spirits fall into two more or less strict categories. There are the somewhat playful spirits who roam in groups and resemble the Cobold in their mischievous ways. They like to play tricks on miners and cause confusion. But they must be treated well since they can become destructive if made fun of or harmed in any way. However, they have also been known to warn miners of impending disasters by knocking on the walls of the shafts.

The second kind of spirit is typified by the Mine Monk (see the commentary to No. 3). He reigns alone in his underground realm, which he regards as his sovereign territory and which he protects against intruders. He must be treated with the utmost respect, and his permission must always be sought before ore is removed from his world or he will punish the intruders with disaster and death.

In the Heilfurth compendium of mining legends (see commentary to No. 1) there are hundreds of legends dealing with Mine Spirits, but other than this Grimm variant (which Heilfurth reprinted in his Introduction) there is no other mention of the figure called Meister Hämmerling. However, in the Heilfurth collection there are scores of other spirits with a wide variety of appearances and functions. For example, a spirit can appear as a large or giant-like figure (50 variants), as a Dwarf (ca. 130 variants), a miner (50 variants), a ghost (1), a foreigner (5), a gentleman (5), an old man (6), a monk (60), a grey figure (7), a white figure (8), a black figure (4), a figure in red (3), the Devil (35), or a Water Nix (3). The Mine Spirit is also thought capable of changing his shape. In the Heilfurth collection he appears as a spider (3 variants), a frog (4), a mouse (13), a bird (7), a horse (6), a swine (1), a goat (5), even as a flame or a light (8). He can appear at any time (13 variants), or during the night shift (14). He can fly through the shafts (1 variant), become invisible (6), or appear only on special holidays (5). He has been known to call out to miners (8 variants), help miners in their work (30), work at night for the miners (18), give assistance when he is called (3), give miners an everlasting oil lamp (12), light the way for lost miners (4), or show miners rich veins of ore (50). Above all, the spirit warns miners of impending disaster (180 variants).

The Mine Spirit can also exhibit a wicked and maleficent nature, especially when miners are guilty of sin, blasphemy, or breaking taboos. When this occurs he hides the miners' clothing or tools (15 variants), frightens miners by pounding, making a racket, or laughing maliciously (25), throws rocks at miners (19), throws a miner into the pit water (1), blows out their lamps (8), attacks miners (6), turns their faces inside out (4), tears off the head of a miner (1), sits on a miner's back (2), buries miners in landslide (5), breathes on miners causing death or injury (8), strangles miners (5), or strikes them blind (1). See C. H. Tillhagen, "Die Bergeistvorstellung in Schweden," in Åke Hultkrantz (ed.), *The Supernatural Owners of Nature*, Acta Univ. Stockholmiensis, 1 (Stockholm, 1961), pp. 123–157; C. H. Tillhagen, "Gruvskrock" ['Mine Spirit' with English summary], *Norveg*, 12 (1965), 113–160; G. Rudolph, "Die Bergmannssage," in *Internationaler Kongress der Volkserzählungsforscher in Kiel und Kopenhagen* (Berlin, 1961), 350–359; G. Heilfurth, *Der Vorstellungskreis vom 'Berggeist' bei Georg Agricola und seinen Zeitgenossen* (Wien, 1967); P. Wolfersdorf, *Die niedersächsischen Berggeistsagen* (Göttingen, 1968); W. Peiter, "Der Berggeist der erzgebirgischen Bergleute," *ZöV*, 2 (1896), 178–180; L. Mackensen, "Berggeister," *HdA* I, 1071–1073; E. Czuray, *Alte Bergwerksgeschichten aus Oberkärnten* (Wien, 1966).

LEGEND NO. 3.    The Mine Monk reigns as sovereign of the underground realm. If he is treated properly he can lead miners to the best veins and give them magical tools and lamps. However, as often happens with gifts from the spirit world, the object comes with a taboo or warning. The taboo is inevitably broken and the magical property of the gift is lost forever. See P. Sartori, "Geschenk," *HdA* III, 715–719.

The appellation "Monk" is probably a secondary development attributable to the hooded cloak the spirit is said to wear. Such hooded cloaks are frequently associated with spirits from the other world. See Nos. 1 and 2 and commentaries.

LEGEND NO. 4.    Mother Holla is a familiar figure in both legends and fairy tales. Especially well known is the Grimm fairy tale of Mother Holla (*Kinder- und Hausmärchen*, No. 24), known internationally also as *The Spinning Woman by the Spring* (AT 480).

In general, legends and fairy tales share many of the same figures, but there is frequently a pronounced difference in their treatment in each genre. The witch of the legend, for example, is a member of a village community who engages in sorcery. In the fairy tale, by contrast, she is a demonic creature who lives alone in the forest and likes to eat children (e.g., Hänsel and Gretel). In legendry, Frau Holla has a variety of names (Holle, Holda, Hulda) and there are related figures such as Mother Perchta (see the commentaries to Nos. 5, 7, 268, and 269).

Mother Holla can be a benevolent figure who helps hard-working girls, but she can also be a demonic leader of the hosts of souls of the damned. She wanders the countryside at night—especially during the twelve nights of Christmas. She particularly watches over spinning maidens and punishes the lazy or those who break taboos associated with spinning. Sometimes she is envisioned as a demonic witch-like creature. See Grimm *DM* I, 222–234; W.

Schwartz, "Perhta," *HdA* VI, 1478–1492 (this essay is marred by an exaggerated and uncritical adherence to the mythological school of folkloric research); K. Paetow, *Frau Holle: Märchen und Sagen* (Kassel and Basel, 1952); K. Paetow, *Frau Holles Weg in deine Seele durch Märchen und Begebnis* (Eschwege, 1956); K. Paetow, *Volkssagen und Märchen um Frau Holle* (Hannover, 1962); V. Waschnitz, *Percht, Holda und verwandte Gestalten: Ein Beitrag zur deutschen Religionsgeschichte* (Wien, 1913); W. E. Roberts, "A Spaniolic-Jewish Version of 'Frau Holle,' " in Fran Utley (ed.), *Studies in Biblical and Jewish Folklore* (Bloomington, 1960), 175–182; W. E. Roberts, *The Tale of the Kind and Unkind Girls* (Berlin, 1958).

LEGEND NO. 5. In this legend, Mother Holla travels around the countryside as a supernatural creature. In this capacity she belongs to a specific category of spirit called by a number of different names depending on the region. For example, there are such figures as Mother Gode, Mother Harke, and Mother Perchta who are thought to be the leaders of hordes of dead souls, frequently those of children who died before being baptized (see commentary to No. 7). Perchta is her usual name in Austria, Bavaria, Baden, and parts of Franconia. See Leopold Schmidt, "Perchtengestalten in Burgundenland," *Burgenläandische Heimatblätter* (1951), Heft 3, 129–142.

LEGEND NO. 6. The Meißen Mountains consist of several peaks reaching 2,400 feet situated about twenty-two miles east of the city of Kassel. See K. Paetow, "Gibt es einen Frau Holle-Mythos am Meißner?" *Hessische Heimat*, 21 (1971), 49–53. See also the commentaries to Nos. 4, 5, and 7.

LEGEND NO. 7. Here Mother Holla is the leader of a horde of dead souls. The appearance of such hordes (see also Nos. 313 and 314) is frequently preceded by a traditional figure who warns the people of the approaching throng of ghosts. Faithful Eckart, about whom Goethe wrote a ballad, is one such figure. The wandering spirits in such throngs are often the souls of murder victims or others who died before their time.

The city clerk of Lucerne, Renward Cysat, who lived from 1545 to 1614, provides a detailed account of such a horde and states specifically that each member was one "whose life ended before the designated time and who did not die a natural death." See R. Brandstetter, *Renward Cysat: der Begründer der schweizerischen Volkskunde* (Luzern, 1909), 40–41.

However, such figures as Holla and Perchta also frequently lead the hordes of souls of children who died before baptism and are thus condemned to wander the earth for eternity. In some legends a child's soul can be delivered if a witness to the procession gives the child a name.

Certain days are particularly auspicious for the appearance of such figures, especially the twelve days of Christmas, beginning Christmas Eve and ending on Epiphany (January 6). F. Mössinger, "Wildweibchen, Holle, und Christkind," *HBV*, 38 (1940), 73–100; W. Roberts, "A Spaniolic-Jewish Version of Frau Holle," in Fran Utley (ed.), *Studies in Biblical and Jewish Folklore* (Bloomington, 1960), 175–182; V. Waschnitius, *Percht, Holda und verwandte Gestalten*, Sitzungsber. der Kaisl. Akademie der Wiss., phil.-hist Kl., 174:2 (Wien, 1913).

LEGEND NO. 8. Gifts from the supernatural world should never be scorned however worthless they might seem at the time, for afterward they often magically turn into gold. However, in the *Sagen* the human protagonist invariably learns this lesson too late—after he has cast the items away.

This motif stresses a theme frequently encountered in legends: Great wealth easily obtained is offered to the protagonist, but it slips through his fingers because he does not show enough respect for gifts from the other world.

In the fairy tale, by contrast, magical gifts are invariably used with great success by the hero or heroine. The supernatural properties help him or her to perform impossible tasks, to defeat superhuman adversaries, to escape pursuers, and the like. See P. Sartori, "Geschenk," *HdA* III, 715–719; M. Lüthi, *Die Gabe im Märchen und in der Sage: Ein Beitrag zur Wesenserfassung und Wesensscheidung der beiden Formen*, Diss. (published) (Bern, 1943). Unfortunately, this excellent work has been out of print for some time.

LEGEND NO. 9. This legend belongs to the larger category of treasure legends (cf. Nos. 124, 158–163, 213, 315–317, and 333–334). The tradition of lost treasure is not necessarily the product of wishful fantasy. Wars and invasions forced many a European prince, bishop, or patrician to hide or bury his treasures to save them from pillaging armies. Not infrequently all witnesses to such a burial perished in the ensuing battle and thus the treasure was forgotten. Such hoardes are traditionally thought to be guarded by ghosts, Dwarfs, demons, mythical beasts, or—as in this case—the White Woman (see commentary to No. 10). On rare occasions—sometimes on specific days of the year such as Epiphany—a fortunate individual is granted access to the treasure.

More often than not, the attempt to take possession of the riches fails because the chosen one does not follow all the prescriptions or because he breaks an imposed taboo. One often finds a mixture of heathen and Christian elements in such prescriptions and taboos. In this case the Spurge Root is the magical implement that permits access to the hidden treasure, but the shepherd, who might have had unlimited access to this source and thus could have been rich for life, fails to understand the warning: "Don't forget the best of all!" Thus, he leaves the magical object behind and is never again able to retrieve it (cf. No. 315).

The Spurge Root (*Euphorbia lathyrus*) is just one of many magical objects thought to have the power of finding hidden treasures. See, for example, H. Biedermann, *Handlexikon der magischen Künste von der Spätantike bis zum 19. Jahrhundert* (Graz, 1968), 332–333; H. Commenda, "Geschichte der Schatzgräber, Teufelsbeschwörer und Geisterbanner in Lienz 1792," *Historisches Jahrbuch der Stadt Linz* (1960), 171–195; Leo Winter, *Die deutsche Schatzsage*, Diss. (Köln, 1928); O. Zingerle, "Schatzsagen und Beschwörung schatzhütender Geister," *Die Schlern*, 4 (1923), 384–387; H. Bügener, "Verborgene Schätze," *Heimatblätter der Roten Erde*, 4 (1926), 80–84; L. Deneke, "Der Schatz im verwünschten Schloß," *Fabula*, 13 (1972), 150–152. For similar traditions from the U.S., see A. Campa, *Treasure of the Sangre de Cristos* (Norman, Okla., 1963); G. T. Hurley, "Buried Treasure Tales in America," *Western Folklore*, 10 (1951), 197–216; J. F. Dobie, "The Dream That Never

Dies," *Folksay* (1929), 64–68. In the West and Southwest of the U.S. one finds more lost mine legends than buried treasure legends. See Byrd Granger, *A Motif Index for Lost Mines and Treasures Applied to Redaction of Arizona Legends, and to Lost Mine and Treasure Legends Exterior to Arizona,* FFC 218 (Helsinki, 1977).

LEGEND NO. 10. *Boyneburg* 'Boyne Castle' has been an important residence of the landgraves of Hesse since the Middle Ages. It is located atop a 1,600-foot peak in the Ringgau region of East Hesse, about twelve miles south of the city of Eschwege. It is only about six miles to the west of the border to the German Democratic Republic.

The revelation of the future in dreams is a nearly universal experience and belief. See M. Förster, "Die altenglische Traumlunare," *Englische Studien,* 60 (1925), 58–93; L. Binswanger, *Wandlungen in der Auffassung und Deutung des Traumes von den Griechen bis zur Gegenwart* (Berlin, 1928); C. H. Tillhagen, *Skrock, tydor, syner, drönmor, orakel* (Stockholm, 1968).

It is striking that three sisters are the passive recipients of the revelations in this legend. More common in fate legends is the role of three sisters as the proclaimers of the future (the Three Fates, the Norns, the Moires, the Weird Sisters, etc.). See the commentary to No. 15.

One of the sisters in this legend becomes the ghostly figure known as the White Woman, who guards the hidden treasures of the castle. The White Woman is one of the more popular figures of German legend, as is the so-called Castle Maiden who is related. See Nos. 12, 25, 123, 222, 228, 268, 315, 318, and 331. See Ignaz Ingruber, "Die weiße Frau," *Osttirolische Heimatblätter,* 1 (No. 16); H. Kügler, "Die Sage von der weißen Frau im Schloß zu Berlin," *Mitteilungen des Vereins für die Geschichte Berlins,* 45 (1928), 57–96; G. Jungbauer, "Die Sage von der weißen Frau," *Deutsche Heimat,* 5 (1929), 421–425; L. Röhrich, *Sage* (Stuttgart, 1966), 13; M. Wähler, *Die weiße Frau: Vom Glauben des Volkes an der lebenden Leichnam* (Erfurt, 1931).

LEGEND NO. 11. Today, the city is called Annaberg-Buchholz, and it lies about twenty-five miles south of Karl-Marx-Stadt (formerly Chemnitz) in the German Democratic Republic. Piel Mountain is now called Pöhl Mountain (*Pöhlberg*). It is an impressive peak, rising 2,700 feet directly above the city.

In North European tradition midnight is the customary witching hour when spirits are active. However, the concept of a Midday Spook (*daemonum meridianum*) is also known, especially in Asia Minor and along the Mediterranean. The notion evidently came from the Near East, spread to Rome and southern France, and then diffused into Europe. See G. Jungbauer, "Mittagsgespenst," *HdA* VI, 414–419; "Meridianus daemon," in Roscher, *Lexikon,* II, 2832; K. Haberland, "Die Mittagsstunde als Geisterstunde," *Zeitschrift für Völkerpsychologie,* 13 (1882), 310–316; O. Schell, "Mittagsdämon, Mittagszauber," *ZVRhWV,* 13 (1916), 262; S. Landersdorfer, "Das daemonum meridianum," *Biblische Zeitschrift,* 18 (1929), 294–303; D. Grau, *Das Mittagsgespenst* (Siegburg, 1960); L. Petzoldt, *DVS,* Nos. 325–326.

LEGEND NO. 12. The Castle Maiden is related to the figure of the White Woman. (See No. 10 and commentary.) The ring of keys she carries has at least two meanings. The Castle Maiden is thought to be the spectral mistress of the castle and thus has keys to all the rooms. However, she is also a Poor Soul, and the keys are the symbol of her need for deliverance.

This particular spirit has the habit of appearing at midday instead of the traditional European witching hour of midnight. She thus fits the category of Midday Spook (see No. 11 and commentary). Ohrdruf lies on the Ohra River about 22 miles southwest of Erfurt. There, a ruined castle overlooks the city.

LEGEND NO. 13.    The motif of the Serpent Maiden who can be delivered by a kiss seems to have originated in Celtic tradition from which it was adapted in late medieval romances. The motif then entered popular tradition on the continent and has become increasingly popular ever since. In this case the Poor Soul who guards the treasure in a deserted castle is often thought to be part serpent and part human. As with any creature from the beyond, she poses a real threat to human beings. Yet, her demand that a human kiss her but three times is by no means an impossible task.

It is a typical trait of legends that success, fortune, deliverance, and the like appear within easy grasp, yet all hopes are quickly dashed. In the fairy tale we find the converse situation. The tasks appear to be impossible, but they are nevertheless accomplished. See E. Frank, *Der Schlangenkuß* (Leipzig, 1928); P. Ducrée, "Die Schlangenjungfrau," *Eifelkalender* (1926), 91–92; E. Hoffmann-Krayer, "Schlangen," *HdA* VII, 1114–1196.

LEGEND NO. 14.    Although a number of variants of this legend have been published, apparently they are all traceable to a single written source. The legend seems never to have been widespread in oral tradition.

Since children who die without baptism are thought to become Poor Souls, ghosts and spooks are frequently encountered in the form of children. For example, a Franconian legend reports that a child, dressed in white and carrying an hourglass, predicts the future (see J. Dünninger, *Fränkische Sagen vom 15. bis zum Ende des 18. Jahrhunderts*, 2nd ed. (Kulmbach, 1964), No. 56, pp. 77–78. Another legend (Praetorius, *Glückstopf,* 510–511) tells of a new-born child prophesying a cold winter and the plague.

The child so heavy that it cannot be lifted from the ground may be an allusion to the story of the Christ child's jumping onto the shoulders of St. Christopher and weighing him down with the burden of all creation. See D.-R. Moser, "Christus als 'Aufhocker?' " *ZsfVk*, 69 (1973), 234–239.

A variant of the Grimm legend, published by G. P. Gath in *Rheinische Sagen* (Köln und Krefeld, 1949), 24–25, adds the final motif that the prophecy came true: "There was an abundant crop of fruit and grain that year but no hands to harvest them for a catastrophical plague decimated the population." However, it is apparent that Gath used the same source as the Grimms (where this final motif is lacking). He evidently added this motif himself for the sake of logic and clarity. Although such an addendum does indeed make the legend far more understandable than the fragmentary account that we have here, folklorists nevertheless frown upon such practices.

LEGEND NO. 15.    This time the treasure found in the ruins of the castle is not money but wine. And here we have a treasure tale linked to a fate tale.

The man's fate is determined by three old men and the funeral procession is an omen for his own impending death. In this tale three Fate Men replace the more common three Fate Women (e.g., the Norns, the Moires, the three fates, etc.). The original meaning of Shakespeare's weird sisters was actually Fate Sisters. See R. W. Brednich, *Volkserzählungen und Volksglauben von den Schicksalsfrauen*, FFC 193 (Helsinki, 1964); R. Wolfram, "Die Schöpfelein, Gottscheer Volksglaube von den Schicksalsgestalten," *Jahrbuch für Volkskunde der Heimatvertriebenen* I (1955), 77–92. There is a widespread belief that when one sees a ghostly funeral procession it is an omen of one's own death. Frequently the person sees himself among the participants in the procession. See P. Geiger, "Der Totenzug," *SAV*, 47 (1951), 71–76.

LEGEND NO. 16.   Giant legends are relatively rare in modern oral traditions for the belief in Giants faded at an early date. One has to distinguish between two basic kinds of Giants in popular tradition. First, there are legends about the mythological Giants, a race of huge beings who inhabit mountain wildernesses and other desolate regions. Second, there are legends about humans of remarkable size and strength.

This legend is what is known as an "etiological legend," from Greek *aitio* 'cause.' An etiological legend is a narrative that explains how characteristic features of the land or its inhabitants came to be. For instance, the large depression in the earth attracted attention and demanded an explanation that the Giant legend supplied. The reason Giants are no longer seen in this area and the reason the Weser has a somewhat reddish color are also explained in this legend.

Huge burial mounds and the remains of megalithic monuments have contributed to Giant legends, as have strange formations of cliffs, mountains, and rivers. Discoveries of fossil bones have also given rise to such legends. See V. Höttges, *Die Sage vom Riesenspielzeug* (Jena, 1931); K. Weinhold, *Die Riesen des germanischen Mythus* (Wien, 1958); C. W. von Sydow, *Jättarna i Mythologie och Folktradition* (Malmö, 1910); J. Broderius, *The Giant in Germanic Tradition*, Diss. (Chicago, 1937); W. Müller-Bergström, "Zwerge und Riesen," *HdA* IXN, 1008–1138; V. Höttges, *Typenverzeichnis der deutschen Riesen- und riesischen Teufelssagen*, FFC 122 (Helsinki, 1937). Regarding etiological legends, see H. Lixfeld, "Ätiologie," *EdM* I, 949–953; M. Schuir, "Aitologischer Schluß," *HdM* I, 46–47.

LEGEND NO. 17.   See the commentary to No. 16. The ruins of the castle of Nidek still stand high above the Hasel River in the Vogesen Mountains of Alsace (see commentary to No. 21), about 30 miles due west of Straßburg. There is indeed a cascading waterfall right next to the castle, and the town of Haslach still lies about five miles downstream. The delightful story of the Giant's Toy is found throughout Germany and Scandinavia. See V. Höttges, *Die Sage vom Riesenspielzeug* (Jena, 1931).

LEGEND NO. 18.   The Giant of this legend belongs to the category of human beings of supranormal strength and size. The sources the Grimms used can be traced back to the medieval historian Notker der Stammerer, who calls the strong man Eishere.

Many regions have their own local strong man; for example, there is Miligedo in Prussia, Hidde in Saxony, Romäus in Villingen, and Haymon in Tyrol. See the bibliography in commentary to No. 16, especially the *Typenverzeichnis* by V. Höttges. See also E. H. Arendt, *Der Riese in der mittelhochdeutschen Epik*, Diss. (Rostock, 1923).

LEGEND NO. 19.   The town today is called Kleinheubach. This is another etiological legend, and it came about in an attempt to explain the conspicuous stone columns in the cliffs along the Main River near the town.

LEGEND NO. 20.   Köter Mountain is located a few miles west of the city of Holzminden, and it offers a splendid view of the Weser Valley and the surrounding countryside.

Several legends have been compacted into this very short narrative. The appearance of the ghostly figure that guards the treasure indicates that he ended his life as a murder victim. According to folk belief, the innocent victim of a violent death becomes a Poor Soul or ghost. See L. Winter, *Die deutsche Schatzsage*, Diss. (Köln, 1925), and St. Hirschberg, *Schatzglaube und Totenglaube*, (Breslau, 1934). See also the commentary to No. 9.

LEGEND NO. 21.   This legend is related to the tradition of the "Emperor in the Mountain" who waits in his underground realm for the day he is to arise and rescue his people (see Nos. 22–28, 292–296, and 315). The Wasgau region is known today as the Vogesen (German) or Vosges (French) Mountains located in the Alsatian region of what is today France. The ruins of Geroldseck can still be visited today.

The kings (with the possible exception of Siegfried) are historical personages who became legendary heroes. Ariovist was the first Germanic chieftain whose name was recorded in history. Caesar describes how Ariovist crossed the Rhine in 71 B.C. to come to the aid of the Sequanes who were being besieged by the Hadueri. He was later (58 B.C.) defeated by Caesar and driven back across the Rhine.

Hermann, known to the Romans as Arminius, led a German army that annihilated the Roman legions under Varus in the Battle of the Teutoburger Forest in A.D. 9.

Wittekind, better known as Widukind, was chief of the heathen Saxons. He led the Saxons in a series of bloody wars against Charlemagne. He was finally subdued in A.D. 785, and on Christmas of that year he was baptized. From this point on the Saxons, who occupied the greater part of present-day Germany, were Christianized—at least in name. See H. Hartwig, *Widukind in Geschichte und Sage* (1951).

The "horned" Siegfried is the famed German hero of the Nibelungen tradition. Whether or not he was an actual historical personage has never been determined with certainty. "Horned" does not refer to horns, but rather to the horny shell that was thought to encase his body. This appellation for Siegfried was a late development (concrete rationalization of magical invulnerability), and is found mostly in the chapbooks and broadsides of the sixteenth century.

LEGEND NO. 22. This and the following legends belong to the famed "Emperor in the Mountain" tradition. It is remarkable how little the Christian concepts of the afterworld come into play in such tales. In this legend the sleeping emperor is Charlemagne, but the same legend is told of other historical figures as well, such as Frederick Barbarossa, Frederick II, Arminius, and Wittekind (see No. 21).

The emperor waits in his underground realm—which is often viewed as a splendid palace inside a mountain—for the day when he is to rise and save his people. Virtually every landscape in Germany has such a mountain or castle where the emperor is said to be sleeping: Odenberg in Hesse, Untersberg (or Wonder Mountain) near Salzburg, and Mt. Kyffhausen in Thuringia are among the most famous.

Similar tales are known in other countries. King Arthur, for example, is said to be sleeping in a hill at Alderly Edge, and Holger Danske sleeps in a hill at Mögeltondern in Denmark. In Germany the legend acquired widespread popularity through the poem "Barbarossa" by Friedrich Rückert (1788–1866). During the days of the Franco-German war (1871), when nationalism was at a high pitch, Germans began to look upon Wilhelm I as the resurrected Barbarossa, and the old tradition attained new popularity. See R. Schröder, *Die deutsche Kaisersage* (Heidelberg, 1893); F. Kampers, *Die deutsche Kaiseridee in Prophetie und Sage* (München, 1896); G. Schultheiß, *Die deutsche Volkssage vom Fortleben und der Wiederkehr Kaiser Friedrichs II* (Berlin, 1911); A. H. Krappe, "Die Sage vom König im Berg," *MSGV* 35 (1935), 76–102; G. Voigt, *Die Kyffhäusersage* (Halle, 1871); J. Häussner, *Die deutsche Kaisersage* (Bruchsal, 1882); J. Häussner, *Unsere Kaisersage* (Berlin, 1884); I. Baudisch, *Das Motiv vom offenen Berg in Sage, Märchen, und Legende*, Diss. (Graz, 1950); D. Ward, "Berg," *EdM* II, 138–146. For Irish parallels see D. MacIvor, "The Legend of Geróid Iarld of Hacklim," *Journal of County Louth Archeological Society*, 14 (1959), 68–81.

LEGEND NO. 23. See the commentary to No. 22. Mt. Kyffhausen is actually a relatively unimpressive range of hills on the south side of the Harz Mountains between the cities of Nordhausen and Sangerhausen. The physical feature that probably gave rise to the legend is a cave on the south side of the range that today bears the name Barbarossa Cave. On the north side of the range, about a mile away, an impressive monument (*Kyffhäuser Denkmal*) has been constructed. Local entrepreneurs have not been lax in making a tourist attraction out of the site.

The first mention of Mt. Kyffhausen as the residence of the sleeping Emperor Barbarossa can be found in the writings of Pastor Johann Rothe of Eisenach who died in 1434. Local traditions later confused Frederick I (Barbarossa) with Frederick II so that both are reported to be sleeping in the mountain. The fact that Barbarossa drowned while swimming in a river during a crusade in 1190 contributed to the tradition that he was not really dead, and that he would someday return.

The motif of the ravens flying around the mountain seems to have been added to the tradition by Prätorius in his *Alectryomantia* in 1681. Whether he heard the motif in oral tradition or invented it himself can no longer be determined with certainty.

LEGEND NO. 24.  This legend belongs to the tradition of the Untersberg, or Wonder Mountain (see Nos. 27–28). A complete version of the legend has been assembled from fifteen manuscripts and chapbook versions from the sixteenth century by W. Herzog, *Die Unterbergsage nach den Handschriften, untersucht und herausgegeben von W. Herzog* (Wien und Leipzig, 1929). The complete legend has also been reprinted in Petzoldt, *HS*, II, 13–21, No. 315. See W.-E. Peuckert, "Dürrer Baum," *HdA* II, 505–515; D. Ward, "Baum," *EdM* I; 1366–1374; M. Andree-Eysn, "Der Birnbaum auf dem Walserfeld," *Bayerische Hefte für Volkskunde* II (1915), 185–188; F. Zurbonsen, *Die Schlacht am Birkenbaum* (Essen, 1940).

In the complete version of the legend, when the emperor wakes after sleeping in Wonder Mountain for centuries, he hangs his battle shield on a withered tree. The tree then sprouts green leaves, the signal for the Final World Battle that is to be followed by a new Golden Age.

LEGEND NO. 25.  In this legend the story of the Emperor in the Mountain has been combined with the story of the Serpent Maiden (see No. 13 and commentary). An interesting concept in these legends is an afterworld that has little to do with Christian belief but which has borrowed elements from classical antiquity, for example, the fire-breathing serpent that guards the entrance to the underworld. The figure of the Serpent Maiden owes much to Celtic tradition.

LEGEND NO. 26.  See Nos. 21–25 and commentaries. Mt. Oden is located a few miles south of the city of Kassel in East Hesse. The name is apparently related to Odin-Wodan, the powerful Germanic divinity, and may thus have been a cult site in heathen times.

LEGEND NO. 27.  See commentary to No. 24. Both the names *Untersberg* and *Wunderberg* are given in this legend, and I have chosen to use the latter form, for it translates more easily into the English 'Wonder Mountain.' I should like to stress, however, that *Untersberg* is the form by which the mountain is known today. Indeed, the folk etymology of *Untersberg* 'under the mountain' probably contributed to the occurrence of the legend in this region. The concept of the other world as an underground realm much like our own, with palaces, gardens, fountains, and considerable splendor, occurs frequently in legendry. See E. Zahn, *Das Jenseits* (Leipzig, 1916); E. Döring-Hirsch, *Tod und Jenseits im Spätmittelalter* (Berlin, 1927).

LEGEND NO. 28.  Charlemagne actually had nothing to do with the region around Salzburg, and consequently the tradition that he is sleeping in the mountain there is somewhat incongruous. The folk etymology *Untersberg* 'under the mountain' (see the commentary to No. 27) evidently contributed to the appearance of this legend in this region. However, the legend is still told in the region today and is even taught to schoolchildren.

LEGEND NO. 29.  A variant of this legend is told in J. G. T. Graesse, *Geschlechts-, Namen- und Wappensagen des Adels deutscher Nation* (Dresden, 1876), 112. See also Petzoldt *HS*, No. 118.

The introduction of the legend is set against the background of historic events. Meinhard II (1237–1295), Count von Tirol-Görz and Duke of Carinthia, had many struggles with bishops and minor counts. After his marriage to the widow of King Conrad IV he acquired new territories in the Upper Inn Valley and also developed a friendship with Rudolf von Habsburg. Meinhard's success in various struggles secured the territories under his control, and he is considered the decisive figure in the establishment of the territory that today constitutes Tyrol. His friend and ally Rudolf von Habsburg was elected king in 1286 and presented Meinhard with the duchy of Carinthia. Count Wilhelm von Scherfenberg, by contrast, appears to have been a purely legendary character.

The legend explains the origins of the family ring of the counts von Aufenstein—as a gift of the Dwarfs. It is thus ultimately supposed to have come from supernatural sources. Noble families liked to tell such stories about themselves for the legends increased the luster of the family name. See, for example, Nos. 35, 41, and 528. See also H. Jungwirth, "Ring, *HdA* VII, 702–724; A. Fourlas, *Der Ring in der Antike und im Christentum* (Münster, 1971).

See No. 30 and commentary for more detailed information on Dwarfs.

LEGEND NO. 30.  The castle of Plesse is located about eight miles north of Göttingen. Today it belongs to the state of Lower Saxony, not Hesse. The Dwarfs of German legendry live in the underworld even, as in this case, when they inhabit the ruins of old castles. The Dwarfs' underground realm is essentially a mirror image of the world above, and such everyday activities as smithing, shoemaking, baking, and brewing take up much of their time. The Dwarfs live in extended families and often have a king. As is the case with fairies of the British Isles, there is frequently an implied connection between Dwarfs and the souls of the dead. Dwarf legends abound in areas where there are caves and holes in cliffs and around the remains of earlier settlements and burial grounds. There are many different names for Dwarfs in various regions, and individual Dwarfs have their own personal names. They are sometimes supernatural creatures who can change shape, become invisible, or even change into animals. But one also encounters the notion that they are exactly like humans, only much smaller.

In this legend, the Dwarfs avoid contact with humans. However, in other legends there is frequently contact, which usually ends when the Dwarfs are insulted or mistreated by humans. Dwarfs frequently give gifts to humans, and they borrow and lend items as well. See I.-M. Greverus, *Die Geschenke des kleinen Volkes*, Diss. (Marburg, 1956) abstracted in *Fabula* I (1957), 263–279.

Dwarfs also occur in Germanic myth and in medieval literature. See H. de Boor, "Der Zwerg in Skandinavien," in *E. Mogk Festschrift* (Halle, 1924), 536–557; A. Lütjens, *Der Zwerg in der deutschen Heldendichtung des Mittelalters* (Breslau, 1911); V. Harward, *The Dwarfs of Arthurian Romance and Celtic Tradition* (Leiden, 1958); W. Müller-Bergstrom, "Zwerge und Riesen," *HdA* IXN, 1008–1138; J. Rühfel, *Der Zwerg* (Dresden, 1923); W. Marwede, *Die Zwergsagen in Deutschland nördlich des Mains*, Diss. (Köln, 1933; printed in Würzburg, 1934); L. Jones, "The Little People," *NYFQ*, 18 (1962), 243–264.

LEGEND NO. 31.   One frequently encounters the notion of Dwarfs using the halls of human residences to celebrate their weddings and festivals. See W. Müller-Bergstrom, *HdA* IXN, 1038, and F. Wilde, "De Unnereerdschen op de Hochtied," *Heimatkunde*, 34 (1923), 18. Goethe also composed a poem on the topic entitled *Zwergenhochzeit* 'Wedding of the Dwarfs.'

The von Eilenburgs were a family of Saxon counts. It is highly likely that their family never actually numbered more than seven, and the curse in this traditional legend became an explanation of the situation.

There is an inconsistency in the number mentioned in the curse and the number in the final sentence of the legend. Since this inconsistency is in the original, I have chosen to translate it just as it is and not correct it.

LEGEND NO. 32.   The town of Elbogen (literally, 'elbow') is today called Loket. It is located on a bend of the Ohře River (formerly the Eger) about eight miles upstream from the city of Karlovy Vary (formerly Karlsbad) in Czechoslovakia. This is an etiological legend that explains the curious rock formations along the river in that region.

LEGEND NO. 33.   Dwarfs not only present humans with gifts, they also borrow items from humans and loan them objects as well. Sites of long-abandoned early settlements, at which there were remains of pots and other utensils, were frequently thought to be abandoned Dwarf communities and doubtless contributed to such traditions. See W. Hirschberg, *Wörterbuch der Völkerkunde* (Stuttgart, 1965), 424–425. See also Petzoldt *DVS*, 433–443.

LEGEND NO. 34.   This is an etiological legend explaining why Dwarfs are no longer seen, and as such documents the fading belief in their existence. Lauri Honko has demonstrated in *Geisterglaube in Ingermanland*, FFC 185 (Helsinki, 1962) that when the belief in spirits is a viable part of a community's daily life it will manifest itself in personal experiences and spirits will be encountered. These encounters will in turn generate first-person narratives that folklorists call "memorates," a term that was coined by the Swedish folklorist Carl W. von Sydow (see commentary to No. 46). When the belief is weak or dying out, the number of such encounters will decrease and finally cease altogether. In this legend the lessening of these experiences contributed to the creation of a narrative explaining why Dwarfs were no longer around.

That the people who had the experience are carefully identified, that precise dates are given, and that the men are described as honest and reliable represent typical elements in belief legends and enhance the credibility of the report. One sees this same process at work in newspaper reports of sightings of flying saucers where it is frequently stressed the person who witnessed the phenomenon was "an engineer," "a trained chemist," and the like, which emphasizes that he/she was not the type of person who would be likely to hallucinate. See L. Dégh, "Flying Saucers and How Folklorists Should Look at Them," *Fabula* 18 (1977), 226ff.

Selbitz and Marlsreuth are villages in the relatively sparsely populated Franconian Forest Nature Park not far from the city of Hof. It is near the point where the borders of East and West Germany and Czechoslovakia meet.

LEGEND NO. 35. The counts von Hoya (the official spelling) descend from the von Stumpenhausen family and were related to the royal lineage of the Welfs. In 1204 Henry von Stumpenhausen settled in the castle of Hoya, which lay on the lower Weser River between the cities of Nienburg and Verden, and from which the family then took its name. The family acquired property by winning border disputes with the diocese of Minden, and in 1384 they acquired the neighboring county of the von Bruchhausen family when that lineage came to an end. Their holdings soon grew into one of the most prominent and powerful counties in northern Germany, occupying the region along both sides of the Weser River right up to the outskirts of Bremen.

The legend offers an explanation for what actually occurred in history. The county was twice divided in two parts because of contesting male heirs—once from 1299 to 1311, and then again from 1345 to 1503. It was in this latter year that the older of the two halves of the house died out. In 1582 the other half died out and the county was then divided between the von Calenberg and Wolfenbüttel lineages. See F. Hellermann, *Die Entstehung der Landeshoheit der Grafen von Hoya* (Bremen, 1912). Hammelmann's *Oldenburg Chronik* is the only source we have for the intervention of Franz von Halle in the affairs of the county.

The theme of the Dwarfs having a banquet in the count's residence probably derives from the practice of setting out food for the spirits to insure their good graces. It is also possible that an attempt to explain the family crest gave rise to this legend. Three gifts from the spirit world that are to be kept in the family's possession constitute a frequent motif in German legends dealing with noble lineages. See Nos. 41, 69, and 71. The families acquire prominence and luster when they are associated with supernatural powers. See H. Rühmann, *Opfersagen des Hausgeist- und Zwergenkultes*, Diss. (Kiel, 1938).

LEGEND NO. 36. The Erz Mountains are a range of peaks separating Czechoslovakia from the German Democratic Republic. The name *Erz* means 'ore,' and there was indeed a great deal of mining in this region along with the related foundries and factories. This legend explains why the Dwarfs were no longer seen there. See the commentary to No. 34. See also H. Schurtz, *Der Seifenbergbau im Erzgebirge und die Walensagen* (Stuttgart, 1890).

LEGEND NO. 37. This legend belongs to the category of Mine Spirit legends. See the commentary to Nos. 2–3. Kutten Mine is in Bohemia (Czechoslovakia) just south of Marienbad (Mariánké Lázně). Idria (Idrija) is a town in the Slovenian region of Yugoslavia about 42 miles west of Ljubljana. German mines once operated in the area.

The practice of leaving food out for the spirits was an actual custom, and it reveals how serious the miners were about the spirits. See H. Rühmann, *Opfersagen des Hausgeist- und Zwergenkultes*, Diss. (Kiel, 1938).

LEGEND NO. 38. The practice of conjuring demons and spirits is well documented in Western Civilization from classical antiquity to the present, and there is a vast amount of literature on the topic. It is rare, however, to find a sorcerer conjuring forth a Mine Spirit. Paul Creuz is one of many local sorcerers who entered the popular tradition. Better known, even achieving international fame, were such figures as Albertus Magnus, Dr. Faust, Paracelsus, and Trithemius von Spanheim, all of them actual historical figures.

From the Middle Ages until well into the seventeenth century, sorcerers were employed at royal courts, and their work was considered scientific. However, with the advent of the Inquisition their work became suspect, and in order to draw attention away from themselves the sorcerers began to make distinctions between scientific or "white" magic and maleficent or "black" magic. The latter, they contended, was practiced by evil women in villages. Such distinctions contributed to the gruesome witch hunts that plagued Europe and the American colonies all through the sixteenth and seventeenth centuries. See F. Byloff, *Das Verbrechen der Zauberei* (Graz, 1902); H. Biedermann, *Handlexikon der magischen Künste von der Spätantike bis zum 19. Jahrhundert*, 2. Aufl. (Graz, 1973). W.-E. Peuckert, *Pansophie: Ein Versuch zur Geschichte der weißen und schwarzen Magie*, 2. Aufl. (Berlin, 1956); M. Schusser, "Beschwörung, beschwören," *HdA* I, 1109–1129; A. Klein, "Der 'Kreuzweg' im deutschen Volksaberglauben," *Blätter für die Heimatkunde*, 6 (1928). For examples from the British Isles, see A. H. Allcroft, *The Circle and the Cross*, 2 vols. (London, 1928); W. H. D. Adams, *Witch, Warlock, and Magician: Historical Sketches of Magic and Witchcraft in England and Scotland* (Ann Arbor, Mich., 1971), reprint of 1889 edition.

Sometimes a book of magic, or a grimoire, is used to conjure spirits not as an instructional manual but rather as a magical item itself. See K. Briggs, "Some Seventeenth Century Books of Magic," *F-L*, 64 (1953), 445–462. Among the favorite handbooks still being published today are the apocryphal *Sixth and Seventh Books of Moses* and *The Egyptian Secrets of Albertus Magnus*. The "precious incense burners" on the table where the spirits appear were part of the apparatus sorcerers used to conjure forth spirits. See M. Schusser, *op. cit.*, 1115. Many of the old grimoires are being reissued today and are earning their publishers considerable profit, as there is a current revival of the occult science throughout the Western world and particularly in the U.S.

LEGEND NO. 39. The notion that, on the one hand, Mine Spirits were frightening figures who could wreak terrible havoc and cause harm and injury to miners, yet, on the other hand, be friendly and helpful, has been a part of folk belief since the middle of the sixteenth century. Both notions are firmly developed in Georg Agricola's famous work *De re metallica* that was published in 1556 (a year after the author's death). See W. Peiter, "Der Berggeist der erzgebirgischen Bergleute," *ZöV*, 2 (1896), 178–180; J. Wahner, "Vom Berggeiste," *Oberschlesien*, 1 (1902), 520–526; G. Heilfurth, *Der Vorstellungskreis vom "Berggeist" bei Georg Agricola und seinen Zeitgenossen* (Wien, 1967); L. Mackensen, "Berggeister," *HdA* I, 1071–1083; L. Petzoldt, *DVS*, 433–443; see also the commentaries to Nos. 2 and 3 for further bibliography and for a delineation of the appearance and functions of Mine Spirits.

LEGEND NO. 40. Although the belief in Dwarfs, Cobolds, and similar spirits predates Christianity in most of Europe, this legend offers an excellent example of heathen-Christian syncretism that developed in later years. Not only does the Dwarf fall to his knees and pray with the girl, he protects her house because she is good and pious.

That this Dwarf lives not in an underground community of similar creatures, but rather in a house in the village, indicates that he fits the category of Cobold or House Spirit (see Nos. 72–79) rather than the category of Dwarf.

That the spirit protects the house against fire indicates that an element of the pre-Christian belief in guardian spirits of house and home has survived in this legend. This function was later taken over by Christian saints. St. Florian is the figure most often invoked to protect a house from destruction by lightning and fire. see L. Petzoldt, *DVS*, 443–447; I. Blum, *Die Schutzgeister in der altnordischen Literatur*, Diss. (Straßburg, 1912); L. Honko, *Geisterglaube in Ingermanland*, FFC 185 (Helsinki, 1962); I. Weiser-Aall, "Germanische Hausgeister und Kobolde," *NdZsV*, 4 (1926), 1–19; H. Rühmann, *Opfersagen des Hausgeist- und Zwergenkultes*, Diss. Kiel (Frankfurt, 1939); A. Johansons, *Der Schirmherr des Hofes im Volksglauben der Letten* (Stockholm, 1964); W. Hävernick, "Wunderwurzeln, Alraunen und Hausgeister im deutschen Volksglauben," *Beiträge zur deutschen Volks- und Altertumskunde*, 10 (1966), 17–34.

LEGEND NO. 41.    This legend combines a family history with the famous theme of midwifery service in the spirit world. As such, the legend becomes a kind of origin myth for the family, tracing their beginnings to a supernatural occurrence.

The von Rantzau family was a prominent noble lineage of Danish descent in Holstein. They took their name from Rantzau Castle in the Wendland region of Holstein. The family is first mentioned in a chronicle that dates from 1226. One of the many prominent family members was Johann von Rantzau (1383–1404), who was an administrator for the Danish crown and who supported the introduction of the Protestant faith in Holstein and Denmark. Another was Josias von Rantzau (1609–1650), who commanded both Swedish and French army units during the Thirty Years' War. He later became governor of Dunkirk.

In 1650 the family was elevated by Duke Frederick III of Holstein to the rank of count. The lineage came to an end in 1734 when Wilhelm Adolf von Rantzau died without heirs. The sudden demise of such prominent families is another occasion for legend-making—in this case to explain the termination of the lineage. See K. von Rantzau, *Das Haus Rantzau: Eine Familienchronik* (Celle, 1865).

It is curious that Dwarfs, Water Nixies, and other spirits are thought to need the services of human midwives to aid in the delivery of their children (see also Legends No. 49, 58, 65–66, 69, and 305 and their commentaries). It is possible that this service was only thought necessary where the woman in labor was a human being who had been abducted to the underground or the underwater realm. Martin Luther retells such a legend in his *Tischreden*. See G. Jungwirth, "Hebamme," *HdA* III, 1587–1603; Peuckert, *DtVSMA* (Stuttgart, 1942), 187–200; Peuckert *Sagen*, 65–69.

The three gifts from the spirit world that become associated with the branches of a prominent family constitute a frequent motif in German legendry. See M. Lüthi, *Die Gabe im Märchen und in der Sage* (Bern, 1943). Of particular importance is the tripartite structure of the functions of the gifts in this legend. As the legend text indicates, the pennies are to insure that the heirs will occupy high positions in government, the herring will assure the other branch of the family success in war, and the distaff will guarantee the birth of many children. Thus, the three branches of the family are destined to represent the three functions of government, warfare, and fertility.

This is the precise trifunctional structure that the French scholar Georges Dumézil has detected in the social structures, religions, and myths of peoples of the Indo-European continuum. Dumézil contends that this tripartite structure was already a part of our civilization during the age of the Proto Indo-Europeans. See G. Dumézil, *Les dieux des Germains* (Paris, 1959). For a summary of Dumézil's theories and scholarship see C. Scott Littleton, *The New Comparative Mythology: An Anthropological Assessment of the Theories of Georges Dumézil*, 2nd ed. (Berkeley, Los Angeles, London, 1973). See also L. Gerschel, "Sur un schème trifonctionnel dans une famille de légendes germaniques," *Revue de l'histoire des religions*, 150 (1956), 55–92.

For a discussion of the motif of wood shavings turning to gold, see the commentary to No. 8.

LEGEND NO. 42. History has otherwise forgotten Hermann von Rosenberg, but his experiences with the spirit world are reported in several printed collections. Rosenberg was a town in what was then the German-speaking region of Bohemia. Today it is the Czechoslovakian city of Rožmberk. For information on the motif of the Wedding of the Dwarfs, see the commentary to No. 31.

LEGEND NO. 43. Winklemann wrote a number of chronicles and journals from which the Grimms acquired a fair number of legends. He died in 1699. This legend seems to be a distorted version of the Oldenburg Horn. A marvelously worked horn of gold, known as the Oldenburg Horn, was once in the possession of King Christian I of Denmark. There was a legend then current about how the horn had been stolen from the Dwarfs who lived under Mt. Osen (actually a hill) near Oldenburg. See H. Dageförde, *Die Sage vom Oldenburger Horn*, Diss. (Göttingen, 1953); F. Ranke, "Wie alt sind unsere Volkssagen?" *Zeitschrift für Deutschunterricht*, 1922, 10–17. See also No. 547.

LEGEND NO. 44. The creature of this legend fits the category of Dwarf since he lives underground, but when he enters the house and takes up residence there he develops into a Cobold figure. See Nos. 72–79. A typical trait of the Cobold is that once he moves into a house he is nearly impossible to get rid of. See Archer Taylor, "The Pertinacious Cobold," *JEGP*, 31 (1932), 1–9.

LEGEND NO. 45. This legend, which has attained a nearly worldwide distribution, was well known in classical antiquity and was retold by Ovid in the *Metamorphosis* (VIII, 611–724). Philemon and Baucis, an elderly married couple living in Phrygia, became noted for their true love. When Zeus and Hermes were wandering through the countryside in human form they found no shelter with the richer inhabitants, but the aged pair received them hospitably. Thus, when the two gods destroyed the rest of the area by flood to punish the inhabitants for the inhospitable treatment, they spared the old couple and changed their miserable cottage into a magnificent temple. Here, the two held priestly offices for the rest of their lives. Finally, when they prayed that they might not be separated in death, they were both changed into intertwining trees.

Thun Lake is located about 17 miles south of Bern in Switzerland.

LEGEND NO. 46. Wunsiedel and Weißenstadt are located in a relatively sparsely settled region near the Czech border east of Bayreuth. This particular account represents a narrative known among scholars of folklore as a "memorate," a firsthand description of an encounter with the supernatural world. See C. W. von Sydow, "Kategorien der Prosa-Volksdichtung," in *Volkskundliche Gaben John Meier zum 70. Geburtstag dargebracht* (Berlin-Leipzig, 1934), 253–268. Reprinted in C. W. von Sydow, *Selected Papers on Folklore* (Copenhagen, 1948), 60–88, and in L. Petzoldt, *Vergleichende Sagenforschung* (Darmstadt, 1969), 66–89. See also L. Honko, "Memorates and the Study of Folk Beliefs," *JFI* I (1964), and D. Ward, "The Little Man Who Wasn't There: Encounters with the Supranormal," *Fabula*, 18 (1977), 212–225.

LEGEND NO. 47. Moss Women belong to the category of Spirits or Creatures of Nature, to which also belong such creatures as Wild Men, Forest Spirits, Mountain Spirits, Big Foot, etc. Such creatures frequently have a wild, half-animal appearance, but the female figures can also be sensual and alluring and often enter into intimate love relationships with humans. See W. Mannhardt, *Wald- und Feldkulte*, 2 Bde., 2 Aufl. (Berlin, 1904–05), who sees the survival of an ancient Germanic worship of nature and its divinities in such figures. See also H. Göttling, *Die wilden Leute und ihre nächsten Verwandten im altdeutschen Schrifttum*, Diss. (Erlangen, 1925); W. Pehl, "Waldgeister," *HdA* IX, 55–62; R. Bernheimer, *Wild Men in the Middle Ages* (Cambridge, 1952).

As creatures of nature, Moss Women possess knowledge of the powers of all plants, and their advice in these matters should be heeded.

A more threatening figure than the Moss Woman is the Wild Huntsman, who hunts Forest Maidens and Moss Women as game. See commentaries to Nos. 48 and 172–173. The legend of the Wild Huntsman chasing Forest Maidens as his prey is widespread throughout Germany, Denmark, Norway, Sweden, and Ireland. The story can assume many oikotypical forms depending on the region, but in essence it tells of a Forest Maiden (Wild Woman, Moss Woman, White Woman, etc.) being pursued by the Wild Huntsman. A human witness sometimes interrupts the chase, saves the woman, and then falls in love with her. Or he witnesses how the Wild Huntsman catches his prey, slays her, cuts up the body, and transports it as he would game on his horse.

The legend was especially popular in Germany during the Middle Ages and was frequently retold in medieval literature: See Lutz Röhrich, *EMA*, II, 5–52; 393–407. See also L. Röhrich, "Die Frauenjagdsage," in G. Megas (ed.), *IV. International Congress for Folk-Narrative Research in Athens* (Athens, 1965), 408–423.

Also widely known is the motif of warding off the Wild Huntsman by chopping crosses into tree trunks. The German folklorist Friedrich Panzer reported witnessing such a practice near his home in Bamberg in the nineteeth century (F. Panzer, *Bayerische Sagen und Bräuche, Beiträge zur deutschen Mythologie* [München, 1848–55], II, 70, my own free translation):

> When watching woodsmen felling trees in our forests, I often saw them take an ax and mark the tree trunk just at the moment it was to fall with six quick strokes, making three crosses. At first I thought they were branding the lumber with their identification marks, but upon inquiry I was told that every trunk that has the cross carved into it just before it falls is sacred. At midnight, when the Wild Horde rushes through the forests making its great racket, the Forest Maidens, the Poor Souls, and the souls of those who died in accidents and who are thus condemned to wander the forests can find safety at these trees. The Wild Men and the Forest Maidens repay the woodsmen for this service by insuring that the trees fall correctly, and they provide safety when they have to travel through the forests at night.

LEGEND NO. 48.    The Wild Huntsman belongs to one of the categories of the more frightening demonic beings in legendry. Two more or less distinct characterizations are known in Germany. First, there is the demonic hunter who is a Lost Soul. He rides with his spectral hounds through forests and over hill and dale (see Nos. 170, 173 and 309–311). Then there is the Wild Huntsman who leads the hordes of Lost Souls across the sky amid the barking of hounds, the roar of wind, and beating of horses' hooves, sweeping up all that lies before them (see Nos. 313–314).

Some scholars—e.g., O. Höfler, "Der germanische Totenkult und die Sage vom wilden Heer," *Oberdeutsche Zeitschrift für Volkskunde*, 10 (1936)—have attempted to link the figure of the Wild Huntsman with the god Wodan. However, Jan de Vries has shown conclusively ("Wodan und die Wilde Jagd," *Die Nachbarn*, 3 [1962], 31–44) that the tradition is known in many societies throughout the world and thus can scarcely represent an exclusively Germanic myth. Similar traditions are known in the southwestern United States where a ghostly cowboy leads a fiery ghost herd across the skies. Reports of contacts with the Wild Horde usually occur in isolated places far from populated regions, and encounters invariably occur in near darkness at dusk or dawn.

It is quite possible that an altered state of consciousness caused by relative sensory deprivation may contribute to such experiences, for experiments have shown that when the senses are understimulated, there is a tendency to hallucinate. For a description of such states see C. Tart (ed.), *Altered States of Consciousness* (New York, 1962).

Similar traditions are known in classical antiquity (see J. de Vries, *op. cit.*). The best summary of the tradition in Germany is offered by K. Meisen, *Die Sagen vom Wütenden Heer und Wilden Jäger* (Münster, 1935).

LEGEND NO. 49.    Saalfeld is on the Saale River in Saxony about forty miles south of Weimar. The town of Breulieb has since become assimilated by Saalfeld. Most people are fascinated by the world of the unknown and are much disposed to believe in underground realms. Contact with these realms is thought to be possible where there are openings in the crust of the earth such as caves, ravines, or ditches. This notion is especially pronounced in the case of bodies of water where the bottom is known to be far beneath the surface of the earth.

Notions that spirits live beneath lakes, ponds, rivers, and seas and at the bottom of wells are encountered in the beliefs and legends of peoples all over the world. Although such traditions have been collected all over Germany, they were especially prevalent in the east—Pomerania, Silesia, and Saxony—where there was contact with the traditions of the Slavic peoples. Water spirits are thought to be both male (Merman, Water Nix, etc.) and female (Mermaid, Water Sprite, etc.). The word *wazzernixe* 'Water Nix' is first documented in the late thirteenth century in a poem by Konrad von Würzburg.

The Water Nix is thought to resemble a handsome young man in appearance, and he is also known for his seductive nature. However, at the same time, he is believed to be a diabolic and terrifying demon. His eyes are said to be fiery, his hair green, and his hands and feet webbed and always icy cold. He devours the children that are born to his human wife, whom he abducted to his underwater realm.

Sometimes a Nix or Merman can be found at the bottom of a well. However, it was the opinion of Swedish folklorist Carl W. von Sydow that such traditions were merely "warning fictions," stories that were invented solely to frighten children and keep them from leaning over the edges of wells. See C. W. von Sydow, "Kategorien der Prosa-Volksdichtung," *Volkskundliche Gaben John Meier zum 70. Geburtstag dargebracht* (Berlin-Leipzig, 1934), 253–268, and reprinted in C. W. von Sydow, *Selected Papers on Folklore* (Kopenhagen, 1948), 60–88.

Sometimes the water spirits demand an annual human sacrifice (see Nos. 54, 57, 61, and 62 and their commentaries).

Female water spirits are also frequently thought of as both beautiful and seductive, and potentially dangerous to humans. The fascination of the poets of Romanticism for such themes contributed to a change in the tradition. Water Maidens became less demonic than was previously the case. They began to be thought of as beautiful and sensitive creatures of nature who invariably fell in love with humans. Especially famous in literature were such figures as Undine and Melusine (see No. 528 and commentary). For further information on the topic see F. Panzer, "Wassergeister," *HdA* IX, 127–191; R. Kühnau, "Wasserdämonen," *MSGV*, 5 (1903), 19–22; P. G. Helms, *Seespuk: Aberglauben, Märchen, Schnurren*, 2nd ed. (Stuttgart, 1965); G. Benwell and A. Waugh, *Sea Enchantress: The Tale of the Mermaid and Her Kin* (London, 1961).

As with Dwarfs, underwater creatures appear to need the help of human midwives when they are ready to deliver their infants (see commentary to No. 41): G. Jungwirth, "Hebamme," *HdA* III, 1587–1603; W. Gubalke, *Die Hebamme im Wandel der Zeiten* (Hannover, 1964).

The motif of the abduction of a human bride is widespread in these legends and is also known in ballads. See P. Bäuerle, *Die Volksballaden von Wassermanns Braut und Wassermanns Frau*, Diss. (Tübingen, 1934). See also L. Röhrich, "Sagenballaden," in *HdVL*, 101–156.

For information on legends in the English tradition see: C. Hole, "Superstitions and Beliefs of the Sea," *Folklore*, 78 (1967), 184–189; Ireland: G. S.

Lane, "Legends of Our Lakes," *The Irish Digest*, 68 (1960), 41; Scandinavia: D. Strömbäck, "Some Notes on the Nix in Older Nordic Tradition," *Medieval Literature and Folklore Studies: Essays in Honor of Francis Lee Utley* (New Brunswick, N.J., 1970), pp. 245–256; East Baltic: A. Johansons, *Der Wassergeist und der Sumpfgeist: Untersuchungen volkstümlicher Glaubensvorstellungen bei Völkern des ostbaltischen Raumes und bei den Ostslaven*, Studies in Comparative Religion, 8 (Stockholm, 1968).

There have been attempts to give rational and/or scientific explanations for the appearance of red waters in lakes and ponds. See, for example, K. R. Fischer, "Das Rätsel der hessischen Blutseen," *Volk und Schule*, 10 (1931), 42–43, who sees algae formations as the ultimate cause.

LEGEND NO. 50. Grödich is a town near Salzburg in Austria.

Wild Women, the female counterparts of the Wild Men, are frequently associated with erotic motifs and they form close relationships with human men. Locally, they are known by a wide variety of names: *Wilde Weibscher, Witte Wiewer, die Saligen*, etc. Mention is already made of them in the twelfth century by Berthold von Regensburg, who points out that they can be helpful to humans if food and drink are left out for them. See K. Beitl, *Wörterbuch der deutschen Volkskunde*, 2nd ed. (Stuttgart, 1955), 547. See also J. Grimm, *DM*, II, 1009; L. Petzoldt, *DVS*, 415–425; L. Röhrich, "Europäische Wildgeistersagen," *RhJb*, 10 (1960), 79–162.

The legend of the wife's surprising the sleeping pair—her husband and the Wild Woman—yet remaining sympathetic toward the lovely creature and even admiring her hair, has a long history in popular tradition. It was printed in Cologne in 1666 in the *Memoires du Maréchal de Bassompierre, contenant l'historie de sa vie*, and is retold by the Grimms in Legend No. 71.

Like many demons of nature, Wild Women have a strong desire to raise human children. The story of the love affair of a nobleman with a maiden from the otherworld (Stauffenberg, Undine, Melusine, etc.) is related and has a widespread distribution (see No. 528 and commentary).

LEGEND NO. 51. For additional information on the Merman and Water Nix, see the commentary to No. 49. Laibach was the German name for the City of Ljubljana, the capital of the Slovenian region of Yugoslavia. Dancing has often been viewed with suspicion in the Christian world, especially among Calvinists, Pietists, and other reform groups. Among some groups even today, social dancing borders the periphery of accepted behavior, and moderation is expected of all participants.

Implicit in this legend, and serving as a warning to others, is the notion that the girl, Ursula Schäferin, was too willing to dance wildly with a stranger. That she had to pay so dearly for her sin was to serve as a severe warning to other young people, and this legend thus served the socialization process.

The extra guest (*der Überzählige*) who shows up at a dance is invariably a demon or the Devil himself in such legends. See L. Kretzenbacher, "Freveltanz und Überzähliger," *Carinthia*, 1 (1954), 843–866; I. Kleine, *Der Überzählige*, Diss. (Göttingen, 1954); L. Kretzenbacher, "Tanzverbot und Warnlegende," *RhJb*, 12 (1961), 16–22.

LEGEND NO. 52.   See the bibliography in the commentary to No. 49.

The concept of the Merman's keeping the souls of the drowned in pots turned upside down is apparently Slavic in origin. See A. Wuttke, *Der deutsche volksaberglaube der Gegenwart*, 3rd ed. (Berlin, 1900), see esp. 48; P. Drechsler, "Der Wassermann im schlesischen Volksglauben, *ZsfVk*, 11 (1901), 201–216; W. Kalak, *Der Wassermann im oberschlesischen Volksglauben* (Ratibor, 1936).

LEGEND NO. 53.   In explaining why the Water Nix is no longer seen, this legend evidently documents a fading belief in his existence. There are a number of variants of this story. See R. Kühnau, "Wasserdämonen," *MSGV*, 5 (1903), 19–22, and H. Jedlitschka, "Der Wassermann und der Fleischer," *Kuhländerin*, 8 (1926), 188–189.

LEGEND NO. 54.   Human attempts to conquer the waters are viewed as audacious and presumptous acts that insult and challenge the water spirits. The notion that bodies of water demand periodical offerings may also play a role in this legend. See the commentary to No. 62.

LEGEND NO. 55.   Although it is believed that many demons and spirits enjoy playing practical jokes and tricks on humans, this kind of behavior is rarely attributed to the Water Nix. See L. Röhrich, *Sage*, 15–25.

LEGEND NO. 56.   Kirchhain is about eight miles directly east of Marburg. The "very deep lake" is in reality scarcely more than a pond. St. Elisabeth was an important saint in Marburg. In addition to the Elisabeth Mill, there is also an Elisabeth Church and an Elisabeth Spring located there. See also Nos. 563–564.

LEGEND NO. 57.   Regarding the motif of challenging the waters by swimming for a wager, see the commentary to No. 54. That the man fell victim to the Water Nix may well represent the survival of the notion that the spirit demanded and received a periodic offering. See also the commentary to No. 62.

LEGEND NO. 58.   Sea-Nymphs, Goddesses of the Sea, and Mermaids were well known in classical antiquity (e.g., Aphrodite, the Nereides, the Sirens).

Dönges is located in present-day Thuringia (German Democratic Republic) just across the border from Hesse. The lake there is now called *Frauensee*, 'Women's Lake,' probably as a result of this legend. The mysterious appearance of a Water Maiden among humans and the love that develops between a man and the spirit is a motif that occurs in many legends and in literature (see Nos. 49 and 528 and commentaries). The attempt of the youth to win the maiden by taking her glove seals her doom.

The blood-red water of the lake may well have come about from a natural physical condition. When ponds and lakes reach a certain saline content and temperature, a bright red algae growth can develop. See K. R. Fischer, "Das Rätsel der hessischen Blutseen," *Volk und Schule*, 10 (1931), 42–43.

LEGEND NO. 59. The belief is widespread that Water Demons can emerge from the depths in the form of a bull, or less frequently as a horse, and graze among the animals on the shore of a lake, pond, or river. The motif was known in Greek antiquity where Poseidon was honored as the creator of the horse and he himself was envisioned in horse form. The motif occurs especially in legends of North Germany. See F. Panzer, "Wassergeister," *HdA* IX, 127–191 and esp. 131–132. See also A. Wirth, "Stier," *HdA* IX, 482–486. The motif also occurs as a miracle in the life of St. Aidanus (see L. Petzoldt, *DVS*, 432). For information on legends from Lake Mummel and nearby Lake Wild, see W. Berg, "Der Mummelsee, der Wildsee und ihre Sagen," *Unterhaltungsbeilage zur Rastatter Zeitung*, Nos. 36–39 (1921), 41.

The motif of trying to fathom the depths of the lake and running into peril in the process appears frequently in legends of lakes. Implicit in such tales is the notion that it is wrong to probe too deeply into the world of the unknown; man was not meant to fathom all, and the attempt to do so is a sin against the mysteries of nature.

One of the most impressive legends of this type was published by K. Reiser, *Sagen, Gebräuche und Sprichwörter des Allgäus* (Kempten, 1894), No. 262, 234. In this legend the man who tries to fathom the depths of the bottomless lake sees a frightful monster rise to the surface, whereupon it warns:

> If thou fathomst me,
> I shall eat thee!

The man is lucky to escape with his life. See also L. Röhrich, *SuM*, 82–85.

LEGEND NO. 60. Although the underground and underwater realms of spirits and demons remain separate from the world of humans, the creatures of these worlds frequently invade the realm of men, posing as humans. Men usually react ambivalently toward these creatures. On the one hand, the spirits represent a danger to their mortal existence, and often to their immortal souls. On the other hand, as creatures of nature, they are viewed with compassion. See the commentary to No. 49. See also L. Röhrich, *Sage*, 15–25.

LEGEND NO. 61. Regarding the water's demand for periodic human sacrifice, see the commentary to Legend No. 62.

The verse in the original German reads:

> *Nix in der Grube,*
> *du bist ein böser Bube,*
> *wasch dir dein Beinchen*
> *mit roten Ziegelsteinchen!*

These verses are sung by children in Germany today as part of a tag game. One of the children plays the Nix and stands in the center of a circle of children. When the verse ends, the child tries to escape. My own daughter, who attended German schools from 1969 to 72, played the game frequently and knew the verses well.

LEGEND NO. 62. The belief that bodies of water demand periodic human offerings is documented in the writings of Gervase of Tilbury who, in his *Otia imperialia* of the year 1214, tells about rivers crying out for their human victims. Furthermore, the belief that there are certain days of the year when a river must have its human victim and that one should not swim on such days is also very old. This led to the practice of trying to placate the water spirits with surrogate offerings. Many such rites have been documented. See R. Wildhaber, " 'Die Stunde is da, aber der Mann nicht,' Ein europäisches Sagenmotive," *RhJb*, 9 (1958), 65–88. For information on Germanic human sacrifices see E. Mogk, *Die Menschenopfer bei den Germanen*, Abhandlungen der phil.-hist. Klasse der sächsischen Gesellschaft der Wissenschaften, 27 (Leipzig, 1909). See also the essay "Menschenopfer," in *RGG* IV, 867–868, and D. Ward, "The Threefold Death: An Indo-European Trifunctional Sacrifice?" in J. Puhvel (ed.), *Myth and Law among the Indo-Europeans* (Berkeley, Los Angeles, London, 1970), 124–142.

The notion that a deceased being can be resuscitated using skeletal remains is an ancient tradition documented in hunting cultures around the world. Hunters of many cultures have been known to save the bones of their game animals, reconstruct the skeletons, wrap them in the animal hide, and send them back to the Lord of the Beasts in the attempt to replenish the supply of animals. See Röhrich *SuM*, 142–194. See also the commentary to No. 302.

LEGEND NO. 63.   It is common in legends for demonic beings to be named after specific physical characteristics they are thought to have. See, for example, L. Röhrich, *Die dämonischen Gestalten der schwäbischen Volks-überlieferung*, Diss. (Tübingen, 1949). Mellrichstadt is in Franconia, not far from the Czech border, near the city of Coburg.

LEGEND NO. 64.   Since millers live and work around streams and millponds it is not surprising that there are many legends told about Water Nixies and millers. See P. Kasparek, "Der Wassermann und der Müller," *Oppelner Heimatkalender*, 13 (1938), 138.

LEGEND NO. 65.   I have not translated the German names Dosten and Dorant because of their alliteration and assonance, and also because it is impossible to determine with certainty the specific plants the names refer to. As is often the case with popular designations of botanical species, one and the same name can refer to a wide variety of plants depending on local usage. H. Marzel ("Dosten und Dorant," *SAV*, 23 [1921], 157–180, and *Geschichte und Volkskunde der deutschen Heilpflanzen* [Darmstadt, 1967], 206–208), the leading authority on popular botany in Germany, identified Dosten as *origanum vulgare*, which would make it identical to pot marjoram. It is an aromatic plant with pink blossoms that grows in rocky soil near forests and can be used as a ground cover. The Grimms identify Dorant as *marrubium*. What is probably meant is *marrubium vulgare* or horehound, an herb used frequently as a pharmaceutical in popular medicine. Marzell, however, identifies Dorant as *linaria*, a form of Toadflax related to Lobelia. Marzell points out that both *origanum vulgare* and linaria are often used in combination to ward off evil spirits, especially witches.

LEGEND NO. 66.  The region in question is in Thuringia in the German Democratic Republic. Regarding the motif of midwife service in the other world, see the commentary to No. 41.

LEGEND NO. 67.  Since the Water Nix is thought to run his underwater household in precisely the same manner as do humans on the surface of the earth, it is not surprising that he has need of the services of a housemaid. More common, however, is the legend of midwifery service in the underwater realm. See the commentary to No. 41.

The words that the maid utters only make sense if one assumes that they were said four years after she returned from the underwater realm. Thus she would have only three years left of the seven that were allotted to her. See Petzoldt, *DVS*, 427.

LEGEND NO. 68.  This legend functions as an explanation (etiological legend) for the origins of the ring with the von Alvensleben family crest. It also explains why half of the family fell into poverty and why that half of the lineage expired.

The imposed taboo against losing the ring is a motif frequently encountered with gifts from the supernatural world. See Max Lüthi, *Die Gabe im Märchen und in der Sage* (Bern, 1943). See also W.-E. Peuckert, *DtVSMA*, 181–186.

The von Alvenslebens were a prominent Prussian family of counts and important political leaders.

The village of Kalbe is in the Altmark region of Magdeburg. It was once a residence for one part of the family. The town of Alvensleben lies about forty miles to the south.

LEGEND NO. 69.  See the commentaries to Nos. 41 and 68.

LEGEND NO. 70.  This legend seems to be a contamination of two well-known legends, "The Wedding of the Dwarfs" and "The Death of the Great God Pan." For the former see the commentary to No. 31. The latter is so named because a version of the legend can be found in the *De defectu oraculorum* (cap. 17) of Plutarch, which tells of voices in the wilderness announcing the death of the Great Pan.

In Europe the legend usually involves a man returning home at night and hearing a tiny voice call out, "Pingeltingel (or some other strange name) is dead." When the man arrives home and reports what he has heard, a maidservant suddenly begins to weep inconsolably. She then runs from the house and is never seen again. It is either explicitly stated or implied that the voice the man heard belonged to some creature from the spirit world (Dwarf, Forest Spirit, etc.). And unsuspected by the household, the maid was also from this world, and the person mentioned was a close relative. Inger Boberg (*Sagnet om den store Pans død* [Copenhagen 1934]) maintains, on the basis of a thorough study of all the extant variants, that the tale was of Germanic origin and that Plutarch somehow heard a version. The story has been recorded in the oral traditions of Germany, Sweden, Norway, Denmark, Brittany,

Flanders, England, Scotland, and Ireland. The British versions invariably speak of the death of a cat or the King of the Cats instead of a demonic creature. See W. Drexler, "Die Epiphanie des Pan," *Philologus*, 52 (1894), 731–732; G. A. Gerhard, *Der Tod des großen Pan*, Sitzungsber. der Heidelberger Akademie der Wiss., phil.-hist. Kl., 5 (Heidelberg, 1915); A. Taylor, *Northern Parallels to the Death of Pan*, Washington University Studies, Humanistic Series, 10 (St. Louis, Mo., 1922).

LEGEND NO. 71. For the three gifts see the commentary to No. 41. For the wife's discovering her husband sleeping with a sprite but choosing not to disturb them, see No. 50. Goethe retells a version of this legend in his *Unterhaltungen deutscher Ausgewanderten (Goethes Werke*, Hamburger Ausgabe, vol. VI, 165).

LEGEND NO. 72. While the Dwarfs live in underground communities away from human settlements, the solitary Cobold takes up residence right in someone's house or barn. He can be a playful, mischievous spirit, or he can be a powerful divinity in whose hands rest the prosperity of house and farm. He is therefore not to be offended in any way. He is especially unhappy when behavioral norms have been violated and he can take revenge by causing cattle to drop dead, crops to fail, or by burning down the barn. In areas where the belief in the Cobold is still intense, his presence is perceived quite frequently and memorates of personal encounters abound. See L. Honko, *Geisterglaube in Ingermanland*, FFC 185 (Helsinki, 1962).

House spirits bearing a variety of personal names appear frequently in the popular literature of the sixteenth and seventeenth centuries (see Nos. 75 and 76). The relationship to house and home can be detected in the etymology of the name *Cobold* 'Ruler of the House,' and he still functions in such a role when the man of the house is away for an extended period. See I. Blum, *Die Schutzgeister in der altnordischen Literatur*, Diss. (Straßburg, 1912); G. Polívka, "Die Entstehung eines dienstbaren Kobolds aus einem Ei," *ZsfVk*, 28 (1918), 41–55; A. Johansons, *Der Schirmherr des Hofes im Volksglauben der Letten* (Stockholm, 1964); A. Taylor, "The Pertinacious Cobold," *JEGP*, 31 (1932), 1–9.

That the Cobold appears with a knife in his back is an indication that, at least in this case, he was thought of as the soul of a man who was once murdered in the house. In this regard he is clearly related to the *Poltergeist* phenomenon.

LEGEND NO. 73. The story of the Cobold that one cannot get rid of no matter how hard one tries is well known. See A. Taylor, "The Pertinacious Cobold," *JEGP*, 31 (1932), 1–9. In this regard he resembles the Mandrake and the *Spiritus familiaris*, or Spirit in the Bottle, each of whom can be gotten rid of only under very specific conditions (see Nos. 84–85). However, a Cobold can sometimes be driven away by too much cursing, reflecting a certain Christianization of the tradition.

LEGEND NO. 74. The motif of offering food to the spirits occurs with many spirits and demons, but it is especially a trait found in Cobold legends.

See H. Rühmann, *Opfersagen des Hausgeist- und Zwergenkultes*, Diss. (Kiel [printed: Frankfurt, 1939]). The foolhardy person who breaks one of the prescriptions in regard to the supernatural world is invariably punished quite severely and is lucky to escape with his life.

LEGEND NO. 75.   The fact that the departing husband entrusts the care of his wife to the Cobold in his absence is a reflection of the original function of the Cobold as Ruler of the House, as the etymology of the name reveals. See commentary to No. 72. See also M. Bringemeier, "Dämonische Wesen in der Hofgemeinschaft," *NdZsV*, 20 (1942), 75–89. The legend has many of the same motifs associated with songs and stories of adultery. See, for example, K. Roth, *Ehebruchschwänke in Liedform* (München, 1977).

LEGEND NO. 76.   The original meaning of the word *Cobold* as 'Ruler of the House' (see the commentary to No. 72) is clearly reflected in the behavior of Hinzelmann. He has definite patriarchal and authoritarian traits: He supervises the servants in the performance of their work; he punishes those who deviate from established behavioral norms; and he generally keeps an eye on all the functions of the residence. He also shows all the other traits that are known to house spirits from popular tradition.

The source the Grimms used, however, was not oral tradition but rather a printed source, *Der vielförmige Hintzelmann* of 1704 (a copy of the original can be found in the university library in Göttingen). A facsimile reproduction was published in 1965 and dedicated to the German folklorist Will-Erich Peuckert on his seventieth birthday. The editors and publishers are not mentioned on the title page or anywhere else in the edition. There were also four additional Hinzelmann books published in the eighteenth century—all of them based on the 1704 edition.

Two questions about the tradition have confronted folklorists working with these materials: (1) Were the adventures and motifs in the 1704 edition taken from the oral tradition, from literary sources, or were they the free inventions of the author? And (2) did the five eighteenth-century books influence later oral traditions? These questions have recently been answered in splendid fashion by Erika Lindig (*Das Hinzelmannbuch von 1704*, Wissenschaftliche Arbeit zur Prüfung für das Lehramt an Gymnasien [Freiburg, 1978]). Lindig was able to show convincingly that although the author used some written sources the book was clearly based on popular oral tradition. Moreover, the five eighteenth-century books did not have a pronounced effect on later popular oral tradition. Lindig also showed that collections of exempla reflecting official theological attitudes toward demons played a dominant role in the history of the tradition.

LEGEND NO. 77.   This legend illustrates the importance of not offending the Cobold in any way since he can cause all kinds of havoc. Being too curious and wanting to catch a glimpse of the Cobold invariably ends in misfortune for the curious one.

The fact that this Cobold becomes a flaming missile and burns down the castle may result from contamination with the figure of the Drâk, a winged dragon-like creature covered with flames. See R. Knopf, *Der feurige Hausdrache*, Diss. (Berlin, 1936).

The name "Knocker" is reminiscent of the word "Tommy-Knocker," the Mine Spirit of British and American legends. Knocking is also a characteristic of the *Poltergeist*, a figure closely related to the Cobold.

LEGEND NO. 78.   Shoes and boots—perhaps because they are constantly in contact with the earth—often play a central role in popular beliefs and rites, especially those concerning health and fertility. See P. Sartori, "Der Schuh im Volksglauben," *ZsfVk*, 4 (1894), 148–180, 282–305, 412–427. They are also prevalent in legends telling of the creatures of the underworld, the Dwarfs. As is the case in this legend, boots are thought to have healing powers. See G. Jungbauer, "Schuh," *HdA* VII, 1292–1353. Boots can even bring peace of mind to the little creatures as attested to by the Swiss legend in which a Dwarf, after being expelled from the region, exclaims, "If I only had my boots, I would have my peace!" (E. L. Rochholz, *Schweizersagen aus dem Aargau*, 2 vols. [Aarau 1856–57], I, 379).

It is common for Dwarfs and other spirits of nature to be named after articles of clothing that they wear (see, for example, "Cappy" in No. 75). Names referring to footwear are not uncommon in German Dwarf legendry. A well-known Dwarf in the Black Forest, for example, was called *Stiefeli* 'Little Boots' (Rochholz, *op. cit.*, I, 377).

LEGEND NO. 79.   This mischievous spirit is not a Cobold, for apparently he spends all his time out of doors. That he appears only as a hand may indicate that he represents the soul of a deceased person. There is a widespread tradition of a hand protruding from the grave. It was thought that when someone who had committed a crime for which he had not been punished during his lifetime died and was buried, his hand would emerge from the grave as though seeking punishment so the soul might rest in peace.

This legend was used to frighten children into behaving and was so used as early as 1552 by Hans Sachs. See L. Schmidt, *Die Volkserzählung* (Berlin, 1963), 225–234, who traces a number of these variants.

Perhaps related are the legends of the chopped-off hand; see the essay "Abgehauene Hand," *HdS* I, 55–56. For English variants of "The Hairy Hand," see K. Briggs, *A Dictionary of British Folktales in the English Language*, Part B, Folk Legends, 2 vols. (London, 1971), II, 532–534.

LEGEND NO. 80.   This legend deals with the widespread phenomenon of the Aufhocker, or Huckup. This is a spirit of widely varying descriptions, who jumps on someone's shoulders usually at night in a dark place, grabs the person around the neck, and rides on his/her back, growing ever heavier, until the victim drops of exhaustion. Traditions of this nature are known in many countries. The fact that the victim is invariably alone, in the dark, and at some spooky spot when the attack occurs may indicate a psycho-physical state induced by fear and auto-suggestion. See F. Ranke, "Aufhocker," *HdA* I, 675–677.

In this legend the Huckup appears in the shape of a ghostly nun, but one can also encounter Dwarfs, Cobolds, the Devil, cats, or Werewolves—virtually any frightening creature can assume this role. See G. Grober-Glück, "Aufhocker und Aufhocken nach den Sammlungen des Atlas der deutschen Volkskunde," *RhJb*, 15/16 (1965), 117–143 (with maps).

LEGEND NO. 81. The Alp, or Nightmare, is one of the truly universal supernatural experiences. Originally, the word "Nightmare" (German "Nachtmahr") did not mean bad dream. Rather, it referred to a feminine creature who jumps upon the chest of her sleeping victim and presses the energy and vigor out of him. She can also ride him around the countryside at night until he awakens in the morning in a state of total exhaustion.

In German tradition the malevolent spirit leaves its human body and travels in the guise of a feather, puff of smoke, mouse, moth, snake, toad, or invisible spirit, entering the room of its victim through an open window, through a keyhole, under the door, etc. Unlike the witch, who acquires her powers voluntarily by choosing to associate with the Devil, the Nightmare is usually thought to be the unwilling victim of outside forces.

In Germany there are a variety of names for the Nightmare, both generic (*Mahr, Mahrt, Alp, Alb, Drud, Trud, Schrättele*) and personal (Walriderske, Doggi, Toggeli, etc.). Often, the experience has an implicit sexual nature that is quite explicit in other traditions, as is the case with the Incubus or Succubus, Lilith, and the like.

In Anglo-American tradition the pressing figure is believed to be an incredibly ugly witch usually known as the "Old Hag." David Hufford ("A New Approach to the Old Hag: The Nightmare Tradition Reexamined," in W. D. Hand [ed.], *American Folk Medicine* [Berkeley, Los Angeles, London, 1976], 73–85) has argued convincingly that a physiological condition common to many people in many places has led to the existence of these traditions. Hufford points out that the victim is usually lying on his/her back with eyes open, and begins to feel a tremendous pressure in the chest area. Efforts to move or yell prove to be in vain for the subject is totally paralyzed. The victim then frequently sees an apparition of an ugly old witch, terrifyingly real as she leans on the victim's chest.

Hufford points out that research on sleep states has shown that during the dream (REM) state the body is virtually paralyzed. He hypothesizes that during an experience of this sort the mind is already in the dream state but the body has not yet received the message. The subject's eyes are still open, but the rest of his body is paralyzed. Since the mind is programmed for dreams in this state, it is especially susceptible to perceiving dream-like apparitions.

More recently, D. Ward has shown ("The Little Man Who Wasn't There: On Encounters with the Supranormal," *Fabula*, 18 [1977], 212–225) that this type of experience is far more common than was previously thought. See also C. Cubasch, *Der Alp* (Berlin, 1877); J. Börner, *Das Alpdrücken, seine Begründung und Verhütung*, (Medical) Diss. (Würzburg, 1855); F. Ranke, "Alp," *HdA* I, 281–305; F. Ranke, "Mahr," *HdA* V, 1508–1512, and C. H. Tillhagen, "The Conception of the Nightmare in Sweden," in W. D. Hand and G. Arlt (eds.), *Humaniora: Festschrift for Archer Taylor* (New York, 1960), 317–329. An excellent monograph on the Nightmare is Gisela Lixfeld, *Der Alp: Analyse eines Sagentyps*, Wiss. Arbeit im Rahmen der ersten Staatsprüfung für das Lehramt am Gymnasium (Freiburg, 1978).

LEGEND NO. 82. The creatures of the spirit world—the Devil, witches, Dwarfs, and Water Nixies, etc.—were thought to be constantly attempting to rob humans of their newborn children and to abduct them to their own underground realms. Thus newborns, especially before they were baptized, were in constant danger and had to be watched closely. Certain apotropaic items in the nursery could help ward off demons, for instance, a Bible, a crucifix, special herbs, and amulets. Children who were in any way mis-shapen, or whose behavior was different or abnormal, were suspected of being changelings.

It is evident that certain relatively common defects of newborn children (Mongoloidism, hydrocephaly, rickets, cerebral palsy, etc.) aroused the suspicion that the child had been exchanged and that the real child had been abducted. In such cases it was considered necessary to force the demonic spirit culprit to come back for its own child.

One method was to beat the imposter unmercifully until the demon took pity on it and came back to fetch it, returning the proper child to its place in the crib. Such beliefs contributed to some of the most inhumane practices known in Europe.

More humane were attempts to get the demonic imposter to express surprise. For example, a mother would perform some peculiar task such as pretending to brew beer in an eggshell. At this point the changeling would jump up in its crib and exclaim: "I am as old as the Bohemian Forest and that's the first time I have ever seen anyone brew beer in an eggshell!" The imposter would thus give himself away.

See H. Ploss, *Das Kind in Brauch und Sitte der Völker*, 2 Bde. (Leipzig, 1884); G. Polívka, "Slavische Sagen vom Wechselbalg," *Archiv für Religions-wissenschaft*, 6 (1903); G. Piaschewski, *Der Wechselbalg: Ein Beitrag zum Aberglauben der nordeuropäischen Völker* (Breslau, 1935); H. Appel, *Die Wechsel-balgsage* (Berlin, 1937).

LEGEND NO. 83. Changelings were usually thought to be fully grown, mature demons who only posed as children to gain access to a human dwelling. Thus, if the supposed infant began to speak in the manner of a fully grown person, it gave itself away. See the commentary to No. 82.

LEGEND NO. 84. The Mandrake is a poisonous form of nightshade (*Mandragora officinarum*) with a forked root that is thought to assume a near human shape. Mandrake has been used as an aphrodisiac since classical antiquity. It was believed that a man who was hanged ejaculated his sperm upon the earth and that from this sperm the Mandrake grew. The legend of how the Mandrake was obtained is strictly a product of fantasy for the Mandrake does not grow in Northern Europe. Doubtless the story was told by the dealers in such items as part of their sales pitch. In Germany they used indigenous plants with a similar root structure (turnips, serpent's garlic, etc.). The roots were carefully dried and the person who possessed such an item took very good care of it, dressing it in velvet and silk, washing it carefully, keeping it in an upholstered box, and the like. It was then supposed to guarantee riches, power, sexual satisfaction, and general happiness.

As early as the sixteenth century, Hieronymus Bock (*Kreuterbuch*

[Straßburg, 1560]) complained about unscrupulous dealers selling such worthless items to gullible people for great sums of money. The German poet, Achim von Arnim, in his novelle *Isabella von Ägypten* tells a suspenseful Mandrake story. See J. Boullet, "Mandragore," *Aesculape*, 1960, pp. 3–37. R. Clark, "A Note on Medea's Plant and the Mandrake," *Folklore*, 79 (1968), 221–231; M. Eliade, "Le culte de la mandragore en Roumanie," *Zalmoxis*, I (1937), 208–225; W. Hävernick, "Wunderwurzeln, Alraunen und Hausgeister im deutschen Volksglauben," *Beiträge zur deutschen Volks- und Altertumskunde*, 10 (1966), 17–34; A. Schlosser, *Die Sage vom Galgenmännlein im Volksglauben und in der Literatur* (Münster, 1912); A. T. Starck, *Der Alraun* (Baltimore, 1917); J. Talley, "Runes, Mandrakes, and Gallows," in G. J. Lawson *et al.* (eds.), *Myth in Indo-European Antiquity* (Berkeley, Los Angeles, London, 1974).

LEGEND NO. 85. The *Spiritus familiaris*, or the Spirit in the Bottle, has been the subject of many literary treatments by such famous authors as Robert Louis Stevenson, Annette von Droste-Hülshoff, Friedrich de la Motte-Fouqué, G. de Nerval, and August Strindberg. The motif also appears in the popular literature of the Near East, most notably in *The Thousand-and-One Nights*. The spirit that is trapped in a bottle or gourd, is generally considered anthropomorphic. However, there are other spirits which take the form of insects; these are trapped in small boxes.

For a discussion of the different forms the spirit can assume, see R. Kühnau, "Gefangene Geister," *Festschrift zum Jahrhundertsfeier der Universität Breslau* (Breslau, 1911), 98–120. See also R. Merrifield, "Witch Bottles and Magical Jugs," *F-L*, 66 (1955), 195–207; P. Beck, "Der Teufel im Glase," *ZsfVk*, 21 (1911), 278–279; W. Werner, *Die Kalendergeschichte bei Grimmelshausen und ihre Zuordnung zum Volkslesestoff*, Diss. (Freiburg, 1950).

LEGEND NO. 86. Although birds' nests are frequently thought to possess supernatural powers, the belief that they can make you invisible is not common in the popular tradition. However, the story told here achieved wide popularity because of the novel by Grimmelshausen that served as the Grimms' source. It can no longer be determined with any degree of certainty whether the *bifolium* that is mentioned in the Grimms' note is intended here rather than a real bird's nest.

In Europe many believe that birds' nests have beneficial powers. This is especially true of nests that are attached to human dwellings such as those of the swallow. For example, a swallow's nest is supposed to bring good fortune and protect one's house against lightning. When the nests have been abandoned, they are removed and ground to a powder for use as pharmaceuticals—thought to be efficacious in the treatment of ailments such as ulcers, cramps, backache, epilepsy, and the like. Sometimes the ground nests are burned as incense—the smoke being inhaled for its healing properties. It is said that if you store bullets in the ashes of a burned swallow's nest they become magical and never miss their mark.

See A. Taylor, "Vogelnest," *HdA* VIII, 1682; A. Taylor, "Schwalbennest," *HdA* VII, 1399–1400; K. Amersbach, *Aberglaube, Sage, und Märchen bei Grimmelshausen* (Basel, 1891–1892); T. Zachariae, "Das Vogelnest im Aberglauben," *ZsfVk*, 19 (1909), 142–149.

LEGEND NO. 87. The brood penny belongs to the category of wish-fulfillment motifs especially common in the oral traditions of oppressed classes. It is related to the motif of the money sack that is always full, the milk pitcher that never runs dry, and so on. Whenever there seems to be no other way to escape poverty and deprivation, people often find comfort in the notion of getting rich by magical means.

It was thought that those people who consorted with the Devil or other demonic creatures could obtain such items. For instance, witches, sorcerers, Jews, and Freemasons were all thought to have brood pennies.

There are numerous ways to obtain these coins, and all the various magical methods of conjuring demons and devils come into play, for example, a circle at the crossroad, blaspheming the sacramental host, grave robbing, and similar acts of sorcery (see No. 38 and its commentary). It was also believed that if you caught the magic serpent on the one day a year it appeared, and then stole its tiny golden crown and put it with your own money, the coins would begin to breed an inexhaustible supply. These coins could also be obtained from such demonic beings as the Nix, the Wild Huntsman, and from Dwarfs.

Certain coins—such as those bearing the date 1777, or any coin that was found at a crossroad—were thought to have this ability all by themselves. The Mandrake Root (see No. 84 and its commentary) was considered a sure means of making coins reproduce themselves.

The motif of the brood coins has often been employed by authors in their literary works. One of the most famous of these stories is Adalbert von Chamisso's *Peter Schlemihls Wunderbare Geschichte*.

The motif has an analogue in the stories from ancient Greece and Persia where the coin always finds its way back to its owner.

See T. Siebs, "Heck(e)taler," *HdA* III, 1613–1624; W. Scurat, "Zaubergeld," *Am Urquell*, 4 (1893), 105–145.

LEGEND NO. 88. This is a variant of the changeling legend (see Nos. 82–83 and their commentaries), in which the Devil himself exchanges his child for a human infant. It is an example of "diabolization," for the Christian Devil here assumes the role previously played by such demonic beings as the Dwarf, the Water Nix, the Witch, and the Wild Woman.

LEGEND NO. 89. Sleeping children are invariably thought to be susceptible to the wiles of the Devil and other demons. The danger is believed to be greatest for infants who have not yet been baptized. See Nos. 82–83 and 88 and their commentaries.

LEGEND NO. 90. This legend has particular significance for students of folklore. Here, the demonic being who exchanges her child for a human infant is depicted as the Spirit of the Rye. Based on this and other legends, as well as hundreds of harvest customs he collected, the German folklorist Wilhelm Mannhardt developed his theory of the *Korndämon* 'Grain Spirit.' In such narratives and related harvest customs Mannhardt saw survivals of an ancient agricultural religion. For instance, he believed that the custom of tying up the last sheaf of the harvest and decorating it as an anthropomorphic figure represented the survival of ancient rites devoted to a divinity of the grain. Moreover, the Spirit of the Rye represented a survival of this same divinity. It was, incidentally, Mannhardt who inspired the English scholar Sir James Frazer to compile his monumental work, *The Golden Bough.*

The famous Swedish folklorist C. W. von Sydow attacked Mannhardt's theories in a number of publications (see below). Von Sydow maintained that the very human trait of putting special emphasis on elements that deviate from the norm (external dominant) results in a celebration of the first and last items in a series. Thus, decorating the last sheaf had, according to von Sydow, nothing to do with ancient religious rites. Furthermore, von Sydow maintained that grain spirits are nothing more than fictitious inventions of adults either to amuse (*Scherzfikt*) or frighten (*Warnfikt*) children so they do not trample the grain.

Of the stories related here, the ones attributed to G. W. Wegener seem to support the contention of von Sydow, for they contain explicit warnings to children to stay away from grainfields. However, the story which the Grimms excerpted from Prätorius seems to support Mannhardt, for here the Rye Spirit is more than a mere fiction; she is truly a demonic being capable of exchanging her offspring for human infants.

Viewed in totality, the evidence shows that such stories were indeed used to keep children away from the grainfields; however, I do not believe that adults freely invented the traditions. It seems much more likely that they used stories and beliefs that were once taken seriously but have since lost their frightening qualities.

The Spirit of the Rye has become especially popular in Germany as a result of Gustav Schüler's ballad, "Die Roggenmuhme," which is based essentially on this Grimm legend.

See W. Mannhardt, *Roggenwolf und Roggenhund* (Danzig, 1865); W. Mannhardt, *Wald- und Feldkulte*, 2 vols., 2nd ed. (Berlin, 1905); W. Mannhardt, *Die Korndämonen* (Berlin, 1868); H. Fink, "Ernte-, Korn- und Almdämonen," *Der Schlern*, 39 (1965), 324–334; D. Jennes, *The Corn Goddess and Other Tales from Indian Canada* (Ottawa, 1957); F. Mainzinger, "Vom Kornmännlein," *Fränkisches Monatsheft*, 8 (1929), 63; L. Mackensen, "Tierdämonen? Kornmetaphern!", *Mitteldeutsche Blätter für Volkskunde*, 8 (1933), 109–121; C. W. von Sydow, "The Mannhardtian Theories about the Last Sheaf and the Fertility Demons from a Modern Critical Viewpoint," *F-L*, 45 (1934), 291–309; C. W. von Sydow, "Die Begriffe des Ersten und Letzten in der Volksüberlieferung," *Folk-Liv*, 3 (1939), 242–254; C. W. von Sydow, "Folkminnesforskningens uppkomst och utveckling," *Folkkultur*, 4 (1944), 5–35.

LEGEND NO. 91. The fact that the Grimms titled this tale "The Two Women from the Underworld" indicates that they believed the women to be underground creatures or Dwarfs. However, Prätorius refers to them as *Bergfrauen* 'Mountain Women.' This latter term is ambiguous in the German language; it could mean either women who live inside the mountain, i.e., Dwarfs, or women who spend their time in the mountains. If this latter meaning is the one intended, the women would belong to the category of Mountain Spirits. Both Mountain Spirits and Dwarfs were thought to exchange their offspring for human infants. See Nos. 47, 82, 83, 88, 153 and their commentaries.

LEGEND NO. 92. This legend is a variant of "The Wives of Weinsperg" (see No. 493 and its commentary). The same legend is told of at least sixty castles in Germany as well as in other countries.

The moving forest that hides an enemy army is another topos that occurs in folklore and literature with some frequency. Its most famous occurrence is in Shakespeare's *Macbeth*. When the witches conjure forth the three apparitions, the third one tells Macbeth that he "Shall never vanquished be until/ Great Birnam wood to high Dunsinane hill/ Shall come against him" (IV, 1, 91–93).

Later as Macduff's army is preparing to attack, a messenger appears and tells Macbeth, "I look'd toward Birnam, and anon, methought, / The wood began to move" (V, 5, 34–35).

As in our legend, the moving forest is the enemy's army that is destined to triumph.

The Christian Mountain here is the same peak that is mentioned in No. 181.

LEGEND NO. 93. This is a variant of the sunken city legends, which in turn belong to the larger category of legends of crime and punishment. Traditions of cities, farmlands, or even continents that sink or are otherwise destroyed are found throughout the world (Brigadoon, Vineta, Atlantis, Sodom, and Gomorrah, etc.). See Nos. 97, 239, 240 and their commentaries.

In areas where grain agriculture is predominant, one most frequently encounters legends in which the sacred substance that is defiled is either bread or the grain itself. However, in areas where dairy farming predominates, the blasphemy is, as in this legend, the defiling of milk and cheese. These legends offer vivid testimony that the prevailing subsistence economy is a dominant concern in the respective regions.

The closing motif of this legend belongs to the category of Poor Souls in need of deliverance. It is a concrete representation of the belief that the sinners will more than likely never be delivered from torment.

See I. Schgör, "Die Sagen von der versunkenen Alpe," *Der Schlern*, 39 (1965), 510; R. Weiß, *Die Volkskunde der Schweiz* (Zürich, 1946), 289; H. Bächtold-Stäubli, "Blümlisalp," *HdA* I, 1434; Paul Geiger, "Blüemlisalp: Ein Beitrag zur Sagendeutung," Sonntagsblatt der *Basler Nachrichten*, June 23, 1929.

LEGEND NO. 94. Legends dealing with competitions between two sorcerers are very rare—and even rarer is the motif of an *alter ego* in flower form. See No. 38 and its commentary.

The lily played a central role in Christian symbolism in the Middle Ages (the Immaculate Conception, etc.) and this was presumably the source of the symbol in legends of sorcerers.

See H. Marzell, "Lilie," *HdA* V, 1300–1301; G. Meinel, "Blume," *EdM* II, 483–495; O. Doering, *Christliche Symbole*, 2nd ed. (Hartig, 1940); Grimm *DM*, II, 689–690; R. Köhler, *Kleinere Schriften* (Berlin, 1900), III, 274–280; M. von Strantz, *Die Blumen in Sagen und Geschichte* (Berlin, 1875).

LEGEND NO. 95. This legend concerns a man who continues to carry on a normal marriage with the ghost of his wife for some years after she has died.

However, the relationship dissolves once again when the husband violates an imposed taboo.

The three sources given by the Grimms are all literary treatments and may in turn owe their existence to a single source. Whenever the story has turned up in other legend collections, it has used one of these literary treatments as its source. The story to my knowledge has never been recorded in the oral tradition.

See No. 458, in which a bereaved husband—the victim of a magic spell—tries to carry on a marriage with the corpse of his wife.

LEGEND NO. 96.   The town of Bretten lies just east of Karlsruhe in Baden-Württemberg. The legend is strictly a local story, but it is still told to this very day in Bretten, where a statue has even been erected in honor of the puppy. Indeed, they still sell postcards there that show a picture of the dog along with the text of a song that begins,

> Es ist ein Hündlein, wohl bekannt,
> Aus rauhem Stein gehauen,
> Zu Bretten an der Kirchenwand
> Am hohen Dach zu schauen.

> 'There is a puppy, quite renowned
> Carved out of solid stone.
> He can be seen in Bretten town
> Upon the wall alone.'

The story related by this song varies considerably from our legend. The city was once besieged by a foreign army and the citizens were on the brink of starvation. In desperation they tried a ruse. They fed the puppy their meager supply of rations until it grew quite fat, and then they sent it out the city gate. When the enemy saw the fat puppy, they assumed there were considerable stores of food left in the city, and they abandoned their siege and moved on—but not before they sent the puppy back with its tail cut off. Thus, the puppy saved the town.

It is entirely possible that both legends were created in an attempt to explain the old proverb (quoted in the legend text) that was no longer understood.

See R. Groll, "Über die Quellen zur Sage vom Brettener Hunde," *Der Pfeifenturm* 6 (1938), 76.

LEGEND NO. 97.   This legend, which is a variant of the sunken city legend (see Nos. 239–240 and commentaries), was collected in Schleswig-Holstein by one of the Grimms' correspondents. It is curious that the oral tradition of the region continued to tell of the epiphany of a saint—unnamed to be sure—long after the area had become Protestant.

LEGEND NO. 98.   Tales of proof of innocence miraculously appearing through the intervention of God at the moment of execution are widespread in Europe. Such stories often appear in collections of *exempla* and were frequently told from the pulpit. See Nos. 261, 360, 479, and their commentaries.

LEGEND NO. 99.   Stories of prospectors making lucky strikes are found in every area where precious ores are found. They are particularly prevalent in the southwestern United States. See No. 9 and its commentary.

Such lucky strikes are frequently made by the unlikeliest of people. It is implicit in such tales that these people have been rewarded by the grace of God. Of course, anyone who misuses this divine gift will inevitably be punished, as we see in this legend.

LEGEND NO. 100.  Since horses were cult objects among Germanic peoples, early Christians, who were intent upon stamping out all traces of the heathen religion, put the stamp of the Devil on all those who made their living from horses. Thus, horse trainers, traders, breakers, and above all skinners were often accused of being in league with the Devil. See G. Freytag, *Das Pferd im germanischen Volksglauben* (Berlin, 1900); G. Neckel, "Über das kultische Reiten in Germanien," *Germania*, 1933. For information on the skinner's trade being considered dishonorable, see W. Danckert, *Unehrliche Leute* (Bern und München, 1963).

The famous sorcerer Dr. Faust is reported to have engaged in horse trading after he enlisted the services of the Devil. See L. Petzoldt, *DVS*, Legend No. 61b.

Of course, anyone who returns from the dead nearly always represents a threat to the living, but if that person worked with horses during his lifetime, he will be considered especially frightening.

LEGEND NO. 101.  In ancient times, oaths were sworn not only to insure that all parties to an agreement would uphold their end of the bargain but also as a means of determining the truth in a dispute or trial. Enforcement of the oath was thus a necessary part of social control, and stories of divine retribution against perjurers abound in virtually every narrative tradition recorded. In Norse mythology, for example, the god Týr must hold his arm in the jaw of the Fenris Wolf as a guarantee for the oath sworn by the Aesir (divine dynasty). When the gods broke their oath, Týr lost his arm. According to the chapbook (*Eine schöne Historie von dem Zauberer Virgilius, seinem Leben und Tod und den wunderbaren Dingen, die er durch Negromantie und mit Hilfe des Teufels vollbrachte*, Frankfurt am Main, n.d.), the Roman poet Virgil had created a metal snake used to discover perjurers. The suspected perjurer would place his arm down the mouth of the snake and then repeat his oath. If the man had perjured himself, the snake would snap the man's arm off. See E. Freiherr von Künßberg, *Rechtliche Volkskunde* (Halle, 1936), 17; G. Kinkel, *Mosaik zur Kunstgeschichte* (Berlin, 1876), 161–243; L. Petzoldt, *HS*, I, 8–18; 343–344.

LEGEND NO. 102.  Judges were believed to function as intermediaries in the judgment of God. If they willfully passed false judgment, their punishment was thought to be immediate and severe. Legends report that false judges are swallowed up by the earth, while others become Poor Souls in dog form or headless ghosts; still others are transformed into trees or fetched by the Devil. See K. Müller-Bergström, "Richter," *HdA* VII, 691–694; Grimm *DRA* I, 378–379; II, 351–369; E. von Künßberg, *Rechtliche Volkskunde* (Halle, 1936), *passim*.

LEGEND NO. 103. The Swiss achieved their independence by forming leagues among themselves, and the first in a long line of such alliances was sworn by the states of Uri, Schwyz, and Unterwalden after the death of Rudolf of Hapsburg in 1291. According to Swiss legend, the leading figures of Waldstätten met upon Rütli Meadow on the west shore of Lake Lucerne (where the town of Seelisberg is located today) in the year 1207. There they swore a sacred oath of allegiance to work together to maintain their independence from the Hapsburg crown. This meeting was thought of as the first Confederation of Swiss states and the forerunner of the later Confederation of the Swiss nation. The allegiance is still referred to today as the *Rütlischwur* 'Oath of Rütli.'

The legend anticipates the torments of Hell that await the man who breaks the oath by depicting him as breathing fire and flame. See Nos. 330, 533, and 534.

LEGEND NO. 104. This legend is based on the widespread motif of the life-token. For instance, an implement or a flower or a tree is decreed to be the symbol of the life of a specific individual. Thus, the chosen object signals the fate of an individual when it gives some sign—the knife rusts, the flower wilts, the tree dies.

K. Bethe, "Sympathie," *HdA* VIII, 619–628.

LEGEND NO. 105. In the days before meteorological forecasts based on scientific information farmers were accustomed to looking at a number of signs to augur the coming weather and to predict the results of the harvest. The spring of this legend was doubtless a valid indicator, for Europe is frequently plagued by rainy summers that are not conducive to bountiful harvests. A gushing spring of course reflects a high water table, which in turn is the result of excessive rainfall.

See D. Ward, "Weather Signs and Weather Magic," *Pacific Coast Philology*, III (1968).

LEGEND NO. 106. This is an etiological legend explaining how an impressive aqueduct came to be. The motif of the suitor who must complete a causeway as a test is related. See Thompson, *Motif-Index*, Motif H 359.1.

LEGEND NO. 107. The concept of an afterworld that is underground or inside a mountain is probably pre-Christian in origin. However, in this legend there is the implicit Christian trait that the inhabitants of this realm are sinners who could not be admitted to Heaven.

See E. Döring-Hirsch, *Tod und Jenseits im Spätmittelalter* (Berlin, 1927); K. Helm, "Entrückung in Sage and Dichtung," *HBV*, 43 (1952), 30–45; D. Ward, "Berg," *EdM* II, 138–146.

LEGEND NO. 108. This is a Redeemer in the cradle legend that has become contaminated with a buried treasure legend. Almost invariably the Redeemer legend is told about a foiled attempt to deliver a Poor Soul. The Poor Soul will then not have a new chance until someone comes along who has been rocked in a cradle made from the tree that is now still a sapling.

Thus, the tale becomes a concrete representation of the interminable torment of the Poor Soul.

The story of the Redeemer in the cradle has a long history dating at least as far back as the Apocrypha of the New Testament. It continued through monks' legends in the Middle Ages and on up to the folk legends of the present day. See F. Ranke, *Der Erlöser in der Wiege* (München, 1911).

LEGEND NO. 109. This legend refers to one of the oldest recorded incidents in German history: the Battle of Teutonberg Forest in A.D. 9. There the Roman army under Varus was destroyed by a confederation of Germanic tribes under the leadership of the Cheruscan chieftain Arminius (Hermann). Thusnelda was the latter's wife.

LEGEND NO. 110. The implication of this legend is that Dwarfs inhabit the inside of the mountain but are never seen.

LEGEND NO. 111. Rivers that stand still or even flow backwards are traditional signs of the divine power of the cosmos. See, for example, No. 351 in which a raging stream becomes calm when a saint's body is transported across it. Such events are, of course, to be classified among the Christian miracles. Flowing water is also used to augur the future. See No. 104 and its commentary.

LEGEND NO. 112. The first part of this legend arose from the attempt to explain a place name. Sunken city accounts are among the most popular of all German and European legends (see the commentaries to Nos. 239–240). Implicit in this legend is the belief that the castle was doomed to sink because of the sins of its inhabitants. In most such legends this theme is stated explicitly.

The second part of the legend serves as a warning to those who wish to fathom the unknown. See commentary to No. 59.

LEGEND NO. 113. This legend is based on the folk etymology that *Ossen* is derived from *Ochsen* 'oxen.' This tale is related to the sunken city legends (see Nos. 239 and 240).

LEGEND NO. 114. The Rhön Mountains are located in East Hesse, south of the city of Fulda. They range south into Franconia.

Small lights that appear in swampy areas were believed to be the souls of sinners, suicides, unbaptized infants, and the drowned. Today the existence of these lights is explained scientifically as swamp gas, fireflies, static electricity, and the like. See P. Samford, "Ignis fatuus," *Scientific Monthly*, 9 (1919), 358–364. See also the commentary to No. 277.

LEGEND NO. 115. Love magic is not merely a narrative motif, it was actually practiced by girls in villages in Europe as well as in other parts of the world. The English antiquary John Aubrey recorded the following ritual in the seventeenth century (ca. 1680):

Young wenches have a wanton sport, wch [sic] they call moulding of Cocklebread; viz. they gett upon a Table-board, and then gather-up their knees and their coates with their hands as high as they can, and then they wabble to and fro with their Buttocks as if the[y] were kneading dough with their A—, and say these words, viz.:

> My Dame is sick & goone to bed,
> And I'll go mould my cocklebread.

The bread thus prepared was fed to a favored male who was then supposed to be attracted to the girl for life. Quoted from Richard Dorson, *The British Folklorists* (London, 1968), p. 9. See also B. Kummer, "Liebeszauber," *HdA* VI, 1279–1297; E. S. Gifford, *The Charms of Love* (New York, 1962). For examples of love charms in the U.S., see Hand, *Beliefs*, No. 4231ff.

LEGEND NO. 116.   See commentary to No. 115. Love magic was feared by the male members of the community, and the practice was considered to be related to the arts of witchcraft.

See K. Baschwitz, *Hexen und Hexenprozesse* (München, 1963).

LEGEND NO. 117.   Christmas Eve was considered an especially auspicious time for love magic. See the reference to cocklebread in the commentary to No. 115.

LEGEND NO. 118.   It was believed that a magic charm could be made from nine kinds of wood. Although the wood could be prepared in a number of ways—boiled, cut, burned, etc.—the most popular method was to create an incense from the wood. This would then be burned at auspicious times as a talisman against witchcraft, demons, and disease or to protect farm animals from harm. It could also be used to summon the powers of nature for acts of sorcery—as is the case in this legend. The charm was thought to be more efficacious if the wood was gathered on Good Friday or at other auspicious times.

See H. Marzell, "Neunerlei Holz," *HdA* VI, 1057–1066.

LEGEND NO. 119.   The art of crystalomancy—divining by crystal gazing—has in recent times become associated with divining the future per se. It is, however, neither a very old nor a very widespread form of divination. It is probably derived from divining the future by looking into a reflecting pool, shiny metal, or mirror (as in Snow White: "Mirror, mirror, on the wall!"). Shiny stones, rock crystal, and the like were among the early divining materials of this kind and were used by medieval court sorcerers.

The glass ball and globes used by fortunetellers today are more recent. They may have developed from the glass beakers of alchemists, although an Oriental source for the practice cannot be discounted. As opposed to most other kinds of divination which could be practiced by anyone, crystal gazing was generally reserved for the practiced sorcerer. That which the sorcerer was supposed to be able to see covered a wide range of objects and events: figures and events from the future; things and peoples in distant places (the first television); angels dressed in white for good news, red or black for bad news; a thief (when one was trying to solve a theft); sites of hidden treasure; and the apparition of a future mate (love divination). The crystal could also be used to counteract the sorcery of a witch.

See G. Kittredge, *Witchcraft in Old and New England* (Cambridge, Mass., 1929), see esp. 185–210; F. Boehm, "Kristallomantie," *HdA* V, 578–594; J. Melville, *Crystal Gazing and the Wonders of Clairvoyance* (London, 1920); G. Roheim, "Spiegelzauber," *Imago*, 5 (1917), 63–71; A. Höck, "Kristallsehen und Schatzgraben," *Hessische Heimat*, 18 (1968), 21–22.

LEGEND NO. 120.    See the commentaries to Nos. 115–118. Of special interest is the fact that the Holy Pentecost is the auspicious time for love magic in this legend. More common for the practice of this kind of sorcery are such periods as the Twelve Nights, Christmas Eve, New Year's Eve, St. Andreas' Eve, and St. John's Day. The Holy Pentecost—as the beginning of the growth period of summer—was, however, frequently associated with fertility rites, and it is thus quite logical that it would also be associated with erotic activities. In France, for example, the Holy Pentecost was the time when young maidens sought love oracles at springs. See F. Sébillot, *Folk-Lore de France*, 4 vols. (Paris, 1904–07), II, 251. See also P. Sartori, "Pfingsten," *HdA* VI, 1684–1697.

LEGEND NO. 121.    The horned goat or ram, especially when black, is considered to be a familiar of the Devil himself. He places it at the disposal of his earthly consorts—sorcerers and witches. There may be a direct line of connection between this belief and ancient Germanic religion (Thor's goats, goat horns associated with lightning bolts, etc.).
    See L. Herold, "Ziegenbock," *HdA* IX, 912–931; H. van Pelt, *Bokkenrijders in de Kempen* (Amsterdam, 1943).

LEGEND NO. 122.    Convents, like bridges, cemeteries, and castles, are the favorite haunts of spooks and ghosts. The Convent Ghost is invariably thought to be the spirit of a former nun. It is possible that the very nature of convent life is conducive to the kind of hysteria that can produce such legends. There has been very little work of a folkloristic nature conducted on this phenomenon. See F. Karlinger, "Über das Sammeln von Volkserzählungen in Klöstern der Romania," *ÖZV*, 71 (1968), 225–227; R. Krebsbach, "Der Schatz am 'Grünen Kloster,'" *Folklore* (Malmëdy), 3 (1923), 107–108; M. J. Eisen, "Die Klöster unserer Heimat," *Eesti Kirjandus*, 21 (1927), 414–415; J. Künzig, "Kloster," *HdA* IV, 1551–1553.

LEGEND NO. 123.    The ghostly apparition of the White Woman is generally thought to be a Lost Soul. She is especially fond of haunting the sites of castle ruins and is frequently envisioned carrying a large ring of keys. This symbol indicates both her ability to control the access to the rooms of the castle and her need for deliverance from her earthly existence. There is a pronounced overlap of this tradition with such figures as Perchta, the Castle Maiden, the Serpent Maiden, the Mountain Maiden, and Mother Holla.
    In the royal house of the Hohenzollerns there is a tradition that whenever a catastrophe is about to strike the family the White Woman appears. Such an occurrence was documented in the palace of Bayreuth in 1486.
    See R. Kühnau, "Über weiße Frauen," *MSGV*, 15 (1913), 186–207. For other White Woman legends see Nos. 4, 10, 12, 16, 222, 224, 268, and their commentaries.

LEGEND NO. 124.  The dove is honored as a sacred bird in many parts of the world, and it is not surprising to find that it plays an important role in the folk beliefs of Europe. In addition to its supposed ability to locate treasure, the dove is often looked upon as the embodiment of a human soul, as a symbol of purity able to ward off evil and disease, and as an important element in love and hunting magic and in many customs and rituals.

See Grimm *DM* I, 122; E. Schneeweis, "Taube," *HdA* VIII, 693–705.

LEGEND NO. 125.  See the commentary to No. 124 for the importance of the dove in divination. Tales of besieged cities and fortresses are still found in the oral tradition of most European nations. See Nos. 135, 257, 376, 382, 398, 406, 448, and their commentaries.

LEGEND NO. 126.  Bell-casting was one of the more difficult and costly trades of the Middle Ages, and legends on the topic abound. Bells were not only considered to be sacred objects, they were thought to have souls and even human voices and were given personal names. They were also believed to have magical powers including the ability to fly to Rome on Good Friday. If the casting of the bell went awry it was not only an embarrassment for the caster, and a costly mistake for the community, it was considered a blasphemy.

This particular legend was reworked into a ballad by Wilhelm Müller in 1826 and has since become very famous in Germany.

See A. Perkmann, "Glockenguß," *HdA* III, 876–877; A. Perkmann, "Glocke," *HdA* III, 868–876; H. Otte, *Glockenkunde*, 2nd ed. (Berlin, 1884); P. Sartori, "Glockensagen und Glockenaberglauben," *ZsfVk*, 7 (1897), 270–274 and *ZsfVk*, 8 (1898), 358–365; J. Pesch, *Die Glocke in Geschichte, Sage, Volksglauben, Volksbrauch und Dichtung* (Dülmen, 1923); E. Erdman, *Die Glockensagen* (Wuppertal-Eberfeld, 1931); P. Sartori, *Das Buch von den deutschen Glocken* (Berlin und Leipzig, 1932).

LEGEND NO. 127.  The full title of Grimmelshausen's novel is *Ratsstübel Plutonis, oder Kunst reich zu werden*, and it was first published in 1672. The indication of cap. 8 by the Grimms in their Sources and Addenda is evidently in error. It should read Nr. 114. The theme of the artisan murdering a competitor or his own journeyman out of envy is a familiar one in legends dealing with a number of trades. See M. Hippe, "Zwei Breslauer Sagen," *MSGV*, 6 (1904), 90–109.

LEGEND NO. 128.  This dramatic story shows the influence of the tradition of the vulgar ballads which were performed by *Bänkelsänger* (mountebanks) and sold on broadsides. The implication is that divine retribution ended the lives of the murderers.

See L. Petzoldt, *Bänkelsang* (Stuttgart, 1973).

LEGEND NO. 129.  Johann Hübner was an historical figure who led a band of robbers in Westphalia. There are a number of such outlaw figures in German legendry, the most famous being Johannes Bückler, better known as Schinderhannes, who headed a band of robbers in the Hunsrück Mountains of the Rhineland. Schinderhannes legends still abound in that area. The best collection of such stories can be found in Petzoldt, *HS* II, 152–181.

It is interesting that the same stories are told about famous outlaw figures throughout the world—Robin Hood in Britain; Jesse James, Billy the Kid, and Bonnie and Clyde in the United States; Cartouche in France; Rinaldini in Italy, etc. Also interesting is the notion of the robber as a social hero who corrects injustices. Such themes have become attached to the traditions of outlaws wherever they have been collected.

See Kent Steckmesser, "Robin Hood and the American Outlaw," *JAF*, 79 (1966), 348–355. M. Zender, "Schinderhannes und andere Räubergestalten in der Volkserzählung der Rheinlande," *Rheinisch-Westfälische Zeitschrift für Volkskunde*, 2 (1955), 84–94; C.-M. Franke, *Der Schinderhannes in der deutschen Volksüberlieferung*, Diss. (Frankfurt, 1958); P. Hugger, *Sozialrebellen und Rechtsbrecher in der Schweiz* (Zürich and Freiburg, 1976).

LEGEND NO. 130.  Eppela Gaila was a famous bandit about whom legends and songs are still told and sung in the region in and around Nürnberg. He too was an actual historical figure and his name was Ekkelein von Gailigen. He was once captured in Nürnberg but managed to escape from the prison. He was later recaptured and executed in the city of Neumarkt in 1381. Unlike other robber figures, Eppela Gaila was transformed into a supernatural being capable of making great leaps with his magic horse.

H. Kunstmann, "Das Rätsel um Eppelein von Gailingen in der fränkischen Schweiz," *Fränkische Blätter*, 4 (1952), 71–72. P. Lücke, "Historisches vom 'Eppele,' " *Bayerland*, 24 (1913), 705–707.

LEGEND NO. 131.  At the end of the Middle Ages, after the decline of the ideal of chivalry, the last knights turned many a crumbling fortress into a secret base for pillaging and plundering. These activities contributed to the narrative traditions surrounding such structures.

LEGEND NO. 132.  This story is a variant of the sunken city legends. See Nos. 239–240 and their commentaries.

Count Isang is apparently a purely legendary figure; he has left no mark in history.

The motif of the servant who brings home a silver serpent when he had been sent to bring a fish alludes to the passage from the Sermon on the Mount: "Or if he [his son] ask a fish, will he give him a serpent?" (Matthew 7:11).

The count who understands the language of the animals after eating the snake is reminiscent of the hero Sigurd (Siegfried) who understands the speech of birds after he tastes the heart of a dragon (*Fáfnismál*, 31–34; *Vǫlsunga Saga*, XIX).

LEGEND NO. 133.  The Isle of Rügen is located off the German coast in the Baltic Sea. It is surprising that the Grimms, who took this account from Prätorius' *Weltbeschreibung* ('description of the world'), did not further investigate it, for the story seems to contain precisely the kind of survivals from the heathen past in which the brothers took such delight. But Jacob makes no mention of this account in his *Deutsche Mythologie*, nor, to my knowledge, did Wilhelm pursue the narrative any further in his many investigations of such themes.

When Prätorius tells his readers that "a Devil was worshipped" on the Isle of Rügen, we can be almost certain that he is talking about a heathen divinity, for it was the practice of the Christian Church and its missionaries to relegate all the pagan gods to the status of devils. Furthermore, when he tells us that a maiden was once drowned there, it becomes apparent that we are dealing with a sacrificial ritual, in which a maiden was offered to the god in question. Drowning was one of the chief means of offering humans to Germanic divinities, especially the divinities of growth and fertility. See D. Ward, "The Threefold Death: An Indo-European Trifunctional Sacrifice?" in J. Puhvel (ed.), *Myth and Law among the Indo-Europeans* (Berkeley and Los Angeles, 1970), 124–142.

LEGEND NO. 134. St. Nicholas was born ca. 270 in Patras in Lycia. He became Bishop of Myra and died ca. 342. In 1087 his bones were transported to the Italian city of Bari. He is honored especially in Russia, in Lothringen, and in all the cities of the Hanseatic League. He furthermore became the patron saint of thieves, of schoolchildren (which is where the Santa Claus tradition developed), and above all of sailors.

K. Meisen, *Nikolaus-Kult und Nikolaus-Brauch im Abendlande* (Düsseldorf, 1931); A. de Groot, *Sint Nicolas* (Amsterdam, 1949); R. McKnight, *St. Nicholas* (New York, 1917).

LEGEND NO. 135. The miraculous escape from besiegement is a favorite theme in European legendry; here it is coupled with an etiological motif explaining the origins of a strange rock formation. See also Nos. 125, 257, 466, 476, 509, 510, and 567.

LEGEND NO. 136. Miracles become more believable if some concrete evidence remains after the event that people can look to for confirmation of their faith. For this reason miracle stories frequently develop around imprints in stone. Such stories are, of course, also etiological in that they were told to explain a curious feature in the landscape.

LEGEND NO. 137. See the commentary to No. 16.

LEGEND NO. 138. See the commentary to No. 16.

LEGEND NO. 139. The Grimms themselves saw a connection between the Jette of this legend and what they considered to be a proto-Germanic form *Jöten* 'giant' (cf. Old Icelandic *Jǫtunn* 'giant'). There is a modern Danish form *joette* 'giant' as well as the Middle English *joten* 'giant' and Old English *eotan*, likewise 'giant.' The form has been linked both with the Finnish word *etona*, *etana* 'snail, slug, worm' (used metaphorically for an evil person) and with Old High German *etan* 'eat' (used to designate a man-eating demon). Neither etymology is wholly convincing. Nor is the Grimms' suggestion that Jette is related to Old Icelandic *Jǫtunn* acceptable, for the German reflex would have to show the root *et-* instead of *jet-*. Apparently Jacob Grimm himself gave up on this etymology for later he merely mentions it as a remote possibility (Grimm, *DM* I, 430, footnote).

See J. de Vries, *Altnordisches Etymologisches Wörterbuch*, 2nd ed. (Leiden, 1962), pp. 295–296; A. Jóhanneson, *Isländisches Etymologisches Wörterbuch* (Bern, 1956), p. 53 and p. 322.

LEGEND NO. 140.   Today Wilten is a section of the city of Innsbruck and is the site of a premonstratenser monastery.

Various regions of Germany have traditions about their local Giants, often giving them personal names. In Prussia, for example, they tell of the Giant Miligedo; in Saxony the Giant is called Hidde; in Swabia he is known as Romäus. In this legend from Tyrol his name is Haym or Haymon. There may be some connection between the Giant here and the legendary Carolingian hero who was called Heimo and who allegedly served in the armies of Charlemagne. His exploits have been recounted in the sixteenth-century chapbook *Heimons Kinder* 'The Children of Haimon.' See Grimm *DM* I, 321 and 437, and II, 574 and 710.

The name Haymon might possibly be linked with the name of the hero Heime, known to us from the cycle of Dietrich epics. Heime was a cruel and demonic warrior who, together with his companion Witege, slayed the hero Alphart in a treacherous manner. The most complete version is told in the Middle High German epic *Alpharts Tod* (ca. 1258).

A number of motifs have been combined in this legend: the battle with the dragon, the removal of the dragon's tongue (a motif known in the epic of Tristan and Isolde as well as in the folktales). The legend also contains the well-known story of a Giant being enlisted to build a large bridge. See I. M. Boberg, *Baumeistersagen*, FFC 151 (Helsinki, 1955). See also the commentaries to Nos. 16–19.

The practice of making an extra-large sarcophagus for the corpses of prominent leaders may well have contributed to beliefs in Giants (see the commentary to No. 216). For more detailed information on Giants see the commentaries to Nos. 16–19.

LEGEND NO. 141.   The bones of prehistoric creatures (mastodons, dinosaurs, etc.) have been uncovered through the ages and have frequently been thought to be the bones of Giants. Such finds have even ended up in churches as relics. The term "Heathen Maiden" is synonymous with Giantess.

The story of the destruction of the world as well as the warning signs leading up to the catastrophe are not exclusively a Christian tradition. They were already well known among pre-Christian Germanic peoples (Ragnarök, Muspilli, etc.). See A. Olrik, *Ragnarök: Die Sagen vom Weltuntergang* (Berlin und Leipzig, 1922).

LEGEND NO. 142.   Bluffs, sheer cliffs, deep narrow canyons, and similar topographical features inevitably stimulate the imagination of those who live near them. Narrative traditions—telling of the leap to safety of unhappy lovers (Lovers' Leap), of some pursued maiden, or even of an animal frequently form around such sites. See Nos. 319–322, 507, 518, 554 and their commentaries.

LEGEND NO. 143. The blasphemy of having an animal baptized may well represent a bowdlerized version of what was originally the motif of sodomy. The belief that intercourse between a human and an animal will result in the birth of a destructive monster is widespread. In ancient Greece, for example, Pasiphaë, the wife of Minos, fell in love with a bull, engaged in intercourse with it, and gave birth to the frightening Minotaur—half human, half bull. See M. P. Nilsson, *Religion of Greece in Prehistoric Times* (New York, 1942), 65–101.

LEGEND NO. 144. Popular tradition preserves a view of the afterworld that does not agree with official Christian teachings. In these older beliefs deceased sinners do not reside in the Christian Purgatory or Hell but exist as shades beneath the surface of the earth, not to be released from this state until Judgment Day. See E. Döring-Hirsch, *Tod und Jenseits im Spätmittelalter* (Berlin, 1927).

Schweidnitz was a German city in Silesia about thirty miles southwest of Breslau. Today it is the Polish city of Świdnica. Officially the mountain bore the name of Mt. Zobten. "Zotten" is a form from the local dialect.

LEGEND NO. 145. This legend combines the motif of a person who has second sight—the ability to see the future—with a Lazarus motif. See K. Schmëing, *Das zweite Gesicht in Niederdeutschland* (Leipzig, 1937).

The man has evidently returned from the dead inasmuch as he has intimate knowledge of an event that transpired on that day two hundred years before. Cf. Nos. 168–170 and 191 and their commentaries.

LEGEND NO. 146. The Huckup, a spirit that jumps upon one's back, growing ever heavier, and resists all efforts to shake it loose is a world-wide tradition much like the Nightmare (see No. 81 and its commentary). The tradition may well owe its existence to a specific psycho-physical state induced by fear, sensory deprivation, drugs, and the like. Indeed, the expression "He has a monkey on his back," which refers to someone addicted to heroin, is probably related. A number of demons, Hobgoblins, Puck, Witches, Cobolds, and Dwarfs, among others, can assume the role of Huckup. Reports of people having had this experience are documented in Germany as early as the fifteenth and sixteenth century.

See G. Grober-Glück, "Aufhocker und Aufhocken nach den Sammlungen des Atlas der deutschen Volkskunde," *RhJb*, 15/16 (1965), 117–143 (with maps showing the distribution); F. Ranke, "Der Huckup," *Bayerische Hefte für Volkskunde*, 9 (1922), 1–33; D.-R. Moser, "Christus als 'Aufhocker?' " *ZsfVk*, 69 (1973), 234–239.

LEGEND NO. 147. The Gottschee region in the Krain area of Yugoslavia is of particular importance for folklorists and Germanists. Gottschee was settled in the Middle Ages by Bavarian farming families. Surrounded by peoples who spoke Slovene, the region became a German speech island isolated from the main body of German-speaking peoples. Thus, the dialect and the folksong and narrative traditions have remained relatively static when compared to the language and traditions of the main body of Germans. See A. Hauffen, *Die Deutsche Sprachinsel Gottschee* (Graz, 1885).

In regard to the realm of the dead sinners being underground in a palace, see No. 144 and its commentary.

LEGEND NO. 148. As belief in Dwarfs faded, the reports of encounters with the tiny people declined and finally stopped altogether. As a result legends developed explaining why the Dwarfs were no longer seen. Such legends invariably indicate the worsening of the human condition, man's inhumanity to other creatures of nature, and developing technology and industry that make the environment less hospitable to man and other forms of life. The tales are thus marked by a tone of nostalgia and elegiac longing for a bygone era.

See W. Müller-Bergström, "Zwerge und Riesen," *HdA* IXN, 1008–1138 (see esp. col. 1117–1119); G. Heide, *Dwarfs in German Folk Legend: An Inquiry into the Human Quality of These Creatures*, Diss. (University of California, Los Angeles, 1976).

LEGEND NO. 149. See the commentary to No. 148.

LEGEND NO. 150. There was a widespread belief that Dwarfs, and other demons and spirits as well, had bird's feet. This belief was early documented in the Talmud, for the farmers of ancient Palestine thought that all spirits and demons had bird's feet. In European tradition curious humans detect the presence of Dwarfs by spreading (as in this variant) ashes on the ground, although other variants tell of the spreading of flour, dung, limestone, gypsum, sand, and the like. Invariably the Dwarfs are offended by the action and this is frequently given as the reason why they are no longer seen. See the commentary to No. 148.

J. Scheftelowitz, *Altpalästinensischer Bauernglaube* (Hannover, 1915), 13; "Aschenspur," *HdS*, 659–664.

LEGEND NO. 151. The Wild Man and the Forest Woman belong to the larger category of Nature Spirits. Wild Men traditions abound everywhere in the world, and sightings of such creatures have been reported in all fifty of the United States. Bigfoot and Sasquatch merely represent the more famous of such beings. In Germany, local regions have given individual generic and personal names to such creatures—*Wilde Leute, Salige Frauen, Holzweib, Moosweib, Wild-Fräulein, Witte Wiewer, Fängge, Fenken,* etc. Such beings are also documented in medieval art. Leander Petzoldt (*DVS*, 415–416) has suggested that such figures owe their existence to the medieval custom of expelling lepers and the mentally ill from human communities, thus forcing them to forage in the wild. Although the reported physical appearance of such creatures varies, the most common report tells of a humanoid creature that is covered with hair, has almost no neck, and is generally somewhat larger than a normal human.

H. Göttling, *Die wilden Leute und ihre nächsten Verwandten im altdeutschen Schrifttum*, Diss. (Erlangen, 1925); F. Ivanetič, "Volkssagen vom Wilden

Mann," *Carinthia* (1875), 182; A. Spamer, "Die wilden Leute in Sage und Bild," *Volkskunst und Volkskunde*, 9 (1911), 117–123; K. Löber, "Wildleute-Orte an der Lahn und im Westerwald," *HBV*, 55 (1954), 141–164; R. Bernheimer, *Wild Men in the Middle Ages: A Study in Art, Sentiment, and Demonology* (Cambridge, Mass., 1952); L. Carlen, "Walliser Wilder Mann: Darstellungen aus dem 16. und 17. Jahrhundert," *SAV*, 55 (1965), 71–73; K. Haiding, "Wildfrauen-Sagen in Österreich," in L. Röhrich (ed.), *Probleme der Sagenforschung* (Freiburg, 1973), 196–203; D. Hufford, "Humanoids and Anomalous Lights: Taxonomic and Epistemological Problems," *Fabula*, 18 (1977), 234–241.

LEGEND NO. 152.   Even apparently harmless contact with the supernatural world or with the world of underground creatures poses dangers for humans. One of these perils springs from the belief that one slips into another time dimension in the spirit world, where a single night can last a hundred years. Noteworthy in this regard is the contrast between the *Märchen* and legend in the treatment of this motif. For example, when Sleeping Beauty awakes from her hundred-year sleep, everything is just as it was before, and she is still young and beautiful. In the legend, however, time in the real world does not stand still during the hundred years, and the person returning to this world is truly a stranger from another time.

See K. Müller-Bergström, "Zwerge und Riesen," *HdA* IXN, 1008–1138.

In popular tradition Heiling is a name that has come to be associated with the king of the Dwarfs (see Grimm *DM*, I, 375). There was also a sorcerer called Hans Heiling about whom a number of legends were told (No. 329). It is possible that popular imagination believed the sorcerer to have been damned to eternal underground existence; that would explain how he came to be linked with the underground creatures.

LEGEND NO. 153.   See the commentary to No. 148. The belief that Dwarfs have magic "fog caps" that render them invisible is widespread in German tradition and elsewhere in Europe. In Germanic heroic tradition a number of Dwarfs are reported to have had such caps. The most famous was the smith Alberich who was defeated by the hero Siegfried. Here, the hero takes possession of the cap and thus acquires the ability to make himself invisible.

See H. de Boor, "Der Zwerg in Skandinavien," *Eugen Mogk Festschrift* (Halle, 1924), 536–557; V. Harward, *The Dwarfs of Arthurian Romance and Celtic Tradition* (Leiden, 1958).

See also W. Grimm, "Über die Elfen," *Kleinere Schriften*, vol. I (Berlin, 1881). This essay, which originally appeared as the introduction to the Grimms' *Irische Elfenmärchen*, is one of the best studies on Dwarfs ever written. For specific information on the fog cap see pp. 452–453, and on the migration of the Dwarfs, see pp. 447–448.

LEGEND NO. 154.   See the commentaries to Nos. 30, 31, 148, and 153.

LEGEND NO. 155.   See the commentaries to Nos. 30, 31, 148, and 153. Dardesheim today is located in the German Democratic Republic, not far from the West German border.

LEGEND NO. 156.   See the commentaries to Nos. 30, 31, 148, 153, and 155. Even though Dardesheim is located near the Harz Mountains, the land around the town is relatively flat. Dwarf Mountain is actually a hill that rises gradually to a height of about 370 feet. It is located to the southwest of the town.

LEGEND NO. 157.   The Dwarf who works alone (or with a limited number of helpers) as a smith belongs to a tradition distinct from the traditions of whole communities of Dwarfs. Frequently, as is the case with this legend, we find a Wild Man in this role instead of a Dwarf. These traditions exist primarily in North and Central Germany where smiths were involved in both the mining and smelting of ores as well as in iron working. In regions such as the Alps where these functions were separate such traditions are lacking.

There has always been a stongly ambivalent attitude toward the smith in Germanic nations. Although he was called upon for help in creating weapons and tools and in healing as well, he was also often feared as an outsider and was never really allowed to be a participating member of community affairs. Indeed, his strange power of transforming red earth into shiny metal as if by magic led to traditions in which the smith was either thought to be demonic himself or to have acquired this power from the world of spirits and demons. The famous smith of Germanic heroic tradition and myths (Wayland, Wieland, Vǫlundr) definitely had traits reminiscent of the Wild Man.

See E. Marold, *Der Schmied im germanischen Altertum*, Diss. (Wien, 1967); E. Marold, "Die gestalt des Schmiedes in der Volkssage," in L. Röhrich (ed.), *Probleme der Sagenforschung* (Freiburg, 1973), 100–111; Jeannine Talley, *The Blacksmith: A Study in Technology, Myth and Folklore*, Diss. (University of California, Los Angeles, 1977).

LEGEND NO. 158.   St. John's Day (June 24) was frequently thought to be the day when hidden underground chambers and caves opened up, and humans—if they were foolhardy enough—could gain access to them then. There is always great danger associated with such ventures, and more often than not the venturesome one has to pay dearly for his or her curiosity.

See S. Hirschberg, "Schatz," *HdA* VII, 1002–1015.

LEGEND NO. 159.   According to folk belief, certain individuals can at certain times be granted limited access to buried treasure guarded by someone from the spirit world. In this case, the Maiden of Will Mountain is evidently a local variant of the White Woman (see commentary to No. 10).

The fact that the spirit throws the nut kernels away and keeps the shells can have several meanings. First, the action attracts the attention of Peter; second, it gives him a reason to follow her; third, it represents the somewhat peculiar behavior characteristic of the spirit world; and fourth, it is conceivable that the spirit has the ability to change the nutshells into solid gold (a motif frequently associated with Dwarfs).

Nuts in general, and the hazelnut in particular, have long been associated with buried treasure in popular imagination. The belief concerning hazelnuts may well be attributable to the golden color of the blossoms. There is a German proverb that says, "Behold, the winter now must go, the hazel spreads its gold upon the snow." A hazel twig is also a favorite divining rod for those seeking hidden treasure.

See H. Marzell, "Hasel," *HdA* III, 1527–1542.

LEGEND NO. 160. The fact that the treasure of this legend is associated with the Thirty Years' War is more than a coincidence. Under the threat of pillaging armies, many a nobleman, bishop, or patrician had treasure buried. See the commentaries to Nos. 158–160.

See also A. Dörler, "Schätze und Schatzhüter in Tirol," *ZöV*, 4 (1898), 225–234; R. Kühnau, "Schlesische Schatzsagen," *MSGV*, 18 (1907), 68–79; L. Winter, *Die deutsche Schatzsage*, Diss. (Köln, 1925); St. Hirschberg, *Schatzglaube und Totenglaube* (Breslau, 1934); M. Cockett, *Magic and Gold: Tales from North Europe* (Oxford, 1971); H. Commenda, *Gesellschaft der Schatzgräber, Teufelsbeschwörer und Geisterbanner in Lienz 1792: Historisches Jahrbuch der Stadt Linz* (Linz, 1960); L. Denecke, "Der Schatz im verwunschenen Schloß," *Fabula*, 13 (1972), 150–152; J. F. Dobie, "The Dream That Never Dies: Oklahoma Treasure Legends," *Folksay*, 1929, 64–68; G. T. Hurley, "Buried Treasure Tales in America," *Western Folklore*, 10 (1951), 197–216; K. Pölt-Nordheim, "Verborgene Schätze," *Schlern*, 4 (1923), 154–155; L. G. Smith, "A True Story of Buried Gold," *Publications of the Texas Folklore Society*, 14 (1938), 259–261; C.-H. Tillhagen, "Gruvsrock," *Norveg*, 12 (1965), 113–160 (with an English summary); B. Granger, *A Motif Index for Lost Mines and Treasures Applied to Redaction of Arizona Legends, and to Lost Mine and Treasure Legends Exterior to Arizona*, FFC 218 (Helsinki, 1977).

LEGEND NO. 161. Buried treasure is inevitably guarded by creatures from the spirit world. Among these are black dogs, generally associated with the Devil and with demons, and the White Woman, who is frequently thought to be a Poor Soul in need of deliverance. The theme of taboos associated with the winning of the treasure is a frequent motif. Often the person is forbidden to speak or, as in this case, to turn around. See B. A. Woods, *The Devil in Dog Form* (Berkeley and Los Angeles, 1958); S. Hirschberg, "Schatz," *HdA* VII, 1002–1015.

A number of legends tell of cherries or cherry blossoms that change to gold. See H. Marzell, "Kirschbaum, Kirsche," *HdA* IV, 1425–1433.

LEGEND NO. 162. See the commentaries to Nos. 10, 158–161. Treasure legends can be divided essentially into two main categories: those that tell of people who actively seek treasures, and those that tell of individuals who accidentally stumble upon the scene. In the case of the treasure seeker, the attempt to recover the treasure comes very close to success but then invariably ends in failure. In the case of the accidental find, the lucky person (usually poor but honest) is frequently successful in recovering at least a small portion of the treasure. However, the attempt to return and recover the rest is never successful. In either case the encounter poses danger for the seeker.

Frequently hidden treasures are said to be revealed but one day a year (often St. John's Day or the Twelfth Day of Christmas). But this text makes no mention of a specific day.

LEGEND NO. 163.   Unlikely items (coal, dead leaves, wood shavings, etc.) frequently turn to gold in folk legends, especially in cases where they constitute a payment from the supernatural world. When the recipient of the apparently worthless gift casts all but one or two of the pieces away, he discovers that they have miraculously turned to gold. When the person rushes back to the site where he cast them away, either he cannot locate the site or the items have vanished. See Nos. 8, 10, and 317 and their commentaries.

LEGEND NO. 164.   It is conceivable that this legend is etiological in nature inasmuch as it was apparently invented to explain a family crest that was no longer understood. The personages mentioned have left little or no mark on history. See E. Stengel, *Die Reichsabtei Fulda in der Geschichte* (Weimar, 1948).

LEGEND NO. 165.   Höxter is located in the Weser Valley in Lower Saxony. Bad Pyrmont lies to the northeast. The legends are etiological, explaining the purpose of the large stones whose original function was no longer understood.

Count Johann T. von Tilly (1559–1632) led campaigns against the Protestants in France and the Turks in Hungary before he was named Field Marshal to the Catholic League in 1620 (at the age of 61). He then organized the armies of the Catholic League and led them in the Thirty Years' War during which he became the most famous of all the generals. He died in 1632 from injuries received while trying to prevent Swedish forces from crossing the Lech River near Ingolstadt.

LEGEND NO. 166.   Marburg is a university city on the Lahn River in Hesse. The town of Wehre is today called Wehrda and is now virtually a suburb of Marburg. The sword dance has been documented in Germanic tradition since Tacitus first described it in cap. 24 of his *Germania*. The motif of using the sword dance as a ruse to stage an ambush is widespread in the traditions of many nations. Curiously, there is no entry for this motif in Thompson's *Motif-Index*.

See K. Meschke, *Schwerttanz und Schwerttanzspiel im germanischen Kulturkreis* (Leipzig und Berlin, 1931).

LEGEND NO. 167.   Bingenheim is on the Horloff River near Bad Nauheim, about 35 miles north of Frankfurt. The Hundred was a political unit that may hark back to the days when Germanic peoples first settled in Europe. The original Hundred evidently consisted of a band of a hundred warriors who had fought together. When the people settled permanently, the Hundred became a territorial unit and political body corresponding somewhat to the later township. During Merovingian times the local official was the Hundred Man. He presided over the session of the Hundred Court, which was assembled periodically during the year, and which all freemen were obliged to attend. The Hundred was also the smallest political unit in pre-Norman England where the Hundred Court was required to meet every four weeks. Regarding Wild Men, see the commentary to No. 151.

See H. Cam, *The Hundred and the Hundred Roles* (London, 1930).

LEGEND NO. 168. This legend is problematic as it could fit into a number of different categories. Since it deals with the oracle of a pending catastrophe, it could be classified as a fate legend (see commentary to No. 145). Certain individuals, such as those born at auspicious times (Twelfth Night, St. John's Day, Walpurgis Eve), or the seventh child of a seventh child, etc., are thought to be gifted with the ability to interpret oracles or otherwise read the future.

Since the figure whose presence signals the catastrophic plague is evidently Death himself this legend could also be assigned to the category of legends of Death and the dead. (See L. Röhrich and I. Müller, "Deutscher Sagenkatalog: X. Der Tod und die Toten," *Deutsches Jahrbuch für Volkskunde*, 13 [1967], 346–397.)

Finally, since the oracle signals the plague, the legend could also be classified in the category of legends of disease and epidemics. There were beliefs in plague demons (Plague Dwarf, Plague Woman, etc.), and customs and rituals meant to placate or drive off such spirits sprang up around them. Epidemics such as the Black Death left a deep and lasting impression on the minds of people and remain the subject for many legends and other popular traditions.

See P. Sartori, "Pest," *HdA* VI, 1497–1522; L. Röhrich, 'Krankheitsdämonen," *Der Schlern*, 24 (1950), 395–397; M. Höfler, "Krankheitsdämonen," *Archiv für Religionswissenschaft*, 2 (1899); M. Bartels, "Über Krankheitsbeschwörungen," *ZsfVK*, 5 (1895), 1–40; B. Lersch, *Geschichte der Volksseuchen* (Leipzig, 1896); J. Nohl, *Der schwarze Tod: Eine Chronik der Pest* (Potsdam, 1924).

A special commission to study the question of an international classification system for folk legends came up with the outline of an international legend index. See "Arbeitsresultat der Sonderkommission der International Society for Folk-Narrative Research," *Acta Ethnographica*, 13 (1964), 130–131.

LEGEND NO. 169. This legend could be assigned to the category of legends of Wild Men and Wild Women, but it could also be called a fate legend as it deals with a successful prophecy. The date, 1644, was less than four years before the end of the Thirty Years' War, one of the most devastating conflicts to have been inflicted on the populace of Europe. The prophecy that had occurred twenty-five years earlier dealt, of course, with the beginning of that war. The creatures and demons of nature are thought somehow to be in tune with the cosmos and thus able to perceive future events.

See L. Laistner, *Das Rätsel der Sphinx* (Leipzig, 1889). See also the commentary to Nos. 46 and 151.

LEGEND NO. 170. This legend belongs to the category of war prophecy legends, a subgroup of fate legends. Reichenberg is a former royal residence in the town of Reichelsheim located on the Nibelungen Road between Bensheim and Michelstadt in the Oden Forest. The ruins of the old fortress are located on a hill overlooking the nearby towns of Oberkainsbach and Niederkainsbach. The ghostly army is reminiscent of the legends of the Wild Huntsman and his wild horde. Indeed, von Rodenstein is one of the traditional Wild Huntsman figures.

See Nos. 47–48, 172–173, and 313–314 and commentaries. See also M. Beth, "Krieg," *HdA* V, 565–574; W.-E. Peuckert, "Weltkriegs-Weissagung," *HdA* IX, 472–495; G. F. Meyer, "Weltkrieg und Volkssage," *Mitteilungen aus dem Quickborn*, 26 (1933), No. 2.

LEGEND NO. 171. This legend has achieved world-wide fame through Richard Wagner's opera of the same name. Wagner combined this legend with No. 561, "The War of Wartburg Castle." The real Tannhäuser was a medieval courtly singer who lived, composed, and performed in the thirteenth century (ca. 1228–1265). His songs are included in the edition of medieval lyrics edited by K. Bartsch and W. Golther, *Deutsche Liederdichter des zwölften bis vierzehnten Jahrhunderts*, 4th ed. (Berlin, 1901), 244–252.

Tannhäuser served at the court of Frederick the Belligerent, Duke of Austria from 1230 to 1246, and the last of the Babenberg lineage to rule. Many of the famous courtly singers of the day served Duke Frederick. Tannhäuser wrote many love songs telling of his erotic adventures, and he also wrote about his exploits during the crusades. After Frederick died in battle, leaving no heirs, political affairs in Austria grew chaotic and Tannhäuser's situation became desperate, a fact he laments vividly in one of his songs. He subsequently sank to the status of a wandering minstrel and finally disappeared entirely from the stage of history. His adventurous existence, however, lived on as the subject of a folk tradition in its own right. A narrative song, on which this legend is based, was recorded on a broadside in 1515, although it had doubtless existed in the oral tradition for many years, for it mentions that Tannhäuser sought the forgiveness and blessings of Pope Urban IV, 1261–1264.

The motif of Venus reigning over a realm of carnal pleasure is related to Celtic fairy traditions, and it was well known in Brittany in the Middle Ages. In German tradition the figure of Venus sometimes becomes contaminated with that of Mother Holla (see Nos. 4–8). Venus Mountain sometimes becomes Hörsel Mountain, which is located in Thuringia and about which a number of other legends are told (see No. 174). Venus and her mountain became the symbol of immoderate carnal pleasure.

Tannhäuser's fate represents the inflexibility of papal rule, for as the song puts it (my own free translation):

> And so, no pope or cardinal
> Should damn a man for his sin,
> No matter how vile his life has been,
> God's mercy he yet may win.

The song and legend clearly reflect some of the antipapal attitudes that prevailed in the Middle Ages due to the investiture struggle that lasted for many years (see No. 489 and commentary). The song doubtless received new popularity as a result of antipapal feelings during the Reformation.

See D.-R. Moser, *Die Tannhäuser-Legende: Eine Studia über Intentionalität und Rezeption kathechetischer Volkserzählungen zum Buß-Sakrament* (Berlin, New York, 1977); F. Rostock, *Mittelhochdeutsche Dichterheldensage* (Halle, 1925), see esp. pp. 12–15; W. Golther, *Zur deutschen Sage und Dichtung* (Leipzig, 1911); D. Koegel, *Die Auswertung der Tannhäuser-Sage in der deutschen*

*Literatur des neunzehnten und zwanzigsten Jahrhunderts,* Diss. (München, 1922); A. N. Ammann, *Tannhäuser im Venusberg* (Zürich, 1964); G. Eis, "Die Sage vom Venusberg bei Rudolf Rebmann," *Studia neophilologica,* 33 (1961), 159–161; R. M. Meyer, "Tannhäuser und die Tannhäusersage," *ZsfVk,* 21 (1911), 1–16; O. Löhmann, "Die Entstehung der Tannhäusersage," *Fabula,* 3 (1960); J. Siebert, *Der Dichter Tannhäuser: Leben, Gedichte, Sage* (Halle, 1934); L. Petzoldt, *Historische Sagen* (München, 1976–77), I, 402–403. I am indebted to Petzoldt's commentary for some of the above information.

LEGEND NO. 172. A. Kuhn and W. Schwartz (*Norddeutsche Sagen, Märchen und Gebräuche* [Leipzig, 1848], Nr. 203) report a similar grave in the Harz Mountains (my own free translation):

In the landscape called Klipperkruge's Garden near Wülperude in the Harz Mountains, people still point to an engraving upon a rock they call Hackelberg's tomb. On it is carved a hunter sitting on a mule, his cloak flowing behind him, accompanied by his hounds. The inscription reads, "March 13, *Anno Domini* 1581."

Hackelberg, like Dietrich von Bern (Theodoric), King Arthur, and von Rodenstein, among others, is thought to be an Eternal Huntsman condemned to the chase forever. Riding his snorting steed and accompanied by barking hounds, Hackelberg leads the wild hunt roaring over hill and dale and sometimes up into the sky, sweeping before him all that lies in his path. Sometimes he leads a horde of Poor Souls in this wild pursuit.

There is no documentary evidence that he ever actually existed. Friedrich Ranke ("Sage und Erlebnis," *Bayerische Hefte für Volkskunde,* 1 [1914], 40–51) tried to explain the legend as based on actual experiences, viz., a temporary psychotic state induced by such physiological ailments as epilepsy (roaring sound in ears, loss of balance, sensation of flying, loss of memory), and he used a famous sixteenth-century report in which the details of such an experience were spelled out to illustrate his thesis. His arguments have met with a great deal of opposition (e.g., A. Wesselski, "Probleme der Sagenbildung," *SAV,* 35 [1936], 131–188; L. Röhrich, *Sage* [Stuttgart, 1966], 5–6). Nevertheless, the universality of the experience may well indicate that it is induced by some form of altered state of consciousness. See the commentary to No. 48.

For another legend featuring Hackelberg, see No. 311. See also R. Wünsch, "Griechischer und germanischer Geisterglaube," *HBV* 2 (1903), 177–192; R. Hünnerkopf, "Der wilde Jäger in Oberdeutschland," *Oberdeutsche Zeitschrift für Volkskunde,* 1 (1927), 34–43; F. Sieber, "Dietrich von Bern als Führer der wilden Jagd," *MSGV,* 31 (1931), 85–124; A. Endter, *Die Sage vom wilden Jäger und von der wilden Jagd,* Diss. (Frankfurt, 1934); A. Büchli, "Wilde Jagd und Nachtvolk," *SV,* 37 (1947), 65–69; R. Christiansen, "Der wilde Jäger in Norwegen," *ZsfVk,* 46 (1936), 24–31; H. Weininger, *Das wilde Heer oder die Nachtjagd* (Landshut, 1863); K. Meisen, *Die Sagen vom wütenden Heer und dem wilden Jäger* (Münster, 1935); J. Mourreau, "La chasse sauvage, mythe exempl.," *Nouvelle école,* 16 (1972), 9–43; G. Roheim, "Die wilde Jagd," *Imago,* 12 (1926), 465–477; P. Sartori, "Der wilde Jäger," *Zeitschrift des Vereins für rheinisch-westfälische Volkskunde,* 24 (1927), 61–63; A. Taylor, "Arthur and the Wild Hunt," *Romanic Review,* 12 (1921), 286–289; J. Zihlmann, "Der wilde Jagd," *SV,* 29 (1939), 51–54.

LEGEND NO. 173.   Tailors belong to the category of craftsmen who pursue a "dishonorable profession," and they are frequently depicted as cowardly, weak, and dumb. See W. Danckert, *Unehrliche Leute* (Bern und München, 1963). The person who mocks supernatural powers invariably pays severely for his foolhardy action. See also the commentaries to Nos. 48 and 172.

LEGEND NO. 174.   Hösel Mountain, better known as Hörsel Mountain, is located near Eisenach in Thuringia. Virtually every demonic being imaginable has been associated with the mountain. The seductive Venus is said to reside there (see No. 171); Mother Holda (Holla) emerges from the mountain during the twelve nights; the White Woman is seen wandering there; the Wild Huntsman emerges from the mountain at sundown; and witches dance on its peak during their sabbaths. But above all, the mountain is thought of as Hell or Purgatory where Poor Souls are tormented. See L. Weiser-Aall, "Hörselberg," *HdA* IV, 400–401.

The appearance of the flames is, of course, related to the notion of the mountain as a place of infernal torment. The souls of the damned are frequently depicted as flames flying through the air (cf. the Ball of Fire in English and American traditions), a concept that grew out of medieval notions of the inferno. See W. D. Hand, "Will-o'-the-Wisps, Jack-o'-Lanterns, and Their Congeners: A Consideration of the Fiery and Luminous Creatures of Lower Mythology," *Fabula*, 18 (1977), 226–233; H. Freudenthal, "Feuer," *HdA* II, 1389–1402; F. Ranke, "Feuermann," *HdA* II, 1405–1411; H. Freudenthal, *Das Feuer im deutschen Glauben und Brauch* (Berlin and Leipzig, 1931); R. Kühnau, "Die Feuermänner," *MSGV*, 5 (1902); W.-E. Peuckert, *DtVSMA*, esp. pp. 173–178.

LEGEND NO. 175.   It was believed that tricks of magic could be practiced both by sorcerers and by spirits and demons in human guise. The magic tricks performed by the servant in this legend are widespread in popular literature (although they are not included in Thompson *Motif-Index*), and here the account has to some degree acquired the jestful nature of the *Schwank* ('merry tale'). The ability to cover great distances in a short period of time has been attributed to a number of sorcerers. Stealing horseshoes so the enemy cannot pursue is a trick typical of such figures as Till Eulenspiegel. See O. Debus, *Till Eulenspiegel in der deutschen Volksüberlieferung*, Diss. (Marburg, 1951).

The horse whose head appears through the window in the tower is known in a number of jests and legends, and a humorous version is told in the Münchhausen collection. The motif is frequently presented as a miracle, and it is associated with the legend of the woman who was thought dead and was buried but reemerged from the grave. See No. 341 and its commentary. A variant of the legend is told by O. von Graben zum Stein, *Unterredungen von dem Reiche der Geister* (Leipzig, 1731), I, 272–274.

LEGEND NO. 176.   The legend of the holy mass of the ghosts is known in virtually every country in Europe (see R. T. Christiansen, *The Migratory Legends*, FFC 175 [Helsinki, 1958], no. 4015). As early as the sixth century Gregory of Tours told the story in his *De gloria confessorum*, and it was repeated circa A.D. 1000 by Thietmar von Merseburg (Chronicon I). The ghosts are frequently reported to march in procession around the church three times before entering, accompanied all the while by ghostly music. All Souls' Eve is a favorite time for such masses, but they have also been reported on Good Friday, Walpurgis Eve (April 30), during Advent, Christmas Eve, New Year's Eve, and at Epiphany. It is said that those who missed attending mass in life are required to make up for it in death.

The mortal who sees the celebration is exposed to great danger. Although, as in this legend, the witness frequently escapes with a minimal amount of damage or injury, he or she may be stricken afterward with a mysterious illness, sometimes even paying for the encounter with his or her life. The motif of the article of clothing that is left behind and found the next morning in shreds upon the graves in the cemetery is almost invariably a part of the story.

A similar narrative is told in some saints' legends where a particular saint witnesses the angels celebrating mass, and there may be a connection between both traditions. See Tubach *Index* (1970), no. 3228; C. Mengis, "Geistermesse, -gottesdienst," *HdA* III, 536–539; H. Ankert, "Die Sagen von der Geistermessen," *ZöV*, 4 (1898), 304–305; O. Schell, "Einige Bemerkungen zu den Sagen von Geisterkirchen und Geistermessen," *Westdeutsche Zeitschrift für Volkskunde*, 8 (1911), 113–119; M. Liebenfels, "Die Mitternachtsmesse," *Blätter für Heimatkunde*, 5 (1927), 76–80; B. Denecke, *Legende und Volkssage*, Diss. (Frankfurt, 1958); P. Foureur, "L'offrande et la messe des morts," *Bulletin de Commission Folklore Chamenois*, 48–51 (1948), 26–27; H. Hungerland, "Die Sage von der Ankumer Totenmette," *Mitteilungen des Vereins für Geschichte und Landeskunde von Osnabrück*, 46 (1924), 387–413.

LEGEND NO. 177.   The dead not only celebrate holy mass (see No. 176), they also participate in festive banquets (see No. 279). The banquet is usually a normal meal served in a normal fashion, but the fare is often quite exquisite and luxurious. The mortal visitor who chances upon the scene is invariably invited to partake and is treated well. He or she is served food or wine but does well not to eat or drink for the fare can turn to flame when it touches the lips. However, a legend from Tyrol reports that whoever eats such a meal releases a Poor Soul.

Frequently, as in this legend, the golden plates and goblets are left behind and the subject becomes wealthy. But in some variants the items change to worthless materials (dung, mud, feathers, etc.) after the participants depart. See C. Mengis, "Geistermahl," *HdA* III, 535–536.

LEGEND NO. 178.   A quick look at European urban architecture from the Middle Ages to the twentieth century will illustrate the fact that the roofer's trade was one of the most dangerous known in Europe. Church steeples, cathedral towers, and city gates have towering roofs that rise hundreds of feet in the air at nearly vertical angles. Roofers were probably well aware of the symptoms and effects of vertigo long before the medical profession even knew it existed. These workers also knew the danger they were all exposed to if one of their number suffered such an attack on the job, for frequently the men were roped together. Therefore, the provision of the law outlined here is thoroughly understandable. A search through various treatises on traditional law, however, yielded no additional information on this topic. Jacob Grimm did not even expound on it in his *Rechtsaltertümer* (*Legal Antiquities*), 4th ed. (Leipzig, 1899). The standard works on trades and crafts likewise provided no additional information.

LEGEND NO. 179. These are two etiological legends attempting to explain the presence of these sculptured crosses. G. Gugitz (*Die Sagen und Legenden der Stadt Wien* [Wien, 1952], no. 126) published a variant of the tale that he thought was unique: A maiden who is betrothed to a knight off on a crusade vows to sit at the base of the stone cross and keep spinning until her beloved returns from his sacred mission. A pilgrim then arrives and informs her of the knight's death. She continues to spin six weeks longer until she dies of a broken heart. The ghost of the pious spinning woman can sometimes be seen at midnight, kneeling before the cross.

Gugitz was convinced that the legend was created at the end of the eighteenth century. There are, however, countless similar legends which tell of a spinning woman at a cross (Baader, *Volkssagen aus dem Lande Baden*, 2 vols. [Karlsruhe, 1851], I, no. 373), as well as on a bridge: F. Panzer, *Bayerische Sagen* (München, 1848–75), II, 207, and J. Künzig, *Badische Sagen* (Leipzig, 1925), 72.

Legends reporting the apparition of ghostly spinning women (at crossroads, in castles, wandering at night) are very common and there is scarcely a collection of European legends which does not have at least one. See Petzoldt *HS*, I, nos. 30a and 30b and notes.

In a number of legends this figure (Mother Holla, see Nos. 4–8) punishes girls who spin after Saturday noon or who break some other taboo associated with spinning. The reference to Colocz in the Grimms' Addenda indicates the fourteenth-century Colocsaer manuscript, a collection of clerical writings.

LEGEND NO. 180. These etiological tales were attempts to explain the name of Buttermilk Tower for the original meaning had been lost. The first legend includes an implicit criticism of the peasants who were wasteful with the buttermilk. The second is directed at the wasteful lords for whom the villagers were forced to perform their socage. The third is a tale of crime and punishment in which the blasphemous act of treating a sow with Christian devotion may be a weakening of the motif of sodomy. See the commentary to No. 143.

It is entirely possible that the name Buttermilk is itself a folk etymology derived from a (Slavic?) word that was no longer understood. The stories were then created to explain the new word. Cf. No. 242 where there is a similar process. Marienburg is today the Polish city of Malbork. It is located about twenty-five miles southwest of Danzig (Gdańsk).

LEGEND NO. 181. Winfried (Old English Wynfrith), later known as Bonifatius (Boniface), was born ca. 673 in Wessex where he became a learned Benedictine monk and head of the monastic school of Nhutscelle (today Nursling near Southampton). In 716 he traveled to Frisia and then to Thuringia for the purpose of establishing Christian missions. His missionary work was extensive and he doubtless contributed to the building of a church at Großvargula, which is located about twenty miles northwest of Erfurt. In 722 he was appointed bishop over all the missionary territories of heathen Germany. In 723 he began his missionary work in Hesse where it is said he chopped down the sacred Donar oak tree in Geismar outside of Fritzlar. The legend reports that he then split the logs himself and used them to build a chapel.

It is possible that his legend about Christ Mountain is a variant of the Geismar legend. Castor Mountain may represent a site devoted to the Germanic Divine Twins—one of whom was called Castor according to *interpretatione romana*. See D. Ward, *The Divine Twins: An Indo-European Myth in Germanic Tradition* (Berkeley and Los Angeles, 1968).

Bonifatius became a very active missionary, founding the sees of Passau, Regensburg, Salzburg, Freising, Eichstatt, Buraberg, Würzburg, and Erfurt. In 742 he became Archbishop of Austrasia (Eastern France), and in 744 he founded the monastery of Fulda, which became the influential center of learning for the German-speaking areas of Europe. In 753, at the age of eighty, he returned to Frisia to have another try at converting those most recalcitrant of all Germanic heathens. On June 5, 754, he and his party were slain during a Frisian ambush on the shores of the Borne River (today in the Netherlands).

See T. Schieffer, *Winfrid-Bonifatius und die christliche Grundlegung Europas* (Freiburg, 1974).

LEGEND NO. 182.   Wanfried lies on the Werra River just west of the East German border near the town of Eschwege (about 45 miles east of Kassel). Regarding Bonifatius, see the commentary to No. 181. The legend of the Devil's Hole is very widespread and is told about virtually every church in Europe that has a hole, an impression, or other irregularity in its wall (see No. 183). See M. Freytag, *Die Sage von den Teufelslöchern bei Jena* (Jena, 1931).

Regarding the maiden with the beard (St. Kummernis), see No. 330 and its commentary.

LEGEND NO. 183.   Although historians know of no battle fought within the church walls of Goslar, the city was nevertheless frequently torn by internal strife and armed conflict and such events could well have contributed to this legend. See K. G. Bruchmann, *Goslar* (München, 1952).

Regarding the motif of the Devil's Hole, see the commentary to No. 182. The motif of walling a cat up during the construction of the church represents more than a mere literary motif. Such sacrifices were common in the Middle Ages. A chicken, dog, cat, or on rare occasions even a human would be sacrificed by being walled up during the construction of buildings, churches, dams, and above all dikes. Remains of such sacrifices are still found when old structures are torn down. The sacrifices were made so that the life force of the victim would be transferred to the structure, giving it extra strength. It was also thought that the sacrifice would placate destructive demons and divinities and ward off floods, fires, and foreign armies.

See G. Schmitt, *Das Menschenopfer in der Spätüberlieferung der deutschen Volksdichtung* (Mainz, 1959); U. Jahn, *Die abwehrenden und Sühneopfer der Deutschen*, Diss. (Breslau, 1884); B. Götz, *Die Bedeutung des Opfers bei den*

*Völkern* (Leipzig, 1933); K. Beth, "Menschenopfer," *HdA* VI, 156–174; R. Stübe, "Bauopfer," *HdA* I, 962–964.

LEGEND NO. 184. This and the previous legend belong to the category of Devil legends. The Devil of the folk legend developed into a creature quite distinct from the biblical concept of Satan or of Lucifer, the fallen angel. Theologians look upon the Devil as an evil force without substance, while folk tradition has made a very concrete figure out of him. In the earliest graphic representations in popular tradition, the Devil appeared as a bird-like demon with wings, beak, and clawed feet. Later, probably as a result of influence from classical antiquity (Pan), he was depicted with the horns and hoofs of a goat. He was also shown possessing fiery eyes, a hooked nose, long fangs, and a hairy face. Later, he was depicted as a handsome, seductive hunter, but with cloven feet. Although the Devil was looked upon as a frightful demon, there was sometimes a certain compassion and sympathy for him (cf., for example, the old and widespread appellation, "poor Devil").

In European legendry a distinct process of diabolization can be detected. That is, the Devil gradually supplanted such pre-Christian figures as Giants, Dwarfs, the Cobold, and the Wild Huntsman. This legend is probably a result of this process. The two main motifs, the Devil as master builder and the cheated Devil, originally belonged to the figure of the Giant.

One of the earliest and most complete stories of this kind is told in Snorra's Edda. While Thor is absent, *Bergrisi* 'Mount Giant' appears and promises the gods that not only will he build Asgard for them but he will finish before the first day of summer. If he succeeds his payment will be the goddess Freyja as well as the sun and moon. The gods, confident that the realm could not possibly be built in so short a time, accept his terms. What they did not know was that the Giant's horse, Swandilfari, was so powerful that it could drag boulders to the site from all over the world with remarkable speed. Three days before the onset of summer only the main gate remained unfinished, and the Giant was working on it with efficient speed. At this point Loki transformed himself into a mare and lured the powerful stallion away (Loki later became pregnant and gave birth to Odin's eight-legged horse). The Giant was unable to keep his end of the bargain, and Freyja and the sun and moon were saved. Thor then returned and slew the Giant. This story turns up later in hundreds of popular legends, and in many of them the builder is not a Giant but the Devil.

See V. Höttges, *Typenverzeichnis der deutschen Riesen- und riesischen Teufelssagen*, FFC 122 (Helsinki, 1937); I. M. Boberg, *Baumeistersagen*, FFC 151 (Helsinki, 1955); G. Roskoff, *Die Geschichte des Teufels*, 2 vols., 2nd ed. (Leipzig, 1869); M. Osborn, *Die Teufelsliteratur des 16. Jahrhunderts* (Berlin, 1893); A. Wünsche, *Der Sagenkreis vom geprellten Teufel* (Leipzig und Wien, 1905); R. Newald, "Die Teufelliteratur und die Antike," *Bayrische Blätter für das Gymnasialschulwesen*, 63 (1927); A. Warkentin, *The Devil in the German Traditional Story* (Chicago, 1937); B. A. Woods, *The Devil in Dog Form* (Berkeley and Los Angeles, 1958).

LEGEND NO. 185. The area in which this legend takes place is located just to the east of Schwäbisch-Gmünd in northern Baden-Württemberg. The ruins of Rosenstein can still be seen overlooking the valley. The report that the cliff with the imprint was blown up by the authorities may well rest on fact. Strange rock formations were known cult sites in heathen times, and for centuries after the introduction of Christianity they remained firmly imprinted in folk memory as places associated with supernatural forces. The Church either tried to associate these forces with the Devil or saw to it that the sites were destroyed.

The fact that the Devil is banished to the bottom of the canyon is reminiscent of the chaining of the Fenris Wolf in Eddic myth. See Petzoldt *DVS*, nos. 18 and 454 and notes for similar legends. See also F. von der Leyen, *Der gefesselte Unhold: Eine mythologische Studie* (Prag, 1908).

Marshy meadows, especially those lying in deep isolated canyons, are frequently considered haunts of supernatural creatures. Indeed, the term Devil's Marsh (*Teufelsklinge*) mentioned in this legend has become the generic term for legends associated with such sites. There are scores of places in German-speaking areas called *Teufelsklinge*. See, for example, Assion *WSF*, Nos. 177 and 195.

LEGEND NO. 186. The widespread legend cycles of the Devil as master builder and the cheated Devil (see commentary to No. 184) serve here as an etiological legend.

LEGEND NO. 187. This legend is also a variant of the Devil as master builder and the cheated Devil complex. See the commentary to No. 184. It is true that Napoleon's armies stripped Germany of countless art treasures and had them shipped to Paris. Many of the items were returned in 1815, the year before this volume of the legends was published. Interestingly, it was Jacob Grimm himself who was sent to Paris after Napoleon's defeat to negotiate for the return of these art treasures, and it is likely that he was personally responsible for the return of this statue (see my Epilogue). Thus we have the curious situation of Jacob Grimm's not only collecting and publishing this legend but also playing an indirect role in its content.

LEGEND NO. 188. This legend belongs to the category of the banished Devil. The tower, today called simply Pont Gate (*Ponttor*), still stands at the northwest entrance through the old city wall of Aachen. The word derives from the fact that there was once a bridge (*ponte*) over the moat at that site. See E. Corr, *Aachener Brunnen und Denkmäler* (Aachen, 1975).

LEGEND NO. 189. The region in this legend lies about thirty-five miles to the southwest of Nürnberg. The remains of an old Roman fort called *Castrum biricianis* in the area evidently gave rise to the legend. The legend is etiological in the sense that it explains the presence of an old structure whose origins and original function had been forgotten. Like the Devil's Marsh (see No. 185), it has become a spooky place.

Objects and phenomena in the environment that deviate from the norm attract attention to themselves and frequently become the subject of legends. The Swedish folklorist C. W. von Sydow has labeled such objects "*externe Dominante*" or external dominating concerns, while the internal concerns (good, evil, crime and punishment, disease, successful harvest, etc.) he has called *"interne Dominante."* The linking of these internal and external concerns, according to von Sydow, produces beliefs and legends. See D. Ward, "The Little Man Who Wasn't There: On Encounters with the Supranormal," *Fabula*, 18 (1977), 212–225, for a discussion of these and related theories.

The motif of the contest between God and the Devil at the beginning of the world is the subject of a wide range of cosmological legends. See Hannjost Lixfeld, *Gott und Teufel als Weltschöpfer* (München, 1971).

The attempt to gain land by some kind of contest is likewise a widespread etiological theme in many legends. There is, for example, the granting of as much land as one can ride around (see No. 524) or plow around (see No. 525) in a given time. Or, as much land is granted as can be covered by a single animal hide, which turns out to be a clever trick (No. 419).

The motif of the Devil's building the wall is related to the theme of Devil as master builder, a theme originally associated with Giants. See the commentary to No. 184.

LEGEND NO. 190.  See the commentary to No. 189. A flat hill overlooking the city of Thale is today called *Hexentanzplatz* 'the Witches' Dance Floor' and no longer 'the Devil's Dance Floor.' See No. 319 and its commentary.

LEGEND NO. 191.  See the commentary to No. 189.

LEGEND NO. 192.  See the commentary to No. 189. Bentheim Palace is located in the city of Bentheim in the Ems Valley, near the Netherlands border.

LEGEND NO. 193.  It is obvious that the Grimms did not want to identify these villages for they referred to them only by their initials. The site of this legend may possibly be the Kössen Valley in the Chiemgau region on the border between Bavaria and Austria.

In every landscape in Germany there are towns that have the reputation of being inhabited by dullards, fools, and/or wicked people. The appellation of Turks or Tartars for such villagers is not uncommon—it reflects the survival of the medieval attitude equating heathens, foreigners, and the Devil with each other. See H. Naumann, "Der wilde und edle Heide," in P. Merker and W. Stammler (eds.), *Vom Werden des deutschen Geistes: Festgabe Gustav Ehrismann* (Berlin und Leipzig, 1955).

Whole villages of Central Europe were often settled by foreign invaders, and legends about such settlements are often xenophobic in the extreme. Some scholars have pointed out that in isolated villages a great deal of inbreeding often occurs, and as a result certain recessive genetic traits can become dominant. I am unable to evaluate the validity of such assumptions.

LEGEND NO. 194.  See the commentaries to Nos. 184 and 189.

LEGEND NO. 195.  During the baroque period when many churches and cathedrals were redone in the prevailing style, it was customary to enclose the baptismal font in an elaborate framework of wrought iron. Baroque craftsmen took special delight in creating optical illusions, for one of the preoccupations of the time was the interplay of illusion and reality. And indeed it was frequently very difficult to follow the design in the wrought iron. In this case the common people explained such creations as the work of the Devil.

LEGEND NO. 196.   Pestorf today is called Pegestorf, and both it and Grave lie on the Weser River about thirty miles upstream from Hameln. Because mills were frequently located in isolated regions and could harness the power in the waters of springs and streams that were once believed to be sacred, the trade of the miller was one that aroused feelings of suspicion among villagers. Mills soon came to be thought of as diabolical and spooky places, and millers were suspected of being dishonorable and in league with the Devil. Small wonder that there are scores of legends telling how millers bargained with the Devil to construct their mills. See No. 184 and its commentary. See also W. Danckert, *Unehrliche Leute* (Bern, 1963), esp. pp. 125–145.

LEGEND NO. 197.   See the commentary to No. 189. The Rhön Mountains lie along the East German border southeast of Fulda.

LEGEND NO. 198.   This legend uses the theme of the Devil as master builder to explain a natural rock outcrop. See the commentaries to Nos. 184 and 189. Reichenbach lies just to the east of Hessisch-Lichtenau in a mountainous region near Kassel, and there is indeed a curious rock outcrop nearby. Such geological formations are sometimes associated with the Devil in the U.S. as well, as, for example, Devil's Postpile in California.

LEGEND NO. 199.   This is another etiological legend (see the commentary to No. 189). Although the area surrounding the Cologne Cathedral is full of chapels and churches (St. Mary's, Holy Apostles', St. Columba's, St. Minontius', the Church of the Antonites, St. Martin's, St. Andreas', etc.), there is, to my knowledge, no Chapel of the Three Holy Kings in the area. However, above the main altar of the cathedral itself there is a famous shrine to the Three Kings. It is evident that one of the chapels within the cathedral once housed this shrine and was called the Chapel of the Three Holy Kings.

LEGEND NO. 200.   Although the etymological explanation that the Grimms suggest in the footnote may not be completely convincing, it is difficult to find a better explanation.

LEGEND NO. 201.   Halberstadt is an important city in East Germany at the foot of the Harz Mountains not far from Quedlinburg. It is a diocese with an important Gothic cathedral. In the local dialect of this region there is no phonetic distinction made between *Lügen* 'lies' and *liegen* 'to lie' (in the sense of a stone lying on the ground). It is thus possible that the story about the Father of Lies (the Devil) came about because of this linguistic confusion, a common occurrence in legendry everywhere (see, for example, No. 242 and commentary). The tossing of a large boulder is an activity associated primarily with Giants rather than with the Devil (see Nos. 16–17 and 135). The motif of the demon enraged at the construction of a cathedral would of course be associated with the Devil from the beginning. Thus we have here a Devil's legend that has adopted a motif from a diabolicized (see commentary to No. 184) Giant's legend.

LEGEND NO. 202.   The Devil is always ready to pounce upon and seize the souls of the unwary. Implicit in this legend is the fact that he is thought to have power only over the sinful. The shepherd here, although setting out on an amorous adventure that just skirts the borders of acceptable behavior in his community, is nevertheless rendered immune to the wiles of the Evil One because he stops on his way to pray to the Mother of God at a mountain chapel.

The Visper is a mountain stream in Switzerland. It flows from Lake Mattmark in the Valais Alps northward, joining the Rhone at the city of Visp.

LEGEND NO. 203.   Bell legends constitute an entire category of European legends (see Nos. 126 and 127). One of the subcategories of these legends is that of the sunken bell. Such legends have an affinity with treasure legends because they deal with valuable lost objects guarded in this case—as are treasures—by demonic beings. The affinity is especially apparent in this legend since the bell in question is made of solid gold. That it sank in a lake that is virtually bottomless stresses the element of its being nearly irretrievable. Moreover, there is not just one demonic being watching over the sunken bell, but a number of them.

Deep and bottomless lakes are thought to be full of numinous powers, and the curious diver who descends into their depths exposes himself to great danger. The black dog that guards the bell is frequently associated with the Devil in legends. (See B. A. Woods, *The Devil in Dog Form* [Berkeley and Los Angeles, 1959].) However, the black horse that emerges from the depths is more reminiscent of legends of water spirits and Nixies than the Devil. Such creatures are thought to belong to the Water Nix, and occasionally one will venture out on dry land (see No. 59 and its commentary).

In many legends bells are depicted as being nearly human. It is possible that the ancient belief in the spirit of the ore is reflected in such notions, although such a contention cannot be proven. In any event, bells are thought to have human voices, and they are baptized and given names. Like children they are susceptible to possession by demons and above all to temptation by the Devil. This danger is thought to be greatly diminished if they are baptized. The fact that the bell in this legend falls to the Devil implies that it happened before it was baptized.

The farmer who plows his field after Vespers on Saturday is guilty of a serious blasphemy, for the Holy Sabbath begins at Vespers on Saturday. In some areas it even begins at noon of that day. The farmer then goes on to compound his sin by cursing and beating the child and the draft animals. He irrevocably seals his doom when he harnesses the diabolic horse to the plow for he who enlists the aid of the Evil One is damned forever. In some respects this legend is a diabolicized Water Nix legend. Nevertheless, the element of the Devil's seizing the bell before it has been baptized is a familiar theme in Devil legends.

The proverb that ends the story is not a common one in Germany, and it has not been included in the Wander collection although there are scores of related proverbs there (K. Wander, *Deutsches Sprichwörterlexikon*, 5 vols. (Leipzig, 1876), IV, 1099–1104). Dassel is in Lower Saxony, between the cities of Einbeck and Höxter.

For bibliography on bell legends see the notes to Nos. 126–127. The German playwright Gerhard Hauptmann wrote a play based on the theme of the sunken bell ("Die versunkene Glocke," 1897).

LEGEND NO. 204.   For information on Henry IV see the commentary to Nos. 489–490. The Schartfeld of this legend is now called Scharzfeld and is located at the foot of the Harz Mountains near Herzberg. Nearby is the town of Pöhlde. Lutterberg is apparently the town in the same region that is called Bad Lauterberg today.

The anticlerical tone of this legend can probably be attributed to the polemic spirit of the Reformation. The chronicle in question was published in 1596 and was probably first recorded during the Reformation period.

It is interesting that the manner in which the Devil punishes the evildoer ultimately serves the cause of good. This aspect of the Devil's activities doubtless contributed to his somewhat ambiguous image in popular tradition (see the commentary to No. 184). The legend also serves to explain how the roof disappeared from the tower in question.

LEGEND NO. 205.   This is an etiological legend explaining why it took literally centuries to build the Cathedral of Cologne. A masterful example of Gothic art, the cathedral was begun in 1248 and the work continued well into the sixteenth century. Construction then ceased and the majestic structure remained unfinished. It was not until the nineteenth century, when the original plans were accidentally discovered, that work was resumed. In 1880 the second of the two towers was finally completed.

LEGEND NO. 206.   This is an etiological *Schwank* that explains how a massive boulder came to lie at a certain spot. There are scores of legends in European tradition dealing with competitions between God and the Devil in which the Evil One invariably ends up second best. Since moving huge boulders was an accomplishment earlier attributed to Giants rather than the Devil, it is likely that this legend was originally told about a Giant. See the commentary to No. 184. Altenburg and Ehrenberg lie on opposite sides of the Pleiße River about fifty miles south of Leipzig.

LEGEND NO. 207.   Priests who are themselves sinners are thought to have no power over the Devil, and thus any attempts they make to exorcise him are doomed to fail. In this legend, as in others, the Devil punishes the sinners and paradoxically serves the cause of good, for the world of spirits and demons is believed to represent a danger especially to those who violate the norms of the community. Thus, the lower world serves to promote social cohesion—at the cost, however, of individual freedom.

LEGEND NO. 208.   Rastenburg was a German city in East Prussia. Today it is the Polish city of Ketrzyn. As with other spirits, the Devil's power ends at sunrise and the woman is thus saved. However, the experience causes her to fall ill, insuring that she does not escape punishment entirely.

The tale of shoeing the sinner was told at a very early date about the concubine of a priest, and it was first recorded around 1200 by Caesarius von Heisterbach (*Dialogus miraculorum*).

See R. Köhler, *Kleinere Schriften*, 3 vols. (Weimar 1898–1900), I, 220 and 568; V. von Geramb, "Die verwunschene Pfarrerköchin," *Blätter für Heimatkunde*, 22 (1948), 20–29; V. von Geramb, "Zum Sagenmotif vom Hufbeschlag," *Beiträge zur sprachlichen Volksüberlieferung: Festschrift für Adolf Spamer* (Berlin, 1953), 78–88; A. Haas, "Die pommersche Sage vom Teufelsroß," *Monatsblatt der Gesellschaft für pommersche Geschichte*, 1 (1927), 6–10; F. Ranke, "Pfaffeneisen," *HdA* VI, 1543–1544; F. Ranke, "Pfaffenkellerin," *HdA* VI, 1544–1547; W. D. Hand, "Witch-Riding and Other Demonic Assault in American Folk Legend," in L. Röhrich (ed.), *Probleme der Sagenforschung* (Freiburg, 1973), 165–176; E. Marold, "Die Gestalt des Schmiedes in der Volkssage," *ibid.*, 100–111.

LEGEND NO. 209.   Motifs of two legend types—the broken oath of betrothal, and the Devil on the dance floor— have been combined into this single narrative. In the former, a man or woman swears an oath that eventually seals his or her doom, for when the party marries another the Devil comes and carries the evildoer off to eternal damnation. In villages where the sole means of support was agriculture betrothals had a special implication, for a young farmer needed a wife and children to help run his farm. Thus, breaking a betrothal oath had serious economic consequences. R. Beitel, *Wörterbuch der deutschen Volkskunde* (München, 1955), 155–156; R. Hirzel, *Der Eid: Ein Beitrag zu seiner Geschichte* (Leipzig, 1902); E. Fehr, "Eid," *HdA* II, 659–672.

In most variants of the Devil on the dance floor the maiden is punished for being too passionately devoted to dancing. When she continues to dance past midnight, the Devil, or some other demon such as the Water Nix (see No. 51), comes and dances away with her and she is never seen again.

The motif of the right of a stranger to the first dance with the bride is especially interesting. It is possible that it represents a weakened form of the ancient custom of granting a stranger the right to sleep with the bride on her wedding night. In early Europe, as well as many other places in the world, the defloration of a maiden was thought to expose a man to the maleficent power of demonic forces. Thus, a priest (in the name of the divinity), a chieftain, or frequently a stranger would be selected to perform this duty in the bridegroom's stead. See B. Kummer, "Geschlechtsverkehr,"*HdA* III, 735–752; E. Fehrle, *Die kultische Keuschheit im Altertum* (Gießen, 1910), 40–46; W. Hertz in *Gesammelte Abhandlungen*, ed. by F. von der Leyen (Stuttgart and Berlin, 1905), 197–212.

Whether the later European custom known as *droit du seigneur* or *ius primae noctis* (right to the first night), that is, the right of the feudal lord to bed all the brides of his fief on their wedding night, is an outgrowth of this belief is a matter of contention. It could merely be the result of a despot's exploitation of the peasantry for his own pleasure. See P. Wilutzky, *Vorgeschichte des Rechts*, 2 vols., (Breslau, 1903), I, 35–39; Grimm *DRA*, I, 525 and 531–532.

LEGEND NO. 210. The Dithmar War from which the soldiers returned was the war that Adolf von Holstein led in 1559 against the Danes to gain the territory for the Duchy of Holstein.

"Wheel of Fortune" is employed today to denote a numbered wheel used in a game of chance. The term originally meant something else. Wheels and disks were sacred symbols in many ancient religions, as, for example, the *rota* of ancient Egypt and the *chakra* of Vedia India. The concept of a disk on which mortals may ride through the air evidently began as an allegory in medieval art and literature. The spinning disk, which was called the Wheel of Fortune (French, *la roue de fortune;* German, *Glücksrad,* etc.), was portrayed as being occupied by four men: one on a throne in the center, one climbing toward the center, one falling off, and one already lying on the ground. The wheel thus became an expression of the *vanitas vanitatum* theme stressing the whims of fate or, as Hamlet put it, "the slings and arrows of outrageous fortune." Out of this allegory grew the tradition of the traveling scholars (i.e., sorcerers) who used such a wheel as a conveyance.

Sorcerers also used a spinning wheel with letters and symbols—also called the Wheel of Fortune—for purposes of divination. The name is also used in astrology.

See W. Anderson, "Glücksrad," *HdA* III, 895–898; K. Weinhold, "Glücksrad und Lebensrad," *ZsfVk,* 3 (1900), 367–369; M. Harmon, "Wheel," in M. Leach (ed.), *Standard Dictionary of Folklore, Mythology, and Legend,* 2nd ed. (New York, 1972), 1171–1174.

It is possible that some element in the human perception appartus enables people to actually see disks flying in the sky. From time immemorial people have observed all kinds of phenomena flying through the skies and have told stories about such apparitions. See L. Dégh, "UFOs and How Folklorists Should Look at Them," *Fabula,* 18 (1977), 242–248. It may be that such apparitions contributed to this and other related legends.

LEGEND NO. 211. This legend shows not only that men can serve as the Devil's advocate but also that, conversely, the Devil can serve as man's advocate. The story is also told as a *Märchen* (AT 821) and is especially popular in the Baltic region. There are at least forty known Finnish variants, twenty-seven Estonian, four Swedish, and a number of scattered variants throughout much of Europe.

The story represents the rather common paradox of the Devil in his pursuit of sinners not only ultimately serving the cause of good but actually acting as the defender of the innocent man. See R. Schömer, "Advocat," *HdA* I, 201–202; "Advocat," *HdS,* 130–131.

Older and more widespread is the related legend of the judge and the Devil. See Röhrich *EMA,* II, 251–278 and 460–471; Rehermann *Predigtexempel,* 158–159, lists eight variants from the exempla literature.

LEGEND NO. 212. "The Dream of the Treasure on the Bridge" (AT 1645) is an old and widespread legend. Variants have been collected in virtually every country in Europe and the theme turns up in literary works from the Orient, even occurring in *The Thousand and One Nights.* The legend may have been brought to Europe during the crusades. The first study devoted to the theme was by Jacob Grimm himself (see below).

The story invariably involves more than the simple sequence of dreaming about a treasure and then going to find it. Rather, as is the case here, it entails the more complex meshing of two different people's dreams that complement each other, and only when the two dreams are put together do they offer the secret of where the treasure is buried. The wealthier of the two men who meet on the bridge disdains information conveyed to him in a dream—in essence he is an Infidel in such matters—and the poor man, who pays attention to portents in dreams, is rewarded and recovers the treasure for himself alone.

The earliest version of the legend in Europe was recorded in 1320 in the verse epic *Der Karlmeinet*. It tells of a Dwarf who appears to a peasant named Hoderich in a dream, telling him that he will experience both love and sorrow as he crosses the bridge that leads into Paris. Hoderich goes there and the prophecy comes true: He is slapped across the face by a stranger but is also told that there is a treasure buried in his home village. He then returns home and recovers the treasure.

See Petzoldt *DVS*, No. 529 and commentary. See also J. Grimm, "Der Traum von dem Schatz auf der Brücke," *Kleinere Schriften* (Berlin, 1866), III, 414–428; Röhrich *EMA*, II, 122–135, 429–438; K. Lohmeyer, "Der Traum von dem Schatz auf der Brücke," *ZsfVk*, 19 (1909), 286–289; J. Bolte, "Der Traum von dem Schatz auf der Brücke," *ZsfVk*, 19 (1909), 289–298.

LEGEND NO. 213. For information and bibliography on treasure legends see the commentaries to Nos. 158–163. It was believed that sunken treasure had to appear periodically—usually every seven years. If one was fortunate enough to be present at that time there was a possibility that one could—with the help of the right combination of words and actions—take possession of the treasure. In a legend from Franconia, for example, if the boys who saw the treasure had made the sign of the cross and uttered the words "In the name of the Holy Trinity!" the treasure would have been theirs. See Assion *WSF*, 113, Nr. 60a. In this case, and in many similar ones, the people present learn what they should have done after the treasure has sunk from sight.

LEGEND NO. 214. The belief that a man can be transformed into an animal is world-wide. In India and Southeast Asia one encounters traditions of Were-tigers, and there are Were-bears throughout the northern hemisphere (see D. Ward, "Bärensohn," *EdM* I, 1232–1235), and even Were-sharks in Polynesia. The prefix "were-" is from Old High German *wêr* 'man' and is cognate with the Latin *vir* (cf. "virile").

Two basic notions have evidently played a role in the evolution of the belief in were-animals. One is the universal belief among hunting peoples that large game animals or predators (bears, wolves, tigers, elk, etc.) have essentially human cores. It is thought that should they choose to walk around as humans, they would only need to shed their animal hides. Conversely, a human donning an animal skin (usually amid chants, music, drugs, etc., to achieve an altered state of consciousness) can actually become—in his mind—the animal. Take, for example, the famous northern Germanic *berserkr* (*beri* 'bear' plus *serkr* 'hide'). They were warriors who worked themselves into a wild state of murderous frenzy thinking they were vicious bears, and it is from them that we get our word "berserk." The *berserkr* were, incidentally, also called *Ulfheðnar* 'wolf-skinned,' indicating a direct relationship with the belief in Werewolves (see E. O. G. Turville-Petre, *Myth and Religion of the North* [New York, Chicago, San Francisco, 1964], p. 61).

The Swedish humanist Olaus Magnus reported in a publication dated 1555 that on Christmas Eve in Sweden and North Germany men used to turn into wolves and roam and plunder in bands, even breaking into beer cellars. They could, he wrote, assume or throw off their wolf-shapes at will (see the essays by O. Höfler cited below).

There are essentially two kinds of Werewolf legends: those in which the victim is the unwilling subject of the transformation, and those in which he actively seeks to transform himself—sometimes with the help of the Devil. The latter group of narratives often assumes Christian traits, but it is not necessarily the more recent. In the case of the involuntary transformation, one often finds a certain sympathy with the poor victim, and attempts are made to release him from his torment. However, in cases where the subject is thought to have purposefully sought the transformation, he is often hanged or burned like a witch, and there is evidence that such executions have actually taken place.

In almost all the variants of the Werewolf motif in which a belt is involved, the transformation occurs by putting the belt *on*, as the Grimms correctly stated in their footnotes. This is doubtless a development from the motif of donning the animal hide. However, G. Schambach and W. Müller (*Niederdeutsche Sagen und Märchen*, 2nd ed. [Stuttgart, 1948], 184) have recorded the belief that the transformation can be accomplished by putting on the belt made from the skin of an executed criminal. This belief is evidently based on a long tradition among Germanic peoples of equating outlaws with wolves (see M. Gerstein, *Warg: The Outlaw as Werwolf in Germanic Myth, Law, and Medicine*, Diss. [Univ. of California, Los Angeles, 1972]).

The Werewolf phenomenon has captured the imagination of laymen and scholars alike and the literature on the topic is prolific. I have, therefore, listed only the most important titles here: A. Bonnez, "Van de weerwulf in't Vrijbusch," *Biekorf*, 62 (1961), 1–5; O. Clemen, "Zum Werwolfaberglauben in Westrussland," *ZsfVk* (1920/22), 141–144; J. Gessler, "De weerwolf: enkele bibliographische aantekeningen," *Volkskunde*, 10 (1951), 64–67; M. Gardiner, *The Wolf-Man, with a Case of the Wolf-Man by Sigmund Freud* (New York, 1971); W. Hertz, *Der Werwolf: Beitrag zur Sagengeschichte* (Stuttgart, 1862); M. Kahlo, "Der Werwolfsaberglaube," *Der Harz*, 2 (1933), 27–30; L. Kretzenbacher, *Kynokephale Dämonen Südosteuropäischer Volksdichtung* (München, 1968); W. Kroll, "Etwas vom Werwolf," *Wiener Studien*, 55 (1937), 168–172; R. Leubscher, *Über die Wehrwölfe und Thiernamen im Mittelalter* (Berlin, 1850); K. Müller, *Die Werwolfssage* (Karlsruhe, 1937); T. Penneman, "De weerwolf von Kalken-Eesvelde," *Volkskunde*, 74 (1973), 141–147; A. Roeck, "Der Werwolf als dämonisches Wesen im Zusammenhang mit den Plagegeistern," in L. Röhrich (ed.), *Probleme der Sagenforschung* (Freiburg, 1973), 139–148; A. Roeck, *De weerwolf in de Nederlandse Volkssage*, Diss. (Löwen, 1967); A. Schäfer,

*Die Verwandlung der menschlichen Gestalt im Volksaberglauben* (Darmstadt, 1905); M. Schuster, "Der Werwolf und die Hexen: Zwei Schauermärchen bei Petronius," *Wiener Studien*, 43 (1931), 149–178; K. Volker, *Von Werwölfen und anderen Tiermenschen* (München, 1972); C. Taylor Stewart, "Die Entstehung des Werwolfglaubens," *ZsfVk*, 19 (1909), 30–51; M.-L. Tenèze, "Quatre récits du loup," in F. Harkort *et al.* (eds.), *Volksüberlieferung: Festschrift für Kurt Ranke* (Göttingen, 1968), 351–367.

There has also been extensive literature in English on the Werewolf. See Ian Dewhirst, "In Search of the Water-Wolf," *Lore and Language*, 4 (1970), 12–14; H. Shoemaker, "Neighbors: The Werewolf in Pennsylvania," *NYFQ*, 7 (1951), 145–155; C. Taylor Stewart, "The Origin of the Werewolf Superstition," *The University of Missouri Studies*, 2 (1909), 1–37; S. Montague, *The Werewolf*, 2nd ed. (New York, 1966); W. Whittlesey, "On the Etiology of Were-wolves," *NYFQ*, 22 (1966), 261–268; M. Kriss, *Werewolves, Shapeshifters, and Skinwalkers* (Los Angeles, 1972).

The following titles are studies of the Germanic berserk phenomenon and its relation to the Werewolf tradition: F. Grøn, *Berserksgangens vesen og åraks-forhold* (Theim, 1929); O. Höfler, *Verwandlungskulten: Volkssagen und Mythen* (Wien, 1973); O. Höfler, "Über germanische Verwandlungskulten," *Zeitschrift für deutsches Altertum*, 75 (1938), 109–115; L. Huchting-Gminder, "Die Berserker der altisländischen Sagas," *NdZsV*, 11 (1933), 239–243; K. Müller-Bergström, "Zur Berserkerfrage," *NdZsV*, 12 (1934), 241–244.

LEGEND NO. 215.    See the commentary to No. 214. There are a number of place names in German-speaking areas formed from compounds with *wolf-*, many of them referring to rocks and cliffs (former cult sites?). It is possible that the Werewolf legends in such areas arose secondarily as etiological stories. See O. Apel, "Der Wolfstein bei Ärzen (in der Nähe von Pyrmont)," *Germania*, 7 (1936), 342–343.

LEGEND NO. 216.    See the commentary to No. 214. The twelve days of Christmas are an auspicious time for the appearance of the hordes of spirits (see Nos. 4–8, 47–48, 172–173, 313–314 and commentaries), but it is unusual for Werewolves to appear in such hordes. The Swedish humanist Olaus Magnus did, however, report that bands of Werewolves roamed and plundered during Christmastide.

LEGEND NO. 217.    The belief in dragons has been recorded throughout history in virtually all regions of the world. European compendia of the earth's fauna, for example, have invariably included dragons with the other reptiles. Even today there is a relatively large number of educated people who believe in the existence of the Loch Ness monster.

Such creatures are certainly the products of man's fertile imagination; nevertheless, they are attributed with the features and abilities of real animals. They reportedly have, for example, the long, twisting body and the deadly venom of the serpent; the armored plates, jaws, and teeth of the crocodile; and the claws and wings of the eagle.

The best treatise on dragons is the essay by Lutz Röhrich that will be forthcoming (as of this writing) in the *Enzyklopädie des Märchens*. I am grateful to Prof. Röhrich for permitting me to consult the typescript from which I have drawn much of the following information. His essay is far more inclusive and detailed than this commentary and the reader is urged to consult it for further information.

Related to the dragon are such creatures as the Basilisk, a sort of lion/griffin creature that can slay men with its glance or its breath; the Sphinx, a winged lion-like beast; and the sea serpents that reportedly inhabit every large body of water in the world.

The dragons that are opposed by the heroes of myth, epic, and folktale are invariably described as having eyes that glow like fire and breath of flames and venom. Moreover, they are frequently envisioned as polycephalic: The dragons of various *Märchen*, for example, are said to have seven heads; Hercules fights the seven-headed Hydra; Thraētona defeats the three-headed Azhi Dahāka; and the biblical dragon Leviathan is likewise seven-headed (Psalms 74:14).

No one can determine for sure just where the tradition of dragon-lore began, and the possibility of poly-genetic origins must be taken into account. Nevertheless, the dragon-traditions of the world share so many common traits that it is difficult to accept the theory of independent invention. One such trait is the association of the dragon with water. In China, where many scholars have looked for the origin of the dragon tradition, it has long been associated with flowing water and is even envisioned as the embodiment of the meandering river, a fact that may have contributed to the positive image the dragon enjoys in China. From India to the west, however—although likewise associated with the flow of water—the dragon is most often considered to be the monster that blocks the supply of water. The divinity or hero is called upon to slay the monster so that men may have access to the life-giving waters. Thus, Indra releases the rivers when he slays Vṛtra (Vedic Myth); in ancient Scandinavia the Midgard serpent embraces the waters that surround the whole world; in Bulgaria and Serbia prolonged droughts are attributed to a dragon that blocks the flow of water—he must be slain if the nation is to survive. See U. Duvoka, "Das Bild des Drachen im bulgarischen Märchen," *Fabula*, 11 (1970), 228–239.

The same configuration of motifs appears throughout European legendry and folktales. In this Grimm legend, for example, the dragon is thought to release the floods each time he vacates his mountain den, and in No. 219 he guards the well and grants access to the waters only when provided with daily rations of livestock. In other variants, the dragon demands the sacrifice of a lovely virgin before he will grant this access. This association of dragons with the flow of earthly waters thus represents one of the oldest mythological traditions known to man and its continuity from the earliest recorded myth and literature to the present is nothing less than remarkable.

Since dragons were believed to control access to the most precious substance on earth, viz., water, it is not surprising that they were also thought to be the guardians of treasure hoards. For example, the proverbial comparison "the miser lies on his wealth like a dragon on its treasure" has been recorded in classical antiquity (Martial, XII, 53, 3; Cicero, *Phädrus*, 4, 21). In Old Norse literature the kenning "dragon's den" was used frequently to indicate a treasure. Likewise the hero Sigurd/Siegfried of Teutonic tradition acquires a great treasure when he slays the dragon.

Dragons are also associated with cosmogonies and with other origin myths. At the beginning of all things, a dragon must be slain so that the universe can be created. Thus, in Babylonian myth the spirit of the great chaos—a dragon—has to be slain by Marduk before the cosmos can be formed. The body of the monster even furnishes the materials for heaven and earth. In ancient Egypt the sun god Re defeats the serpent of darkness, thus permitting the creation of the cosmos. Similarly at the founding of cities or institutions, dragons must be slain so that order can be established. The city of Alexandria, for example, was reportedly founded after a dragon had been slain at the site.

The gods are not the only dragon-slayers; the heroes of epics and legends must also defeat formidable dragons before their great reputations can be heralded throughout the lands. Sigurd, Lancelot, Iwein, Tristan, Wigalois, Dietrich, and Titurel are all medieval European heroes who are renowned dragon-slayers. And there are still other heroes who must do battle with the monsters in order to liberate captive maidens. Among these are Jason, who liberates Medea by slaying a monster; Theseus, who defeats the Minotaur and frees Ariadne; Perseus, who defeats the sea-dragon and wins Andromeda; and the heroes of countless fairy tales.

In Christian tradition the dragon has become the embodiment of evil and is one of the forms the Devil himself sometimes assumes. As such, he invariably represents a less formidable opponent than the dragons of myth and legend. St. Michael, who expels the dragon of evil from Heaven, and St. George, who slays the wicked dragon, are the best known of the saints reputed to have slain dragons. Hagiographic literature knows scores of others. See G. Frenken, *Wunder und Taten der Heiligen* (München, 1925), pp. 58–60, for a listing of such saints.

The English word "dragon" is a borrowing from the French form, which was in turn a borrowing from the Latin. Ultimately the word was acquired by the Romans from the Greek *drakon* 'the one with sharp glances.' Among other documented forms are such words as Old High German *traccho*, Old Norse *dreki*, Anglo-Saxon *draca*, and Old English *dreke*. This latter form yielded the modern English reflex "drake." Thus, the original Greek word entered the English language at two different times, producing both reflexes "drake" and "dragon." An older indigenous Germanic term is preserved in the tautological German form *Lindwurm*, both parts of the compound meaning 'serpent.' The combined form arose when the meaning of the word *lind* had been forgotten. The German form survived longest in remote Alpine regions where it has been recorded in the twentieth century.

See L. Mackensen, "Drache," *HdA* II, 364–404; E. Mogk, "Drache," Hoops *RL*, I, 485–486; C. -M. Barbeau, "The Old-World Dragon in America," *Proceedings of the 29th International Congress of Americanists* (1952), 115–122; D. Burkhart, "Zum Drachenkampfthema," *Zeitschrift für Balkanologie*, 5 (1967), 146–159; C. Gessner, *Schlangenbuch* (Zürich, 1589); R. Bauman, "A Sixteenth-Century Version of the Dragon-Slayer," *Fabula*, 11 (1970), 137–193; Grimm *DM* II, 573–576; P. Cassel, *Drachenkämpfe: Archäologische und mythologische Auslegungen* (Berlin, 1868); S. Erdész, "Drachentypen in der ungarischen Volksüberlieferung," *AE*, 20 (1971), 85–128; C. Gould, *Mythical Monsters* (London, 1886); M. Gutch, "Saint Martha and the Dragon," *F-L*, 63

(1952), 143–203; H. Du Bose, *The Dragon* (London, 1886); A. Haas, "Pommerische Drachen und Lindwurmsagen," *Pommerland*, 10 (1925), 21–24; E. S. Hartland, *The Legend of Perseus* (London, 1894–96); K. Michel, "Der Drache im Volksglauben," *HBV*, 23 (1924), 112–113; E. Siecke, *Indras Drachenkampf nach dem Rig-Veda* (Berlin, 1905); E. Siecke, *Drachenkämpfe: Untersuchungen zur indogermanischen Sagenkunde* (Leipzig, 1907); G. Róheim, "The Dragon and the Hero," *The American Imago*, 1 (1939–40), 40–69, 81–94; G. Róheim, *Drachen und Drachenkämpfer* (Berlin, 1912); E. Ploss, *Siegfried-Sigurd, der Drachenkämpfer* (Köln und Graz, 1966); M. W. de Visser, *The Dragon in China and Japan* (Amsterdam, 1913); G. E. Smith, *The Evolution of the Dragon* (Manchester and London, 1919); H. Dübi, "Von Drachen und Stollenwürmern," *SAV*, 37 (1939), 141–164; P. Deimel, "Der Drachenkampf bei den Babyloniern und in der heiligen Schrift," *Orientalia*, 5 (1922), 26–34; A. G. von Hamel, "Tristan's Combat with the Dragon," *Revue Celtique*, 41 (1924), 331–349; J. Tatlock, "The Dragons of Wessex and Wales," *Speculum*, 8 (1933), 223–235; Leo Winter, *Die deutschen Schatzsagen*, Diss. (Köln, 1925); K. Dalla Torre, "Die Drachensage im Alpengebiet," *Zeitschrift des österreichischen Alpenvereins* (1887), 208–226; W. Lange, *Der Drachenkampf*, Diss. (München, 1939); J. Fontenrose, *Python* (Berkeley and Los Angeles, 1959); T. Daly, *The Decadence of the Dragon* (Boston, 1961); H. Gehrts, *Das Märchen und das Opfer* (Bonn, 1967); E. Ingersoll, *Dragons and Dragon Lore* (New York, 1928; reprinted: Michigan, 1968); I. Lämmermann, *Drachendarstellungen in Literatur und Kunst des Mittelalters*, Diss. (Wien, 1968); H. Mode, *Fabeltiere und Dämonen*, 2nd ed. (Leipzig, 1977); L. Schmidt, "Sichelheld und Drachenzunge," *Fabula*, 1 (1958), 19–25; P. Zinck, "Drachen und Lindwurmsagen," *Mitteldeutsche Blätter für Volkskunde*, 6 (1931), 177–193, 221–229; C. Lecouteux, "Der Drache," *Zeitschrift für deutsches Altertum*, 108 (1979), 13–31.

LEGEND NO. 218. Winkelried is a legendary Swiss national hero second only to William Tell in popularity among the Swiss. He is said to have been a hero in the famous Battle of Sempach (July 9, 1386) where the Swiss preserved their independence with a resounding victory over the Austrians.

There is no evidence that such a man ever actually existed. The story of his fateful encounter with the dragon is a migratory legend that attached itself to his heroic personage. See the commentary to No. 217. See also E. Theuner, "Die Schlacht bei Sempach und die Sage von Winkelried," *Preußisches Jahrbuch*, 58 (1886), 283–303; O. Kleißner, *Die Quellen zur Sempacher Schlacht und die Winkelriedsage* (Göttingen, 1873); J. Bürkli, *Der wahre Winkelried* (Zürich, 1886).

LEGEND NO. 219. See the commentary to No. 217 in which I call attention to the old and widespread motif of the dragon blocking access to water and of its demands for offerings.

LEGEND NO. 220. The names of the heroes of this legend indicate an antiquity greater than the sources the Grimms used. Such supposed antiquity has led a number of scholars to speculate that this legend is a euhemerized version of a Dioscuric myth. For a survey of this scholarship see D. Ward, *The Divine Twins: An Indo-European Myth in Germanic Antiquity* (Berkeley and

Los Angeles, 1968). A pair of brothers is also associated frequently with the *Märchen* of the dragon slayer (AT 300), and with the tale of the Two Brothers (AT 303). See K. Ranke, *Die zwei Bruder: Ein Studie zur vergleichenden Märchenforschung*, FFC 114 (Helsinki, 1934). See also H. Gehrts, *Das Märchen und das Opfer* (Bonn, 1967).

LEGEND NO. 221. This legend is remarkable in that it not only tells of a mythical serpent queen, it tells of her having control over the fertility and prosperity of the farm and farm animals. It is tempting to infer that this legend represents the survival of an ancient Germanic myth of a serpent cult, but there is precious little corroborating evidence to support such an inference. Although snake cults are found in almost every part of the world—and for Europe they are especially well documented in the Baltic region—there is very little evidence of such having existed among Germanic peoples.

However, in German folk belief there is a widespread notion that snakes can bring good fortune, that they are guardians of house and home, and that they can even be the alter egos of the inhabitants—that is, if harm befalls the snake harm can befall a member of the household. This relationship is reflected in Grimm *Märchen* No. 105. See B-P, II, 459–464.

The fact that the serpent queen gives her crown to the maiden is more than a mere symbol of good will. The serpent's crown was considered to be one of the more powerful items of magic in the world. It or the jewel set within it guaranteed fertility, prosperity, wealth, and even immortality.

See E. Hoffmann-Krayer, "Schlange," *HdA* VII, 1114–1196; C. Olbrich, "Das Milchtrinken der Schlangen," *MSGV*, 6 (1904), 67–72; W. D. Hand, "Children and Snakes," *Krzyzanowski Festschrift* (1968), 889–900; J. B. Deane, *The Worship of the Serpent Throughout the World* (London, 1833); J. Fergusson, *Tree and Serpent Worship* (London, 1868); C. S. Wake, *The Sun and the Serpent* (London, 1905).

LEGEND NO. 222. Osel Mountain is today called Hessel Mountain *(Hesselberg)*. It is an impressive peak overlooking the Sulzach River just a few miles east of Dinkelsbühl. This legend shows the clear interrelationship of legends of the White Woman, the Castle Maiden, and the Serpent Maiden. The ring of keys is a concrete symbol of the maiden's need to be released from her ghostly existence. See Nos. 10–13 and commentaries.

LEGEND NO. 223. The Wasgau is the former name of the Vogesen Mountains of Alsace (known in English and French as the Vosges Mountains). The castle of Nothweiler lies right on what is today the Franco-German border north of Straßburg. This is also a legend in which the three related spirits, the White Woman, the Castle Maiden, and the Serpent Maiden, are combined into a single figure. See Nos. 10–13 and commentaries.

LEGEND NO. 224. This legend combines the motif of the Castle Maiden (White Woman, etc.) with the theme of the Redeemer in the cradle, a motif which offers graphic and concrete evidence of the great length of time the Poor Soul must wander the earth waiting for deliverance. See F. Ranke, *Der Erlöser in der Wiege* (München, 1911). See also No. 108 and commentary.

LEGEND NO. 225. Although there are countless beliefs regarding sneezing, the dangers it poses, and the incantations needed to counteract such forces, this legend is only indirectly associated with this complex of beliefs. The sneeze here represents the occasion for the utterance "God bless you!" which, more or less by chance, is the formula that—if repeated three times—releases the Poor Soul from its torment. However, there are a number of legends in which the spirit's presence can be perceived because it sneezes. See P. Sartori, "Niesen," *HdA* VI, 1072–1083.

LEGEND NO. 226. See the commentary to No. 225.

LEGEND NO. 227. For the sneezing formula as a charm of deliverance, see the commentary to No. 225. For spirits who appear at midday, see Nos. 7, 11, 12, 229, and their commentaries.

LEGEND NO. 228. Sorge today lies just over the border to East Germany in the Harz Mountains. Here, the Castle Maiden continues to haunt the area long after the ruins of the castle have disappeared. See Nos. 10–13.

LEGEND NO. 229. Legends frequently tell of unusually severe punishment for breaches of behavioral norms. They thus serve as stern warning to children as well as others and are an important device in the socialization process. Although such behavioral models clearly contribute to social cohesion, they certainly inhibit the freedom of the individual.

It is interesting that this spirit appears at noon rather than at midnight. Although most hauntings occur at midnight, the witching hour, there are spirits who prefer midday. This concept, known in Rome as the *meridianus daemon*, probably originated in the Near East, spreading to Rome and the Mediterranean and into France and Germany.

See G. Jungbauer, "Mittagsgespenst," *HdA* VI, 414–418; K. Haberland, "Die Mittagsstunde als Geisterstunde," *Zeitschrift für Völkerpsychologie*, 13 (1882), 310–318; O. Schell, "Mittagsdämon, Mittagszauber," *ZVRhWV*, 13 (1916), 262–265; D. Grau, *Das Mittagsgespenst* (Siegburg, 1966).

LEGEND NO. 230. This legend is essentially etiological in that it explains the origin of a strange rock formation on the cliff. But it is also a warning to children to honor their fathers and mothers. Moreover, it is an effective illustration of the beliefs regarding the power of the spoken word, especially when uttered in the form of a curse. When a curse is uttered in a legend it is invariably fulfilled. See K. Beth, "Fluch," *HdA* II, 1636–1652. See also No. 231.

LEGEND NO. 231. In this legend the transgression of the fourth commandment is punished in an unusually severe manner. It serves not only as a warning to children to honor their fathers and mothers but also as an illustration that one should not foolishly utter a curse that one will later regret, for the power of the spoken word is believed to be irreversible. See the commentary to No. 230.

The inclusion of the exact details, the date of the boy's death, the names of the people living in the house at the time the legend was recorded, the imprints of his feet that were left behind, etc., is typical of the style of narration of legends as it lends credence to the factual nature of the account. Legends are invariably told as factual accounts, and there are many devices that are used to intensify the credibility of the stories.

LEGEND NO. 232.   This legend is of particular significance to folklorists for a number of reasons, not the least of which is the fact that one early version has preserved part of the text of the dance song (dance ballad? see below) to which the participants allegedly danced. The first documentation of the event, by the monk Lambert of Hersfeld in 1075, is nearly contemporaneous to the event itself, which is said to have occurred in the village of Kolbeck (Kölbigk) during the reign of Henry II, 1002–1024 (see the commentary to No. 482). Lambert tells of one of his monks who had participated in the infamous dance of "Collebecce" and as a result suffered from chronic and severe tremors.

News of the event disseminated rapidly through all of Europe. Beggars and vagabonds soon claimed to have been participants in the event and carried beggars' letters in Latin attesting to this. The content of one such letter is related by William of Malmesbury in his *Gesta regum Anglorum* of 1140. That the document cited by him dates from the eleventh century is attested to by the fact that it mentions the son and daughter of the priest of Kolbeck—something that would not have been possible after the Gregorian reforms (ca. 1075, see No. 489 and its commentary). In later versions, as is the case here, the daughter was replaced by the sexton's sister.

The story became a favorite text for priests to read from the pulpit and it is accordingly found in many exempla (F. Tubach, *Index Exemplorum*, No. 1419; E. Rehermann, *Das Predigtexempel*, 156, twelve variants). Especially interesting is a version written by the French church historian Ordericus Vitalis, ca. 1130, in which he quotes the following words as part of the song that was supposed to have been sung by the participants as they danced:

> Equitabat Bovo per silvam frondosam
> Ducebat sibi Merswinden formosam.
> Quid stamus? Cur non imus?

> 'Bovo rode through the forest green
> Led by Merswind the Beautiful.
> Why are we standing here? Why don't we go?'

Folksong scholars have long sought to unravel the mystery of this song and have speculated that it is a stanza from an early dance ballad. In a recent monograph devoted to the topic, Ernst Erich Metzner (*Zur frühesten Geschichte der europäischen Balladendichtung. Der Tanz von Kölbigk* [Frankfurt, 1972]) has linked the text to the cycle of ballads associated with Dietrich von Bern (Theodoric the Great). Metzner also surveys the literature on the topic. See also D. Ward, "The Origin of the Ballad: Urban Setting or Rural Setting?" in P. Conroy (ed.), *Ballads and Ballad Research* (Seattle, 1978), 46–52; Petzoldt *HS* I, Nr. 58 and the notes on 356.

The dance described in this legend may have been an actual event, viz., one of the famous dance epidemics that swept Europe in the Middle Ages. Hypnotized by the rhythms of the music and their own movements, dancers would fall into a deep trance and continue to dance for days until they dropped from complete exhaustion. See A. Martin, "Geschichte der Tanz-krankheit in Deutschland," *ZsfVk*, 24 (1914), 113–134, 225–239.

LEGEND NO. 233. This legend as well as the preceding ones deals with blasphemy and retribution, or crime and punishment—one of the largest categories of folk legends. Such stories provided graphic illustrations of what the results of blasphemous acts and sins could be and thus served as behavioral models. One of the most blasphemous sins in the eyes of Christian villagers was defiling the Holy Sabbath by working on that day.

See W. Treutlein, *Das Arbeitsverbot im deutschen Volksglauben* (Bühl, 1932); L. Röhrich, "Tabus in Volksbräuchen, Sagen und Märchen," in H. Lederer and J. Seyppel (eds.), *Festschrift für Werner Neuse* (Berlin, 1967), 8–23.

LEGEND NO. 234. This legend is widely known in Innsbruck where the rocky crag called Frau Hütt towers above the north side of the Inn Valley. As the legend indicates, children are still warned not to waste bread and food or they will suffer the same fate as Mother Hütt. At one time bread was considered to be a nearly sacred substance and defiling it in any way—letting it get moldy, throwing it away, using it for purposes other than food, etc.—was considered serious blasphemy. Indeed the defiling of the bread represents a whole category of European folk legends.

See Nos. 235–241 and commentaries. Cf. No. 93 where there is blasphemy related to milk and cheese. See also F. Eckstein, "Brot," *HdA* I, 1590–1659; M. Währen, *Unser täglich Brot in deutscher Geschichte und im Volksbrauch* (Bern, 1951); M. Währen, *Brot seit Jahrtausenden* (Bern, 1953); F. Binder, *Die Brotnahrung: Auswahl-Bibliographie zu ihrer Geschichte und Bedeutung* (Ulm, 1973); B. Schnittger, "Brot," in Hoops *RL*, I, 330–331.

LEGEND NO. 235. Regarding the defiling of bread, see the commentary to No. 234.

LEGEND NO. 236. The region in which this legend occurred is today part of Czechoslovakia. Regarding the defiling of bread, see the commentary to No. 234. Entire cities and castles sinking from sight as punishment for sins is a widespread motif in legends. See, for example, Nos. 112, 132, and 239–240.

LEGEND NO. 237. The trampled bread producing blood is evidently a Christian motif equating the bread with the Eucharistic host that represents the body of Christ. Injuring the bread is tantamount to injuring the divinity. Whether pre-Christian concepts of a grain divinity are reflected in this notion can no longer be established with any degree of certainty. The German folklorist Wilhelm Mannhardt assembled a great deal of evidence in support of his theory that the Germans worshipped a divinity of the grain in pre-Christian times and that survivals of this practice can still be perceived in beliefs, customs, and legends.

See W. Mannhardt, *Die Korndämonen* (Berlin, 1868). See also the commentaries to No. 234 and especially No. 90.

LEGEND NO. 238.  Widespread in German legends is the theme that if the dead are not buried in proper fashion they will become restless spirits. However, linking this motif with the defiling of bread is not a common occurrence in legendry.

LEGEND NO. 239.  Tales of the destruction of cities, countries, castles, convents, etc., because of the sinful ways of the inhabitants (Sodom and Gomorrah) are among the oldest and most familiar legends known to man. There are essentially three main categories of such legends: (1) the mythological traditions of the great world flood after which the world had a new beginning; (2) the destruction through the wrath of a divinity by means of fire, flood, earthquakes, and the like; (3) the case of cities sinking out of sight—in many cases being replaced by a lake, the sea, or marshes. In German legends this third category is the most popular and it is the one with which we are dealing here. In the Will-Erich Peuckert Archives in Freiburg, Germany, there are literally thousands of legends excerpted under the heading *versunken*, indicating that this is one of the most frequently collected of all legend types.

Sunken cities sometimes reappear on certain days of the year, or once every hundred years (Brigadoon), but they are doomed to sink again beneath the surface. The cities invariably sink because of the sins of the inhabitants, which include such things as defiling bread, greed, failure to feed the starving, vanity, sexual promiscuity, and the like. Stavoren was probably never a prosperous city as this legend indicates, but it does indeed exist. It is a tiny community of a few houses surrounding a lighthouse on the south side of the Zuyder Zee in the Netherlands.

There are a number of similar legendary cities along the Baltic and the North Seas: Arkona, Rethra, and the most famous of all, Vineta. The latter evidently comes from the name of Jumneta, the name of a castle that once stood on the island of Wollin off the Pomeranian coast. It was destroyed by the Danes in 1098, and its disappearance evidently contributed to the legend.

See W. Anderson, "Sintflut," *HdA* VIII, 6–11; W.-E. Peuckert, "Sodom und Gomorrha," *HdA* VIII, 21–25; R. Andree, *Die Flutsagen* (Braunschweig, 1891); G. Gerland, *Der Mythos von der Sintflut* (Bonn, 1912); F. Schmarsel, *Die Sage von der untergegangenen Stadt*, Diss., Kiel, 1913 (published: Berlin, 1913); J. Riem, *Die Sintflut in Sage und Wissenschaft* (Hamburg, 1925); K. Schuchhardt, *Arkona, Rethra, Vineta* (Berlin, 1926); A. Hofmeister, "Die Vineta-Frage," *Monatsblatt der Gesellschaft für Pommersche Geschichte und Altertumskunde*, 46 (1932); H. Henning, *Von rätselhaften Ländern: Versunkene Stätten der Geschichte* (München, 1925); O. von Holzhausen, "Eine fränkische Vineta," *Fränkische Heimat*, 5 (1926), 442–443; A. Kettner, "Das schlesische Vineta," *Die Heimat*, 2 (1923), 19–21; F. Erfurt, "De sage von het verval van de stad Stavoren," *Nederl. Tidscrift f. Volkskunde*, 42 (1938), 50–56; F. Gebhardt, "Das versunkene Schloß," *Mainbote*, 15 (1930), 38–39; A. Burkhardt, *Sagen und Märchen vom Ostseerand* (Rostock, 1965); R. Hennig, "Die Lösung des Vineta-problems," *Pommerland*, 10 (1925), 260. W. Maurer has recently written an excellent monographic essay on sunken cities—"German Sunken City Legends," *Fabula*, 17 (1976), 189–214. See also the commentary to No. 93.

LEGEND NO. 240.  See the commentary to No. 239. The motif of the ring recovered from the fish's stomach is especially popular in Germany due to its inclusion in Schiller's ballad, "Der Ring von Polycrates," and in the medieval verse epic *Gregorius auf dem Steine* (ca. 1188) by Hartmann von Aue (motif here is a key instead of a ring). It is, however, an ancient and widespread motif that may have originated in India. It is spread throughout the Middle East, occurs in rabbinical literature, and in folktales. It is retold by Paulus Diaconus in his *History of the Bishops of Metz*.

See A. Wünsche, "Die Sage vom Ring des Polycrates in der Weltliteratur," *Allgemeine Zeitung München* (Beilage), Nos. 179, 180, 185, 188 (1893); R. Köhler, *Kleinere Schriften*, II, 209; J. Künzig, "Der im Fischbauch wiedergefundene Ring in Sage, Legende, Märchen und Lied," *Volkskundliche Gaben: John Meier Festschrift* (Berlin, 1934), 85–103.

LEGEND NO. 241. These are actually four separate legends that the Grimms excerpted from four different sources and presented here as a unit, a practice which folklorists of today would frown upon. Each of the narratives shares not only the motif of the transformation of the bread to stone, but also the theme of the need to show charity to the poor and starving. The motif of bread turning to stone doubtless came about through the attempt to give concrete representation to the words Christ is reported to have delivered in his Sermon on the Mount: "Or what man is there of you, whom if his son ask bread, will he give him a stone" (Matthew 7:10).

The theme of bread as a sacred substance that should not be defiled is also stressed in these narratives. See the commentary to No. 234.

St. Kastulus is not one of the better known saints in Germany. There are, to my knowledge, only two churches devoted to him in all of Germany. He was the treasurer of Emperor Diocletian who ruled from A.D. 284 to 305. An early convert to Christianity, Kastulus offered asylum to persecuted Christians in his own home. He was subsequently arrested and—according to the legend—buried alive. His relics were later brought to Moosburg in Bavaria, and in 1604 they were moved to the church in Landshut.

LEGEND NO. 242. Hatto I was Archbishop of Mainz from 891 to 913. He was a very powerful figure in the political scene of his day and legends show him in a very negative light (see Nos. 468 and 469 and their commentaries).

The tower in the legend was built on an island in the Rhine near Bingen, and it still stands there today. In medieval times its function was that of a toll gate, exacting fees from ships that wanted to pass. Accordingly it was called *Mautturm* 'toll tower' (Old High German *mût* 'toll'). The word *maut*, however, was gradually replaced in German by the word *Zoll* 'toll.' The original meaning of *maut* was gradually forgotten, and it became, via the process of folk etymology, *Mausturm* 'Mouse Tower.' This story was thus invented—on the model of other mouse legends then extant—to explain the name. A similar legend had earlier been recorded by Thietmar von Merseburg (975–1018) in his *Chronicon* (Bk. 6, cap. 49).

Leander Petzoldt (*HS* I, 346–347) suggests that the mice are thought to be the souls of the victims of Hatto's holocaust and thus represent an example of the human soul in mouse form, a theme known in other legends (see Nos. 248 and 433 and their commentaries).

This legend achieved widespread popularity, and it was soon told in a number of European lands about various despotic rulers. Variants have been recorded in Austria, France, England, Denmark, Poland, and Russia.

See F. Liebrecht, "Die Sage vom Mäuseturm," in F. Liebrecht, *Zur Volkskunde: Alte und neue Aufsätze* (Heilbronn, 1879), 1–16; S. Feist, "Die Sage vom Binger Mäuseturm," *Zeitschrift für den deutschen Unterricht,* 9 (1895), 505–511; R.-D. Kluge, "Die Sage von Bischof Hattos Mäusetod im alten Russland," *Mainzer Almanach* (1968), 142–154; W. Mannhardt, "Zur Sage vom Mäuseturm," *Zeitschrift für deutsche Mythologie,* 3 (1855), 307–320; B. Beckmann, *Von Mäusen und Menschen: Die hoch- und spätmittelalterlichen Mäusesagen* (Bremgarten, 1974). Rehermann (*Das Predigtexempel,* 154) lists nine variants from exempla literature.

LEGEND NO. 243.   Isolated places, especially where there are breaks in the earth's surface leading underground—ravines, ponds, lakes, caves, and especially marshes where people can scarcely walk (see No. 185 and commentary)—are considered to be the haunts of ghosts and other spooks. Legends about such places frequently develop secondarily to provide causes for the numinous atmosphere that seems to prevail at such sites.

It is possible that the name *Bubenried* 'Boys' Marsh' did not come from the legend, but rather the legend came from the name (see commentary to No. 242). The German folklorist Will-Erich Peuckert (*Sagen: Geburt und Anwort der mythischen Welt* [Berlin, 1965]) has correctly noted that the numinous quality of the impression such places have on the human soul belongs to a primary mythological realm of human experience.

See also Sigmund Freud, "Das Unheimliche," *Imago,* 5 (1919), 297–310; Rudolf Otto, *The Idea of the Holy* (London and New York, 1939), a translation of *Das Heilige,* 30th ed. (München, 1936); R. Beitl, *Im Sagenwald* (Feldkirch, 1963).

LEGEND NO. 244.   The fact that the attempt to explain names produces legends (see Nos. 242–243) has long been noted. Indeed, the frequency of this occurrence lends support to Friedrich Max Müller's highly disputed contention that myths are *nomina* and not *numina* (see his essay "Comparative Mythology," reprinted in R. Dorson, *Peasant Customs and Savage Myths* [London, 1968], II, 67–119). According to Müller, the first myths were not about divine forces and beings, but rather about enigmatic names, phrases, and metaphors. That such linguistic elements indeed generate narratives cannot be disputed.

LEGEND NO. 245.   The story of the Pied Piper of Hameln was first made available to the English reader early in the seventeenth century by Richard Verstegan in his *A Restitution of Decayed Intelligence* (Antwerp: Robert Bruney, 1605; second printing, London: John Norton, 1634). Indeed, it is from this account that we have the name "Pied Piper":

> There came into the town of Hamel in the countrey of Brunswyc an od kynd of compagnion, who the fantastical cote which hee wore beeing wrought with sundry colours, was called the pyed pyper; for a pyper hee was, besydes his other qualities.

The story continues in the familiar pattern of the piper ridding the town of its plague of rats:

> . . .the townsmen . . . offred him far lesse then hee lookt for: but hee therewith discontented, said hee would haue his ful recompense according to his bargain . . . wherevpon he betakes him again to his pype, and going through the streets as before, was followed of a number of boyes out of the gates of the citie, and coming to a hil, there opened in the syde thereof a wyde hole, into the which himself and all the children beeing in number one hundred and thirty, did enter.

The Grimms fashioned their own version of the narrative by combining materials from a variety of sources. Curiously enough, to my knowledge, their version has never before been translated into English, although it together with Verstegan's account did form the basis for Robert Browning's famous poem on the topic. It was also made available to the English-speaking world in Andrew Lang's translation of a nineteenth-century French adaptation by Charles Marelles (A. Lang, *The Red Fairy Book* [London, 1890]). The story has subsequently been adapted in countless children's books, films, radio dramas, etc.

For all its fantasy, the legend evidently has a kernel of truth. The documented evidence points to an event that happened on June 26 in 1284—the date almost never varies in any of the chronicles and manuscripts reporting the event. The earliest account is a manuscript found in nearby Lüneburg dating circa 1435. However, it was copied from a source dated 1370.

This and other early versions of the legend report nothing of a plague of rats or any successful attempt to rid the town of such. Instead, they merely report that someone marched into town on June 26 (St. John and Paul's Day) in 1284 and marched away with 150 of the town's children.

The motif of the ratcatcher who rids the town of a plague of rats or other vermin (cf. St. Patrick in Ireland, etc.) is a legend in its own right (see Petzoldt *DVS*, Nos. 75–79) and was first appended to the Hameln story in the Zimmer Chronicles of 1557. The various sources for the legend (manuscripts, chronicles, stained-glass windows, inscriptions, oral tradition) have been compiled into a single volume by H. Dobbertin, *Quellensammlung zur Hamelner Rattenfängersage* (Göttingen, 1970).

There have been countless attempts to solve the riddle of what particular historical event might have given rise to the legend. Among them are the following: There was a battle at Sedemünde in the year 1260 in which many of the young men of the town of Hameln were lost. Moreover, a children's crusade moved through the area in the thirteenth century and it is conceivable that many of the children of Hameln were recruited for it. There is furthermore documentation of a dance epidemic (St. Vitus' dance; see the commentary to No. 232) having struck the area in the Middle Ages. There is also a report of a number of Hameln families being recruited to colonize East Prussia and of their being lost at sea en route. Others have speculated that floods, plagues, ritual murder/suicide (cf. Jonestown, Guyana, 1978) may have given rise to the legend.

The most convincing of all such attempts was made by W. Wann (*Die Lösung der Hamelner Rattenfängersage*, Diss. [Würzburg, 1949]). Wann showed that Bishop Bruno of Olmütz had sent emissaries into Lower Saxony in the thirteenth century to recruit families to colonize his Bohemian diocese. A comparison of city records of Hameln and Olmütz reveals a startling agreement in the family names recorded in each place, indicating that Hameln was one of the places where successful recruiting had taken place. Thus, if Wann is correct, a number of Hameln families marched off in the thirteenth century never to return.

See also H. Spanuth, *Der Rattenfänger von Hameln* (Hameln, 1951). Spanuth found the Lüneburg MS in 1936. H. Dobbertin, *Wohin zogen die Hämelschen Kinder?* (Hildesheim, 1955); W. Woeller, "Zur Entstehung und Entwicklung der Sage vom Rattenfänger von Hameln," *ZfdPh*, 80 (1961), 180–206.

LEGEND NO. 246.   The legend of the ratcatcher existed prior to and separate from the pied piper story of Hameln. It is related to such famous accounts as St. Patrick's driving the snakes from Ireland. See the commentaries to Nos. 245 and 247.

LEGEND NO. 247.   The man who charms the snakes, ridding the land of them, only to fall victim himself to the snake queen or king is a favorite legend in German-speaking areas. It is especially well represented in Bavaria, but it is also known in Lower Saxony and Mecklenburg. The snake queen or king is frequently reported to be a white snake, sometimes with a crown. It is the last snake to be charmed and invariably takes the snake charmer with it into the flames (pit, water, etc.). "The snakes can be driven out in this manner, but someone will have to sacrifice himself in the process" is the way a legend from Gottschee puts it (A. Hauffen, *Die deutsche Sprachinsel Gottschee* [Graz, 1895], 98–99).

The legend is a very old one, having early been recorded in all its detail in the narrative that forms the framework to the great Sanskrit epic, the Mahābhārata.

Lutz Röhrich investigated the variants of this legend and came to the startling conclusion that the contemporary legends represent a more primitive tradition than the Sanskrit epic. This finding is of great theoretical import for comparative studies, for Röhrich has shown convincingly that the dates when a tradition was recorded have very little to do with age and relative chronology. See L. Röhrich, "Die Sage vom Schlangenbann," in F. Harkort *et al.* (eds.), *Volksüberlieferung: Festschrift für Kurt Ranke* (Göttingen, 1968).

See also W. Porzig, *Das Schlangenopfer, aus dem Sanskrit übersetzt* (Leipzig, 1924), and Rehermann *Predigtexempel*, 155, for a variant from exempla literature. See also Petzoldt *DVS*, Nos. 48–50 and their commentaries.

LEGEND NO. 248.   The separable soul in the form of a mouse was first set down in the eighth century by Paulus Diaconus (see No. 433). The notion of a separable soul is certainly very old and is encountered in nearly every culture on earth. It probably arose independently in various places because of the universality of the dream experience. In regard to the *Trud* (Nightmare) mentioned at the end of the legend, see the commentary to No. 81. See also "Albmaus," *HdS*, 272–276.

LEGEND NO. 249.   The girls in this legend are thought to be Nightmares, that is, spirits who invade the bedrooms of their victims and weigh upon their chests until they have pressed the very life force from their bodies (see No. 81 and its commentary). Noteworthy here is the belief that only the souls, which leave the girls' bodies as puffs of smoke, are capable of performing this act.

In this legend the girls are not the innocent victims of demonic forces. With the help of a magic incantation, they seek actively to drive their souls from their bodies so they might plague the farm youth. The implication in this and similar stories is that they have acquired such powers by trafficking with the Devil or other demonic forces.

LEGEND NO. 250.   This legend deals with the ancient notion of the separable soul. Many peoples of the world share the belief that the soul has the ability to leave the body in the form of an animal, a puff of smoke, a feather, or the like. The body of the person in such a state is as if dead, and if the soul cannot find its way back the subject will not revive. Often the person whose soul goes wandering is thought to be a Nightmare who torments people in their sleep.

In this legend, there is no mention of what the soul of the girl is up to during its wanderings. However, the cat is a favorite alter ego of witches, and the implication is that she is up to no good. A hollow tree is a favorite place for such spirits to hide their bodies when the soul goes on its wanderings.

See O. Lauffer, "Geister im Baum," in *Volkskundliche Gaben: John Meier Festschrift* (Berlin and Leipzig, 1934), 104–120; O. Tobler, *Die Epiphanie der Seele in deutscher Volkssage* (Kiel, 1911); H. Boesebeck, "Verwünschung und Erlösung des Menschen in der deutschen Volkssage der Gegenwart," *NdZsV*, 5 (1927), 88ff, and 6 (1928), 15ff; L. Laistner, *Das Rätsel der Sphinx*, 2 vols. (Berlin, 1889); I. Paulson, "Swedish Contributions to the Study of Primitive Soul-Conceptions," *Ethnos*, 19 (1954), 157–167; A. Schaefer, *Die Verwandlung der menschlichen Gestalt* (Darmstadt, 1905); H. Lixfeld, "Die Guntramsage (AT 1645A)," *Fabula*, 13 (1972), 60–107.

LEGEND NO. 251.   The Grimms have combined three different legends in this narrative, all of them dealing with witches. We have already seen that, although they possess human attributes, many of the creatures of legendry—dwarfs, Water Nixies, Wild Men, and the like—are nonhuman. Moreover, they live in a realm or dimension separate from the human. By contrast, the witches of legendry are mortal human beings who have acquired superhuman characteristics. Others who fit this category are warlocks, sorcerers, signers of Devil pacts, wandering scholars, and, in European folk imagination, Free Masons. Curiously, the witch of the fairy tale, for instance in Hänsel and Gretel, is a different kind of creature. She is a demon who lives alone in the forest and likes to eat children. In the legend she is a member of the human community, most frequently of an agricultural village.

The notion of women having occult powers is certainly older than Christianity, but the idea of the maleficent woman who gets her supernatural powers from the Devil is one that developed in Christian times. It was believed that if a woman wanted to acquire those powers, she had to enter into a compact with the Devil, engage in sexual intercourse with him, and be initiated at one of the wild orgies known as witches' sabbaths. These were believed to be staged on mountaintops at midnight during certain nights of the year, the eve of St. Walpurgis' Day (May 1) being one of the favorite times and, of course, All Hallows' Eve (October 31) being another. Virtually every community in Germany has a hill in its vicinity where the witches would supposedly convene periodically to engage in their disgusting orgies. After cohabiting with the Devil, the initiate would bear the mark of the Devil's bite, the *stigma diaboli*, for the remainder of her life, and such marks—any blemish or birthmark would do—were considered positive proof of guilt at witchcraft trials.

With the help of magic potions witches could fly on their poles or broomsticks. They were also believed to be able to transform themselves into rabbits, cats, moths, bats, or any animal they so chose. They could also supposedly direct their maleficent magic at their neighbors—and their victims would then suffer the most harm where they were most vulnerable. In agricultural villages, where witches were believed to be especially active, it was thought that they could destroy crops through ice, frost, or hail, cause milk-producing animals to drop dead, magically steal the milk and butterfat from cows, cause sexual impotency in man and beast, and engage in all kinds of havoc. Indeed, the English word "butterfly" appears to derive from the notion that a witch could change herself into such a creature to steal milk from cows. The German word *Schmetterling* (a borrowing from the Slavic *smetana* 'butterfat,' 'cream') has the same origin.

The German word for witch is *Hexe*, and as early as the ninth century it was glossed as *hagazussa* 'hedge or fence rider.' The Old Norse word for witch, *tunridha*, has the same meaning and refers to the witch's ability to fly.

The origins and development of the complex of beliefs about witches are difficult to trace. It is certain that indigenous concepts of women practitioners of magic (Old Norse *seiðr* 'witchcraft') became combined with the learned notions of sorcery and of demon summoning which trace their origins back to classical antiquity. This bipartite nature of the belief in witches continued through the centuries; scholarly treatises existed side by side with the beliefs of the masses. Although the two traditions overlapped to a large degree, they were never identical. Thus, the folk legend remains the very best source for folk notions about witches and must be used—even today—to supplement the older written sources.

In a marvelous bibliography (cited below) Joseph Hansen assembled the titles of the hundreds of learned treatises that appeared in the Middle Ages. Hansen also compiled a total of 740 papal bulls, issued between the years 1258 and 1526, that were directed at the practice of sorcery and witchcraft. These bulls had little effect in German-speaking areas until Pope Innocent VIII issued the papal bull of December 5, 1484, that unleashed the Inquisition in Germany and made the practices of sorcerers and witches its main target.

The bull gave the theologians Jakob Sprenger and Heinrich Institoris the authority to carry out trials against heretics and against those who sold their souls to the Devil in exchange for diabolic power. On the basis of the many learned writings of their predecessors, these two men compiled the most complete treatise on witchcraft up to that time: *Malleus maleficarum* 'The Witches' Hammer' (1487). The novelty of this treatise was its focus on the maleficence of women. Although speculation about the malevolence of village witches had been around for a long time, the *Malleus maleficarum* saw the danger almost exclusively in women. The age of the witch-hunt began.

The literature on the topic of witches and witchcraft is vast; there are literally thousands of titles. I have thus chosen relatively few of the total number to include here: W. H. D. Adams, *Witch, Warlock, and Magician* (Ann Arbor, 1971, repr. of 1889 ed.); C. Alderman, *A Cauldron of Witches: The Story of Witchcraft* (New York, 1971); B. Alver, *Heksetro og Trolldom* (Bergen, 1971); H. Auhofer, *Der Hexenwahn der Gegenwart* (Stuttgart, 1965); T. Aylesworth, *Servants of the Devil* (Reading, Mass., 1970); J. Caro Baroja, *The World of Witches* (Chicago, 1964); K. Baschwitz, *Hexen und Hexenprozesse* (München 1963); H. Biedermann, *Hexen: Auf den Spuren eines Phänomens* (Graz, 1974); L. R. Booker, *Ghosts and Witches of Martin County* (Williamston, N.C., 1971); R. L. Brown, *A Book of Witchcraft* (New York, 1971); R. Byrne, *Witchcraft in Ireland* (Cork, 1967, 3rd ed. 1973); R. Cavendish, *The Black Arts* (New York, 1967); W. B. Crow, *A History of Magic, Witchcraft, and Occultism* (London, 1972); H. Döbler, *Hexenwahn: Die Geschichte einer Verfolgung* (München, 1977); E. Fehrle, *Zauber und Segen* (Jena, 1926); G. B. Gardner, *Witchcraft Today* (London, 1954); H. Haag, *Teufelsglaube* (Tübingen, 1974); P. Haining, *The Anatomy of Witchcraft* (New York, 1972); C. Hansen, *Witchcraft at Salem* (London, 1970); J. Hansen, *Quellen und Untersuchungen zur Geschichte des Hexenwahns und der Hexenverfolgung im Mittelalter* (Bonn, 1901); R. Hart, *Witchcraft* (London, 1971); C. Hole, *A Mirror of Witchcraft* (London, 1957); C. Honegger, *Die Hexen der Neuzeit* (Frankfurt, 1978); G. L. Kittredge, *Witchcraft in Old and New England* (Cambridge, 1929); A. C. Kors and E. Peters, *Witchcraft in Europe, 1100–1700* (Philadelphia, 1972); J. Kruse, *Hexen unter uns: Magie und Zauberglaube in unserer Zeit* (Hamburg, 1961); O. Lauffer, "Die Hexe als Zaunreiterin," *Volkskundliche Ernte: Festschrift für Hugo Hepding* (Giessen, 1938), 114–130; H. C. Lea, *Materials Toward a History of Witchcraft* (New York, 1957); A. Macfarlane, *Witchcraft in Tudor and Stuart England* (New York, 1970); M. Summers (trans. and editor), *Malleus Malificarum* (London, 1928); E. Maple, *The Dark World of Witches* (London, 1962); J. Michelet, *La sorcière* (Paris, 1952); E. Mudrak, *Grundlagen des Hexenwahns* (Leipzig, 1936); M. A. Murray, *The God of the Witches*, 4th ed. (Oxford, 1973); M. A. Murray, *The Witch-Cult in Western Europe*, 4th ed. (Oxford, 1971); V. Newall, *The Encyclopedia of Witchcraft and Magic* (London, 1974); V. Newall, *The Witch Figure: Katharine Briggs Festschrift* (London, 1973); L. Paine, *Witches in Fact and Fantasy* (London, 1971); W.-E. Peuckert, *Pansophie: Ein Versuch zur Geschichte der weißen und schwarzen Magie*, 2nd rev. ed. (Berlin, 1956); R. H. Robbins, *The Encyclopedia of Witchcraft and Demonology* (New York, 1959); B. Rosen, *Witchcraft* (London, 1969); A. Runeberg, *Witches, Demons, and Fertility Magic* (Helsingfors, 1947); J. B. Russell, *Witchcraft in the Middle Ages* (New York, 1972); A. Wittmann, *Die Gestalt der Hexe in der deutschen Sage*, Diss. (Heidelberg, 1933); Rehermann *Predigtexempel*, p. 159, lists nine versions from exempla collections.

LEGEND NO. 252.   Stories of innocent people witnessing the witches' sabbath abound in legendry. After all, reliable reports of the practice have to exist in order to give credence to beliefs and legends.

Invoking God's name counters the magic of witchcraft and dispels the assemblage at a witches' sabbath. See No. 251 and its commentary.

LEGEND NO. 253.  This legend deals with the feats of a practiced sorcerer. See the commentary to No. 38.

LEGEND NO. 254.  Regarding sorcerers and their feats, see the commentary to No. 38.

LEGEND NO. 255.  The "shirt of need" is an inadequate yet accurate translation of the German *Nothemd*. Like magic caps that could make one invisible, magic cloaks that enabled one to fly, the shirt of need was thought to make soldiers magically invulnerable to all bullets and weapons.

The pictures on the shirt in this legend are not explained, but it was believed that both divine and diabolic forces had to combine to produce the necessary magic effect. The man with the helmet and the beard is thus probably St. George, the patron of all soldiers. Images of St. George were frequently carried into battle on coins or on medallions. Moreover, such magic shirts were also called "St. George Shirts" and they bore an image of the saint in front. The other picture is evidently of the Devil himself, for it was believed that all such magic forces were essentially diabolic in nature, and the forces of the dark had to be harnessed to those of the light to make the magic effective.

As in this legend the means of making such a shirt are very complex and involve powerful forces. For example, it is thought that a pure virgin (or seven pure virgins, etc.) had to work through the night on Christmas Eve or before dawn on Good Friday, that the power of the Devil had to be invoked through incantations, or that the spinning went on through the night "in the Devil's name." If the magic did not work, it was then believed that the maidens who worked on it were not undefiled.

The German poet Ludwig Uhland wrote a ballad called "Das Nothemd" on this theme. See G. Jungbauer, "Hemd," *HdA* III, 1709–1745; P. Sartori, "Georg, hl." *HdA* III, 647–657.

There is a strikingly similar practice that has been documented among the Sioux (Western Dakota) Indians of the American plains. They would paint their ghost shirts, as they called them, and then dance themselves into a frenzied trance, believing that the garments rendered them invulnerable to bullets. The ghost shirt was part of the ceremony of the ghost dance that originated among the Northern Paiute (or Paviotso) Indians and spread among most of the Plains Indians. See R. Lowie, *Primitive Religion*, reprint edition (New York, 1952), 185–189.

LEGEND NO. 256.  These are actually three legends the Grimms combined into a single narrative. Concerning the art of making one invulnerable to weapons, see the commentary to No. 255. Occult talents are rarely confined to a single area of activity, thus it is not surprising that the man who knew the secret of making himself invulnerable also knew how to read the future. Regarding "second sight," see the commentary to No. 119.

LEGEND NO. 257. The hunter who acquires the ability to shoot at a target and never miss or who acquires magic bullets is one of the most popular German legends. It was used by Carl Maria von Weber as the basis of his famous opera, *Der Freischütz*.

The man who acquires such an ability does so, however, by entering into a pact with the Devil or other dark forces, forfeiting his immortal soul in the process. Thus, in legends the stories about such hunters invariably end tragically; in the *Märchen*, on the other hand, acquiring this ability helps lead the hero to everlasting happiness.

The number of magic ways of acquiring this ability are countless, but the most common method of obtaining a magical weapon involves nailing the sacramental host to a tree and shooting a bullet through it. The host then begins to bleed and the blood is believed to transform the weapon into one with magical power. To acquire magic bullets one shoots three times into the heavens and when three drops of blood fall from above one must catch them in a cloth. This cloth is then burned in an earthenware jug, and when the bullets are to be cast, these ashes are mixed with molten lead that has previously been acquired from stained glass windows in churches. The whole process is thought to be made more effective if the molten lead is poured into the mold through the eye sockets of a skull of an executed criminal.

See E. Seemann, "Freigewehr, Freikugel, Freischuß, Freischütze," *HdA* III, 2–22. For treatments of this theme in world literature, see the entry "Freischütz," in Frenzel *Stoffe*, pp. 188–189.

LEGEND NO. 258. Both the miller and the hunter of this legend had evidently acquired the secret of magic bullets from demonic forces (see the commentary to No. 257). Only by using even more powerful magic was it possible for the hunter to overcome the miller.

LEGEND NO. 259. Although doubles and alter egos abound in folk legends, the story of the Devil's trying to deceive someone by creating such an illusion is not common.

See V. Meyer-Matheis, *Die Vorstellung eines alter ego in Volkserzählungen*, Diss. (Freiburg, 1974).

LEGEND NO. 260. Evil spirits are thought to be able to take on the characteristics of living people and thus become their doubles. Such an apparition can be a portent of death for the person involved or can merely be an evil trick played by a spirit. On some occasions the appearance of a double can mean the separable soul of the individual has left the body and can then be perceived as a separate being.

See V. Meyer-Matheis, *Die Vorstellung eines alter ego in Volkserzählungen*, Diss. (Freiburg, 1974).

LEGEND NO. 261. This belongs to the category of executions of the innocent. Such legends are invariably miracle legends, that is, the innocent person about to be executed predicts that some sign will be given (presumably by God) after the execution indicating that the party involved was innocent. As such, they are related to the legends of trial by ordeal in which the divine sign is given at the trial rather than at the execution.

See Nos. 98, 360–361, and 465. The theme is especially well known in exempla literature. See Tubach *Index*, No. 4697; W. Müller-Bergström, "Unschuld," *HdA* VIII, 1443–1451.

LEGEND NO. 262. Sometimes the ability to see things from the other world can be a curse rather than a blessing. See H. Meier to Bernd, *Das zweite Gesicht im Volksglauben und in Volkssagen*, Diss. (Göttingen, 1952).

LEGEND NO. 263. Portents of death are many and varied in the traditions of every nation in the world. Although they exist as superstitions, their validity can be attested to in legends that tell how the portent came true. See P. Geiger, "Todesvorzeichen," *HdA* VIII, 993–1010.

For literally hundreds of such portents in American belief, see Hand *Beliefs*, II, Nos. 4874–5531.

LEGEND NO. 264. Death is the one incontrovertible fact of life, and thus any attempt to avert the portended fate invariably ends in failure. This theme is present in almost every fate legend.

See P. Geiger, "Todesvorzeichen," *HdA* VIII, 993–1010; A. Jaffé, *Geistererscheinungen und Vorzeichen* (Zürich, Stuttgart, 1958).

LEGEND NO. 265. Noise coming from a grave has been reported not only as a death omen but also as an indication that any epidemic currently raging will continue to claim victims for some time to come. See P. Keller, *Grab des Aberglaubens*, 5 vols. (Frankfurt and Leipzig, 1777–86), III, 92. In German folk belief, when a church quakes and rumbles as if it were going to collapse, it is considered an omen that the clergyman or sexton will soon drop dead. See A. Meiche, *Sagenbuch des Königreichs Sachsen* (Leipzig, 1903), No. 156, 121. See also G. Jungwirth, "Pfarrer," *HdA* VI, 1565–1568.

LEGEND NO. 266. Bells represent just one of many portents of death. See the commentaries to Nos. 263–264. See also J. Pesch, *Die Glocke in Geschichte, Sage, Volksglauben, Volksbrauch und Dichtung* (Dülmen, 1923); P. Sartori, *Das Buch von den deutschen Glocken* (Berlin und Leipzig, 1932).

The fact that the woman does not brush the clothes until seventeen weeks after the funeral was also a prescription of German folk tradition. See G. Jungbauer, "Kleid," *HdA*, 1458–1512 (see esp. 1502–1503). The period varies in different areas.

LEGEND NO. 267. See the commentaries to Nos. 263–264.

LEGEND NO. 268. For information on the White Woman see Nos. 4, 10–12, 16, 123, 222, and 224 and their commentaries. Although the ghostly figures of women who roam the countryside fall into neat categories such as the Castle Maiden, the White Woman, Mother Holla, etc., there is, as here, a great deal of contamination of one legend type with another in these traditions.

Bertha (Berch, Perchta, etc.) is a variant of these figures and is encountered in the Alpine regions of Bavaria and Austria. She is reported to be about during the Twelve Nights and, above all, on the Eve of Epiphany, i.e., the Twelfth Night. She watches over spinning girls and punishes children who do not behave. But she is also thought—like the Christkind—to reward good children by bringing Christmas presents. Her name has been documented as early as the ninth century in various Old High German words for the Twelfth Night: *Giperahta naht, perhtenaht,* and *Berhtag.* She is also believed—like the Wild Huntsman and Mother Holla—to be the leader of a troop of Lost Souls. A plural form (Die Berchten, Perchten) was sometimes used to designate the ghostly members of her entourage. At one time it was a widespread practice for people to don Perchten masks during Carnival and other festivals, but the custom survives today in only a few isolated places.

See M. Andree-Eysn, *Volkskundliches aus dem bayrisch- österreichischen Alpengebiet* (Braunschweig, 1910); M. Andree-Eysn, "Die Perchten im Salzburgischen," *Archiv für Anthropologie,* 3 (1905), 24–37; H. Fink, *Verzaubertes Land: Volkskult und Ahnenkult in Südtirol* (Innsbruck und Wien, 1969), 368–370; E. Kranzmyer, "Name und Gestalt der Frau Bercht im südostdeutschen Raum," *Bayerische Hefte für Volkskunde,* 12 (1940), 55–62; W.-E. Peuckert, *Deutscher Volksglaube des Spätmittelalters* (Stuttgart, 1942), esp. pp. 97–102; H. Moser, "Neue Beiträge zur Geschichte des Perchtenlaufens," *Bayerische Hefte für Volkskunde,* 12 (1940); L. Schmidt, "Perchtengestalten im Burgenland," *Burgenländische Heimatblätter,* 3 (1951), 129–161; L. Kretzenbacher, *Santa Luzia und die Lutzelfrau* (München, 1959).

LEGEND NO. 269.    See the commentaries to Nos. 5, 7, 10–12, and 268. The grotesque ending of this narrative—using a plowshare and chain to sew up the torso of the victim—is an almost infantile exaggeration. It is conceivable that the legend was told essentially as a warning to children who then fashioned it into a ludicrous exaggeration in an attempt to disarm the demonic qualities.

LEGEND NO. 270.    The Türst, Posterli, and Sträggele are all well-known local demons in the Swiss tradition. They have become bogeyman figures used to frighten children into behaving so they won't wander off. These demons have assumed a number of diabolic forms in Swiss legends and customs. For example, the Türst is said to ride through the countryside in a red wagon on the eve of St. John's Day. The Sträggele is an ugly witch seen sometimes in the guise of a monstrous cat, sometimes as a Wild Woman, and sometimes as a Wild Huntress. The figures have become popular carnival demons depicted in some areas by men in costumes and masks.

The word Türst is related to MHG *turst* 'bold,' 'reckless.' Karl Meuli (see below) assumes that Sträggele is related to OHG *scrato* 'demon,' 'Nightmare,' and MHG *Schrätel* 'house spirit.' Even though he was able to come up with an analogous case of a shift in Alemannic from Sk- to St-, the etymology is not convincing. Much more likely is that Sträggele is related either to Latin *striga* 'witch' or to MHG *strageln* 'to strike.' Posterli is much more difficult to trace. There are scores of possibilities, none of which is totally convincing. See K. Meuli, "Masken, Maskereien," *HdA* V, 1744–1852.

LEGEND NO. 271.    The Night Hunter is another name for the Wild Huntsman and *Rüttelweib* is a local name for the Moss Woman (see Nos. 47–48 and

172–173). I have translated this latter form as "shaking woman" on the basis of New High German *rütteln* 'to shake.' However, there is the possibility that an earlier form meant 'to clear away or uproot trees,' a meaning that would be in keeping with the central motif of this legend. *Reuten* and *roden*, both of which mean 'to make a clearing' (cf. Proto-Germanic *rothon*), are possibly related.

LEGEND NO. 272.   Again the Grimms have combined two separate memorate accounts into a single narrative—a practice frowned upon by contemporary folklorists. The man with the slouch hat, long beard, and grey cloak is not identified, although he is clearly a spirit from the other world. Often the Wandering Jew (see No. 344 and its commentary) appears in similar guise.

In Nordic tradition when Odin appeared among mortals (frequently to intervene in a battle) he was described as having the same appearance as the apparition in this legend. There are many such appearances of Odin among men described in Saxo Grammaticus, *Gesta Danorum* (*History of the Danes*). There is, however, no further evidence to support the contention that this legend represents the survival of an account of the epiphany of Odin-Wodan.

See G. K. Anderson, *The Legend of the Wandering Jew* (Providence, R.I., 1965).

LEGEND NO. 273.   The spirit of this legend belongs to the category of the Huckup, a demon who jumps upon a victim's shoulders and back. There is no way to dislodge the creature and he continues to grow ever heavier, forcing the victim to carry him until total exhaustion sets in. See No. 146 and commentary.

LEGEND NO. 274.   The Chimmeke belongs to the category of Cobold or House Spirit (see Nos. 72–77 and their commentaries). Although they are frequently playful, friendly, and helpful creatures, if they are offended Cobolds can become very dangerous as this legend attests. Chimmeke (with variant forms (Chimke, Chim, Jimmeken) is a local appellation for the Cobold especially in Pomerania, but also in Mecklenburg and in Posnań. The name Chim also turns up in the records of seventeenth-century witch trials as an appellation of the Devil. Jacob Grimm thought the name was a variation of the personal name Joachim (see below). Ludwig Laistner (see below) saw a relationship with *hiemk* and *hemeke*, Low German words for 'cricket.' This latter etymology is especially appealing since the cricket is thought to be a form that the Cobold was able to assume. Interesting is the question of where Walt Disney came up with the word "Jiminy" for the name of the conscience-spirit in the form of a cricket in his film *Pinocchio*. The name sounds remarkably like the form Jimmeken mentioned above. It is conceivable that expressions such as "By Jiminy," "Jumpin' Jiminy," and even "Jiminy Cricket" influenced Disney's choice of name. "By Jiminy" is thought to be a folk-etymology for the invoking of the twins: "By Gemini." (See D. Ward, *The Divine Twins* [Berkeley and Los Angeles, 1968], p. 31). However, I would not rule out the possibility that, somewhere along the line, the English language picked up the equivalent of the German "Jimmeken the Cricket." See F. Ranke, "Chimken," *HdA* II, 36; Grimm *DM* I, 417; L. Laistner, *Nebelsagen* (Stuttgart, 1879), 334.

Crickets were also believed to be the souls of the deceased (cf. Dickens' story *The Cricket on the Hearth*). See also K. Riegler, "Grille," *HdA* III, 1160–1169.

LEGEND NO. 275. The area in question lies near the Nibelungen Road near Reichelsheim in the Odenwald. The inclusion of specific personal and place names and of specific dates and times is a typical narrative trait that storytellers employ to enhance the credibility of their accounts. The screaming spirit of this legend belongs to the generally undifferentiated category of demonic spooks that haunt isolated marshes, ravines, cliffs, and the like. See Petzoldt *DVS*, 402–403, for a discussion of such creatures. See also R. Beitl, *Im Sagenwald* (Feldkirch, 1953).

Related to the screaming spirit is the so-called Hay-Man (Hehmann, Hoimann, He-hehmann, etc.), a spirit who calls out to lonesome wanderers at night, frightening them terribly. He is thought to punish those who poach game and steal wood from the forests.

See J. Hanika, "Zur Hehmannsage," *Stifter Jahrbuch*, 6 (1959), 253–257; B. Ortler, "Die Sage vom Glursner Juzer," *Die Schlern*, 24 (1950), 83–84; E. Rath, *Der Hehmann* (Wien, 1953).

LEGEND NO. 276. It is difficult to determine if this tale, which the Grimms extracted from a sixteenth-century literary text, was ever a popular legend. The appearance of devils, demons, and ghosts in the guise of monks is familiar in exempla literature. See Tubach *Index*, Nos. 1615, 1647, 4245, and 3372. See also A. Becker, "Die Speyerer Mönchsüberfahrt von 1530," *Blätter für pfälzische Kirchengeschichte* (1930), 65–60.

The coach in flames is a concrete representation of its infernal qualities. The medieval concept of souls burning in Hell obviously gave rise to this motif. See H. Freudenthal, *Das Feuer im deutschen Glauben und Brauch* (Berlin and Leipzig, 1931). For American parallels see J. Q. Anderson, "The Legend of the Phantom Coach in East Texas," *WF*, 22 (1963), 259–262.

LEGEND NO. 277. The small fiery lights seen in isolated places at night have a variety of names in various languages. In English they are called Will-o'-the-Wisp, De Wull er de Wust, Waller-Wups, etc., in German *Irrlichter*, *Irrwisch*, Swedish *irrbloss*, Dutch *dwaallicht*, French *feu follet*, Italian *fuoco fatuo*, etc. As a phenomenon they should probably be kept separate from a variety of other fiery spirits that are larger and more threatening (balls-o'-fire, jack-o'-lanterns, and so on). The existence of such lights over swampy areas and elsewhere has been scientifically explained as swamp gas, fire flies, St. Elmo's fire, and static electricity, so there can be little doubt that natural phenomena have contributed to supernatural traditions in this case. See P. Samford, "Ignis fatuus," *Scientific Monthly*, 9 (1919), 358–364.

It is generally believed that these apparitions are the flaming souls of sinners, suicides, the drowned, and unbaptized infants. Consequently one encounters traditions in which attempts are made to baptize the spirits. Often the apparition will veritably hypnotize a wanderer, who is then compelled to follow and will eventually be lost in the wilderness.

The girl who frivolously taunts the spirits with the satirical verse is

*Commentary · 403*

acting in a foolhardy manner according to folk belief, for the creatures of the other world are always a potential threat to humans. The girl, and her family as well, pays dearly for her reckless attitude. The story, of course, serves as a warning to others to treat the creatures with greater respect.

See W. D. Hand, "Will-o'-the-Wisps, Jack-o'-Lanterns, and Their Congeners: A Consideration of the Fiery and Luminous Creatures of Lower Mythology," *Fabula*, 18 (1977), 226–233; F. Ranke, "Irrlicht," *HdA* IV, 779–785; W. W. Newell, "The Ignis Fatuus, Its Character and Legendary Origin," *JAF*, 17 (1904), 39–60; T. W. Tally, "De Wull er de Wust (The Will-o'-the-Wisp)," *Tennessee Folklore Society Bulletin*, 21 (1955), 58; K. Amersbach, *Licht- und Nebelgeister: Ein Beitrag zur Sagen- und Märchenkunde*, Programmschr. (Baden-Baden, 1907).

LEGEND NO. 278.    See the commentary to No. 276.

LEGEND NO. 279.    Sites of old castles, monasteries, palaces, and the like are frequently thought to be haunted by the spirits of the dead. Sometimes these spirits are found inside mountains, living a purgatorial existence. In legendry, mortals frequently stumble upon such situations just as a banquet or party is being held. Although the human guest may be treated well by the ghostly hosts, the encounter—as is the case in all such encounters with the other world—poses a considerable danger for the subject. See the commentary to No. 177.

LEGEND NO. 280.    The ruins of Lichtenberg Castle still stand high upon a peak overlooking the valley town of Ingweiler (today called Ingwiller in French). The castle lies about forty miles northwest of Straßburg. For information on the apparition of lights see the commentary to No. 277.

LEGEND NO. 281.    The German term *Wafeln*, here translated as "wafeling," is limited to the Low German dialect areas. It is not restricted to the usage in this tale, for in general it means 'to spook.' The term is related to Old Saxon *valfia*, *vâfersyne*, ON *Vafra*, *vofa*, MHG *waberen*, all with related meanings of 'being in motion,' 'wandering around,' 'appearing to one.' ON *vofa* is glossed with the Latin *spectrum* 'vision,' Old Saxon *vâfersyne* with *spectaculum* 'scene of action,' and OS *vâferlic* with *theatralis* 'theater,' 'site of action.' In the OHG Tatian (210, 3) the related term *wabarsiunu* is used for the apparition of the dead emerging from their graves at the crucifixion.

See Grimm *DM*, III, 278; L. Laistner, *Nebelsagen* (Stuttgart, 1879), p. 248; see also C. Mengis, "Umgehen," *HdA* VIII, 1320–1321.

LEGEND NO. 282.    At certain times of the year ghosts inhabiting the remains of old castles and other ruined structures can be seen engaging in many of the activities they knew during life—parties, banquets, and the like. However, their apparent pleasure is misleading for they are suffering the torment of lost souls. The mortal who stumbles upon such a scene is usually treated well, but he or she must carefully heed the taboos that are either explicitly stated or implied. The woman in this legend is forced to break the imposed taboo and pays dearly for it. See also Nos. 177 and 279 and commentaries.

LEGEND NO. 283. If the reader has read a substantial portion of the legends in this collection, he or she will realize that many, if not most, of the legends are reactionary in nature in that they support the established order and give frightening examples of the punishment that befalls anyone who transgresses that order. The established powers even helped to disseminate this kind of manipulative lore—often via the exempla that were recounted from the pulpit—to prevent the populace from questioning the *status quo.*

In this legend, however, a member of the exploitative powers is punished for sins committed against a member of the oppressed class. Although such legends are relatively rare, they occur frequently enough to give a breath of fresh air to a number of collections of legends.

An anthology of such carefully selected legends has been published in the German Democratic Republic: R. Wossidlo and G. Schneidewind, *Herr und Knecht: Antifeudale Sagen aus Mecklenburg* (Berlin, 1960).

LEGEND NO. 284. The Grimms have again combined two separate legends into a single narrative. The first short report is given in a Low German dialect; the site is accordingly somewhere in Northern Germany—exactly where cannot be determined. The second legend takes place near Erbach in southern Hesse. The fiery figures are reflections of the medieval notion of the fiery torment suffered by sinners in the inferno of Hell. Some were thought to suffer the same torment when they were required to wander the earth as Poor Souls. See H. Freudenthal, *Das Feuer im deutschen Glauben und Brauch* (Berlin und Leipzig, 1931).

LEGEND NO. 285. For information on Will-o'-the-Wisps see the commentary to No. 277. This legend involves one of the dominating concerns of farmers in German village society. In most German-speaking lands the farmers do not live on their farmland but rather in villages, and they have parcels of land here and there in the surrounding territory. These parcels have been carefully surveyed and marked off with border stones. In past centuries, because the farmers in these lands lived a marginal existence, every square foot of land was of crucial significance, hence the concern over border stones and the accuracy of the surveyors' measurements. Stories such as this were told to remind the surveyors that eternal punishment awaited them if they did not perform their duties with complete honesty.

LEGEND NO. 286. For the importance to German farmers of land measurements and border stones see the commentary to No. 285. The man who moves a border stone—presumably for his own gain—is guilty of one of the most blasphemous crimes known in village society. Moving such stones in the dark of night was not a difficult task, and enforcing sanctions against such actions was nearly impossible. It is thus not surprising that terrifying legends were devised as stern warnings against such acts. A man who was guilty of such activities was condemned to wander the earth for all eternity as a demonic ghost. As in this legend, contact with spirits of the dead involved mortal danger.

See F. Ranke, "Grenzfrevler," *HdA* III, 1157–58. Such stories are not limited to German-speaking lands. See, for example, O. Bö, "Deildegasten," *Norveg*, 5 (1955), 105–124.

LEGEND NO. 287. This is an etiological legend that arose no doubt when the inhabitants of the area were confounded by the curious zigzag pattern of the border. Thus this story was invented to explain how it came about. Such legends explaining borders are common in German legendry. See No. 288 and the commentary.

LEGEND NO. 288. I have translated the name Kluß Pass into Klausen Pass, since that is the name by which it is known today. The highway that leads from Glarus to Altdorf over the Glarn Alps in Switzerland goes through this pass, and the Schächen Valley opens up to the west. This legend, like No. 287, is etiological in nature, explaining how the present border came to be. However, the story was not freely invented; it is instead an international migratory legend that can be traced back to classical antiquity.

Sallust (*Bellum Jugurthinum*, cap. 79) tells the story of the dispute between the cities of Carthage and Cyrene regarding their mutual border. Since there were no natural barriers, such as streams, mountain ranges, or ravines, they could not agree on a territorial border. Thus, they went to war to settle the issue. When the war proved inconclusive they decided each side would choose a party to set out on foot from each of their cities, and the place where they met would then become the border.

The Carthaginians chose two brothers named Philänus who set out at a high speed, while the Cyrenean party progressed at a leisurely pace. When the two parties met, the Cyreneans realized they were in trouble and complained bitterly. They then made the following suggestion: either the Carthaginian brothers should allow themselves to be buried alive at the place they thought should be the border, or the Cyreneans should be permitted to continue to the place they thought would be a fair border and then themselves be buried alive. Much to the surprise of the Cyreneans, the Carthaginian brothers consented to be buried alive at the spot where the parties had first met, and there the border was drawn. Other versions of this story were later told by Valerius Maximus and Pomponius Mela in the first century A.D.

Evidence that there was indeed a border dispute between Uri and Glarn as early as 1196 is outlined in a letter from the Landgrave Otto of Burgundy.

See L. Röhrich, "Eine antike Grenzsage und ihre neuzeitlichen Parallelen," *Würzburger Jahrbücher für Altertumswissenschaft*, 4 (1949/50), 339–369, reprinted in Röhrich *SuM* 210–234; W. Müller-Bergström, "Grenze," *HdA* III, 1137–1157; O. Moser, "Der Grenzlauf," *Die Kärntner Landmannschaft*, 7 (1960), 4–8.

LEGEND NO. 289. Entlebuch is both a town and a region lying southwest of Lucerne. Such regional battles were not uncommon among the cattle-herding villages of Switzerland, and there may be some historic validity to the legend.

LEGEND NO. 290. Objects which deviate from the norm attract attention to themselves (von Sydow's external dominant), and often special supernatural power is attributed to such items. See the commentary to No. 189.

LEGEND NO. 291. St. Boniface indeed engaged in missionary work in Thuringia where he established a number of churches and chapels. See the commentary to No. 181. It was then the practice not always to build churches in villages; often they were constructed in isolated spots in wilderness areas. This was done not only to provide the focus for pilgrimages, but often because such sites had been sacred places to the recently converted heathen. It was a clever device of the missionaries to place the chapels in places where people were accustomed to going for religious devotion.

LEGEND NO. 292. This is a rather fragmentary version of the emperor in the mountain legend. See Nos. 21–23 and 26–28. The Kassuben region is an area of the lower Vistula settled by Wendic tribes of the same name. Lauenburg, now called Lębork, lies about forty miles west of Danzig (Gdańsk), which is presently located in Poland.

LEGEND NO. 293. Swan Mountain (Schwanberg) is in Styria, south of the Austrian city of Graz, as the Grimms indicate in their footnote.

LEGEND NO. 294. Eilenhausen is today called Eilensen and lies directly east of Dassel in the Solling Forest of Lower Saxony. In many similar fate legends such signs indicate not only that a great battle will ensue, but that it will be the final World Battle—reminiscent of the *Ragnarök* of Nordic tradition.

See Petzoldt *DVS*, Nos. 20–21; A. Olrik, *Ragnarök: Die Sagen vom Weltuntergang* (Berlin und Leipzig, 1922); P. Althaus, *Die letzten Dinge* (Leipzig, 1933); F. Zurbonsen, *Die Schlacht am Birkenbaum* (Essen, 1940); O. Lauffer, "Schicksalsbaum und Lebensbaum im deutschen Glauben und Brauch," *ZsfVk*, 45 (1935), 215–230. See also the commentary to No. 295.

LEGEND NO. 295. Modern folk belief in Germany corresponds remarkably with notions recorded in Old Norse myths that the end of the world will be preceded by specific signs.

See the commentary to No. 294. See also F. von der Leyen, "Weltanfang und Weltende in der Dichtung der Germanen," *Bayerische Hefte für Volkskunde*, 4 (1919), 226–237; E. Nöth, *Weltanfang und Weltende in der deutschen Volkssage* (Frankfurt, 1932).

LEGEND NO. 296. Frederick I (Barbarossa) drowned as he was bathing in a river while on a crusade (see the commentary to No. 494). It took months for word of his fate to reach his homeland, and since he did not return, the tradition arose that he had been captured by the Turks. (The word "Turk" was often used in the Middle Ages as a generic term for all the heathens of the Near East.) Thus, a tradition developed that he would someday return. This tradition then grew into the emperor in the mountain legend, which stated that Barbarossa was alive and well and living underground but would someday arise and lead his people once again. There are similar traditions about great leaders everywhere—the accounts that Hitler is living in Argentina, or that Franklin D. Roosevelt is not really dead, etc., belong to this category of legends. See the commentaries to Nos. 21–28.

LEGEND NO. 297.   See the commentaries to Nos. 21–23, 26–28, 292, and 296.

LEGEND NO. 298.   It is not only emperors and kings who live underground waiting for the day of their triumphant return; national heroes are thought to do the same thing. In this legend the story is retold about three generations of the Tells of Switzerland—William, his father, and his son. Although William Tell was an historical figure, most of the stories told about him are migratory legends that have become attached to the Swiss national hero. Even the famous motif of shooting the apple from his son's head had been told earlier in Persia in the twelfth century, and it has been recorded in most European countries. See E. L. Rochholz, *Tell und Geßler in Sage und Geschichte* (Bern, 1877); H. G. Wackernagel, *Altes Volkstum der Schweiz* (Basel, 1956); L. Stunzi, *Tell: Werden und Wachsen eines Mythos* (Bern, 1973).

Historians generally agree that the historical Tell was not nearly the noble figure that legend has made him out to be. For the more famous legend of William Tell, see No. 518.

LEGEND NO. 299.   In order to include as much material in their collection as possible without making it overly long and cumbersome, the Grimms fell into the questionable practice of supplementing their written sources with information they had recorded from oral tradition. And they did this not in supplementary notes but rather by weaving this data directly into the narrative. In this legend the practice proved most unfortunate, for the account now presents two distinct kinds of creatures from the spirit world.

First, there are mountain spirits who reign high up in the mountain fastness, as far from human settlements as possible. The imagination of Alpine cowherds has projected a situation analogous to their own lives upon these mountain creatures. They are thought to be the lords of the herds of wild chamois that graze among the highest Alpine peaks. The concept of the mythical lords of game animals is an ancient notion found among hunting peoples all over the world. See the commentary to No. 302.

The other creatures of this legend are Dwarfs who live underground in the vicinity of human dwellings (see Nos. 21–46, 148–156, 302–304). See I. Bergheer, "Gemse," *HdA* III, 630–632.

The best article on the topic of the spirits of the wilds is Lutz Röhrich "Europäische Wildgeistersagen," in Röhrich *SuM*, 142–194 (originally in *RhJb*, 10, [1962], 79–162). See especially the excellent bibliography in the footnotes.

LEGEND NO. 300.   This is an etiological legend explaining why pine nuts are found only in nearly inaccessible places. It also expresses a mild protest of the oppressed classes. See the commentary to No. 283.

LEGEND NO. 301.   The belief that there is a realm where the most beautiful game animals reside in a kind of paradise is widespread among hunting peoples around the world. The well-known "happy hunting grounds" of some American Indian peoples belongs to this concept. See Röhrich *SuM*, pp. 156,

188, and 315. It is often thought that the "Lord of the Beasts" reigns over this paradise. See the commentary to No. 302.

LEGEND NO. 302. The Alpine hunter's encounter with the spirit who is lord of the chamois belongs to a cultural phenomenon documented among hunting peoples the world over. In modern times it represents the survival of relatively ancient religious concepts. The mythic-religious notion of the "Lord of the Beasts," the patron protector of game animals, must have been present among the earliest Europeans at a time when they were still exclusively hunters and gatherers.

The lord—either male or female—knows all the animals individually, and he or she alone may select the animals the hunters may take. The lord must be treated with proper reverence as the success of the hunt is entirely in his or her hands. The Lord of the Beasts is also the originator of all hunting magic and through good will has taught man this art. The lord is thus a friend of the hunter; however, if offended in any way he or she can become a powerful enemy and prevent everyone from taking game animals.

The lord is thought of both as an anthropomorphic being and as an animal. The two notions are not at all contradictory, for it is well documented that hunting peoples invariably believe that the animals they hunt have essentially human cores. In some cases it is believed that each species has its own individual lord, so that among a given hunting people it is possible to find a lord of the elk, of the bear, the fish, and so forth.

Also part of this cultural complex are rituals involving the reconstruction of skeletons in the belief that these animals will be restored to life and returned to the realm of the beasts and its lord. Survivals of this concept also occur in German legends. See No. 62 and commentary.

For literature on the more universal aspects of the Lord of the Beasts, see W. Bogoras, "The Chuckchee, II. Religion," in *The Jessup North Pacific Expedition*, Memoirs of the American Museum of Natural History, 11 (Leiden and New York, 1907); A. Dirr, "Der kaukasische Wild- und Jagdgott," *Anthropos* 20 (1925), 139–147; U. Holmberg, "Über die Jagdriten der nördlichen Völker Asiens und Europas," *Journal de la Société Finno-Ougrienne*, 41 (1926); U. Harva, *Die religiösen Vorstellungen der altaischen Völker*, FFC 125, Helsinki, 1938; D. Zelenin, *Der Kult der Ongone in Sibirien* (Moskau and Leningrad, 1936); H. Baumann, "Afrikanische Wild- und Buschgeister," in *Festschrift für B. Ankermann, Zeitschrift für Ethnologie*, special issue, 70 (1938), 208–239; H. Findeisen, *Das Tier als Gott, Dämon und Ahne* (Stuttgart, 1956); A. Friedrich, "Die Forschung über das frühzeitliche Jägertum," *Paideuma*, 2 (1941/43), 20–43; A. E. Jensen, *Mythos und Kult bei Naturvölkern* (Wiesbaden, 1951); C.-E. Edsman, "Studier i jägerens religion," *Annales Academiae Regiae Scientiarum Upsaliensis*, 2 (1958), 33–94; A. Hultkratz (ed.), *The Supernatural Owners of Nature: Nordic Symposium on the Religious Conceptions of Ruling Spirits and Allied Concepts* (Stockholm, 1961).

For information on the European survivals of this ancient cultural pattern, see W.-E. Peuckert, "Der Alpenjäger," *ZfdPh*, 78 (1959), 337–349; L. Röhrich, "Europäische Wildgeistersagen," *RhJb*, 10 (1959), 79–162; L. Röhrich, "Die Sagen vom Herrn der Tiere," *Internationaler Kongreß der Volkserzählforscher in Kiel und Kopenhagen* (Berlin, 1961), 341–349; E. Mudrak, "Herr und Herrin der Tiere," *Fabula*, 4 (1961), 163–174; I. Paulson, "Wald- und Wildgeister im Volksglauben der finnischen Völker," *ZsfVk*, 57 (1961), 1–25; I. Paulson, *Schutzgeister und Gottheiten des Wildes in Nordeurasien* (Stockholm, 1961); V. Voigt, "Elemente des Vorstellungskreises vom Herrn der Tiere im ungarischen Volksmärchen," *AE*, 11 (1962), 391–430; K. Sälzle, *Tier und Mensch, Gottheit und Dämon* (München, 1965); R. Grambo, "The Lord of the Forest and Mountain Game in the More Recent Folk Traditions of Norway," *Fabula*, 7 (1965), 33–52.

LEGEND NO. 303.    See Nos. 30–35 and commentaries.

LEGEND NO. 304.    This legend is composed of elements from a number of legend types cleverly woven into a single narrative. First we have a treasure legend that makes use of a magic flower (see No. 9 and its commentary) to open the mountain; next we have a Dwarf legend (see Nos. 30–35); and finally, since the site of the treasure is Mt. Kyffhausen, there is an allusion to the emperor in the mountain legends (see Nos. 21–23, 25–26, 28, and 296–297). Since it was common knowledge that Mt. Kyffhausen was the resting place of the sleeping emperor, there is the implicit notion in this tale that the great treasure there is Barbarossa's hoard.

Mt. Kyffhausen is a peak on the southern side of the Harz Mountains near the town of Sittendorf. Atop the mountain today stands a monument to the sleeping emperor. Nearby is Questen Castle and the town of Questenberg.

The legend of the sleeping emperor has been invoked by political leaders throughout German history as a metaphor for the sleeping German nation and has consequently acquired ideological overtones.

Jacob Grimm thought that the unnamed flower of this legend was the Forget-me-not. See Grimm *DM* II, 1152. See also H. Marzell, "Blume," *HdA* I, 1431–1434; G. Meinel, "Blume," *EdM* II, 483–495.

LEGEND NO. 305.    For information on the Water Nix see Nos. 49, 51–69 and commentaries.

LEGEND NO. 306.    Today, Schwarzach Castle is in Baden, not the Palatinate.

Lakes, ponds, and rivers represent openings in the surface of the earth leading to the mysterious underground realms where the supernatural spirits reside. These spirits are a constant threat to those who come too close to the shore. Although such legends may have been told to children to keep them from playing too close to the water's edge, they represent more than mere "warning fictions" (von Sydow). There are diverse legends that tell about the myriad number of spirits who live beneath the surface of the water and what happens to humans who either fall in and drown or are abducted and taken beneath the surface.

In East Germany there exists a belief, evidently a Slavic influence, that the souls of the drowned are kept trapped in pots turned upside down (see No. 52). There is also a common belief that the souls of the abducted and drowned are condemned to spend all eternity in the watery depths. Some traditions even report that the souls of the drowned become fish. Other legends report that it is the task of drowned souls to work constantly, pumping subterranean waters to the surface of the earth, thus keeping the earth's waters circulating. The bell pealing beneath the surface indicates the notion of some kind of life at the bottom of the lake.

See C. Mengis, "See," *HdA* VII, 1558–1568; F. Panzer, "Wassergeister," *HdA* IX, 127–191.

LEGEND NO. 307.   Epfenbach is a tiny village located in the Kraischgau region, which lies east of Heidelberg and about ten miles north of the city of Sinsheim.

Stories of water maidens emerging from the depths and fraternizing with and being loved by mortals were popular in the Middle Ages and are probably even older. The story of the water sprite Melusine was recorded as early as circa 1390 by Jean D'Arras in his *Histoire de Lusignan*. Such motifs served as genealogical legends enabling royal houses to trace their lines back to supernatural origins.

The topic was picked up by many of the chapbooks that were popular throughout Europe in the sixteenth century. The German poet Johannes Fischart also gave literary treatment to such a legend (see No. 528 and commentary, and see also No. 58). The motif became especially popular in the age of Romanticism (see, for example, the novella *Undine* by Friedrich de la Motte-Fouqué, written in 1811), and it is likely that these stories had their effect on popular oral tradition. Such stories presuppose at least an ambivalent attitude toward the creatures of the supernatural, for while the spirits are thought to be potentially dangerous, they are also thought to have a very human side.

Whether such traits have always been present in folk legendry (cf. the legends of the Dwarfs) or whether they arise only as a by-product of fading belief cannot be determined with certainty. However, it is certain that where belief in such spirits is intense, their frightening, demonic characteristics predominate.

See the commentary to No. 306. See also J. Kohler, *Der Ursprung der Melusine Sage* (Leipzig, 1895); K. Heisig, "Über den Ursprung der Melusinensage," *Fabula*, 3 (1959), 170–181; K. von Spiess, "Die Sagen von der Fisch- oder Schlangenjungfrau," *WZV*, 46 (1941); Frenzel *Stoffe*, see entries "Melusine" and "Undine."

LEGEND NO. 308.   This legend reflects the belief that a drowned person is condemned to lead an existence as a Poor Soul in the realm of demonic beings. It is also believed in some areas that the body of a drowned person will not surface unless extraordinary forces are at work—in this legend it occurs only with the help of sorcery. See the commentary to No. 306.

LEGEND NO. 309.   The Eternal Huntsman is reminiscent of the Wild Huntsman (see No. 48 and commentary). While the Wild Huntsman is usually thought to lead his horde of lost souls through the heavens, the Eternal Huntsman is more often a solitary figure on horseback who rides through the forest accompanied only by his hounds.

In the legends of the Eternal Hunter, the main stress is his being a Poor

Soul condemned to hunt for eternity because of some blasphemy he committed in life. In the legends of the Wild Hunter, on the other hand, the stress is more on the demonic and threatening aspects of the apparition. There is, of course, a great deal of overlap between the two traditions. See G. Jungwirth, "Jagd, Jäger," *HdA* IV, 575–593.

The legend of the Eternal Hunter also forms the core of the legend of St. Humbertus. See A. Wrede, "Hl. Humbertus," *HdA* IV, 426–434; L. Huyghebaert, *Sint Hubertus: Patroon van de jagers in woord en beeld* (Antwerpen, 1949).

LEGEND NO. 310.   In the seventeenth century removing anything from a forest was considered poaching since all such land was the property of noble families. Thus, collecting acorns was seen to be both a sin and a crime. In this legend the spirit has been condemned to be an Eternal Huntsman—and headless at that—not because of his excessive desire to engage in the hunt, but for his sins in general.

Headless spirits in European and American folklore are invariably thought to be revenants and Poor Souls. This particular punishment is inflicted in cases where the sins have been especially heinous or blasphemous. The notion prevails that if a criminal is guilty of crimes severe enough to warrant beheading but has escaped this punishment, he will be damned to become a headless ghost.

Headless beings were documented in Iceland as early as the Middle Ages, but there the figures were thought to be living corpses rather than headless ghosts (see E. Mogk, "Altgermanische Spukgeschichte," *Neue Jahrbücher für das klassische Altertum, Geschichte und deutsche Literatur*, 43/44 [1919], 103–117).

Headless spirits and divinities were widely known in ancient Egypt as well as in classical antiquity. See K. Preisendanz, "Akephalos," *Beihefte zum alten Orient*, 8 (1926), 6–17.

The earliest documented reference to a headless spirit in Germany was in a sermon written by Geiler von Kaysersberg, ca. 1505, who mentions such spirits as being members of the Wild Horde. There are additional reports later in the sixteenth and seventeenth centuries. See W. Lerche, "Kopflos," *HdA* V, 215–230. Headless spirits are also well known in the popular traditions of India. See W. Crooke, *An Introduction to the Popular Religion of Northern India* (Allahabad, 1894), 159–162. The headless ghost tradition is a favorite in American legendry as well. See W. D. Haden, *The Headless Cobbler of Smallett Cave* (Nashville, 1967); I. Rodger, "The Headless Horsemen," *JFI*, 2 (1965), 266–271.

LEGEND NO. 311.   Hackelberg is one of the figures who has become a Wild Huntsman in German legendry (see No. 172 and its commentary). Here, however, we are told how he died and how his death was prophesied in a dream. In so doing, the legend draws upon the international migratory type of "The Dream of the Wild Boar." It is a typical fate legend, for it first reports the prophecy of death, then goes on to the apparent escape from the prophesied death, but at last relates the ultimate triumph of a terrible fate that can never be averted.

A similar legend from antiquity was documented by Herodotus (I, 36–45), who states that a wild boar of great size and strength was reported to be living on the slopes of Mt. Olympus. Atys, son of Kroisos, wanted to slay it and made plans for a hunt. Kroisos, however, then received a warning in a dream that a wild boar would kill his son by means of an iron lance, and he forbade his son to partake in the hunt. Atys ignored the advice, arguing that a boar had no iron lance and even if it had there were no hands to wield it. During the hunt they indeed raised the boar and one of the youths cast his lance at it. However, the beast dodged and the lance sped on, striking Atys and killing him.

The variant the Grimms have published here is clearly a more effective account, for Hackelberg's refusal to participate in the hunt seems to insure that he will certainly evade his fated death. Thus, the tragic irony of the denouement is all the more effective.

It is possible that this more "correct" version represents a tradition that is older than Herodotus. See H. Meier, *Die Hackelbergsage*, Diss. (Göttingen, 1954); W.-E. Peuckert, *Geburt und Antwort der mythischen Welt* (Berlin, 1965), see esp. pp. 33–34; C.-M. Barbeau, *Les rêves des chasseurs* (Montréal, 1950). See also Grimm *DM* III, 280.

LEGEND NO. 312.   This is a delightful tale with a number of humorous elements. It is based on the belief—documented as early as the twelfth century—that the Wild Hunt was accompanied by witches who would blow horns signaling its approach. It was also thought that witches could easily change their shape into such nocturnal flying creatures as the owl. This tradition was somehow combined with a convent ghost legend. The rather humorous and disparaging treatment of the hysteric nuns may well represent a post-Reformation, Protestant viewpoint. However, the inclusion of the motif of the successful exorcising of the spirit by the Capuchin monk does not support such an inference. I know of no other legend that mentions the figure of Toot-Osel, and I have never encountered a ghost quite like her in European legendry.

Hackelberg is one of the traditional Eternal Huntsman figures of German legendry. He was believed to have haunted the region around Mt. Hösel (see Nos. 172, 311, and their commentaries).

LEGEND NO. 313.   This legend combines the motifs of the Wild Horde and a fate legend. As is always the case in such stories, the attempt to avert the fated death is doomed to fail. See Nos. 7, 47–48, 172–173, 309 and their commentaries.

There are a number of popular beliefs regarding horses as death omens. See Hand *Beliefs*, No. 5233ff.

LEGEND NO. 314.   Faithful Eckhart is the traditional benevolent figure who appears on the scene to warn people to take cover just before the Wild Horde rages past. Goethe wrote a ballad ("Der getreue Eckhart") on the topic that has become very popular in German-speaking lands. See No. 7 and its commentary. See also Nos. 48 and 309.

A raging horde of creatures traveling over hill and dale and even through the air is a nearly universal supernatural experience. Similar traditions are known in the southwestern United States where a ghost herd of cattle led by a ghostly horseman (who in life caused cattle to stampede) rages over the grasslands and deserts. The fact that this event occurs in desolate areas at dusk or in the dark may indicate that an altered state of consciousness induced by sensory deprivation contributes to the universal nature of the experience. See the commentary to No. 48.

A similar tale from antiquity was documented by Herodotus (who died in 425 B.C.). Moreover, Pausanias wrote the following words around A.D. 150 about the plains of Marathon:

> All night long the neighing of horses and the sounds of battling warriors can be heard on these plains. He who dares to go there to have a closer look at the events will not escape unharmed.

Quoted from K. Meisen, *Die Sagen vom Wütenden Heer und Wilden Jäger* (Münster, 1935), 20–21.

See also W. Mannhardt, *Wald- und Feldkulte*, 2 vols. (Berlin, 1875), I, 82–85 and 123–128; Petzoldt *DVS*, notes on pp. 393–394; R. Wünsche, "Griechischer und germanischer Geisterglaube," *HBV*, 2 (1903); H. Plischke, *Die Sage vom wilden Heere im deutschen Volk*, Diss. (Leipzig, 1914); J. de Vries, "Wodan und die Wilde Jagd," *Die Nachbarn*, 3 (1962), 31–45.

LEGEND NO. 315. This is a treasure legend featuring the magic flower that opens underground chambers and the motif "Don't forget the best of all." See Nos. 9 and 304 and the commentaries.

The town of Wehren is today called Wehrden. It lies on the Weser River about eight miles south of Höxter in Lower Saxony. Godelheim lies about two miles north of Wehrden. The maiden of the legend fits the category of Castle Maiden—frequently thought to be a Poor Soul who watches over treasure. See Nos. 10–13 and 222–224.

This legend is typical of many treasure legends in that the task of recovering great wealth seems to be very easy but nevertheless ends in failure. In *Märchen* one frequently encounters the opposite—the task seems impossible but the protagonist nevertheless succeeds, often with the help of magic powers.

LEGEND NO. 316. Wernigerode today is a relatively major city in East Germany. It lies on the north side of the Harz Mountains.

In most treasure legends the greedy seeker of wealth nearly succeeds but ultimately must fail. However, since the shepherd in this variant is not only poor but also good and pious he is given access to the treasure, and he manages to recover a substantial portion of it. Nevertheless, the unlimited wealth that he might have had is denied him because he was ignorant of the prescriptions associated with the treasure. See the commentaries to Nos. 124, 158–163, and 213.

LEGEND NO. 317. The Ilse River flows through steep canyon walls between two of the highest peaks in the Harz Mountains and is one of the most scenic spots in the whole area. This legend is a variation on the maiden's leap stories associated with such areas all over the world (see Nos. 320–321, and cf. the countless lovers' leap traditions in the U.S.).

The gift of the apparently worthless items—in this case fir cones and acorns—that later turn to gold represents one of the most common motifs in German legendry. The recipient invariably throws almost all of the material away, retaining only a small amount. This motif again stresses a trait common to legendry in general—that although eternal bliss seems to lie at one's fingertips it always remains just out of reach. Ilse, the maiden who guards the treasure, belongs to the category of Castle Maiden. See Nos. 10–13, 222–224, and 315.

LEGEND NO. 318. The county and city of Glatz once belonged to Bohemia, but they are today a part of Poland and are called Klodzko. The city is located about 50 miles south of Breslau (Wroclaw), just north of the Czech border. Nearby are the Riesengebirge 'Giant Mountains,' one of the last great wilderness areas in Central Europe.

The Heathen Maiden of this legend with her feats of strength is, of course, a Giantess. It defies all logic that the icon and relics of a Heathen Maiden, who allegedly practiced incest, should end up in a church. It is conceivable that the original meanings of the relics were forgotten after the area became Lutheran. The attempt to explain them would then give rise to this etiological legend. One could even further speculate that the tradition was invented by Protestant clergymen in an attempt to discredit the sacred relics rather than have them removed from the church.

LEGEND NO. 319. The Grimms have combined five separate legends under this heading. Each of them is an etiological narrative attempting to explain a single physical feature in the landscape. The city of Thale is located on the edge of the Harz Mountains near Quedlinburg in the German Democratic Republic, and there is indeed a cliff near the city called *Roßtrappe* 'the Horse's Hoofprint.' Across from the cliff rises a hill called not the Devil's Dance Floor but rather *Hexentanzplatz* 'the Witches' Dance Floor.'

In the first legend, the drowned maiden becomes a frightening spirit of the deep, a familiar motif in German legendry (see No. 306 and commentary).

Steep, jutting cliffs naturally attract attention, and people take pleasure in attaching adventurous stories to such sites. Should the formation also bear some mark or indentation, one can be assured that a story concerning an attempted leap across the ravine will have been woven around it. For example, in Höllenthal Ravine outside of Freiburg there rises a sheer cliff called *Hirschsprung* 'Stag's Leap.' According to local legend a magnificent stag once saved itself from a relentless hunter by making a courageous leap across the chasm.

Virtually every type of legendary character imaginable attempts these leaps, elk, deer, maidens, heroes, famous people, gods, saints, Giants, witches, the Devil; the list is virtually endless.

See H. Pirchegger, "Der Jungfernsprung," *ZsfVk*, 45 (1935), 112–119; E. Stemplinger, "Fußspur," *HdA* III, 240–243.

LEGEND NO. 320. See the commentary to No. 319. Ballenstedt and Harzgerode lie in the eastern part of the Harz Mountains in the German Democratic Republic. There is a small village actually called *Mägdesprung* 'Maiden's Leap' located between the two cities, and a sheer cliff overhangs it.

Such legends are not of course limited to Germany. There are thousands of such rock formations in the United States, for example, and many lovers' leap legends—usually about Indian lovers—are told about them. See J. Brunvand, *The Study of American Folklore* (New York, 1968), p. 97.

LEGEND NO. 321.   In this group of legends the maiden's leap becomes a Christian miracle. See the commentaries to Nos. 319–320. The village and castle of Oybin are located right on the Czech border in the easternmost part of the German Democratic Republic.

LEGEND NO. 322.   See the commentary to No. 319.

LEGEND NO. 323.   Hidde is the local name for a Giant said to have lived in Saxony. See the commentary to No. 140.

The story of the dim-witted man who mistakes one species of animal for another is a favorite among the numbskull stories of popular tradition (AT 1319A–M). Indeed, the following story picked up by the German Press Agency (dpa) and published in the *Badische Zeitung*, No. 178 (4/5 August 1979), indicates that it still enjoys some popularity:

Battista Toninelli noticed that the watchdog that he had purchased at the marketplace of the city of Brescia in northern Italy had unusually large paws and short ears, and that it was also strangely quiet for a dog. After it had broken its line and bitten him on his leg, Toninelli called his vet. When the latter appeared he told Toninelli, "Man, you bought yourself a young lion!"

Even though the news account mentions the man's name, the story is most probably fictional. News agencies are constantly acquiring stories from popular tradition and publishing them as fact.

LEGEND NO. 324.   Nordhausen and Ilefeld lie on the southern slopes of the Harz Mountains just over the border of the German Democratic Republic.

Whether the ritual practiced by the youths was mere hazing for its own sake, an initiation rite, a healing ceremony, or some other kind of ritual cannot be determined from this text alone. Painful rituals of this sort are known to occur often in initiation ceremonies. Furthermore, it has been well documented in a number of societies that when a significant event takes place—for instance, the placing of a border stone—the occurrence must be deeply impressed upon the memory of the participants. Thus, hazing, beatings, and other painful rites frequently accompany the commemoration. Friedrich Nietzsche has written about such practices in his famous essay "The Genealogy of Morals."

The practice of "pulling through," that is, pulling a human body through a narrow opening in a hollow tree, through the looped roots of a tree, through vines or holes in rocks is a healing process frequently observed the world over. In such rites the disease is supposed to be divested and transferred from the sufferer to the tree, vine, or rock. It is also possible that the idea of symbolic rebirth is present in such rituals. The rebirthing process is believed to return the patient to the pure state of infancy and thus to health.

See M. Eliade, *Das Mysterium der Wiedergeburt: Initiationsriten, ihre kulturelle und religiöse Bedeutung* (Zürich und Stuttgart, 1961). W. D. Hand, " 'Passing Through': Folk Medical Magic and Symbolism," *Proceedings of the American Philosophical Society*, 112 (1968), 379–402.

LEGEND NO. 325. Three motifs associated with Giants are found in this legend. There are two etiological motifs explaining how the giant stones got to the top of the mountain and how the castle was constructed—the Giant as master builder (see No. 184 and commentary). Secondly, there are relics of the Giant in the form of huge bones. Finds of prehistoric fossils of such creatures as mastodons have given rise to legends of this sort (see the commentaries to Nos. 16 and 141). Finally, there is the legend of the Giant's Toy (see No. 16).

LEGEND NO. 326. Here we have two etiological legends explaining the red color of the water of the lake. However, a more scientific explanation tells us that a combination of the right temperature and the right saline content produces algae that turn the color of water red. See K. R. Fischer, "Das Rätsel der hessischen Blutseen," *Volk und Schule*, 10 (1931), 42–43.

Egeln and Westeregeln lie about twenty-two miles northeast of Quedlinburg. The Hackel is a hill that rises about 700 feet and dominates the otherwise flat landscape.

LEGEND NO. 327. Many Giant legends have been invented to explain Germanic burial sites. The term *Hünegrab* 'Giant's grave' is still used to designate such sites. See the commentary to No. 16.

See also Petzoldt *DVS*, 447–448; H. Seger, "Die Denkmäler der Vorzeit im Volksglauben," *MSGV*, 6 (1904), 1–13; J. R. Broderius, *The Giant in Germanic Tradition*, Diss. (Chicago, 1932).

LEGEND NO. 328. The Helpful Dead are known best in the *Märchen*, especially in AT 506, *The Grateful Dead*. Although in legends the dead are usually frightening creatures who pose great dangers for the living, as with any creature from the spirit world they can also be helpful.

See O. Schweber, *Der Tod in der deutschen Sage und Dichtung* (Berlin, 1876); R. Kleinpaul, *Die Lebendigen und die Toten in Volksglauben, Religion und Sage* (Leipzig, 1898).

LEGEND NO. 329. The area in which this legend occurs lies in present-day Czechoslovakia. Hans Heiling was one of many legendary figures who was thought to have signed a pact with the Devil. The tradition of such figures extends to the very earliest era of Christianity in Rome and Greece. As early as the first century A.D. there was a story told concerning one Cyprianus who conjured forth the spirits of the underworld to help him win the love of Justina (see L. Radermacher, *Griechische Quellen zur Faustsage*, Sitzungsbericht der Akademie der Wissenschaften in Wien, phil.-hist. Kl., 206: 4 [Wien-Leipzig, 1927]).

From the ninth century we find the story of the slave of Proterius. He denies Christ and conjures forth the Prince of Hell who appears with a contract that the slave signs "with his own hand" (see L. Rademacher, *ibid.*). The slave later repents, performs forty days of intense penance, and is saved by a miracle.

From the tenth century on, the legend of Theophilus gained great popularity. He was deposed from his office as a canon, and growing bitter, denied Christ and his mother, and signed the Devil's contract "with his own blood." Later, after he repents and prays for the intervention of the Virgin Mary he is saved. See L. Kretzenbach, *Teufelsbündner und Faustgestalten im Abendland* (Klagenfurt, 1968).

The number of such Faust figures is nearly endless. Besides Dr. Johannes Faust himself, there are legends about such figures as Paracelsus, Albertus Magnus, Trithemius von Sponheim, and Agrippa von Nettesheim. Then there are scores of such figures that are known locally in the European oral tradition. Hans Heiling is such a figure, as is Paul Creuz from Legend No. 38. Also known were Dr. Johann Anton Kittel of Bohemia (see A. Ohorn, "Dr. Faust in Böhmen," *Kalender fürs deutsche Landvolk* [1927], 77–79). In Poland, Pan Twardowski achieved fame and notoriety comparable to that of Faust in Germany. In Rumania we have Dr. Salomonar, and Master Krabat was known among the Wends (see L. Kretzenbacher, *Teufelsbündner und Faustgestalten im Abendland* [Klagenfurt, 1968], for information on these and similar figures). In the Tyrol people still tell of Pfeiffer Hiusile who sold his soul to the Devil (see H. Holzmann, *Pfeiffer Huisile: Der Tiroler Faust* [Innsbruck, 1954]).

It seems likely that people have long been fascinated with such figures because their behavior is the exact opposite of the customary mores stressed in most legends. The pious Christian is supposed to accept all things on faith and not probe too deeply into forbidden realms; thus human curiosity is looked upon as a sin and is invariably punished in folk legends. An alternative is represented by the curious and scholarly man who cannot resist the temptation to probe into the unknown—even if he has to associate with the frightful powers of the dark to do so. Of course, the theme that he does so often for purely selfish reasons is usually present, for legends are supposed to present negative examples of antisocial behavior. Nevertheless, a certain grudging (pious Christians would say perverse) admiration for the probing spirit seems to lie behind much of the popularity of such figures.

See also G. Hendel, *Von der deutschen Volkssage zu Goethes "Faust"* (Weimar, 1967); H. Henning, *Faust in fünf Jahrhunderten* (Halle, 1963); P. Palmer and R. More, *The Sources of the Faust Tradition* (Oxford, 1936); R. Petsch, *Faustsage und Faustdichtung* (Darmstadt, 1966).

LEGEND NO. 330. Hagiographers will recognize this story as the legend of St. Kümmernis. Many versions set the tale in Portugal where the king tries to force his daughter to marry a heathen. The princess is desperate to escape this fate and prays to God to make her ugly. God grants her wish and she grows a beard. In a towering rage, the king has his daughter crucified. The addition of the Poor Minstrel theme in this legend is found exclusively in the German variants.

The story is told throughout Europe, although the name varies according to the locale. There are such forms as Kumini, Comeria, Wilgefortis (from *virgo fortis*), Hülpe, Liberata, Souci, Ontkommer, etc.

The most convincing of the many attempts to explain the legend and its origin has been made by Gustav Schnürer and Josef Ritz (*Sankt Kümmernis und Volto Santo* [Düsseldorf, 1934]). They trace the legend to the Byzantine Romanesque period, when it was common in iconography to depict Christ on the cross as a triumphant king with a golden crown, splendid robes, and even jewel-studded shoes. This tradition spread west into Italy, where an excellent and influential example is the altar painting of the *Volto santo* ('sacred countenance') found in the Cathedral of Lucca. Copies of this painting later appeared in woodcuts distributed on prayer sheets and other religious handbills that found their way across most of Europe. In the sixteenth century when depictions of Christ in a loincloth and a crown of thorns dominated popular iconography, the fully clothed and crowned figure was no longer understood, and it was thought to be the picture of a bearded woman. The etiological legend of St. Kümmernis was then invented.

See also A. Wrede, "Kümmernis," *HdA* V, 807–810; P. Rehorn, "Der hl. Kummernus oder die hl. Wilgefortis," *Germania*, 32 (1887), 461–480; K. Weinhold, "Sanct Kummernuss," *ZsfVk*, 9 (1899), 322–324; F. Gorissen, "Das Kreuz von Lucca und die heilige Wilgifortis/Ontkommer," *Numaga*, 15 (1968), 122–148; L. Kretzenbacher, *Heimat im Volksbarock* (Klagenfurt, 1961).

LEGEND NO. 331.  This legend, like many others in the collection, is about the "Castle Maiden/White Woman" figure. See Nos. 10–12, 25, 222, 224, 228, and their commentaries.

The story, in providing an example of a foreign overseer's exploitation of his subjects for his own carnal pleasure, gives expression to social grievances. However, even though it stresses this note of protest, the legend does not demand any action against arbitrary despotic forces. Instead it leaves the punishment of sins to the supernatural forces that condemn sinners to an eternity on earth as Poor Souls.

The fact that St. Michael's chapel marks the site where the maidens fled into the ravine is a further indication that punishment and reward were thought to be in the hands of divine forces. St. Michael is known above all as the one who weighs the good and evil in the souls of the deceased. The results of the weighing determine whether the final destination will be Heaven or Hell. Michael, as the Archangel that cast the Devil-dragon from Heaven at the Apocalypse, is also revered as the protector of the innocent against sinful and diabolic forces.

See A. M. Renner, *Der Erzengel Michael in der Geistes- und Kunstgeschichte* (Saarbrücken, 1927).

LEGEND NO. 332.  Regarding Lake Mummel, see No. 59 and its commentary. The lake does not really lie in Murg Valley as this legend indicates, but rather at the head of a valley running parallel to it. The area is in the Black Forest near Baden-Baden. As the Grimms' source as well as the style indicate, this version is a literary treatment of what must have once been a genuine folk legend. It clearly reflects the age of early Romanticism in which it was written. Nevertheless elements of earlier ages are perceptible in the story.

The late medieval period, during which many of the once chivalrous knights were reduced to marauding and pillaging, left a deep and lasting impression on the German populace. After the once glorious castles and fortresses had been reduced to overgrown ruins, it was quite natural that these isolated and spooky sites would become the focal point of stories that gave expression to the long-remembered age when cattle and crops were exposed to the whims of the marauding robber barons. This legend, like many others, although expressing a degree of social protest, is nevertheless content to leave punishment to divine forces.

LEGEND NO. 333.  Reichenau (today called Bogatynia) lies on the border where the German Democratic Republic, Poland, and Czechoslovakia meet. Today it is part of Poland. The fact that the peddler is both poor and pious is the reason he has been selected to be the recipient of the treasure. See Nos. 9, 124, 158–163, 315–317.

The mouse is representative of supernatural forces in a number of legends (see Nos. 242, 248, and 433). Mice are thought to be the epiphany of the human soul in many legends as well as a form the Nightmare can assume during its nocturnal meanderings. They are also thought to have a close relationship with Elves, Dwarfs, and other underground creatures. In the Rhineland, for example, it is said that Elves feed their mice gold (P. Zaunert, *Rheinische Sagen*, I, 249). Dwarfs are also thought to be able to change themselves into mice. Since Dwarfs and Elves are frequently thought to be the guardians of treasure it is not surprising to see mice in this role as well. There are instances of mice showing men where treasure is located, and although this is not a common motif, it does occur in some collections. See K. Landsteiner, *Reste des Heidenglaubens in Sagen und Gebräuchen des niederösterreichischen Volkes*, Progr. (Krems, 1869), 152; O. Tobler, *Die Epiphanie der Seele in deutschen Volkssagen*, Diss. (Kiel, 1911), 17–18.

In some legends a mouse can function as a *Spiritus Familiaris*. Elsewhere it is believed that every gold piece placed inside a mousehole will breed another one during the night. See R. Riegler, "Maus," *HdA* VI, 31–60. Cf. Mot. B562.1: animal shows man treasure.

LEGEND NO. 334.  In the fourteenth and fifteenth centuries, when European cities were vying with one another in the construction of majestic cathedrals, it was commonplace for the craftsmen's guilds to contribute funds, labor, and skills to the project. Their contributions were frequently commemorated by the depiction of the guild symbols in stained-glass windows or in the stone walls and columns of the completed structures. The stone engravings of this legend were evidently such symbols, but the reason for their being there had been forgotten, and this story was told to explain them.

LEGEND NO. 335.  This legend consists of three parts that have been combined into a unified and powerful narrative. It was not done by the Grimms, however, for the combined form was in their source. It is probable that the linking of the separate tales had already occurred in oral tradition. First, there is the story of the master thief, then the invitation to the gallows, and last, the invitation to appear before God's judgment.

The tricks played by the master thief are nearly endless, and many of them have been incorporated into the international tale type AT 1525. Curiously, the trick with the crutches is not included in either the Aarne-Thompson index of tale types (FFC 184) or in Thompson *Motif-Index*. It is, however, widespread in narratives about thieves (see, for example, Petzoldt *HS*, No. 475b; and J. Künzig, *Badische Sagen* [Leipzig, 1923], No. 353).

The nobleman's foolhardy invitation to the corpse hanging from the gallows represents a version of the international legend type, Death comes to dinner (Don Juan). The earliest literary treatment of this legend is found in the drama told by Tirso de Molina, *El Burlador de Sevilla y convidado de pietra* (1630), and the most famous is Mozart's opera *Don Giovanni* (1787).

The story tells of the heedless man who invites a corpse (a skull, a skeleton, a statue in a graveyard, etc.) to dinner. Later there is an ominous knock on the door and the corpse appears. This tale was a favorite of priests and ministers, and as it was read often from the pulpit, it turns up in countless exempla collections (see L. Petzoldt, *Der Tote als Gast: Volkssage und Exempel*, FFC 200 [Helsinki, 1968]).

The invitation to appear before the judgment of God rests upon the very human desire for and belief in ultimate justice, especially when the institutions of man fail to achieve this end. The tale also draws upon the passage in the Old Testament (Joel 3:2) which tells that the final judgment will be held in the valley of Jehoshaphat: "I will also gather all nations, and will bring them down into the valley of Jehoshaphat, and will plead with them there for my people. . . . " And again in Joel 3:14, "Multitudes, multitudes in the valley of decision: for the day of the Lord is near in the valley of decision."

In folk legends the right to invite a guilty party to appear before God's judgment in the valley of Jehoshaphat does not have to wait until Judgment Day; it can occur at any time (often a specific period of time is mentioned, as in this legend). A sinner is approached by a man (or a ghost, or spirit—often the sinner's victim) and told that although justice of this world has failed, he will yet have to appear before the judgment of God in the valley of Jehoshaphat. Frequently, the man extending the invitation has himself been unjustly punished by the institutions of man, and he invites his judge or prosecutor to appear in the valley of decision.

The legend also becomes a fate legend and accordingly the attempt to avert the prophesied fate, which at first is apparently successful, is nevertheless doomed to fail.

The fact that a Lithuanian is accorded the duty of being the hangman is based on the belief that a foreigner had to perform this duty. See A. Keller, *Der Scharfrichter in der Kulturgeschichte* (n.p., 1921).

See also S. Harding, "Die Vorladung vor Gottesgericht nach Walliser Quellen," *SAV*, 52 (1956), 10–18; and W.-E. Peuckert, "Josaphat Tal," *HdA* IV, 770–774. The best single work on this entire complex of motifs is L. Petzoldt's monograph *Der Tote als Gast* (cited above).

LEGEND NO. 336. This story is another variant of the invitation to the gallows (see the commentary to No. 335).

Hanged criminals were denied the privilege of any kind of burial and left on the gallows to rot. Thus, it is not surprising that the criminals had been hanging there "for years." This fact, of course, makes the later appearance of the guests at the inn especially frightening.

The rational explanation at the end of the legend occurs in many folk legends (see Röhrich *Sage*, 3–5).

Rehermann *Predigtexempel*, 136, lists five variants from exempla literature. See also L. Petzoldt, *Der Tote als Gast*, FFC 200 (Helsinki, 1968).

LEGEND NO. 337. This is a variant of the Devil as master builder and the cheated Devil legends. See the commentary to No. 184.

LEGEND NO. 338. This is essentially the same legend as No. 210 (see the commentary to that tale). An etiological addendum has been appended to explain the origin of the Corpus Christi chapel near Erfurt. Traveling scholars were thought to be sorcerers in league with the Devil (see the commentary to No. 503). See also L. Weiser-Aall, "Fahrende Schüler," *HdA* II, 1123–1124.

The great flying disks on which the German students travel is reminiscent of the flying saucers of contemporary tradition. People have seen things flying in the sky from the beginning of recorded history and probably long before that. Reports of horsemen, flaming swords, crucifixes, great disks, and the like roaring through the skies abound in the chronicles and histories of Europe. Because of the nature of human perception it is possible for people to have all kinds of experience with such apparitions.

See D. Ward, "The Little Man Who Wasn't There: On Encounters with the Supranormal," *Fabula*, 18 (1977), 212–225. See also L. Dégh, "UFOs and How Folklorists Should Look at Them," *Fabula*, 18 (1977), 242–248; M. Berger, *The Supernatural: From ESP to UFOs* (New York, 1977); J. Michell, *The Flying Saucer Vision* (London, 1974).

LEGEND NO. 339. The site of this legend is in present-day Poland. It is an etiological tale explaining the origin of the drainage canals. The story is unusual in that the guilty party who agreed to the contract with the Devil is not the one who is punished. Rather, the onus falls on the unsuspecting workers assigned to the project. It is thus an effective reminder that any contact with the Evil One—even where one is totally unsuspecting—is potentially dangerous.

LEGEND NO. 340. The transformation of a human into a tree is a motif encountered in mythology (Daphne) and in fairy tales (e.g., variants of AT 425M and AT 516). However, in legends this kind of transformation is rare. When it occurs it is considered a diabolic curse from which the victim needs to be delivered. More common in legends is the notion that trees contain spirits of the deceased.

See D. Ward, "Baum," *EdM* I, 1366–1374; H. Marzell, "Baum," *HdA* I, 954–958; O. Lauffer, "Geister im Baum," *Volkskundliche Gaben: John Meier Festschrift* (Berlin und Leipzig, 1934), 104–120.

LEGEND NO. 341. The story of the woman who is buried and then brought back to life was already familiar in classical antiquity. Chariton of Aphrodisias (ca. A.D. 200), for example, tells the story of Kallirrhoë, a prominent citizen of Syracuse, who when thought dead was buried, but was then awakened by grave robbers.

In Germany the story became attached to the von Adochts, a prominent Cologne family. The earliest documentation of this version is in the Koelhoff Chronicle (*Die Cronica van der hilliger Stat van Coellen*), which was printed in 1499. The legend is based on the deep fear people have of being buried alive, and laws requiring a certain time to elapse between death and burial are based on such fears. The story was told about Richmodis von Adocht, and it became very popular in oral tradition in and around Cologne.

Variants of the story were printed on broadsides, and engravings illustrating the event were also circulated. For example, an illustrated story on a handbill was printed in the year 1604 by the Cologne engraver Johannes Bussenmacher. The woman in the story is called Richmuth von der Adoicht and the year is given as 1357.

The linking of this tale with the miracle of the horse in the loft probably came about in an attempt to explain the crest of the Hackeney family who lived in Cologne around the year 1500. The name Hackeney means 'horse,' and they adopted a pair of horses in the family crest. The miracle story was then invented (on the model of extant narratives) to explain the crest when the meaning of the family name was no longer understood, for the association of Hackeney with horse is no longer immediately apparent in the German language.

See Petzoldt *HS*, I, Nr. 20a, 350–351; J. Bolte, "Die Sage von der erweckten Scheintoten," *ZsfVk*, 20 (1910), 353–383; J. Hertel, J. Bolte, and A. Andrae, "Zur Sage von der erweckten Scheintoten," *ZsfVk*, 21 (1911), 282–285; H. v. Hentig, *Der nekrotrope Mensch* (Stuttgart, 1964); L. Röhrich, *EMA*, I, 415–428.

The story has also continued to exist as a newspaper legend and as a vulgar ballad. See L. Petzoldt, *Grause Thaten sind geschehen* (München, 1968), Nos. 1 and 7. Horses appearing in lofts and on steeples and the like is also a *Schwank* motif and occurs in traditions about Till Eulenspiegel and Baron von Münchhausen. It also occurs in other legends as a *Schwank* motif. See No. 175 and the commentary. I am indebted to the works of L. Petzoldt (see above) for much of this information.

LEGEND NO. 342. One of the most widespread legends, and one that is still common today, concerns the appearance of the double of a human being. The basis for many such stories is the belief that a person's soul can separate from the body at the time of death. This double—the Germans call it the *Doppelgänger*—is often perceived by family and townspeople not as a ghost or spirit, but as a perfectly normal human being.

In many legends, if a man sees his own double it means that he will die soon. In this legend, however, the appearance of the double is a clear indication that the person has just died.

See Vera Meyer-Matheis, *Die Vorstellung eines alter ego in Volkserzählungen*, Diss. (Freiburg, 1974). See also No. 259 and commentary.

LEGEND NO. 343. The area in question lies just southeast of Stettin in Pomerania. In 1624 the area had been ravaged by the Thirty Years' War.

Although talking birds occur regularly in fairy tales (e.g., "Faithful John," AT 516), their occurrence in legends is relatively rare. However, birds are traditionally thought to be omens of future events. In ancient Rome the behavior of birds was observed in great detail as ominal magic. The appearance of certain birds near residences is also said to augur future events, frequently death.

See A. Taylor, "Vogel," *HdA* VIII, 1673–1679; E. Ingersoll, *Birds in Legend, Fable and Folklore* (New York, 1959). See also Hand *Beliefs*, 5279–5336; P. A. Travis, "Bird Lore of New York State," *NYFQ*, 1 (1945), 197–204; J. K. Strecker, "Folk-Lore Relating to Birds," *Publications of the Texas Folklore Society*, 7 (1928), 25–37.

LEGEND NO. 344.   The legend of the Eternal Jew has been popular in Europe since the Middle Ages. It was first documented in the thirteenth-century *Chronica Majora* by the English monk Matthew Parisiensis. He tells of a Jewish door guard at the palace of Pontius Pilate who tried to make Jesus hasten his steps by beating him as he bore the cross. Pilgrims returning from the Holy Land in the thirteenth century also brought with them the tale of a Jew who could not die and who was thus forced to wander eternally because he mistreated Christ at the crucifixion.

In 1602 the material of the legend was published as a chapbook in Germany, *Kurtze Beschreibung und Erzehlung von einem Juden mit Namen Ahasverus* 'A Short Description and Story of a Jew by the Name of Ahasver.' This is the first time that the name Ahasver is used for the Eternal Jew in print. It was taken from the Book of Esther, where it appeared as the Hebrew version of the name of King Xerxes of Persia. Xerxes' Jewish wife, Esther, successfully thwarted a pogrom planned by his vizier Haman. Jews celebrate this event every year with the Feast of Purim, during which appropriate passages from the Book of Esther are read aloud to the accompaniment of noisy celebration. Non-Jews chancing upon this ceremony misunderstood the role of Ahasver, and thinking him a Jew, adopted him in their lore as a symbol for all the Jews.

The chapbook, which spread through all of Europe in a number of variants, tells the story of Ahasver the cobbler. On the fateful day when Christ is on his way to be crucified he leans his cross against the wall of the cobbler's shop and stops to rest. Ahasver, fearing that his house will be cursed by the presence of a condemned criminal, flies into a rage telling the wretched man to get himself and his cross away from his property. The cobbler is then condemned to wander for all eternity or until Judgment Day.

Popular legends tell that he is constantly wandering around the world, but that he returns to the same places once every hundred years. Because he is able to recall names and events that have nearly been forgotten by everyone else he thus reveals his identity. He frequently informs people that things have become progressively worse in the last hundred years, and he thus becomes the symbol for a constantly changing and deteriorating world. It is said that he is permitted but one hour's rest each day, and one legend states that he walked around a table all night at an inn.

He appears as an ancient spectral figure with grey hair and beard and is clad in old worn clothes. He is also said to have nails in the soles of his boots in the shape of a cross. Upon seeing him, a girl once exclaimed, "Jesus!" at which point he struck his chest with his fist and sighed. Frequently, as in this legend, he tells villagers that the next time he comes by their village will no longer exist.

See Petzoldt *HS*, II, 272–273; H. Lixfeld, "Ahasver," *EdM* I, 227; W.-E. Peuckert, "Jude, Jüdin," *HdA* IV, 808–847; A. Soergel, *Ahasver-Dichtungen seit Goethe* (Leipzig, 1905); J. Gaer, *The Legend of the Wandering Jew* (New York, 1961); G. K. Anderson, *The Legend of the Wandering Jew* (Providence, 1965); J. Peletová, *Die Sage von Ahasver in der deutschen Literatur*, Diss. (Prague, 1920); L. Neubaur, *Die Sage vom ewigen Juden*, 2nd ed. (Leipzig, 1893); A. Schmidt, "Das Volksbuch vom Ewigen Juden," *Beiträge zur Entstehungsgeschichte des Buches* (Danzig, 1927); E. Dal, "Ahasverus in Dänemark," *JbVlf*, 9 (1964), 144–170; B. af Klintberg, "The Swedish Wanderings of the Eternal Jew," *Fourth World Congress on Jewish Studies* (Jerusalem, 1968), 115–119; J. J. Gielen, *De wandelnde Joode in Volkskunde en letterkunde* (Amsterdam, 1931).

The Eternal Jew has been the subject of scores of literary treatments by such authors as Goethe, Schlegel, Lenau, and Chamisso. Wordsworth wrote about him in *Song for the Wandering Jew* (1800); Shelley, *The Wandering Jew, or the Victim of the Eternal Avenger* (1806), and Hans Christian Andersen, *Ahasverus* (1848). See Frenzel *Stoffe*, pp. 15–19, and T. Kappstein, *Ahasver in der Weltpoesie* (Leipzig, 1906). He also puts in an appearance in Franz Werfel's play *Jacobowsky and the Colonel*. The most recent literary adaptation of the legend is Pär Lagerkvist's *Ahasverus död* (Stockholm, 1960).

LEGEND NO. 345. The epiphany of God as a wanderer on earth, while not a common motif, occurs now and again in legend. His role here as a vengeful divinity, although not in keeping with the tenets of Christianity, is nevertheless known in popular tradition. See No. 45 and its commentary for a similar theme dating from classical antiquity. For information on towns and villages that have sunk beneath the waters or the surface of the earth because of the sins of their inhabitants, see No. 239 and its commentary.

LEGEND NO. 346. This is an etiological legend explaining how the weeping willow tree came to be the way it is. There are a number of such legends throughout Europe, and they almost invariably involve Christian themes, e.g., the weeping willow dropped its branches so it could hide the Holy Family from Herod's soldiers (Slavic, Dutch, and German variants); the weeping willow drooped its branches over Mary as she wept on Christ's grave (from Transylvania); the willow witnessed the crucifixion and has never stopped mourning (Italian, German). There are also many variants of this Grimm legend throughout Europe.

See Oskar Dähnhardt, *Natursagen*, 4 vols. (Leipzig und Berlin, 1909–12), II, 41, 201, 230, 290; H. Marzell, "Weide," *HdA* IX, 241–254.

LEGEND NO. 347. The location of the icon, its physical environment, and the peculiarities of human perception can actually produce the illusion described in this legend. See, for example, J. J. Gibson, *The Perception of the Visual World* (Boston, 1950).

LEGEND NO. 348. Christian icons have long been placed at the edges of cliffs, atop mountains, and deep in wilderness areas where they have subsequently become the object of pilgrimages. Such sites were frequently chosen because they had been places of worship in heathen times, and early missionaries wisely kept such sacred traditions going, merely changing the names of the divinities in question.

In this case, the local populace could not imagine how the statue came to be in its location on the cliffside and this delightful etiological legend was invented to provide an explanation. The area in question is in southern Switzerland not far from the Matterhorn.

LEGEND NO. 349. The Grimms have combined two etiological Christian miracle legends here into a single narrative. The rather cryptic passage that, just before the church was ready to be consecrated, work suddenly stopped and was not resumed for thirty-six years doubtless explains an actual delay that happened during the construction of the church. Calamities such as famines, epidemics, wars, invasions, etc., have frequently caused such havoc that even nearly finished buildings were abandoned.

LEGEND NO. 350. In popular Christian belief there is a widespread tradition that God often reveals his sacred oracles through animals, and such motifs are especially popular among animal husbandmen. This legend is also etiological in that it gives an explanation for the mysterious ruins.

St. Stephan is celebrated as the first martyr of all Christendom, as he was, according to legend, the first disciple of Christ to have been put to death for his faith. St. Stephan's Day (Dec. 26) is celebrated with great festivities in some areas, especially in Catholic Ireland.

LEGEND NO. 351. The Grimms have combined three saint's legends into a single narrative. This is again unfortunate, for the first legend is evidently about an entirely different saint from the one in the second and third legends. The first Notburga was born circa 1265 in Rattenberg on the Inn River east of Innsbruck. The Grimm legend was taken from the same source that functions as her official *vita*. This account depicts her as a maidservant working on a dairy farm. Accordingly, the iconography of the area shows her holding a milk pitcher and wearing an apron. She was the patronness of all maidservants and was invoked by them in time of need. She was also invoked for help at childbirth and for curing diseases in farm animals. It was said that she was especially pious, kind, generous, and charitable, and that she was ready and willing to sacrifice all she had to help those in distress.

Much less is known about the Notburga from the Neckar Valley. The church at Hochhausen on the Neckar, which lies about 35 miles upstream from Heidelberg, was once devoted to her memory, but it has since become a Protestant church. In the crypt there is a flat stone covering a tomb on which is carved the image of a maiden with one arm, holding a serpent. Preserved also are two panels of what was once a large altar triptych depicting her career.

In the last Grimm legend she is said to have been the daughter of King Dagobert. This is evidently Dagobert I (see the commentaries to Nos. 438–440), the Merovingian king of Austrasia from 623 to 628 and king of all the Franks from 630 to 639. He was defeated by the heathen Samo, king of the

Slavic Wends. In the Grimm sources the latter is the heathen to whom Dagobert wanted to give his daughter in marriage.

See W. Pfaundler, *Die heilige Notburga* (Wien, 1962); H. Huth, "Die Geschichte des Altares in der evangelishen Kirche von Hochhausen am Neckar," *Nachrichtenblatt der Denkmalpflege in Baden-Württemberg*, 5 (1962).

LEGEND NO. 352. Legends telling of sacred structures being built with precious materials are widespread in German-speaking areas.

Here, the first legend attempts to rationalize the practice, while the second legend attributes the excess to the sinful heathens. Both legends reflect an age when such wasteful practices were looked upon with distrust.

Frederick III was crowned Holy Roman Emperor by the pope in 1452—the last of the German kings to be accorded this distinction. Although construction of St. Stephan's in Vienna was begun in 1304, more than a hundred years before Frederick's birth, construction was still going on during his reign.

LEGEND NO. 353. The Grimms felt a duty to include everything in their collection that could be called "German legends," and thus they made no attempt to suppress this and the following example of the ugliest kind of prejudice and racism.

The belief that Jews engaged in the ritual murder of Christian children was first documented in 1253, and in the following centuries 150 official accusations of such practices were filed with the authorities. These beliefs were hideous beyond description, and the legends and rumors that they generated were directly responsible for some of the grisly pogroms and other atrocities suffered by Jews at the hands of Christians through the centuries. The Holocaust of the Third Reich was the culmination of this madness.

In the Middle Ages it was thought that Jews not only sacrificed Christian children but also used the blood in making Passover bread, and that they engaged in other cannibalistic practices. Other beliefs included virtually every kind of Anti-Christian blasphemy imaginable, from desecrating the sacramental host to crucifying children. The Christian Church evidently did little or nothing to stop the spread of such lies. Indeed, there is evidence in some cases that it was instrumental in both the origin and dissemination of these tales.

Nevertheless, in the nineteenth century there was a concerted effort to discredit these scurrilous accounts, and the traditions seemed to be on the way to extinction. But they re-emerged in the twentieth century—even before Hitler—and after 1933 they erupted with a vengeance in such Nazi publications as *Der Stürmer*.

It is ironic that the early Christians themselves were the victims of similar prejudices. The Romans, probably because they misunderstood the Holy Eucharist, accused the Christians of practicing blood sacrifice and cannibalism. After all, the Christians themselves claimed that they consumed the blood and flesh of Christ while taking the Holy Eucharist.

See D. Chwolson, *Die Blutanklage und sonstige mittelalterliche Beschuldigungen der Juden* (Frankfurt, 1901); W.-E. Peuckert, "Jude, Jüdin," *HdA* IV, 808–833; Petzoldt *HS*, II, 297; H. Oort, *Der Ursprung der Blutbeschuldigung gegen die Juden* (Leiden/Leipzig, 1883); M. Stern, *Die päpstlichen Bullen über die Blutbeschuldigung* (München, 1900); K. Thieme, *Judenfeindschaft* (Frankfurt, 1963).

LEGEND NO. 354. Regarding the scurrilous accusations of blood sacrifices made against the Jews, see the commentary to No. 353.

LEGEND NO. 355. Although this story is etiological in nature and explains the incongruity of horseshoes nailed up in a church, it is also a powerful story of sin and retribution. The count was guilty of a number of blasphemies, not the least of which was choosing to go to a tavern instead of to church on a Sunday morning. Drinking to excess to win a gold chain to flatter his vanity was also a blasphemy. Finally, of course, the count's drunken high jinks that interrupted the church service were a mortal sin.

Ellrich and Klettenberg lie on the south side of the Harz Mountains, just inside the East German border.

See E. Goez-Roetzel, "Der Schuldbegriff in der deutschen Volkssage der Gegenwart," *NdZsV*, 6 (1928), 129–158; L. Röhrich, "Tabus in Volksbräuchen, Sagen und Märchen," in H. Lederer and J. Seyppel (eds.), *Festschrift für Werner Neuse* (Berlin, 1967), 8–23.

LEGEND NO. 356. This short legend combines three themes: an etiological legend explaining the irregularities in the wrought iron as well as the origins of the monastery; a miracle legend in God's giving his sign through the blossoming roses; and a tale of sin and retribution resulting in insanity for the unrepentant sinner. As with famous outlaws such as Johann Hübner (No. 129) and Eppela Gaila (No. 130), specific robber barons were accorded fame and notoriety in popular tradition. However, though outlaws were often shown to have certain positive traits such as courage or a desire to help the poor, etc., robber barons were generally depicted as blasphemers with no redeeming qualities whatsoever. Only when these barons were repentant—as is the case in this legend—were they allowed to show a positive side.

The blossoming of a dried branch or twig is one of the favorite miracle motifs in European legendry. See, for example, No. 171.

LEGEND NO. 357. The site of this legend is in the steep Aare canyon near Meiringen, just east of Brienz in central Switzerland.

LEGEND NO. 358. This legend owes its existence to the misinterpretation of a strange tombstone engraving. Carved on the stone lid of a tomb in the cemetery of Petersberg are the reliefs of the man buried in the tomb and of his wife. Somehow their heads became chipped away. The legend was then related as an explanation.

The reliefs and statuary in cemeteries have produced scores of similar legends in Germany (see, for example, Nos. 581 and 585, and their commentaries) and presumably elsewhere. See M. Wähler, "Denkmale als Ausgangspunkt für Sagen," *Volkswerk: Jahrbuch des Staatlichen Museums für Deutsche Volkskunde* (1943), 99–114.

LEGEND NO. 359.   Schweidnitz was formerly a German city, located just south of Breslau in Silesia. Today it is the Polish city of Swidnica.

The punishment described in the legend is not simply a motif of oral literature. It was an actual practice in the late Middle Ages and is a variant of the humiliating punishment that debtors and other sinners received when they were chained or pilloried to the cathedral or city hall in full view of all the citizens. In especially severe cases they would be left to starve.

In Augsburg in 1409, for example, four priests were suspended in a cage from Perläch Tower. They were set out on a Saturday and by the following Thursday three of them were dead, followed swiftly by the fourth the next day (A. F. Oefele, *Rerum boicarum scriptores* [Augsburg, 1763], I, 614, quoted by Grimm *DRA*, II, 323–324). Similarly, in 1411 a criminal was carried up on a ladder and placed (on the city hall?) where he could not climb down—he starved to death (*Anzeiger für Kunde der teutschen Vorzeit*, 2 [1832], 256).

LEGEND NO. 360.   This legend is related to the reports of miraculous signs of innocence that are often thought to occur during or after the execution of alleged criminals. For instance, it rains from clear skies because God is weeping (see No. 361); a tree stump becomes a blooming myrtle; milk flows from the body of the victim instead of blood; a withered twig produces roses; a white dove flies from the neck of a decapitated victim, etc. See W. Müller-Bergström, "Unschuld," *HdA* VIII, 1443–1451.

In this legend the sign of the rainbow does not signify innocence, but it does indicate the forgiveness of God.

LEGEND NO. 361.   See the commentary to No. 360.

LEGEND NO. 362.   Even today such miracle legends remain some of the most popular oral narratives, especially in Catholic areas. From the Middle Ages on, such stories were collected in the so-called "miracle books" (*Libelli miraculorum, Mirakelbücher*, etc.).

See H. Delehaye, "Les premiers *Libelli miraculorum*," *Annales Boll.*, 29 (1910), 427–234; G. Schreiber, *Deutsche Mirakelbücher: Zur Quellenkunde und Sinngebung* (Düsseldorf, 1938); G. Mensching, *Das Wunder im Glauben und Aberglauben der Völker* (Leiden, 1957); O. Weinreich, *Gebet und Wunder* (Stuttgart, 1929); G. Eis, *Altgermanische Beiträge zur geistlichen Gebrauchsliteratur* (Bern und Frankfurt, 1974). Rehermann *Predigtexempel*, p. 158, lists four variants from exempla collections.

LEGEND NO. 363.   The Grimms end Volume I of their collection with this delightful tale of the three old men. The story is told throughout northern Germany, Scandinavia, and North America in a number of variants. Sometimes it occurs as a jest, other times as a *Märchen* or legend, and in recent years as a popular joke. It is included in AT as Type 726, *The Oldest on the Farm*. The story invariably has an intensification of the theme of old age culminating in the figure of the Great Grandfather. Here are a few examples from current oral joke traditions.

Two old men in their nineties are asked to what they attribute their great age, and they reply, "Clean living—no tobacco, no sex, no alcohol . . ." Just then a great racket breaks out upstairs, and the visitor asks, "What's that!" "Oh, don't pay it no mind," says one old man, "it's just Gramps. He always raises hell when he gets drunk."

Another version: Three very old men are sitting on a bench and someone comes by and asks them their secret of long life. The first two reply that they lead clean lives—no sex, no alcohol, no tobacco. The third, however, admits that he engages in sex at least four times a day, and drinks and smokes to excess. When he's asked how old he is, he replies, "Twenty-nine!"

A third version: Three old geezers are sitting on a bench, and the first laments that only last year he could still jog ten miles a day but now he can't do better than two. The second complains that it's the same with him—last year he could ride his bike twenty miles a day, but now he can barely make five. The third and oldest of all says he knows just how they feel. "This morning at 6:00 A.M.," he says, "I stopped by to visit my girlfriend, and she said, 'Why you lustful old goat. You were just here two hours ago!' That just goes to show you, when you get old your memory begins to fail."

Hannjost Lixfeld (see below) contends that the more serious variants—the ones providing a model for a healthy diet and clean living—are probably the oldest, and that the reversal of the main theme into a joke is a product of more recent years. See H. Lixfeld, "Die drei Alten (AT 726)," *EdM* I, 383–387.

See also J. Bolte, "Die drei Alten," *ZsfVk*, 7 (1897), 205–207; A. Wesselski, "Alters-Sinnbilder und Alters-Wettstreit," *Archiv Orientální*, 4 (1932), 1–122. Richard Dorson includes a variant in his *Negro Folktales in Michigan* (Cambridge, 1956), No. 145.

ABBREVIATIONS

| | |
|---|---|
| AE | *Acta Ethnographica*. Academiae Scientiarum Hungaricae. Iff. 1952ff. |
| Assion *WSF* | Assion, Peter. *Weiße, Schwarze, Feurige: Neugesammelte Sagen aus dem Frankenland*. Karlsruhe, 1972. |
| AT | Aarne, Antti, and Thompson, Stith. *The Types of the Folktale*. 2nd revision. FFC 184. Helsinki, 1964. |
| B-P | Bolte, Johannes, and Polívka, Georg. *Anmerkungen zu den Kinder- und Hausmärchen der Brüder Grimm*. Leipzig, 1913–32. |
| E-B | Erk, Ludwig, and Böhme, Franz M. *Deutscher Liederhort: Auswahl der vorzüglicheren deutschen Volkslieder nach Wort und Vers aus der Vorzeit und Gegenwart*. 3 vols. Leipzig, 1893–94. |
| EdM | Ranke, Kurt, ed. *Enzyklopädie des Märchens: Handwörterbuch zur historischen und vergleichenden Erzählforschung*. Vol. Iff. Berlin and New York, 1977ff. |
| FFC | Folklore Fellows Communications. Iff. Helsinki, 1910ff. |
| F-L | *Folk-Lore: A Quarterly Review of Myth, Tradition, Institution and Custom Being the Transactions of the Folk-Lore Society*. Iff. 1888ff. Later called *Folklore*. |
| Frenzel *Motive* | Frenzel, Elisabeth. *Motive der Weltliteratur*. Stuttgart, 1976. |
| Frenzel *Stoffe* | Frenzel, Elisabeth. *Stoffe der Weltliteratur*. 4th edition. Stuttgart, 1976. |

| | |
|---|---|
| Grimm *DM* | Grimm, Jacob. *Deutsche Mythologie.* 3 vols. 4th edition. Berlin, 1875–78. |
| Grimm *DRA* | Grimm, Jacob. *Deutsche Rechtsaltertümer.* 2 vols. 4th edition. Leipzig, 1889. |
| Hand *Beliefs* | Hand, Wayland D. *Popular Beliefs and Superstitions from North Carolina.* 2 vols. Durham, N.C., 1961–64. |
| *HBV* | *Hessische Blätter für Volkskunde.* Iff. 1902ff. |
| *HdA* | Hoffmann-Krayer, E., and Bächtold-Stäubli, Hanns, eds. *Handwörterbuch des deutschen Aberglaubens.* 10 vols. Berlin and Leipzig, 1927–42. |
| *HdA* IXN | *Nachtrag* 'Addendum' to the above title. This constitutes the second half of vol. IX. |
| *HdM* | Mackensen, Lutz, ed. *Handwörterbuch des deutschen Märchens.* 2 vols. Berlin and Leipzig. 1930–40. Publication ceased after the entry "Gyges." |
| *HdS* | Peuckert, Will-Erich, ed. *Handwörterbuch der Sage.* 3 fascicles. Göttingen, 1961–63. Publication ceased after the third fascicle with the entry "Aufwachsen und Abnehmen der Gestalt." |
| *HdVL* | Brednich, Rolf Wilhelm; Röhrich, Lutz; and Suppan, Wolfgang, eds. *Handbuch des Volksliedes,* 2 vols. München, 1973–75. |
| Hoops *RL* | Hoops, Johannes, ed. *Reallexikon der Germanischen Altertumskunde.* 4 vols. Straßburg, 1911–19. |
| *JAF* | *Journal of American Folklore.* Iff. 1888ff. |
| *JbVlf* | *Jahrbuch für Volksliedforschung.* Iff. 1928ff. |
| *JEGP* | *Journal of English and Germanic Philology.* Iff. 1902ff. |
| *JFI* | *Journal of the Folklore Institute.* Iff. 1964ff. |
| *KHM* | Brüder Grimm. *Kinder- und Hausmärchen.* 6th edition (*Ausgabe letzter Hand* 'definitive edition'). Berlin, 1857. |
| *MSGV* | *Mitteilungen der Schlesischen Gesellschaft für Volkskunde.* Iff. 1900ff. |
| *NdZsV* | *Niederdeutsche Zeitschrift für Volkskunde.* Iff. 1923ff. |
| *NYFQ* | *New York Folklore Quarterly.* Iff. 1945ff. |
| *ÖZV* | *Österreichische Zeitschrift für Volkskunde.* NS Iff. 1947ff. This is a continuation of *Wiener Zeitschrift für Volkskunde.* |
| Petzoldt *DVS* | Petzoldt, Leander, ed. *Deutsche Volkssagen.* 2nd edition. München, 1978. |
| Petzoldt *HS* | Petzoldt, Leander, ed. *Historische Sagen.* 2 vols. München, 1976–77. |
| Peuckert *DtVSMA* | Peuckert, Will-Erich. *Deutscher Volksglaube des Spätmittelalters.* Stuttgart, 1942. |
| Peuckert *Sagen* | Peuckert, Will-Erich. *Sagen: Geburt und Antwort einer mythischen Welt.* Berlin, 1965. |
| Rehermann *Predigtexempel* | Rehermann, Ernst. *Das Predigtexempel bei protestantischen Theologen des 16. und 17. Jahrhunderts.* Göttingen, 1977. |
| *RGG* | Galling, K., ed. *Die Religion in Geschichte und Gegenwart.* 7 vols. 3rd revised edition. Tübingen, 1957–65. |
| *RhJb* | *Rheinisches Jahrbuch für Volkskunde.* Iff. 1950ff. |
| Röhrich *EMA* | Röhrich, Lutz. *Erzählungen des späten Mittelalters und ihr Weiterleben in Literatur und Volksdichtung.* 2 vols. Bern and München, 1962–67. |
| Röhrich *Sage* | Röhrich, Lutz. *Sage.* 2nd revised edition. Sammlung Metzler. Stuttgart, 1971. |
| Röhrich *SuM* | Röhrich, Lutz. *Sagen und Märchen: Erzählforschung heute.* Freiburg, Basel, Wien, 1976. |

| | |
|---|---|
| Roscher *Lexikon* | Roscher, W. H. *Ausführliches Lexikon der griechischen und römischen Mythologie.* 6 vols. Leipzig, 1884–1973. |
| *SAV* | *Schweizerisches Archiv für Volkskunde.* Iff. 1899ff. |
| *SFQ* | *Southern Folklore Quarterly.* Iff. 1937ff. |
| *SV* | *Schweizer Volkskunde.* Iff. 1911ff. |
| Thompson *Motif-Index* | Thompson, S. *Motif-Index of Folk-Literature.* 6 vols. Copenhagen, 1955–58. |
| Tubach *Index* | Tubach, F. C. *Index Exemplorum: A Handbook of Medieval Religious Tales.* FFC 204. Helsinki, 1969. |
| *WF* | *California Folklore Quarterly.* I–V. 1942–46. This was continued as *Western Folklore,* VIff, 1947ff. |
| *WZV* | *Wiener Zeitschrift für Volkskunde.* XXV–XLIV. 1919–39. This is a continuation of *Zeitschrift für österreichischen Volkskunde. WZV* was later continued as *Österreichische Zeitschrift für Volkskunde.* |
| *ZfdPh* | *Zeitschrift fur deutsche Philologie.* Iff. 1869ff. |
| *ZsfVk* | *Zeitschrift des Vereins für Volkskunde.* I–XXXVIII. 1891–1928. This was continued as *Zeitschrift für Volkskunde,* XXXIXff, 1930ff. |
| *ZöV* | *Zeitschrift für österreichische Volkskunde.* Iff. 1895. This was continued as *Wiener Zeitschrift für Volkskunde.* |
| *ZVRhWV* | *Zeitschrift des Vereins für Rheinisch- Westfälische Volkskunde.* Iff. 1940ff. This was continued as *Rheinisch-Westfälische Zeitschrift für Volkskunde,* Iff, 1945ff. |

1 2 3 4 5 6 7 8 9 10 11 12 13  90 89 88 87 86 85 84 83 82 81

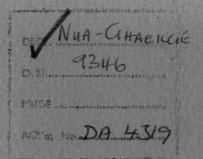